COLLECTED PAPERS

VOLUME FOUR

COLLECTED PAPERS

VOLUME FOUR: TOWARD A GENERAL SOCIAL SCIENCE

KENNETH E. BOULDING

LARRY D. SINGELL, EDITOR

COLORADO ASSOCIATED UNIVERSITY PRESS
BOULDER, COLORADO

COLORADO ASSOCIATED UNIVERSITY PRESS
BOULDER, COLORADO

Copyright © Kenneth E. Boulding 1974

Colorado Associated University Press
1424 Fifteenth Street
Boulder, Colorado 80302

Library of Congress Card Number 77-135288
ISBN 87081-053-7

CONTENTS

v

INTRODUCTION

Many years ago I became convinced that all social sciences were fundamentally studying the same thing, which is the social system, though, of course, from different points of view. Since that time I have put a lot of work and effort in trying to find that "same thing." This volume is one fruit of that effort.

Almost as a byproduct of this activity I got involved in general systems, which in a sense is an attempt to discover the basic underlying patterns of the "same thing" that all the sciences are studying. Out of this enteprise emerged the Society for General Systems Research, which continues to prosper. The enterprise of establishing a general social science has never found a similar institutional framework and continues as the amiable eccentricity of a handful of individual social scientists.

Whatever general social science it may be that emerges from this volume may be summarized very briefly. In the first place it must be dynamic, that is, a perception of patterns of the four-dimensional space-time continuum in society. Equilibrium I am firmly convinced is unknown in the real world in any field. It is valuable only as a heuristic device and as a substitute for something better that is not available, that is, real dynamics, though its value in this respect is not to be despised. An equilibrium model should always be seen as a special case of a more general dynamic model and the real world as a profoundly disequilibrium system in continuous dynamic process. There are several kinds of dynamic models, such as simple mechanical ones like celestial mechanics and econometrics, cybernetic models which include feedback either stabilizing or destabilizing, which lead into open systems, equifinality, or teleological models guided by images of the future, and so on. Random elements are very important in social systems and cannot be left out. Whether there is "real" randomness I will leave to the philosophers; that there is epistemological randomness, that is, uncertainty, no one can deny. Hence, all dynamic models become less secure as we move them further into the future and I hold very strongly that the best way to prepare for the future is to prepare to be surprised.

Evolutionary models also have great applicability to social systems and I am at present working on a book which seeks to explore how far the neo-Darwinian evolutionary models can be applied to society. Ecological models are, of course, simply a subset of evolutionary models. Dialectical processes I hold have a somewhat limited application and tend to be dominated by evolutionary processes. This is the main argument in my book, *A Primer on Social Dynamics* (The Free Press, 1970).

I distinguish three major subsystems of society, which I have called the threat system, the exchange system, and the integrative system (Chapter 13). These, of course, all interact but are distinct enough to be identified as threads in the fabric. Political science I regard mainly as the study of legitimated threat, economics as the study of legitimated exchange, sociology as primarily the study of the integrative system, though it gets into generalized exchange and more subtle forms of threat. The social system tends to be dominated by images, that is, cognitive structures, especially by images of the future, which act cybernetically, constantly guided by perceived divergences between the real and the ideal. The dynamics of society, therefore, can be summed up very largely as human learning. This in turn is dominated by the demographic processes of birth, death, and the transplanting of images from one generation to the next. Values and preferences play a critical role in this process, for in the human race for the most part these are not genetically given but are learned, which increases the complexity of the system enormously. In the learning process cognitive structures grow towards values which themselves are learned. Economic growth, for instance, is largely a learning process; capital is merely human knowledge imposed on the physical world.

As I read over this volume it does seem to hang together. There is inevitably some repetition, especially in the later chapters, but in the great phrase from Alice in Wonderland, "What I tell you three times is true." In a sense the capstone, which is a general theory of social evolution, to which this whole volume is a prelude, is missing, but this I am chiseling away at now.

Again, I would like to thank Professor Larry Singell for his untiring labors in editing these volumes.

Boulder, Colorado 1974   Kenneth E. Boulding

A CONCEPTUAL FRAMEWORK
FOR SOCIAL SCIENCE

Papers, Mich. Acad. of Sci., Arts and Letters,
37 (1952): 275-282

A CONCEPTUAL FRAMEWORK FOR SOCIAL SCIENCE

THE noble concept of the unification of science has always attracted the imaginative thinker. It is a concept, however, which has proved disappointing, and perhaps even positively dangerous in practice. It has led either to grandiose overall systems like those of Bacon and Compte, which remain empty because the bulging and slatternly corpus of knowledge obstinately refuses to fit the neat corsets of the system builders, or it has led to something much more dangerous—pseudo-systems which have been satisfying to the mind without being sufficiently true to reality. The Aristotelian system was one such. In the social sciences there are the Marxian system and also that of Veblen. Both these represent premature syntheses in social science—integrations of bad economics, bad sociology and anthropology, bad political science. Nevertheless, because they are syntheses they exert remarkable power over the minds of men, to the ultimate detriment of intellectual progress. They are comfortable mental inns on the long dark road of knowledge; it is little wonder that men seek their warmth and shelter, and that they settle down in them and refuse to continue their journey.

For all its dangers, however, the impulse to integrate will not be denied. It may well be that we move fastest along our narrow specialized trails. Still, the trails are converging. There are three signs of this convergence. One is the development of hybrid specializations. In the natural sciences, for instance, physical chemistry developed between physics and chemistry some three or four generations ago; biochemistry, biophysics, astrophysics, and geophysics are latecomers. In the social sciences the first hybrid to develop was social psychology (political economy, alas, was stillborn), and there are signs that we may be on the threshold of separate disciplines of economic sociology, economic psychology, and political psychology. The second sign of convergence is the development of applied fields which cut across the specialized disciplines. Labor relations, for instance, is a field which cuts across economics, sociology, social psychology, psychology, law, political science, and engineering. International relations is a field which cuts across economics, political science, social psychology, sociology, and law. In the process of contributing to an applied field the specialized disciplines can hardly avoid contributing to one another. Finally, even in pure theory there are signs of increasing dissatisfaction with the narrow models of the pure disciplines. Especially is this true in economics, where we are beginning to realize, for instance, that the firm is not merely an economic institution maximizing profit, but is a complex social organism with sociological, psychological, and political aspects which must be brought into view if an adequate theory is to be developed. All these signs suggest that the time may be approaching when, in spite of the dangers involved, a new attempt at synthesis needs to be made. It is not the purpose of this short paper to make such a synthesis! Nevertheless, some lines may be indicated along which a synthesis seems to be growing.

The theoretical structure of virtually every science consists of, first, a theory of some *individual*, which is the basic unit of study of the science, and, secondly, a theory of *interaction* among these individuals. The individual is the unit of behavior of the science, behavior being defined as the change in the individual in response to changes in its environment. Thus the physicist studies electrons; the chemist, atoms and molecules; the biologist, cells, organs, and organisms; the psychologist, organisms in terms of their behavior as aggregates; the sociologist, groups, families, and churches; the economist, firms and banks; the political scientist, towns, counties, and states. The study of the behavior of individuals in response to changes in their environment inevitably leads to the study of *interaction*, for the environment of any one individual consists of other individuals. Behavior, therefore, is always interaction; a change in one individual constitutes a change in the environment of others, which in turn constitutes a change in the environment of the first.

There is emerging from a great many different sciences something like a general theory of an individual, or of behavior on the one hand and a general theory of interaction on the other. By this I do not mean that we expect to find a *single* theory into which individuals as diverse as electrons, molecules, cells, rats, men, families, nations, philosophies, poems, and universes can all be put. Such a theory would either have to be so general as to be contentless or it would be a strait-jacket into which reality would have to be forced. What is emerging is not a single theory of immense generality, but, rather, a continuum or a spectrum of theoretical structures and concepts—not necessarily in one dimension—in which the theoretical structure of one science overlaps with those of related sciences, and all throw some sort of light on one another. In a similar way I believe a general structure of the theory of interaction is likewise beginning to emerge from a number of different sciences.

At the base of the theory of the individual is the concept of behavior itself, that is, of predictable change in response to a controlled environment. At the level of physics and chemistry even the definition and the taxonomy of the individual are determined not by direct observation but by a study of behavior; what is observed is usually an entirely different thing from the individuals (e.g. atoms, electrons, protons, and mesons) which are being studied. Nobody has ever observed an atom, much less one of the smaller particles; their existence is inferred from certain regular patterns of behavior, and their classification depends not on the direct observation of differences in appearance but on the observation of differences in behavior. This is true largely even at the level of cytology and bacteriology; the taxonomy of bacteria depends mainly on their reactions rather than on their appearance through a microscope. As we rise in the scale of complexity of the individual the taxonomic structure comes to rest more and more on direct observation, and less on reaction; nevertheless, there is a question here whether the significant taxonomies do not always rest on reaction classifications and whether the purely observational taxonomies in the biological and social sciences are not sometimes misleading.

Probably the next most general concept which is encountered in the theory of the individual is that of homeostasis, that is, the interpretation of behavior in terms of some equilibrium state which the individual "seeks" to maintain. The theory of valency in physical chemistry is an example of this principle at a very simple level, that is, an interpretation of the behavior of atoms or ions in terms of stable electron rings. At the level of the biological organism the concept is most illuminating. Even at the simplest levels of life the behavior of the organism in response to changes in its environment can be interpreted largely in terms of the attempt to restore an optimum condition in physical and chemical terms. As we rise in the scale of complexity the number of "homeostatic" mechanisms in the organism ever increases, until in the human body their number runs into dozens—or, if we count mental processes, perhaps into hundreds. Thus we have equilibrium values of such variables as body temperature, blood count, sugar concentration, water concentration, acidity, and calcium concentration; a disturbance from the equilibrium value due to a shift in the external environment sets off a chain of reactions which have the effect of insulating the body, and especially the most delicate structures, such as the brain, from these external changes. If we go into a cold room our teeth chatter, we stamp up and down

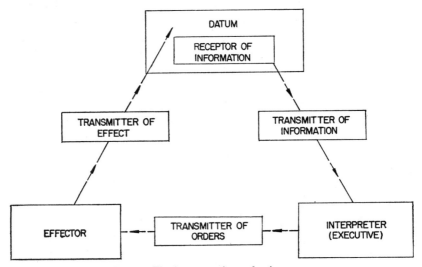

FIG. 1. The homeostatic mechanism

and so on—exercises some of which are involuntary, and some semivoluntary, but all of which are designed to release heat from the muscles. If we go into a hot room we become lassitudinous, the sweat glands open, respiration increases and so on—all these reactions being designed to cool us off.

Any homeostatic mechanism requires six parts, as shown in Figure 1. There must first be the *datum*—the object of stabilization. Suppose we take as an example the homeostatic control of house temperature by a thermostat. The datum in this case is the temperature of the air around the thermostat. Secondly, there must be a *receptor* of information about the datum—the thermostat itself. There must be a *transmitter of information* from the receptor to an *interpreter*—in this case the wire connecting the thermostat to the furnace control. There must likewise be a transmitter from the inter- preter of the information to an *effector* (the furnace) and a transmitter of the effect from the effector (the pipes and radiators) back to the datum. Then, if there is a divergence between the actual and the equilibrium value of the datum, this information is received and trans- mitted to the interpreter, which sets in motion the effector, which affects the datum in a direction calculated to diminish the divergence between the actual and the ideal value. Thus, if the house is cold (temperature below the set value), the thermostat registers this fact, transmits it to the furnace control, which sets the furnace in motion, which heats up the house; if the house is too hot, the thermostat registers this information, transmits it to the control, and shuts off the furnace. The mechanism may, of course, be much more complex than this, even in such a simple thing as a furnace control, but the system described is the basic element in all such arrangements, and anything which can be described as an organism, whether biological or social, will have arrangements of this kind.

I shall give two examples from the social sciences—the firm and the state. The firm is an organism consisting of an interpreter (the executive), who receives information through the accounting system, the budget system, the market-research system, Kiplinger letters, gossip on the golf course, and so on. As a result of his interpretation of this information certain decisions are made which are transmitted to the production and sales organizations and result in certain actions. These actions produce effects on the datum (sales, prices, and profits), which in turn are picked up by the receptors and trans- mitted to the executive as information, which again produce decisions. The simplest possible theory of the firm is the theory of "homeostasis of the balance sheet," in which we suppose that there is some compo- sition of the balance sheet which the firm wishes to maintain. Then changes in the data, occasioned, for instance, by sales of goods, are transmitted to the effector in the form of a message to *replace* (by production) the goods sold; this replacement restores both the goods and the money items in the balance sheet to their initial level.

At the political level we can suppose also that there is some "state" of an organism, such as a nation, at which discontent is a minimum.

A divergence from this happy condition results in discontent, which is eventually transmitted through the political and constitutional machinery into a need for action on the part of government (the effector)—the action presumably being directed toward reducing the discontent and restoring the body politic to contentment.

It should be observed that every homeostatic mechanism involves cycles. The amplitude of the cycle depends mainly on the sensitivity of the mechanism. If the mechanism is highly insensitive, large cycles will be set up because of the lag between the receptor and the effector. If some elements of the system are too sensitive, there is also a possibility of large cycles; generally, however, most cycles are the result of inadequate sensitivity. Thus the many cycles which are observed in economic and social life may be regarded as the result of an inadequate homeostatic mechanism; the so-called business cycle is largely a result of inadequate homeostatic mechanism in the monetary and fiscal system; the "war cycle" is a result of the absence of homeostatic mechanisms in international relations; the cycle of liberal and conservative governments in a two-party system may also be regarded as a homeostatic cycle.

Homeostasis does not, of course, exhaust the theory of the individual; indeed, it represents only the very first approximation. We cannot be content with merely observing that some state is maintained; we must raise the question of *what* state is maintained. Answers to this question involve problems of growth and decay, of learning and accretion, of survival and evolutionary development. Such questions arise in connection with almost any organism, from the simplest biological organism to the most complex social organization. The social sciences have given far too little attention to them; especially is this true of economics, where the theory of the firm remains at a level of static equilibrium (maximization), is only just beginning to advance toward a theory of a homeostatic mechanism, and has scarcely begun to include theories of growth and decay life cycles, and learning. It is hardly an exaggeration to say that in the world of the economists man never learns anything; he just knows it already. Thus there is practically no discussion in economic literature with which I am familiar of how business men become aware of the nature of the demand which faces them.

I now pass on to the second broad field of theory in which integration seems to be taking place; this is in the study of the interaction of individuals and populations of individuals. In the study of individual behavior we assume that the environment is given, independent of the individual himself, and that we can examine the response of the individual to changes in that environment without worrying about the effect of this response on the environment itself. Where the individual is small in relation to his environment, this aspect of behavior is usually sufficient. Where, however, we are considering a whole system, and especially when there are few individuals interacting, we must recognize that the environment of each individual consists of other individuals, and that each individual itself comprises part of the environment of others. Ecology is the general science which studies these interactions, that is, which studies whole systems of individuals. Its general principles apply not only to biological systems but also to social systems. Any system, in fact, which can be regarded as a system of interacting populations can be regarded as an ecosystem. The general theory of such systems is formally quite simple, though the topology of particular systems may present numerous difficulties. If there are n populations, $x_1, x_2 \ldots x_n$, interacting, we simply write the equilibrium magnitude of each population as a function of the size of all the others. This gives us immediately a set of n equations which can theoretically be solved for the n unknowns to give a general equilibrium value for each population. There may, of course, be various restrictions placed on the solution; we may not admit negative values, for instance, zero being the lower boundary of each variable, or there may be lower boundaries established by "niches" which shelter some populations from the rigors of interaction.

These complexities, however, are nothing compared with the complexities introduced when the interaction is not direct, in the sense that the responses are to changes in the present environment, but indirect in the sense that the responses are to uncertain expected future changes in the environment. This is a problem which rarely if ever arises in the biological sciences, since it is essentially a phenomenon of consciousness—even of a fairly advanced level of consciousness. In human interaction, however, the problem of uncertainty and anticipation must be faced; the environment to which an individual reacts is not merely an external but an internal, subjective environment. It is at this level that we run into the type of problem considered in the economic theory of oligopoly or, more generally, in the theory of games.   It is clearly of enormous importance in political science and in the study of group interaction of any kind.   Unfortunately, the difficulty of the subject is at least as great as its importance; still, it is a rapidly developing field and holds great promise for the future.

I am not proposing this twofold scheme of the theory of the individual on the one hand and of interaction on the other as a complete framework for all science, or even for all social science; there are many studies which do not easily fit into it, especially in psychology. I believe, however, that, like the framework provided by the periodic table in chemistry, it may serve to point up new directions of inquiry by providing a structure in which there are some obvious missing segments.   I have found this to be true in my own field of economics.   I would be surprised if it is not true of others.

THE PRINCIPLE OF PERSONAL RESPONSIBILITY

Rev. Soc. Economy, 12, 1 (Mar. 1954): 1-8

THE PRINCIPLE OF PERSONAL RESPONSIBILITY

If we were to seek the one thing on which all those who count themselves Christians agree, it is that the greatest of the Christian virtues is love. Love is the heart of the Gospel, the essence of salvation, the most precious attribute of God. It is when we come to interpret the meaning of love in daily life, however, that we run into the dilemmas and the disagreements. For Christian love is not merely an emotion, an agreeable warmness or liking for people and things, even though its emotional attributes must not be neglected. We are commanded to love all men, even our enemies, but we clearly cannot feel the same depth of emotion towards all the two billion inhabitants of the earth that we feel to those who are near to us. Even in terms of intimate relationships the meaning of love is not always clear — where, for instance, in our relationships with our children, between total permissiveness and authoritarianism is the best expression of parental love? When we come to consider the less intimate relationships of economic life — our relationships with the butcher and baker, the sales clerk and cleaning lady, the employee and the boss, the income tax collector and the far-away state, the problem of the right expression of love in action becomes even more difficult. Still more difficult is the question of our relationship with those millions of the unseen who serve us and whom we serve in the vast web of commercial relations — the coffee grower of Brazil, the sheep rancher of Australia, the tin miner of Bolivia. In a simpler day one's "neighbor" was literally someone who was "near" and most economic connections involved personal contact. Today the world has become a neighborhood, thanks to improvements in com-

munications; but in very consequence of this the simple ethics of
neighborhoodliness have become less adequate to deal with its problems. We affect, and are affected by, the actions of people we neither
see nor know. Under these circumstances not only is it difficult to
feel love for these blank faces; but even if we persuaded ourselves to
feel, what *difference* would this feeling make to our actions? This is a
critical and indeed an embarrassing question for those of us who profess to be moved by Christian love, for if there is no way of expres-
sing this love in action, and if it makes no difference to our behavior,
then it is a false emotion hardly removed from self-deception.

One attempt to reduce the unmanageable claims to love to reasonable dimensions is through attempts to define and limit responsibility.
The idea of responsibility is certainly not to be identified with love, but
perhaps it is a reasonable first approximation, especially in dealing with
the complex relationships of economic life. Or if we look at the matter
from the point of view of different levels of abstraction we may say
that responsibility implies a certain extension of self, in that we are
concerned for the welfare of others as well as for ourselves; and it is
precisely this extension of self which is implied in the concept of love.
Love and responsibility do not imply, it should be observed, pure altruism. We are not commanded to love our neighbor and hate ourselves,
but to love our neighbor *as* ourselves. Indeed one sometimes suspects
that the love of these miserable selves of ours, whose ugliness and
weakness we know all too well, is much harder than the love of our
superficially attractive neighbors!

We must beware, however, of two different meanings of the term
"responsibility." Responsibility *to* someone is a very different thing
from responsibility *for* someone. The latter might be called *internal* responsibility. It rests on an inner sense of concern for the other person
and at least a partial identification of his interest with ours, a sharing of
his joys and sorrows. Responsibility *to* someone is a very different
matter. We might call it *external* responsibility. This concerns the
ultimate locus of power and the structure of organization. We are responsible *to* the people who can put us out of our job if we don't satisfy them!

Responsibility *to* may be thought of in both formal and real terms.
Confusion of thought frequently arises because the real power relationships in society do not correspond very closely to the formal structure
of organization. Thus in an American university the formal power relationships generally flow from the trustees or governors to the presi-

dent to the deans to the department heads to the faculty. The president is formally responsible to the trustees, the deans to the president, and so on. Formally, therefore, the president is not responsible to the faculty, as he is, say, in an Oxford college. Nevertheless one suspects that the informal power structures do not differ very greatly in widely differing formal types of institutions, and that in fact an American university president has little more power over, and is almost as much subject to opinion of his faculty as, say, the Warden of All Souls. If I may venture an even more delicate example, if we compare the actual power structures in episcopal and congregational forms of church organization, which formally are so different, we might find them much more similar than the formal difference would suggest. Authority, Chester Barnard has argued, is granted from below and not from above. The cycnic might argue that advancement in episcopal churches comes by pleasing the Bishop and in congregation churches by pleasing the people; but in fact the parish priest who outrages his congregation is likely to find himself unpopular with the Bishop, and the congregational minister who outrages the leaders of his denomination is likely to find himself in trouble with his congregation.

I do not want to suggest, however, that formal responsibility is unimportant. Indeed, the central point of my argument is that one of the principal objectives of political structures, customs, and organizations is to identify the various forms of responsibility. That is to say, it is desirable that we should be responsible *to*, in both a formal and an informal sense, those whom we are responsible *for*. I do not put this forward as a single absolute objective, for there may be other objectives of social and political organization which compete with it, and a due balance must be struck. Nevertheless I suggest that this is one objective which must be considered in the evaluation of organizational structures, and one which has a high ethical content. If we are responsible for, but not responsible to any group of people the relationship is both difficult and dangerous. Even if we are men of the utmost good will the relationship can easily degenerate into an insensitive paternalism which either corrupts or drives to revolt those in subordinate positions. If we are not men of good will the relationship can easily descend into the blackest tyranny. But the important point is that good will itself is not necessarily enough to protect us from the dangers of inadequate or improper organization. In the highest sense love can only exist between equals, and when we attempt to exercise love towards inferiors, or towards those who are unreservedly in our power, or towards those in whose power we are, the relationship falls short of the highest ideal, and becomes at best pity or submissiveness, and at worst sentimentality and toadying. And while I would not want for a moment to deny that there are real virtues which are less than love, it is important not to mistake them for love.

The implications and ramifications of the theory of responsibility outlined above would carry us into all spheres of human life, and cannot be developed in a short paper. It leads clearly in the direction of non-authoritarianism in family life, and towards democratic institutions in political life. The main concern of this paper, however, is with economic life. What, especially, is the significance of the institution of the market in regard to the responsibility of the individual both to and for the people who are affected by his decisions, and what is the relation of the structure of economic responsibility to the structure of economic power?

I shall argue, perhaps with some appearance of paradox, that the market under conditions approaching pure competition is an institution of high ethical value, in that it provides a check on concentrations of economic power and goes a long way towards accomplishing that union of responsibility and power which I have put forward as a prime object of human organization. I shall also argue, however, that the institutions of the market, and the kind of behavior which is involved in commercial life, are inadequate to generate the *motivations* of responsibility and of concern for others which are both desirable in themselves and necessary as a cement of the social fabric.

Consider for a moment the difference between an institution like a business enterprise which exists primarily in a market environment, and an institution like a state, an army, or an established national church which does not. The prime difference between them is that the former must depend for its survival on the voluntary cooperation of the individuals who are related to it, whether as workers, capitalists, suppliers, or customers, whereas the latter depends for its survival on its power to coerce individuals into cooperating with it. This is the old controversy between the carrot and the stick. The "market" organization survives, if it does, because of its power to persuade those related to it that it "pays" them to continue the relationship. It must attract workers by offering them at least as good wages and conditions of work as they can get elsewhere. It must attract customers by offering them goods or services as good and cheap as they can get elsewhere. It must attract investors by offering them a rate of return at least as good as they can get in comparable occupations. And in a well-operating free market there is always an "elsewhere" — this is the essence of the concept of pure competition as the economist understands it, and this is how competition limits the power of the organiser or the entrepreneur. In a very real sense, therefore, the business man is responsible *to* those persons who are affected by his actions, in the sense that he is in their power as much as they are in his. If he cannot offer workers the "going wage" or consumer the "going price" he will not be able to attract them to his shop. A market-determined organization therefore can only survive by satisfying human wants — at least those wants which can be expressed through the market. The organization must be *serviceable,* at least in this restricted sense, if it is to survive.

There are, of course, important qualifications of this too-optimistic view of the market, with which most economists are familiar. Monopoly (or monopsony) represents a kind of knot, kink, or distortion in the general field of economic relationships, or a toll-gate in the network of economic communications which enables some individuals to capture and exploit power-positions which otherwise competitive forces would erode away. Furthermore needs are not quite the same thing as wants, especially those wants which can be expressed in the market. There are collective needs which are unsuited to market expression, and for this reason government — and a tax system — is necessary in spite of the inevitable element of coercion involved. Indeed Baumol[1] has suggested that there might be a species of "voluntary coercion," where we have something (like paying taxes) which we are all willing to do if everybody does it but are not willing to do *unless* everybody does it.

It is also true that there are substitutes for the market environment in the case of political organization like states, and that political democracy can best be understood in these terms. There is a world of difference between the absolute state, whether of Louis XIV or of Malenkov, in which the citizen has virtually no choice of rulers and no say in decisions, and the democratic state in which the citizen can lawfully depose his rulers and can write indignant, and frequently effective letters to his congressman. The vote of the citizenry is the "market" for the product of the democratic state, and it plays much the same role in modifying the power of the state that the consumers or the labor market does in modifying the power of the business man. The congressman is "responsible to" his constituents because they have

[1] W. J. Baumol, *Welfare Economics and the Theory of the State.* Harvard, 1952.

the power to throw him out of office at the next election. Similarly the business man is in a sense "responsible to" his workers and his customers because they likewise have the power to throw him out of office by shopping elsewhere. In the latter case the power is not so visible, and hence not so well understood, as it results in a removal of the office from the businessman rather than the removal of the businessman from office; but it comes to the same sort of thing.

One value of this way of looking at things is that it points to the "politicising" of business through the rise of labor unions, collective bargaining, "co-determination" and so on as in a sense a *substitute* for the market. These things are most likely to arise therefore in periods when the market as an institution is functioning poorly, either because of monopoly or because of deflation and depression. If the worker *cannot* get a job elsewhere he feels acutely his inferior power position and is strongly motivated towards unionism as a "countervailing power." Thus unionism can be regarded as an attempt to make employers responsible *to* their workers, or in other words to put the workers in a better power position *vis a vis* the employer. It must be pointed out however that an active labor market does much the same thing, and that if it had not been for the inability of capitalist economies to maintain continuous active labor markets over the past hundred years or so the motivation for the rise of the labor movement would have been much weaker. One interesting and difficult question in this regard is whether in the dynamic processes of society the attempts to provide political substitutes for the market do not themselves weaken the ability of the market to function properly, and so set up a social dynamic process which will eventually eliminate the market. This is the basis of the "Schumpetrian pessimism" about the future of capitalism. All one can say I think is that the pessimistic view is at least not proven, and that we still have opportunities to find a set of institutions which will stabilize the market as an institution by remedying its vices without leading to its destruction.

There is yet another, and perhaps more fundamental reason, for qualifying the optimistic view of the market as a spreader of power and allocator of responsibility. It is that market behavior and market institutions — that is, commercial life — frequently leads to the development of a type of personality which mistakes the abstractions of commerce for the realities of existence, and hence loses much of the richness of full human relationship. The exchange relationship is by its very nature abstract, and indeed it owes its success to its very power of being abstract. When we make a purchase from a store clerk we do not enter into a full and intimate relationship with him. Even the relationship of employee to employer, though it is richer and more complex than that of simple commodity exchange, is still exchange, and still falls far short of the richness and complexity, say of the marital relationship. And this is as it should be: the worker-employer relationship is not the same as the son-father relationship, and any attempt to make it so will create frustration and resentment on both sides. There must be economy in human relationship if *large* fabrics of society are to exist at all, because if we are to have relationships with *many* people these relationships must be limited and abstract rather than full. There is danger, however, in a predominantly commercial society, that people will take economic behavior as the measure of all things and will confine their relationships to those which can be conducted on the level of the commercial abstraction. To do this is to lose almost all richness or purpose in human life. He who has never loved, has never felt the call of a heroic ethic — to give and not to count the cost, to labor and not to ask for any reward — has lived far below the peak levels of human experience. Economic man dwells in Limbo — he is not good enough for Heaven or bad enough for Hell. His virtues are minor virtues: he is punctual, courteous, honest, truthful, painstakingly, thrifty, hardworking. His vices are minor vices — niggardliness, parsimoniousness, chicanery. Even the covetousness of which he is often accused is a playful and innocent thing compared with the dreadful covetousness of the proud. On the whole he escapes the deadly sins, for his very vulgarity saves him from pride (how much better, for instance, is the commercial vulgarity of Coca Cola than the heroic diabolism of Hitler). But he misses also the Great Virtue, and in that he is less than Man, for God has made man for himself, and he has an ineradicable hunger for the Divine, the heroic, the sanctified and the uneconomic.

What this means, I think, is that if the market is to be a stable and fruitful institution in society it must be hedged around with other insitutions of a non-market character—the home and the school and the church. For here and only here can the *motive* of responsibility develop. It is only as we are ourselves loved — by our parents, our mentors, and by our God — that we gain the capacity to love. "We love Him because he first loved us" is no pious platitude; it is one of the deepest truths of life and existence. It is the great task of economic and political institutions to place limitations on power, that we may be checked when we are moved to evil. But these institutions are not adequate to move us towards good. We must achieve the right distribution of power, so that power does not corrupt the will. But we must also grow towards the right will, which is His Will. This I conceive to be the great earthly task of religion; not so much to prevent us from doing wrong as to make us eager to will the good.

NOTES ON THE INFORMATION CONCEPT

Exploration (Toronto, Ont.), 6 (1955): 103-112

NOTES ON THE INFORMATION CONCEPT

The first question I wish to raise in this paper is the relation of the information or 'message' concept to the concept of 'knowledge'. It is clear, I think, that we cannot regard knowledge as simply the accumulation of information in a stockpile, even though all messages that are received by the brain may leave some sort of deposit there. Knowledge must itself be regarded as a structure, a very complex and frequently quite loose pattern, almost like an enormous molecule, with its parts connected in various ways by ties of varying degrees of strength. Messages are continually shot into this structure; some of them pass right through its interstices (in at one ear and out the other) without effecting any perceptible change in it. Sometimes messages 'stick' to the structure and become part of it. Thus the message 'the King is dead', if it is believed, will 'stick' in the sense that it becomes part of the structure and will be given out (without, of course, ceasing to be part of the structure) when the appropriate question is asked. Rote learning especially is of this nature. When a student 'learns' that Washington is the capital of the United States we mean, no doubt among other things, that if asked in an examination what is the capital of the United States he will reply 'Washington'. One of the most interesting questions in educational theory and practice is under what conditions does information 'stick' in this way, and under what conditions does it fail to 'take hold' of the structure of knowledge.

There is, however, another possible impact of messages on knowledge which might be called 'reorganization'. Occasionally a message does not merely stick to the structure, but hits some 'nucleus' that knocks the props out of a large area of the structure and effects a very radical re-organization of the mental structure itself. This 'mental structure' which I have called 'knowledge' is the subjective 'perception of the world and one's place in it'—perception not in the sense that everything in the structure is immediately and presently perceived, but in the sense that it can be recalled if necessary. Normally the messages received do not change the basic pattern of the structure. Indeed, there is a lot of evidence that the structure itself may be thought of as exhibiting 'homeostasis'—that is it *resists* change, and is deaf to messages which conflict with its pattern. Anyone holding a strong belief or prejudice reacts to messages which conflict with this belief by *disbelief of the message* rather than by readjustment of his mental structure. Occasionally however a message which is inconsistent with the basic pattern of the mental structure, but which is of such a nature that it cannot be dis-believed hits the structure, which is then forced to undergo a complete reorganization. In this way a very small 'cause' can produce very large 'effects' if the conditions are right. Thus a man who has an old and trusted friend may find a letter or overhear a conversation which reveals that the friend is in fact deceiving him; a man who has devoted his life to a particular theory may come across information which is incontro-vertibly inconsistent with it. In such cases radical re-structurings of 'knowledge'—that is, the way in which the universe appears to be and operate—are likely to occur.

Some light is thrown on the problem of the impact of messages on the knowledge structure by a theory of signal detection recently developed by a group of mathematicians and psychologists at the University of Michigan. The problem is one of great interest and universality. A 'signal' is a non-random event set in the middle of a succession of random events (noise). All events, however, are events: they do not come along with tags around them saying 'I am a signal' or 'I am a random event'. The problem therefore of how to tell when any given event is random is a difficult one, and indeed is incapable of exact solution. The most we can do is to discuss the probability of detection as related to the probability of a 'false alarm'. In general there are four possible situ-ations relating a detector to a signal: (1) He may say there is a signal when there is one (a hit); (2) he may say there is a signal when there isn't (a false alarm); (3) he may say there isn't a signal when there is (a miss); (4) he may say there isn't a signal when there isn't (a negative hit, or a correct rejection). It can then be shown that for any given level of intensity of the signal relative to the noise by which it is surrounded there is a function relating the probability of a hit with the probably of a false alarm under 'optimum' behaviour. This is called by Tanner the 'signal detection curve'. The cautious operator will get few hits, but will also give few false alarms; the reckless operator will get many hits, but will also give many false alarms. It can also be shown that the degree of 'recklessness'—that is, the position of the detector on the signal detection curve—depends not only on the intrinsic probability of the presence of the signal but on the 'payoffs' (relative rewards and penalties) associated with the four possibilities. The detector will be more reckless the greater the intrinsic probability that the signal is present, the smaller the rewards for correct rejections and the smaller the penalties for false alarms, and the greater the rewards for hits and the penalties for misses.

The implications of this theory for many fields of inquiry are startling, yet seem to be inescapable. In the theory of perception it destroys the notion of a clear psychophysical 'threshhold' of signal intensity above which the signal is perceived and below which it is not. All perception is only probable, and the greater the probability of hits the greater the probability also of false alarms. Where the signal-noise ratio is as large as it is in most ordinary experience, the probability of a hit will be very great and the probability of a false alarm very small at normal levels of cautiousness. Even here, however, extreme recklessness will produce false alarms, as the divergent testimonies of witnesses of an accident clearly show. This theory throws considerable light on the phenomenon of hallucination. In a society which believes generally in ghosts, penalties for false alarms are small and rewards for hits are large, so people see ghosts. In a rationalistic and skeptical society the rewards for perceiving, or at least for talking about mystical and non-rational experience are small, and the penalties for false alarms in this area are great, and it is little wonder that the subtler messages of the inward life are missed. Even the 'objectivity' of science is reduced to a matter of probability and payoffs, for the perception of anything cannot be divorced from the valuations which surround the act of perception. The whole concept of a 'fact' really disappears: all that is left are messages in noisy channels, and the interpretation of these messages as 'facts' depends in part on the value system of the observer.

Thus the above theory has important implications both for the problem of the validity of knowledge (which is the basic problem of epistemology) and for the problem of the validity of ideals (which is the basic problem of ethics) and also for the problem of the viability of organizations, which in a way is the basic problem of politics.

What I have called 'knowledge' up to this point is 'what somebody thinks he knows'. A question naturally arises as to whether it makes sense to ask if 'what a person thinks he knows' is 'true'—that is, in terms of the simple model, whether any concept of correspondence can be developed between the subjective mental structure and something to which it relates outside. In terms of the simple model this may reduce to the question of whether it is the whole system which exhibits homeostasis. Thus in the simple example of a thermostat, the 'control' gives its directions to the furnace in accordance with its 'perception' of the nature of the divergence between the actual and the ideal value of the temperature. Suppose now that the control itself gets disconnected from the receptor, or suppose that the control exhibits great insensitivity to messages received, or gets 'reckless' and gives many false alarms, so that it continues to 'believe' that the temperature is 'too low' and so continues to give orders for heat even when in fact the temperature is 'too high'. Here we have an example of homeostasis of the 'subjective knowledge' rather than of the system as a whole, and such a system is unlikely to be viable—i.e., because of its failure to maintain homeostasis in the 'real' variables these variables may exceed the critical limits beyond which the system may not survive—the house may burn up or the angry householder may call a repairman and disconnect the erring control.

There are really two problems (at least) involved here: one is the question of the correspondence between 'subjective' and 'objective' knowledge as perceived by some outside observer—the difficulty here being that the subject's subjective knowledge can only be derived by a response of some kind—i.e., has to be inferred—and the factors which lead to 'erroneous' knowledge may also lead to 'erroneous' response. There is the famous story of the 'talking horses' which were in fact motivated by slight movements of the trainer, not by understanding the questions. When the trainer 'asked' the horses whether they in fact understood the questions of course they said 'yes!' The other question, which may be easier to solve and is not, I think wholly unrelated to the first, is what is the optimum degree of sensitivity or ability to maintain homeostasis of the 'subjective knowledge' structure itself from the point of view of the viability or survival potentiality of the whole organization. It is clear that there can be both too much and too little sensitivity to message input: if we 'believe' every message (i.e., adjust our subjective knowledge structure accordingly) this is optimum for the whole system only if the messages are uniformly reliable (i.e., if there is no 'noise' or other distortion in the receptor or the receptor-control channel).

If the messages that come to the control are not wholly reliable it may have to develop a capacity for 'criticism'—*i.e.*, the ability to select the impact of messages on its knowledge structure. This is a most important characteristic of the human organism, and indeed of almost all living organizations, and one where they are clearly superior to the thermostat! We are constantly rejecting or reinterpreting the messages which come to us by the senses: we do not belive that a stick in a glass of water is 'really' bent, we do not (if we are educated) believe that the sun 'really' goes round the earth every day, we do not (if we are nice people) believe every evil report about our friends, and so on. Some degree of permanence in the knowledge structure is clearly desirable, or the world would dissolve into a heap of incoherent impressions—automobiles would get bigger as they approach us, rooms would change shape as we walked through them, people around us would dissolve into shapes and noises, and the world would become a nightmare of chaos. Too much homeostasis on the part of the knowledge structure again however is not optimum—the blind who lead the blind fall into the ditch they did not know was 'there'. It must be emphasized that the notion of an optimum degree of sensitivity of the knowledge structure, useful as it may be, begs some of the ultimate metaphysical questions, and is not even a sufficient model on the level of simple observation, but it is at least a place to start from in the analysis.

Signal detection theory throws some light on this problem of the 'critique of messages', in that it points to the importance of the value or 'payoff' structure in determining the conditions under which messages will affect the knowledge structure. If the rearrangement of our knowledge structure is in itself painful, as it frequently is, a strong bias is given towards *not* detecting signals which involve such rearrangements if detected. From the point of view of the viability of the organization we can postulate that there is some 'optimum' payoff subjective structure. Divergence from this optimum weakens the organization, in that it distorts the detection of signals away from that which is most likely to maintain the organization. The inherent instability of dictatorship, for instance, arises because the dictator is apt to impose severe penalties for messages which do not conform to his own knowledge structure, and hence neither receives them nor hears them, even though they may be of vital importance to his survival. It is a most dangerous business for an executive to surround himself with yes-men.

Our present difficulties in regard to Communism may also be interpreted in part with this theory. We seem to be proceeding on the assumption that the penalties for false alarms are very slight (that is, that it does not much matter if we say that people are dangerous when they are not) and that the penalties for misses are very great (saying that people are not dangerous when in fact they are). Consequently we are in danger of raising so many false alarms that we destroy our own internal morale and security because of a false estimate of the payoff structure. A similar problem faces us in the control of economic fluctuations. Random ups and downs (noise) occurs in all economic series. The question is when do we interpret a given movement as a 'depression' necessitating action. This is actually a surprisingly difficult problem—there have been quite severe depressions which even experts did not recognize as such until they were almost over. By and large the labour groups feel that penalties for false alarms (saying there is a depression when there isn't, and hence probably falling into some inflation) are slight, whereas the penalties for a miss (saying there isn't a depression when there is, and so falling into unemployment) are great. Business groups and especially rentier groups are more apt to feel that the penalties for a false alarm are heavy, and for a miss are not so great. The difference in the perception and in the policies advocated by these groups can largely be attributed to these differences in the subjective payoff structures.

In the explanation of the *development* of organizations, their homeostatic mechanisms and their payoff structures, models of adaptive or revolutionary change must play an important role. There are at least two such models; the evolutionary model of mutation and natural selection familiar in biology, and the 'adaptive mechanism' model based on the assumption of step functions which has been developed by W. R. Ashby in *Design for a Brain*. It is difficult to put any predictive content into the natural selection model because of its extreme dependence on hindsight—the 'survival of the fittest' after all means only the survival of the surviving if 'fitness' is simply fitness to survive, and the idea has little content unless survival value can be spelled out in terms of other variables or characteristics of a system. This is not the place to try to put content into evolutionary theory; nevertheless two interesting propositions may be suggested which throw some light on the development of communication among organisms. Any ecological system tends to set up cycles in the populations of its components. Unless its population cycles are damped a species is in grave danger of extinction, simply because there is a 'point of no return' on a downswing which may be reached if, for instance, conditions worsen suddenly while the population is at an ebb. An important element in the damping of these cycles, or in raising them above the danger level, and therefore an important element in the survival of a species, is the development of redundancy or 'playfulness' in its behaviour patterns—*i.e.*, the development of activity of a ritualistic nature which makes no direct contribution to the business of physical survival—food getting, breeding, and so on. The play of animals, the courtship of birds, the somnolence of reptiles and the innumerable ritualistic activities of man may therefore make an important contribution to the survival of the species, simply because they give it a kind of 'reserve' to fall back on when conditions get bad. A species on the other hand that devotes all its available time and energy to the serious business of food, shelter, and breeding may increase in numbers to the point where a sudden worsening of conditions wipes it out completely. This is a principle, oddly enough, which was familiar to the classical economists, for both Ricardo and Malthus pointed out that it was only the existence of conventional luxuries in the subsistence level which prevented the growth of the human population to the level of sheer animal survival.

It has been suggested that communication and language itself arose as a 'redundancy' and turned out to have survival value on that account as well as on account of the extension of organization which it permits. Be that as it may, it is also true that the survival of organizations may depend on the development of redundancy in their communications channels. Any crisis in an organization requires a great extension of internal communication if the crisis is to be overcome. An organization therefore in which there are no informal relationships, no chit-chat and small talk, no redundancy in intercourse and in which the communication channels are filled close to capacity with their normal loads will find that it is thrown into confusion and anarchy when a crisis demands an exceptional amount of internal communication which the system is not designed to take. Undercapacity operation in normal times is almost a prerequisite for the survival of crises, and an organization which is too efficient streamlines itself towards the exit.

The evolutionary model is not the only way in which we can construct models of 'adaptive mechanisms'. Ashby in *Design for a Brain* has shown with remarkable force how the introduction of 'step functions' into a model can simulate forms of adaptive behavior which are highly characteristic of living organisms. An organization in this model is thought of as a set of variables operating according to some system of dynamic relationships in a field which is *bounded* by a set of *critical values,* a critical value of a variable being one at which the whole system takes a 'step' into a new set of dynamic equations and starts off on a new tack. If this new tack carries the system to another critical value, another 'step' will be taken and the system will go off on yet another tack. This process will be repeated until the system 'finds' a set of dynamic equations which bring it to an equilibrium position *within* the range of critical values of *all* the relevant variables: within this field the system now exhibits simple homeostasis (*i.e.*, stable equilibrium), a small disturbance simply setting in motion changes in the variables which restore the equilibrium. Even if the step-processes by which the equations of the system are changed when the critical variables are reached are random an astonishing simulation of 'teleological' behaviour is engendered by the system, on the simple principle of 'if at first you don't succeed, try something different'. If now it were possible to introduce into the model a 'critical faculty' in the sense that the change in the equations of the system when the critical values are reached is not random but selective according to some principles derived from past experience, we have a model which would probably come as close to human behaviour as a model could get.

From the theory of a single organization we should go on, of course, to a theory of interaction. Here we are likely to encounter a principle of great generality—that models of interaction among many organizations can be constructed without too much difficulty, but that models of interaction among few organizations are very difficult to construct and to handle. The reason is that interaction among the many can be treated by models in which the effects of the behaviour of a single organization on its own environment can be neglected except for simple cumulative changes. Organizations can of course 'foul' their environment if their metabolic processes result in a diminution of food supply and the increase in excrement. Thus automobiles are the excrement of General Motors and labour and raw materials are its food supply, and if it is to survive it must have sewermen in the shape of a sales force and food supply in the shape of a labour market. When there are many interactors however the environment of each can be treated as passive and not as itself an organization even though it may consist in part of many other organizations. What this means I think is that the input or output of an organization from or to its environment can be treated as matter or energy and not as information—hence it follows the simple laws of cause and effect, aggregation and disaggregation: small causes produce small effects, and so on, and there is nothing of the alarming property of information systems which enable small causes occasionally to produce large effects or large causes small effects.

When, however, we consider models of interaction among few organizations we can no longer neglect the fact that the output-input relationships include not only material or energy transfers but also information transfers, and it is this fact which makes the theory so difficult. We run into this problem in economics, for instance in the theory of 'oligopoly' (competition among the few). It is extremely important in international relations, and in 'small group theory' in group dynamics or in social psychology. It may also turn out to be important in physiology where the theory of feedback systems is proving to be a useful tool in understanding otherwise mysterious phenomena.

There seem to be some interesting problems in regard to the relation of information to communication. The communication phenomenon may be divided into two distinct types: unilateral communication in which information passes in one direction from one organization to another or to many others, and bilateral communication, or discourse, in which information passes in both directions between two, or among a number of organizations. The problems of the first seem to be largely encompassed in simple information theory, even the problem of 'mass communication' where the information passes from one source to many recipients. Even mass communication however contains certain elements of discourse—letters to the editor, surveys of radio or television audiences, market surveys, and so on, and it would certainly seem that a theory of discourse or conversation is the general case of which unilateral communication is simply a special case where the feedback to the originator is zero. In common experience two patterns of discourse are clearly visible—a dynamically unstable pattern which leads to mutual modification of the subjective knowledge of all parties towards a common structure. The first pattern is 'war', and it is deplorably common. It may be seen in the squabbles of children, in the price of advertising wars of firms, in international relations, and sometimes in party politics. The second pattern is 'discussion' and it is seen frequently, though not always, in science, and in the operations of any harmonious political or social system. It should not be impossible to develop models which possess one or the other of these dynamic properties and from them to throw some light on the vital practical question of how to transform 'war' into 'discussion'.

We are here touching upon subjects of great importance to all the social sciences, though at present little developed. Communication theory should be of great importance to the study of the sociology of knowledge. It may well be the centre of the coming rehabilitation of political science, foreshadowed perhaps in the stimulating work of Karl Deutsch. It should be of importance in statistics and in the theory of scientific methodology—the prime task of statistics, after all, is to organize data in such a way that it 'communicates', in that complex masses of material can be presented to the mind in a manner which brings out their significance. It might even be argued that communication is the task of all scientific method—to organize and extend the various universes of human experience in an orderly and communicable manner. Science is shorthand, even if shorthand isn't science!

Information and communication theory may be of more importance in economics than most economists now recognize. Up to the present I can think of only one economist of any standing whose prime concern has been with the impact of communications on the economy—the late Harold A. Innis—and he was never able to present his thought in a way that carried weight among professional economists. Nevertheless, the study of the sources and spread of economic information, the way in which information changes the subjective knowledge of their economic environment of various actors and so affects their economic behaviour— these may well be the keys to a successful dynamic economics that will enable us to solve the highly mysterious problem of the rates of transmission of economic behaviour through the economy, for example in inflation or depression. And as Innis also suggested, the wider dynamic processes of society involved in the rise and fall of nations, empires, religions and civilizations may also be closely related with the dynamic laws of the information and communication process.

Economics has not only things to learn from information theory—it may also have something to give. Insofar as economists have been concerned with expectations and uncertainty, they have inevitably been involved in the information concept, though often without realizing it. At least one economist—G. L. S. Shackle, in *Expectations in Economics* has made an important contribution to the uncertainty concept in the shape of the 'potential surprise function' as a substitute for the conventional probability approach. The improbable is not quite the same thing as the surprising, and yet it is the surprise rather than the probability aspect of information which is significant from the point of view of the knowledge structure. An important consequence of Shackle's theory is that behaviour under conditions of uncertainty is likely to be governed by two 'focus-outcomes' representing the maximum and minimum values of the outcomes after discounting by a 'surprise' factor. The theory of games would then indicate that the lower focus outcome dominates the situation—that is, that our behaviour is limited by our fears of the worst rather than by our hopes of the best.

GENERAL SYSTEMS THEORY: THE SKELETON OF SCIENCE

Management Science, 2, 3 (April 1956): 197-208

GENERAL SYSTEMS THEORY—THE SKELETON OF SCIENCE

General Systems Theory[1] is a name which has come into use to describe a level of theoretical model-building which lies somewhere between the highly generalized constructions of pure mathematics and the specific theories of the specialized disciplines. Mathematics attempts to organize highly general relationships into a coherent system, a system however which does not have any necessary connections with the "real" world around us. It studies all thinkable relationships abstracted from any concrete situation or body of empirical knowledge. It is not even confined to "quantitative" relationships narrowly defined—indeed, the developments of a mathematics of quality and structure is already on the way, even though it is not as far advanced as the "classical" mathematics of quantity and number. Nevertheless because in a sense mathematics contains all theories it contains none; it is the language of theory, but it does not give us the content. At the other extreme we have the separate disciplines and sciences, with their separate bodies of theory. Each discipline corresponds to a certain segment of the empirical world, and each develops theories which have particular applicability to its own empirical segment. Physics, Chemistry, Biology, Psychology, Sociology, Economics and so on all carve out for themselves certain elements of the experience of man and develop theories and patterns of activity (research) which yield satisfaction in understanding, and which are appropriate to their special segments.

In recent years increasing need has been felt for a body of systematic theoretical constructs which will discuss the general relationships of the empirical world. This is the quest of General Systems Theory. It does not seek, of course, to establish a single, self-contained "general theory of practically everything" which will replace all the special theories of particular disciplines. Such a theory would be almost without content, for we always pay for generality by sacrificing content, and all we can say about practically everything is almost nothing. Somewhere however between the specific that has no meaning and the general that has no content there must be, for each purpose and at each level of abstrac-

[1] The name and many of the ideas are to be credited to L. von Bertalanffy, who is not, however, to be held accountable for the ideas of the present author! For a general discussion of Bertalanffy's ideas see *General System Theory: A New Approach to Unity of Science, Human Biology*, Dec., 1951, Vol. 23, p. 303–361.

tion, an optimum degree of generality. It is the contention of the General Systems Theorists that this optimum degree of generality in theory is not always reached by the particular sciences. The objectives of General Systems Theory then can be set out with varying degrees of ambition and confidence. At a low level of ambition but with a high degree of confidence it aims to point out similarities in the theoretical constructions of different disciplines, where these exist, and to develop theoretical models having applicability to at least two different fields of study. At a higher level of ambition, but with perhaps a lower degree of confidence it hopes to develop something like a "spectrum" of theories—a system of systems which may perform the function of a "gestalt" in theoretical construction. Such "gestalts" in special fields have been of great value in directing research towards the gaps which they reveal. Thus the periodic table of elements in chemistry directed research for many decades towards the discovery of unknown elements to fill gaps in the table until the table was completely filled. Similarly a "system of systems" might be of value in directing the attention of theorists towards gaps in theoretical models, and might even be of value in pointing towards methods of filling them.

The need for general systems theory is accentuated by the present sociological situation in science. Knowledge is not something which exists and grows in the abstract. It is a function of human organisms and of social organization. Knowledge, that is to say, is always what somebody knows: the most perfect transcript of knowledge in writing is not knowledge if nobody knows it. Knowledge however grows by the receipt of meaningful information—that is, by the intake of messages by a knower which are capable of reorganizing his knowledge. We will quietly duck the question as to what reorganizations constitute "growth" of knowledge by defining "semantic growth" of knowledge as those reorganizations which can profitably be talked about, in writing or speech, by the Right People. Science, that is to say, is what can be talked about profitably by scientists in their role as scientists. The crisis of science today arises because of the increasing difficulty of such profitable talk among scientists as a whole. Specialization has outrun Trade, communication between the disciples becomes increasingly difficult, and the Republic of Learning is breaking up into isolated subcultures with only tenuous lines of communication between them—a situation which threatens intellectual civil war. The reason for this breakup in the body of knowledge is that in the course of specialization the receptors of information themselves become specialized. Hence physicists only talk to physicists, economists to economists—worse still, nuclear physicists only talk to nuclear physicists and econometricians to econometricians. One wonders sometimes if science will not grind to a stop in an assemblage of walled-in hermits, each mumbling to himself words in a private language that only he can understand. In these days the arts may have beaten the sciences to this desert of mutual unintelligibility, but that may be merely because the swift intuitions of art reach the future faster than the plodding leg work of the scientist. The more science breaks into sub-groups, and the less communication is possible among the disciplines, however, the greater chance there is that the total growth of knowledge is being slowed down by the loss of relevant communications. The spread of specialized deafness means that someone who ought to know something that someone else knows isn't able to find it out for lack of generalized ears.

It is one of the main objectives of General Systems Theory to develop these generalized ears, and by developing a framework of general theory to enable one specialist to catch relevant communications from others. Thus the economist who realizes the strong formal similarity between utility theory in economics and field theory in physics[2] is probably in a better position to learn from the physicists than one who does not. Similarly a specialist who works with the growth concept—whether the crystallographer, the virologist, the cytologist, the physiologist, the psychologist, the sociologist or the economist—will be more sensitive to the contributions of other fields if he is aware of the many similarities of the growth process in widely different empirical fields.

There is not much doubt about the demand for general systems theory under one brand name or another. It is a little more embarrassing to inquire into the supply. Does any of it exist, and if so where? What is the chance of getting more of it, and if so, how? The situation might be described as promising and in ferment, though it is not wholly clear what is being promised or brewed. Something which might be called an "interdisciplinary movement" has been abroad for some time. The first signs of this are usually the development of hybrid disciplines. Thus physical chemistry emerged in the third quarter of the nineteenth century, social psychology in the second quarter of the twentieth. In the physical and biological sciences the list of hybrid disciplines is now quite long—biophysics, biochemistry, astrophysics are all well established. In the social sciences social anthropology is fairly well established, economic psychology and economic sociology are just beginning. There are signs, even, that Political Economy, which died in infancy some hundred years ago, may have a re-birth.

In recent years there has been an additional development of great interest in the form of "multisexual" interdisciplines. The hybrid disciplines, as their hyphenated names indicate, come from two respectable and honest academic parents. The newer interdisciplines have a much more varied and occasionally even obscure ancestry, and result from the reorganization of material from many different fields of study. Cybernetics, for instance, comes out of electrical engineering, neurophysiology, physics, biology, with even a dash of economics. Information theory, which originated in communications engineering, has important applications in many fields stretching from biology to the social sciences. Organization theory comes out of economics, sociology, engineering, physiology, and Management Science itself is an equally multidisciplinary product.

On the more empirical and practical side the interdisciplinary movement is reflected in the development of interdepartmental institutes of many kinds. Some of these find their basis of unity in the empirical field which they study, such as institutes of industrial relations, of public administration, of international

---

[2] See A. G. Pikler, Utility Theories in Field Physics and Mathematical Economics, *British Journal for the Philosophy of Science*, 1955, Vol. 5, pp. 47 and 303.

affairs, and so on. Others are organized around the application of a common methodology to many different fields and problems, such as the Survey Research Center and the Group Dynamics Center at the University of Michigan. Even more important than these visible developments, perhaps, though harder to perceive and identify, is a growing dissatisfaction in many departments, especially at the level of graduate study, with the existing traditional theoretical backgrounds for the empirical studies which form the major part of the output of Ph.D. theses. To take but a single example from the field with which I am most familiar. It is traditional for studies of labor relations, money and banking, and foreign investment to come out of departments of economics. Many of the needed theoretical models and frameworks in these fields, however, do not come out of "economic theory" as this is usually taught, but from sociology, social psychology, and cultural anthropology. Students in the department of economics however rarely get a chance to become acquainted with these theoretical models, which may be relevant to their studies, and they become impatient with economic theory, much of which may not be relevant.

It is clear that there is a good deal of interdisciplinary excitement abroad. If this excitement is to be productive, however, it must operate within a certain framework of coherence. It is all too easy for the interdisciplinary to degenerate into the undisciplined. If the interdisciplinary movement, therefore, is not to lose that sense of form and structure which is the "discipline" involved in the various separate disciplines, it should develop a structure of its own. This I conceive to be the great task of general systems theory. For the rest of this paper, therefore, I propose to look at some possible ways in which general systems theory might be structured.

Two possible approaches to the organization of general systems theory suggest themselves, which are to be thought of as complementary rather than competitive, or at least as two roads each of which is worth exploring. The first approach is to look over the empirical universe and to pick out certain general *phenomena* which are found in many different disciplines, and to seek to build up general theoretical models relevant to these phenomena. The second approach is to arrange the empirical fields in a hierarchy of complexity of organization of their basic "individual" or unit of behavior, and to try to develop a level of abstraction appropriate to each.

Some examples of the first approach will serve to clarify it, without pretending to be exhaustive. In almost all disciplines, for instance, we find examples of populations—aggregates of individuals conforming to a common definition, to which individuals are added (born) and subtracted (die) and in which the age of the individual is a relevant and identifiable variable. These populations exhibit dynamic movements of their own, which can frequently be described by fairly simple systems of difference equations. The populations of different species also exhibit dynamic interactions among themselves, as in the theory of Volterra. Models of population change and interaction cut across a great many different fields—ecological systems in biology, capital theory in economics which deals with populations of "goods," social ecology, and even certain problems of statistical mechanics. In all these fields population change, both in absolute numbers and in structure, can be discussed in terms of birth and survival functions relating numbers of births and of deaths in specific age groups to various aspects of the system. In all these fields the interaction of population can be discussed in terms of competitive, complementary, or parasitic relationships among populations of different species, whether the species consist of animals, commodities, social classes or molecules.

Another phenomenon of almost universal significance for all disciplines is that of the interaction of an "individual" of some kind with its environment. Every discipline studies some kind of "individual"—electron, atom, molecule, crystal, virus, cell, plant, animal, man, family, tribe, state, church, firm, corporation, university, and so on. Each of these individuals exhibits "behavior," action, or change, and this behavior is considered to be related in some way to the environment of the individual—that is, with other individuals with which it comes into contact or into some relationship. Each individual is thought of as consisting of a structure or complex of individuals of the order immediately below it—atoms are an arrangement of protons and electrons, molecules of atoms, cells of molecules, plants, animals and men of cells, social organizations of men. The "behavior" of each individual is "explained" by the structure and arrangement of the lower individuals of which it is composed, or by certain principles of equilibrium or homeostasis according to which certain "states" of the individual are "preferred." Behavior is described in terms of the restoration of these preferred states when they are disturbed by changes in the environment.

Another phenomenon of universal significance is growth. Growth theory is in a sense a subdivision of the theory of individual "behavior," growth being one important aspect of behavior. Nevertheless there are important differences between equilibrium theory and growth theory, which perhaps warrant giving growth theory a special category. There is hardly a science in which the growth phenomenon does not have some importance, and though there is a great difference in complexity between the growth of crystals, embryos, and societies, many of the principles and concepts which are important at the lower levels are also illuminating at higher levels. Some growth phenomena can be dealt with in terms of relatively simple population models, the solution of which yields growth curves of single variables. At the more complex levels structural problems become dominant and the complex interrelationships between growth and form are the focus of interest. All growth phenomena are sufficiently alike however to suggest that a general theory of growth is by no means an impossibility.[3]

Another aspect of the theory of the individual and also of interrelationships among individuals which might be singled out for special treatment is the theory of information and communication. The information concept as developed by Shannon has had interesting applications outside its original field of electrical engineering. It is not adequate, of course, to deal with problems involving the semantic level of communication. At the biological level however the informa-

[3] See "Towards a General Theory of Growth" by K. E. Boulding, *Canadian Journal of Economics and Political Science*, 19 Aug. 1953, 326–340.

tion concept may serve to develop general notions of structuredness and abstract measures of organization which give us, as it were, a third basic dimension beyond mass and energy. Communication and information processes are found in a wide variety of empirical situations, and are unquestionably essential in the development of organization, both in the biological and the social world.

These various approaches to general systems through various aspects of the empirical world may lead ultimately to something like a general field theory of the dynamics of action and interaction. This, however, is a long way ahead.

A second possible approach to general systems theory is through the arrangement of theoretical systems and constructs in a hierarchy of complexity, roughly corresponding to the complexity of the "individuals" of the various empirical fields. This approach is more systematic than the first, leading towards a "system of systems." It may not replace the first entirely, however, as there may always be important theoretical concepts and constructs lying outside the systematic framework. I suggest below a possible arrangement of "levels" of theoretical discourse.

(i) The first level is that of the static structure. It might be called the level of *frameworks*. This is the geography and anatomy of the universe—the patterns of electrons around a nucleus, the pattern of atoms in a molecular formula, the arrangement of atoms in a crystal, the anatomy of the gene, the cell, the plant, the animal, the mapping of the earth, the solar system, the astronomical universe. The accurate description of these frameworks is the beginning of organized theoretical knowledge in almost any field, for without accuracy in this description of static relationships no accurate functional or dynamic theory is possible. Thus the Copernican revolution was really the discovery of a new static framework for the solar system which permitted a simpler description of its dynamics.

(ii) The next level of systematic analysis is that of the simple dynamic system with predetermined, necessary motions. This might be called the level of *clockworks*. The solar system itself is of course the great clock of the universe from man's point of view, and the deliciously exact predictions of the astronomers are a testimony to the excellence of the clock which they study. Simple machines such as the lever and the pulley, even quite complicated machines like steam engines and dynamos fall mostly under this category. The greater part of the theoretical structure of physics, chemistry, and even of economics falls into this category. Two special cases might be noted. Simple equilibrium systems really fall into the dynamic category, as every equilibrium system must be considered as a limiting case of a dynamic system, and its stability cannot be determined except from the properties of its parent dynamic system. Stochastic dynamic systems leading to equilibria, for all their complexity, also fall into this group of systems; such is the modern view of the atom and even of the molecule, each position or part of the system being given with a certain degree of probability, the whole nevertheless exhibiting a determinate structure. Two types of analytical method are important here, which we may call, with the usage of the economists, comparative statics and true dynamics. In comparative statics we compare two equilibrium positions of the system under different values for the basic parameters. These equilibrium positions are usually expressed as the solution of a set of simultaneous equations. The method of comparative statics is to compare the solutions when the parameters of the equations are changed. Most simple mechanical problems are solved in this way. In true dynamics on the other hand we exhibit the system as a set of difference or differential equations, which are then solved in the form of an explicit function of each variable with time. Such a system may reach a position of stationary equilibrium, or it may not—there are plenty of examples of explosive dynamic systems, a very simple one being the growth of a sum at compound interest! Most physical and chemical reactions and most social systems do in fact exhibit a tendency to equilibrium—otherwise the world would have exploded or imploded long ago.

(iii) The next level is that of the control mechanism or cybernetic system, which might be nicknamed the level of the *thermostat*. This differs from the simple stable equilibrium system mainly in the fact that the transmission and interpretation of information is an essential part of the system. As a result of this the equilibrium position is not merely determined by the equations of the system, but the system will move to the maintenance of any *given* equilibrium, within limits. Thus the thermostat will maintain *any* temperature at which it can be set; the equilibrium temperature of the system is not determined solely by its equations. The trick here of course is that the essential variable of the dynamic system is the *difference* between an "observed" or "recorded" value of the maintained variable and its "ideal" value. If this difference is not zero the system moves so as to diminish it; thus the furnace sends up heat when the temperature as recorded is "too cold" and is turned off when the recorded temperature is "too hot." The homeostasis model, which is of such importance in physiology, is an example of a cybernetic mechanism, and such mechanisms exist through the whole empirical world of the biologist and the social scientist.

(iv) The fourth level is that of the "open system," or self-maintaining structure. This is the level at which life begins to differentiate itself from not-life: it might be called the level of the *cell*. Something like an open system exists, of course, even in physico-chemical equilibrium systems; atomic structures maintain themselves in the midst of a throughput of electrons, molecular structures maintain themselves in the midst of a throughput of atoms. Flames and rivers likewise are essentially open systems of a very simple kind. As we pass up the scale of complexity of organization towards living systems, however, the property of self-maintenance of structure in the midst of a throughput of material becomes of dominant importance. An atom or a molecule can presumably exist without throughput: the existence of even the simplest living organism is inconceivable without ingestion, excretion and metabolic exchange. Closely connected with the property of self-maintenance is the property of self-reproduction. It may be, indeed, that self-reproduction is a more primitive or "lower level" system than the open system, and that the gene and the virus, for instance, may be able to reproduce themselves without being open systems. It is not perhaps an important question at what point in the scale of increasing complexity "life" begins. What is clear, however, is that by the time we have got to systems which both reproduce themselves and maintain themselves in the midst of a throughput of material and energy, we have something to which it would be hard to deny the title of "life."

(v) The fifth level might be called the genetic-societal level; it is typified by the *plant*, and it dominates the empirical world of the botanist. The outstanding characteristics of these systems are first, a division of labor among cells to form a cell-society with differentiated and mutually dependent parts (roots, leaves, seeds, etc.), and second, a sharp differentiation between the genotype and the phenotype, associated with the phenomenon of equifinal or "blueprinted" growth. At this level there are no highly specialized sense organs and information receptors are diffuse and incapable of much throughput of information—it is doubtful whether a tree can distinguish much more than light from dark, long days from short days, cold from hot.

(vi) As we move upward from the plant world towards the animal kingdom we gradually pass over into a new level, the "animal" level, characterized by increased mobility, teleological behavior, and self-awareness. Here we have the development of specialized information-receptors (eyes, ears, etc.) leading to an enormous increase in the intake of information; we have also a great development of nervous systems, leading ultimately to the brain, as an organizer of the information intake into a knowledge structure or "image". Increasingly as we ascend the scale of animal life, behavior is response not to a specific stimulus but to an "image" or knowledge structure or view of the environment as a whole. This image is of course determined ultimately by information received into the organism; the relation between the receipt of information and the building up of an image however is exceedingly complex. It is not a simple piling up or accumulation of information received, although this frequently happens, but a structuring of information into something essentially different from the information itself. After the image structure is well established most information received produces very little change in the image—it goes through the loose structure, as it were, without hitting it, much as a sub-atomic particle might go through an atom without hitting anything. Sometimes however the information is "captured" by the image and added to it, and sometimes the information hits some kind of a "nucleus" of the image and a reorganization takes place, with far reaching and radical changes in behavior in apparent response to what seems like a very small stimulus. The difficulties in the prediction of the behavior of these systems arises largely because of this intervention of the image between the stimulus and the response.

(vii) The next level is the "human" level, that is of the individual human being considered as a system. In addition to all, or nearly all, of the characteristics of animal systems man possesses self consciousness, which is something different from mere awareness. His image, besides being much more complex than that even of the higher animals, has a self-reflexive quality—he not only knows, but knows that he knows. This property is probably bound up with the phenomenon of language and symbolism. It is the capacity for speech—the ability to produce, absorb, and interpret *symbols*, as opposed to mere signs like the warning cry of an animal—which most clearly marks man off from his humbler brethren. Man is distinguished from the animals also by a much more elaborate image of time and relationship; man is probably the only organization that knows that it dies, that contemplates in its behavior a whole life span, and more than a life span. Man exists not only in time and space but in history, and his behavior is profoundly affected by his view of the time process in which he stands.

(viii) Because of the vital importance for the individual man of symbolic images and behavior based on them it is not easy to separate clearly the level of the individual human organism from the next level, that of social organizations. In spite of the occasional stories of feral children raised by animals, man isolated from his fellows is practically unknown. So essential is the symbolic image in human behavior that one suspects that a truly isolated man would not be "human" in the usually accepted sense, though he would be potentially human. Nevertheless it is convenient for some purposes to distinguish the individual human as a system from the social systems which surround him, and in this sense social organizations may be said to constitute another level of organization. The unit of such systems is not perhaps the person—the individual human as such—but the "role"—that part of the person which is concerned with the organization or situation in question, and it is tempting to define social organizations, or almost any social system, as a set of roles tied together with channels of communication. The interrelations of the role and the person however can never be completely neglected—a square person in a round role may become a little rounder, but he also makes the role squarer, and the perception of a role is affected by the personalities of those who have occupied it in the past. At this level we must concern ourselves with the content and meaning of messages, the nature and dimensions of value systems, the transcription of images into a historical record, the subtle symbolizations of art, music, and poetry, and the complex gamut of human emotion. The empirical universe here is human life and society in all its complexity and richness.

(ix) To complete the structure of systems we should add a final turret for transcendental systems, even if we may be accused at this point of having built Babel to the clouds. There are however the ultimates and absolutes and the inescapable unknowables, and they also exhibit systematic structure and relationship. It will be a sad day for man when nobody is allowed to ask questions that do not have any answers.

One advantage of exhibiting a hierarchy of systems in this way is that it gives us some idea of the present gaps in both theoretical and empirical knowledge. Adequate theoretical models extend up to about the fourth level, and not much beyond. Empirical knowledge is deficient at practically all levels. Thus at the level of the static structure, fairly adequate descriptive models are available for geography, chemistry, geology, anatomy, and descriptive social science. Even at this simplest level, however, the problem of the adequate description of complex structures is still far from solved. The theory of indexing and cataloging, for instance, is only in its infancy. Librarians are fairly good at cataloguing books, chemists have begun to catalogue structural formulae, and anthropologists have begun to catalogue culture traits. The cataloguing of events, ideas, theories, statistics, and empirical data has hardly begun. The very multiplication of records however as time goes on will force us into much more adequate cataloguing and reference systems than we now have. This is perhaps the major unsolved theoretical problem at the level of the static structure. In the empirical field there are still great areas where static structures are very imperfectly known, although knowlege is advancing rapidly, thanks to new probing devices such as the electron microscope. The anatomy of that part of the empirical world which lies between the large molecule and the cell however, is still obscure at many points. It is precisely this area however—which includes, for instance, the gene and the virus—that holds the secret of life, and until its anatomy is made clear the nature of the functional systems which are involved will inevitably be obscure.

The level of the "clockwork" is the level of "classical" natural science, especially physics and astronomy, and is probably the most completely developed level in the present state of knowledge, especially if we extend the concept to include the field theory and stochastic models of modern physics. Even here however there are important gaps, especially at the higher empirical levels. There is much yet to be known about the sheer mechanics of cells and nervous systems, of brains and of societies.

Beyond the second level adequate theoretical models get scarcer. The last few years have seen great developments at the third and fourth levels. The theory of control mechanisms ("thermostats") has established itself as the new discipline or cybernetics, and the theory of self-maintaining systems or "open systems" likewise has made rapid strides. We could hardly maintain however that much more than a beginning had been made in these fields. We know very little about the cybernetics of genes and genetic systems, for instance, and still less about the control mechanisms involved in the mental and social world. Similarly the processes of self-maintenance remain essentially mysterious at many points, and although the theoretical possibility of constructing a self-maintaining machine which would be a true open system has been suggested, we seem to be a long way from the actual construction of such a mechanical similitude of life.

Beyond the fourth level it may be doubted whether we have as yet even the rudiments of theoretical systems. The intricate machinery of growth by which the genetic complex organizes the matter around it is almost a complete mystery. Up to now, whatever the future may hold, only God can make a tree. In the face of living systems we are almost helpless; we can occasionally cooperate with systems which we do not understand: we cannot even begin to reproduce them. The ambiguous status of medicine, hovering as it does uneasily between magic and science, is a testimony to the state of systematic knowledge in this area. As we move up the scale the absence of the appropriate theoretical systems becomes ever more noticeable. We can hardly conceive ourselves constructing a system which would be in any recognizable sense "aware," much less self conscious. Nevertheless as we move towards the human and societal level a curious thing happens: the fact that we have, as it were, an inside track, and that we ourselves *are* the systems which we are studying, enables us to utilize systems which we do not really understand. It is almost inconceivable that we should make a machine that would make a poem: nevertheless, poems *are* made by fools like us by processes which are largely hidden from us. The kind of knowledge and skill that we have at the symbolic level is very different from that which we have at lower levels—it is like, shall we say, the "knowhow" of the gene as compared with the knowhow of the biologist. Nevertheless it is a real kind of knowledge and it is the source of the creative achievements of man as artist, writer, architect, and composer.

Perhaps one of the most valuable uses of the above scheme is to prevent us from accepting as final a level of theoretical analysis which is below the level of the empirical world which we are investigating. Because, in a sense, each level incorporates all those below it, much valuable information and insights can be obtained by applying low-level systems to high-level subject matter. Thus most of the theoretical schemes of the social sciences are still at level (ii), just rising now to (iii), although the subject matter clearly involves level (viii). Economics, for instance, is still largely a "mechanics of utility and self interest," in Jevons' masterly phrase. Its theoretical and mathematical base is drawn largely from the level of simple equilibrium theory and dynamic mechanisms. It has hardly begun to use concepts such as information which are appropriate at level (iii), and makes no use of higher level systems. Furthermore, with this crude apparatus it has achieved a modicum of success, in the sense that anybody trying to manipulate an economic system is almost certain to be better off if he knows some economics than if he doesn't. Nevertheless at some point progress in economics is going to depend on its ability to break out of these low-level systems, useful as they are as first approximations, and utilize systems which are more directly appropriate to its universe—when, of course, these systems are discovered. Many other examples could be given—the wholly inappropriate use in psychoanalytic theory, for instance, of the concept of energy, and the long inability of psychology to break loose from a sterile stimulus-response model.

Finally, the above scheme might serve as a mild word of warning even to Management Science. This new discipline represents an important breakaway from overly simple mechanical models in the theory of organization and control. Its emphasis on communication systems and organizational structure, on principles of homeostasis and growth, on decision processes under uncertainty, is carrying us far beyond the simple models of maximizing behavior of even ten years ago. This advance in the level of theoretical analysis is bound to lead to more powerful and fruitful systems. Nevertheless we must never quite forget that even these advances do not carry us much beyond the third and fourth levels, and that in dealing with human personalities and organizations we are dealing with systems in the empirical world far beyond our ability to formulate. We should not be wholly surprised, therefore, if our simpler systems, for all their importance and validity, occasionally let us down.

I chose the subtitle of my paper with some eye to its possible overtones of meaning. General Systems Theory is the skeleton of science in the sense that it aims to provide a framework or structure of systems on which to hang the flesh and blood of particular disciplines and particular subject matters in an orderly and coherent corpus of knowledge. It is also, however, something of a skeleton in a cupboard—the cupboard in this case being the unwillingness of science to admit the very low level of its successes in systematization, and its tendency to shut the door on problems and subject matters which do not fit easily into simple mechanical schemes. Science, for all its successes, still has a very long way to go. General Systems Theory may at times be an embarrassment in pointing out how very far we still have to go, and in deflating excessive philosophical claims for overly simple systems. It also may be helpful however in pointing out to some extent *where* we have to go. The skeleton must come out of the cupboard before its dry bones can live.

SOME CONTRIBUTIONS OF ECONOMICS TO THEOLOGY AND RELIGION

Religious Education (Nov.-Dec. 1957): 446-450

IT MIGHT surprise, and even annoy, a good many economists to contemplate the possibility that economics might have something to contribute to theology or religion. Economics grew up in the essentially secular atmosphere of eighteenth century rationalism. Adam Smith, the unquestioned founder of the discipline, was a close friend of David Hume, and shared most of his rationalistic prejudices. On the other side, Mammon has never had much of a reputation among the religious, and the pursuit of wealth has generally been regarded as somewhat dangerous to spiritual virtue. As economics has developed it has tended to become more abstract, more mathematical, more remote from the higher as well as from the lower passions of mankind, more concerned with an abstract system of commodities and less with the rich complexities of human personality. What then, we might ask, can a highly abstract system of thought regarding the relationships of commodities have to do with religion, which deals with human life, history and experience in its fullest height, depth, concreteness, and confusion?

Nevertheless no person, and no discipline, is too lofty to learn. Economics, grubbing around at the roots of the tree of knowledge, brings up insights within the framework of its narrow world which are of the same stuff as the brave questions which make the fine flowers of ethics, philosophy, and religion. Many of the concepts which economics has developed within its little universe — exchange, production, consumption, distribution, and above all, *value,* are little clear shadows, as it were of great, vague, universal concepts which lie above them. And by clarifying the relationships of his narrow abstract world, the economist may at the same time — often unknown even to himself — be clarifying the larger, vaguer, and more difficult relationships of the great world of universal concepts.

Consider, for example, the concept of Value. Adam Smith worried about the paradox of Value in Use and Value in Exchange — why did water, which was absolutely necessary to existence and of enormous value in use, have so little value in exchange, and why did diamonds, so obviously a piece of vanity and feminine foolishness, with so little value in use, have so great a value in exchange? It took a hundred years to answer the question clearly, though the answer is simple; water being plentiful, a little more means little to us, and it is on the significance of the little more (marginal utility) that value in exchange rests, not on the significance of the total stock or supply (total utility). Diamonds, on the other hand, being scarce relative to the demand for them, have little total utility but a high marginal utility. What this means is that it is not the basic *preference* system which determines values-in-exchange, or relative values, as much as the relative *scarcities* of the things valued. As W. S. Gilbert sings "His wise remarks, like precious stones, derive their value from their scarcity!" The economist simply points out that all things derive their (relative) values from their scarcities, not merely from people's preferences. We cannot therefore deduce the basic preference system merely from relative values, without knowing something about the relative scarcities of the things valued.

This principle holds as well for abstract virtues and vices and for the more profound and holy objects of value as it does for more humble commodities. We may hold some ideals or principles high in our scale of relative values not so much because we have a great preference for these things as because they are scarce in our culture. Thus the harsh, cruel cultures of Europe, which through history have been ruthless, vindictive, and loveless, repressing domestic affection and treating children with brutal punishment and discipline, have responded avidly to Christianity as a religion of love, not so much perhaps out of the love of love as out of its scarcity. In the gentler, more easygoing and permissive culture of Asia, on the other hand, where love, at least in childhood is plentiful but where goods are scarce and families large and crowded and living in very close quarters, a religion of love has had less appeal and a religion of courtesy like Confucianism, or a religion of withdrawal into an inward world like Buddhism appeals to qualities which again derive high value from their natural scarcity in the culture.

The economist thus sees relative values as established by relative scarcity, and relative scarcity in turn established by the relative ease of difficulty with which the quantity of the valued object can be increased. From this arises the extremely important concept of *alternative cost,* which may be defined as the amount of one thing which must be sacrificed in order to obtain a unit of another. Alternative cost is itself a result of some basic scarcity in "resources." If there were no limitation in resources we could have all our cakes and eat them too, and we could have more of one thing without giving up anything of another. Where resources are limited, however, as in this life at least they always are, alternative cost inevitably raises its dismal head. More guns means less butter, more butter means less cheese, more churches means less schools, and more piety means (perhaps) less art. The fact that we have only twenty-four hours a day to spend, and only one earth to exploit, and only so much knowledge to draw on, and only so much equipment and stocks of goods previously accumulated, imposes on all our activities, from the lowest to the highest, the iron law of alternative cost. It is a law all the more important because of its golden exceptions. Sometimes we move in a realm of blessed complementarity in which more of this means not less but more of that! After an hour in the classroom the students (we hope) know more, but — strange miracle — the teacher knows more too! An ex-

pression of love increases love all around, both of the giver and of the receiver. Cells multiply by dividing in the magical mathematics of life, genes print their images on the chaos around them and organize inert matter into organisms of vast complexity. It is as we ride these waves of complementarity that we break through the grim laws of conservation and scarcity, and emerge with evolution and with economic development, with knowledge and civilization and organization.

Over the short run however scarcity and alternative cost hold sway. We value highly what we must sacrifice a lot to get, or high costs mean high prices. The relationship however is a curiously indirect one. High costs do not *cause* high prices. I might make a solid gold cadillac at a cost of a million dollars, but I might then have to dispose of it for a paltry hundred thousand. High costs however beget scarcity, and scarcity begets high prices. One interesting conclusion follows from this analysis. It is that if unit costs are unaffected by the quantities of goods produced, then relative values are quite unaffected by any change in "demand" or preferences. A change in preferences changes the relative *quantities produced* but not the relative *values* of the goods. If there is a switch in demand from tea to coffee, for instance, there will of course be an eventual decline in tea production and an increase in coffee production. If these changes however produce no change in relative costs, so that no matter how much is produced the sacrifice of a pound of tea releases resources which can then produce, say, three quarters of a pound of coffee, then the shift in outputs will go on until the relative prices have returned to what they were before the switch in demand. Thus though the first impact of the switch in demand will be a fall in the price of tea and a rise in the price of coffee, the effect of this price change is to discourage tea production and to encourage coffee production, and as the output of tea diminishes its price will rise, and as the output of coffee increases, *its* price will fall. This process will go on until the relative prices are equal to the relative costs, at which point it will not pay to switch resources from tea to coffee any longer.

Tea and Coffee may seem to be a long way from the Great Values — Freedom and Justice; Goodness, Truth and Beauty; Courage, Patience, Modesty, Serenity, Vigor, Sensitivity; Faith, Hope, and Charity. The principles which govern the relative evaluation of the great values however are not essentially different from those which govern the evaluation of the small. In spite of the difficulties in measurement the great values are all at least capable of degree. It makes sense to say that this person has more patience, but less vigor than that person, or that this culture has more freedom but less justice than that culture. We are not really much better off than this in the measurement of the quantities of the goods of commerce; there is a deceptive appearance of accuracy in the pound of tea, as there is also in the accountants' figures, but this is appearance only; behind the figures lie a morass of quality differences for which no objective measurement is possible. It is just about as hard to say whether there is more automobile in a Volkswagen Microbus than there is in a Plymouth station wagon as it is to say whether there is more freedom in Russia than in Spain.

In the Great Values as well as in the small, therefore, the economist will look for certain fundamental relationships. What are the relations of complementarity and competitiveness? What are the alternative costs? How much freedom must we give up in order to achieve a certain increase in social justice? Must a certain amount of truth be sacrificed on occasion in the interests of love? Are there some values the pursuit of which actually *increases* the others? These are important questions, for the moral philosopher if not for the theologian. They are questions however which come directly out of the mode of thought of the economist. They relate to what an economist would call the opportunity functions of the Great Values. The Great Values as well as the small are subject to the basic laws of scarcity; we cannot have

enough of them all. So with these as with others we face a problem of *choice*. And the theory of choice is the peculiar concern of the economist.

If the economist, then, has anything special to say in the area of the Great Values it is that values, whether great or small, are always the result of acts of choice. Values do not "exist" independently of the actions of a valuer; they are quantities which are conveniently descriptive of acts of evaluation. It is these acts which exist, not the values. The "price" of a commodity is not a physical quantity like its weight; it is a quantity descriptive of an act, either of exchange or of evaluation, and is meaningless without the actor. The economist, therefore shifts the discussion of value from the value as a "thing" to the evaluation as an act.

Let us look for a moment then at the economists concept of the "act" — that is, of "economic behavior." The actor is seen in the midst of a "field of choice," or a set of alternatives. Action always involves the selection of one among a number (perhaps a very large number, perhaps not) of *possibilities*. One of the economist's great interests is the exact description of the field of choice, and the delineation of the boundaries between the possible and the impossible. Most of the functions or curves which are the stock in trade of the economist — demand curves, cost curves, and the like — are "possiblity boundaries" which divide a certain field into two parts — a possible set and an impossible set. Over the whole field of choice (or at least over its most relevant parts) the economist postulates a *value ordering*. This simply means that if we have a set of possible situations, A,B,C — etc., then we can *rank* these in an order of "betterness and worseness," just as a teacher, for instance, may rank a class of students in a class list "first," "second," "third" and so on. Economic behavior then consists simply in the selection of the "best" — that is the "number one" selection in the value ordering of the relevant field of choice.

Ethical behavior, however, is not essentially different from economic behavior, for ethical behavior too involves choice among selections according to some value ordering. When we distinguish ethical from "unethical" behavior, or "higher" from "lower" standards of behavior we are in effect *evaluating the value orderings* themselves. *All* behavior involves value orderings; the murderer decides that the elimination of his victim is the "best" out of all the possible states of the world which are open to him, the martyr decides that his own death is the best of the possible states which are open to him. It is the ethical judgment which argues that the first value ordering is "low" and the second is "high." An individual usually is faced with a hierarchy of value orderings. Thus I may say that A is better than B for "me" but that B is better than A for my family, or that C is better than D for my family but D is better than C for the nation, or that E is better than F for the nation but that F is better than E for the world at large. Each of these value orderings is characteristised by a frame of reference (the self, the family, the nation, the world). Generally speaking ethical theory argues that the larger the frame of reference the "higher" the ethic and the better the value ordering. This rule is not without conceivable exception, however, and the choice of the appropriate frame of reference presents real and difficult problems.

The apparatus of economic analysis, especially the use of opportunity function and indifference curves, can be used to clear up many cases of ethical confusion. Ethical confusion arises when many different points of the field of choice are "bracketed" at the top of the value ordering, or are very close together at the top, so that a very slight shift in preferences or in opportunities may produce large shifts in the decision. The shifts in the communist party line, or the shifts in behavior on the outbreak of war, are examples of dramatic shifts in the *position* chosen because a relatively slight shift in the nature of the opportunities may bring a radically different set of positions to the top of the value ordering. This further emphasizes the proposition that what is

actually *selected* as best is apt to depend more on the opportunities than on the preferences. The same set of basic preferences may produce widely differing behavior as opportunities change.

Besides its contribution to ethical theory economics also has an important contribution to make to the sociology of religion and the study of the church as an institution. The economist's basic abstraction of the social institution is that of the "firm," which derives revenue from the sale of a product and is able to produce the product because out of the revenue it can reward the factors of production sufficiently to induce them to make this particular product and not some other. The church as an institution has many of the aspects of a firm. It produces a spiritual rather than a material product (church buildings and furniture come under the heading of plant and equipment rather than of product) nevertheless it is not unreasonable to suppose that the financial contributions which give the organization its revenue are paid "for something" which the contributor receives. Out of these revenues the church must pay what is necessary to attract resources over and above those which are attracted by the purely internal rewards of service. The "success" of the church as measured by the worldly standards of size, membership and income depend on its power to attract revenue on the one hand, and its power to attract resources on the other.

The question what is the "spiritual product" of the church is one of great interest not only to the sociologist of religion but also to the theologian. The truth seems to be that there are many such products; the church is not a single-product firm, but it produces many different products, some of which do not appear in its official prospectuses! People may contribute to the church out of a sheer desire for sociability, or respectability, or acceptability. They may go to church for spiritual entertainment from the minister and the choir, much as they would go to a concert or a play. They may support the church because it is a symbol of a larger culture — for instance of a national or a language group within a large cosmopolitan culture. They may support the church because they think it is good for their children in some ill-defined way. Or they may support the church because it provides for specifically religious needs — for religious instruction, for salvation, for personal spiritual help. Or the church may be the expression of an individual discipleship and commitment to a person or an ideal. One suspects that the purely "religious" product of the church is a fairly small part of its total social product, even though this may be the ostensible excuse for its existence as an institution.

The question of the organization of the church to supply spiritual products is also somewhat within the purview of the economist. Are there increasing returns to scale — that is, can large churches supply spiritual products (and attract support) more easily, and with less unit expenditure of resources, than small churches? The answer here seems to depend on the nature of the product; churches which give their numbers respectability, acceptance, emotional security and so on probably have increasing returns to scale and easily become large: churches which appeal to highly special needs or exceptional devotion have diminishing returns to scale and tend to stay small. This is of course the difference between the "church" and the "sect." The ecological competition of churches is thus not very dissimilar from that of firms. Thus in the transportation system we have the railroads, which are something like the Catholic Church (hierarchical, ritualistic): we have the large automobile firms, General Motors, Ford, Chrysler which may perhaps be compared to the great Protestant denominations — Presbyterians, Methodists, Baptists. But we also have sectarian modes of transport (Volkswagens, Renaults, down to three wheelers, motor bikes, bicycles and electric wheelchairs) which correspond to the smaller and more specialized sects from the Quakers to Jehovah's Witnesses. If theologians are offended by these comparisons I must remind them that even the greatest spirit must inhabit a body, and that bodies are all subject to the laws of the body!

When it comes to questions of high theology, to the great concepts of salvation and redemption, the work of the Living God in history, the nature of Christ and the Holy Spirit, the theological nature of the Church, and so on we would hardly expect a discipline as earthy as economics to make any great contribution. Nevertheless there may be insights from economics which are valuable even here. One reflects, for instance, that all creativity — in art, in music, in architecture, in literature — involves *economizing* — that is making the most of a set of limitations, allocating scarce resources, equating marginal gains to marginal losses. It is *because* the artist is limited by his material that art exists; all creativity is making the best of a bad job, and if there is no bad job to be made the best of — that is, no scarcity, no limitation — there is no art, only formless and cancerous growth. Even when art seeks to escape from one set of limitations (as for instance in modern painting) it must accept another set; otherwise it is mere random dabbling. In contemplating the mystery of the Creation of all things, then, and of their Creator, we may not be surprised to see the same principle at work, and to find the Infinite, in the interests of creation, take on finitude, and the Immortal take on mortality.

RELIGION AND THE SOCIAL SCIENCES

In: *Religion and the State University,*
Erich A. Walter, ed. Ann Arbor, Mich.:
University of Michigan Press, 1958, pp. 136-155

Religion and the Social Sciences

The great drama of man's history has a long and continuous main plot in which the principal theme is the tension between the sacred and the secular aspects of life. This struggle is not a simple dialetic in which, for instance, the secular enlightenment gradually overthrows the sacred gloom, but a complex web of interacting strands as first one, then the other aspect of life rises to dominance in constantly changing forms—priest over peasant, king over priest, prophet over king, priest over prophet, emperor over priest, pope over emperor, princes over pope, people over princes, preachers over people, professors over preachers. The development of man's whole image of the universe can be interpreted in terms of a tension between the heroic vision—the wild leap of the poetic imagination, the awe in the presence of Revelation—and the prudential vision—the common-sense view of things, the wisdom of practical men. On the whole this tension between the secular and the sacred has been a creative tension, each constantly reproving the excesses of the other, though there have been times when it has become excessive and destructive.

We are now contemplating a single scene in this enormous drama. The set is the campus of a state university in the United States; the time is A.D. 1957. (It is interesting to note that the number 1957 is part of a series with a sacred origin.) We have come late to the play, as inevitably we must; we find our seats— no, worse, we find ourselves pushed onto the stage from the wings, for we are not spectators but actors. We fumble for our programs: What has gone before? How much do we have to know of what has gone before, and of what is still going on in other theaters, in order to get the hang of the plot and to know what is going on now?

Our first clue is the set itself. The architecture is strangely miscellaneous; surely an amorphous mixture of the sacred and the secular. If there is an emotional center to the campus it is likely to be a bell tower with no church attached. This is deeply symbolic: the sterile phallus. There is likely to be some Gothic or quasi-Gothic architecture, recognizably a sacred type. The building, however, that looks like a cathedral turns out to be a library, and the one that looks like a chapel turns out to be a gymnasium. Detailed inspection reveals no building on the campus used primarily for religious purposes, except perhaps something called, enigmatically, a Y. The conclusion seems to be that we have here an institution in which the secular is completely dominant, and in which the sacred is present only in vestigial forms and organs. We must be careful, however. On the edge of the campus, pressing in on all sides, are buildings that are quite clearly sacred, both in form and in use. We count at least a dozen churches and perhaps two or three building. Furthermore, we find them crowded and prosperous, bursting with activity. Looking at the matter in some detail, we find that on one or two campuses there are even chapels, just built or projected. On other campuses there remains a certain hostility to religion; this, however, is diminishing, and the prevailing attitude toward religion might be described as a slightly bewildered friendliness. We might conclude that we are here witnessing a turn-of-the-tide phenomenon; that a high watermark of secularism has been reached somewhat earlier and that the tide of religion is once more coming in.

Now we must look at some of the previous scenes. The idea of a university itself comes from the previous high watermark of the Sacred, the thirteenth century. If we visit the older universities of Europe, we shall find them occupying the sets of the previous act, and at the center of the set is always a large chapel. The medieval university was primarily a religious institution, modeled on the monastery, and the monastic flavor lingers in the architecture and in some of the customs. Today, however, the chapel is little more than a tourist attraction—students rarely visit it, and it plays little or no part in the life of the college. Between the thirteenth and the twentieth century a great tide of secularism has washed over the whole world. The story is a familiar one—the Reformation, which broke the unity of Christendom and yet renewed the vigor of the society; the Renaissance, which was an infusion of a strong current of ancient secularism; the Discoveries, which brought the whole world into a geographical unity; the Enlightenment; the rise of nationalism and democracy, and finally the enormous enlargement of man's view of the universe and of his power over it through science. The American state university is a monument to nationalism, to democracy, to the separation of church and state, and to science and technology. Its saints are Copernicus, Galileo, Kepler, Newton, Adam Smith, Dalton, Darwin, Freud, and Einstein, and perhaps Washington and Jefferson.

Here again, however, the plot is not so simple as it seems. The tide of secularism is full of strange eddies; it not only draws its springs from sacred waters but carries them on its surface far and wide. Medieval Europe, which we westerners parochially think of as the then known world, was in fact a tiny peninsula on the edge of the great world of Islam, sprawling across the hemisphere from Spain to the Philippines. The cultural explosion that carried Europe to a position of world dominance by the nineteenth century is a good illustration of the creative tension between the sacred and the secular. It can be argued that it was a revival of religion in the Reformation and Counter Reformation that set it off—a revival fed continuously by the rise of new sects in Protestantism and new orders and movements in Catholicism. Even the saints of secularism are strangely religious; both Galileo and Copernicus were unmistakably Catholic Christians, Newton was obsessed by theology, Dalton was a devout Quaker, Faraday was a Sandemanian preacher, Priestley was a Unitarian minister, Darwin was a man of natural piety, Einstein a mystic. The apparent breakup of the medieval religious unity was in fact the

beginning of the great age of world expansion of Christianity—
to all the Americas, to important missionary enclaves in Asia
and Africa. Coming closer to the present scene we find that one
of the most striking long-run trends in the history of the United
States has been the rise of organized religion. The United States
was founded at the height of the Enlightenment; the founding
fathers were almost to a man deists and rationalists. I have seen
one estimate that at the time of the Revolution not more than
4 per cent of the people of the American colonies were actively
associated with any organized church. This figure may be un-
duly small; however, there seems to be evidence for a very
steady rise in the proportion of church members in the population from a rather small figure in the mid-eighteenth century
to about 60 per cent today.

Where then—to come to the main topic of this chapter—do
the social sciences stand in this complex historical pattern? The
rise of social science is one of the most striking, and perhaps
one of the most far-reaching, movements of the twentieth century. Its origins, of course, go far back into social thought and
philosophy. The peculiar characteristics of the movement that
enable it to qualify for the holy name of "science," however, are
quite recent. I would argue that Adam Smith developed the
first over-all "system" of social science in his theory of the
equilibrium of a price system. Quantification comes even later.
The modern census began in the eighteenth century, but it is
not really until the twentieth century that the collection of
social information becomes deliberate and massive. Statistics
owes a great deal to, and has done a great deal for, the social
sciences, but this, too, mostly in the twentieth century. Sociology, anthropology, and psychology, as organized professions
and departments of learning, are creations of the second half of
the nineteenth century. The twentieth century has also seen the
rise of applied social sciences into professions with professional
schools in the universities to propagate them. Schools of public
administration, business administration, journalism, and social
work, and institutes of human relations, labor relations, and
international relations can all be regarded as applied social
science institutions, much as schools of engineering are mostly

applied physical science and schools of medicine and dentistry are applied biological science. Social science is even creeping into professions and professional schools that previously had little to do with it. Industrial engineering tends to become less and less distinguishable from business administration; schools of medicine get interested in social medicine, in public health, in psychosomatic and psychiatric medicine. Nursing is presumably at least half applied social science.

I think it must be argued that the social sciences historically ride firmly on the secular side of the secular-sacred seesaw, even more so than the natural sciences. It is extremely hard to think of antireligious persons or even nonreligious persons among the great names in the natural sciences. This is perhaps because the natural sciences compete with religion only at its periphery. Religions, especially those which rest on sacred books, have always tended to give sacred sanction to the ideas of the physical world which were prevalent at the time of their founding. These ideas of the physical world, however, are the accidents of religion—they rarely form its central core. Thus, while Copernicus and Galileo are upsetting to the church, in that they destroy the literal validity of much of the physical imagery of the Bible, they upset the imagery rather than the image, and insofar as the new ideas of the physical universe inspire awe and wonder at its grandeur, they are actually friendly to some of the deepest religious emotions. The extension of the universe, both in time and in space, away from the cozy three-storied, four- or five-thousand-year-old universe of the Bible into the billion-galaxied, four-billion-year-old universe of today's image should make man more, not less, ready to fall on his knees in wonder and adoration at such great majesty and splendor. As we penetrate more deeply into the intricate machinery of life, here again a sense of awe is neither unseemly nor unnatural.

The great object of study of the social sciences, however, is man. (A sociologist has recently described his science as the improper study of mankind!) The subject matter of the social sciences lies closer to the heart of religion than does the material of the natural sciences. The views which religion holds of the nature of man are not peripheral, for all religion concerns itself deeply with the regeneration, improvement, or salvation of man, and consequently its views as to what should be done about him must be rooted firmly in certain views about his nature. The possibility therefore arises of competitive relations between the views held on the nature of man by religion and by social science. A further possibility for competition arises because in their applications both religion and social science conceive themselves as performing a therapeutic role not only on the individual but on society as a whole. A church that lays down the law on usury runs into disagreement with the economist; a church that lays down the law on divorce runs into disagreement with the sociologist; a church that claims divine right for kings runs into disagreement with the political scientist, and a church that claims to divide human actions sharply into sins and virtues may run into disagreement with the psychoanalyst.

In view of the potential competition, therefore, between religion and social science, it is not surprising to find that on the whole the great figures in the social sciences have been frequently indifferent or even hostile to religion. Adam Smith, like his friend Hume, might be classified as a deist, but his attitude toward religion was at best quizzical. He looks at the church as a kind of spiritual business, meeting certain human needs which no doubt need to be met, but always in danger of creating an artificial demand for its products by arousing enthusiasm. His recipe for "that pure and rational religion, free from every mixture of absurdity, imposture, or fanaticism, such as wise men have in all ages of the world wished to see established" is, as we might expect, free competition among sects so that each has to moderate its doctrines in the direction of sweet reasonableness in order to attract adherents from the others. I have never been able to detect the slightest interest in religion in Ricardo's writings. Malthus, it is true, was a clergyman, and this fact seems to have given him some slight qualms about birth control, but apart from this, religion seems to have made singularly little impact on his thought. Keynes was a thoroughly secular character. Marx, of course, like Freud, was actively hostile to religion.

The sociologists have been more interested in religion than

the economists, as one might expect, but apart from Max Weber and Durkheim, it is hard to think of outstanding figures who have paid much attention to it, and I doubt if there are more than a dozen sociologists in the United States today who regard themselves as specialists in the sociology of religion. The one sociologist who has taken religion very seriously is Sorokin, and perhaps partly because of that very fact he is looked upon with a good deal of suspicion by his professional colleagues. In psychology, likewise, there has been little attention paid to religious experience except when it takes pathological forms. There was very little follow-up from the pioneering work of William James's *Varieties of Religious Experience*, and apart from Allport's study of student religion, there seems to be little interest in the matter among modern psychologists. Yet in spite of all this, religion flourishes as it has not done perhaps since the seventeenth century!

Anthropologists, by reason of their very subject matter, have been much interested in primitive religion, for religion, as one of the earliest parts of the intellectual life to develop, forms a large part of the culture of primitive peoples. With some exceptions, however, anthropologists have been also indifferent or hostile to the religion of their own culture—perhaps because of a certain habit of nonparticipation in the cultures which they have investigated and a not wholly justified identification of advanced with primitive religion.

The aversion or indifference of many social scientists toward religion may arise in part because of the difficulty of transferring from one abstract role to another when the subject matter with which the two roles are concerned exhibit so many similarities. The role of the scientist is marked by aloofness from the subject matter which he investigates and an assumption of an ideal of objectivity. By contrast, the role of the religious person is marked by deep involvement with the subject matter, by commitment and dedication to it, by reverence and obedience. The role of the scientist is like that of the musicologist and critic—a questioning, inquiring attitude, holding nothing sacred, approaching the object of inquiry as an "outsider." The role of the religious person is like that of the artist, identifying himself with his material, willing of course to use objective knowledge, but always being willing to transcend it in the act of identification. It is not surprising, therefore, that there seem to be few people who are capable of sustaining both roles, as they seem to involve contradictory values. Nevertheless, tolerance of apparently contradictory roles may be one of the principal sources of creativity in the individual.

My main thesis is that the traditional hostility or indifference of social scientists to religion is a historical accident, arising from the peculiar circumstances of the period when the social sciences developed, and that, if certain misconceptions can be overcome, we should be able to enter a period of mutually beneficial interaction between these two great areas of human life and experience. We can think of these two areas as slightly overlapping regions of our social space. Each consists of a "core" of more or less professional, full-time practitioners, with a penumbra of persons affected in greater or less degree by the web of interaction within the region. At present the "cores" of the two regions overlap little; there are a few Catholic social scientists; there is some interaction among social scientists and professional churchmen, both in the denominations and in such bodies as the departments of the National Council of Churches. There are also certain strong currents of ideas which permeate our whole society—the ideas of Marx, Freud, and Keynes, for instance, exercise influence on many who have never read them or who do not even know their names, and similarly the influence of Barth, Niebuhr, and Tillich spread out far beyond the relatively narrow circle of their own readers. On the whole, however, the overlap is small; economists, psychologists, sociologists, and anthropologists pursue their professions, teaching, reading, writing, meeting, without being much aware of what is going on in the world of religion (or even of what is going on in neighboring sciences). Similarly, the religiously minded go on their own way, preaching, teaching, writing, worshipping, conferring, without much regard to what goes on in the little world of the social scientists. The two areas differ in that religion has a very large penumbra, reaching out in varying degrees of involvement and interaction into almost the whole society, touching all classes, poor and rich, intellectuals and laborers, whereas the penumbra of social science is much smaller, reaching beyond the intellectual classes only in a very attenuated form, and consisting mainly of students, most of whom have only a very casual contact. The difference may be stated in the form that religion is sustained by a general, non-specialized community (the church); social science is sustained by a specialized community of academics and intellectuals. Social scientists have classes, social workers have clients, but only preachers have congregations!

Let us then explore some conditions under which a greater degree of interaction between these two social regions would be mutually beneficial. The most essential condition of such inter-course is a widely shared belief in the complementary, or at least noncompetitive, nature of the two areas. As long as even one side visualizes the other as a "threat," interaction will be discouraged, and defense will be sought in isolation. Important in this connection also is whether one party visualizes itself as a threat to the other. Here is an area where few or no studies have been made and where a little social-scientific inquiry might be very fruitful. One may venture a tentative hypothesis that on the whole the churches do not see themselves either as threatened by, or as a threat to, social sciences, either at the core or at the penumbra, whereas many social scientists visualize social science as something of a threat to the churches; hence, expect the churches to see social science as a threat and, hence, see the churches as at least potentially hostile to social science. Both the complacency of the churches and the arrogance of the social scientists may, of course, be due to ignorance; at the present stage of this interaction, however, one suspects that the obstacles lie more on the side of the social scientists than on the side of the churches. This may not last. As the churches become more aware of the "threat" of social science, their attitudes may harden.

In situations of this kind a clear delimitation of boundaries can lessen tension and prepare the ground for interaction. As long as each does not feel secure within a certain "home base," there will be mutual suspicions. This delimitation would take the form of a recognition of the different levels of abstraction at which the two processes operate. Social science on the whole is an attempt to apply mechanical and mathematical models to the behavior of men and societies. This is a useful abstraction, and the power of social science lies precisely in its ability to abstract from the immense complexity of the human organism those elements that permit the construction of rather simple mechanical models. The danger of abstraction, of course, is the danger of mistaking the abstraction for the reality and hence elevating the model into a metaphysic.

Religion on the other hand is not an abstraction, but a practicum—an area of human life, experience, and practice in all its complexity, both present, past, and to come. To revert to a previous analogy, that of music: there is a "science" of music, which includes both its physical mechanics and its social mechanics. There is a physics of sound and a sociology of the symphony. Both these are necessary to the full understanding of the phenomenon; neither are strictly necessary to the practice or the enjoyment of music. Religion similarly encompasses an area of experience—in prayer, in worship, in liturgy, in revival meetings, in meditation and devotion, and so on. This likewise requires a mechanics—in this case a mechanics of communication and emotion, of social involvement and individual values. The practice and enjoyment of religion, however, like that of music, is not necessarily dependent on the underlying mechanics. This is not to say that in both cases understanding may not lead to enrichment of the experience, though I have known cases where an overintellectual understanding destroyed the enjoyment of music, and there are even more cases where an obsession with the mechanics of religion has prevented the enjoyment of its practice. Where this happens, however, it is because of a failure to appreciate the difference between abstraction and reality, or because of a fear of reality which prevents a person from plunging into it and giving himself to it, and which leads to the substitution of the safe abstraction for the dangerous reality. To use still another figure, it is no doubt useful for a swimmer to know the mechanics of swimming, but nobody ever learns to swim by just studying the mechanics. To learn to swim, we have to get in the water.

There is here a very interesting problem of the relation of science to practice which might be described as the relation of explicit to implicit knowledge. The swimmer swims largely because of implicit knowledge. He could not formulate his knowledge of hydrodynamics in terms of differential equations, and it would not help him to swim better even if he could, in spite of the fact that his actions depend on the implicit solutions of some very complex equation systems. On the other hand, airplanes fly and submarines swim because of explicit knowledge; an airplane does not fly like a bird, nor does a submarine swim like a fish. This is because we have discovered that by the application of much simpler systems than are generally present in living organisms, it is possible to do simple things better than the living organism. Because living organisms have to do such enormously complex things as growing and reproducing, they have to have an immensely complex machinery, and because they then have to use this complex machinery for doing simple things like locomotion, they do these simple things rather badly. Hence, no living organism uses the wheel, the piston, and the screw as part of its biological apparatus mainly because devices which require a high degree of mechanical accuracy can only be made, they cannot be grown.

The business of science is explicit knowledge; the power which comes from this kind of knowledge arises out of the possibility of applying it at its own system level—that is, its own level of simplicity. Mechanics is very useful for making machines, but if we are ever to duplicate living organisms—as one day I expect we will—we will have to have explicit knowledge about the processes of life which we do not have at present. Art and skill, on the other hand, involve implicit knowledge—the application of unconscious systems in which the organism is able to control parts of its environment because of an elaborate system of information fed out from and back into the system. Thus, the potter who throws a pot on a wheel adjusts the pressure of his fingers to the feel of the clay by a complex "cybernetic" process in which deviations of the performance of the clay from the "ideal" in the mind of the potter are perceived and almost instantly corrected by movements of the hand.

One of the great difficulties in the application of the social sciences is that the subject matter of the social sciences largely consists of behavior involving the use of implicit knowledge of social systems. These systems, however, are immensely complex—quite beyond, in their complexity, the ability of simple mechanical systems to describe. On the whole, however, social science has not risen much above the level of simple mechanical systems in its theoretical models. The explicit systems of the social scientist, therefore, are very imperfect substitutes for the implicit systems on which most human behavior is based.

The church, like all social organizations, tends to operate with implicit rather than explicit knowledge of its social environment. The question as to what use can the social sciences be to the church then resolves into the question, whether there are any areas in which an explicit knowledge of social fact or relationship derived from the peculiar techniques of the social sciences can improve upon the implicit knowledge which comes out of common-sense experience and casual observation. The answer to this question would certainly seem to be "yes" in some limited areas. The survey method, for instance, can be applied to derive explicit information about the population of the area which is served by a church or a group of churches— information which may be of great importance in planning the work of a church, in visitation, in planning buildings or new locations, in identifying its "constituency," in pointing the way to needs which it might serve and which it is not now serving. These things may sound trivial, and perhaps they are. Whatever else a church is, however, it is also an organization, existing in a certain environment, drawing its sustenance from the fact that it meets certain human needs and is therefore able to attract resources to itself. There seems to be no loss in becoming more self-conscious of the nature and environment of the organization, even though all these matters may properly be regarded as secondary in the minds of the "core group" of the church.

The question of explicit knowledge of the internal functioning of a church organization is perhaps more delicate. In every organization there is a formal hierarchy of some kind, but also an informal system of communication and influence, and the two systems do not usually coincide. A skilled social anthropologist should be able to go into any organization, such as a church, and by studying the patterns of communication and influence, develop a picture of the organization as an explicit role structure. It might be doubtful whether he would find out more than a well-placed individual within the organization would know; on the other hand, it might well be that much more goes on than any single individual is aware of.

Another point at which the social sciences can be—and are —helpful to the church is in the field that might be called applied religious ethics. All religions include some kind of an ethic, and in the advanced religions the development and inculcation of the ethic is conceived as a major task of the church. Religion is thought of as containing a set of general ethical principles which have to be applied in the situations of daily life as well as in the observance of specifically religious ordinances. As the world changes around us, however, so do these applications of the religious ethic change—new techniques, new products, new ways of life constantly pose new ethical problems, and if the church is to remain in touch with the life of its people, it must help them to solve these new problems. This is perhaps less pressing in churches whose life consists mainly in ritualistic pursuits and otherworldly hopes, but for most American churches, the problem of social ethics has been one of substantial interest. It is interesting to note that the interest in this problem in the Roman Catholic church has closely paralleled the development of the "social gospel" in the Protestant churches, and also that a common interest in the social applications of Christian ethics has been one of the main sources of the ecumenical movement in Protestantism.

If the ethical judgment is to be mature and informed, it must be based on a firm knowledge of the consequences of various kinds of human action or political policy. It is one of the objectives of social science, however, to increase explicit knowledge of social systems and relationships, and this increased knowledge cannot fail to have an effect on the ethical judgment. As an illustration of this point, we might observe the change in the social doctrines, especially of Protestant churches, which has come about as the result of increasing sophistication in regard to economics. In the middle of the nineteenth century, the prevailing social doctrine was one of classical laissez faire; preachers united with economists to laud the benefits of free trade and the magic of property. Toward the end of the nineteenth century, "Christian Socialism" in various forms became popular. The roots of this are to be found not so much in Marx as in the "romantic" revolt against the coldbloodedness and calculatingness of capitalism—as represented, for instance, by Ruskin and Carlyle, William Morris, and Charles Kingsley. It is the contrast between the mechanical coldness of laissez faire market capitalism and the warm, familistic love ethic of the New Testament that really produces this revolt. By the end of the nineteenth century, this had produced the "social gospel" as represented by preachers like Gladden and Rauschenbusch, and by the various social action agencies of the churches. The British Labour party and the American "New Deal" owe much to this "social gospel" movement—British socialism has been described as Methodist rather than Marxist socialism, and the New Deal owes a great deal intellectually to a group of reforming economists of the early twentieth century (H. C. Adams, Ely, Commons), who in turn were much affected by the movement for "social Christianity."

In the mid-twentieth century again, the "social gospel," as represented, say, by the pronouncements of the Department of Church and Economic Life of the National Council of Churches or by the writings of leading Christian social philosophers like Reinhold Niebuhr and John Bennett, has become more sophisticated, partly of course under the impact of the momentous events of the times, such as the rise of Hitler and Stalin, but also under the impact of criticism from professional social scientists. Christian social thinkers have come more and more to realize that familistic forms of organization may not be suitable for large groups, that there is a real and difficult problem of power and responsibility in society, that a "profit system" does not necessarily imply Scrooge-like behavior, and that all problems are not solved by turning them over to co-operatives, labor unions, or the benevolent mother-state. The rise of the Keynesian economics has opened up the possibility of remedying the major defects of an unregulated market economy by the fairly simple means of government policies that do not involve serious loss of individual freedoms or the manipulation of men. Such a movement in social science inevitably has a profound impact on the judgments and preachments of social ethics.

In other areas also, a wider knowledge of the social field inevitably leads to modifications of the ethical judgment. In their teaching on sexual ethics and family life, for instance, the churches can hardly fail to be affected by Malthusian and Freudian theories, even though they would be under no necessity to swallow them whole. They can also hardly fail to be affected by the growth of explicit knowledge of the facts of sexual behavior as represented, for instance (however imperfectly), by the Kinsey studies. Ethical judgments on race relations, both inside and outside of the churches, have likewise been profoundly affected by the work of social scientists. Insofar as prejudice might almost be defined as judgments in social ethics derived from highly limited and restricted fields of experience, the expansion of the field of experience which the methods of social science opens up inevitably has a corroding effect on prejudice. The churches have to make their own adjustments to this widening of the field of knowledge. As it is hard for the church to move much ahead of its members, these adjustments are often difficult. They are, however, necessary and creative.

I now come to the very delicate and difficult problem of the contribution that religion can make to social science. The very suggestion that religion might make some contributions to social science will be resented by many social scientists, especially by those whose vocational drive into the social sciences arose out of a rejection of the religion in which they were brought up. It must be admitted also at the start that many excellent and creative social scientists have been indifferent or even hostile to religion. There is no law which says that a man must be religious in order to be a good social scientist. Indeed, there might well be cases in which devotion to religion actually stood in the way of that objectivity of mind and devotion to truth at all costs which is supposed to be—and sometimes is—the mark of scientific inquiry. This problem, however, is not peculiar to religion. If any ideology is held in such a way that a threat to the ideological system is perceived—even subconsciously—as a threat, either external or internal, to the person holding it, devotion to the ideology will be a handicap in the discovery of truth. This is true of the communist ideology; it is true also of materialist or atheist ideologies, as well as of religious ideologies. The strait jacket into which scientific inquiry is forced by the ideology of dialectical materialism is well known—the destruction of free scientific inquiry in Russia has been one of the most shocking fruits of communism. It is not so easy for us to see that we may have a strait jacket of our own—a kind of secular, nationalist materialism which likewise sets limits to scientific inquiry that does not follow the established high roads. There is a quasi religion of "scientism" which by rejecting all psychic or spiritual phenomena severely limits the scope of scientific inquiry.

Religion differs sharply, however, from these atheistic and materialistic "faiths" in that it consists not merely in an ideology but in a set of practices and special experiences. There is really no equivalent, for instance, either in communism, national secularism, or scientism for the practices of prayer and worship. These represent one of the worlds of human experience, just as music or art or science itself is a world of human experience. If this is rejected out of hand as invalid or uninteresting, this rejection severely limits the field of social-scientific study. We may say, therefore, that one important contribution of religion to the social sciences is to give it a field of study and inquiry. For reasons which may be found in the sociology of the social sciences themselves, this is perhaps the most neglected field in the whole subject matter of social sciences. Psychologists make very little attempt to study religion as an aspect of human behavior; sociologists have done very little work on the church as a social organization. A world of fascinating subcultures within the framework of American society awaits the social anthropologist, and religion, as an outgrowth of small group interaction, has been shockingly neglected by the social psychologist. Even the economist might find it profitable to look at the influence of the churches on economic behavior.

This neglect of an important field of study is merely one facet of a serious problem in the sociology of the social sciences, arising out of the narrow field of personal experience of the social scientist himself. Social scientists, like any other occupational group, form a subculture within the larger society. They are, moreover, a rather small and narrow subculture —not quite so narrow as that of the Amish, perhaps, but almost comparable. This subculture has its own sublanguage, its own rituals, such as the publication of articles in quasi-liturgical form (coefficients of correlation and statistical tests of significance are nice examples of social science liturgies), and its communications are very largely internal to the group —even casual and social communications. Furthermore, this subculture is middle class, academic, largely cut off from contact with wageworkers or farmers, and is transmitted from the old to the young through the power which the old have over the promotion and professional advancement of the young. As a result of this, the social scientist tends to have less and less firsthand, intimate, face-to-face contact with people in the other subcultures around him. He consequently tends to concentrate his investigations within his own or closely related groups—experimental human psychology and social psychology, for instance, is almost wholly confined to the behavior of college sophomores—or his contacts with other groups are made on the basis of such an impersonal relationship as the questionnaire or the interview. This inevitably leads to a narrowing of his field of social vision, and it becomes very hard for him to escape the prison of his own subculture. Of all the social scientists, anthropologists live most intimately with other cultures. Here, however, there has been a strong tradition of studying remote cultures, so that while we know a great deal about the Ubangi, we know very little about

Jehovah's Witnesses. Also, one wonders whether the limitations of the intimate personal experience of the anthropologist in the cultures of his own civilization do not at times blind him to certain qualities of richness and depth in more primitive cultures.

Few social scientists will quarrel with the proposition that religion should provide subject matter for social science investigations. Many will not follow me in the assertion that for the healthy growth of social science we need maturely religious social scientists. I base this assertion, however, on two grounds. The first is that, as religion is part of the whole experience of mankind, the social scientist who does not participate in it is cut off from a deep and meaningful area of human experience and is in this sense maimed. Now, of course, a maimed person may be a very good scientist; the blind and the halt also serve, and these deficiencies can be overcome. But who would argue that they are an advantage! Similarly, the social scientist who is deaf to music and blind to art may be excellently skilled in his profession, but there will be something lacking in his person. Not that I would press the argument too far—otherwise, we might find ourselves arguing that we must sin the more that knowledge may abound! But where a large area of human experience is rejected or neglected, surely it can be argued that there is a deficiency.

The other argument is that as social science develops, the problem of the ends of human activity become increasingly pressing, even for social scientists. Knowledge, we write over our schoolroom doors, is power, and power is power unto salvation or unto damnation, depending on how we use it. As long as man is relatively impotent, the problem of what to do with the power he does not possess remains academic. With the growth of power, the problem of its use becomes of increasing importance. We see this in the physical sciences, where the question of the use of the powers which knowledge has unleashed has become perhaps the most critical question of our age. The power which the social sciences may unleash, however, may be ever more terrible—power to control the minds and actions of men, both individually and in the mass;

the power of indefinite corruption of the integrity and individuality of sovereign man. We cannot therefore rest neutrally with the question, "How do people get what they want?" We cannot even assume that it is ethically neutral to help people to get what they want. As social science develops, the critique of ends becomes ever more important, and the question, "Do I (or does anybody) want the right things?" becomes insistent and inescapable. It is precisely this critique of ends, however, which is the great moral task of religion. The future of science, and especially of social science, may depend on our getting better answers than we now have to the question of when ignorance is bliss—or, as a matter of fact, what bliss is anyway! And bliss, curiously enough, is one of the great subjects of religion.

I am not, of course, advocating religious tests for the employment of professors of social science—religious tests, like so many others, test the test rather than the testee, and even from the point of view of the health and vigor of religion itself, the secularization of academic (and political) institutions has been a great gain. We have only to compare, for instance, the remarkable vigor of the Lutheran churches in this country with their debility in Scandinavia to see the futility of trying to impose religion by external sanctions. One does not make people musical by forcing them to go to concerts, nor does one make people religious by forcing them to profess religion. Religion must make its own way and be judged on its own merits; the very breath of coercion will destroy it. It is not necessarily a bad thing to have a few atheists around a university, even if it is only to prove that there is religious freedom (a few communists, incidentally, might also be used to prove that there is political freedom). But there is a great opportunity today for fruitful intercourse between religion and social science, and if the university should not force this, at least it should be able to provide some facilities.

The application of religion to the social sciences must be left to the social scientists themselves. With the application of social science to religion, however, the university might well be positively concerned. One can visualize, for instance, a research institute in this area, somewhat analogous, shall we say, to institutes of industrial relations, which would bring together social scientists from different fields for the development of both theoretical and empirical research in the area of religious experience, practices, and institutions. Such an institute would be difficult to staff at present, and it would run into some difficult problems of public relations, both inside and outside the university, for its members would have to deserve the confidence of both the academic and the religious communities. The development of such a research center would do much to encourage the kind of interaction which I have argued is desirable; it would also bring the university closer to its ideal of studying the universe.

SECULAR IMAGES OF MAN
IN THE SOCIAL SCIENCES

Religious Education, 53, 2 (Mar.-April 1958): 91-96

Secular Images of Man In the Social Sciences

SCIENCE DERIVES both its success and its limitations from its abstract nature. It is the ability to abstract from the endless riches of the real world a slim, stripped, elementary system that gives science its cognitive power, and that enables it to detect relationships which otherwise would be hidden in the gross complexities of reality. On the other hand, there is danger also in the abstraction, for we may come to mistake the abstractions for the realities which they shadow. This is not so important perhaps in the physical sciences, where the simple mechanical relationships which are the principal substance of the sciences correspond closely to the types of systems which they represent. I always rather envy the physicist, because physics is so trivial.

As we move through the biological to the social sciences, however, we find increasingly that the abstract system remains mainly on the mechanical level, whereas the reality which it purports to describe and interpret moves to systems of increasingly higher orders and complexities, about which we know extraordinarily little. We really know little about growth, we know practically nothing about awareness and I'd say we know absolutely nothing about self-consciousness, that is, as systems. We are a long way yet from making a self-conscious machine. Nevertheless, because we are ourselves self-conscious machines or at least self-conscious systems, we have a sort of inside track which gives us, I think, perfectly genuine, although rather disreputable knowledge. This is the kind of knowledge that is expressed in the humanities — the sort of knowledge of human nature, for instance, which is found in Shakespeare. The sacred images of man rest heavily on this "inside" knowledge — it is from this indeed that they derive much of their power.

The social and behavioral sciences move uneasily between the two kinds of knowledge — abstract knowledge of precise reproducible systems, which is the fruit of science, and immanent knowledge of the self and (by extension) of others, which is the fruit of the humanities. It is no exaggeration to say that the more "scientific" the social sciences become, the further they remove themselves from man, and the more they live in self-contained abstract systems. On the other hand the closer they get to their subject matter the more they borrow from the insights of the humanities (often without much acknowledgment). As we traverse the spectrum from, say, econometrics to psychonanalysis we shall find that at the one extreme there is scarcely anything that can be called an image of man at all, and at the other an image which borrows heavily from art and literature, and has slight claims to be "scientific" in the narrow sense of the word.

Econometrics studies a completely abstract universe of economic quantities — prices, wages, outputs, inputs, etc. The basic abstraction here is the *commodity:* the one feature which all economic quantities have in common is that they are descriptive of the world of commodities. There are really no *people* in this world at all. There is an abstract activity called *labor,* and there are presumably objects which are prodded into this abstract activity by the receipt, or the promise, of an equally abstract bundle of commodities called a wage, but these objects can hardly be dignified by the name of men. Similarly, there are equally abstract decision-machines which relate investment decisions to various other elements of the system, but these likewise can hardly be dignified by the name of business men. As a matter of fact, I expect in the next 25 years that many of these will be replaced by electronic calculators. I have often used the analogy of astronomy. In the middle ages (I've been given to understand perhaps this is a libel!) people thought that planets were moved by angels. As astronomers studied the movements of the planets, however, it eventually became clear that the angels were so well behaved that they could be replaced by differential equations, and nobody would know the difference. In fact *anything* that is sufficiently well behaved can be replaced by a set of differential equations. In a similar way econometrics plots the course of economic quantities through time much as the astronomers plot the course of astronomical quantities, and the fact that these things are moved by man is of about as much interest to the econometrician as the angels are to the astronomers. If the quantities bear stable relationships to each other then the system can be propounded that reproduces the course of these quantities through time and can be used for predicting their

future course, and the men who happen to move them are of no more interest than the angels are to the astronomers.

Carrying on now from econometrics into economics proper we notice perhaps an increasing interest in human behavior as such, in addition to the behavior of prices and other economic quantities. Economists have had a certain continuing interest in the problem of what constitutes "rational" behavior. And here I must say a little word in defense of poor old economic man, who is the most misunderstood creature in the whole history of thought. Rational behavior is *calculated,* but it is not necessarily either selfish or self-centered. There is nothing to prevent economic man from being as altruistic as he wishes, provided only that he is deliberately altruistic. No economist has ever supposed that man is actuated by financial motives alone. Adam Smith, for instance, takes great pains to point out that non-financial motives are essential to the understanding of differences in the financial rewards of different occupations. He also points out, that he thought clergymen should be badly paid because "nothing but the most exemplary of morals can give dignity to a man of small fortune." Thoreau and Saint Francis perhaps are almost the ideal types of the economic man preferring deliberately, calculately, occupations of low financial reward because of the large non-financial rewards in communion with nature or with God which they provided. One could argue, I think, that the banker, for instance, isn't an economic man at all, but is a strictly anthropological man, a member of a tribe with all sorts of taboos and traditional regulations.

This interest in rational behavior has led to a considerable development in theory which I don't want to go into here but which all depends on the general principle that rational behavior consists in looking over a field of possible alternatives and ordering the field as one orders a class list and then simply selecting the "top of the class," that is, picking out what you regard as the first place in the field. This is a simple principle yet is far-reaching in its application. We shouldn't criticize it, I think, because it perhaps doesn't encompass the heights and depths of human glory and despair; it isn't intended to.

When the field of choice can be specified rather exactly, particularly when it can be represented by continuous functions, with specific properties, the theory of rational behavior can be given a good deal of content and interesting conclusions can be derived from it. We do this, for instance, in what in economics we call the theory of the firm, which isn't the theory of any firm anybody was ever in, but it's useful for drawing broad conclusions and it's particularly useful for passing examinations with!

In recent years attempts have been made to extend rational behavior theory into cases where the field of choice is uncertain — that is, where the various possible positions cannot be specified completely at the time the choice is made, but where there are some known aspects of each position that imply certain other aspects with a greater or less degree of uncertainty. In the last ten years an extremely interesting body of theory has grown, partly out of economics, but mostly out of pure mathematics, which is called the theory of games. In some application of this, which are called the decision theory, we have quite a large body of analysis which deals with this problem. It's a problem of great practical importance because all actual decisions are made in the face of various degrees of uncertainty and hence theories which assume certain outcomes aren't very realistic. The problem of the measure of uncertainty has turned out to be surprisingly difficult. An even more difficult problem is the problem of the criterion of rationality. One of the difficulties of the decision theory is that there are about half a dozen alternative standards of what rational behavior is supposed to be — under uncertainty some people want to maximize expected values, some people want to minimize potential regret, some people want to make the decision which will be best if the worst happens. This is what is called the minimax; this means marrying the wife who will be most acceptable

at eight o'clock on Monday morning, not the one who will be most wonderful at twelve o'clock on Saturday night. Some people argue it means maximizing the chance of survival and Herbert Simon has argued for what he calls "satisficing" which is, I suppose, really the theory of complacency. This means getting along with the reasonably good. All these and more have been suggested as criteria of rational behavior. Then what do we do if the process of decision-making is unpleasant, so that we choose not to choose? This is the theory of teetotalism. It is clear that once we leave the nice, safe, but not very significant ground of maximizing behavior in the selection of perfectly known choices, the theory of decision-making flies off in all directions. The case is still worse when we introduce second and third parties into the picture, as we have to do in the theory of oligopoly (few sellers) in economics, or in the theory of games. Here what is rational for A to do depends on how he thinks B will react to his decision, and when C is brought into the picture a vast horizon of coalitions or various degrees of stability opens up: A and B may gang up against C, but C may woo away either A or B, and the game goes on. The theory of decision-making actually has some quite practical fruit in what is called Operations Research — which is a way of substituting mathematics for intuition, and there's a lot to be said for this.

As economics moves toward the study of economic institutions — labor unions, collective bargaining, regulation of public utilities, and the like, we find it edging over toward the other social sciences, and especially toward sociology. At this point I must confess leaving my field of peculiar competence, and you don't have to believe a word I say from now on. Even an amateur in the other social sciences, however, can detect the same pattern of abstraction which we have found in economics. There are sociological quantities just as there are economic quantities, and much of the work of the sociologist is devoted to defining, detecting, and seeking for relationships among them. That is, what the sociologist studies is not people but data. This is fundamental. Data rarely have anything to do with people. I recall one case at a midlewestern university which will be nameless, where the prize investigator for the Department of Sociology disliked people so much that she made up all her questionnaires and never interviewed anybody at all! And this went on for years before it was found out! The sociologist perhaps has this advantage over the economist: where the economist is mainly interested in equilibrium — in the theory of the firm, for instance, the firm maximizes something and then lives happily ever after, just like the princess in the fairy tale, — the sociologist is much more interested in dynamics. This means, for instance, that the sociologist's family never lives happily ever after — it always staggers from crisis to crisis and the theory is always conceived in terms of crisis and adjustment. The economist I think can learn something from this. One also has a suspicion that this may be also true of the firm.

The position can at least be defended that the sociologist is really no more interested in people than is the economist and that just as the economist inhabits a kind of astronomical universe of commodities and economic quantities, so the sociologist inhabits a universe of institutions, groups and organizations, etc., which he sees as a fairly self-subsistent set of relationships. The fact that *people* create and operate institutions and organizations, live in ecological regions, and generally activate his variables is of secondary interest to the sociologist. A basic tool of the sociologist is the interview, survey, or questionnaire, in which the investigator obtains answers to a long list of questions from a respondent. It might be thought that this would indicate an interest in people; a respondent, however, is a much more abstract and tenuous concept than a person. The sociologist's concept of man, in fact, seems to be that of a question-answering machine, and though this unquestionably reaches further into the complex reality than the input-output machine of the economist, it is far from the fullness

of truth. Nevertheless I want to emphasize again that it is the abstract nature of the concept which makes it useful, and which makes it possible to perceive relationships among these abstractions which are in some sense true of the concrete reality, but which cannot be perceived without the process of abstraction.

Moving now into social psychology, we find the same principles of abstraction at work. The basic concept here is that of the *role* — a pattern of behavior which fulfills the expectations of the performer and of those who surround him. The role however is not a person either: indeed, the abstract nature of the concept can be readily seen when we reflect that the same role can be occupied by a number of different persons in succession, and that a single person can occupy a number of roles. The role, of course, is affected by the occupant — the square peg in a round role makes the role squarer. It is also affected by those who communicate with it, directly or indirectly. Thus the role of the President of the United States has been created not only by the Constitution, but by all those who have occupied it, by those who have surrounded it, and by those who have written about it. The role, however, is behavior-determining as well as behavior-determined. What we do does depend on our conception of the job or position which we occupy. A person is conceived as a set of intersecting roles. I, for instance, am a professor, a lecturer, a writer, a father, a husband, a son, a Quaker, an economist, a recorder player, and President of the Society for General Systems Research. Add up the roles, define the behavior which is expected from each, note the various conflicts and complementarities, the amount of time and energy given to each, and you have the Person; at any rate you have Homo Sociopsychologus. Homo Sociopsychologus however is just as much an abstraction as Homo Economicus. Homo Economicus seems perhaps to be too much inner-directed, as he spreads out the field of choice on the screen of his image, orders it on a value scale and then picks out the best position, like a man in a restaurant picking a French pastry off a tray. Homo Sociopsychologus seems to go to the extreme of other-direction, as he charts his way through a maze of roles which he seems to take, largely without question, from other people, always taking whatever is on the tray that is handed to him. Both these abstractions, it is clear, fall short of the rich complexity of Homo Sapiens.

The question of the image of man in the various branches of psychology proper is a field in which I am an amateur but I might however briefly indicate the application of my main thesis — that of the essentially abstract nature of the social scientific image of man. Experimental psychology, whether of animals or humans, deals mainly with the behavior of living organisms as a whole, as distinguished from biology which investigates the parts and the structure of organisms. Its conceptual and theoretical framework however is still essentially abstract; just as the economist inhabits a universe of economic quantities, so the psychologist inhabits a universe of psychological quantities — of stimuli and responses. If Homo Economicus is a choosing machine and Homo Sociopsychologus a question-answering machine, and Homo Sociopsychologus a set of mirrors and matching blocks, Homo Psychologus Experimentalis is a stimulus-in-the-slot machine, capable, it is true, of making a certain amount of change and of delivering a considerable repertoire of responses, but still basically a "black box" which we explore by observing what outputs correspond to what inputs.

The *Homo* of the more speculative and theoretical psychologists, like Kurt Lewin and the Gestalt school seems to live by solving abstract puzzles and perceiving equally abstract patterns. Lewin developed the theory of what I would call the "quandary" or what the psychologists call "conflict." Lewinian man is Homo Economicus Dynamicus: he moves toward his preferred positions, but the extent of the movement depends on the distance of his objective and the nature of the obstacles which he encounters. Whereas Homo Economicus surveys the field of choice from a god-like vantage point and selects the most favored position, Homo Economicus Dynamicus travels painfully over the field, drawn towards various objectives by forces of differing strength. An interesting insight which this view affords is that the quandaries in which the subject is pulled toward two equally attractive goals (like Buridan's ass between the two bales of hay) are easily resolved, for they are dynamically unstable — the donkey eats first one and then the other. Quandaries however in which the subject is repelled by two equally undesired states are dynamically stable: This is the ass between two skunks — as he moves away from one he is repelled by the other. There is a certain inference here that there may be two species of Homo Economicus: one is guided by the principle of moving towards what he likes, the other by the principle of moving away from what he doesn't like. One chooses the greater good; the other, like some theologians, the lesser evil. The conclusion is, of course, that the first resolves his quandaries easily and moves to his optimum position in a fine glow of mental health. This is Homo Economic proper, as economists have always understood him. His unhappy brother who minimizes bad instead of maximizing good is constantly getting into insoluble quandaries which lead to frustration, aggression, and mental breakdown.

The images of man in clinical psychology and psychoanalysis are still extremely abstract and they are even rather unrepresentative abstractions, as they are largely abstracted from the sick bed and the couch.

While I am listing the intellectual species of man I must put in a commercial for my own favorite — Homo Eiconicus. In my book *The Image,* I have argued that the behavior of living organisms, and especially the behavior of man, is a function not of the stimulus but of the "image," that is, the whole cognitive structure. Between the input and the output stands the image — modified by the input, fathering the outputs. I suggest that the image can be studied as an abstract entity, built up out of messages, filtered through a screen of values and built up into a structure containing both a "field" — an image of space, objects and time, relationships and also. a "value ordering." Behavior, on this "eiconic" theory, consists in moving towards the most highly valued part of the image of space-time. This is, of course, just as formal and abstract as the others, but it perhaps moves a step nearer reality from those theories which confine themselves to purely mechanical relationships.

It would be presumptuous to attempt in a short paper to evaluate the significance of the social sciences for religious education and this, of course, is not my purpose. The practice of religious education has already been profoundly affected by the rise of the social sciences, and will be affected still more in the future. The only purpose of this concluding note is to sound a modest note of warning. Religious education deals with one of the subtlest and most complicated processes in the world — the growth of the Image, both in the child and in the adult. We will be fooling ourselves if we think that we "understand" this process, in the sense for instance that we "understand" a chemical reaction, or the circulation of the blood, or even the operations of the price system. Here we are dealing with the symbolic image in its highest development and the growth of this image is subject to strange spurts and reversals. Social science to date, I think, says very little about this process. Until it does, we should be hesitant to jump to conclusions from the essentially "lower" and simpler systems of social science. This is in no way to disparage these simple systems; indeed, I believe that the rise in social science is a great step forward toward more secure knowledge of man and society, and it is bound to increase man's power over himself and his society, for good and ill. Through it he can release himself from the grip of "social forces" just as natural science has increased man's independence of "natural forces." Its achievements, while solid, must not be over estimated. It may be able to save us from depressions, from certain forms of social disorganization, from certain forms of mental illness, and perhaps eventually even from war and revolution. It cannot now, and perhaps will never, know enough about the symbolic systems of the human organism to save our souls, without which it profits us not to gain the whole world.

THE KNOWLEDGE OF VALUE
AND THE VALUE OF KNOWLEDGE

In: Ethics and the Social Sciences, Leo R. Ward, ed.
Notre Dame, Ind.: Notre Dame University Press, 1959, pp. 25-42

The Knowledge of Value
and the Value of Knowledge

This paper is essentially an application of parts of the theory of the Image, as outlined in my book by that title.[1] I should therefore begin by sketching the framework of this basic theory.

What I mean by the "Image" is the *cognitive structure* or "subjective knowledge" possessed by an organism or organization. The image is seen in its most clear and developed form in man, but the interpretation of the behavior of all the lower forms of life, even down to the one-celled organism, involves simpler forms of an image concept, and the understanding of the behavior of social organizations likewise calls for the concept of a structure of images in its component organisms. The image, then, is the "view of the universe" held by an organism. This "view" may be fairly simple in the case of an amoeba, consisting of little more than a dim awareness of the distinction between food and not-food, between a time to eat and a time to divide, or perhaps between danger and not-danger. In the case of man the image is extremely complex. It includes elaborate images of time and space, images of the self and of other persons, images of objects and their properties, images of predictive laws (what will happen if—), images of language and skills, and so on. Though confined in the nutshell of his body, man is indeed king of infinite space; the galaxies and the eons, the

1. *The Image: Knowledge in Life and Society,* University of Michigan Press, 1956.

round world and all that therein is, the triumph and tragedy of
the human heart, are all within him as well as outside him, por-
trayed on the enormous many-dimensioned screen of his image.
There is a great difference, of course, between the image of an
untutored savage and the image of an Einstein. A rough notion
of his immediate territory in the case of the first expands into the
extended and complex relational image of the second. Even so the
gap between the simplest human image and the most complex
image of the lower animals is even more enormous; only man, for
instance, has a clear image of time, of his own birth and death; only
man is able to develop complex relational images and measurements.

Within the image a distinction may be made between the "image
of fact" and the "image of value." The image of fact is the "field"
of the image — the world of space, time, objects, persons, and relationships. The image of value consists of an *ordering* of parts of
the field of the image. By an ordering I mean simply the arrangement of the objects or parts of the field of the image in a rank order — first, second, third, etc., like a class list. There are many
images and scales of value — many different orderings, that is, of
various parts of the field of the image. Thus the scale may be aesthetic — building A is ranked above building B on the scale of
beauty. The scale may be hedonistic: sausage gives me more pleasure than bacon. Without getting into the subtleties of pleasure and
pain, the scale may be one of simple personal preference — I prefer the Volkswagen to the station wagon. It may be a scale of ethical value: I may rate one pattern of life ethically superior to another. The scales may have various referents: I may say, for instance, that A is better than B for me, but that B is better than A
for my community, or my country, or the world at large. It is clear
that there are a large number of value scales, many of which overlap, and which order different parts of the field of the image: the
concept of an ordering, however, is common to them all. We do
not have to suppose that the whole field of the image is ordered in
value scales. Many value scales consist only of "first, second, also
ran." Over large parts of the field we are indifferent; all the objects rate equally, which is really to say there is no value scale at
all. At different times and places the value scale spreads over different parts of the field. Thus among astrologers I suppose that

Saturn is regarded as a "worse" planet than Venus. I confess I am homocentric enough to think Earth a "better" planet than distant and chilly Pluto, but for the most part I throw no value ordering over the solar system. Most Americans, I imagine, regard the Russian satellites as "worse" than the American variety, and Russians no doubt reverse this order; future generations may class such value orderings with those of astrology. No matter what and when the valuation process, however, and no matter how lofty or how low its frame of reference, the process itself always consists in matching a set of ordinal numbers with parts of the field.

My main interest in *The Image* was the theory of behavior, rather than of the image itself. I suppose there that the behavior of organisms or organizations consists not in a mechanical stimulus-response pattern, but rather in a response to the image. A *decision* involves the selection of part of the field of the image representing the possible future which is highest valued (first in the ordering) of the dominant value ordering. Stated a little less carefully, we might say that an organism moves towards the highest valued part of its image of the future. Thus as long as in my image of space and time my home has the first place in the dominant ordering, I stay at home: when, say on Monday morning, my office has the highest value, I go to the office. Sometimes strange places like New York or South Bend move into top place, on certain dates, and I accordingly move to these places and times. What is true of my behavior, however, is no less true of the lowly amoeba, as it rejects the grain of sand and embraces the grain of food. The concept of the *dominant* value ordering involves the further concept of an ordering of the value orderings themselves. Thus from the point of view of sheer fleshly pleasure I may rate staying in bed on Sunday morning higher than going to church: from the point of view of ethical conduct I rate going to church higher than staying in bed. Which I do depends on which of these value orderings is itself rated highest; the fleshly man stays in bed, the ethical man goes to church. In any case, behavior is quite incomprehensible without a complex of value orderings: a mere image of fact will never lead to behavior, but merely to vegetative inactivity in any place where one falls.

We can now go on to inquire how the image — both of fact and of value — is formed. At this level of analysis I simply avoid the question of the psycho-physical material substance of the image, which is just as well because we know practically nothing about it! That there is some relation between the cognitive content of the image and the material architecture of the nervous system I do not doubt, but what this relation is I do not know, nor does any other mortal know. I am sure that the relation is highly complex, and the evidence suggests that in ways we cannot now visualize the correspondence between the mental content and the molecular and electrical structure of the organism is a correspondence of wholes rather than of parts, in a type of system which as yet we simply do not understand. Be that as it may, the problem of psycho-physical correspondence is fortunately irrelevant at the level of abstraction at which I am operating.

The raw material of the image consists of *information inputs* — information simply being defined as improbable patterns without further inquiring patterns of what substance. Information inputs come from two sources: some come from outside the organism, or rather from outside the image itself, from sense receptors, proprioceptors, or even from more subtle sources. Some however come from within the image itself. This self-generation of messages by the image is the work of the *imagination,* which "bodies forth the forms of things unknown." This self-generation of messages is peculiarly the property of the human image: there may be foreshadowings of it among the higher animals, but it is not until the image and the corresponding messages become largely symbolic in nature that the imagination can develop. This distinction between symbolic and non-symbolic messages is of great importance, and is perhaps the most important single distinguishing mark which separates mankind from the animals. Thus suppose I am in a room and hear a voice speaking behind me. I interpret the sound waves which reach my ear, and the corresponding disturbance, whatever it is, in the nervous system, first of all as a *sign* of someone's presence in the room: I may even recognize the voice as that of an old friend. A dog can do as much. When, however, I listen to what the voice is saying, and understand that the person is talking about things of which I have no direct knowledge, and perhaps no previous knowledge; when the voice describes places where I have never been so that I can picture them, or relates experiences which I have never had, or abstract relations which I have never previously understood, the messages are symbolic. This is an experience denied even to the most intelligent of the lower animals.

One of the interesting things which has emerged from modern studies of perception is that what we usually think of as "sense data" are not "data" at all, but are highly learned interpretations of sense messages which are fitted together into our images of time and space. This learning goes on in early infancy — probably from birth, or even before — so that we are not much conscious of it. The learned character of the interpretation of sense messages is shown by people who, for instance, receive their sight as a result of an operation in adult life after having been blind from birth. It often takes months, or even years, for these people to fit their new sense into their old world; they indeed see "men as trees walking" even though physiologically their sight may be perfect.

Messages, whether from internal or external sources, may affect the image in four ways. Most of the innumerable messages which impinge on us in the course of a day simply pass right "through" the image, like an electron through a molecule, without changing it. Most sense messages, especially when the body is not in motion, make little or no impact on the image of the room where we are sitting. As every teacher knows, a great many symbolic messages likewise are capable of passing through the structure of the student's image and leaving it unscathed! In the second place the message may simply add to the structure of the image, as in rote learning; we learn in school that the sun is 93 million miles from the earth (probably without examining the evidence very closely!) and ever afterwards we can regurgitate this "fact" on call. In a somewhat more involved way messages may extend or clarify our existing images, without producing any fundamental reorganization. Thus we visit a new place: we have an indistinct idea of what it is going to be like before we go, but having been there and seen it we now have a clearer and more distinct image of it. Finally messages may hit some kind of "nucleus" of the image and effect a drastic reorganization. This happens in a dramatic form in conversion: it happens on a smaller scale when we re-evaluate a person, a situation, or a theory. This may be called the "restructuring" of the image.

The image exhibits a good deal of resistance to restructuring, especially where the parts involved are high on some significant value scale. Thus suppose messages reach me to the effect that a highly valued friend, whom I have previously pictured as an upright and honorable man, is in fact a scoundrel. My first impulse is to reject the messages as untrue; my image of the authority of the messages, or of the source of the messages, may be easier to shift than the image of my valued friend. Suppose now however that similar messages come from many different sources, and from sources which I have hitherto always found to be reliable. As these messages cumulate there comes a point where I can no longer accept the "messages are untrue" explanation of the incompatibility between the messages and the image, and my image of my friend undergoes a drastic reorganization. The resistance of the image to restructuring must not be regarded as necessarily undesirable; indeed, were there not such resistance the world would dissolve into a kaleidoscope of meaningless and contradictory messages. Nowhere do we see this more clearly than in sense perception: we only get along in the world by constantly disbelieving the clear evidence of our senses. Thus we do not believe that the stick becomes bent when we put it in water, and if the pattern of an automobile on our retina is growing larger we do not interpret this to mean that the automobile is suffering a strange and uniform increase in size — we get out of its way fast! Similarly we interpret a constantly shifting pattern of lines and shadows as a quite stable and stationary room, even as we walk across it; we interpret another shifting pattern of light and shade and sounds as a person, and so on. In the realm of theories and ideas also we progress towards knowledge only as we hold reasonably fast to that which we have; the person who is blown about by every wind of doctrine, and who is convinced by everything that he hears or reads no matter how contradictory to his previously held opinions, is not likely to proceed to a mature and well-considered point of view.

On the other hand too great resistance to restructuring of the image is also dangerous, and is a sign of mental ill-health. At the extreme we have the schizophrenic whose image is so tight and self-consistent that it resists all change, so that all messages which are inconsistent with it, whether external or internal, are simply rejected out of hand. In extreme cases even sense messages are controlled by the image, so that the unfortunate person only sees, hears or even touches what his image tells him, and he retreats into a world of hopeless hallucination, having lost touch altogether with the "real" world both outside him and within. There are many pre-schizophrenic types in active life, of which the fanatical communist is a good example, whose images are so rigid that no contradictory message can get through to them.

Where the image does change and grow, and is from time to time restructured we must look to the inconsistencies for an explanation — either inconsistencies between various parts of the image, which come to be perceived through the internal message system, or inconsistencies between messages and the image. Just what constitutes inconsistency, however, is hard to spell out. Logical inconsistency is only one aspect; many people seem to have quite stable images which are logically inconsistent! There seems to be a kind of aesthetic consistency which at times dominates "mere" logic, or perhaps constitutes a higher logic. Then there is perhaps some over-all valuation function of the image — that wherever reorganization threatens to give us a "worse" image in some over-all sense it is strongly resisted, and hence the stable image will exhibit something like a maximum of over-all value, at least in the small.

II

I now come to the main thesis of this paper, which is that the value image — that is, the various ordering systems by which the parts of the field of the image are ranked — is created and developed, added to and restructured in much the same way that the "image of fact" or the field of the image is itself created and developed. From the point of view of the genetics and growth of the image, therefore, there is not a sharp distinction between the image of fact and the image of value: both are an integral part of the image, both exhibit consistencies and inconsistencies, both are

capable of addition and of restructuring, and the growth patterns
of both are always limited by the nature of the messages received
and by the nature of the existing image. It is highly probable that
in the growth of the organism from its very beginnings in the fertilized egg images both of fact and of value are present together;
were this not so it is difficult to see how growth or any form of organic behavior could be possible. The gene clearly carries some
kind of a blueprint even in the earliest stages; it certainly has
"know-how" of a most elaborate kind, even if it does not have conceptual knowledge, nor does it seem to have any learning ability.
Furthermore this "know-how" implies a value image: there are
some lines of cell growth which it "prefers" and others which it cuts
off in the sculpture of the organic structure. How the gene does this
we do not know: from what it does, however, we must presuppose
something not wholly unlike, though still very different from a "decision process." Once the organism has developed to the point of
awareness, even far below the self-conscious level, it is aware of
comfort and discomfort, danger and safety, and these constitute
primitive value orderings according to which it moves in its dimly
perceived world. Even in such lowly organisms as the molds and
slimes we observe behavior which seems inexplicable without some
kind of primitive awareness and a primitive value ordering of some
complexity, as when large numbers of free cells come together to
form complex and differentiated spore-bearing structures.

As we move towards the symbolic and self-conscious level of organization the image correspondingly becomes enormously more
complex, in its valuational aspects as well as in its over-all field.
At lower levels the value image may be confined to some kind of
comfort-discomfort or pleasure-pain scale, though even at these
levels it may be more complex than we think — there is self-sacrifice in the interests of a higher cause, for instance, even at the
level of the cell! No matter what the biological origins, however,
it is clear that as we approach the symbolic and self-conscious
image in man the value image also becomes symbolic, and is increasingly divorced from the simpler biological values. On the one
hand this leads to people starving in the midst of an abundance of
nutritious but unaccustomed food, and on the other hand to the
noblest behavior of the martyr or the saint. In man there is a

strong tendency for the symbolic image — those things which we have learned by hearing the words or symbols of others — to become dominant. Where there is a complex hierarchy of value orderings, however, the "lower" ones can never be wholly neglected; at the unconscious level or under stress they may take over, and human behavior is nearly always the result of a complex pattern of intersecting and shifting value systems. Purity of heart, alas, is one of the rarest of virtues, and when this purity is obtained by throwing out the higher value systems, it can become pure evil.

We have observed that the growth of the image depends not only on the messages received, but also on its present structure, for present structure always sets some kinds of limits on future growth; thistle seeds do not grow into fig trees, puppies do not grow up into lions, firms rarely grow into churches, or churches into nations, or banks into hospitals. As a special case of this general principle we are coming increasingly to realize that the growth of the image of fact in any individual is governed in part by his existing value orderings, and that change in value orderings likewise is governed in part by reorganizations of the image of fact. This is true, as we noted earlier, even in what we used to think of as "simple" perception. We see the world the way we do, instead of in some possible alternative way, because in some sense it "pays" us to do so. In the theory of signal detection, for instance, it has been shown that the chance of a person detecting a signal, failing to detect it, or giving a false alarm, depends on the "payoffs" (rewards or punishments, or value orderings) associated with each contingency. If penalties for false alarms are great, or rewards for correct interpretations are small, there will be few false alarms but also many "misses." Thus we might almost say that we learn to interpret the barrage of messages from the senses as a three-dimensional world of space and a one-dimensional world of time because if we do not do this we bump into things and hurt ourselves!

Thus in the development of the image a large part is played by a process which might be called *confirmation*. Because the image always includes relations, it can be used as an instrument for predicting the consequences of behavior decisions. Thus if I have an image of a room with myself in it at a certain spot, and also a (largely subconscious) image of my powers of walking, I can decide to walk across the room; my image then includes a prediction of what will happen to the messages I receive as I carry out the decision. If the messages as observed and recorded do not correspond to the images as predicted, then the image is extremely likely to be revised. Suppose, for instance, that as I start to walk across the room, I suddenly run into an invisible wall. It is clear that the messages do not correspond to the prediction, and the image must be revised. I conclude, perhaps, that what I thought was a room was in fact a mirror, or a picture, or perhaps I conclude that there actually is an invisible wall across it. In any case, my previous image is bound to be revised, because of "disappointment" — that is, the failure of predictions to be confirmed. If the prediction is confirmed, then of course the image which gave rise to it is reinforced. A prediction which leads to decision and action, however, always implies that the field of the prediction has a value ordering. If I decide to walk across the room, it is because I want to get to the other side, like the celebrated hen in the riddle. This means that the other side of the room at that time is higher on my value scale than the place where I am. If now my prediction is disappointed, whether by bumping into an invisible wall or by finding that when I get to the other side of the room I don't like it there at all, the value image as well as the field is reorganized. I may decide that the other side of the room is not where I want to be and this side comes uppermost in the value ordering. A good deal of the fabled wisdom of the East consists in the good advice to want what you get rather than to try to get what you want, on the grounds that it is easier to change the value ordering than to encounter repeated disappointments in the field. We see therefore the total image built up as a result of a complex process of message reception, reorganization, prediction, confirmation and disappointment, in which the value image and the image of fact are continuously and inseparably intertwined.

The elaborate images of science are no exception to this rule. The processes of confirmation here are more elaborate, and the value orderings perhaps less explicit than in ordinary life. Scientists form a subculture within the larger society, and this subculture has its own prevalent value orderings. A theory gains acceptance if it rates above competing theories in the value ordering of the

scientific subculture: we can say if we like that those theories succeed which are "pleasing" to the scientist — bearing in mind that
this "pleasing" is not merely an arbitrary emotional glow, but involves the fulfillment of certain rather elaborate predictions, the
development of certain proved attitudes, and the ability to command a hearing. Even science however is not exempt from sociology, especially on matters where perception is difficult. The extreme dependence of marginal perceptions on the value orderings
of the perceiver raises difficulties even in astronomy, where it has
been suggested that the long controversy over the existence of canals
on Mars may be due to the fact that only the sharp-eyed young can
see them, whereas the dimmer-eyed old have the professorships and
carry the prestige! The difficulties of research into extra-sensory
perception arise out of much the same situation.

III

To say that all images arise from the complex interaction of mes-
sage-inputs with the existing image of fact and of value does not
mean, of course, that there is no distinction between fact and fancy,
illusion and falsehood, right and wrong. It must be emphasized
that the image can be considered at many different levels of abstraction. In the foregoing I have been dealing with it as an object
of observation, and discussing the principles which govern its origins and growth much as one might discuss, say, the principles
which govern the origins and growth of an organization, or of a
plant. I have not said anything — and on the whole I shall try
(probably unsuccessfully) to avoid saying anything about the ultimate truth of the image. Epistemology here faces a very serious
dilemma, that what is *meant* by the "truth" of an image is the correspondence between the image and some reality outside it, which
would continue to exist no matter whether anyone had an image
of it or not: to this extent I am a correspondence theorist. On the
other hand we can never in fact compare an image with an external reality, for all we can ever compare are images with images.
The truth of an image must always be in some sense an inference.
Questions of truth and falsehood therefore can also be discussed

at various levels of abstraction, below the ultimate level of correspondence with external reality.

The image is not arbitrary; it makes a difference whether we hold "truer" or "falser" images, even though absolute truth may elude the purely rational grasp. If my image, for instance, tells me that gravity does not exist, and in consequence I jump off a cliff, then no matter how elevated my thoughts on the way down something fairly unpleasant is likely to happen at the bottom. There are images, that is, which lead to disaster, and others which, we hope, do not. At one level, it certainly seems legitimate to call those which do not lead to disaster "truer" than those which do. In this rather narrow and abstract sense, however, it is clear that value images are just as much subject to judgments of truth and falsehood as are images of fact. If my value ordering is based exclusively on my immediate physical sensations of comfort, so that I always value the immediately comfortable more highly than the immediately uncomfortable, and model my behavior accordingly, this also will lead to disaster, simply because it is sometimes necessary to be uncomfortable in order to survive. Similarly if my value ordering is confined entirely to the states of my own person, so that I treat all others merely as means to my own ends, this too is likely to lead to disaster in the complex interaction of social relations and personal character, for without love the human organization shrinks, decays, and eventually disintegrates.

Let me make quite clear that I am not *equating* survival value, or even the mere absence of disaster, with ultimate truth. I do not presume in this essay to inquire into the ultimates and absolutes. What I am arguing is that on the humbler ground where "truer and falser" in regard to the image relate merely to the pragmatic workability of the image, there are processes of validation even if there is no automatic touchstone of truth, and that *these processes of validation apply just as much to the value image as they do to the image of fact*. At this level, at any rate, the "knowledge of value" is not a different kind of thing from the "knowledge of fact"; both are arrived at by much the same kind of processes, both are an integral and necessary part of the image, both are worked out and tested in behavior, in prediction, in consequences, in confirmations, both grow and develop in the way that the whole image grows and develops. It is a leap of faith, of course, from this proposition to the proposition that the knowledge of values is knowledge of a real, objective world, and that values can be true or false in the sense of correspondence to some outside reality. This leap of faith, however, is no greater than the one required in believing that the image of fact likewise corresponds to a real, objective world and that knowledge of fact likewise implies that there is something there to know. In neither case can we ever compare directly the image with the correspondent reality, for as we have seen only images can be compared with images. In both cases, however, there are processes of validation or confirmation, some of which operate on very simple, unsophisticated, common sense levels and others of which require an elaborate theoretical system and experimental controls.

Even though the processes of validation are much the same in all parts of the image, the difficulties of validation differ markedly from one part to another. There are some parts of the image where validation is easy, as, for instance, in the common-sense image of objects in space and time, because confirmations are direct and rapid. There are other parts where validation is difficult because of the complexity of the relations involved and the slowness with which they operate. Ease of validation usually results in extensive *agreement* about the image — that is, the image is a public image widely shared by indefinitely large numbers of people. Where validation is difficult there is more likely to be disagreement: the public image breaks up into subcultural groups, with each subculture bearing a public image which is shared by its own members but not with others. Here again I do not want to equate the existence of a widespread public image with its ultimate truth: one cannot deny the possibility that widely shared images may be wrong. Forty million Frenchmen *can* be wrong; even an image which is shared by the whole human race *might* be wrong. Nevertheless the wide sharing of a public image is part again of the *process* of validation, even if it is not an infallible test of truth.

A peculiarly difficult problem arises for epistemological theory — and indeed, for social and mental health — in the case of *self-validating images*. Self-validating images are of two kinds. There are those which validate themselves because they control the process of validation in the individual; these might be called self-justifying *illusions*. There are others which validate themselves because they give rise to a corresponding reality outside the image; the image creates the world to which it corresponds. The self-validating image in its first form is perhaps the most distinguishing mark of mental illness. The schizophrenic actually sees, hears, and even touches the illusions which his diseased image bodies forth: the paranoid who thinks that everyone is his enemy interprets even kindness as hidden hostility, and no matter *what* he experiences he will interpret it into his diseased and distorted image. Frequently, however, a diseased image creates its own reality: the paranoid not only misinterprets friendship as hostility; because he does this he behaves in such a way that friendship *turns* into hostility. Indeed, part of the psychological treatment of mental disease consists in creating an "artificial" environment for the patient in which "reality" in the shape of professionalized personal relationships remains unaffected by the patients' behavior, so that the self-validating *social* process at least is cut off. One finds similar phenomena in economic and political life: the "paranoid" nation that believes that everyone is hostile towards it acts in such a way as to transform what may have been initially an illusion into a reality — everybody does become hostile towards it! Similarly in economic life, if everyone believes there is going to be an inflation, individuals seek to protect themselves against this by trying to shift their assets out of money and into goods or stocks, and the result, of course, is the very inflation which was feared. Similarly the fear of depression can lead to one, the fear of war can lead to one, the fear of dictatorship can lead to one. A large part of the problem of social institutions and policy consists in setting up institutional barriers to these self-justifying processes — stabilization devices in economics, federal government in politics, and so on.

The phenomenon of self-justifying images also crops up in the value image. Indeed, it is not too much to claim that every culture is built around a set of value images which the culture then proceeds to protect by setting up institutions of validation. Because of the symbolic nature of much of the value image in man, much of its validation likewise comes from symbolic sources — especially from the approval or reproof of those whose good opinion is im-

portant to us. An important part of the confirmation of value
images lies in the perception of congruence between the value
images of the person and those of the "reference group" with which
he is surrounded. In a closed group therefore the value image is
likely to be fairly stable, and is perpetuated from generation to
generation by the institutions which support and propagate it —
the family, the church and the school. The situation is not as simple as this, of course: in the experience of the growing child strong
ambivalences are developed, especially under the stricter regimes of
child-rearing, and *rebellion* is not infrequent, with rejection of the
value image of the culture and the acceptance of competing images:
even children reared in a good Catholic environment occasionally
become Quakers, and *vice versa!* If, however, the subculture can
eject the rebels and if it has a sufficiently high birth and conversion
rate, it can maintain itself even in the midst of strong and even
hostile competing cultures. The astonishing persistence of the
Amish eighteenth-century culture in the midst of the aggressive
secular culture of modern America is a case in point. Incidentally,
this perhaps explains in part why the church in a monoreligious
culture like that of Scandinavia or Spain compares very unfavor-
ably in internal vigor with the same churches in a polyreligious culture like the United States. In a monoreligious culture the church
has to absorb its rebels; in a polyreligious culture it can easily eject
them.

To say that the value image is partly self-validating within a culture is neither to condemn it nor to deny its ultimate validity. We
have seen that even in the image of fact some degree of rigidity is
necessary if the image is not to collapse into a jelly of unorganized
information. There is unquestionably some optimum point or range
of rigidity and degree of self-validation in the value image as well
as in the image of fact. The firm structure which is not impervious
to challenge seems to be the desirable form. And there is certainly
no lack of challenge to the value image, even within fairly tight and
closed subcultures. The challenge, especially in a pluralistic society,
may come from an outside culture. A good example of a change
in the value image of a culture under such challenge is the development of an explicit social ethic in both Catholic and Protestant

Christianity in the latter half of the nineteenth century, a movement which is certainly not unrelated to the challenge of secular
social faiths, whether liberal or socialist. The challenge may even
come from a *past culture;* the challenge of Greece and Rome as
revealed in their surviving literature and architecture had a lot to do
with the Renaissance, and the challenge of Biblical Hebraic culture
as embodied in the Bible had something, at least, to do with the Reformation. This is perhaps one reason for the paradox that a culture which rests heavily on sacred scriptures and records of the past
is often so surprisingly dynamic and vigorous: the constant challenge of the past on the present continually renews it. The challenge may also come from prophetic individuals within the culture.
There are from time to time in history individuals who are not
caught in the deterministic dynamics of their own culture, but who
seem to have access to outside reservoirs of moral reality. We are
here approaching the phenomenon of Revelation.

From all these sources, challenges continually come to existing
value systems; the challenge, of course, may be rejected, or it may
be accepted in whole or in part. It is not difficult to see in this
process something strongly akin to the general process of validation
of the image, difficult and complex and long drawn out as the
process may be. At least in this regard we travel hopefully. It is
only proper humility to confess that we know very little about the
ultimates and absolutes: it is sheer cowardice, however, to maintain with some modern philosophers that these matters are of no
concern to us, or are "nonsense propositions" not worth troubling
our minds about. We are not given perfect knowledge, but it is
not unreasonable to hope for sufficient knowledge. When this is
perceived, it is cause for thankfulness and adoration.

IV

This brings me, very briefly, to the last part of my title. If the
subject of the knowledge of value is a touchy one, that of the value
of knowledge is doubly so. It is almost treason in the groves of
academe to suggest even that the question exists. It is part of the
value image of the academic community that any extension of

knowledge, in any direction, by anybody, is intrinsically good, and that more knowledge is always to be preferred to less. As far as this is a prejudice, I must confess that I think it is a noble prejudice, and it is one that I share. I detest secretiveness; I harbor the feeling that no decent person would *want* to do classified research whether for government or business, however much other values might impel him towards it. The concept of an open fellowship of seekers after knowledge is one of the most precious gifts of science; by comparison the beastly secretiveness of the totalitarian or military state, or of the mystagogue or the quack is repugnant to the mind and spirit.

Nevertheless there is a problem of the *economy* of knowledge. In the modern world especially we cannot know everything. We are hampered not only if we know things that aren't so, but also if we know things that aren't *necessary*. What is "necessary" is of course a tricky and delicate question, and the above proposition is capable of monstrous perversion. We do *not* want a world of slick technicians, trained rather than educated, knowing only their own little corner of the universe and indifferent to the great concerns and cosmic responsibilities of man. There is a famous passage in Sherlock Holmes where the good Watson reproves the Master for his ignorance of astronomy, and Holmes defends himself by saying that he cannot afford to carry any surplus knowledge in his profession, and that the question of whether the sun goes round the earth or the earth goes round the sun is a matter of utter indifference to him. In that argument I confess I am on the side of Watson! There are things which we should know simply because of our status as men — these are the things which are the proper core of liberal education. What these things are, of course, is open to discussion, and the need to replace the mediaeval synthesis with a new trivium and quadrivium appropriate to the vastly expanded knowledge of our day is one of the central questions of modern education. This core of necessary knowledge, however, is a minimum, not a maximum. Even as we go on into the specialized disciplines the problem of the necessary core remains; if we insist on what is not necessary we are doing grave harm to the educational process. What this means is that the growth of the image itself is subject to the evaluative and critical process; the value ordering extends not only over the existing field, but over potential future fields. At some points, much as I hate to admit it, ignorance is, if not bliss, at least good economy. This is a problem which has received too little attention in the academic community, perhaps because each specialist has a strong vested interest in his own specialty and tends to think that this, at least, must be part of the necessary core of knowledge! We must come to recognize, however, that the planning of a curriculum is an ethical problem, and that the more clearly this is recognized, and the more earnestly explicit value systems and ethical principles are sought after in this regard, the more likely we are to achieve "balanced growth" (that elusive ideal of the economics of development!) in knowledge.

ORGANIZING GROWTH

Challenge, 8, 3 (Dec. 1959): 31-36

ORGANIZING
GROWTH

Unconscious evolution, conscious direction—or both

■ AS WE LOOK around the world, both of nature and of man, we observe two broad types of growth and change. The first might be called organizational growth. This is the kind of growth that transforms the egg into an embryo, the embryo into a fetus, the fetus into a young animal, the young animal into a mature animal and the mature animal into a corpse. It is the type of growth also which transforms an idea into a plan, a plan into a proposal, a proposal into a young organization, a young organization into a mature organization and a mature organization into extinction.

The second might be called ecological or evolutionary growth. This is the process by which in the mutation and selection of innumerable individuals, each following its own pattern of organizational growth, the whole pattern and composition of individuals changes. Atoms give rise to molecules, molecules to viruses, viruses to cells, cells to animals, and animals proliferate and differentiate themselves on the long road that leads through fish, reptiles and mammals to man. Man in turn forms families, tribes, states, corporations, churches, businesses, trade unions, federations, and so on, in a pattern of ever-increasing complexity and richness.

Measuring either of these forms of growth is a matter of some difficulty. In the case of organic growth, we usually have some rough measure of the size of the organism or organization—normally, weight or volume in the case of the organism, and members, capital value or net worth in the case of the social organization. But no single measure is ever quite satisfactory. In the case of the biological organism, a mere increase in weight is obviously not "growth" in the same sense as the orderly "balanced growth" of the youngling into the adult.

Similarly, organizations can exhibit obesity of the membership list and firms can have inflated balance sheets. In most cases, however, it seems not to be too difficult in practice to distinguish "true" from "false" growth and to get a measure which is good enough to indicate at least the direction.

Youth and vigor

Organizations can renew their youth and vigor in ways which do not seem to be open to the higher animals. Because men die, organizations need not. Death (and retirement) removes persons from the organization and permits their replacement with younger and perhaps more vigorous types. Consequently, the very processes which result in the death of the biological individual may perpetuate and even augment the species or the organization.

A good deal of current world controversy between communism and capitalism, and also what may be even more important in the long run—subcontroversies within each of these world systems—revolves around the relative merits of organizational versus ecological growth patterns as applied to the economic system.

The classical "capitalist" pattern of economic growth is ecological rather than organizational. New economic species are supposed to arise through the mutational activities of the entrepreneur, who creates a new type of commodity, an improved method of producing an old commodity, or an improved form of organization. These improved forms feed voraciously on the profits which their temporary market situation gives them and grow at the expense of older and less-advanced forms. Railroads dispossess the stagecoach, and the bus and the truck displace the railroad, much as the mammals displaced the reptiles.

The competition of all producers for "food" in the shape of consumer purchases insures, ostensibly, that only the ablest and most progressive forms of economic organization will survive. The price mechanism, which operates to shower profits on those who are most successfully meeting the needs of consumers, likewise operates to remove these profits as soon as maturity and conservatism make them unnecessary. The test of survival is the ability to sell, and it is hoped that the ability to sell corresponds closely to the desirability of the sale.

In the classical "Communist" pattern, on the other hand, society is conceived as a single organization or a "one-firm state." The survival of any particular suborganization or pattern of production within this giant body depends not so much on its ability to command income from sale of product, as on its ability to command a budget allotment in the over-all plan.

Ability to conform

Growth in this case originates with that group at the top of the hierarchy which has control of the budgets of the whole society. In such a society the "success" of an organization depends, in part at any rate, on its ability to conform to the plan sent down from the central agency.

Neither of these ideal types exists or ever has existed; but they are useful extreme concepts with which reality may be compared. Even in the most capitalist of countries there has been a considerable attempt at self-conscious control of the destinies and growth of the society by those in government who felt themselves peculiarly responsible for the whole. In the United States, for instance, commercial policy, land policy, immigration policy, reclamation policy, educational policy, and even military policy have constantly been framed with the rapid development of the society in mind; in part, our success may be due to good fortune, but good management has at least played *some* part in it!

By contrast, Communist societies are not as monolithic as they seem at first glance. Traces of the market institution exist everywhere in overt or covert form, and the will of the planners is frequently frustrated by the intractability of the planned–especially in agriculture. This is not to deny, of course, the very real differences between the two types of society. But it is by no means inconceivable that these differences will become less as time goes on.

Capitalism has certainly shown a remarkable capacity for developing institutions of centralized control without losing the essential flexibility of the market economy. Communist societies seem to be more hag-ridden by dogma and subject to more ideological rigidity. But even Russia under Lenin adopted a New Economic Policy of limited free markets, and Poland at least seems to be moving in that direction under its present rulers.

There may be very good reasons for this hope of convergence of communism and capitalism. If biological systems are anything to go by, both ecological and organizational growth play an important part in the over-all pattern of development. There are large elements of unconscious organization in the body which bear some analogies to a price system. The growth of the body is not planned in detail by the central planning committee of the genes; it follows certain loosely defined "payoffs." The heartbeat and the growth patterns of the body are wholly outside self-conscious central direction.

There seems to be an optimum combination of unconscious and conscious processes in any organism, and this may be true also in the social organization. Whatever the position of the balance, however, a balance there must be, in the social as well as the biological organization. It may be, indeed, that as organizations become larger and more complex, more and more of the ordinary operations must be taken over by unconscious and automatic processes.

When it comes to the question of the relation of different social systems to economic growth, it is clear from the record that a system's position on the ecological scale tells us very little, in itself, of the system's growth performance. Both capitalist- and Communist-oriented systems have shown high rates of growth, and both have also shown stagnation. As far as growth is concerned (quite apart from the human costs of growth in terms of violence, insecurity and repression), Communist Russia has done well. Communist China, if reports are to be trusted, has done very well; Poland and Hungary rather badly; and East Germany very badly.

On the other side, the United States has done very well, along with Japan and West Germany. Conversely, most of Latin America has done quite badly.

It is clear that the essential ingredients for rapid economic growth may be present—or may be absent—in almost any type of economy; neither the free market nor the planned economy can guarantee it.

Ecological growth, whether in the biological or the sociological world, depends on the number of viable mutations. In social life, the mutant is the innovator—the man who does something different from what has been done before, or is being done around him. The institutions of a society, even a free market society, may be such that the mutant is penalized to the point where no innovation pays off. Then there will be no economic growth.

Will to grow

Similarly, in organizational growth the combination of the will with the power to innovate is crucial. Organization concentrates power in the upper echelons of the organizational hierarchy. If the powerful have a strong will to grow, as in Russia and Communist China, the power and the will may move together, and high growth rates will result. A large proportion of resources will be devoted to human and material investment and, in spite of the almost inevitable inefficiency of very large-scale organizations, the society will move forward. The concentration of power, however, increases the chance of serious mistakes, such as the forced collectivization of agriculture in Russia, Britain's African groundnuts and even, dare we say it, the Edsel!

The problems of organizational growth are not confined to Communist societies. Indeed, communism can be seen as just a very extreme case of that "organizational revolution" which has created General Motors, the U.S. Air Force, the United Mine Workers, the American Medical Association, the University of California and the National Council of Churches. The crucial long-run problem here is whether the large organization can develop techniques of role-filling, especially in the process of promotion toward the higher roles, which avoid the perpetuation of a smug and conservative oligarchy through the continual promotion and replacement of like by like.

Weight of tradition

In this respect, most large organizations are still too young to tell whether this problem can be solved. The Catholic Church and, to some extent, the British ruling class solve this problem by encrusting the roles themselves with so much weight of tradition and authority that the occupant hardly matters. In the more insecure and less well-established roles of the big corporation or the Communist state, a poor occupant can ruin both himself and the organization. The problem does not arise as long as the first generation of leaders is in power, as these are the innovators and creators and, clearly, the organization would never have grown had they not been capable of organizing its growth.

As time goes on, however, the problem becomes more and more acute. Of the large American corporations, only American Telephone & Telegraph seems to take this problem much to heart, and it is by no means certain that AT&T can solve it.

The problem of succession in a Communist state, with its immense concentration of power in the hands of the hierarchical leader, is even more frightening, as the case of Stalin illustrates dramatically. Even the problem of the aging and deterioration of the occupant of a powerful role becomes more intractable as organizations grow in size, and one ends with the horrible vision of a world's destiny in the tremulous hands of a small group of sick, old men.

For these reasons, if for no others, I confess to a certain prejudice in favor of ecological growth and the kind of institutions which permit it. It is the imperceptible forces which, in the long run, are often the stronger. "The tumult and the shouting dies, the captains and the kings depart." Conquerors and dictators flash like shooting stars across the backdrop of history, but the great tidal movements of intellectual, technical, economic and social change sweep on.

Population explosion

The invention of DDT, by controlling mosquitoes and thereby setting off a human population explosion in the tropics, may have more impact on human history than the Russian or Chinese revolutions. This does not mean, however, that man's attempts to control the destiny of his societies and his race are all doomed to total frustration.

It is the mission of the intellect to make the latent manifest, and to bring out into the light of conscious knowledge what has been lurking in the dark. A people that thinks it knows where it is going, and has a clear idea of its future, has an advantage over one that does not, even though its image may be false and its prophets deceivers.

We will not get anywhere without a ticket to somewhere, and though mankind has had plenty of tickets to nonexistent places, to nirvanas and heavens and utopias and classless societies, the search for the right ticket continues.

Because of the almost complete irreversibility of the growth of knowledge, therefore, it may be that the long run lies with organization rather than evolution and that intelligence will once more mold a whole universe to its heart's desire. This, however, is a long run indeed, and for the moment wisdom seems to require some bets on both sides. ■

A THEORY OF SMALL SOCIETY

Caribbean Quarterly, 6, 4 (1960): 258-269

A Theory of Small Society

THE theory of a small society is only a special case of the theory of society as a whole, so we must start with the general case. I am not going to define society, except to say that I am considering human societies rather than animal societies, and that I think of a human society as any group of people which is interesting ; exactly what makes one group interesting and another group not interesting I do not propose here to examine.

The first concept I wish to develop is that of the *state* or condition of a society, as it exists at a moment of time. Here we imagine that someone takes a flashlight photograph of the society with all its relevant conditions, variables and parts. This will include, in the first place, certain stocks which exist at this moment of time in the society. There is the human population, classified by age, sex, education, character, religion or any other relevant personality variable. Then there are stocks of physical assets, land, buildings, and apparatus ; stocks of social institutions and organisations, schools, firms, governments, churches, families ; stocks of knowledge and ideas and skills in the population. It is clear that the list might be extended almost indefinitely, and what we include in the list will depend to a large extent on the type of studies that we wish to pursue. The economist studying the economic dynamics of a society will include one set of things ; the sociologist and the anthropologist and the psychologist will include other things. In the description of the state there are not only stocks, there are certain flows : birth and death rates, rates of production, consumption and depreciation of all kinds of commodities, rates of formation or destruction of organisations, rates, in fact, of addition to and subtraction from any item that is important in the stock.

The problem of the dynamics of society is how we get from the state of today to the state of tomorrow. If we can do this in a regular and unequivocal way, we can then get to the day after tomorrow and the day after that and the day after that, proceeding indefinitely into the future. It may be, of course, that tomorrow's state depends not only on today's state, *but on yesterday's* state and the state of the day before yesterday and the day before that. In many cases we shall find this to be true. Nevertheless, the fundamental principle remains, that if we can get from today till tomorrow, if we understand how tomorrow grows out of today, then we have gone a long way towards understanding the dynamics of a society.

One very important determinant of tomorrow is the flows of today. If, for instance, births exceed deaths today, there will be more people tomorrow than there were today. If production exceeds consumption today, there will be more physical goods in existence tomorrow than there were today. This principle can be applied to any element in the stock. If the rate of production of high school graduates today, for instance, exceeds their death rate, there will be more high school graduates tomorrow than there are today.

Another very important principle is that the *flows* of today are related to the *stocks* of today. If, for instance, there is a large proportion of women of fertile age in the population, the birthrate is likely to be higher than if there was a small proportion. If there are a lot of literate and educated people in the population, the output of goods is likely to be higher. If the population is very religious, there will be a large production of churches ; if the population consists mainly of farmers, there will be a large production of agricultural commodities.

These dynamic processes are extremely complex, and it is hard to trace them out. The character and abilities of a person aged, say 50 today, is a result not only of the state of yesterday and the day before, but is a result of all that has happened to him and to the society in the past 50 years. The state of any society today therefore, depends not only on its state yesterday, but on its whole past history and especially on its history in the past 70 or 80 years which produced the people of the society today.

In studying the dynamics of a society, we need to pay special attention to what we might call the transmitters of culture : the people of today are what they are because of the influences which have made them so—these influences include their parents, the families in which they grew up, the teachers who taught them, the preachers who preached to them, the friends and acquaintances who have communicateed with them constantly all their lives. Many anthropologists and social psychologists lay a great deal of stress on what happens in the first few years, or even in the first few months of life. While this effect can be exaggerated, it nevertheless remains very important, and it is hardly an exaggeration to say that conditions in the family are one of the main determinants of the character and of change in that character. If we want to change the character of a society, the people we must change are the mothers and the fathers who are training the next generation. We must not underestimate, however, the influence of schools, churches, boys clubs and even universities. It may be true that the predispositions of character are set in early childhood, so that whether a man is grasping or generous, fearful or courageous, dependent or independent, may depend much on what happens to him as a very small child. The thoughts, ideas, and actual patterns of behaviour, however, are determined largely by what happens in somewhat later years, especially in the years of adolescence. Early childhood may predispose us to certain things, but by and large it is adolescence that disposes us. In understanding the dynamics of a society, we must also be constantly on the look out for the creators, as well as the transmitters of culture. The prophets, the poets, the historians, are the people who very often create the culture which is thenceforward transmitted by more ordinary spirits.

One of the problems of the theory of the society, is how to simplify the enormous complexity of these dynamic processes. Some writers, like Karl Marx, have tried to simplify them by aggregating people into classes, and postulating a quasi-mystical succession of classes. Another attempt at simplification is to take one particular strand of the network, like economics, or religion, or philosophy, or politics, and to suppose that everything else depends on this one strand. All these are oversimplifications, that get less realistic as time goes on and society gets more complex. I must confess in regard to the theory of society that I am an eclectic. Even though there are within society some sub-systems which obey certain dynamic principles of their own, nevertheless the whole great web weaves and interweaves into a pattern of great complexity. We cannot say that any one strand determines the other. The development of economic life and institutions is an important strand, and this often affects the other aspects of life in society, such as the family, religion and the state. Nevertheless these non-economic elements in society have an inner dynamic of their own which often proceeds almost independently of what is happening in the rest of the society, and in turn leads to impacts upon other sub-systems. We can argue indefinitely, for instance, about whether the Reformation was a cause of Capitalism, as Max Weber suggested, or whether it was the rising capitalist class that gave strength to the Reformation. This is like arguing which came first, the chicken or the egg. Occasionally some strand in the social web develops a dynamic of its own which takes it far away from the development of other strands, and develops inconsistent movements within the framework of society. These inconsistencies can slow down or even arrest the development of a society— as when, for instance, the dynamic of its religious ideas goes counter to the dynamic of its technology. Sometimes, however, all the separate strands seem to be working in the same direction, and when that happens the society will change rapidly.

Another method of dealing with the complexities of social dynamics, is to postulate an *equilibrium* to the system, and to suppose then that the dynamic process leads eventually to this equilibrium. An equilibrium system is one in which tomorrow is exactly like today—that is, in which the dynamic processes of today, produce a tomorrow which is no different from today. In this case, all the flows in the society are only just sufficient to maintain the state of the stock unchanged. On the whole societies which have approximated an equilibrium condition, have been fairly simple. Almost all advanced societies since the dawn of history, have been in process of rapid and continuous change. Our own society especially for the last two hundred years, has been going through a process of rapid change which is unprecedented in the whole history of mankind. It is hardly surprising therefore, that some writers question the value of the equilibrium concept, in a world that is as dynamic and is apparently as far from equilibrium as this one. Nevertheless the concept of equilibrium is an important tool of the social sciences, as indeed of all sciences, and I am prepared to defend it. The study of equilibrium, tells us where the present processes are going to take us, and even if this future state is a long way off. Also if we know the equilibrium, we know the general long-run *direction* of change, for equilibrium is what we are moving towards.

Let me take an example from the equilibrium of populations. It is not too difficult to develop a dynamic theory of population growth. We know for instance that if births exceeds deaths, that is, if the birth rate exceeds the death rate then the population will grow. We know also that anyone who is forty-nine today, will either be 50 next year or he will be dead; by means of relatively simple assumptions about future birth and survival rates, it is possible to project the numbers and the composition of the population for several years ahead. These projections are not predictions, and are easily falsified; indeed the failure of population predictions in the past 20 years has been spectacular; nevertheless we do know something about the future of population. We know, for instance, that population cannot grow forever—sooner or later must come the day of reckoning and an equilibrium population. I calculated recently that if the world population continues to grow at its present rate of about 2 per cent. per annum, it will only take a little over 700 years, for there to be standing room only over the whole earth—oceans as well as land. Even if we were to try to solve this problem by shooting people off into space, it would take only a little over 8,000 years for the whole astronomical universe two billion light years in diameter, to become solid with humanity. It is clear that achieving an equilibrium population is not a problem for the remote future. In many parts of the world it is a problem which must be tackled in the present generation. Now, however, we are gripped by a certain iron law of mathematics; in an equilibrium population the expectation of life of the average individual is related directly to the birth and death rates. If the birth rate is at its physiological maximum of about 45 per thousand, and the death rate is correspondingly high, the expectation of life cannot be more than about 22 years—to put the same thing in another way, if we want an equilibrium population with an expectation of life of 70, we cannot have a birth rate and death rate of more than 14 per thousand. To put the same thing in still another way, if we have an equilibrium birth rate with a high expectation of life, and if everybody marries, then the average family cannot be more than two children, especially if all children survive into maturity.

An equilibrium population, with an average expectation of life of a little over 20 years, is a population in abject misery. If we are to have successful society with an equilibrium population, then we must eventually face the problem of population control. There is no escape from this conclusion; this does not mean of course, that we have to endorse one method of limiting population over another. The particular techniques of family limitation, are largely irrelevant to this problem. It is significant for instance, that two countries which have been fairly successful in family limitation are Ireland and Austria. Both of these are strongly Catholic countries. What is important here is not any particular techniques, so much as the whole moral attitude toward the family. There must be a sense of responsibility and desire for high quality rather than quantity, which pervades the society as a whole.

Looking out towards the still larger horizon we may ask ourselves the question as to whether a permanent high level society is possible in any case. We have to admit, I think, that with present techniques it is not. The economic development and the remarkable progress of the last two hundred years have been achieved only at the cost of running down the store of geological capital. We have burnt coal and oil, we have mined ore and scattered the products all over the earth. This is a process which might be called social and economic entropy, by analogy with the great concept of the second law of thermodynamics. Man finds a world in which things are concentrated. The processes of his life, however, result in diffusion. Both energy and ores have become less available for subsequent generations.

Fortunately the case is not hopeless. We have indications that a high level technology is possible which does not depend on exhaustible resources. We are living through a period in which mankind has a fighting chance to achieve such a technology. Atomic energy has enormously pushed back the frontiers of the limitations of power although it is a costly and dangerous method of producing power under present techniques. The possibilities of the direct utilization of solar energy are real and it is highly probable that this problem may be solved even within the present generation. The problem of the diffusion of ores is more troublesome. Even here, however, we are developing processes like the fixation of nitrogen from the air and the production of magnesium from the sea which offer escape from the seemingly inevitable processes of diffusion.

These questions are important from the point of view of the dynamics of society. Because if no long run high level equilibrium is possible then all our economic development, all our progress, all our civilisation are ultimately doomed to frustration. Human progress then becomes a mere flash in the pan of geological time, an insignificant era of exploitation of natural capital resources, between two long periods of miserable scratching for existence in the forests. An ecologist has recently written a spine-chilling article in which he compares mankind as a species to the pioneer species which first invade an environment, expand in population with great rapidity, but are destroyed by their own success because the environment which they can use is exhausted, and then other less ambitious species come along to inherit the earth. The proposition that the meek inherit the earth may be more true than it is comforting. One resents all the more resources which are wasted in war and in luxury when one realises that the present era represents a never to be repeated chance of establishing the permanent high level society which we all desire and that every wasteful use of resources makes the chance of success somewhat smaller.

All that I have said up to this point applies to all societies, to the small as well as to the large. Let us now turn to the question of the peculiar problems of the small society. The first question to ask is why are there small societies at all? This might be called the boundary problem. Why is the great universe of mankind split up into nations, classes and groups within nations? Why are some of these large and some of them small? What determines the boundary between one and another? I have recently revived an old interest in astronomy and I have been exploring the, for me, new constellations of the southern sky. In looking through the Atlas of the Stars, I find somewhat to my surprise that the number of constellations in the whole sky is almost exactly equal to the number of nations in the United Nations. There are eighty-eight constellations in the sky; there are eighty-two nations in the United Nations. It is clear that there is still room for the West Indies—though not much! It is a mere accident, of course, that the numbers should correspond so closely. It is an amusing accident also that the Great Bear should occupy the position in the celestial sphere almost identical with that of Russia on the globe and that lying to the west of it is the great constellation of Hercules. Nevertheless, it is no accident that there is about the same number of constellations in the sky as in nations on the earth, for the constellations are not in the galaxy nor are nations on the earth; both are products of the minds of men. If we ask why the globe of the sky is divided by man into these little pieces, and why the great globe of humanity likewise is divided into little pieces, the answer is much the same.

The first answer is that this division is a result of the smallness and inadequacy of the human imagination. Our minds are too small to grasp the great constellation of the whole sky. They are likewise too small to grasp the great constellation of humanity. As a result we find it necessary to break up these great systems into small parts in the hope that the parts will be small enough for our minds to grasp and that perhaps we may build up the great system out of the small.

The second answer is kinder to the dignity both of the constellations and of the nations. It is that man is a great pattern-maker, and that these patterns are not arbitrary, but are perceived as patterns by many different men of diverse times and cultures. These *gestalts*, as the psychologist calls them are an integral part of man's relationship with things, and even if they are in man rather than in the things, this does not detract from their reality and importance. Thus men in many climes and ages have looked at Orion as it rises now like a great celestial symphony in the west, and have detected and enjoyed in that region of the sky much the same pattern. Casseopeia and the Big Dipper, Auriga and Pegasus stand out with almost equal vividness. On the other hand, there are many constellations which defy the most lively imagination, and others which one itches to rearrange. Similarly, with the nations and societies of mankind; some nations are great constellations in time, space and culture, clearly marked off by the inner integrity of their own pattern from the rest of the world. Others may be less clearly marked off, and others again may be in need of rearrangement. The patterns, however, are not arbitrary; the great brocade of mankind is not a plain patternless sheet.

There is a third principle which governs the boundaries of societies and nations which also applies to the stars. This is the principle of perspective. When we look at the landscape or at the sky the near things look large and important and the far things look small. The sun is a miserable little star as stars go—but not to us! The same happens when we look at the social landscape. Those people and things which are close to us, our own family, our circle of friends, our job, our country look large, and the things which are far from us look small. It is not unreasonable, therefore, to see a pattern in near things which we do not see in the far. Even though, therefore, we know that perspective is an illusion in the landscape as well as in society, nevertheless it is one of the illusions by which we live and it must be respected.

I must confess that when I was a young man I was very impatient of nationality and of this division of the great world of mankind into what seemed to me arbitrary and meaningless constellations. I was impatient too of the waste of resources which the quarrels of nations involved and of the desolation which followed their idiotic wars. I longed to be a world citizen,

I longed to see the day, in the noble words of Tennyson, "When the war drums throb no longer and the battle flags were furled in the parliament of man, the federation of the world". I think perhaps I became an American partly because this was as close as I could get to becoming a world citizen and that being a member of any smaller society gave me claustrophobia.

Now that I am in middle life I must confess that I am somewhat more tolerant of nationalism and especially of rising nationalisms. I see that it is necessary for people to have an identity, and for individuals to find a home even though the nations, like the constellations, exist in the minds of man. Nevertheless they fulfil a purpose there. If nations are the result of the smallness of our minds, very well then—we have small minds and the world must be adjusted to it. Furthermore, just as the small constellation is a useful tool to the study of the great constellation of the sky, so the nation may also be a useful stepping stone to the development of that sense of the oneness of all mankind which I am sure we all desire.

Every individual needs to belong to some group with which he can identify, of which he can say "this is what I am". The nation helps to satisfy this need. I am not convinced that the nation is the *only* thing which can satisfy this need. As man develops he becomes part of many groups, each of which satisfy a certain need of his being, and it may be that we are moving towards the time when the nation is no longer an emotional necessity and when man will find his identity partly in his occupation, partly in his faith, partly in groups of common interest and allocation. As we move towards a world in which everybody is a professional, men will perhaps find in their professional specializations that identity which previously they needed the nation to supply. We are, however, a long way from this golden age, and in the meantime the nation has an important part to play, both in organising the world and in meeting psychological needs.

It is an interesting, and to me an unresolved question, as to whether there is anything that might be called an equilibrium set of nations of different sizes. Is there any reason to suppose, for instance, that a nation will conform to one boundary rather than another? Certainly one would expect homogeneity to be a factor. Nevertheless there are many nations which are extremely heterogeneous, which have more than one language, more than one religion and more than one culture and more than one level of economic life. There have been nations which have split into two or more. There have been nations which have come together in a larger federation and unit. Perhaps the most essential factor here is the intensity of communications. Where we have a group of individuals who communicate a great deal with each other but less with people outside, there we have the raw material for the nation. Where one nation is divided into two non-communicating groups, it may be ripe for splitting. Where the people of two nations communicate frequently with each other, but less with the outside world, they may be ripe for federation and union.

The boundary problem concerns all nations, large or small, and it may still be felt that we have not yet reached the problems of the small society. The greatest difference between large societies and small societies is that the smaller a society the more important is its external environment. For humanity as a whole there is no external environment as yet, though space travel may alter this! For large nations like Russia and the United States, the external environment is a matter of secondary importance though even in these cases it is still a very important factor. The smaller we go in national size, however, the more important the external environment becomes, and it is perhaps the theory of the external environment which is peculiarly the theory of the small society.

I distinguish four elements in the external environment. The first consists of the market opportunities which are open to a society, the economist summarises these under the concept of the *terms of trade*. These opportunities determine the possibility of enrichment through specialisation. The real income of a small society depends not only on its per capita output of what it produces; it also depends on how much it can get in exchange for what it produces. The income of a small society will be greater the higher the prices of its exports and the lower the prices of its imports.

The second element in the environment of a society consists of its opportunities for emigration and immigration. This is the import or export of people. Emigration ordinarily reduces the rate of increase of the population. Immigration usually increases this rate. Where a society is really at the subsistence level, emigration may not help its population problem because for every emigrant that leaves more children survive to maturity. It must be remembered also that emigration and immigration change the composition of the population as well as its size, emigration frequently adversely, immigration favourably. A society with large emigration tends to lose some of its most able and active members in the prime of life. A society which receives immigrants receives energetic adults whose "cost of production" have been met by other societies.

The third element in the environment of a society consists of its organisational connections. The small society is a locus of parts and segments of larger organisations. Corporations, federal or imperial governments, churches, United Nations organisations, and so on, have segments within the small society. These parts lead both into and out of the parent body. In some cases they may be a disadvantage to the small society in that they drain its resources out, in other cases they may be an advantage to the society because they feed resources in. A small society, however, always has to face the problem that it exists in a world of large organisations and that these are going to penetrate it.

The fourth element in the environment of a society consists of the information outflows and inflows. These are important because they build up the image of the society both within it and outside it and hence affect the behaviour of both individuals and organisations. The information inflows and outflows are important also because they affect the knowledge and the skills of a people of the society. A society which was completely isolated from information from the outside world would find its pace of change very slow, and the first step towards social and economic development is often an accelerated inflow of information.

I have to confess that I know very little about existing small societies, and I propose to create a totally imaginary small society to illustrate some of the principles which I have developed. Any resemblance to any existing small society is a *gestalt* in the mind of the reader. This small society I shall call the Hesperides, or the Fortunate Isles. It is well known that in classical times these islands lay west of the Pillars of Hercules and were largely populated by duppies. They have an ideal climate where winter never comes. They have had a sad history. At the moment of observation they are looking forward to a more hopeful future, to economic development and political self-control. I use the term self-control advisedly rather than independence because if one is honest one has to admit that the small society cannot be truly independent in the sense of not being dependent on the rest of the world. Indeed one could argue that in this day independence is an illusion even for the largest society. The existence of the Hesperides as a nation is complicated by the existence of at least three sub-constellations. We have first Hesperidaica, a self-contained island of about a million and a half people who, in the opinion of the other islanders are also very self-contained. Then we have Hesperidad, and the Hesperikids, a group of small islands among which is the last remaining outpost of the Roman Empire—Hesperidados. We should also possibly include an island which is almost wholly surrounded by land known as Hesperidiana. These islands are united, or possibly divided, by a common language, a certain amount of common history and certain common traditions. It is an interesting question as to whether the common language is a uniting or a dividing force. The difficulty of the common language is that it enables people to think they understand each other. There are some notable examples of nations which are united by *not* having a common language and which stay together because neither part understand what the others are saying about them. The Hesperides are poor, but they are not *that* poor. They are at least rich enough to have traffic jams, ulcers and neuroses. Still they want to be much richer and are not at all satisfied with their present levels of living.

One of the big questions at the moment is whether they will get richer together or apart. This is by no means clear. Hesperidaica is small, but there are ten countries which are smaller in the League of Imaginary Nations. It is not surprising therefore to find some Hesperidaicans who think that Hesperidaica could go it alone. Moreover Hesperidaica has been thriving, under a capitalist-socialist government, and is at least a going concern, and it is not sure whether it wants to exchange a going concern which it knows for a more heterogeneous larger unit of more doubtful future which it does not know. Hesperidad is the richest of the islands but the kids are quite a problem as kids usually are. Hesperidad is a more heterogeneous society, racially and religiously than Hesperidaica and this opens up fine possibilities of political impasse. Hesperidiana, unfortunately, worships false gods which are placated with vodka rather than with rum, which is the sacred beverage of the islands. To complete the picture we should add that the islands are highly dependent on world trade, and that their main exports still consist of products of tropical agriculture, though mineral extraction is of increasing importance and manufacturing is beginning. A large proportion of the population consists of poor farmers, working on farms which are too small to give them a decent living or to permit the use of advanced methods. The islands used to be very unhealthy, which kept their population in check. Now, however, they have been hit by an information input of medical knowledge and practice which has made them very healthy, and has greatly reduced their death rate, but not their birth rate. Population therefore is rising at an explosive rate. The islands have long been colonies of a world empire, but empire having become both unfashionable and unprofitable, the mother country is somewhat ambivalently trying to push them out of the nest, while perhaps wanting to have them home occasionally for Christmas. What we seem to be witnessing, to vary the metaphor, is the natural childbirth of a nation, without many of the violent pangs which have in the past accompanied such births. The question before us is what might be the dynamics of such a society. Where might it go from where it is? What might be its future dynamic path?

We might distinguish three general possible paths. The first let us call the road to ruin. Population grows unchecked, doubling every twenty-five years. Emigration cannot keep pace and in any case skims off the cream of the people. Farms are sub-divided and sub-divided until the country produces far more people than it can take and the people crowd into huge city slums where there is large-scale unemployment. Education collapses under the strain of poverty and the flood of children. Superstition and ignorance increase, along with pride. Self-government means that every pressure group has to be placated, and there is less and less discrimination between high and low quality products whether bananas or people. This ends in a famine, an insurrection. The regiment shoots down the mob and establishes a military dictatorship. Foreign investments and gifts dry up; the islands are left to stew in their own misery and the world in effect draws a *cordon sanitaire* around them. That the road to ruin is a real road, and a distressingly wide and available one, is shown by the example of some nearby islands which have gone a long way down it.

The second part is the road to nowhere. This means keeping things much as they are; not disturbing existing relationships; desperately trying to keep pace with population growth by emigration, a little industrialisation, and perhaps, family planning, and keeping pretty tight hold of mother. This may be better than the road to ruin, but also it may be a road that is closed. Things have moved too far, too many hopes have been raised, and people will not be content simply to stand still. The road to nowhere slips imperceptibly into the road to ruin; it may be that it is no longer possible for the islands simply to stay where they are: they must either go forward or go backward.

Third part is the road to somewhere. This is a hard road to find—a straight and narrow road indeed, and it is by no means easy to travel; nevertheless it exists and it is not beyond the wit of the Hesperidians to find it. Like all straight and narrow roads which lead to salvation, it requires first a vision. There must be a belief that the road exists, and there must be a vision of what lies at the end of it and of the sacrifices and difficulties that lie in the way. This vision must be widespread in the society. It is not enough to have it confined to the few; it must be a vision which is contagious, which can inspire even the simple and unlettered with hope for their own and for their children's future. It must be a realistic vision. It must not be frittered away in ancient recriminations and in false hopes.

The key to the future of a small society is a vision of the *quality* of human life. The greatest resource of any society is the human resource, and in a small society this is of overwhelming importance. A small society cannot hope to rely on sheer weight of numbers, or wealth of natural resources. If it is to find a place for itself in the world, it must rely on the quality of its life and product. The first priority of a small society, therefore, must be its human resources and investment in the quality of these human resources. There is already something to build on. The Hesperides have a reputation for political maturity, for a certain rugged independence of the individual, and for certain habits of mutual help and co-operation. The first priority then must be education, and education of the right kind. This should be education of the whole community, adults and children alike; the local school must become a community centre, encouraging creativity and independent thinking as well as the more formal skills of literacy and mathematics. The education must have a moral and spiritual as well as an intellectual base; it must be directed towards the ideal of quality in all phases of life, and especially in family life and in the raising of children. Quality, not quantity, must be the slogan everywhere. The vision should inspire the most able and idealistic young people to go into teaching, especially into elementary teaching. The budget should be strained to make teaching more attractive financially, and the most highly honoured of all the professions—only thus can the society hope to escape from the trap of a self-perpetuating, poverty-breeding culture, transmitted from generation to generation, from parents and grandparents to children, and from these in turn to their children and grandchildren.

At the political level there must be a realistic appraisal of the bargaining position of the islands of the world. The islands do not have much bargaining power, and do not have much of a monopoly position; nevertheless, they are in a good position to take advantage of the goodwill of the richer countries, especially if the islands can broaden the base of their cultural and political connections and sources of support. One would like to see them developing political ingenuity, not merely copying the no doubt excellent institutions of the past, but branching out into new ways of solving the age-long political problem. Could we visualise perhaps a research institute instead of the traditional upper house of the legislature?

Finally, the islands must find themselves in the world society and must stand for something in the world. The islands already have one great achievement to their credit: they are among the first countries to belong to the human race. The establishment of a society in which nobody need feel an alien because of the accident of his physical type or skin colour seems almost within reach. This is something to be proud of and something which must be cherished and developed. The islands' intellectual and spiritual horizon has been limited by the accident of empire. They are too little aware even of their near neighbours, and have little sense of belonging to a world society; this must change. They must stop straining every nerve to get into the nineteenth century, and must look instead to the 21st century which is almost upon us and which the present generation of children will have to manage. We are moving with great rapidity into a world frighteningly different from that even of our fathers, a world of great danger but also of great promise, with space travel, automation, atomic energy and perhaps with immense new powers over the forces of life. The islands have already caught the vision of the human race; they must now catch the vision of the world society. They should be leaders of the movement for world government and world order, for this is on the road to somewhere for all humanity. This is a hard road, but it is not an impossible one, and if the vision can be caught, the road can be travelled.

POLITICAL IMPLICATIONS OF GENERAL SYSTEMS RESEARCH

In: *General Systems Yearbook,* Vol. 6, Ludwig von Bertalanffy and A. Rapoport, eds. Ann Arbor, Mich.: Society for General Systems Research, 1961, pp. 1-7

POLITICAL IMPLICATIONS OF GENERAL SYSTEMS RESEARCH*

Whatever is not chaos, is system, and wherever there is system, there can be knowledge. Wherever there is subjective knowledge—what I have elsewhere called an image—there are expectations. Even the amoeba "expects" the particle which it accepts to be "food," and "assumes" the particle which it rejects to be "not-food." Where expectations are persistently fulfilled, it is reasonable to suppose that the image on which they are based is "true" in the sense that it represents knowledge of a system of which the knower is a part, or which the knower can observe. When expectations are disappointed, there is a presumption that something is wrong with the image on which they were based.

Two points of possible confusion should be cleared up here. The first is that systematic knowledge, or knowledge of systems, is not necessarily given by mere logical consistency of the image. An image may be without internal contradictions, and yet the expectations which it generates may be disappointed. It is even possible for an image to have internal inconsistencies, and yet to generate expectations which are at least fulfilled often enough to reinforce the image. As we move toward the higher symbolic images, this case becomes not uncommon, though as a scientist, one has a certain blind faith in the preposition that "true" systems cannot be internally inconsistent. The second point is that expectations do not have to be precise in order to be systematic. Most expectations in ordinary life are fairly vague—that is, we expect something within a certain range of likelihood. I expect the weather tomorrow, for instance, to be something like what it is today. For most expectations we have what G. L. S. Shackle[1] calls a "potential surprise function." There is a certain range of values over which we will not be at all surprised; outside this range, potential surprise increases to the maximum of utter dumfounderment. Thus, writing in the middle of December, I shall not be surprised if tomorrow's temperature in Ann Arbor is anywhere between, say, 15° and 50° F. I would be a little surprised if it turns out to be -10° F. or 60° F.;

I would be very much surprised if it were -25° or 75°, and I would be utterly astonished if it were -50° or 110° F. One might postulate that there is a degree of astonishment (failure of expectations) which constitutes "system breakdown" and which necessitates a revision of the image which produced the "false" expectations. Within the upper and lower limits of system breakdown, we have a range of fulfillment of expectations, or of potential surprise, which is "image maintaining." Thus in the above example, my image of the Ann Arbor climate would be severely shaken if tomorrow's temperature were above 75° or below -25°; with this range I might be surprised, but I would regard the surprise as "unusual," and the condition which produced it as an exception to an otherwise intact system.

It is one of the main concerns of science to narrow the range of potential surprise and also the range of image-maintaining perceptions in its systematic expectations. These ranges are never reduced to a point; even in the case of the solar system, that beau ideal of the system builder, there are slight disappointments in the astronomers' expectations of the positions of the heavenly bodies. It takes only a very slight disappointment, however, to cause astronomers to look for a revision of the system—perhaps the inclusion of an unknown planet, perhaps a revision of some of the basic constants. It takes much greater disappointments to make us look for systems revision in the loose systems of ordinary living and fairly large disappointments to make even social scientists revise their image of social systems. There are no qualitative differences, however, between the loose systems and the tight, the vague and the precise; it is all a matter of the size of the range of image-maintaining expectations.

It is by systems, therefore, that we live, both in daily life and in the laboratory. We use systematic knowledge whenever we proffer a handshake, drive a car, build an oil refinery, design a machine, predict an eclipse, or shoot off a sputnik. There are, however, at least four levels of systematic knowledge, even apart from the matter

*This paper was given as a presidential address to the Society for General Systems Research at the meetings held in conjunction with the American Association for the Advancement of Science in Indianapolis, December 27, 1958. It would have appeared in the 1959 volume but for an invitation extended to Professor Boulding to spend a year as Visiting Professor of Economics at the University of the West Indies, Kingston, Jamaica. It is presented here in its original form, unrevised, because it speaks as eloquently of the present as it did of the recent past. Professor Boulding's further thoughts on the subjects raised here have been formalized and, by the time this appears, should have been published as Conflict and Defense: A General Theory, by Harpers, New York.

1. G. L. S. Shackle, Expectations in Economics, (Cambridge, Eng., 1949).

of the looseness of the systems involved, levels which involve both "understanding" and power.

The first level is that of the purely empirical system, based on frequently observed connections. These involve the kind of knowledge on which bodily skills are based. When we throw a ball, use a knife and fork, drive a car, or operate a machine, we are using "knowledge" of a kind, even if it resides in the lower structures of the nervous system, and this knowledge leads to certain expectations which are usually fulfilled. Thus, when we get into a car and turn on the switch and the engine starts, we are using a simple empirical system. If it refuses to start, we expand the system, perhaps by pulling out the choke, perhaps by calling a mechanic. Most of the systems by which we operate in daily life are of this kind, even the systems by which we perform intricate tasks and make complex decisions. They need not involve anything in the way of "understanding" the deeper systems on which they are based. We can drive a car without having the slightest idea what makes it go. We can play tennis without any knowledge of ballistics, and we can direct a firm or even a nation without any explicit knowledge of social systems.

At the second level we have what might be called mechanical construction systems. These involve the kind of knowledge which would enable us to build a house or a machine from a blueprint. They involve a fairly meticulous ability to translate symbol into some physical reality and to follow instructions or plans. Such systems differ from the first only in that whereas in the first a systematic connection between acts, events, or objects is all that is postulated (like turning the key and starting the engine), in the second there is a connection (equally empirical) between symbols and events or objects. One can take a blueprint and build a machine without in any way understanding why it is built the way it is. We can go on to distinguish a third level, which might be called engineering systems. These involve the kind of knowledge which would enable us to design a machine. Here we have clearly moved over a significant watershed; there is a degree of understanding and of knowledge of "inner" systems involved in this skill which is not involved even in the building of a machine from a blueprint. It is possible to design quite workable machines, however, with only a very sketchy knowledge of the theory behind them, and especially with a merely empirical knowledge of many properties and connections. Thus a clockmaker may design a clock without knowing why the pendulum swings in a constant period, or why springs have the properties which make them so useful.

We should therefore distinguish a fourth level of systematic knowledge which forms the basis for the designs of the third level. This might be called the theoretical level. Pure science is concerned mainly with this level. Here the inquirer is never satisfied with merely empirical laws or connections; he always wants to go "behind" these empirical laws and develop theoretical systems which have these laws as essential properties. Thus Boyle's Law is a purely empirical relationship relating the temperature, volume, and pressure of a gas; as such, however, it is not much more than a refined and quantified system of the first level. With the molecular theory which operates at the fourth level, however, we can not only derive Boyle's Law for a perfect gas, but can even develop more complex laws which predict in fair measure the behavior of actual gases. General Systems Research of course operates mainly at this fourth level, interested as it is in theories and models which have application to more than one empirical field. It is at least not an absurd ambition to wish to go even beyond this level, as the general systems which underlie the whole empirical world come more and more clearly into view, and to postulate a fifth level—as yet hardly existing—at which "systems of theoretical systems" can be discovered. If such exist, then the design of theoretical systems may be systematized, just as theoretical systems themselves inspire the design of engineering systems. This goal is still far off, perhaps, but it is at least near enough to be worth keeping somewhere in sight. As we approach it we should be able constantly to improve our ability to construct theoretical systems in all fields.

There is little doubt that the most important fruit of the improvement of general theoretical systems would be the development of more adequate theoretical structures in the sciences of man and society. Here we face an empirical universe that seems at first sight almost hopelessly complex and chaotic; as we view with the mind's eye the rise and fall of nations, of spiritual and material empires, of the complex tides of economic life, and of the mental and emotional powers of an individual man, our first impression may well be one of complexity verging on chaos, and we may despair of ever finding systems in this multitudinous turmoil. Neither society nor the individual, however, is purely random in movement, and it is the basic faith of social and behavioral science that the non-random elements can be expressed in systematic form.

The major difficulty in the study of social systems is that they are essentially symbolic systems, or what I have elsewhere called "eiconic" systems. That is to say, they are systems in which "images"—the cognitive structures of persons—enter in a quite essential way. Images are systems of extreme complexity and delicacy, especially at the symbolic level. The subtle relationships and nuances of poetry and music, the adrenalin-like symbols of patriotism and religion, the summary-symbols which condensed into a single stereotype or index (often at great cost in accuracy) an enormous mass of otherwise indigestible information, all are part of a system capable of sudden discontinuities and apparently wild disturbances—but still not random! There is a system—or one should perhaps say there are systems—of aesthetics, of morality, of loyalty and commitment, and though we see these but as in a glass darkly, we have some hope that one day they may be made exquisitely and mathematically explicit. At present, however, we have hardly more than the raw beginnings of a mathematic of symbolic systems—perhaps because traditional mathematics is a language inordinately poor in verbs (it really has little more than a few variations on the verb "to be"!)

In saying that social systems are essentially symbolic, I do not wish to deny the usefulness and limited validity of "mechanical" systems or models of various aspects of social life which abstract from this symbolic character of the system and postulate a set of simple functional relationships among various social variables. All the "higher" systems in some sense "enclose" the lower systems[2]—that is, a "lower" system is always a legitimate abstraction of certain aspects of a higher system. Thus the human organism has a geography (anatomy, mechanics of levers and muscles), chemical systems, information systems, growth systems, and so on) as well as involving a symbolic and eiconic system of great complexity. Thus it is quite legitimate to abstract from the social system a "price system," as economic theory does, and to postulate a set of equations which "determine" the price system in a rather mechanical way, in spite of the fact that actual prices are quoted or accepted by "people" in the light of highly complex images going far beyond the dimensions of the economic abstraction. Similarly Lewis F. Richardson's[3] theory of arms races is again a purely mechanical system, based on assumed functional relationships between rather abstract variables related to national defense, yet in spite of the absence of any eiconic considerations, it is extraordinarily useful in interpreting certain sets of historical events.

I now come to the main theme of this paper, after what is I fear a long introduction. This theme is the possible political effects of the rise of systematic knowledge of social systems, whether of a mechanical or a symbolic nature. This is an area where there must frankly be some speculation, and I may be accused of writing science fiction rather than science. Nevertheless the problems themselves are of such intrinsic importance that we cannot wait upon perfect knowledge; furthermore these problems are already upon us, and

unless we devote thought to them, even at the cost of some speculation, the far-reaching consequences of certain modern movements in systematic theory and practice may catch us unaware.

The basic problem may be presented as follows. In the past, political decision making (in which I would include not only the decision of politicians, but also any decision made in the role of a responsible head of a large organization) has on the whole been at the first level of systems operation. This is not to deny that there has been some engineering, for instance in the framing of constitutions and the setting up of administrative procedures, or even that there have been some vague theoretical structures. On the whole, however, the ships of state have been steered with much the same kind of rude empirical knowledge by which we drive a car—with this additional hazard, that the images which govern political behavior have been extremely tolerant of disappointment of expectations, and highly resistant to change, with a range of image-maintaining variation so great that it frequently leads to the destruction of the system. That is to say, political decision makers have a strong tendency to develop a "false" image of themselves and their environment, and of the system in which they are operating, because of the extreme tolerance of their images for messages which register disappointment or incompatibility with the existing image. It takes a big shock (like Sputnik) to change a political image. Consequently, it is easy for political decision makers to make their decisions in the light of images which are so far from reality that the decisions which they father are disastrous, or even fatal.

We are now, I think, beginning to witness the rise of political and social images of a somewhat different order than those previously held. These new images are based on more elaborate, explicit, and "sophisticated" theoretical structures, and also on more elaborate, more quantitative and more specialized information systems than have been available in the past. Let me cite as an illustration the development of a new image of economic policy in the past generation, based on Keynesian theory and on national income statistics. Before 1929, economic information was fragmentary and was collected mainly as a by-product of other activities such as the collection of taxes and import duties. The prevailing image which guided economic policy was that of a largely self-regulating economy in which the functions of government were confined to maintaining law, order, and the rights of property, with a little protection for those groups with sufficient political pressure. It took a great depression to shatter this image; shattered, however, it was and in its place grew the

2. See K. E. Boulding, General Systems Theory, the Skeleton of Science. (Management Science, Vol. 2, No. 3, April 1956, pp. 197-208.)
3. Lewis F. Richardson, Generalized Foreign Policies. (Brit. Journ. of Psychology, Monograph Supplement No. 23, June 1939.)

image of a basic responsibility of government for economic stability, however loosely that might be defined. This basic responsibility, however, can only be exercised first, if there is an elaborate economic information system, especially in regard to the size, composition, and distribution of national income or product; and secondly, if there are some fairly explicit and well-founded images of the quantitative effects of various types of government action such as raising or lowering taxes, tightening or loosening credit, and so on. It would be too much to claim that these conditions are perfectly fulfilled. Nevertheless we are certainly much closer to their fulfillment than we were, say, thirty years ago.

It is not only in government that a movement has been gathering that progresses towards decision making based on more explicit theoretical systems and on specialized information collection. In business enterprises, especially the larger ones, a similar process has been going on, even if this is sometimes reflected more in the size of the staff organization rather than in its quality. We have seen a persistent tendency for "research"— that is a professionally oriented activity of a presumably scientific nature—to spread from chemistry and engineering and the "production sciences" towards marketing research, operations research, organizational research, and so on, which impinge much more directly on the basic decision-making functions of the responsible directors. In the last ten years, we have seen the rise of something variously called "management science" or "administrative science," which brings fairly sophisticated mathematical theory even into the sacred precincts of those ultimate decision-processes which have hitherto been regarded as the peculiar mystery and prerogative of the boss himself. We must not overestimate the extent of this movement: it is a cloud no bigger than a man's hand, but one of substantial portent.

At this point I may well be asked, "This is all very well, but is it General Systems?" In so far as General Systems is a hope rather than a reality, of course the answer is "no". Nevertheless, there is something abroad that might be called a "systems movement," of which the Society for General Systems Research is merely one aspect, or perhaps merely a symptom! To describe the movement in detail would require another paper; it is reflected in such new journals as Management Science, the Administrative Science Quarterly, The Journal of Operations Research, and the Journal of Conflict Resolution; it is reflected in institutions like the Mental Health Research Institute at the University of Michigan, and in the Rand Corporation at Santa Monica. It is reflected in the new computer industry. It is reflected in intellectual developments such as Game Theory, Decision Theory, and the various ramifications of Operations Research. It is this larger

"systems movement" with which I am principally concerned, and I shall argue that the political consequences may be very great, and that the political questions which it raises are of the first magnitude.

The first question is that of the impact of the systems movement on the locus of political power and influence. There is a certain tendency for the political power to concentrate in those elements of society which have the type of scarce knowledge required for the political decisions of that society. By political decisions I mean as before those decisions which affect the lives of many people and have large social consequences. The concept of political power is a more difficult one; we can perhaps define it for the moment as the ability to make political decisions, and we may roughly quantify this by defining the extent of a political decision as the number of people it will affect weighted by some measure of the intensity of the effect. Where the ability to make political decisions requires access to scarce knowledge— knowledge, that is to say, which is not widely distributed, or generally available, or which has some peculiar institutional means of transmittal from generation to generation—then there is a strong long-run tendency for the possessors of this knowledge also to occupy key positions in the political power structure. If those who occupy positions in the institutional structure which give them political power do not possess the requisite knowledge to make "good" decisions, they will tend to make "bad" decisions, and in the long run these bad decisions will operate to remove these people from positions of power. We can thus think of a "normal" political power structure which corresponds to the distribution of the requisite scarce knowledge among the population, somewhat as the economist thinks of a "normal" price system. The actual distribution of political power, like the system of market prices, may not correspond to the normal distribution, but if it does not, there will be persistent forces tending to bring the actual structure into conformity with the normal structure. The normal structure itself, of course, is continually changing under the long-run impact of change in techniques, institutions, and knowledge, but the actual structure is continually chasing it.

Thus, in the Middle Ages churchly and knightly knowledge bestowed power on its possessors and transmitters; the ruler is a knight, his advisor, visier, or minister is frequently a priest or imam. With the rise of commercial and legal knowledge to increasing importance in an age of expanding commerce, the locus of political power shifts towards the possessors of commercial and legal knowledge; even though military men still hold positions of titular power, the power of kings and aristocrats declines, and of lawyers and businessmen rises. The question I would like to raise—I do not pretend to answer it—is whether we are not now passing to a condition in which the significant scarce knowledge is "systems knowledge"—that is, abstract and scientific, rather than commercial and legal knowledge—and whether therefore the locus of political power will not gradually shift towards those trained and skilled in this newly significant kind of knowledge.

As long as systems knowledge remains in the natural and even in the biological sciences, one may hazard a guess that it presents only a small threat to the existing political power structure. Physical and biological scientists can be treated as hired hands, provided certain amenities are observed. The kind of knowledge which they possess still has about the political significance of that of the armorer or the gunsmith, the architect or the navigator. It is a kind of knowledge which the wielders of political power can use, even if they do not understand the theoretical systems on which it is based. Moreover the wielders of political power can rely on the personal allegiance of most scientists to the national and folk cultures in which they are embedded. In their personal lives and in their political allegiances, natural scientists are generally no more sophisticated than the people around them. Indeed, the abstract nature of their professional lives sometimes makes them quite unfitted for political life, and when they do venture into economic and political affairs, the naïvete of their opinions is frequently painfully apparent. Hence the political unimportance of a Galileo or an Oppenheimer, or even of such organizations as the Federation of Atomic Scientists, or the Society for Social Responsibility in Science. A natural scientist who breaks the bounds of his scientific abstraction and who even seems to challenge the powers that be is likely to be broken by them, and it is little wonder that most scientists retreat into the quiet harbors of their laboratories and professional journals and rarely venture forth on to the uncertain, stormy seas of political power. There is even probably a certain self-selection of personality types among those who elect to make a career of science. It would be merely insulting to assert that men become scientists because they hate people, but there is a slight sting of truth in the insult. Science, even social science, if a fine refuge—a sort of new monasticism—for those who cannot bear the complexity and richness—and wickedness—of the world of intricate personal and political relations.

Now it may well be that social and behavioral scientists are no better than natural scientists in their fixation on abstractions and their flight from the responsibilities of power. Nevertheless, there is a difference in the subject matter of the abstractions which may make the difference between politically significant knowledge and politically unimportant knowledge. As we move towards the discovery of "truer" knowledge of social systems—by which I simply mean images of social

systems with smaller and smaller ranges of system-maintaining surprise—the success of actual social systems in the ecological successions of human history will depend more and more on the extent to which they are governed by decisions based on these more "sophisticated" images, and on the complex systems of information-collection and analysis which support them. As long as all political decisions were made by "folk knowledge" alone, one could reasonably suppose that the rise and fall of systems was mainly governed by chance—a system (e.g., a nation, an empire or a church) that had a succession of "good" rulers making "good" decisions, largely by accident, flourished, whereas one with a succession of "bad" rulers and "bad" decisions declined or perhaps even perished. Thus, the Roman Empire might reasonably be regarded as a historical accident, and its fall as a restoration of the normal state of things. The situation might be complicated by the phenomenon of "returns to scale"—a few good rulers might raise a nation, for instance, to a size where its mere size gave it an advantage that it took a lot of misrule to destroy. In such a system, however, there would be no persistent selective factor at work, and the rise and fall of empires might well be accounted for on the majestic principles of chance.

An organization which operates according to a "superior" systems-knowledge, however, will have a persistent bias in its favor. The rise of systematic knowledge in the natural sciences has given a persistent bias in favor of systems based on this knowledge as over against systems based on "folk" knowledge of a less accurate nature, so that "folk cultures" are in full retreat everywhere before the penetration of "scientific" cultures. It is not unreasonable to suppose that this principle will also hold true for organizations based on more scientific knowledge of social systems as opposed to those based on folk images of society. Thus in this sphere as in any other, the transition from a folk image to a scientific image marks a change in the over-all system of human history and gives a persistent bias to the course of events in favor of those societies based on the more accurate knowledge-processes.

If this is so, however, the specialized knowledge of social systems may become "politically relevant" in a way that the specialized knowledge of nature systems is not. Whether this is in fact the case depends somewhat on the "salability" of such knowledge—that is, on whether an unspecialized ruler can base good decisions on answers to questions presented to subordinate social scientists, or on information volunteered by them. We do not know enough about the nature of the social systems involving unspecialized decision makers and subordinate "staff" social scientists to know whether these are in fact superior to those in which the specialized social-systems-knower is himself the ruler. If the latter turns out over the long run to be more efficient, we are in for a substantial revolution in the locus of political power! In any case the locus is likely to be substantially disturbed by the rise of knowledge of social systems, even though we may not be able to predict now in which direction.

Another large question which again it is easier to raise than to answer is that of the impact of social systems knowledge on the "engineering" of political life—that is, on the institutions, constitutions, forms and habits of political organization and behavior. We naturally have a special interest in the problems which are likely to be raised—and which are already being raised—for democratic institutions. On the whole, the assumption of democratic theory is that the skills of government are "folk skills" which every concerned citizen is capable of appraising and which most citizens are capable of performing if called upon to do so. The extreme form of this assumed universality of governmental skills is the selection of officials from the citizens by lot, as in some of the ancient Greek republics. In modern democracies there is at least a process of selection of rulers by party convention and election, and if this at times resembles the ancient trial by ordeal, at least the candidates must endure public discussion of their merits, so that some visible evidence of capability is an asset.

Becoming more acute all the time, however, is the problem of how do the "people" control the specialists, whose very language is so esoteric that it cannot be understood by more than a handful of the elect? This problem has arisen visibly in connection with atomic energy; here, almost for the first time, we have a major technical development which is wholly the product of a non-folk subculture (that of theoretical physicists), and which is terrifying remote from the workshop-tinkerer and the amateur inventor and engineer. Here major policy decisions have to be made, which profoundly affect the lives not only of the citizens of one country but of the whole human race, under the circumstance that only the expert understands the language in which the decisions have to be couched. There is little wonder that the public attitude is one of a despairing apathy. Anyone who attends an operations research or a management science conference, however, finds himself in a world that to the outsider is just as esoteric as that of the atomic physicist—yet what is being talked about may be the essential raw material of vital political decisions which in a previous generation were discussed avidly around the cracker barrel.

Most of what might be called "ordinary" democratic theory assumes (implicitly if not explicitly) that the kind of knowledge which is required to make political decisions, and still more important, to judge them, is not "scarce," is not the sole possession of a specially trained class, and is available to all who take the trouble to acquire a reasonably general education. Suppose now that a decision rests on the solution of a set of equations so complicated that only a major computer can handle them and only a Ph.D. can understand the solution when it is presented. How can this be reconciled with democratic institutions? In gloomier moments, one imagines a new Dark Age, with Science as the Church and the military as the king, and the people as helpless pawns, pushed around by decisions in which they cannot participate, because they cannot understand the processes or the images on which they are based. Even worse, one visualizes a neon-lit dark age of the manipulative society, in which the instruments of formation of character and opinion (forged, of course, by social science!) are so firmly in the hands of a ruling elite that their tyranny is unshakeable. Even if the tyranny were benevolent, it would still be tyranny, and if it were malevolent it would still be unshakeable. This is a political nightmare from which one might well wish to wake up screaming. Does the tree of knowledge, as it grows and ramifies into ever more complex branches and systems, ever become the tree of life, or does it always remain a tree of death and destruction, giving more power to evil and making corruption all the more efficient?

At least part of the answer to this probably unanswerable question lies in a third set of implications of systems analysis. These are the implications of self-conscious knowledge of social systems for science itself as a social system. Science is a subculture within the framework of a larger society; indeed, it is a subculture which to some extent transcends national and local societies, penetrating the folk cultures out of which it has grown as the roots of a tree penetrate the various varieties of soil and subsoil which support it. The scientist, however, in his personal life is part of the folk culture in which he has grown; the American scientist is an American, the Russian scientist is a Russian; there are scientists who are Communists, or Moslems, or Hindus, or Christians. It is evident that science as a culture is not rich enough to be self-subsistent; that is to say, science can be a subculture; it cannot, at least up to the present, be a culture. There are no "scientific" societies, and perhaps there never will be.

Nevertheless science everywhere presents challenges to the folk cultures which support it and which it to some extent supports. The relations between the scientific subculture and the folk cultures in which it is embedded may be one of symbiosis, but it is a rather uneasy symbiosis. The uneasiness reflects itself in an ambivalent attitude towards science and scientists on the part of the non-scientific population, a result perhaps of the feeling that the very triumphs of science are undermining the system on which the folk culture rests. Thus in a day when physical science almost everywhere is putting a large amount of its resources and energy into plans which are likely to lead to the destruction of the human race, it is not wholly surprising that in a recent survey in the Middle West, some 14% of high school students regarded scientists as "evil". Among scientists themselves too there is moral confusion, leading sometimes to the perversion of science itself. We see this most clearly in Russia, where in spite of the claims of the society to be "scientific" in fact even basic science is frequently perverted (as in the Lysenko incident) to fit the Marxist "folk culture."[4]   Nevertheless, even in the freer atmosphere of the United States, a scientist who is suspected of an unqualified loyalty to truth will find himself in serious trouble.

I suspect that we are moving towards a major crisis in science, or at least in the scientific subculture. Most scientists today are personally committed to images of social systems which are essentially at the "folk" level. As a result, they are committed to institutions and to social systems which their own discoveries may have made obsolete. Thus it is highly probable today that national defense, which for many generations of mankind has at least provided occasional islands of security in a troubled world, is now no longer workable as a world system. Nevertheless most scientists are still committed to national defense as a system, and if they are not, they will find it hard to continue being scientists. Of all people, however, scientists should be most susceptible to new knowledge of social systems. Naïvete is an unstable virtue; like virginity, once it is lost, it is lost for ever. We can hardly suppose that scientists will retain their naïvete about social systems for ever.

If they lose their naïvete, however, this will intensify the already existing strains between the scientific subculture and the various national folk cultures. Russian scientists may begin to lose their faith in Marxism; American scientists may begin to lose their faith in militarism. The world of science inevitably transcends national boundaries and national loyalties, for it rests on a loyalty to truth which dominates all other loyalties. If scientists believe this today, however, they will have to say it under their breath, like Galileo, otherwise they will not be given security clearance.

It seems clear that a fairly major struggle between science and the various national folk cultures is highly probable. As long as scientists submit to the commitments of the folk culture they will be tolerated, or even encouraged. Such submission, however, will destroy the inner integrity of science itself. I am not suggesting that a new Marx will arise to cry, "Scientists of the world, unite: you have nothing to lose but classified research," simply because this is as false as the famous statement which it parodies. Scientists have a lot to lose in any conflict with a national culture, for they are supported by it, not only economically but emotionally. It is dangerous to exchange the loyalty to what is for loyalty to what is yet to be (even though this is the essence of the moral claims of religion). One can only hope that knowledge of social systems may progress to the point where a true dynamic can be perceived, and where we may see not only the goal of a world society which is more secure and satisfactory than the one in which we now live, but also a road which leads there. Without this I venture to predict that the present world social system leads to the corruption, and perhaps to the extinction of science, if not of man himself.

4. The case of Communism is so fascinating that it must at least be mentioned, even though it deserves a paper to itself. Marxism is an interesting example of a pseudo-science. It is a rather logical and self-subsistent system which is in fact a highly special case, to which reality rarely if ever corresponds. It is analogous to the "ptolemaic" or "phlogiston" theories, representing a premature systematization of social systems. In spite of its scientific inadequacies, however, it illustrates in a most alarming manner the theses of this paper. First, it has in parts of the world led to an abrupt shift in the locus of political power from the possessors of the "obsolete knowledge" of the czars and mandarins to the possessors of the "new knowledge" (the Communist Party). Secondly, it has led to a tyranny which, if not unshakeable, is at least firmly based. In the third place, it has had profound effects on the social system of science—elevating it in status and corrupting it in detail. If a "false" social system can do so much, how much greater will be the powers of "truer" social systems!

THE ETHICAL PERSPECTIVE

In: *Issues of High Moment in Our Changing Economy.*
New York: National Council of Churches, 1962, pp. 35-44

THE ETHICAL PERSPECTIVE

Three Economic States of History

By a heroic process of simplification, we can divide human history into three economic states which we might describe in modern Western terminology as pre-civilized, civilized, and post-civilized or "developed." Between these three states stand the two great transitions, the first great transition from pre-civilized to civilized society, the second great transition from civilized to developed society. The first great transition began, perhaps, some eight thousand years ago with the domestication of plants and animals and the beginning of agriculture. This got well underway about 3,000 B.C. with the rise of the first cities and the beginnings of civilization itself. Civilization almost by definition is what goes on in cities. Civilization, then, depends on two factors—the surplus of food from the food producers, which is given by agriculture, and a political and coercive organization adequate to take this surplus away from the food producers and to use it to feed armies, artisans, priests, philosophers, artists, and kings. Simple, one-sided coercive organizations which seem to have existed in the very earliest civilization soon gave way to rival coercive organizations and we have the phenomenon of war, which is almost as characteristic of the age of civilization as the city.

The first great change is not, of course, a continuous process. At times it occurred rapidly; there were long periods of stagnation; there were periods in particular parts of the world of retrogression. In general, the change probably proceeded more rapidly during peace, that is, when there was a monopolistic coercive organization, and was frequently reversed by war, that is, by the development of rival coercive organizations. From 3,000 B.C. on we have a long history of the rise and fall of empires and the building and destruction of cities. There is a long, slow spread, however, of civilization from its origins in Egypt, Sumeria, and the Indus until now it spreads over the whole world and pre-civilized society exists only in scattered fragments. The last great pre-civilized continent, Africa, became civilized only in the last hundred years.

Now, hard on the heels of civilization, comes the second great change to the developed society, a state of society which will be as different from civilization as civilization itself is from pre-civilized society. As the origins of civilization can be traced back to the beginnings of agriculture, the origins of the developed society can be traced back to the beginnings of organized science and technology. We are still in the middle of the second great change and we cannot tell at the moment where it is leading us. It may lead us, of course, to total destruction or it may lead us to a state of man almost beyond our imagination. The United States is probably the country furthest advanced towards the developed society, although Western Europe, Japan, Australia, New Zealand, the Soviet Union, and some others are close on its heels.

On the whole, the developed society is strikingly a product of the temperate zone; the tropics still rest squarely in the age of civilization. The major characteristic of the movement towards the developed society is a long, persistent increase in the productivity of labor in a large number of different fields. In agriculture, for instance, whereas in almost all societies of classical civilization it took about 80% of the people to feed the 100%, today in the United States we can feed everybody with less than 10% of the population and pretty soon it will be 5%. In countries like China, India, and Indonesia which are in the "civilized" stage, the agricultural population still represents something like three-quarters of the total. In the production of almost all manufactured goods, the same process is discernible. Only in the rendering of services, in such professions as haircutting, teaching, and preaching, does technology lag, and even here, important changes seem to be on the way. The movement to developed society is characterized by the disintegration of many of the characteristic institutions of civilized society. The city is visibly disintegrating and war has become unmanageable. These are merely symptoms of the magnitude of the ·change.

Problems for Today's Christians

For the Christian living in the twentieth century, the change presents two rather different sets of problems. There is first the problem of the place of religion in general and Christianity in particular in the developed society, that is, in the third state of man. The Christian ethic, moreover, has been an important element in the origins of this movement. It has been argued that we can trace the whole movement from civilization to the developed society back to the Benedictines, who were almost the first intellectuals who worked with their hands. In classical civilization work was regarded as degrading; only the leisured, that is, the exploiters were permitted the status and privileges of a civilization. It is to the great credit of Christianity that it changed the ethic of work. The fact that its Founder was a working man, not a prince like the Buddha, had a profound impact on its whole ethic. Furthermore, Christianity was a powerful agent in destroying animism (the attribution of special powers to material things) and in, therefore, permitting the rise of mechanical power. Be this as it may, the fact is that the movement towards the developed society had its origins in Christian culture although, once it had begun, it could be imitated by non-Christian societies.

The Marxists believe that religion is a passing phase in man's development, characteristic, perhaps, of the age of civilization, but that the age of post-civilization, which they call Communism, will be an age in which all religious cobwebs are swept away and in which pure rationality, science, and social control render religion unnecessary. Evidence against this view, however, is presented by the quite astonishing vitality of religion in the most developed countries. In the United States we have observed a steady rise in church membership and, I think, in the political power of religion almost since the foundation of the Republic. There may be doubts about the quality of this movement, but there can be no doubts about its quantity.

Religion is Changing, Not Withering

Far from withering away, in an age of science and technology, religion seems to be more necessary to man than ever. It does, however, change its form; it is no longer the "opiate of the people," a device to keep the poor quiet and content with their miserable lot. It is, rather, a "consumer good" in an affluent society providing man with human fellowship and Divine assurance in a large, complex, and mechanized world. In the United States religion has not only become a consumer good, as the slogan, 'Go to the church of your choice," indicates; it has become a consumer good for which there is evidently a very substantial demand.

Religion achieved its power, however, not by threats of hellfire but by the promises of spiritual rewards, beginning on this earth. It has passed out of the hands of what I would call the "threat system" and has become part of the "promise system." This, I suspect, is part of a very fundamental change from "mere" civilization to the developed society, for in this society, the threat system becomes unworkable and we have to rely on exchange and on mutual concern as the major mechanisms for holding societies together. Further evidence of the persistence of religion into the developed society is the extraordinary vitality of religion in the Soviet Union where 44 years of atheistic socialism have, if anything, rejuvenated the church.

In thinking about the relevance of the Christian ethic to the present state of man, we must, therefore, look forward to the developed society even though we do not yet know what it really looks like, for as yet, I believe, we have not even reached the mid-point in the change. Indeed, just as we have had many varieties of civilized societies, we may likewise have many varieties of developed societies. The Soviet Union and the United States, for instance, are proceeding along very different paths even though they are both clearly proceeding towards a developed society. As yet we do not know whether the end product will be approximately the same. One can certainly detect signs of convergence. The United States has been moving towards more self-conscious control of economic development and the Soviet Union, we hope, has been moving tentatively in the direction of greater political and economic liberty. The reconciliation of liberty with control is perhaps the greatest problem of each society, and it may well be that the final solutions will not be dissimilar. It is equally possible, however, that there will be wide divergences in the final result. Whatever the social, economic, and political institutions which will finally emerge, however, it is certainly the faith of the Christian that religion will continue to be relevant. What Rufus Jones once called "the double search" of man for God and God for man, and the ultimate unslakeable thirst of man for truth and righteousness is not going to pass away merely because we get rich. It is perhaps because the great religious questions are unanswerable that they will continue to be asked as long as man is around to ask them.

I regard, therefore, the historical connection between socialism and atheism as largely an accidental one, arising out of the peculiar intellectual history of the 19th century. It is perfectly possible to visualize a theistic socialist society and an atheistic capitalist one. In any case, the difference between socialism and capitalism is much less than the difference between the developed society and the undeveloped or "merely" civilized society. In spite of important differences, even today the United States is much more like the Soviet Union than either of them is like China or India.

Recommendations Appropriate to Time and Place

Even though we can predict with some assurance that religion will continue to show vitality as we move towards a developed society, we will have to face the fact that its particular ethical recommendations may have to change. The fundamental ethical principles may be unchanged, but fundamental principles always have to be translated into particular recommendations which are appropriate to the time and place. To take but a single example: at least in its Catholic manifestation, the Christian ethic is ostensibly unfavorable to the control of population and even some Protestant groups are not far behind the Roman Catholic Church in the disfavor with which they regard the deliberate control of the number of children. This is an ethic which is appropriate to the world of undeveloped civilization in which death rates are high and in which birth rates, therefore, must also be high. In a period when there is no death control and when the very survival of mankind depends on its fecundity, an ethic of familism and fruitfulness is highly appropriate.

No civilization has survived, I think, without the family being a vigorous institution in it, whether Christian or not. In the developed society the role of the family is more dubious. If we have death control we must have birth control, and fecundity can easily ruin us. Indeed, one of the great dangers of the world today is the impact of certain developed techniques on the undeveloped civilized countries. These techniques have enormously reduced the death rate but the birth rate remains high. Under these circumstances, these countries suffer a rate of population increase which can easily be fatal to them, as 2-4-D is fatal to the dandelion. It can be argued also, however, on the other side that the basic Christian principle of family responsibility is all the more necessary in a developed society. No merely mechanical methods are wholly successful in controlling population; ultimately population control must rest on the sense of moral responsibility, not only to society as a whole, but also within the family circle. It is significant, for instance, that, of all Western countries, it is puritan Catholic Ireland that has been most successful in population control since it learned its terrible lesson in the famine of 1846.

Ethic of Love Becomes More, Not Less, Important

It can be argued on the more positive side that, as we move towards the developed society, the Christian ethic of love becomes

more, not less, important. Civilized society virtually has to support
itself by coercion and exploitation; this is almost the only way in
which it can survive. In developed society, by contrast, exploitation
of man by man becomes obsolete. We find, to put it crudely, that
we can get a hundred dollars out of nature for every dollar we can
squeeze out of man. Hence, the exploitation ethic, which has been
the reality underlying the fine phrases of civilization, itself becomes
obsolete. The greater our potential for riches, the more necessary
becomes an ethic of love in order to realize them.

The richer we are, the more likely we are to find ourselves in
social situations which correspond to what the game theorists have
called the "prisoner's dilemma." This is a situation in which, if both
parties to a relationship are "good," they are both very well off. If,
however, one party is good and the other is bad, it may pay the
good party to become bad, so that we move to a position in which
both parties are bad; under these circumstances they are much worse
off than they would be if both parties were good. In order to get
from the "both bad" to the "both good" stage, it is necessary, however, to have a sense of community. It is necessary, that is to say,
for the parties to act, in a certain sense, as if they were one. In
other words, the more love there is in a society, the less chance there
is of the "prisoner's dilemma" moving everybody into the worst of
all possible worlds. We see this particularly in the case of our conflict
with the Russians. The absence of love between us is moving us both
rapidly into a position where we are going to be enormously worse
off than we could be if we loved each other a little.

Even more relevant to the Christian ethic is the proposition that
as we move towards the developed society, it becomes necessary not
merely to love but to love our enemies. In a society in which, because
of technical development in weaponry, defense has given place to
deterrence, the only real possibility for stability in the system lies
in what I have called "enemy-supportive behavior." Two firms in
duopoly, each of which can destroy the other, refrain from doing so
because they know that the struggle may ruin both of them. It is
true, of course, that enemy-supportive behavior on the part of one
party alone may not be sufficient to guarantee the stability of the
system. Enemy-supportive behavior on the part of one party, however,
may produce enemy-supportive behavior on the part of the other.
This is where the ethic of the cross clearly becomes relevant. It is
the willingness to lay down one's life for another which breaks the

prisoner's dilemma and permits systems of affluence and power to realize themselves instead of destroying themselves. Impotence does not require sacrifice; it is not only power that makes sacrifice meaningful. Economic development, therefore, makes an ethic of sacrifice meaningful in a way that it is not in a poor and impotent society.

Guides to Transition Concern Us Most

So far, we have considered mainly the relevance of the Christian ethic in the society towards which we seem to be moving and which, in part, we have already realized. If we are to guide ourselves through the transition we must keep this end in view. Nevertheless, the ethical problems of the transition itself are the ones that concern us most as individuals, because this is the period in which we happen to be living.

The problems of the transition itself are different from the problems of the final state, if, indeed, there is a final state. We are living in the period of most rapid technological, social, and political change that the human race has probably experienced to date. The problems of adjusting to this rate of change are very great. They are primarily learning problems. It is literally true today that anyone in middle life spent his youth in a world that has totally passed away. We learn about the world, however, in our youth and we seldom change our view of it. Most people, therefore, are living in a totally unreal world and this is the greatest potential threat to the continuance of the change.

It is very hard to learn in rapidly changing systems. We learn ordinarily from the stability of the world, not from its instability. We learn, for instance, to walk and comport ourselves in regard to physical movements because the gravitational constant is mercifully stable. If it fluctuated from day to day, we would experience extraordinary difficulty in adjusting ourselves to it. The constants of our social systems, however, are changing all the time and with appalling rapidity. It is little wonder that we find it hard to learn to walk in society.

In the face of this enormous rate of change, where does the question of ethics stand? A biblical ethic is, after all, a stable ethic and it can be argued that this is inappropriate in a world of enormous change. It is easy to sit in the seat of the scornful and to poke fun at the ethic of nomads and sheep herders, hillbillies and itinerant preachers, and to ask how can the ethic of these people be relevant to the complex world of the day. The world of the Bible, however, was not a stable world. It was a world of constant upheaval, of disaster and of recovery. In the midst of this world of insecurity and tension, the Jews found not merely an ethic but the author of All Good. It is not surprising, therefore, that the Bible speaks to us today in spite of the enormous intensification and complexity of our problems.

The Meek Shall Inherit

Two elements in the Biblical ethic seem peculiarly relevant for today's world, the ethic of repentance and the ethic of meekness. Both of these can be gathered under the single heading of the ethic of learning: "Teach me thy way O Lord." By repentance we become willing to unlearn, to trace our way back however painfully from the blind alleys and the false paths. Through meekness we become willing to learn. The meek inherit the earth because they are adaptable and learn fast. The strong, and those who have refused to negotiate except from strength, have usually perished. In a period of rapid change only the fast learners know what the world is like. This is why the proud are scattered in the imagination of their hearts, the mighty are cast down from their seats, and the humble and meek are exalted.

In the light of the Christian ethic, the outlook for the United States is very bleak. We have, it is true, pioneered in the movement towards the developed society. The pioneer, however, is not always the one who enjoys the fruits of his pioneering. This looks like one of the occasions when the meek are once more going to inherit the earth, and the United States and the Soviet Union are not among the meek. If they destroy each other, as seems all too probable at the moment, it may well be the poor and humble people of the tropics who will carry on the process of change if the setback is not too great. Whatever happens, I think the Christian ethic will still be relevant. In an age of civilization it may well remain an interim ethic applicable only to those who have in some sense renounced the world in their own time and who are deeply alienated from the time in which they live. In the developed society, it becomes, I think, a relevant ethic, without which the society probably cannot survive. To my mind, this is the real meaning of the Second Coming of Christ, His coming power in the hearts of men, because only this kind of life is consistent with the technology of society. In this immensely difficult and dangerous transition through which we are passing, it is Christ, the inward teacher, to Whom we must turn, for only in His light can we perceive that an old world has passed away and that a new world is struggling to be born. In a sense, it is the great mission of the Christian to identify himself with the world that is not yet, confident that neither things present nor things to come can separate him from the love of God.

What Is the Individual Christian to Do?

In the terrible dilemmas and agonizing frustrations of our time what, then, is the individual Christian to do? The Christian ethic does not attempt to give a rule for every occasion. It is not a manual of etiquette or of arms. It arises out of an encounter with the living God. It is a spirit not a letter. We encounter the living God, however, in our vision of history and in our image of the nature and purpose of man, as well as in the dailiness of life. The Christian in these difficult days more than ever must learn to live in two worlds at once, the world of time and the world of eternity. In the world of time, he must usually carry on his daily duties in the setting of the existing institutions of church and state as faithfully and consistently as he knows how to do it. In the light of eternity, he must see the dead church in the terrible radiance of the living Christ, the church historic defending its privileges, clutching its property, proclaiming that false comfort that is short of repentance, hating peace, fanning the cold war, supporting privilege, blocking the road to education and to development, and at the same time feeding the hungry, clothing the naked, sheltering the poor, binding up the wounds of the world, and proclaiming in however faltering a voice the Lord whom she betrays. Similarly, in the light of eternity the Christian will contemplate his nation with agony, as a destroyer of children, the wielder of monstrous threats, and the planner of genocide, as well as an expression of common concern and community responsibility, more efficient, more widespread and less discriminating than the church. A man's enemies, as Jesus said, shall be those of his own household. In the light of eternity we must see our own church, our own state, our own friends as our deadly enemies whom we must love and for whom we must suffer.

These formulations, you may say, are all very well, but what shall we do? Each person must find the answer to this question in the light of his own agony. If he has no agony let him seek the answer in the newspaper column of Advice to the Lovelorn, not in the Christian ethic. For the Christian ethic flows from the agony of the cross, repeated continually in the life of man. But out of the agony can come surprisingly different answers. For some it is to stay home and mind their own business, to be little centers of life and joy and cheerfulness. For others, it may be to go on doing what they are doing now, to do their duties in their small ways as they see it. For others it may mean a revolution in their way of life. A peace march, a freedom ride, a new job, a renunciation of even church and state, and any or all of these may be wrong as well as right. But we can at least ask at the end of each day "what have we done for man," and what we have done for man we have done for God.

THE RELATIONS OF ECONOMIC, POLITICAL AND SOCIAL SYSTEMS

Social and Economic Stud., 11, 4 (Dec. 1962): 351-362

The Relations of Economic, Political and Social Systems

The raw material of social systems is the history of mankind. The record of history, however, is no more than raw material. In order to have knowledge of social systems we must abstract out of the almost infinite complexity of this record those elements which exhibit enough regularity to be subject to analysis. Social systems, that is, are essentially abstractions from reality; without these abstractions, however, we cannot hope to understand reality. A system is anything that is not chaos, and even though history seems highly chaotic at times, we have an intuitive feeling that it is not pure chaos. If it is not chaos, there is system in it, and if there is system in it, there is some hope that the system may be perceived and understood.

All systems potentially consist of three elements which might be labelled necessity, chance, and freedom. In the case of systems which have worked themselves through time into a virtual equilibrium, the elements of chance and freedom are practically non-existent and the element of necessity is all that remains. The solar system is a good case in point. In the formation of this system there may well have been important elements of chance which determined how many planets there should be, how large they should be, and in what orbits they should lie. In so far as the system was created it will have elements of freedom in it also, but this we must leave to the theologians. At present, however, the elements of chance and freedom have almost been eliminated, with the notable exception now of political astronomy. It is necessity that rules the stars or, at least, the planets. Their orbits can be described by difference or differential equations of only the second order. Given the position of the solar system yesterday and today, we can theoretically find an equation which will predict exactly its position tomorrow; given today and tomorrow, we can then predict the next day, and so on indefinitely into the future. It is this stability in the relationship between the positions of the system in successive time periods which constitutes *necessity* in mechanical systems and which gives us, therefore, the power of prediction. We can predict eclipses because they belong to a system in which the elements of chance and freedom are almost wholly eliminated.

As we move from the physical into the biological systems, the element of chance becomes more important in the dynamic process. We cannot predict the life history of an infant of any kind in the way that we can predict the movement of the planets. We can predict a limited range of life histories

but we cannot tell in advance out of this limited range which one will be realized. We know that a kitten will not grow up into a dog, but his life history
as a cat has many possible variations, none of which can be predicted in advance. It may be a hungry alley cat or a sleek house cat; it may be ferocious
or gentle, depending on its experiences. In a living organism we may, perhaps, regard its genetic constitution as embodying the element of necessity
in its development, for its genetic constitution is something which it cannot
change. Its development depends also, however, on environmental factors,
some of which may be subject to necessity but many of which can only
be attributed to chance. Systems of this kind are called "stochastic" systems
and they are by no means absent even in physics. As we move from the
physical through the biological into the social sciences, however, the stochastic element becomes more and more important. Such systems may be expressed by stochastic equations in which there is some random component;
money invested at a constant rate of interest in a safe bank grows, according
to a simple law of necessity, at a constant rate of growth. Money invested
in speculative enterprises grows according to a stochastic system. There
may be a constant growth component in it, but from day to day or from
year to year a number is picked, as it were, out of a hat and added or subtracted. The actual day-to-day course of the system, therefore, is fundamentally unpredictable, even though the general tenor of its way may be predicted.

The third component of general systems, freedom, is virtually unknown
at the physical level except in mixed socio-physical systems. It begins to become important as we reach the higher organisms in biology and it becomes
of great importance in social systems. By freedom I mean that element which
is introduced into the system by the existence of knowledge structures, or
images, and especially by the existence of an image of the future. Freedom
is the process by which an image of the future is consciously realized. If
I am in Jamaica in December, 1961, it is not because of any mechanical necessity, such as that which moves the planets, for my movements are too complex to be described by differential equations except, perhaps, of an infinite
degree. Nor is it satisfactory to explain my appearance in Jamaica on the
grounds that my movements constitute a random walk. I may flatter myself,
but I am pretty sure that my movements around the face of the earth do
not have the mathematical characteristics of a purely random path, that is,
a path in which the direction, extent, and changes of movement are determined by the throw of the dice. The mere fact that I return home again
occasionally is sufficient to destroy the random walk explanation, simply because a random walker returns home much less often than I do. There must,
therefore, be some other explanation of my movements, and this can only
be found in the fact that I have an image of the future at any moment of
time and that I tend to act in such a way as to make the future conform
to my image. If my image of the future involves going to Jamaica in December, 1961, sometime before this date I will make preparations; I will

buy a plane ticket; at the right time I will go to the airport, get on the plane, and eventually arrive in Jamaica. There are, of course, stochastic elements in this process which may interrupt it; I may have a heart attack, the plane may crash, or the world may come to an end; these stochastic elements, however, lurk in every system, but it is one of the great objects of knowledge to lessen their incidence and to lower their probability.

We must recognize, therefore, that in any system which has an important element of freedom in it, knowledge about the system always changes it. We run into this even in the physical sciences in the famous Heisenberg principle, according to which the attempt to inform ourselves about the position or velocity of an electron changes its position or velocity. As we move towards the social sciences, knowledge about the system and information collected from the system becomes a more and more important part of the system itself. This does not mean, however, that knowledge is impossible or that the systems are uncontrollable. Indeed, the possibility of control of social systems arises only as knowledge about them increases. I am by no means a Marxist and, indeed, I regard Marxism as a very dangerous simplification of social dynamics, but I have a lot of sympathy with what Engels called the "leap from necessity into freedom." We begin to make this leap when our knowledge of social systems rises to the point at which some sort of control becomes possible so that the future is no longer solely in the hands of necessity and chance. We can then form images of the future of society as well as of our own personal lives which have some chance of coming about, a chance which is great enough to make it worthwhile pursuing conscious efforts towards the future that we have in mind. The more inaccurate our knowledge of the social system, of course, the less the element of freedom in it; we may think that we are directing our actions towards a certain future when, in fact, our actions have the effect of taking us away from this future rather than towards it. Nevertheless, the idea that we can plan for a future of society as well as in our own personal lives is, perhaps, one of the most important ideas of the nineteenth century, and it is an idea that we owe in no small measure to Marx himself.

If we are going to reduce the almost inconceivable complexity of human history to manageable, systematic form, we must break up the social system, at least conceptually, into sub-systems, recognizing, of course, but at the same time keeping in the back of our minds, the fact that these sub-systems are not independent and that they constantly interact with each other. A large number of these sub-systems may be identified, but I propose to discuss only four of them which I regard of primary importance. These four I shall label populations systems, exchange systems, threat systems, and learning systems. In all of these we can trace the same three general elements of necessity, chance, and freedom.

In population systems we consider, first of all, the total stock of all those objects or items which are significant from the point of view of social systems. We may consider also the composition of the stock, that is, its division into various significant categories. Then we consider the dynamics of the stock, that is, its change through time, as this is determined by additions to and subtractions from the stock. The fundamental law of necessity in such a system is that the increase in any stock over a period of time must be equal to the additions to the stock less the subtractions from it, or "births" into it minus "deaths" out of it. This identity is a mechanical necessity which can be avoided neither by chance nor by freedom.

The most significant population system is, of course, the population of human beings themselves. It is possible to make projections of human population and its distribution by area, race, sex, or any other composition by assuming fairly simple relationships between births, deaths, immigration, emigration, and so on into the various groups. These projections represent the element of necessity in population systems; they all take the form of saying that, if certain parameters of the system remain the same, then its course will be as projected. These projections, however, are not predictions because of the chance elements in the system. The parameters themselves, such as the age-specific birth and death rates, are always subject to unpredictable change, and those who believed that the population projections were, in fact, predictions have been grievously disappointed by the experience of the last twenty-five years. Nevertheless, the projections are important, for they give us the range of possible futures and they enable us to make propositions of the form, "If there is no change in these parameters, then the future will be like this." We can say, for instance, to use a very crude example, that if the population of Jamaica continues to increase at its present rate, it will double, roughly, every forty years. Population systems also enable us to make projections about the distribution and composition of populations. Cohort analysis enables us to predict, within reasonable margins of error, what the age composition of the population is likely to be in the future. In the United States, for instance, the fact that there were so many more babies born in the forties than there were in the thirties has now created a crisis in the educational system because of the distortion in the age distribution of the population. This is a crisis which was both predictable and predicted. On the other hand, it is extremely dangerous to assume that birth and death rates will continue at present rates or will follow any prescribed course into the future. The failure of the population predictions of the forties were based largely on this mistake.

It is not only to human populations, however, that population analysis applies. It can be applied to anything which has a stock and which has additions to or subtractions from that stock. It can be applied, therefore, to the whole world of capital goods and of commodities; it can be applied even to such things as ideas and images. The famous proposition that capital can only increase if production exceeds consumption is identical in form with the basic identity of all population analysis. A good deal of the theory of economic development rests on this identity. The rate of capital accumulation can be increased only by increasing production or by diminishing con-

sumption. Frequently, the latter is the only alternative open. So we run into
the iron law of development; that development implies parsimony, whether
involuntary or imposed.

It is clear that population systems broadly interpreted cover a large part
of the field of social dynamics; nevertheless, they do not cover it all. As we
move from demography into economics, for instance, we find that the concept of exchange becomes more and more important. Exchange systems
may, perhaps, be regarded as a sub-division of population systems as they
essentially involve the redistribution of existing stocks of things among
people. Exchange systems, however, have peculiarities of their own which
perhaps justify their classification as a special sub-system. Exchange is a
basic form of human interaction; it is basic, not only to economic life, but
also to all social relationships, such as marriage, friendship, and all kinds
of collective action. We think of it fundamentally as an exchange of "goods"
and its basic proposition is, "I will do something good for you if you will
do something good for me." It is a positive-sum game in which all parties can
be better off, but it is also a curious mixture of co-operative and competitive
elements. It is co-operative in so far as there is gain to both parties; it is
competitive in so far as the distribution of this gain depends on the terms
of trade, that is, on the ratio of exchange, and any movement in the ratio
of exchange makes one party relatively better off and one party relatively
worse off than they were before.

Exchange systems can become seriously disturbed by changes in the
medium of exchange. Inflation or deflation in the monetary system, for instance, disturbs the whole system of exchange because of the fact that many
exchange relationships involve a time interval between one transaction and
its reciprocal transaction. Exchange, of course, always consists of two transfers or transactions, but these do not have to occur at the same time. In a
debt relationship, for instance, or in the implicit exchange among the generations in which the middle aged support the young in expectation that
they themselves will be supported when they are old, and support the old
in repayment of the support that they received when they were young, there
is a substantial time interval between one transfer and the transfer which
completes the exchange. If, in the interval, there is a general social change,
for instance, in the price level, the whole system of transfers over time is
disturbed. Inflation discriminates against the creditors, deflation against the
debtors, and economic development can easily discriminate against the generation that initiates it. Marriage and friendship both may be wrecked by
disappointment in deferred exchange, though in this case, the commodity
may simply be affection or approval. Political parties and political structures,
likewise, are involved in this time exchange; a political party makes promises
and, if these are not fulfilled, the voters may take their revenge at the next
election. The whole dynamics of society and the dynamics of population
systems themselves are profoundly affected by the operations of the exchange
system. Thus, the great depression in the United States, which resulted fun-

damentally from a breakdown in the exchange system, had profound effects on the birth rate, on future populations, and on the accumulation of capital.

Exchange systems, again, have certain elements of necessity in them. The relative price structure, for instance, is not arbitrary and cannot be changed at will without severe repercussions on the society. The closer we get to perfect competition, the greater the element of necessity in the system and the more all-pervasive and compelling is the "law of supply and demand." We cannot force the price structure away from some equilibrium position without producing serious consequences in the way of shortages and surpluses of commodities. As we move towards monopoly, and especially towards oligopoly or bilateral-monopoly, however, the element of chance in the system becomes more important. Where we have bargaining, there will be a range of prices at which a bargain may be struck, but there is no way of predicting in advance where within this range the bargain will actually be found. Under these circumstances there is a genuinely stochastic element in the dynamics of a price system which cannot be neglected. There are also, however, elements of freedom in it. The equilibrium price structure is not an absolute necessity; it can be changed under appropriate governmental action and pressure. It can be distorted by price control and by taxation. Within limits, the consequences of these distortions can be predicted, and the control of the price system may well be an instrument by which we move towards some image of the future. We may wish, for instance, to make vice expensive and virtue cheap, and we may be able to do this both through the tax system and through direct prohibitions or encouragements. We may look into the future and decide that some commodity, for instance, water, which is plentiful now, is going to be scarce in the future. We may wish, therefore, to distort the present price system in order to anticipate the future scarcity. The present price system, for instance, affects the course of future technology; if we make something expensive it is likely to be economized. This is one argument, for instance, for distorting the price system in favour of higher money wages. Then a "disequilibrium" system would create dynamic change. Even though high wages create unemployment, it may be better to have unemployment than low wages because, if labour is scarce, it will be economized and it is the economizing of labour which constitutes the essence of economic development. These elements of freedom in the price system are not well understood or worked out, but they undoubtedly exist, and the more explicit we can be about them the better our policy is likely to be. The argument that the price system must lie wholly in the realm of necessity is not, I think, acceptable to modern ears.

We have still by no means encompassed all the relationships of society and here, again, even though what I have called "threat systems" may be viewed as a special case of exchange systems, they nevertheless present so many peculiarities that they deserve to be singled out for special treatment. An exchange system is based on a transfer of goods, a threat system on the transfer of "bads." An exchange system, as we have seen, is based on the proposition "If you do something good for me, I will do something good for you." A threat system is based on the proposition, "If you do not do something good for me I will do something bad to you." Threat systems are the basis of politics as exchange systems are the basis of economics. Political power fundamentally is based on threats. Actual political life, however, is made up of a curious mixture of exchange systems and threat systems. In part, and perhaps in the largest part, government is always by consent, that is, by exchange. We give up some of our personal sovereignty to the state, as we give up some of our personal income in taxation because we feel that the state does something for us in exchange. It gives us protection, identification, an enlarged personality, and other benefits and, in so far as it does this, the system may quite properly be regarded as a system of exchange. This, however, is not the whole story. Man early discovered that threats were a powerful method of social organization. We can, indeed, conceive of classical civilization as essentially a threat system based on the fact that, with the invention of agriculture, the food producer produced more than he could eat himself or rather, than he needed to eat himself, and that with the food surplus the ruler was able to feed an army or a coercive organization which would then compel the food producer to give up the food that would feed the agent that coerced him. As long as this is unchallenged, this is a very stable social system. As the civilizations of the Mayans and of Mohenjodaro testify, the threat, of course, need not always be a physical one. It can also be spiritual. Many of the early civilizations seem to have been based on spiritual threats, that is, on the capacity of a priesthood to threaten people with spiritual damnation, if they did not turn over their food surpluses to the social organization.

Slavery in the early colonial system was a good example of the threat system in an almost pure form. With the surplus which the slave produced over his subsistence, the master could employ a coercive power with which he could threaten the slave's life. As long as the slave preferred slavery to death, and as long as the master was able and willing to use the means of coercion at his disposal, the system continued. The demise of the system occurred, not so much because of any internal instability, but because of the fact that both its moral and its economic base were eroded by the development of more profitable systems of social organization, namely, a system of exchange. An exchange system is fundamentally more productive than a threat system simply because the exchange of goods encourages the production of goods, whereas the threat of ill discourages the production of goods. While a one-sided threat system is internally stable, threat systems in themselves develop instability because of the fact that they become, not one-sided but bi-lateral. The proposition, "If you do not do good to me, I will do bad to you," becomes "If you do bad to me I will do bad to you." It is hard to keep a monopolistic threat system intact, and, against one threat system, another threat system tends to be aroused. Threat systems, therefore, constantly decline into war systems or deterrence systems which seem to have an inherent instability in them. This is the main reason for the rise and fall of civilizations, and the long cycles which have characterized human development for the last five thousand years. We are now at the extreme end of this period in which the threat system has become so universal that it threatens to destroy us all.

Any account of social dynamics would be incomplete if it did not include learning systems. Learning, of course, is involved in all the other systems but here, again, it has peculiarities of its own which make it desirable to single it out. A learning system may be defined broadly as a social process by which the image of the world possessed by the individuals of the society comes to change. At each moment each individual has an image of the world which includes an image of space, of time, of the past and the future, of his role in society, of things that are expected of him, the things he expects of others, his obligations and his rights, and so on. This image largely determines his behaviour. If people find themselves in situations where their behaviour does not reinforce their image, then either their image must change or they will find themselves in a new situation. If a man thinks he is Napoleon and acts as if he were Napoleon, when in fact he is not, he will soon find himself segregated in a mental hospital in which his role is acceptable. We might add that if he thinks he is Napoleon when he is Napoleon he finds himself at Saint Helena. Society moves and changes by an enormous interaction of images, behaviours, disappointments, role fulfilments or unfulfilments, and the constant interaction of images on society and society on the images.

The most significant thing that has happened, perhaps in the whole history of mankind, is the formalization and systemization of the learning process itself in what we know as science. This has resulted in an enormous acceleration of change in the image. In folk culture the image is very resistant to change. If messages are received which are inconsistent with the image, they are generally rejected. Because of this stability in the image, a primitive society in which the processes of learning are not specialized, provided that it is left to itself, is likely to be very stable and will reproduce itself generation after generation. The specialization of the learning process has introduced an enormous dynamic into human society in the last four hundred years and has now placed us in a pace of social change so rapid that now we go through in a single year a change in the basic parameters of the social system at least equivalent to what took a thousand years in the age of classical civilization.

This specialization of the learning system offers both great hope and great danger to mankind. It offers hope because it is only out of this specialization that we can hope to understand the nature of social systems and, hence, move from the realm of necessity into the realm of freedom. It is only by the specialized activities of the knowledge seekers, especially in the social sciences, that we can hope to understand the social system sufficiently well to be able to control it and to be able to move into a positive image of the future through our own volition and policy. Otherwise, we are merely slaves of necessity or victims of chance. On the other hand, the very specialization of the learning process and the rapidity of change make it all the more difficult to understand and especially to get widespread understanding of the nature of the change itself. Let us imagine what the world would be like if the parameters of the physical systems in which we operate changed as rapidly and as unpredictably as the parameters of the social systems. Suppose, for instance, that on Monday the gravitational constant was low, whereas on Tuesday it was high; we would literally never know how to get out of bed. On Monday we fly through the window and Tuesday we would crack our head on the floor. To live at all in a world like this we would have to have an elaborate system of scientific information; we would have to have a gravimeter by the bedside to tell us before we even got up whether to make a desperate leap or a gentle movement.

This, however, is precisely the fix we are in in social systems. Their significant parameters such as, for instance, the price level, the productivity of labour, the range of the deadly missile, or the proportion of communications received outside the family, change constantly and often with great rapidity. Under these circumstances, it is extremely difficult to know how to operate and it is not surprising that we make serious mistakes. Under these circumstances too, however, it is all the more important to devise accurate and unbiased methods of sifting information and of condensing information into forms which are readily appreciated. We desperately need a social systems equivalent of the gravimeter by the bedside. In economics we have this to some extent in the form of national income statistics. It was still possible in the United States in 1931 to argue about whether there was a depression or not. Today, we cannot have a turndown for two or three months without this fact coming to the attention of all the significant decision-makers in this society. In international systems we have not yet reached this position; we have, in fact, a system of information which is almost designed to be corrupted. Both diplomats and intelligence agencies produce an extremely biased picture of the truth, by nature of the social system which they themselves inhabit, and until we can get more accurate and more "scientific" information in international systems the chance of handling them well is very slim.

In religious systems, in family life, and in the broader learning process by which the images, skills, and ideas of society move from one year to the next our information processes are not organized at all. Because of this, public expenditures, especially in the field of health, education, and welfare, are usually made very inefficiently. In the United States, at any rate, we seem to have a very fundamental principle, that while we are willing to spend a lot of money to see that public funds are spent honestly, we will not spend a dollar to see that they are spent wisely. Until this situation is rectified, one must remain highly sceptical about the advantages of any substantial expansion in the public sector, even in the most developed economies of the

capitalist world. As a corollary one might say that there is no socialist country
in which an expansion of the private market sector would not result in a
marked increase in economic efficiency, even though this might not result
in the desired rate of social change.

I should perhaps, add a fifth system to the four I have already outlined,
though I am hesitant to do this because we understand so little about it. The
four systems outlined above, however, do not encompass an important social
phenomenon which could variously be described as social integration, affection, altruism, or even by the simple word "love." Love systems are those
in which the individual comes to identify his own desires with those of
another. These are important in the explanation of the institution of the
family, of the church, and of nationalism, of the phenomena of philanthropy
and self-sacrifice, and of all those areas of life where we do not merely exchange or threaten but in which we *identify*. A sense of identification, of
course, participates in both exchange and threat systems; the love of country,
like the love of a spouse, has elements of exchange in it or perhaps even of
threat. These elements do not encompass the whole picture, however, and
I suspect that we have to include an autonomous element of integration if
we are to obtain a full description of social systems.

The complaint may be made with some justice that I have not dealt adequately with the title of the paper, in that my classification and hierarchy
of systems does not correspond closely to the division between the economic,
the political, and the social. My only defence to this charge is that I believe
that the distinctions I have made are more elemental and important than
the usual distinctions on which the customary division of the social sciences
are based. It is true, of course, that economic systems concentrate around the
phenomenon of exchange, and, if we like, we can identify exchange systems
with economics. Economic systems cannot wholly be understood, however,
apart from the economic operations of the government, especially through
the systems of unilateral transfers in taxes and subsidies. In order to understand this element in the economic system we have to invoke either threat
systems or love systems. The budgets of states are arrived at by an extremely
complex process of exchange, threat, and philanthropy; the same is true, as
a matter of fact, for the budget of individuals.

Similarly, even though we may wish to make a certain identification of
political science with threat systems, these also do not quite encompass its
traditional field. Government is by consent as well as by threat; in order to
explain government by consent we have to introduce either exchange systems
or love systems. We consent also because we identify our own interest with
those of the coercer. Even in international relations where we might suppose
that threat systems reign supreme we find that there are examples of the
systems of stable peace, for instance between the United States and Canada,
in which the threat system has been so completely overlaid by other relationships that it has ceased to be important or, at least, visible.

Social systems are less clearly demarcated traditionally from political or economic systems. This has always caused difficulties, for the sociologist has never quite decided whether he is studying everything about the social system or whether he has a demarcated field within it. Sociologists like George Homans attempt to make exchange the basis of all social relationship. I suspect this is quite inadequate and that even in the most elementary forms of social interaction, threat systems and love systems are important and that all these, of course, exist in the setting of population systems and learning systems. It would certainly be tidy if the sociologist could be designated to study love systems as the core of his discipline, that is, the systems by which integration takes place. To put the matter in another way, the principal subject of sociology would then be alienation which is, of course, the opposite of integration. This division of labour is probably too tidy and most sociologists would object to it. However, it does seem to me that the problem of how, in the course of social interaction, we learn or fail to learn to identify with other people and with other organizations is peculiar to the "sociological" part of social systems.

As for the interaction among these various systems, it would take, of course, a large volume even to summarize them. I will take but a single example from the problem of economic development. Economic development as a process can be described fairly accurately by means of population systems. Its principal measure is the increase in *per capita* income which is, of course, the birth rate of commodities per person or the amount of commodities to which the average individual gives birth in the course of a year's activity. There is a somewhat mechanical economic theory of economic development which is essentially an application of population analysis, arising out of the assumption that income is a function of total capital and that the increase in capital is a function of the differences in income and consumption. This mechanical theory, however, is descriptive rather than predictive. In order to give it flesh and blood we must have some notion about the role of the exchange system, especially are reflected in the price structure, in this process. We must know also something about the role of threat systems, that is, the possibility of the use of the coercive power. On the whole, it may be said that the capitalist development rests on exchange systems and socialist development on the threat systems, but this, as usual, is too simple a point of view and many modifications would have to be made. It can be said also, I suspect, that a prerequisite of economic development is a certain minimum of social integration. Economic development always involves costs to certain parts of the population. It is a painful process which may involve a gross injustice to a whole generation who sacrifice for growth in order that the next generation or so may enjoy the benefits. Such a system is impossible unless there is a strong sense of social identification. In traditional capitalism the sense of identification is supposed to be found through the family. The present generation is expected to be parsimonious because the parents identify with the children or even the great-grandchildren who will enjoy the fruits of the parsimony. The family, that is, is a love system extending through time. Socialist development attempts to expand this sense of identification to the whole society, at least as embodied in the élite party. There is a thin dividing line, however, between love systems and threat systems and there is a constant tendency for one to pass into the other. Thus, capitalist development has seldom proceeded very far without the exercise of police power, and socialist development seems to be even more dependent on coercion, as the record of Stalin shows. It is in the study of the subtle interweaving of these various systems of society, therefore, that the best hope of understanding of social systems and, therefore, ultimately, their control lies.

SOCIAL JUSTICE IN SOCIAL DYNAMICS

In: Social Justice, Richard B. Brandt, ed.
Englewood Cliffs, N.J: Prentice-Hall, 1962, pp. 73-92

Social Justice in
Social Dynamics

I propose to approach the problem of social justice as an economist and social scientist in a manner somewhat different from that which is customary among the philosophers. The philosopher treats the concept of justice as essentially a normative concept. He is concerned with abstract notions of what is right, good, and just. He is concerned with what ought to be, not necessarily with what is. These normative discussions are important and I would not for a moment wish to decry their value. There is, however, another point of view from which the problem of social justice can be examined. This might be called the *positive* or *operational* point of view in which social justice—or at least the image of social justice as it exists in the minds of the members of society—is an essential variable in determining the dynamic processes and the evolution of that society.

By "social dynamics," I mean neither more nor less than social evolution; that is, the whole great process by which a society moves from Monday to Tuesday to Wednesday and so on. Social evolution is, of course, a process of extreme complexity. It can be illuminated, however, by theoretical models which are drawn essentially from the processes of biological evolution. Although there are great differences between biological evolution and social evolution, there are important similarities as well. The most important point of similarity is the fact that the notion of ecological succession and of a dynamic based on mutation and selection applies to both. Biological evolution can be regarded as a succession of short-run biological equilibria of the ecosystem. A pond, for instance, can be regarded as an equilibrium system of interacting populations of different chemical and biological species. This equilibrium is likely to survive small disturbances. If, for instance, ten per cent of one kind of fish are taken out of a pond, the proportions among the populations of the different species in the pond will be upset, but it is likely that in a year or two they will be re-established. Yet even in the absence of external forces, the equilibrium will gradually change over the long run because of certain irreversible factors in the very processes by which the equilibrium is maintained. The metabolic processes of life, for instance, absorb carbon from the air and the pond gradually will fill up and become a swamp. Mutations occur in the genetic materials of the different organic species. Most of these disturb the equilibrium for a while and disappear. Occasionally, however, one appears which gives the organism—and eventually the species—an advantage so great that a *new* and lasting population equilibrium takes the place of the old. Sometimes the ecological revolution is swift and dramatic: a small change in the environment produces a drastic change in the population of species. The precarious equilibrium of the forest and the prairie in the Middle West before the advent of civilization was an interesting example of this point.

Society, likewise, may be thought of as a large pond filled with interacting populations. In addition to biological and inorganic species, there are social species such as automobiles, schools, gas stations, teachers, clubs, philosophers, corporations, states, missiles, and ideas. It is the last of these which constitutes the essential difference between a social system and a biological system and between social evolution and biological evolution. Below the level of the human species, ideas or images are present only in a very rudimentary form: there are instincts that are genetically determined and behavior patterns which may properly be attributed to images—that is, to cognitive structures within the organisms concerned. These images, however, are not learned from experience, but are built into the organism by the growth process which is guided by the genes. The bird builds its nest and the spider spins its web because in some sense it "knows" how to do this, but this knowledge has not been created by a learning process and has not been erected by experience. The image, the instinct, is built into the organism itself by its genetic processes of growth.

The principle of learning from experience begins to appear in the evolutionary process only with the higher animals. A cat, for instance, behaves like a cat not only because of its genetic constitution but also because it has learned things from its mother as a kitten. In a very real sense, cats have a culture in a way that insects do not. In the development of the human species, however, still another principle comes onto the evolutionary stage. The human nervous system is capable of creating symbolic images and modifying and transmitting these images through speech. Cats teach through signs; humans teach through symbols. This seemingly small change has resulted in an enormous acceleration of the pace of evolution. Under the impact of man, the face of the earth and the composition of its species changes at a pace a hundred or even a thousand times greater than it had done previously. This pace accelerates all the time as social evolution produces more and more complex social forms.

One may be tempted to ask, "But what does this have to do with social justice?" The answer is that the images that men have of themselves and of the society around them—because of their impact on human behavior—are an important, indeed, almost a dominant element in the course of social evolution. In these images the idea of social justice plays a significant role. In an earlier work,[1] I developed a theory of human behavior (or at least a way of looking at it) as consisting essentially of setting in motion a course of events which is intended to carry the person into the most highly valued of his images of potential futures. This is, of course, an economist's way of looking at the matter: to regard behavior as being fundamentally subject to choice. Choice is a process by which we scan a number of possible futures and allot some ordinal numbers such as first, second, third, etc., to elements of this set, and

[1] *The Image* (University of Michigan Press, 1956).

pick out the element which is labeled first. All that is strictly necessary for this process is that we divide the set of possible futures into two sub-sets, one of which we label first and the other second. If the set labeled first contains only one element, this constitutes the chosen future and we behave accordingly.

The future, of course, does not always turn out as we expect, for the choice of a future does not necessarily guarantee it. The future, however, is determined by the choices that we make. That is, there will exist a set function relating the chosen future to the actual future. Thus suppose that F_1, F_2, . . . F_n is the set of images of the possible future, and G_1, G_2, . . . G_n is the set of actual futures. The choice of, say, F_1, does not necessarily mean that we shall proceed into the identically corresponding actual future G_1; it does mean, however, that for any F_1 that we select, there is some G_j which corresponds to it. For many choices, there is a high probability that G_j will, in fact, be the same as G_1, but this is not necessarily true.

If, for instance, I find myself lecturing at Swarthmore on March 19 of a certain year, it is because at some earlier time I had an image of time and space in which, out of all possible futures, my lecturing in Swarthmore on March 19 was labeled first in my value system. Because of this value preference, the formation of which is irrelevant here, I performed certain acts—such as telephoning a travel agency, picking up a plane ticket, driving to an airport, getting on a plane, and so on—all of which were designed in my image of cause and effect to make the image of the future correspond with the actuality. Without having formed and selected the image "in Swarthmore on March the 19th," I would certainly not be there. But the mere fact of my having the image, and of setting in motion certain behavior to realize it, did not guarantee that the image and the actual future would correspond. As I write this on March the 9th I must recognize a certain possibility that I will not be at Swarthmore on March the 19th. I may be taken ill; trains and planes may be immobilized by strikes, or Swarthmore may be hit by a nuclear bomb before that date. In the absence of extraordinary events, however, I shall be somewhat surprised if the actual future does not correspond to my image.

How does the image of social justice fit into this pattern of human behavior? My visit to Swarthmore is clearly—in my own eyes —good, or I would not go. I am not sure, however, that I have thought of this particular activity as being just or unjust either socially or individually. I might feel, I suppose, that it is unjust that I should be asked to give this lecture when Professor X obviously would have given a much better one. On the other hand, Professor X may have already been asked and refused, in which case the injustice is lessened. It may even be that the organizers of this lecture believed that, in fact, I am the best person to give it. In this they may be unwise and mistaken, but error, or lack of wisdom, does not constitute injustice. It may be also that the reward which I will get for the lecture, both the honorarium and the pleasure I will receive at being among old friends at Swarthmore, is more than I deserve. On the other hand, I am not sure that I can provide an operational definition of the concept of desert. If we all get our deserts, as Hamlet said, "Who should 'scape whipping?"

It may be that my total reward for giving this lecture is larger than the smallest amount for which I would have consented to come. In this case, I am getting what the economist calls *economic rent* or *economic surplus,* and this is perhaps in some sense unjust. If it is unjust, I must confess, it is a burden that I will bear with some equanimity. It is clear from this that my concept of social justice played a very small part in making the decision to come and give a lecture about it. This fact demonstrates that the image of social justice is not a universal element in that valuation process by which men come to decisions. There are, however, some choices in which the image of social justice plays an important part, and it is these which we must identify if we are to examine the role which the image of social justice plays in the dynamics of society.

Before proceeding in full cry after these decisions in which the image of social justice is significant or even dominant, let me pause for a moment to look at the role which is played in decision-making by the perception of divergences between a perceived real situation and a perceived ideal situation. The concept of perceived divergence between real and ideal values also plays a dominant role in the explanation of the behavior of what have come to be called *cybernetic* systems, or control systems. A thermostatic system, for instance, has an ideal temperature at which it is set, say 70°. It has a thermometer which enables it to "perceive" the actual temperature. If the actual temperature falls below the ideal, the system sets in motion behavior to warm things up. If the perceived actual temperature rises above the ideal, the system sets in action behavior which will result in cooling things down. This is the principle of homeostasis which is of such great importance in understanding what Cannon called the "wisdom of the body." This principle can also be invoked to explain a great deal of human behavior at the cognitive or affective level. We keep our friendships in repair by much the same process by which we keep a constant temperature in our bodies or in the house: if a friendship is cooling below our ideal level, a letter, a telephone call, or a Christmas card may warm it up. If a friend is getting a little too affectionate and demanding, there are many ways of increasing the social distance which will cool him down.

The wisdom of the spirit, of course, consists in knowing where to set the ideal. A purely homeostatic mechanism is—within wide limitations—quite indifferent as to where the ideal is set. My home thermostat will maintain a steady temperature anywhere between fifty and eighty degrees. It is up to me to set it at the level which best reconciles the claims of health, vitality, and comfort. As we move toward social systems, the problem of where to set the ideal becomes of increasing importance. There is what may be called a homeostatic apparatus within the social system, which acts to reduce divergences between perceived actual and ideal values. In this homeostatic sense, social justice is an ideal; that is, it is something divergence from which is perceived and acts as a cue to behavior.

The perception of divergence between the perceived real value and the ideal value of any important psychological variable—that is, of any variable which is strongly related to utility or general satisfaction—may be labeled *discontent*. In this sense, discontent can be regarded as the prime mover of man to action provided that his image of cause and effect permits him to believe himself capable of such action as to reduce the divergence between the perceived real and the ideal. We may notice a point here, the importance of which will be clearer later. The divergence between the real and the ideal may be reduced by acting so as to manipulate the real. But it may also be reduced by adjusting the ideal. This is the way of renunciation—of wanting what you get, rather than getting what you want. It is traditionally associated with Eastern philosophies, and if adopted it is a powerful deterrent to rapid change.

The adjustment of the ideal is not, of course, necessarily "irrational." If activity results in a continued failure to reduce the gap between the perceived real and the ideal, a person may follow one of three courses. He may change his perception. This may be dangerous if the perception differs much from something which we can call reality, but, on the other hand, it is also comforting. A man may say that his wife really loves him in spite of that fact that she continually hits him over the head with the frying pan. Modern studies of perception indicate that what we think of as sense data are, in fact, so strongly guided by existing beliefs and by our value system that we cannot afford to dismiss as immediately invalid the alteration of perception in response to homeostatic failure. Only one cheer, however, for this solution; we do well to be suspicious of it and to give at least two cheers for the second alternative, which is the readjustment of the ideal. At its worst, this can be a retreat into apathy or into criminality. But somewhere along the line, as the bloom of youth is knocked off us by our contact with the world, we make this kind of adjustment. The third reaction, and the only one for which I am inclined to give three cheers, is that of finding a new course of behavior and of developing a more accurate image of cause and effect. Faced with homeostatic failure, the schizophrenic adjusts his perceptions, the weak man hauls down his ideals, and the hero puts in a new furnace and insulates the house. The wisdom of the spirit consists in the knowledge of the proper proportions of these three responses—the blind eye, the struck flag, and the renewed effort.

Now let us return to the concept of discontent and its relation to social justice. The crucial distinction here—both from the point of view of the definition of social justice, and also from the point of view of its impact on the general dynamics of society—is the distinc-

tion between what might be called personal discontent on the one
hand and political discontent on the other. These are distinguished
mainly by the reactions they arouse. Personal discontent is the individual's dissatisfaction with his place in society, created by his
perception of a gap between his present condition within the framework of his society and the position which he feels he might attain
through his own efforts. Personal discontent, therefore, drives the
individual to seek a new situation within the existing framework.
It does not drive him to seek to change the framework itself. If he
is discontented with his income, he looks for a better job, he goes to
night school, or he tries to marry a rich woman. If he is discontented with his marriage, he arranges for a divorce. If he dislikes
the town where he lives, or if he cannot get along with his neighbors, he moves. Personal discontent is the muscle which moves
Adam Smith's hidden hand. It has profound impact on the dynamics of society. It diminishes one occupation and increases another.
It raises the population of one place and lowers that of another.

The political consequences of personal discontent may be pro-
digious, but they are indirect. The individual's political discontent
has direct political consequences. Political discontent is discontent
with the framework of the society in which a man operates. It may
arise because of his inability to deal with personal discontents. He
may have failed in his own efforts to improve his position: his new
job is no better than the old, the new town and the new neighbors
present all the old problems, his new wife turns out to be just as
unsatisfactory as the old one. A purely rational individual, under
these circumstances, might seek more fundamental means of assuag-
ing personal discontent, such as religion or psychoanalysis. Failing
this, however, or even after this, personal discontent may be re-
directed at the social framework. His failure to deal with his own
discontent, he argues, cannot be the result of a personal deficiency
or of ill-considered decisions. It must be the result of larger external
forces—"the system." Political discontent does not always have to
have disreputable origins, however; it may be, and frequently is, an
expression of the noblest and the most altruistic motives. Political
discontent is frequently found in persons whose personal satisfac-
tions are of the highest, but who are observant and sensitive and

who identify themselves with those who seem to be ill-treated or unhappy or unjustly served by the society—even though these others may not feel personal discontent with their treatment by society; yet even this form of political discontent may be said to arise from the individual's personal failure: his inability to do in a personal capacity what he would like for others. This failure, however, has a much more noble origin than the political discontent which arises out of merely personal failure to improve one's own position.

Whatever the sources of political discontent, its effects are frequently similar. It manifests itself in agitation for some kind of political or social change. The word *agitation,* itself, derives from a very accurate analogy. The politically discontented individual acts, as it were, to increase the Brownian movement of society, to stir up discontent in others in the hope that the increased movement of large numbers of individuals will eventually effect a change in the social vessel which holds them. Political discontent, therefore, is expressed in organization, meetings, propaganda, pamphlets, and—in its more extreme form—armed rebellion. All wars, in fact, as distinct from piracy and freebooting, must be regarded as expressions of political discontent. In some ways, the political party, the election, the letters to the editor, the pamphlets, the speeches, the processions, the sit-downs, the sit-ins, and other forms of nonviolent resistance must be regarded as an organizationally superior substitute for war. The characteristic of political discontent is struggle. This is in marked contrast to the reaction to personal discontent which is adjustment, to which such struggle as there is is merely incidental.

The concept of social justice, because it is largely irrelevant to the satisfaction of personal discontent, seems to be irrelevant to a very large area of social life. The concept of social justice is quite fundamental, however, to political discontent, for it presumably represents an ideal state of society from which the existing state is perceived as a significant divergence. It is this divergence between the existing and the ideal state of society which is perceived as the motivation for homeostatic change. Even here, however, the ideal contains a good deal more than the concept of justice. A good deal of thinking about war and peace at the moment, for instance, re-

flects the view that, in the present stage of military technology, it
would be worthwhile paying a good deal in injustice for the establishment of a stable peace. Although war has historically been
one of the ways in which men have attempted to correct what they
perceive as injustices, at the present time it may be that war has
become too expensive and too dangerous as a means of moving the
world toward a more just order. Similarly, there may be a conflict
between the claims of social justice and the desire for economic development. In certain societies, a higher rate of economic development may be achieved by riding roughshod over the more delicate
issues of social justice. A similar competitive relationship may exist
between justice and freedom. Freedom and justice are hard to measure, but it does seem that one may be expanded at the expense of
the other. The institutions of justice inevitably limit much of the
freedom of some, and some of the freedom of all. It may be argued
that this limitation of the freedom of some is in the interests of
greater freedom for all, but this conclusion is by no means necessary.
It can easily be shown that an over-meticulous concern for justice
can easily interfere with peace, order, economic growth, and freedom.
An obsession with "fair" shares may inhibit the growth of the total
social product, may lead to costly conflict, or may severely limit the
freedom of action of the individuals in the society.

It is clear from the above that political discontent has a good
many dimensions, depending on the object of discontent. If there
is discontent with the anarchy of violence and war which results
from the present social system, political agitation will be directed
toward the establishment of world government. Discontent with
the rate of economic growth may lead to agitation for a self-conscious economic program for the creation of political institutions to
promote growth. Discontent with restrictions on personal liberty or
with the subordinate position of a particular people or race may
lead to agitation for civil liberties, national liberation or civil rights.
Discontent with the distribution of the privileges and burdens of
society—the feeling that some are getting more than they deserve
and some are getting less—may lead to agitation for progressive income and inheritance taxes, or even for expropriation of property.
These last two forms of political discontent are the most closely

allied to the concept of social justice. The concept of justice is profoundly two-dimensional. It encompasses, on the one hand, what
might be called "disalienation," that is, the idea that nobody should
be alienated from the society in which he lives. This is the aspect
of justice which is reflected in the struggle for equality: the equality
of individuals before the law, the equality of racial and religious
groups in the culture as well as before the law and, in its extreme
form, equality of income. The concept here is a familistic one—
society is conceived as a great family from whose table not even the
humblest of her members shall be excluded.

The second dimension of justice is the concept of *desert*. In a just
society, each gets what he deserves, neither more nor less. It is this
concept which gives rise to a productivity theory of distribution
according to contribution, and leads to the view that he who does
not contribute to the social product does not deserve any reward
out of it. There is considerable tension between these two dimensions of justice. In general, they cannot both be satisfied. Many
sit down at the table of society who do not deserve to be there and
many eat from it who have not made any contribution. On the
strict desert theory, the young may be admitted on the grounds that
they will make a contribution in the future, and the old may be
admitted on the grounds that they have made a contribution in the
past. However, this leaves the question of the sick, the incompetent,
and the mentally deficient. We face the dilemma, therefore, that if
everyone gets his deserts, some may be driven from the table; and
if everyone comes to the table, some may not get their deserts. In
practice, this seems to be resolved by the establishment of a social
minimum as reflected, for instance, in the poor law, in social
security, and in various welfare services. The principle of desert
may come into play above this social minimum. That is to say,
society lays a modest table at which all can sup and a high table at
which the deserving can feast. This general principle can be traced
in almost all practical efforts to solve the problem.

The establishment of this principle, useful as it is, leaves a very
great many problems unsolved. It is one thing to establish the
principle of a social minimum; it is quite another thing to determine where this minimum shall be set. It may be set at the utmost

limits of Malthusian rigor—a bare table with bread and water and
no propagation. It may be set higher with more sympathy, but also,
perhaps, with less long-run validity as in Speenhamland and in aid-
to-dependent-children. Then, above whatever minimum has been
set, the principle of to each according to his deserts may be permitted to prevail. Within these limitations of the principle, however, a wide range of controversy is possible. There is an almost
universal consensus that an unrestricted market economy will give
the rich more than they deserve. Hence, many countries impose
progressive taxation designed, not with universal success, to diminish the divergence in income between the rich and the poor. The
actual schedule of taxation in any country and the rate at which
it progresses seem to depend largely on historical accident. There
is no clearly ideal tax schedule, and there is a strong tendency for
almost any schedule, once established, to persist. There may be
political discontent with existing schedules, especially among the
members within the upper brackets, but it seems to be very hard to
translate this discontent into political action and into legislative
results. The agitation to limit tax rates in the United States to 25
per cent of income, for instance, has achieved nothing. It is very
hard to make the poor and the middle class who make up the
majority feel a great deal of sympathy for the worries of the rich,
and hence the rich in a democratic society have little political
bargaining power.

Political discontent is, then, a powerful agent of social change.
It is, indeed, the principal agent of what might be called "manifest"
social change, in which the course of society is deliberately directed
toward a self-conscious end. The dynamics of a society cannot be
understood without reference to the prevailing images of a political
future. As in the case of an individual, however, the images of the
future may not be realized even though they are an important
element in determining it. This is even more true in the case of
social dynamics than it is in the dynamics of individual behavior.
We do not go anywhere unless we have a ticket, and what is
written on the ticket determines where we will go. But in society,
even more than in the case of the individual, what is written on the
ticket is not necessarily where we end up; the latent forces in the

dynamics of society often confound even the explicit plans of the politically discontented. Thus, the Christian image of a heavenly kingdom has helped to organize a good many earthly societies which have not in themselves borne much resemblance to Zion. Similarly, the communist image of a classless society has, in fact, created totalitarian and highly stratified dictatorships. The Mormon vision of a community of latter-day saints led to the establishment of the State of Utah, which maintains a level of crime and divorce comparable to other less professedly virtuous communities.

That part of political discontent which is related to ideals of social justice is sometimes a very important agent of social change, and sometimes not. A very important problem in the theory of social dynamics is to determine those circumstances under which discontent takes a personal rather than a political form and those under which political discontent aspires after social justice rather than order, growth, or freedom. There are many puzzling problems here. It cannot be assumed, for instance, that just because people are poor they will be discontented, either personally or politically. History records the existence of many peoples whose misery and exploitation have been deplorably stable and who have not given any expression of personal or political discontent. One might venture on the proposition that there is very little discontent below a certain level of poverty simply because people do not have the energy to question their lot and merely drag out an existence from day to day on their meager resources. Above this level, it may take a large improvement in conditions to diminish discontent again, as a little improvement only raises the appetite for more. Another hypothesis is that any worsening of conditions will increase discontent even if people are fairly well off to start with. The individual comes to think that he merits what he is accustomed to; hence, any worsening of his condition is a serious threat to his self-esteem. A subordinate hypothesis may then be formulated: threats to our self-esteem are the principal source of discontent, either political or personal.

A third hypothesis is that discontent, once generated, can take either a personal or a political form, depending upon the opportunities and chances of success. In a rapidly advancing society in which individuals can, with a little effort, easily participate in the general wealth, most discontent will be personal and will express itself in efforts on the part of the individual to advance his position within the existing social framework. A society, on the other hand, which is stagnant or declining will be likely to generate political discontent, for the individual who attempts to solve his problems by purely personal means will be met with considerable lack of success. This will upset his self-esteem which can only be restored by attacking the social framework.

A fourth closely related hypothesis is that if the individuals of a society perceive that political change within it is easy, whether this is in fact so or not, the discontent will be likely to take a more personal form. Thus in democracies political discontent is likely to be mild, whereas in totalitarian or autocratic societies the very suppression of political activity leads to an intensification of political discontent.

Political discontent perhaps can be subdivided further into revolutionary discontent and constitutional discontent. Constitutional discontent expresses itself, as the name implies, within the constitution of the society: it may seek to effect a change in personnel or a change in party, but not a change in the essential political system. If discontent cannot be expressed constitutionally, it will be expressed in revolutionary ways. Revolutionary discontent despairs of adequate political change within the existing constitution of society and, therefore, sets out to change the constitution itself. The degree of intensity of political discontent is important also: a mild political discontent is likely to express itself constitutionally, whereas an intense political discontent is likely to express itself in revolutionary form. The more intense the discontent, the more likely is its expression to be violent.

The next problem is to determine the mode of political discontent: that is, the circumstances under which it is likely to be directed against anarchy and war, against poverty and the failure of economic growth, against restrictions on freedom or on dignity, or against social injustice. This clearly depends upon the nature of the image of the existing society and of the divergence between this image and the ideal image. Political discontent will be directed toward those elements in society which are felt to diverge most from the ideal. If the society is orderly and war is perceived only as a peripheral activity, the problem of order and anarchy will not receive much attention. Similarly, if the society seems to be progressing satisfactorily toward greater per capita income, there will not be much pressure for general economic reform. In a society which is both orderly and progressing but in which there are large divergencies between rich and poor, or in which there is discrimination between some class or group, political discontent will mainly take the form of a demand for social justice.

This gives rise to an interesting question: is social justice an ideal which becomes important only in societies which are already orderly and progressing, or is it prominent in the political discontent even of disorderly or stagnant societies? This cannot be answered without reference to the facts of history. One suspects that there is some tendency for a dominant order of this kind: that a strong political discontent directed at social injustice is only likely to arise in those societies which are relatively orderly and progressive, and that the demands for social justice may be low in disorderly and poor societies. A possible exception to this is in those societies which have developed, as it were, a habit of political action. In such societies, if the problems of order and progress are not well solved, political action will still divert itself into the quest for justice.

The relation between discontent and action is not, itself, an invariant one. When a society has a deep interest in politics and its human energy is not "diverted" into religion, art, domesticity, or economic advancement, a small amount of political discontent may produce a disproportionate amount of political action. Under these conditions, the quest for social justice may actually prove to be inimical to that very order and progress which permitted the quest. The difficulty here is that the ideal of social justice is less easily defined than other political ideals. It is all too easy to perceive disorder or economic stagnation, and it is—perhaps—easy to perceive gross injustice. The fine definition of justice, however, is extremely difficult and there is a wide range of social states over which controversy can range. Under these circumstances, the quest for social justice may actually endanger the very order and progress which permitted it. In the struggle about the final distribution of a cake, the cake itself may be thrown to the ground and lost. One sees this even within the family where the quest for personal justice among the children not infrequently results in a bitter and quarrelsome situation in which many of the values of family life are lost. Each, in trying to get his fair share, diminishes the total that is to be divided.

We may conclude by some historical illustrations of these principles. It can be argued that from about 1880 on in the countries of northwest Europe and in the United States, the quest for social justice became a very important element in political discontent and had a profound effect on the political activities of these societies. These societies were already rich and had been—for the most part—getting richer rapidly. These societies enjoyed a high measure of internal order within this period and, until very recently, war affected them only peripherally. Constitutional rights and individual freedoms were well-developed, and the great constitutional battles against autocratic government had been won. There existed, however, a strong habit of political action and advanced institutions for legislation. It is not surprising, therefore, that the political action, on the whole, took the form of a demand for social justice which, in turn, played a dominant role in the legislative activities of these societies. In the United States, which was advancing most rapidly, discontent still took a personal rather than a political form. The American labor movement, for instance, by contrast with European labor movements, was fundamentally an expression of personal discontent. The American union, especially the craft union of the American Federation of Labor, was not an instrument to change society or even the rules of society, but an instrument by which its members bargained for better incomes. As late as the Great Depression, the American Federation of Labor was still denouncing social security. Although the socialists had some influence in the union, they were never able to dominate it. In the European democracies, however, because the class structure was more rigid and the general rate of development not as high, the opportunities for individual advancement were fewer. It is not surprising, therefore, that the discontent took a more political form and that the labor movement in Europe gave rise to the social democratic parties of later years. Yet even in Europe, the discontent generally took a constitutional rather than a revolutionary form, because of the relative lack of alienation of the mass of the people from the institutions of society. It has been the most advanced countries in Europe, with the exception of France, which have retained the institution of the monarchy. And France, perhaps, is the exception that proves the rule, for her economic development, until very recently, has been erratic, localized, and unsatisfactory.

Another interesting case study in the pathology of social justice is agricultural policy. With economic development, the proportion of the population engaged in agriculture has continually diminished so that it is now a relatively small minority in all advanced countries. In spite of this, legislative activity devoted to promoting social justice for agriculture has continually increased, and large sums are spent to subsidize what is a relatively small part of the population. Psychoanalytic roots can, perhaps, be found for this behavior: many city dwellers have rural parents, grandparents, or great-grandparents; the move to the city may reflect a rejection of rural life and rural values, which is, in a sense, a rejection of the parent, the guilt for which has been compensated for by agricultural subsidies. Part of the explanation lies in a certain constitutional lag which has resulted in gross over-representation of agricultural populations in the legislatures—for example, in the American Senate. This is not sufficient to account for the phenomenon of agricultural subsidy, however, since nearly all these subsidies required the support of city voters. The rationale of agricultural policy can only be explained by an appeal to social justice. The farm interests have made much of the fact that per capita incomes in agriculture are only about half what they are in industrial pursuits. Support, therefore, is enlisted under the concept of parity, or of equality for agriculture. Such aid to agriculture, however, has generally taken the form of price supports. These, in fact, create more injustice than they rectify, for they inevitably subsidize the rich farmer more than the poor. The poor farmers are those who have little to sell; a better price does not much better their condition, but it benefits greatly those who have a lot to sell. Agricultural price policy, then, has been an attempt to legislate social justice, the effects of which are very likely to be perverse. Nevertheless, it is the appeal to social justice which must be invoked to explain the action.

Another example of an appeal to social justice with unintended consequences is the history of the minimum wage. Minimum wage legislation is usually argued on an appeal to the principle of a social minimum. Yet the short-run effects of a minimum wage are very likely to be the pushing of considerable numbers of people below the social minimum, for many of these who previously had employment below the new minimum wage will now be unemployed. The long-run effect of a minimum wage, however, may be a technical reorganization of the affected industries which would not otherwise have taken place, and which will eventually enable them to reabsorb workers at or above the minimum wage. What is designed to be an instrument of social justice turns out to be an instrument of economic development from which social justice, as a by-product, may eventually emerge.

The essentially subordinate status of social justice as a goal of rational political discontent is illustrated by the principle that any group will find it eventually unprofitable to redistribute income toward itself at the cost even of the smallest decline in the rate of economic development. For any group which succeeds in such a redistribution there will be some year in the future beyond which it will be worse off in an absolute sense because it effected the initial redistribution in its favor. The general conclusion seems to be that social justice is something that we ought to have but that we should not want too badly, or else our craving for it will dash it from our lips and, in our eagerness to snatch it, we shall spill it.

Because many problems which appear to be problems of distribution are, in fact, problems of relative growth, there exists the danger that their treatment as problems in distribution may destroy the growth which would solve them. This may be true in large measure even of the chief problem of the world today: its division into rich countries and poor. This is a problem which can be solved, not by redistributing the riches of the rich to the poor but by making the poor productive. The rich can, and should, play an important role in the task, but the more important role must be played by the poor countries themselves: they must reorganize their societies so as to permit rapid economic development. This may seem at times like a hard and ungenerous doctrine, but it is, unfortunately, all too true. In a very real sense, justice is something that only the rich can afford. Only as the poor become rich can social justice, in any of its meanings, be established. But this is not primarily a matter of present distribution, but a matter of eventual participation in the organization and productivity of a high level society.

Lest I seem to have come out against social justice, let me add a word in its defense. There are processes in the development of a society which may be self-defeating because they violate the sense of social justice. A good example is the type of economic development in Cuba before the Castro revolution. Although it raised the per capita income of Cuba above that of any other Latin American country, it eventually destroyed itself because it violated the sense of social justice in so many people. The benefits of development were enjoyed by about twenty per cent of the people; the rest benefited little and in some cases even went backward. Discontent, which under more favorable circumstances might have found personal channels, under these conditions was channeled into purely political forms—both on the part of the peasant who felt cut off from opportunities for advancement in such a society, and on the part of his middle-class sympathizers. It remains to be seen whether the new and very different dynamic which has resulted from the revolution can, in fact, solve the problem of economic development together with the problem of social justice.

Economic development is not just a process of growth: it involves the radical reorganization of society itself. There is a stage, however, in any process of economic development at which only part of the society has been transformed. At this stage, since there are likely to be wide disparities of income between the transformed parts and the untransformed parts of the economy, development seems to have been purchased at the expense of social justice. This may be seen on a world scale today: in the eighteenth century, the per capita income in the richest country was probably not more than four or five times the per capita income of the poorest; now, the per capita income of the richest country is about forty times the per capita income of the poorest. This is not the result of exploitation but because of different rates of growth. When this disparity occurs within a society, it creates considerable strains within the social framework. The poor will inevitably become more discontented as they observe the increasing riches of the rich. If this discontent can express itself in personal terms and the process of development is such that the poor can better their condition through individual effort, political upheaval may be avoided. This was the pattern in Britain and the United States. It is also the pattern in Russia, where the Communists were able to persuade the working class to accept a sharp reduction of real income over a period of more than twenty years. This can happen only if the society can develop an ideology which prevents the poor from being alienated. If the poor are alienated, they will eventually overthrow the rich. This may bring the whole process of development to an end—as it seems to have done, for instance, in Mayan civilization. If the poor are led by the middle-class, however, the process of development could easily continue under new social forms.

These considerations underline the close relationship between the two concepts of social justice: disalienation and equality. Equality is a luxury of rich societies. If poor societies are to maintain any kind of peak achievement or civilization, they simply cannot afford it. Without sharp inequalities, we would not have had the Parthenon or the cathedrals or the great cultural achievements of any of the past civilizations. With the coming of the great revolution and what I have called post-civilization, however, equality becomes feasible as a social ideal. Equality, that is, is one of the fruits of development. On the other hand, if there is alienation, the inequality which inevitably develops in the process of development may arrest that development through political discontent. Social justice, therefore, is not a simple and a single ideal of society, but is an essential part of a great complex of social change for which some things may have to be sacrificed at times and which itself, in turn, may need at other times to be sacrificed for greater goods.

THE SOCIETY OF ABUNDANCE

In: The Church in a Society of Abundance,
Arthur E. Walmsley, ed. New York: The Seabury Press,
1963, pp. 9-27

THE SOCIETY OF ABUNDANCE

The most important changes in the condition of mankind are probably the long, steady transitions in which there is a slow but persistent development in one direction in some central variable over a long period of years. Changes of this kind, like the growth of a plant, are not easy to perceive, and our image of man's history is frequently colored by the more dramatic changes such as wars and revolutions which take place quickly, but which may not be so important in their long-run effect, because they do not have a consistent direction.

For the past three hundred years or so, man has been subject to long, persistent change which I have called elsewhere "the second great transition." The first great transition was, of course, the passing from precivilized to civilized societies, which began with the invention of agriculture and the domestication of livestock perhaps eight thousand years ago, and which culminated in the development of political and coercive skills which concentrated the fruits of agriculture into cities. This also was a long, slow process extending over hundreds and, indeed, thousands of years. We are now in the middle of a change in the state of man certainly as large as and perhaps even larger than the transition from precivilized to civilized societies. In order to dramatize this stage I have sometimes described it as a change from civilized to postcivilized society. If this word is too shocking because of our long association of civilization with the good society, we can call the new state of man into which we are moving the "developed" society.

Whatever we call it, we must recognize that the developed society is as different from the society of classical civilization as classical civilization was from the precivilized societies which preceded it. What we call, rather innocuously, "economic development" is nothing more than an enormous revolution in the state of man, perhaps the greatest revolution which he has so far undergone. The spectrum of human societies is of course fairly continuous, and any classification is somewhat arbitrary; nevertheless, the grouping into savage, civilized, and developed societies is at least a workable starting point.

The key variable in explaining the transition from one of these states to the next is the efficiency of human labor in producing the basic needs of subsistence, that is, in providing the essential energy requirements of the human organism. Food is the most important element in the means of subsistence, while shelter and clothing, by cutting down calorie loss, are also important. If we take the family as the basic unit, we may say that precivilized, or savage societies are characterized by the fact that it takes a family roughly full time to produce the means of subsistence for itself, and it produces no surplus over and above what it must consume in order to stay alive and to reproduce. This seems to be the case in most food-gathering or hunting-and-fishing societies. With the invention of agriculture and the domestication of crops and livestock,

it became possible for a single family to produce more subsistence than it needed to keep itself alive and reproducing. This
surplus of the means of subsistence is not in itself a sufficient
condition to produce civilization, though it is a necessary one.
Obviously the cities cannot be fed unless the food provider
produces more food than he and his family can eat. Cities and
civilization, however, are the product of the agricultural food
surplus plus a political organization usually involving some coercive means which can extract the food surplus from the food
producer and use it to feed the kings, armies, priests, philosophers, and artisans who make up and construct the city. The
surplus upon which classical civilizations were built was astonishingly small. Even at the height of the Roman Empire, for
instance, which may be taken as the ideal type of classical
civilization, it probably took about 75 per cent of the population to feed the total, which meant that only 25 per cent could
be spared for urban employments. This is still the case today in
those countries of the world that are regarded as underdeveloped, such as Indonesia, which is about at the level of development of the Roman Empire at its height. It is hard for us, especially those who are nurtured in the traditions of classical
education, to think of the Roman Empire as a poor country,
but in fact its population, extent, and per-capita income were
probably similar to those of present-day Indonesia, which is one
of the poorest countries in the world.

The technology of classical civilization is largely a "folk"
technology; it is based on the slow accumulation of traditional
knowledge which is transmitted primarily through the family.
Even the beginnings of science in Babylonia and Greece
affected the technologies of these societies very little. Folk
technology, however, has a limited horizon. It does not involve

much division of labor in the learning process; it tends to be conservative and rigid; and it is not surprising, therefore, that once the step from precivilized to civilized society has been made there are still long periods of technological stagnation. The early civilization of the Indus at Mohenjo-Daro appears to have been technologically stagnant for almost a thousand years, and even the Roman Empire seems to have stagnated from the time of Augustus to that of Constantine. It was, indeed, the fall of the Roman Empire in the West that laid the foundation for the next technological advance. The so-called Dark Ages, from the fifth to the tenth centuries in Western Europe, saw such fundamental inventions as the water wheel, the stirrup, the horse collar, and the rudder, none of which the Romans had.

The origins of the second great transition, like all origins, are obscure. It has been attributed to, among others, the Benedictines of the sixth century A.D., who pioneered in certain aspects of agricultural and mechanical technology. The suggestion here is that the Benedictines were the first intellectuals who worked with their hands. The technological stagnation of classical civilization depends in part on the sharp separation between the intellectual and the manual laborer. In a society where the life of the mind is supported by the labor of slaves, there is no incentive either on the part of the slave or on the part of the master to improve the efficiency of labor. It was only as Christianity raised labor to a dignity which it did not possess in classical times or in the great Asian civilizations that the possibility of improving the efficiency of labor by taking thought first entered the world. A considerable part of the explanation of the great historic difference between the development of Asia and of Europe may lie in the fact that, whereas the religious teachers of Asia were princes and philosophers, Jesus was a carpenter and St. Paul was a tentmaker. Christianity was the first proletarian religion, and because of this, even when it reached power and affluence, it still found a place for physical labor as an activity consistent with the dignity and purpose of man—*laborare est orare.*

Whatever its origins, from about the sixth century on we can detect the beginnings of a long, slow, but persistent increase in the productivity of labor, partly, as Adam Smith observed, arising out of the specialization of labor itself, but more importantly arising out of the activity of "philosophers or men of speculation whose trade it is not to do anything, but to observe everything, and who upon that account are often capable of combining together the powers of the most distant and dissimilar objects."

By the seventeenth century the movement which only the utmost refinements of historical hindsight can perceive in the Dark Ages comes in full view. "God said, 'Let Newton be,' and there was light." Science, like a chain reaction, develops as an enormous and irreversible expansion in human knowledge, extending its domain to one field after another. Hand in hand with the explosion of knowledge comes a similar explosion of know-how. New sources of energy—steam in the eighteenth century, electricity in the nineteenth, atomic energy in the twentieth—give man enormous new powers. The story is familiar and need not be recapitulated. What is happening here, however, is a long, steady increase in the productivity of human effort, mainly because of man's ability to learn and to teach. We see this manifested dramatically in agriculture. In classical civilization, as we have seen, it took three-quarters of the people to feed the whole; in modern America we can produce all the food we need with 10 per cent of the population, perhaps even with 5 per cent, thus releasing more than 90 per cent to produce the conveniences and luxuries of life.

It is important to realize that we are still in the middle of this transition and there are no signs as yet of its impetus diminishing. If anything, we seem to be in the accelerating phase of the change, and it is probable that we have not yet reached the midpoint. We have only begun, for instance, to devote substantial resources to research and development itself. Much of the development of the previous centuries was on a haphazard and almost accidental basis, and involved an astonishingly small amount of actual human resources. Today we are devoting billions of dollars to the explicit purpose of technical change. We may not be doing this very wisely, but even the most wasteful application of resources of this kind can hardly fail to produce substantial results. We often gain the impression, from the way history is taught, that the Industrial Revolution was something that happened in the eighteenth century. Nothing could be further from the truth. The eighteenth century saw some quickening of the rate of change, though it could be argued that the increase of the rate of change has been fairly steady from the sixth century on and that the eighteenth century represents no great watershed. This we can leave the historians to dispute. What is indisputable is that the revolution in the state of man which is due to science and technology is a process still continuing at an accelerated pace, and the end is nowhere in sight. The wildest excesses of science fiction are probably not adequate to describe the possible state of man which may emerge from this enormous transition.

Merely because we have been observing a long and steady historical process extending over some hundreds of years, with only occasional reversals, it is tempting to fall into the belief that this process is automatic and irreversible. This belief would be a dangerous illusion. Any trend, no matter how long it has been going on, is the result of certain underlying conditions, and if these conditions change, the trend can come to an end or be reversed. There are a number of pitfalls which lie in the path of the second great transition, and it is by no means a foregone conclusion that man will achieve the society of abundance toward which he seems now to be moving. The most obvious pitfall is the possibility of nuclear war, which could easily be an irretrievable disaster. Even if we avoid general nuclear war, the continuance of the present arms race and, still more, its extension represent a burden on the back of mankind which may, in the long run, make all the difference between achieving the abundant society or falling back into an even more primitive state than man's present condition. The world-war industry now consumes resources estimated at about $120 billion a year; this is equal to the total income of the poorest half of the world's population. Even though some of this goes into research and development, which spills over into civilian and humane uses, the bulk of it from the point of view of the development of mankind as a whole is sheer waste— and it is a waste which we cannot afford.

The second pitfall along the road of the transition is the inability of man to control the growth of his own population. At the present rate of reproduction we will reach "standing room only" in a little over seven hundred years, and long before that time there will have to be a drastic change. Technology alone cannot exorcise the Malthusian demon. If the only thing that can check the growth of population is misery, then no matter how advanced our technology the ultimate end is merely

194
BOULDING: COLLECTED PAPERS

to permit a larger population to live in misery. This is what I sometimes call "the utterly dismal theorem." The conscious control of population, however, in a way that is consistent with human dignity and privacy is still an unsolved problem. At present the price of population control is high, no matter how it is approached. The two countries of the world that seem to have been most successful in restricting the growth of population are Ireland and Japan. In Ireland this is achieved by late marriages and a strict Puritan-Catholic culture that imposes strong sanctions against sexual indulgence. In Japan the solution seems to be through abortion, though in both countries there is a strong familistic morality. Whatever the price of population control, it will eventually have to be paid, and we should be concerned to see that the price be as low as possible.

The third pitfall along the road to the abundant society is the possible failure to achieve a permanent high-level technology. The high incomes of the twentieth century have been achieved largely by drawing on our geological capital in the form of fossil fuels (coal, oil, gas) and ores. This means that our present technology is ultimately suicidal, and that, indeed, if we do not move to another technical level, the more economic development we have in the undeveloped parts of the world, the sooner will come the evil day when all geological capital is gone and all mines and wells are exhausted. If by that time we have not achieved a permanent high-level technology, man will have to step back into a technology based on what the earth can grow by the use of current solar energy. Whether this permanent technology is high-level or low-level depends in large measure on the use we are making of the present opportunity.

Fortunately there are signs that a permanent high-level technology, released from dependence on geological capital, is at least just below our horizon. To the present time, the economic system has been mainly "entropic," in the sense that man has taken stores of energies of concentrated materials and has dissipated and diffused these in seas and in dumps throughout the world. The soil, the seas, and the atmosphere are the only permanent sources from which man can draw what materials he needs. Two technical developments of the twentieth century—one the Haber process for the fixation of nitrogen from the air, and the other the Dow process of extracting magnesium from the sea—point toward a new kind of technology in which we will be able to use energy in order to concentrate the diffuse materials of the ocean and the atmosphere. This may ultimately release us from dependence on exhaustible mines. At the moment, however, we are putting very little energy into research and development in these areas, and it may be that we do not have much time. Geologically speaking, the whole present era of extraction of fuels and ores is only a flash in the pan, a mere moment of time. It may be a moment, however, long enough to permit man to transform the stored resources of the earth into knowledge and information which will enable him to dispense with them. The present time must be regarded as a unique moment in the history of this planet. We have at most a few centuries to make the transition to a permanent high-level technology, and if we fail to do this, man will fall back to scratching a meager living from the soil in an exhausted and mined-out world. The critical nature of the present time makes one all the more resentful of the resources wasted in the world war industry and makes disarmament one of the major priorities of man.

It may well be that when we see this second great transition in its perspective, we shall perceive in it not one revolution but

two: the second, however, following so close upon the heels of
the first that they seem to be part of the same process. The first
might be called the "energy revolution," and the second the
"information revolution." The energy revolution is perhaps the
more obvious, and certainly the per-capita use of energy in a
society for human concerns correlates well with its per-capita
income. If in modern America per-capita incomes are of the
order of twenty times what they were in classical civilization,
a major explanation of this phenomenon is that Americans use
so much more energy per head. Insofar as this energy is derived
from fossil fuels, or even from uranium, it is not, as we have
seen, capable of sustaining a high-level society indefinitely.
While it lasts, however, our riches are clearly due to it. It is a
commonplace that one modern man has a hundred mechanical
horses to do his will. The growth of abundance follows the
ability to utilize different forms of energy other than man's
muscles: first, livestock, including human slaves; then the wind
and moving water; then coal, oil, and, finally, atomic fission.
The permanent high-level society will probably have to be based
either on the energy released by fusion or on the use of solar
energy, which is practically the same thing.

Energy, however, is not the whole story. Life uses energy to
segregate entropy, that is, to build up more and more complex
structures with less randomness, more order and structure, and
less probability than the world around them, at the cost of
increasing disorder elsewhere. Society does likewise, and the
high-level society uses its energy in order to create little islands
of diminished randomness and increased structure: food,
homes, cities, art, and religion. The information revolution is
a revolution in the efficiency of the teaching-learning process
and the spread of knowledge—knowledge being to information

what capital is to income. The major information revolution of the first great change was the invention of writing, which enormously increased man's power of communication across time and space and permitted the organization of empires and the development of history in the consciousness of man, by liberating mankind from the impermanence of the spoken word. The invention of printing played somewhat the same role in the second great transition as the invention of writing did in the first. It permitted a great increase in the diffusion of knowledge, and hence paved the way for the scientific revolution which followed it. Science itself, however, is now the major source of the information revolution. It is a relatively small subculture based on an extensive communication and learning process of a peculiar kind. In folk culture the basic image of the world is stable. For unnumbered generations, for instance, the Navajo believed that rain dances would cause rain. The image of the world is stable in spite of disappointments partly because it is reinforced with the coercive powers of sacredness, but also because disappointments can usually be explained away. If we perform a rain dance and it does not rain, there must have been something wrong with the dance; and as rain dances are very complicated, a careful searching of the heart and the memory will usually find something wrong with them. In a folk culture, therefore, whatever happens tends to confirm one's image of the world. If the image is that rain dances cause rain—which is, incidentally, a scientific proposition whether true or not, that is, a testable proposition about the empirical world—then in a folk culture almost everything that happens confirms the image. If, following a rain dance, it does rain, this of course confirms the belief that rain dances cause rain; if it does not rain, the dance is examined, something wrong is found, and thus also is confirmed the belief that a rain dance *properly performed* causes rain.

There is enough similarity here to what goes on in a science laboratory—where the student is expected to make the experiment come out right, and where, if it does not come out right, the assumption is that there was something wrong with the experiment—to make us a little uneasy about the sociology of the scientific community. Nevertheless, by and large the success of science is the result of the fact that, by contrast with folk culture, in the scientific subculture the image of the world is not stable, and disappointment or failure of experience to correspond with what our image of the world led us to expect, results not in a rejection of the experience or a rejection of the inference which led to the expectation, but rather in a readjustment of the image of the world itself. An experiment may be little more than a simplified rain dance, but the fact that it is simplified is all-important. If the experiment turns out unexpectedly, as did the famous Michelson-Morley experiment on the velocity of light, we cannot deny the experience or the inference, and hence we must reorganize our image of the world.

One of the most significant developments of the last one or two hundred years is that the energy revolution, or the increase in the per-capita use of energy, has come increasingly to depend on the information revolution, that is, on the scientific subculture. The domestication of animals, the invention of the horse collar, even the invention of the wheel, the water wheel, and the windmill, possibly the early steam engines, grew out of folk culture. It is extremely unlikely, however, that the folk culture could have discovered electricity, and it is impossible that it could have discovered atomic energy. Indeed, we can say that the information revolution has taken command and that the energy revolution now depends on it.

The information revolution, furthermore, has aspects which are significant for economic abundance and which go beyond the mere provision of more energy. In the past generation we have seen the development on an astonishing scale of information-processing and problem-solving machines, that is, computers. The development of the high-speed electronic computer is likely to have an impact on human life and organization at least equal to that produced by the inventions of writing or printing. It is not impossible, indeed, that the long-run impact will be greater than that of any previous change in the organization of the information process. Nonhuman sources of energy increase abundance by adding power, as it were, to the human muscle; nonhuman information-processing and problem-solving machines increase abundance by adding power to the human mind. The importance of this is clear. It is mind, not muscle, that produces abundance; the elephant has a lot more muscle than man, but in the absence of man it has no means of harnessing energy outside its own muscular system because its mind (that is, its information-processing and problem-solving system) cannot go much beyond its muscular environment. It is the glory and the peril of man that his mind has leaped far beyond the environment of his own body to take in the secrets both of the stars and of the atoms. With what might be called the folk powers of his mind he perceived the value of fire, he harnessed animals to his will, and he harnessed the winds and the waters. Now, because of the information revolution, he can expand the powers of his own mind. A computer is to a mind what, say, a power saw is to a muscle. It does not replace it or even compete with it, but it enormously expands its capability.

The development of automation in industry is but one phase of this information revolution and in the long run perhaps not even the most important phase. It does represent, however, a movement which is going to have a substantial impact on the developed economies, especially, in the course of the next generation. The production of commodities involves the application of both energy and information to the earth in order to change the form of its materials from a less structured to a more structured form. In primitive craftsmanship man provides both the energy and the information for this process out of the resources of his own body alone; this is the boy whittling a stick or primitive man shaping an arrowhead. Man soon begins to shape things into tools which economize the use of his energy. Then, as we have seen, he begins to draw on nonhuman sources of energy which further increase the productivity of his effort. Now he is at the stage of economizing on the information process itself, which gives him, as it were, an additional leverage. Aristotle's vision of the shuttle that moves by itself and the lyre that plays itself has already largely come to pass. The extension of human powers in information-processing and problem-solving is something, again, of which we have seen only the beginning, and we cannot prophesy its end.

Even though we cannot see the end of this great process, we have a certain obligation to look twenty-five or fifty years ahead to ponder the kind of society likely to be emerging by that time. It is clearly a society in which the whole structure of human activity is very different from what it was in classical civilization, or even from what it is now. In classical civilization roughly

80 per cent of the population was in agriculture or other rural pursuits and about 20 per cent in all other occupations. In the United States today we have a little over 10 per cent in agriculture, about 30 per cent in manufacturing, and about 60 per cent in what might be called the "tertiary" occupations—the professions, trades, and so on. There is little doubt that this trend will continue, and in fifty years we may reasonably expect— short of disaster—to have all our food produced by perhaps 5 per cent of the population or less; to be producing all our manufactured goods with perhaps 15 or 20 per cent; and to have 75 per cent at least of the population in tertiary occupations. There are some who quail before this prospect and who visualize automation as producing massive and intractable unemployment. This view seems to me mistaken; I see no reason why, given proper economic policy, we cannot employ as many people as we wish. We are moving rapidly toward what we might call a service economy in which a relatively small proportion of the labor force will produce all the "things" that we need, and the great bulk of us will be providing services for each other. Nobody as yet has spelled out in detail what an economy of this kind would really look like and exactly what we would do for each other. To what extent, for instance, would we expand professional services? To what extent would we expand the more unskilled services? One of the worrisome problems of an economy of this type is what happens to the demand for the labor of the unskilled and those who are not capable of acquiring skill. The economy into which we are moving seems to demand a high level of education and skill from almost everybody, and unskilled and untrained labor is rapidly diminishing in importance. It is disquieting, for instance, that the general rate of unemployment, while too high

to be comfortable, is not too high to be tolerable; when we examine this carefully we find that unemployment is largely concentrated among the unskilled Negroes and among youth, especially unskilled youth. We may find ourselves by the year 2000 with a society in which there is no place for the unskilled or the untrainable, and how we give these people the moral status which their position as fellow human beings demands may turn out to be one of the major ethical problems of our day.

In spite of these difficulties I am prepared to assert that the balance sheet of the information revolution on the whole is enormously positive. Furthermore, there is no retreat; there is no way back to Eden. Once we have eaten of the tree of knowledge, a flaming sword bars our return to the innocence which is born of ignorance. Because there is no road back to Eden, the only way that we can take is forward to Zion—toward the great hope which man has always had of a kingdom of heaven on earth. We can discern the outlines of Zion more clearly perhaps than any previous generation, and it has become for us more than an eschatological hope or even a utopian dream; it has become a city set on the hill of the future toward which there now seems to be a road.

The road, as we have seen, is strewn with pitfalls. Nevertheless, our ability to avoid the pitfalls depends in large measure on the continued progress of the information revolution. The achievement of stable peace and disarmament depends on the accomplishment of a certain intellectual task in the understanding of international systems and of an educational task in modifying men's images of the world. The solution of the population problem likewise depends on the accomplishment of an intellectual and educational task. Even more clearly, the development of a permanent high-level technology depends on the solution of certain intellectual problems. These are all part of the information system, and our hope of achieving the present transition without disaster must largely be based on our ability to develop still further the information revolution in which we are engaged. Unfortunately we are not doing well at this; we are not putting our intellectual resources in the field where the problems lie, namely, in the study of social systems; and if war, peace, and population seem such pitfalls today it is largely because we leave these areas to folk culture and do not allow the information revolution to penetrate them. One of the major needs of our time is to devote a massive effort to research in peace, population, and stable high-level technology, and if we delay this too long it may become too late.

In the midst of this enormous transition, and in these centuries which are the most critical in the four-billion-year history of this planet, the Christian will be impelled to ask where stands his own faith. A change as enormous as that through which we are now passing cannot fail to make an impact on every aspect of man's life and thought. We must recognize humbly that the great transition began in a Christian civilization. We may, it is true, trace the origins of science back to the Greeks and the Babylonians, and this torch was handed on mainly through Islam rather than through medieval Christianity. Medieval Christian Europe was, indeed, an obscure peninsula on the edge of the great civilization of Islam. Islam, however, died upon the vine, or perhaps Tamerlane killed it. At any rate it was Europe and its American extension that produced Galileo, Newton, Dalton, Darwin, and Einstein. This, I think, was no accident. Those whose faith is in the Word made flesh are well equipped to initiate and to receive an information revolution. To many this great process of transition which came out of Christian civilization seems likely to supplant not only civilization but the religion out of which it grew. We would certainly expect to find the institutions of Christianity undergoing great sociological modification in the course of a transition in the state of man as profound as that which leads to the abundant society. Sociological transformation, however, is nothing new to Christianity, which has a remarkable ability to take different social forms from, say, the Caesaropapism of Byzantium to the fierce individualism of the Adventist sects. At the core of the Christian faith, however, is not a philosophical doctrine or a scientific theory, but a particular historical event—the resurrection—of unusual symbolic significance. The historical evidence is unlikely to receive much addition, and the symbolic significance is unlikely to be affected by mere affluence, which is powerless before the inescapable necessity of death. I suspect, therefore, that the transition to abundance will not greatly affect the historical and symbolic core of Christianity, much as it may affect its external organization. Furthermore, it may well be that it is only as we move toward the abundant society that the ethic of the New Testament becomes more than a holy ambition for the few; it becomes a necessity for society at large. In the nuclear age we must learn to love our enemies, painful as it is to acquire this skill. The control of population must rest ultimately on a deep personal acceptance of moral responsibility, and the progress of science and technology themselves depends on deep respect for the truth and a high standard of personal integrity.

There are those who disapprove of the abundant society, seeing in it only a universal opportunity for excess, licentiousness, vulgarity, and decadence. We must admit that this indeed could be its shape, and a society of abundance might well be one in which the dignity of mankind is lost. If this were to become true, I am sure that the abundance would not endure. It is a Christian hope, however, that man is capable of heaven even on earth, and that he has within him the potential even to endure bliss.

GENERAL SYSTEMS AS A POINT OF VIEW

In: Views on General Systems Theory
Mihajlo D. Mesarovic, ed. New York: John Wiley and Sons,
1964, pp. 25-38

GENERAL SYSTEMS AS A POINT OF VIEW

(A Small Cry of Distress, from a Not Very Mathematical Man)
I'm like a rat within a maze,
When faced with sigma's i's and j's,
And problems soon become enigmas
When wrapped in i's and j's and sigma's.

K. B

I teach a course in general systems as part of the Honors Program of the University of Michigan.* I get an excellent cross section of the undergraduate seniors taking the Honors Program in a wide variety of departments. After taking it one year, a student came to me and said, "I haven't learned a thing in this course but I have got a new point of view." I confess I was encouraged by this remark and felt that the course had probably been justified. I hoped, of course, that the student had picked up a certain amount of information at least about some of the more exciting intellectual developments which are going on in our day. I presume he must have learned something or he would not have obtained a new point of view. I must confess, however, that giving a new point of view rather than imparting information as such is one of the main objectives of the course, which is exactly why I have called it "general systems."

I have implied above that general systems is a point of view rather than a body of doctrine. In the future it may develop into a body of doctrine, for it is difficult to find any intellectual movement which does not. Perhaps, indeed, this is inevitable and indeed desirable. One cannot remain forever perched on a point of view, however pleasing the prospect, and one must go down and occupy the land. At the moment it would be presumptuous to claim that there is any clearly defined body of theory which could be identified with the name "general

*It is listed in the University of Michigan catalog (1962/63) as College Honors

systems." Nevertheless there is a general systems point of view and there is what DeSolla Price has called "an invisible college," of people who recognize each other as possessing this point of view. What I wish to do, therefore, is to try to identify some of the main elements of the point of view even though this may represent the first slippery step toward a body of doctrine and may, indeed, reveal the distressing fact that there is not one point of view in general systems but a large number.

Any point of view depends on certain value presuppositions and positions of the viewer, for we all view the world from some high-valued peak within our own welfare function. Things which we value more highly loom more closely in our mental landscape. This I call the iron law of perspective. I know of no real escape from this iron law. Even the attempt in the world of art to look at things from all sides, as the cubist does, sometimes ends up by looking at them from no side at all, and results in breaking up order into something perilously akin to chaos. Even if our welfare function sets a high value on the virtues of objectivity and a Cartesian clarity, we still view the world from a perspective, for those things which are clearly quantifiable and orderly will occupy the foreground, and we will relegate Celtic twilights, mystical experience, and all things of clouded and brooding significance to the jungle edges of our tight little intellectual clearing. The only way to bend the iron law of perspective is to know as well as we can the point from which we view. Then we can at least know intellectually, even if not perhaps viscerally, that the looming foreground is not as large nor the shadowy background as small as it seems to us. Not even general systems, broad as its landscape claims to be, can escape this iron law, and we must therefore look frankly at the value presuppositions which are likely to lead to a general systems point of view.

The first of these presuppositions is a prejudice in favor of system, order, regularity, and nonrandomness (all these words being roughly synonymous), and a prejudice against chaos and randomness. Along with the poets, the general systems type of person has "rage for order," as Austin Warren has called it. He will certainly be fond of mathematics, almost certainly fond of music, and he may have a half-ashamed passion for the eighteenth century.

The next prejudice is a simple corollary from the first, that is, the whole empirical world is more interesting ("good") when it is orderly. It is to the orderly segments of the world, therefore, that the general systems man is attracted. He loves regularity, his delight is in the law, and a law to him is a path through the jungle.

Now comes the main article of the general systems faith, for the first two, after all, he shares with many scientific specialists; that is, the order of the empirical world itself has order which might be called order of the second degree. If he delights to find a law, he is ecstatic when he finds a law about laws. If laws in his eyes are good, laws about laws are simply delicious and are most praiseworthy objects of search. The critic may perhaps argue that the hunger and thirst after this order of the second degree is merely a passion for the familiar. The general systems man, he will say, is the sort who would be reminded of Pittsburgh even in the middle of Bangkok, simply because both are cities and have streets with people in them. The critic (I somehow visualize him as a historian in a high collar) has a passion not so much for order and familiarity as for things that are peculiar, unique, strange, and disjoint. As a general systems man, I will visit him in his lonely eyrie, but even there I will probably be reminded of something—much to his annoyance. To avoid circumlocutions, let me call my general systems man a generalist and my high-collared historian a particularist. The generalist rejoices when he sees, for instance, that in all growth patterns there are significant common elements, such as nucleation, structural adjustment in the parts of the system, diminishing returns to scale, and ogive curves. A particularist brushes this aside and rejoices in the fact that the growth of the flower is so different from the growth of a crystal, or the growth of Rome so different from the growth of Athens.

Because of his rage for order, our generalist is likely to set a high value on quantification and mathematization, for these are great helps in establishing order. There is, therefore, a prejudice in their favor and a desire to use them as far as (or even farther than) they can usefully go. Even the most passionate generalist, however, is likely to admit that there are elements of the empirical world, such as aesthetics, love, literature, poetry, human relations, religion, etc., which resist quantification and yet are orderly in their own bizarre fashion. The generalist, however, has a strong desire to discover a continuum, which he enjoys perceiving, between quantifiable and nonquantifiable order. He sees poetry as a nonrandom sequence of words, music as a nonrandom sequence of notes, different in kind but not in form from any nonrandom sequence of numbers.

Order is always perceived as an abstraction from the complex flux of reality. It is indeed usually seen as a relation among abstractions themselves, such as numbers, lines, or spaces. The difference, perhaps, between the general systems man and the pure mathematician is that, whereas the mathematician is content with the mere perception and demonstration of abstract order, the general systems man is interested in looking for empirical referents of these systems and laws of abstract order, for it is this ability to perceive the infinite particularity of the empirical world as examples of an abstract order which gives that world its unity and, indeed, makes it in some sense "good." To justify the ways of God to man is an important task, even for atheists, and it is done by tracing the golden threads of abstract order through the infinitely fragmented dark and light mosaic of the world of experience.

Thus the mathematician is content with having discovered the exquisite abstract order implied in the exponential function and the elegant properties of the strange number e (2.718). The general systems man seizes upon this as the expression of a general law of growth at a constant rate, of which over short periods there are innumerable examples in the empirical world, whether this be the growth of a crystal, of a living body, of an organization, of a whole economy, or perhaps of the universe itself. The mathematician devises an equation which describes a familiar ogive curve; the general systems man regards this as a pattern which is repeated over and over again in the empirical world, as we move from one equilibrium system to another at a different level. The mathematician sees the solution of simultaneous equations as a problem in abstract order; the general systems man perceives this as descriptive of the equilibrium of an ecosystem or of a price system. The mathematician develops difference equations or differential equations as expressions of a relationship among purely abstract concepts; the general systems man considers them descriptive of a large class of dynamic processes, whether one which keeps the planets in their courses, one which determines the movement of a falling body, or one which describes the movement of an economic system through time. Not all mathematical equations or relationships have empirical referents. I find it hard to conceive, for instance, any real empirical referent to the series of prime numbers, although I have one student who is working on this problem. When an empirical referent can be found, however, there is great rejoicing in the general systems heaven.

The process of finding empirical referents to formal laws can easily take either one of two possible directions. We may find some elegant relationship in the world of abstract mathematics and then look around the world of experience to see if we can find anything like it, or we may patiently piece out a rough empirical order in the world of experience and then look to the abstract world of mathematics to codify, simplify it, and relate it to other laws. A good example of this phenomenon is "Zipf's law." Zipf was a Professor of German at Harvard who conceived a passion for counting things and for plotting the frequencies of organized distributions on double logarithmic paper. A purely empirical law seemed to emerge which showed that almost all organized distributions—e.g., the size of cities, the frequencies of words, the intervals between notes in music, or the distribution of income—when plotted on double logarithmic paper turned out to be a straight line. Following this purely empirical observation, which itself may be open to some questioning, several attempts have been made, the most successful perhaps by Herbert Simon, to develop mathematical models which will produce organized distributions having this property. Going to the other extreme, we find whole branches of mathematics which have been developed by pure mathematicians without even a thought of empirical referents which have later turned out to be of enormous significance in exploring the more refined aspects of the empirical world, especially in physics. Even in the social sciences, the mathematical theory of convex sets was developed long before it turned out to have an important empirical referent in linear programming. The value system of the general systems man is, therefore, different from that of the pure mathematician. The famous Cambridge toast, "Here is to pure mathematics, and may it never be any damned good to anybody," has been reworded by him to "Here's to pure mathematics, and may it soon be good for something" or "Here's to empirical regularity, may we soon find a mathematical excuse for it." Whatever his other virtues, the general systems man is irretrievably impure in his tastes and his fundamental value system.

Simply because any point of view implies perspective as we have seen, and perspective is illusion interpreted to mean reality, the interpretation may break down. The near things may be perceived as large, and the far things as small *in fact*. A point of view, therefore, implies certain dangers of misperception, and the general systems point of view is no exception to this rule. The general systems man, if he is honest, must admit these dangers and be prepared to face them. Some of the dangers are obvious and are avoided fairly easily; others are more subtle and require a highly sensitized perception.

An obvious danger frequently pointed out is that an interest in the whole empirical world and the attempt to view this world as a whole lead to superficiality and dilettantism. The whole empirical world in our days, at least, is far beyond the capacity of any one mind to know. My wife has a standard formula, for which I endeavor to be grateful, for deflating me whenever my general systems visions soar too high. She says simply, "If you are going to be the great integrator you ought to know something." Even the most renaissance of renaissance men in our days cannot hope to know more than a very small fraction of what is known by somebody. The general systems man, therefore, is constantly taking leaps in the dark, constantly jumping to conclusions on insufficient evidence, constantly, in fact, making a fool of himself. Indeed, the willingness to make a fool of oneself should be a requirement for admission to the Society of General Systems Research, for this willingness is almost a prerequisite to rapid learning.

One obvious safeguard against the worst forms of superficiality is a firm foundation of knowledge in at least one empirical discipline. Before the general systems man takes off into the outer space of his ignorance, he ought at least to have a launching pad in some discipline where he can reasonably claim to be an expert. He must have the courage not merely to take refuge in a well-tended little plot of specialized knowledge but he should also feel that his most important and most secure contributions comes when he brings back and applies to his own specialized fields the insights which have come to him during his aerial surveys of the whole empirical universe. The ideal general systems man must be willing to talk nonsense outside his own field but must be equally unwilling to talk nonsense inside it.

A danger less readily perceived, but perhaps characteristic of the whole scientific enterprise, arises because the "rage for order" leads to the perception of order where, in fact, no order exists. Alex Bavelas has reported (orally) some experiments in which he has given his subjects random sequences or patterns, for instance, sequences drawn from a table of random numbers, and asked them to deduce any law or principle which governs the sequence. His subjects almost invariably not only see order in these random sequences but also vigorously defend the order which they have perceived when he challenges it, and they become angry with him when he suggests that sequences are, in fact, random. I once had a sad experience in teaching business cycles when I began by asking the class to plot random sequences on a graph, the sequences being derived, for instance, by throwing dice or by pulling numbers out of a hat. Such sequences, when plotted, have all the appearance of time series of most economic variables, and I confess my objective was to shatter the naive faith that the student might have in the strictly nonrandom character of economic fluctuations. Unfortunately, my experiments backfired. One student, who was something of a gambler, thought that he did, in fact, perceive a law in the sequence of throws of dice and spent most of the semester trying to find what it was. He did not, as far as I recall, get a very high grade in the course, and I never did find out whether his researches paid off financially.

It may be, therefore, that the same rage for order which produces a sonnet produces, in its pathological form, the rigid and compulsive gambler at the slot machine. In its pathological forms, too, the rage for order creates race prejudice, stereotyping, international conflict, MacCarthyism, and so on. Unfortunately, I know of no very good remedy for this except a constant watchfulness. As far as I know, there is no absolutely secure way of testing the randomness of any finite sequence. All empirically perceived regularities, therefore, have a degree of ambiguity in them, and in some cases, especially in social systems, the ambiguities are so severe that the problem of accurate social perception seems almost impossible. William Gamson, for instance, of the University of Michigan, has reported (orally) that the Cuban crisis of October 1962 reinforced almost in everybody his image of the international system which he had previously held, no matter how inconsistent these images might be. In the extreme case of the schizophrenic, *all* the messages which he receives reinforce the unreal image of the world which he possesses, and even much that passes for normal behavior is perilously close to this pattern.

Our particularist critic now seems to have turned from a high-collared historian into a soft-shirted semanticist. There is a certain intellectual syndrome that includes both general systems and general semantics, improbable as this may seem. Actually, this may turn out to be a very useful combination. The insistence of general semantics on the particular, even to the extent, perhaps, of extending the semantic incantation to "this general system is not that general system," is nevertheless a useful corrective to the more pathological expressions of the rage for order. To talk about truth at all, and to hold conversations about it, we must look for general systems. Nevertheless, it is useful to heed William Blake who said that truth always lies in minute particulars. Too much obsession with the particular, however, and too much semantic nervousness may prohibit conversation altogether, and might even make pictures disintegrate into pointilliste patterns. As Alice in Wonderland so sagely remarked, "What is the use of a book [or for that matter a world] without conversations and pictures?"

If the rage for order has its dangers, a passion for order of the second degree and for the laws of laws, no doubt, exposes us to double jeopardy. A grave danger here is that of drawing false analogies. Analogy seems to have a bad name among philosophers, and though I know of no good study of what makes an analogy false, I am aware that this may simply indicate my ignorance of current philosophical literature. Even the analog computer in these days seems to have been fighting a losing battle with its digital brother, although there are some signs that its greatest usefulness may still lie in the future. Among general systems men the words "homology" and "homomorphism" are "good words," which seem to avoid the unfortunate histories associated with the word "analogy." I must confess that I am not quite sure of the exact difference between analogy and a homology, except that analogy is a bad homology and homology is a good analogy.

The confusion of thought here arises, I suspect, because it is not so much the analogy that is bad as the system which is derived from it. Wherever man is faced with an empirical system of some kind, he has an uncontrollable urge to produce a mental system or an image in his mind which is a model or an explanation of the empirical system he encounters. Empirical systems in the outside world are very complex and, as we all know, it is extremely hard to find out what is their true systematic nature. It is not surprising, therefore, that we argue by analogy from systems we know, or think we know, to systems we think we do not know. Thus, primitive man encounters a strange world of trees, animals, and objects of all kinds which clearly have some systematic properties but whose mysteries he cannot fathom. He is conscious also of himself as a complex system which is guided, however, by the mysterious unity of the "me." It is not surprising, then, that he argues by analogy from himself to the inanimate world, and populates this world with spirits. As he learns that he can placate and move other men by suitable language, it seems reasonable to him that he can also placate the spirits of trees, rocks, and animals by suitable language. Because of the ambiguity of all systems, it takes him a long time to learn that this method is ultimately disappointing. Nevertheless, animism may justly be regarded as the first general system, and the fact that we now regard it as false does not negate the fact that it was a remarkable achievement of the human mind at an early stage.

In the physical sciences, the method of analogy ("What would I feel like if I were a flying stone") has largely been superseded by the development of theoretical systems which are very closely tied to their own particular referents. The internal logic of the theoretical system is tested by reference to the formal principles of mathematics to be sure that the logic comes from its own internal structure and is not borrowed from some system outside. Logic alone, however, will not guarantee that a theoretical system has the right relationship to its empirical referent. To insure such correspondence, the system or the theory must be *tested* against its supposed empirical referent. The fundamental principle of all such testing is to create expectations of the future by means of careful inference from the supposed system and then simply to observe whether this expectation is disappointed or fulfilled. In the experimental method, the expectation is created by acts on the part of the investigator; in the observational method, the expectation is created by projections of past history of the dynamic system. All of this is familiar in the philosophy of science. It is not surprising under these circumstances that physical scientists especially are suspicious of general systems, simply because their own success has been the result of their breaking away from false methods of analogy. The biological sciences, likewise, seemed to have achieved their greatest successes by developing highly special systems with narrow empirical referents, and here again suspicion of general systems as the bearer of false analogies is understandable.

It is in the social sciences, perhaps, that we are most plagued with false analogies and yet have the greatest hope from true ones. The damage done by false analogies has been enormous. In political science, for instance, a great deal of thinking has not risen much above propositions of the type, "The body has a head, therefore, the state must have a king." Social Darwinism is a case of application of a false analogy from the biological sciences to systems which are much more complex. It is an example, indeed, of how dangerous can be the application of an empty theory from one discipline into another discipline. What might be called vulgar evolutionary theory, as summed by the slogan "the survival of the fittest," is an almost completely empty theory, for, if we ask what the fit are fit for, the answer, of course, is to survive; so the theory is a theory of the survival of the surviving, which does not tell us very much. The application of theory of this kind to the social sciences is so misleading as to be positively disastrous.

The dangers of analogies are, of course, not confined to those analogies that cross the disciplines, for even within a single discipline, we still find ourselves in grave errors as a result of what might be called animistic analogy. A good example of this is to be found in economics. One of the major problems of our day is the tremendous gap that exists between systematic economics, or the image of the economy in the minds of the professional economists, and "folk economics," which is the image of the economy in the minds of practically everybody else. Folk economics argues largely by analogy from individual experience to the economic system as a whole, and these analogies are nearly always false and almost invariably result in fallacies of composition. In systematic economics, for instance, expenditure and receipts are exactly the same thing, as one person's expenditure is always somebody else's receipts. In folk economics, which argues by analogy by the individual to the total system, expenditure can be different from receipts. In systematic economics, the national debt is seen clearly as equivalent to the government securities held by the public and, hence, an important constituent of the financial system capable of being used as an instrument of cybernetic control. In folk economics, the national debt is seen simply as a burden and a moral evil to be gotten rid of as soon as possible. It is hardly an exaggeration to say that the attitudes engendered by folk economics are enormously costly in that they prevent the proper operation of our economic system, and it is quite conceivable that they might even be disastrous. Even the social scientists, therefore, do not have to be persuaded that analogy is dangerous.

I seem to have made general systems sound so dangerous that I almost appear to be putting forward a motion for the dissolution of the Society for General Systems Research. I must confess, however, that this is something of a rhetorical trick. It is now Act V, and I must rescue my heroine from villains who have threatened her. The crucial question is, "At what point does the method of special theoretical systems and empirical testing break down?" I argue that it breaks down at two points. One is at the point of the Heisenberg principle of indeterminacy where the information that the investigator is endeavoring to extract from the system has the same order of magnitude of the system itself, so that information cannot be applied to or withdrawn from the system without changing it. This principle was first noticed in physics, but it is of increasing importance as we move up through the biological to the social sciences. We frequently cannot investigate the living organism without killing it, we cannot make a statement about the economic system without changing it, we cannot ask a man a question without changing his opinion, and we cannot put an anthropologist into a tribe without changing its culture. In other words, we have to recognize the fact that we do not have an outside observer, but that the investigator is always an intimate part of the system and cannot make his own observations or develop and propound new knowledge without changing the system that he is investigating.

The second point of breakdown in the classical scientific method of special systems and empirical testing occurs in the study of systems that are in themselves probabilistic or stochastic, and in which the nature of the order itself is not deterministic (i.e., events occur with the probability of one), but in which (in the essential nature of the system itself) events occur with the probability of less than one. In such a system, a single observation tells us nothing about the probability of the occurrence of the event observed. The method of the testing of expectations, therefore, breaks down simply because the expectation is that of a probability of an event, not of its certainty. In October 1962, for instance, we managed to avoid a nuclear war, but this fact in itself tells us nothing about whether the probability of nuclear war at that time was 5% or 95%. Even if the probability had been 95%, we might still have picked the one white ball out of the bag with 19 black balls in it, and the mere fact that we picked a white ball out the bag tells us nothing about how many black balls there were. Physical systems in the small range, biological systems in the middle range, and social systems throughout their whole range are of this probabilistic nature, and also have Heisenberg principles built right into them. The two properties, indeed, seem to go along together.

We now see the success of the method of special systems and empirical testing in physics as a fortunate accident, and, as a result, the fact that the systems investigated were gross in nature and with a very small probabilistic element. For Heisenberg systems where information and the observer are of the same order of the magnitude of the system, and for the closely related probabilistic systems, the method of general systems is a necessity. Weak and dangerous as it may be, it is the only avenue open to us towards greater knowledge. This explains, I think, the increasing interest in simulation in both social and biological sciences. Where systems cannot be investigated without changing them profoundly, and where they cannot be tested because of the probabilistic elements involved, the only road to knowledge left is that of simulation, that is, the construction of grosser systems which have some kind of one-to-one relationship with the systems we really want to investigate, and which are so gross that they can, in fact, be investigated. It is perhaps too much to claim that the method of simulation is a child of general systems, but it is certainly highly consistent with the general systems point of view.

The great problem here is how to defend ourselves in the case of ambiguous systems and ambiguous perceptions from the danger of allowing value presuppositions to govern our perception of the system. The great psychological problem is the rigidity of the image, and it is associated with values which seem to be involved with the identity of the person. People often construct their own personal identity around some ideology to which they give assent. When a man says *I am* a

Baptist, or a Republican, or a Communist, he is, in effect, identifying his person with the ideology which he holds. A threat to the ideology, therefore, is seen as a threat to the person, and it is not surprising that it is strongly resisted. Under these circumstances, we become immune and deaf to any messages which seem to contradict the ideology. Either we reject the inferences which gave rise to the disappointed expectations or we deny that expectations have, in fact, been disappointed, because of the ever-present ambiguity in the interpretations of the message inputs.

I argue that there are two closely related remedies for this disease. One is the lessening of the ambiguities in perception itself largely through the quantification, indexing, and systematic processing of large quantities of information. A good example of this process is the impact of the development of national income statistics which were pioneered in the National Bureau of Economic Research in the 1920's, taken over by the Department of Commerce in the 1930's, and became, as it were, public property and a familiar element in political discourse in the 1940's. This has made our perception of economic fluctuations much less ambiguous. In 1931 it was still possible for quite intelligent people to argue about whether or not there was a depression. Herbert Hoover, indeed, in his memoirs says that apple selling became very profitable at this time, and a lot of people went into it. In the 1960's no such argument is possible. There are, of course, very real problems of interpretation and measurement, some of which are indeed inherently insoluble. Nevertheless, we now cannot have a downturn in the economy for even two or three months without most people in decision-making positions being aware of it, and this awareness in itself creates a strong desire to do something about it. One of the great needs of the present is a similar information processing system in international systems. At the moment we rely on a hopelessly obsolete way of information collecting and processing, involving diplomats, the CIA, and a State Department almost entirely innocent of social science, all of which contribute to a magnificent system for the corruption of information. It is not surprising that the international system works so badly and is so fantastically dangerous.

The second line of defense against the misperception of ambiguous systems is the general systems point of view itself. If analogy is dangerous and leads to the development of untrue systems, the remedy is not to throw it overboard altogether, for there are situations in which no other method of systems development is open to us. The remedy for false analogy is not *no* analogy but *true* analogy. This involves the development of a critique of analogy and a theory of simulation.

Although we are still unfortunately a long way from this goal, it is, nevertheless, one of the principal concerns of the general systems enterprise. It has been said before that the business of science is to detect similarities amid apparent differences, and differences amid apparent similarities. If the first is a peculiar task of the generalist and the second the particularist, this merely points out the fact that these two views are complementary rather than competitive.

Let me now return to the question which was implicit in my opening statement, as to whether general systems should, in fact, be taught especially to undergraduates or even graduate students. Some may argue that general systems is a heady brew likely to distract students from the main business of acquiring competence in their own particular field, and that, even if it is justified at all, nobody without at least two Ph.D.'s should be allowed to touch it. I confess that I have had one or two experiences with students which indicate that the danger is not wholly unreal. It is possible for students of a certain type to get so caught up with the excitement of the general systems point of view that they try to introduce it prematurely and inappropriately even into a Ph.D. dissertation. The acquisition of a specialized discipline always involves a certain amount of heavy, dull work, and it is to be expected that occasionally a brilliant but not too solid student will kick over the traces and try to take the short-cuts to knowledge which the general systems approach may seem to offer. Even good advice and firm handling may not wholly eliminate this risk. Nevertheless, I believe that this is a risk worth taking. Dullness and a lack of a sense of significance are the greatest enemies facing the intellectual life. It is a terrible commentary on our whole educational system that we still take the eager young minds which come out of high school and knock all the eagerness and enthusiasm out of them by the long grind that leads to a Ph.D. Creativity in the sciences as well as in the arts comes from a combination of excitement, hard work, and discipline. In our educational system it is easier to teach discipline than excitement, and the discipline often destroys the excitement. If a general systems point of view can be developed alongside the acquisition of a specialized discipline, it will enrich the work in the discipline itself, simply because of the intellectual excitement that the general systems pont of view can engender. What we are in danger of losing in our universities is a feeling that a great intellectual task is still to be accomplished. Intellectual excitement is generated at the point where the individual feels that what he is doing is advancing, in however small a degree, some intellectual task. Excitement, of course, is not a substitute for solid achievement, but it is a very good complement, and it seems to me we are in much more danger from dullness than from overstimulation. I am not suggesting, of course, that only the general systems point of view creates intellectual excitement. A student can get a great sense of excitement from being on the frontier of a particular discipline. A general systems point of view is, however, important in creating a feeling of intellectual community and of a common task, and in this sense the excitement that it generates may be peculiarly beneficial.

THE PLACE OF THE IMAGE
IN THE DYNAMICS OF SOCIETY

In: Explorations in Social Change, George K. Zollschan
and Walter Hirsch, eds. Boston: Houghton-Mifflin and London:
Routledge and Kegan Paul, 1964, pp. 5-16

The Place of the Image in the

Dynamics of Society[1]

"The dynamics of society" may seem like merely a pretentious way of talking about history. It is, however, history with a difference; history conceived not as narrative or chronicle, not even as a connected story or tale, but history conceived as a system, that is, as a social system with emphasis on regularities and patterns as well as discontinuities and gaps.

Social systems are, of course, very different from physical systems. The difference is so great that some people have denied that social systems exist at all. This would be a confession of intellectual defeat, however, which I am not prepared to make. The patterns of history may be almost infinitely complex but they are patterns. To deny any pattern to history is to deny any possibility of influencing the future, for influence can only come by following the pattern. In this matter of the interpretation of history, we indeed go between Scylla and Charybdis, the one being the council of despair that refuses to find any pattern or system in the ongoing flux of man and society; the other being the self-assured cockiness that sees patterns where they do not in fact exist. Perhaps the latter is in fact the greater danger. The human mind has a craving for patterns. Anarchy and randomness are abhorrent to us and we have a profound tendency to organize the unorganized, whether this is in sense data, in historical sequences, or in the labor market. We must constantly be on our guard, therefore, against inadequate, incomplete,

[1] An earlier form of this chapter was given as an address before the Public Relations Institute, Cornell University, August 10, 1961.

and premature patternings of history. Nevertheless, without patterns, we cannot live and without some interpretation of history, we cannot guide our actions intelligently. Perhaps even a false guide is better than none at all.

The great difference between social and physical systems is that social systems contain information, images, and symbols as essential elements, whereas physical systems can generally be described completely without these variables and aspects. The basic concept of any dynamic system is that of a succession of "states." A state of the system is a complete abstract description of the relevant variables of a system as they exist at a moment in time. It is like a frame on a reel of film. The dynamics of a system consist, in the first place, of the succession of states, as frames succeed one another in a movie. The system can be dynamically described, that is, reduced to "law" if any one state can be deduced in its entirety from a finite number of preceding states. The simplest case, of course, is where the state on any one day bears a constant relation to the state of the previous day — the "day" here being, of course, any arbitrary unit of time. This is what we mean by a difference equation of the first degree. If there is a constant relation between the state of the world on Monday and the state of the world on Tuesday, and if we are given the state of the world on Monday, we can proceed to deduce the state of the world on Tuesday. Then, given the state of the world on Tuesday, we can deduce the state on Wednesday. Thus we can go on indefinitely and project the whole system indefinitely into the future, or for that matter, back into the past.

In difference equations of the second degree, the state of affairs on, let us say, Wednesday, depends not only on the state on Tuesday, but also on the state on Monday. Systems as simple as this are adequate to describe the whole glorious counterpoint of celestial dynamics. It is little wonder that the success of astronomers in predicting celestial events is the envy of all other sciences. When we are looking for systems and patterns in history, therefore, we are looking for something like difference equations, that is, stable relationships between the past and the present. The economist, for instance, looks for a stable relationship between the household expenditure of today and the income of yesterday. This in one form is the consumption function. In social systems, however, we must reckon with the fact that simple dynamic relationships of this kind do not exist in a truly stable form. There may be temporary stabilities which are helpful in short-run predictions; there are, however, virtually no long-run stabilities of a simple order.

We can, indeed, think of human history as determined by difference equations of an infinite degree. Today depends not only on yesterday or even on the day before yesterday, but on all previous yesterdays. A relationship of this complexity is not only too complex to handle but is theoretically incapable of giving prediction. A dynamic system of

an infinite order is one which we are incapable of discovering because
the discovery of stable dynamic relationships can only take place if there
is experience over a period of time longer than the order of the relationship. We could never hope to discover, for instance, whether the relationship between Monday and Tuesday was stable if our whole experience was limited to these two days. We never, indeed, obtain certainty
in our knowledge of these relationships. There is a small probability, as
the philosophers have pointed out, that the sun will not rise tomorrow.
The probability of the truth of a dynamic relationship, however, increases
very rapidly with an increase in the number of cases. If from our observance of the relation between Monday and Tuesday, we venture to predict
on Tuesday on the basis of this relationship what will happen on Wednesday, and our prediction is fulfilled, we will be justified in thinking that
this might have been an accident. If, however, our prediction is fulfilled
also on Thursday, Friday, Saturday, and on a number of succeeding
days, confidence in the original law relating yesterday to today will be
strongly fortified.

A single disappointment, however, can shatter a law, and in history
(that is, in social systems), these disappointments are extremely frequent.
To give but a single example, in the United States and indeed in the
Western world generally, it was observed that a peak in the price level
came roughly in 1815, in 1865, and in 1919. A long cycle of from 50
to 60 years called the Kondratiev, was postulated on this experience.
On the basis of this observation in the *Encyclopedia of the Social Sciences*
about 1934, the very distinguished economist, John R. Commons, predicted
that prices would continue to fall until 1952, after which they would rise
again. Needless to say, this prediction was very far from the truth and
it is apparent today that the Kondratiev was largely an accident. To give
another example, Mr. Sewell Avery of Montgomery Ward on the basis
of the experience of 1919–1920, expected a sharp depression after the
end of the second World War. In this expectation, he was disappointed
at considerable cost to the corporation which he directed.

The difference between social and physical systems is not confined
to the complexity and order of the difference or differential equations
which govern them. Social systems are characterized by at least two
other peculiarities which differentiate them very sharply from simple
physical systems, such as celestial mechanics. The first characteristic
is the predominance of "threshold" systems in which small causes can
sometimes produce very large consequences. The second characteristic is
that social systems are what I call "image-directed," that is, there are
systems in which the knowledge of the systems themselves is a significant
part of the system's own dynamics and in which, therefore, knowledge
about the system changes the system.

In view of the fact that social systems are the creation of the human
organism, and especially of the human nervous system, it is not surprising

to find that the closest analogue to the threshold quality of social systems is to be found in the neural networks of the human nervous system. The essential element of a threshold system is something like a neuron — an element which has inputs and outputs but in which the output depends upon the sum of the inputs reaching a certain threshold. It would be more accurate to say that some function of the inputs must reach a certain threshold as the function does not have to be simply additive. As long as the threshold is not reached an addition to input produces no output whatever. The moment the threshold is reached, there is an output. In the case of the neuron as far as we know, this output is fairly standardized. We can, however, postulate elements of as great complexity as we wish. A system of this kind is represented in Figure 1 where the square boxes represent "neurons" or threshold elements. The number in each box is the "height" of its threshold elements. Thus, suppose we assume that each of the threshold elements of Row 1 receive 20 units of input. Only Element A will "fire." It will produce an output of 20 which it will pass along the lines marked by the arrows to the next row of threshold elements. As will be seen from the figure, only Element C in Row 2 will fire, and the process will again pass along the lines marked by the arrows to the third row of elements. In this row, both

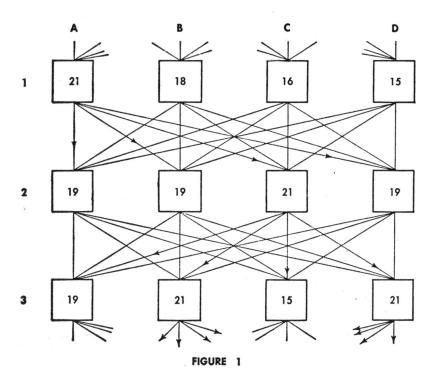

FIGURE 1

Elements B and D will fire, which may mean, of course, that still more elements will fire in Row 4 when this is reached.

It is obvious that systems of this kind are very complex, although some of their properties have been explored by the mathematical biologists. These are systems in which, if I dare quote Browning,

> Oh, the little more and how much it is
> And the little less, and what worlds away!

It was for the loss of a nail, we remember in the nursery rhyme, that the kingdom was lost. There are times in history when a very small change in output can cause one threshold unit to fire which otherwise would not have fired and the whole course of history is changed. It is this among other things which makes prediction so difficult in the social sciences. If we are to be able to predict in social systems, we must know a good deal about the thresholds of the threshold units involved. Unfortunately, this information is often very hard to come by. The higher the threshold, the harder it is to find out where it is. The elements that correspond to neurons in the neural network are, of course, persons in the social system; the firing of a neuron corresponds to the decision of a person — a decision, that is to say, is output of some kind, usually of communication or of information, which follows from the cumulative result of a number of past inputs. These outputs result only, however, when the past inputs accumulate over some threshold. Where the thresholds are low, the behavior is repetitive and easy to find out about. Every morning, for instance, men stagger into the bathroom and shave. This is a very low-level decision. In fact, some people deny the name of decision to these habitual reactions. However, there is input in the shape of the alarm clock and the information which reaches us from our physical surroundings and this is sufficient to carry us over the threshold of behavior. It may be, indeed, that on Saturday morning, the threshold is not reached and we do not shave.

The situation is further complicated in social systems by the fact that the decisions of different persons have different weights. In Figure 1, I have supposed all the threshold elements to be equal in the sense that each one is connected with the next set by an equal number of lines of communication. In social systems, this is not true. There are some elements which are connected to very many others, other elements connected to only a few. The decisions of a sharecropper in Mississippi or a shoeshine boy in New York are communicated to a very small circle of other persons. The decisions of a Kennedy or a Khrushchev are communicated to hundreds of millions of people and may affect the lives of all of them. This is because communication in social systems is neither a uniform nor a random effort but is organized into role structures and organizations. An organization, in fact, has been defined as a set of roles linked by lines of communication.

At this point there are two extreme views of the nature of social systems between which we have to pick our way. On the one hand, there is the purely mechanical view that the nature of a role occupant is quite unimportant and that the decision is determined by the role structure itself. The course of history in this view is determined by great impersonal social forces and the actual decisions of the decision-maker, no matter how exalted, are relatively unimportant. At the other extreme, we have the "great man" theory of history in which the decision of those placed in powerful roles is regarded as all-important and history is written largely in terms of the character and peculiarity of kings, dictators, generals, and prophets. Karl Marx may be regarded as representative of the one extreme and perhaps Thomas Carlyle of the other.

The truth clearly lies somewhere between these two extreme positions. Exactly where it lies, however, is hard to say. We can certainly distinguish large and apparently impersonal forces which operate on the dynamics of social systems. Such things as changes in climate, the discovery of new lands, the accumulation of knowledge and skill, and the growth of population seem at times to be almost independent of the human will. In what Baumol has called "the magnificent dynamics" of the classical economics there is little place for individual decision. In the Malthusian system, for instance, if we once accept the initial premise that the only effective check on the growth of population is starvation and misery, then no matter how grandiose our images or how reasonable our decisions the end is the same. We may illustrate this perhaps in Figure 2. If the system of decision points is triangular in the sense that the number of decision points continually declines in the course of time, then no matter what the path of the system, it all follows down to the same end. It cannot be doubted that systems of this kind exist. It is also clear, however, that the social system of mankind as a whole, up to the present rate, has not been a system of this kind. If anything, indeed, it is a reverse triangle; that is, the number of decision points continually increases with time so that the system becomes less and less determinate in a mechanical sense, hence, the path becomes more and more important.

We now come to the second great peculiarity of social systems, which is that they are to a considerable extent determined by the images we have of them and the knowledge we have about them. They are, that is to say, in part image-determined. It is very important to say "in part" image-determined because there are mechanical elements, independent of the image, of great importance in any social system and we neglect these at our peril. I recall an old Peter Arno cartoon of a very jolly party in an airplane which is about to crash into a cliff, the caption being "My God, we're out of gin!" The future of that small social system could be deduced from its physical environment quite independently of any images of its own future which it might possess. Social systems, therefore, are always mixed systems in the sense that they combine both the

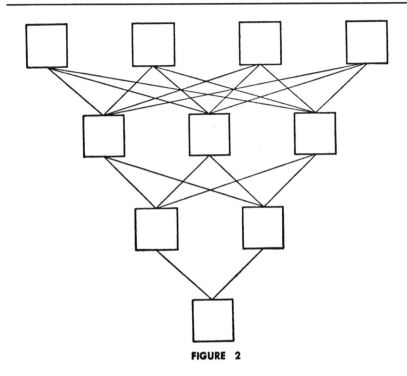

FIGURE 2

mechanical and image-determined elements. One may venture a guess that as the knowledge of society increases, the image-determined elements in social systems become more important. That is, as I said in my book, *The Image* , there is a strong tendency for the latent to become manifest. Man begins with an image of a world which has really very little to do with his actual environment or the actual system in which he lives. To some extent, these images may be self-reinforcing and where this is the case, he does not change them easily. It occasionally happens, however, that he is disappointed and is aware of his disappointments and, under these circumstances, there may be a change in the image towards "reality." I would rather leave the question of what is meant by reality to another time, or even to another person. Our common-sense notions, however, that some images may be truer than others, are probably not wholly illusory.

Even images which are in some sense false, however, produce marked effects upon the dynamics of society. Dr. Fred Polak in his great book, *The Image of the Future* , has brought together an impressive array of historical evidence to indicate that one of the major elements, perhaps indeed the most important single element, which governs the dynamics of particular societies is the nature of the image of the future which prevails in them. One might even extend this concept to the behavior of the individual. If we contrast, for instance, the behavior of the graduate student with that of the bum, we will see pretty clearly that the principal difference is in the image of the future. The graduate student has a long-run image of the future in which he sees himself enjoying certain rewards as a result of the pains and efforts he is now enduring. The bum has hardly any image of the future beyond that of the immediate moment, or if he has any image, it is so depressing that it is repressed. Polak's major point is that in the dynamics of a society, the principal factor is not so much the particular content of the image of the future as its quality of optimism or pessimism. A society which has a negative or pessimistic image of the future is likely to be disorganized and its image of the future is all too likely to be fulfilled. On the other hand, the society which has an optimistic image of the future, even though this image may be quite unrealistic, will be well organized and will go forward into some future, although not necessarily the future of its image. An excellent illustration of this principle is to be found in the remarkable degree of coherence and organization present among the Millenialist and Chiliastic sects like Jehovah's Witnesses or the Seventh Day Adventists. Here we have a group of people with a highly positive image of their own future of a strictly metaphysical or trans-empirical kind. It is an image not shared by most of the population and a great many people would regard it as unrealistic or even ludicrous. The fact, however, that it is positive and full of hope means that in this world, these subcultures are well organized and, in fact, move toward a positive and desirable future even in this world, in spite of the fact that their basic image of the future is other-worldly. The strength of the Communists likewise depends upon their having a highly positive image of the future. This does not differ so much from that of the Millenialist as we might think. Even though the golden future of the Communist image is ostensibly in this world, it is so remote that it might just as well be in another.

Examples of self-justifying images of the future are very common in economic life. It is a commonplace of economics that if everybody expects a rise in prices, everybody will act so as to bring the rise in prices about, and the same goes for the expectation of falling prices. If most businessmen expect a depression, they are likely to behave in such a way as to bring it about. If there is a general expectation of economic development, this is also an important element in bringing it about. And, by contrast, if people have a strong impression that any attempt to better their own position will fail, they are likely to be apathetic and unwilling to exert themselves in new enterprises. The general level of aspiration of the people, as many writers have pointed out, is perhaps the largest single element in the psychological substratum of economic development. In a slightly different area, the expectations of war and peace, likewise, are frequently self-justified. Where we have two countries such as the United States and Canada which are genuinely at peace in the sense that not even the threat of war is used as an instrument in their relationship, the total absence of the expectation of war justifies itself. There are no preparations for war and virtually no possibility of war. On the other hand, the strong expectation of war almost invariably produces it, for this leads to an arms race, which eventually leads to an intolerable situation in which one side or the other precipitates overt conflict.

A question of great importance is the extent to which men's images can be deliberately manipulated and hence, insofar as images determine the future, the future itself can be manipulated. The "cause" of our images is to be found in our total experience. The growth of the image follows a process which is related to biological growth. It is, however, very different from biological growth in the sense that is peculiarly subject to symbolic changes. This is the prime difference between man and the lower animals. The lower animals undoubtedly have images and they may even have dreams. These images, however, are derived from direct experience and are not derived from symbols about experience. A dog can have an image of chasing a rabbit after he has once chased one; he can never derive an image of chasing a rabbit from hearing someone talk about it or reading about it in a book. A human being, by contrast, can derive images of things of which he has no direct personal experience. I have never been to Australia but I have read about it and as a result I have a fairly clear image of what it is like. If I went to Australia I am sure there are some things which would surprise me, for the image derived from symbols is never quite as vivid or as accurate as the image derived from direct experience. I would, however, be very surprised if I was very surprised. It is the essentially symbolic nature of the human image which dominates the social system. It is this which makes human history so profoundly different from any other record of events or any other temporal system. Because of this, the image-makers are a profoundly significant element in society when it comes to the interpretation of social dynamics. These are the writers, the preachers, the teachers, the politicians, the orators — and even the advertising and public relations men!

It is easy to acknowledge the importance of the role of the image-maker in society; it is not so easy to understand or to assess it. The difficulty here is that we are dealing with symbolic systems and these are systems we understand very little. We are unquestionably dealing with threshold systems of a kind, but we do not really know what the inputs and outputs are and we know even less about what determines and constitutes the thresholds themselves. What is it for instance, that gives a symbol power? Duns Scotus "fired France for Mary without spot" and the Virgin, as Henry Adams saw so clearly, built some of the greatest monuments of the human spirit. A Middle-western Protestant of 1961 is not similarly fired. Under the sign of the crescent, the Arabs almost conquered the world, and shifted the center of civilization from the Mediterranean toward the Persian Gulf. I must confess that the Koran which moved so many, moves me very little and I find it hard to enter even by the gates of empathy into an experience that is at the same time so profound and so remote. Now it is nationalism and communism that seem to fire men to devotion and action. Tomorrow, these, too, may seem hollow and unrewarding.

The problem is that the image is not merely an aggregate of information, it is a structure — a structure, moreover, of great complexity and many dimensions. Its complexity is so great that there is a powerful urge to simplify it, and the symbol is the simplification of the image. A symbol, that is, is something which stands for or evokes an image of much greater complexity than its literal self. At a common-place, statistical level, we see it in such concepts as the price level, which reduces a massive list of individual prices to a single number. Similarly the flag invokes a complex and emotionally rich image of national history and the cross invokes a similar rich image of Christian experience, martyrdom, and doctrine. Our image is as frequently clarified and made more powerful as a spring of action by the loss of information as it is by the gain. We have, for instance, a profound tendency to try to reduce a multi-dimensional reality to a single linear dimension. We have a strong urge, for instance, to reduce the almost infinitely dimensioned variety of the human character to a single dimension of good and bad. Even worse, we set up a point on this continuum and divide all mankind into two boxes — the good guys and the bad guys, the right people and the wrong people, the ins and the outs, the good families and the riff-raff, the free world and the Communists, the whites and the negroes. The stereotyping of the image inevitably leads to a loss which can sometimes even be measured in economic terms. The trouble with discrimination is that it is undiscriminating — that is, it discriminates according to an unreal and false set of criteria.

We must, however, at least be modestly humble at this point. There is no litmus paper of truth. There is no simple way of identifying the truth of the image. In theory, indeed, there is no way at all, for images can only be compared with images; they can never be compared with reality. In practice, I think there is a certain skill at truth, and the least we can say is that a demand for it produces a certain supply. One suspects, perhaps, that the main difficulty with the provision of truth is the absence of demand, rather than any basic inelasticity in the supply.

When one thinks of the image-makers, one thinks also, unfortunately, of lies. And the question arises, therefore, what is the power of a lie in determining a course of the dynamics of a society. Goebbels believed, of course, that the bigger the lie, the more often and the more loudly it was shouted, the better chance it had of being believed. There is, unfortunately, a certain amount of evidence to justify this hypothesis. On the other hand, truth has a certain advantage which the lie does not. The lie may be found out, whereas the truth cannot. That is, the lie cannot be found to be a truth and the truth cannot be found to be a lie.

The lie, that is to say, can only be justified within the symbolic system —
it cannot be justified outside it in the cold school of hard experience. I
think, therefore, that we are justified in assuming a certain "outability"
of truth and that Lincoln's favorite aphorism that you can't fool all of
the people all of the time is ultimately truer than Goebbel's belief.

One circumstance, however, must require withdrawal at least in part
of the optimism of the previous paragraph. When the image is self-
justifying, what does it mean to say that it is true or false? In a world
of fairy wishing-caps what would happen to the truth? This is a real
problem and one stands, indeed, on the edge of an abyss — the abyss
of fairyland — a horror where all dreams are true and in which, therefore,
there is no truth. The only escape from this nightmare, I think, is the
faith that images are self-justified only in the short run. The belief that
prices are going to rise may cause prices to rise for a while, but not
forever. Eventually, the underlying reality of the world must impose
itself on the self-justifying realities of the image. It is a very real problem in social organization, however, as to how we defend ourselves
against self-justifying images. These may only be justified in the short
run, but the short run can be a desperately long space of time. To
paraphrase Lincoln again, we can fool too many of the people too much
of the time. The record of history is full of great expectations that were
self-justified for a while but which eventually were disappointments.

I may seem at this point almost to be arguing for the mechanical
interpretations of social systems which are so attractive in their seeming
objectivity, and so free from the corruption of dreams. The image of
the social system as mechanical, however, is itself a retreat from reality,
for social reality is more complex than any mechanical system can possibly describe. Mechanical views of history, like those of Marx, are therefore likely to lead to results that are as perverse and dangerous as those
which stem from the efforts of the liar, the propagandist, and the deliberate perverter of the truth. The Communists are certainly better inten-
tioned than the Nazis, but they may have caused just as great a sum
of human misery, and even the most selfless efforts of Christian missionaries have occasionally accomplished disintegration and disaster for
the societies which they have influenced. What I am pleading for, therefore, is not a return to clear — and therefore false — mechanical views of
history, it is rather that we should dedicate ourselves to a long, slow
task, the task of developing true images of social systems, true in the
sense that they conform to the nature of man himself and to his potentialities — which I believe are greater than any that we have yet brought
to light. They should be true also in the sense of giving us skill in the
handling of our society. I do not believe that I have ever asked of the
image of a social system that it would enable us to foretell the future.
It is not too much to ask of such an image, however, that it give us a
guide to present action and certain reasonably secure conditional expectations. What we ask from the image is a reasonably accurate measure of

possible futures that we can choose among. I do not believe either that we are a helpless pawn of destiny or that we are the masters of our fate. The truth lies somewhere in between. We have real choices, but the choices are within a limited menu. The menu perhaps grows longer all the time, but it is always limited. It should be the great business of the science of society to learn the limits of this menu — to learn what we cannot have as well as what we can have, and hence, to guide our choice into those areas which are not only desirable, but realizable.

The most important property of man's image, however, is his ability to change it. Without this, we may be trapped in images which are self-reinforcing even though they are not self-justifying. The image, that is to say, is reinforced in defiance of experience. It is the skill of learning which is the greatest hope of the human race. It is the will to learn which is its greatest question mark. If the image-maker conceives his role as that of the printer, printing his image upon the plastic minds of mankind, then he betrays his function as a teacher. For the teacher is not an imprinter; he is one who cooperates with the inward teacher, the will to learn, the mysterious inner forces of growth and development of the image within the personality of the individual. Unless there is a basic respect for the individual image, the image-maker, whether preacher, politician, writer, ad-man, or even professor, becomes the mere propagandist who may actually destroy the tender buds of true knowledge and so help to imprison mankind behind the terrible walls of false images. It may be true that man has mostly lived in these prisons — prisons of superstition, magic, ideology, priest-craft, party lines, and thought control. But I believe he was not made to be so imprisoned; it is for this hope that man can and must break out of his image prisons into that "free world" of the future for which we think he was made and toward which his potentialities impel him. In this world there is only one loyalty, loyalty to the truth. It is a difficult and painful loyalty to possess, especially in a world that recognizes it so little. In this loyalty, however, there lies, it seems to me, the only image of the future which is truly creative, and it is a future which we do not wholly have to wait to enjoy. No man, I think, in this world can live wholly free from lies but he can love the truth and direct the current of his mind and life towards it. If this sounds like moralizing, I will not deny it; I would only point out that values are an essential part of the image and constitute, indeed, that aspect of it which is most influential in affecting behavior and the dynamic course of society.

THE COMMUNICATION OF LEGITIMACY

Channels (Western Mich. Univ.), Spring 1965: 24-28

The Communication of Legitimacy

One of the most important and at the same time most puzzling strands in the great web of society is that which constitutes the legitimacy of human relationships. It is this which makes the difference between the policeman and the bandit, the pretender and the king, the heretic and the orthodox, the bastard and the heir. Without legitimacy, no complex and continuing operation of social life is possible. Social relations become one-shot jobs, single acts of violence or even of exchange, without any continuing pattern. The struggle of rival systems of legitimation is by far the most important conflict in society, and the one with the most far-reaching consequences. The conflict of ideologies which seems so important in the world of today is only a special case of this much larger and continuing conflict of different ideas of legitimacy. Without legitimacy, armed might and the ability to carry out threats is usually as costly, if not more so, to the threatener as it is to the threatened. Hence the whole threat system, that is, the organization of social life by means of threats, rests on a foundation of bluff, and unless this is reinforced by strong feelings of the legitimacy of the threat system, the threats will be defied and the whole system fall in ruins. Legitimacy is something which is even superior to the law itself, for if the law is regarded as illegitimate, by a wide section of society, as for instance the prohibition law was regarded, it will be flouted and its enforcement will be impossible, and the law itself eventually will have to adjust to the prevailing ideas of what is legitimate. Even though the law is in many ways an embodiment, perhaps a delayed embodiment, of the general concept of legitimacy in a society, it is sometimes regarded as legitimate to break and defy the law. What all this means is that legitimacy is not a static phenomenon; the concepts of what is and is not legitimate are in constant flux, and different legitimacies are in continued conflict.

In view of the overriding importance of legitimacy as a social concept, it is astonishing how little attention has been paid to it and how little we really know about it. I am aware of no general theory of legitimacy, and indeed there seems to be astonishingly little interest in the problem among social scientists. Perhaps this is because there is no simple, abstract act or class of acts which constitutes the establishment and maintenance of legitimacy. In the case of economics, we have a relatively simple act, the act of exchange, around which almost all of economics is built. In the case of the strategic sciences, again we have a relatively simple act of the threat, around which again a science can be built. Legitimacy, however, is conveyed, built up, and eroded in innumerable ways, and by a great variety of acts, the common quality of which is not easily recognized. Legitimacy, furthermore, is a concept which is very hard to quantify, even though concepts of "more" or "less" certainly apply to it. The United States, for instance, has a lot of legitimacy in Hawaii and practically none in Okinawa, and almost certainly a negative quantity, if we could measure it, in Vietnam. Furthermore, legitimacy is like the air around us—we only notice it when it is withdrawn. The more legitimacy a system possesses, the less noticeable it seems to be. It is only when legitimacy is questioned or destroyed that we notice it.

In any study of legitimacy, the problem of how it is communicated must, obviously, be in the forefront of consideration. Here again, the problem of the unnoticeability of legitimation is very striking, because legitimacy is communicated mainly in the things we all take for granted. It is communicated also to a substantial extent at the non-verbal level. The handshake or the equivalent greeting in other cultures, which seems to be an almost universal cultural trait, is an interesting example of a social ritual which essentially is directed towards the communication of legitimacy. The handshake symbolizes equality, symmetry in the human relationship. That is, the essential character of the act is not changed if the parties are reversed, and this implies reciprocation, that is, what A does to B, B does to A. Even where the parties are in a hierarchical power relationship, at the moment of the handshake they stand on an equal footing. This is a reflection of a very profound social truth, that communication can only take place among equals, and that for organization, communication is necessary. Hence a purely hierarchical relationship of superior and inferior cannot create organizations except of a fairly primitive kind. This is perhaps the most fundamental reason for the decay of the legitimacy of the inferior-superior-relationships, as symbolized, for instance, in the reverential gesture—the bow, for instance—with which we approach a king. The contrast between the bow of a courtier acknowledged by a slight inclination of the monarch's head and the handshake of the president is a profound symbol of two sharply different systems of legitimacy.

Another aspect of the communication of legitimacy is pomp or state, the ceremonial or ritual which is designed to establish the legitimacy of a hierarchical organization. In architecture, the Roman portico, the processional mall, and the Gothic spire alike have the primary function of communicating importance. Indeed, the use of architectural symbols in communicating legitimacy is worth a volume in itself. A great many architectural forms which otherwise seem completely nonfunctional become understandable when we conceive them as symbols of legitimation. Imagine, for instance, the Capitol building in Washington without a dome, that otherwise useless excrescence. It would convey no message of importance, no sense of the building being a focus or peak of human activity. The psychoanalytically oriented might continue the speculation on the dome as a female symbol (the government as the nurse of the welfare state) and the spire as a male symbol, whether in the form of the church or the bank, penetrating and fertilizing the mysterious universe. Both the dome and the spire, however, whatever their sexual significance, are symbols of saliency. The fact that these objects are decorated with corbel, cusp, crocket, and pillar is likewise of great significance. These decorations are like the wreath which the conquered place on the brows of the conqueror. They are symbols of the necessity to endow power with legitimacy and with the ornaments of beauty. One of the great problems of modern architecture, incidentally, is to recover the function of ornament. In the long retreat from Ruskin, who regarded ornament as everything, to the extreme functionalists who denied all function to ornament whatever, architecture lost a sense of the true function of ornament as a symbol of the great web of legitimacy.

Clothing is another interesting example of the nonverbal communication of legitimacy. In a democratic and equalitarian society, everybody dresses alike. Differences in clothing, as reflected for instance in loud shirts and ties, reflect only individual eccentricity, and even these communicate a good deal about status. The uniform, as in the armed forces, emphasizes both the equality—indeed, almost the cipher-like equality—of those in the same rank, and also, of course, emphasizes the differences among ranks. A strongly hierarchical organization such as an army would be almost impossible without a constant reminder in the form of clothing of the nature and legitimacy of the hierarchy. The gold braid and what is sometimes irreverently called "scrambled eggs" of the higher ranks are like the dome of the Capitol, a constant reminder of saliency and status.

A very interesting study could be made of the clothing of the clergy as a symbol of changing systems of legitimacy. The use of the word "the cloth" in English to describe the clergy collectively is itself a fascinating symbol. In a hierarchical religion we respect not the man but the cloth, that is, the clothes, he is wearing, because the clothes symbolize the role and it is the role that we respect rather than the occupant as such. In a priestly religion, the inadequacies of the person of the priest in no way diminish his capacity to perform his role. The traditionally feminine character of clerical clothes is also very interesting, symbolizing the comforting, reassuring, motherly role of the clergy in society. This is seen most clearly, of course, in the soutane or the robes of monastic orders (skirts rather than trousers), but we see it even in the vestigial feminine symbol of the clerical collar. The abandonment of clerical garb by a large number of Protestant ministers in the United States is an interesting symbol of a profound change in the clerical role, involving the abandonment of hierarchy, the abandonment of priesthood, and the development of the clerical role as essentially not very different from that of a social worker. In modern Protestantism, the cleric is no longer a priest, and he no longer has a vocation but a profession or occupation.

The clothing of the medical doctor would also provide an interesting sidelight on the communication of legitimacy. While the frock coat was the prime symbol of status, surgeons insisted on performing their operations in it, even at the cost of an enormous toll in mortality. Today the white coat has become the status symbol, and is worn by a good many people in places where it is no longer functionally necessary. The decline of the academic gown is also a symbol of a profoundly changing system of legitimacy. Like the cleric, the professor is no longer a race apart. He no longer has a divine aura around him. This is reflected in the fact that he, too, is indistinguishable from anybody else by reason of the clothes that he wears, except that by convention he is allowed to be a little shabbier and down-at-heels than other people of comparable status.

Changing styles in the communication of the legitimacy of wealth also make a fascinating study. As long as the legitimacy of wealth itself is unquestioned, it tends to be expressed in ostentation and extravagance and what Veblen called "conspicuous consumption." If, however, the legitimacy of wealth is questioned in society, conspicuous consumption disappears and its place is taken by inconspicuous consumption. We saw this, for instance, in Tokugawa Japan, where wealth was legitimate for the lord but not for the merchant, so that as the merchants became wealthy they had to disguise this fact behind mean housefronts and dismal outdoor clothing. Similarly in our own society, the Marxist attack on the legitimacy of private wealth has at least been moderately successful in driving it, as it were, underground into Foundations. In a society in which the principal repository of legitimacy is the middle class, ostentatious housing and even more ostentatious clothing are completely outmoded. In their housing, clothing, and deportment, even the wealthy have to say, in effect, "Well, we are all buddies together, aren't we?" Even in his own generation a man like Hearst was regarded as something of an eccentricity.

When we come to verbal forms of communication, we see here a strong tendency for the ornaments of language, like those of buildings or clothes, to convey legitimacy. The decline of a status language, the decline, for instance, in English of the second person singular, which was reserved normally for people of inferior or familiar status, is a symbol of a profound change in the structure of legitimacy. The Japanese today face a very interesting problem of a language which is exquisitely adapted to express shades of hierarchy in a society in which hierarchy has largely lost its meaning. All this points up a very important principle, that legitimacy is almost always conveyed by indirection. Nobody stands up and begins every sentence with "I am legitimate," simply because this would destroy his legitimacy. Nevertheless, every channel of the communication process is permeated with the symbols of legitimacy, and it is high time for these symbols to receive careful and systematic study. In the long run all power, even of money and weapons, resides in the ability to conform to the underlying symbolic system by which legitimacy is conveyed, created, and destroyed.

THE DIFFICULT ART OF DOING GOOD

Colorado Quarterly, 13, 3 (Winter 1965): 197-211

The difficult art of doing good

As far as I know, nobody has ever written a general history of doing good. Nevertheless, the subject is of considerable importance to any-one who is interested in the overall dynamic processes of society. The general subject of benefaction, if we may translate the expres-sion into Latin to make it more impressive, clearly falls into two parts: philanthropy or charity on the one hand and social action on the other. Neither of these has been studied with the attention that each deserves in the light of their increasing importance in the social system. Philanthropy is at least as old as the beggar, who must be a pretty ancient institution. In the form of the support of children and old people, it is certainly as old as the family. Social action is perhaps a more modern notion, certainly in the sense of an organized political movement, although prophets have tended to give good advice to monarchs and those in authority for a long time. Philanthropy may be distinguished from social action in that philanthropy involves the making of some kind of grant, gift, or assistance from one person or institution to another within the existing general framework of society, whereas social action seeks to do good by changing the framework of society itself through changing its laws, its constitution, or its customs.

Both of these represent well-recognized and identifiable social phenomena. Nevertheless, the amount of careful study which they have received is astonishingly small. I participated a couple of years ago in a study of the economics of philanthropy sponsored by the National Bureau of Economic Research which, as far as I know, was almost the first study of its kind. Anyone who seeks a theory of philanthropy in the literature of social science will have to look far and wide. Many historical examples of social action of course have been studied, but I know of no attempt to bring these together into a general pattern or a general theory.

Behind this neglect of the subject there may lie the fact that doing good is not always approved. Over large areas of our society at least, the expression "do-gooder" is opprobrious. We may remember W. S. Gilbert's Bad Baronet of Ruddigore as a comic type of all robber barons who endow philanthropies. He was forced under the provisions of an ancient curse to do a crime every day. But, as he says, "I get my crime over the first thing in the morning and then, ha! ha!, for the rest of the day, I do good, I do good, I do good. Two days since, I stole a child and built an orphan asylum. Yesterday, I robbed a bank and endowed a bishopric," and so on. Even the late C. S. Lewis, who is certainly on the side of the angels, remarked in his *Screwtape Letters* about a certain lady "who lives for others—you can always tell the others by their hunted expression." The beggar's whine often conceals a muttered curse and even foreign aid is rarely loved without ambivalence by its recipients.

Our somewhat mixed attitude toward philanthropy may arise because doing this kind of good is always a privilege of the relatively rich. Those who give always have a higher status than those who are given to. The cynic might argue that every gift is, in a sense, paid for by a grant of status from the recipient. Our defensiveness against the "do-gooder," especially in the form of Lady Bountiful, may therefore be part of a quite legitimate dissatisfaction with the status system, even though it may also be inspired by simple envy, malice, and cantankerousness on the part of the ungrateful and undeserving poor.

There are many reasons, therefore, why in these days mere philanthropy tends to have a rather bad press and social action has received more social approval. In part, this arises because of a widespread recognition that charity, as such, or what the national income accounts might describe as private transfers, is likely to be inadequate, both in quantity and in quality, to solve the problem which creates the need for it. Charity, it has often been said, satisfies the consciences of the rich before it satisfies the hunger of the poor. There has therefore come to be an increasing demand for supplementing, if not replacing, private charity with organized public transfers through the political machinery of society. Thus, the item in the national income accounts of the United States, which is called "government transfer payments to persons" and includes such things as Social Security and veterans' benefits, was a negligible 0.9 percent of the gross national product in 1929 and is now running about 6 percent of the gross national product, or about thirty-four

billion dollars a year. Even if we deduct the personal contributions
for social insurance, about ten billion, we are still left with a hand-
some twenty-four billion, which is well in excess of the total of
private charity.

The term, "social action," itself is a little ambiguous. It may
mean the development of a political movement among the "non-
professionals," such as the movement which led to the establishment of prohibition or that which characterizes the civil rights
movement or the peace movement at present. The motivation here
is philanthropic in the sense that it does not arise so much out of
personal interest or out of hope of receiving personal benefits, but
rather out of a general feeling of what is good for society. It is this
aspect of social action which is most visible. It is this which leads
to the parades, the banners, the letters to Congress and what might
be called the organized moral pressure groups. A good deal of
legislation, however, which profoundly changes the social system
is not the result of social action in the above sense, is not the result,
that is, of professional politicians reacting to pressures from the non-
professionals, which we may call "social action I," but is the result
of a spontaneous perception of a social situation and a social need
on the part of the professionals—the politicians and civil servants
themselves. This is "social action II." The social security system of
the United States, for instance, did not come into being as the result
of social action of the first kind; that is, there was no great political
campaign among the non-professionals. Rather, it was the result of
a perception of the social situation among the professionals, that
is, the civil servants on the one hand who drafted the legislation
and the congressmen who themselves perceived a need and who
passed it. Not long before the first social security legislation was
passed, indeed, the organized labor movement had been quite
apathetic about it, or even hostile, and in no sense could we say
that the people who were going to benefit from this legislation had
organized themselves in order to produce it.

Often, of course, the two kinds of social action are mixed and
changes in the legal or other institutions of society occur because
of a mixture of political pressure from the non-professionals and
a perception of the situation on the part of the professionals. There
may well be some kind of optimum mixture here. A movement for
social action, which is entirely in the hands of non-professionals

often wastes the energy which it develops because of the fact that it is only through the professionals that an actual change in legal structures, at any rate, can be achieved. The peace movement, for instance, has unquestionably suffered from the fact that it has been frequently unable to express its objectives and ideals in terms which the professional politicians could perceive as practical policies.

Sometimes indeed, as in the case of prohibition, a strong movement for social action outside the professional politicians has resulted in a situation in which they are pressured into a solution which perhaps a maturer judgment would have rejected. The social actionist who is not a professional politician tends to see things in terms of black and white. The politician, by his very nature, turns all things to tattle-tale grey.

There are many reasons, therefore, why a rational critique of doing good is at least worth a try even though it is hard to come by. We cannot sustain the proposition that because doing good is virtuous in the mind of the doer it is thereby exempt from criticism. A man who says some mothers are bad is not necessarily against motherhood. Indeed, it is indiscriminate momism which brings motherhood into disrepute. Even among sacred things, some sacred things are better than other sacred things. A mere motivation to do good, therefore, is not necessarily enough to justify the results. It is highly necessary, then, to rescue benefaction from undiscriminating blame or praise.

One suspects, indeed, that it is our refusal or inability to criticize intelligently the doing of good that leads to a general cynicism and a denial of the possibility or desirability of doing good which is much more destructive than even the most naive efforts of the do-gooders. Such cynicism is destructive because it denies an essential part of man's nature—his need to identify with others, his need to expand his interests and concerns beyond the confines of his own body, and to participate in what I have called the "integrative system"—that aspect of society which deals with status, legitimacy, honor, love, affection, respect, compassion, and so on. Benefaction then is not something casual or spurious; it arises from the very nature of man and society, and cannot be denied. The cynic who denies it indeed may be in danger of having his child turn out a saint out of sheer reaction against the denial of something so true and fundamental!

A critique of benefaction may imply that we are not putting the right proportion of our total resources into it and also that we are not directing our benefactions to the right ends and are not distributing our effort wisely. It can rest on a demonstration that the results of benefaction are ineffective or poor by the standards and values of the benefactors themselves, or it can go further and challenge the values by which these results are judged. In any case, nobody can claim exemption from criticism merely because of his good intentions, neither the private donor nor the philanthropic foundation, nor the government, nor the social worker, nor the organizers and supporters of social movements and pressure groups. Otherwise, doing good may be the enemy of doing better.

We can start, perhaps, with a brief glimpse at philanthropy, especially as it is expressed in private gifts, in philanthropic foundations, and in government subsidies and transfer payments. The economist distinguishes fairly clearly between the "exchange economy," in which every quid gets a quo and in which, for each party to a transaction, something is given up and something received, and what might be called the "grants economy" in which money, goods, services, or other benefits are disbursed in unilateral transfers without any obvious return to the disburser. Philanthropy, whether personal, public, or private, falls very clearly in the sphere of the grants economy. The growth of the grants economy, both domestically and internationally, has been spectacular in the last generation. Yet economists mostly continue to teach and to talk as if the exchange economy were all that really mattered.

There may be a more subtle reason for this neglect of the grants economy. It is that economists know what to do with exchange, whereas they do not know what to do with grants. In the exchange economy, for instance, we can use profits or profitability as at least a first approximation to a measure of the worth of an undertaking. In the world of business, which is dominated by exchange, 6 percent per annum is better than 5 percent unless there are good reasons to the contrary, which of course there may in some cases be. In the grants economy, there is no such easy measure of success or failure, even at the level of first approximation. If the Ford Motor Company produces an Edsel, it is soon apparent that a mistake has been made simply because the Edsel is (or was) a phenomenon of the exchange economy, so that if not enough people buy it and if its production is unprofitable, it will soon cease to be made. If the Ford Foundation, however, produced the equivalent of an Edsel, how would anybody ever find out? There is no simple measure of profit or loss for a foundation. Its decisions have to be made without any clear guidelines and also without any clear standards by which the results of these decisions may be judged.

In the grants economy it is not quite true that the wheel that squeaks the most gets the grease, but, in the mysterious process by which decisions regarding grants are made through the complex interaction of grantors and grantees, there is certainly no obvious guarantee that the ultimate decision will be wise. Furthermore, there is little protection against the making of mistakes simply because, even if we do make mistakes, it is very hard to find out that they are mistakes in fact and nothing bad happens to the man who made the mistake as a result of making it. Nevertheless, the allocation of resources which goes on in the grants economy, and this is particularly true of the resources devoted to research and development, may have a profound effect on the whole future course of the society. Indeed, we may say that while we have strong defenses built into the social system itself against gross misallocations in the exchange economy, simply because if we have such gross misallocations we soon become aware of the fact through the operation of the price system, in the grants economy there is no such mechanism. This indeed is a solid reason against too much reliance on the grants economy, and it is a particularly solid reason against giving the grantors of grants a monopoly in any particular field. In education, for instance, it is highly desirable to have private schools which operate mainly through the exchange system, to offer competition to public schools which operate through the grants economy. Countries, indeed, in which the state has a tight monopoly of education almost always underinvest in this field. At the other extreme one would certainly not advocate turning education wholly over to the private sector. Here again, what we are looking for is an optimum mixture.

Some rather narrow-minded economists have argued that it is illegitimate to inquire whether grants are bad or good just as they do not inquire whether purchases, for instance, are misguided. According to this view, the man who gives the beggar a dime or the government who gives pensions or foreign aid is beyond criti-

cism just as the man who buys gin rather than gospels is beyond
criticism, at least by the economist as such. This position seems to
be too extreme, though it must be admitted that, once we abandon
it, it is hard to stop short of a total ethic which would prescribe
and proscribe everything and which would almost have to be arbitrary and imposed. If preferences themselves are to be criticized,
both on the part of exchangers and on the part of grantors, this
amounts to saying that poetry *is* better than pushpin, that it is
better to buy a good house and raise a decent family than to raise
hell in riotous living and dissipation, and that it is better to make
grants for universities and for research than it is to build elaborate
palaces and pleasure gardens for the delight of princes. Whatever
the difficulties of a rational critique of preferences, whether for
purchases or for grants, the plain fact is that we do criticize preferences all the time. There may not be agreement about tastes, but,
in spite of the Latin tag, there is a great deal of disputation about
them. We cannot, indeed, understand the dynamics of society at
all unless we realize that very few people are neutral in regard to
the tastes of others. It is hard to maintain a pure cultural relativism
and ethical neutrality in the face of Dachau or Auschwitz. The
many difficulties of a rational critique of preferences should not
lead us to abandon the task but rather to pursue it more vigorously.

The first obvious task is to evaluate doing good by the values of
the doer himself. Any action which makes things worse by the
values of the actor himself obviously has something wrong with it.
If giving money to beggars makes us feel guilty and miserable, we
will probably stop doing it or do it only under duress. Equally, of
course, a Scrooge in whom the wells of compassion have run dry
and who attaches importance only to his own gains will likewise
find philanthropy unacceptable. Philanthropy arises out of identification of the giver with the recipient. It is a part, therefore, of
what I have elsewhere called the integrative system. Even in its
lowest form of pity, there is an implication of identification of one
person with another so that the objective woes of B are reflected,
as it were, in the subjective woes of A. We relieve the necessities
of the poor for very much the same reason we do not allow our own
children to starve—because they are, in some sense, part of us.

All charitable organizations rely for their support on their ability
to produce a feeling of identification on the part of their donors

with the work or objectives of the organization. This identification is often a little arbitrary and depends on the accident of past experience. Thus, Americans are much more willing to give to the support of orphanages in Korea than they are to give to support orphanages in, shall we say, Somalia because our involvement in the Korean war has given us a lively interest in Korea and an identification with its problems which we do not feel toward Somalia. We shall feel free to criticize the pattern of identification itself later. Criticism, according the the values of the actor in this case, leads only to a conclusion that a "bad" gift is one which has been made as a result of an identification created through ignorance or fraud. The question here is only would we regret the gift if we knew all the facts. We cannot quite leave the matter in this way, which shows the weakness of the principle of only valuing action by the values of the actor. New information frequently causes a change in the nature of the identification and in the value system of the actor himself. The value system, that is, is not something which is stable, but is something which changes constantly under the impact of experience.

The critique of social action by the values of the actor may be even more useful than a critique of philanthropy. In the mind of the social-actionist, his action is intended to produce certain consequences, and it is often not too difficult to find out from him what consequences he regards as desirable. If the action produces different, or opposite, consequences from what is intended, then clearly there is something wrong with it even in the mind of the actor himself. Thus, the temperance movement arose in the nineteenth century as a result of putting a highly negative value on drunkenness which, especially in the light of the increased danger from drunkenness in industrial and mechanical society, seems to be very reasonable. This value system produced a social movement which eventually concentrated on the establishment of a single political and legal objective—that of prohibition. In the United States, this was successful, and I recall indeed, in my Methodist childhood in England, how at that time we looked to the United States as the great moral leader in this field whose example would shortly be followed by all wise countries. This image was soon falsified—prohibition turned out to have alarming side effects and, in the long run, it may have even increased the problem of alcoholism rather than solved it. As a social movement, the temperance movement was so shattered by the failure of prohibition that even though the problem remains a real one, and indeed a desperately serious one, there is really no social movement to cope with it with the possible exception of Alcoholics Anonymous and a small movement for research in alcoholism, and the moral enthusiasm which once went into the temperance movement now goes into movements for nuclear disarmament or civil rights. The history of the temperance movement indeed is a sobering (pardon the word) example of how a social movement may succeed in imposing a solution which, in fact, fails to solve the problem, even by its own values.

Even in what I call "social action II," which is motivated by the awareness of a situation by the professional politician or civil servant rather than by pressure from a lay social action group, the possibility of failure by the standards of the actor himself is very real. I am not familiar enough with the drug addiction laws of the United States to know whether they were, in fact, drafted by professionals. I suspect they were. In any case, they reflect an approach to the situation which quite manifestly fails to solve the problem, even by the values of those who support and enforce the laws.

Foreign aid is a good example of a quasi-philanthropic enterprise on the part of the United States government which has very little in the way of a popular social action movement behind it, for it is indeed one of the least popular policies of the government. It arises mainly because of an image of the world in the minds of the professionals in the State Department, in Congress, and in the White House which wants to see a large number of viable, independent nations which are friendly toward us. If foreign aid leads to corruption and to unstable and unfriendly governments, it will be criticized even by those who are now mainly responsible for creating the program. Similarly, if public housing leads to a violation of the principles of neighborhood ecology, to what one social worker described as "filing cabinets for live bodies," and if it results in social breakdown, delinquency, and crime, it is not difficult to criticize the programs by the values of those who created them. Similarly, if aid to dependent children leads to the development of self-perpetuating poverty cultures where the aided children grow up to expect aid for their children and where unemployment becomes the accepted way of life, here again, criticism is possible by the values of those who have created the program.

I am not suggesting that all the criticisms I have suggested here are necessarily valid. Many of them, indeed in many cases, are not. What I am trying to point out is that the criticism of social action by the values of the actors themselves is a large field open to the social sciences. The crucial question here is whether our analysis of social systems and our skill in the social sciences is refined enough first, to enable us to detect what are the values of the actors and secondly, to help us find out what are the probable consequences of the programs which the actors have initiated. This involves first, an adequate social theory by which our information as it comes in from society can be interpreted; secondly, it demands an adequate system for the collecting and processing of information about social systems; and third, it requires an adequate system of feedback by which information can be fed back into the theory to test it and to modify it constantly in the direction of realism.

It would be foolishly optimistic to think we have reached this state of affairs. We still have a long way to go in social theory. Information collection and processing of data from social systems is woefully inadequate simply because we do not put enough new resources into this, and perhaps because of this the modification of our images of social systems in the direction of reality does not take place fast enough and sometimes, indeed, does not take place at all. Nevertheless, the situation is not hopeless. The social sciences are somewhat in the position of the farmer who refused the services of an extension agent on the grounds that he knew how to farm twice as well as he was doing already. I would argue indeed that what we are facing here is a pretty clear misallocation of resources in the grants economy. It is pathetic how little research is put into our action programs. We seem to have a firm conviction in this country that we will put any amount of money into seeing that money is spent honestly, but we will put nothing into seeing that it is spent wisely. We have an elaborate system of public accounting to see that money is spent according to rule; we put practically no effort into inquiring whether the rules make any sense.

Even without challenging, therefore, the existing values of most of the people who make our policies, I would put in a very strong plea for what might be called Action Oriented Research, directed at social systems. I have argued elsewhere that we are suffering in this country and in the world at large from a massive misallocation of our intellectual resources as between the study of physical and biological systems on the one hand and social systems on the other. Our problems these days are mainly in social systems. Yet, we persistently put the bulk of our effort into the physical or even biological systems which merely, as it were, provide the conditions and the framework within which the social systems operate.

I was impressed with this fact when a few years ago I was a member of the committee which was supposed to advise the State of California on the social and economic consequences of the California water plan. This plan had been in preparation for ten years by engineers and at the end of this time it occurred to somebody that perhaps some social scientists ought to look at it. Even a relatively casual glance at the problem revealed that the engineers were treating it as a purely physical problem: how to get water from Northern to Southern California.

Even in the first hour or two of looking at the problem the social scientists could raise questions which should have been raised ten years before, about, for instance, the pricing systems on water use, the possibilities for water-saving inventions, the wasteful use of water in agriculture, the relation of the water plan to distribution of incomes, the political structure of decisions on water in the legislature, questions even about whether a major effort should not be put in a totally different technological direction, for instance, along the lines of long-distance ocean transportation of water in enormous submarines. These questions were not raised because engineers are not taught to think in terms of social systems, but only in terms of physical systems.

If we turn to flood control, we find a similar situation. We treat floods not as a problem of social systems, for instance in how to zone the flood plain, but in terms of physical systems—how to prevent floods. As a result, we have spent over four billion dollars in creating a high probability of major disasters in the next fifty years because we treat the river as a physical system and as an enemy at that instead of treating the river-man complex as a socio-physical system.

We can go down the line in almost all other fields of policy, whether it be agriculture policy, housing policy, transportation policy, social security, public assistance, and even the war against poverty, and we shall find that we are treating these problems without adequate information, without adequate research, and without an adequate conception of the social system within which the problem is set. There is a story running around about the man who said, "I hear there is a war against poverty, where do I surrender?" This illustrates the absurdity of treating poverty as an enemy to be fought instead of treating the abolition of poverty as a skill to be learned.

The case is even stronger when it comes to national defense and the international system. The fact that we have put the bulk of our intellectual resources into the development of weapons (some 60 percent of the research and development effort in this country goes into the military) has meant not only that we deprive the other areas of our society of problem-solving capacity but that even in the field of the international system itself, we have created a situation of fantastic and terribly dangerous insecurity. By contrast, we put practically nothing into the study of peace as a social system, we put extraordinarily little into the study of social change, or into the study of the learning process by which the views of the world and value systems change. Yet, these things are crucial to the operation of the international system and even in the relatively short run may be more important than weapons. Even without challenging the existing values, therefore, it is abundantly clear that our ability to do good either to ourselves or to the world is enormously hampered by our sheer ignorance of the social systems in which we operate. I would not suggest for a moment that this ignorance can be removed simply by spending money on social science. I do argue, however, that we are not farming this particular plot half as well or even a tenth as well as we know how to do it and that even the mere application of existing knowledge would make an enormous difference.

Even with this, however, I am not satisfied. It is not sufficient to leave existing values unchallenged. Any ethical system implies an orderly criticism of existing values. For my generation, at least, as I hinted earlier, Hitler destroyed ethical relativism, that Olympian stance from which we observe, "Some people eat their grandmothers and some don't; how interesting!"

We constantly find in the history of mankind that at some point or other somebody rears back and says, not merely, "These are my values," but "These ought to be your values." Such a challenge usually meets with some kind of response. It may be that the challenger's values are accepted—it may be that they are rejected. But, without this process of constant challenge and response in value systems the history of mankind is wholly inexplicable. We could not explain, for instance, the phenomenon of the rise of the great world religions, such as Christianity, Islam, or Buddhism, or even the rise of the secular faiths of communism or nationalism, without supposing a constant process of challenge to existing values and response to that challenge.

Even in our own times, we have seen such phenomena as the rise of social insurance and of progressive taxation, the rise of world organization, and the collapse of colonialism, which cannot possibly be explained except in terms of a response to a challenge to existing values. In part, it is true, this comes about as a result of a reappraisal of our image of the world of fact. Thus, the collapse of colonialism is certainly not unconnected with the gradual realization that, in the twentieth century at any rate, an empire is a burden rather than a benefit to the imperial power and that the way to get rich is to stay home and mind your own business well. Nevertheless, there has also been a profound change in basic values —a slow growth of a world integrative system and a sense of a community of mankind transcending nation and sect. Without understanding this, we cannot understand at all what is going on in the world.

This process of value change can be observed and studied just as any other element in the social system of which it is an essential part. This is not to say, of course, that we can find some simple "litmus paper" which will tell us by an easy formula whether any particular set of values is "right." All we can do is submit to a constant testing process of challenge-acceptance or challenge-rejecttion. If, however, we can find some patterns in this process, it should be possible to speed it up, or at least make it less costly. If there is any single ethical principle in this pattern, it is the principle of being willing to learn. Ignorance, that is an unrealistc view of the world, always leads eventually to disaster. If the disaster is not fatal, we can sometimes learn from it, as indeed the Japanese have learned an enormous amount from the Second World War and the United States learned a great deal from the great depression.

We are now faced, however, with possibly irretrievable disaster, and the question, therefore, whether we can learn without disaster has become acute. The method of science is the best weapon we know of learning without disaster, by testing directly our image of the world and constantly modifying this image in the light of the result of our testing. We can do this in social systems just as we can in physical systems, even though we may not be able to do it so accurately. It is the unwillingness to learn that leads to disaster, but how do we produce the will to learn?

Perhaps a partial answer to this question is found in another pattern which one detects in the slow development of an orderly, universal structure to the integrative system. The grants economy today is a crazy quilt of social security, private gifts, missions, foreign aid, United Nations special funds, and the like. It is the visible who receive grants, not the deserving. Some integrative systems, such as world communism, have turned out to be astonishingly weak. (The great unity of the working class turned out to be worth nothing when Russia had to decide between helping China and slowing down her own development.) The integrative system of science is astonishingly weak; chemists in rich countries do not tax themselves to build labs for chemists in poor countries, though scientists have tried to build lines of communication across national and ideological barriers, as in the Pugwash conferences. Even these however are financed by the generosity of non-scientists!

Religion is stronger than science as a grants economy, but even here when the chips are down, rich American Christians do not stint themselves much for the benefit of their fellow Christians in poor countries. (We would rather build fancy tax-exempt churches at home.) The other world religions have a negligibly small grants economy. The nation emerges as by far the strongest integrative system and the biggest organizer of grants, yet the nation is a unit so arbitrary—and so dangerous to mankind—that one wonders if its integrative power is not based on an illusion which will one day suddenly be found out. In all this, however, one can perhaps hope to perceive a pattern—the gradual emergence of the planetary view, the emergence of mankind as a structured integrative system where the near indeed are dear, but where the far are not altogether excluded from the great network of inclusive human concern and responsibility. And as we learn to love and to perceive the great pattern of mankind, so also we may learn to learn.

I find it a little depressing that Confucious saw most of what I have been trying to say with admirable clarity twenty-five hundred years ago. As he says in the *Analects*, "Love of goodness without the will to learn casts the shadow called foolishness; love of knowledge without the will to learn casts the shadow called insensibility; love of candor without the will to learn casts the shadow called rudeness; love of daring without the will to learn casts the shadow called turbulence; love of firmness without the will to learn casts the shadow called eccentricity." The shadows indeed are long shadows and in the words of the song that seems to haunt the younger generation, "When will they ever learn, when will they ever learn?"

But we do learn, however painfully and slowly, and in that lies the best hope of mankind for doing good to itself.

THE MENACE OF METHUSELAH: POSSIBLE CONSEQUENCES OF INCREASED LIFE EXPECTANCY

Jour. of the Wash. Acad. of Sci., 55, 7 (Oct. 1965): 171-179

The Menace of Methuselah: Possible Consequences of Increased Life Expectancy*

In the past ten years we have been witnessing an extraordinary explosion of biological knowledge. It seems not unreasonable to suppose, indeed, that in the field of biology we are now in the position corresponding to where we were in the field of nuclear energy in about 1900. We know that life has a code; we know that the building up of the body or the phenotype of various living organisms is done by information carriers; and we have a pretty fair idea what the code is. If past experience is any guide, this information should begin to result in profound practical results in a couple of generations. In 1900, we knew that nuclear energy existed, but we did not have the slightest idea as to how to tap it. Today we can almost say that we know the code of life; we just don't know how to write it. The possibility, however, of quite radical changes in our control over biological processes is something which every student of the future has to take into account.

One of the greatest mysteries of biological systems is aging. In the short run, the biological system is an open system, in von Bertalanffy's sense. That is, it consists of a structure which we might almost describe as a role structure, the role occupants of which are constantly changing. In the body of any organism, the particular atoms which comprise the body are continually changing; the structure, however, remains much the same, just as in a flame the atoms are continually moving from one zone to the other but the zones remain constant.

Flames do not age. They go out when they have no more fuel or when the environment is disturbed; but if fuel and oxygen are continually provided, there is no reason why a flame should not last forever. The flame, indeed, in many cultures has been a symbol of immortality. The body is likewise an open system, but it seems to have certain irreversible processes at work in it, which eventually change the nature of the system. Part of these processes are the processes of growth, the element in the biological organism which assures that we do not simply maintain the open system of the baby, but change this gradually to the adult. We really understand very little about this. It may be the same growth process that produces aging, which is a kind of negative growth, or it may be quite a different process. All we seem to have at the moment is a few speculations regarding the accumulation by irreversible processes of certain substances in the body, but at present we certainly don't know enough about aging to do anything about it. If indeed, however, as one suspects is the case, aging is built into the organism by its genetic information system, the possibilities of intercepting this information and changing it seem to open

* An address before the Washington Academy of Sciences on March 18, 1965.

up, even though the techniques of doing this are as inconceivable today as the techniques of nuclear energy were in 1900. It may be, of course, that this is a pipe dream, that some fatal Heisenberg Principle will be discovered which will deprive us of the opportunity of putting new information into the system; but at the moment, at any rate, there seems to be no nonexistence theorem to this effect, and the possibility of the discovery of the Fountain of Youth is perhaps just around the corner.

If the aging process were really understood and controlled, this would open up the possibility of an almost indefinite expansion of the human life span. Up to the present, all improvement in medicine has only enabled more people to live to be aged. The probability of living to be seventy is much greater today than it was a hundred years ago; the probability of living to be a hundred is no greater at all, and may even be less. Once we crack the aging barrier, however, there seems to be no reason why the process should not be slowed down indefinitely, and why man should not remain in full vigor for centuries. Bernard Shaw, with the uncanny insight of the artist, foreshadowed something like this in his "Back to Methuselah," though the methods which he proposed were more akin to Christian Science than to modern biology.

One caution must be added here, against undue hopes of immortality. Old age is by no means the only cause of death, and even though we have had remarkable success in eliminating causes of death in the young, we have not eliminated them completely. A particularly intractable cause of death which is not closely related to age is accidents; and even if we eliminated all causes of death except this, the existence of an accident rate would prevent the expectation of life from shooting off toward infinity. Indeed, at the present accident rate, even if all other causes of death were removed, the average expectation of life would probably not rise

much above two or three hundred years. Even this relatively modest extension, however, as we shall see, would create an enormous crisis.

All this, of course, is science fiction. In these days, however, one seems to have to read science fiction in order to keep up with the news. What is certain is that any major extension of the span of active human life would create a crisis for the human race almost beyond imagining. Even if there is the slightest possibility of such an event, we should begin to think about it now and to prepare ourselves for the totally new, wonderful, and terrifying world which this possibility opens up. What I am trying to do in this paper is little more than social science fiction. Our knowledge of social systems is still fairly primitive, and our knowledge of any system whatever beyond the limits of the variables which we have experienced is precarious. We do know enough about social systems, however, to be able to make at least speculative projections of these extreme values.

The essential problem arises because society has an age-specific role structure, and if the age distribution of the population does not correspond to the role structure, various tensions and difficulties arise. There is one role for the new-born baby, another for the ten-year-old, another for the teenager, another for the college student, another for the person of middle age, another for the aged. This is true of occupational roles; we do not expect a teenager to be a college president, or a grandfather to be an office boy. Age specificity is even more important in other roles. The five-year-old is most unlikely to be a parent, and it is a rare woman who gives birth to a child after the age of sixty. We expect children to play hopscotch; we do not expect elderly bankers to do the same. The one item of information which tells us more about anybody than anything else is the date of his birth. The age specificity of roles is not, of course, absolute. There is a certain amount of flexibility. Occasionally we find a man of thirty becoming a college president, or a child prodigy giving a concert, or a man of eighty becoming a father. For each role in society we may have perhaps a ten-year margin in regard to the age that can occupy it. Even when all allowance is made for this flexibility, however, the age specificity of roles is a limiting factor of enormous importance.

We are perceiving at the moment, especially in the tropical countries, a little foretaste of what a major upset in age distribution can bring about. In large parts of the tropical world, there was a drastic decline in infant mortality in the years around 1950, due mainly to the introduction of chemical insecticides and the subsequent control of malaria. In some countries in less than two years the infant death rate was halved. As a result we now find in many countries enormous cohorts of teenagers, almost twice as many as their somewhat elder brothers and sisters. The impact of this is only beginning to be felt in urban unemployment, juvenile delinquency, and the general disruption of these societies, and this is something which is likely to increase and become a world-wide problem in the next ten years, as these youngsters enter the labor market. The effects on traditional societies are going to be particularly disruptive. If twice the usual number of teenagers are seeking to enter the role structure of a traditional society, it is hard to see how it can avoid being blown to pieces. Either half the teenagers will have to be driven out of it into the cities, or there will be widespread disruption and maladjustment.

At the other end of the scale, we find that even the increase in the number of the aged has created severe social problems. In the ancient world, old age was a respectable and honorable role, mainly because so few people survived to it, and scarcity gave value. In the modern world, where almost everyone survives into his seventies, the aged become of little value to society, they have no clear role, they

become disorganized, they tend to be segregated, and old age begins to take on terrors which it did not have in an earlier society. I was struck when I was in Korea with the extraordinary serenity and beauty of the faces of the old people in the villages, by contrast with the anxiety, the striving after a false youthfulness, and the pathetic discontent of so many old people in our own society. In the traditional society, if you succeeded in living to be old, you had something to look forward to. In modern society it is so easy to live to be old that there is nothing much to look forward to, and this can easily have a disintegrating effect on the whole of life.

What might be called the traditional age-specific role structure in society has been developed over the course of human history to fit in with pre-scientific mortality tables. Even the relatively small changes in age distribution which have occurred in the present century have created severe problems. Imagine, then, the kind of problems which would be created if large numbers of people started to live to be a hundred and fifty or two hundred, or even five hundred. This would create a set of wholly unprecedented problems, simply because the age-specific role structure would be unable to adjust fast enough to correspond to the age distribution. It would create problems not only for the old but for the young, because of the fact that it is not the absolute age structure which matters so much as the relative age structure, that is, the proportion of people of different ages. In a society in which everyone lives to be seventy, the equilibrium proportion of children and young people up to adolescence is about a quarter of the total population. In a society in which everybody lives to be a hundred and eighty, this would fall to a tenth of the population. If we can imagine a society in which the average age of death is a thousand, only one percent of the population in equilibrium would be under the age of ten. Formal education, assuming that this ended in the twenties as it does now, would be a very small part of the total human enterprise, and it is almost inconceivable for us to imagine a set of age-specific roles which would correspond to such longevity.

On the positive side of the picture, one may point to the fact that while longevity would create enormous problems, it would also increase the power of the human race, one would hope, to deal with these problems. In terms of simple economics, economic development is impossible if the average age at death is below a certain figure, at a guess about thirty. Under these circumstances, half the population is under the age of fifteen, the working force is a small fraction of the population, and the sheer requirements of transmitting the culture from such a small adult population to such a large child population are so great that there is nothing left over for growth, development, and change. An absolutely necesary prerequisite for economic development is an increase in the average age at death, and one suspects that this was a major factor in the extraordinary and apparently irreversible development which followed the invention of agriculture and the domestication of plants and animals. The difference between the average age at death of Paleolithic and Neolithic man may not have been more than five or ten years, but this small margin was enough to insure that Paleolithic man, in effect, stagnated for an inconceivable length of time. The moment man entered the Neolithic, he began an irreversible and accelerating process of development, simply because he now lived long enough, thanks to more secure and adequate food supplies, so that he did not have to spend all his time and energy in simply transmitting his culture to the next generation. A substantial increase in longevity, such as we are contemplating here, would release even more resources for growth and development, assuming, of course, as I am

doing throughout, that the increase in longevity is accomplished without any substantial impairment of the physical or mental powers.

Let us now take a brief glimpse at some of the organizations and institutions of society which are likely to be affected by a substantial increase in longevity— let us say, modestly, to two hundred years. The first of these is obviously the family. A substantial increase in longevity would correspondingly reduce the childbearing and child-raising function of the family. If the population is eventually to reach equilibrium, each couple will not be able to average much more than two children. One can imagine, therefore, a couple marrying, say, in the twenties, having all their children raised and independent by the time they are fifty, and then enjoying say a hundred and fifty years more of childless married life. It would be surprising if this did not produce some strains, especially if sexual activity remained unimpaired for most of this period. It would not be surprising to see the development of new forms of household arrangements, for instance joint families on the Oneida Community plan, or even a rise in monasticism, or perhaps a retreat to the desert and the hermits' caves. One certainly wonders what will happen to the sense of kinship, even with a stationary population. By the time a man gets to be two hundred, he will have quite a lot of descendants, and how interested he will remain in his great-great-great-great-great-grandchildren is a little hard to predict. The economics of the family certainly changes somewhat under this kind of structure. Inheritance will become a relatively unimportant aspect of income redistribution, and any great expectations will indeed be long deferred. Wages and salaries are likely to be the only form of income which will be adequate to support most persons, though the pattern of retirement on the death of one's parents would probably become the dominant model, as it would only be very late in life, say at about a hundred and seventy-five, that anything would be inherited.

The effect on other organizations, such as businesses, universities, or government departments, of a substantial increase in longevity, would be even more drastic than on the family. In the family, at least, the main difference in reorganization would be over fairly early, and after that the reaction would be optional. In the case of the organization, there is a much more age-specific role structure, with each level of the hierarchy corresponding roughly to a certain age group. It is even written in the American Constitution that the President must be over thirty-five. Because of the fact that income, status, and responsibility usually rise with age, an individual can make economic progress even if the society does not. The rate at which his income and status are likely to increase, however, depends on the age distribution. There are always fewer roles in the higher levels of a hierarchy than in the lower levels. If the mortality at each age was such that the number of survivors at each age group corresponded to the number of places in the hierarchy, everyone who survived would be automatically promoted, and those who don't survive presumably don't mind. Even the present decline in mortality in middle age has created real problems, as now there are far more individuals in each age group than there are positions in the hierarchy which correspond to the age group. If everybody lives to be seventy, there may be only one position at the top of the hierarchy which is appropriate for the age, and a very large number of frustrated and disappointed seventy-year-olds will be found at the lower levels.

An increase in longevity, to say two hundred, would accentuate this problem enormously. The average rate of rise of income and status is likely to be lower, the greater the average age at death. If the average age at death is two hundred, the rate of rise in income and status per-

haps for the first hundred years of life will be almost negligible, and the prospect of being an assistant professor for a hundred and fifty years might daunt the most enthusiastic of academics. It is the propensity of the old, rich, and powerful to die that gives the young, poor, and powerless, hope. When death is postponed, so is promotion. This will unquestionably introduce enormous psychological strains, which might well threaten the functioning of large hierarchical organizations.

The effect on the educational system would not be confined to the general effect on organizations. Knowledge tends to grow at such a rate that a professor easily finds himself obsolete even in his fifties, and certainly the Ph.D. could hardly be regarded as a union card for university teaching for a hundred and seventy-five years, again assuming that intellectual vigor was unimpaired with age. The contrast between the distinguished and the undistinguished would be enormously accentuated. Imagine the universities today scrambling for Adam Smith and Ricardo, still in their prime at the age of two hundred or so.

In a society of Methuselahs, formal education would become a very small part of human activity. In some ways, this might be desirable. As scarcity develops value, the scarcity of children and young people would make them highly valuable to society, and a great deal would be put into their education. It would almost certainly happen, for instance, that formal education would be extended many years beyond what it is now. We might very well expect it to go on for forty or fifty years if the life span increased to two hundred. Whether this would really increase the competence of the human race is a nice point on which I would not venture an answer.

The impact on savings, insurance, pension plans, and indeed economic life in general would certainly be drastic. The consumption function in any society is highly dependent on the age distribution.

By and large, the young and the old consume more than they produce and those in middle life produce more than they consume. If the proportion, both of the young and of the unproductive old, is small, with the present psychology at least, the consumption function is likely to be very low. Unless, therefore, there are deliberate attempts to offset this in the form of government expenditures or budget deficits, there is very likely to be a chronic state of deficient demand and unemployment. A man who lives to be two hundred would be able to accumulate enormous amounts of capital by saving a relatively small proportion of his income each year. Suppose, for instance, he were saving on the usual kind of pension plan, by which he saved, say 10 percent of his income; and suppose his income averages $10,000 a year. In a working life of two hundred years, with interest at 5 percent, he would accumulate $358,000,000. Even if the rate of interest were only a modest 1 percent, he would still accumulate $145,000. If there were only a few Methuselahs in a society, and if they had an inclination towards thrift, it would not be long before they had gathered unto themselves most of the wealth of the economy. Indeed, this problem is not unknown. In the Middle Ages, the church and its constituent bodies operated as Methuselahs, a monastery, for instance, being theoretically immortal; and in many countries the church did in fact acquire so much of the wealth that it was eventually dispossessed. In Swift's wonderful chapter on the Struldbrugs in *Gulliver's Travels*, which is the first, and still the best, essay on this "copious and delightful" subject, as Swift calls it, he says, ". . . if it had been my good fortune to come into the world a *struldbrug*, as soon as I could discover my own happiness, by understanding the difference between life and death, I would first resolve, by all arts and methods whatever, to procure myself riches. In the pursuit of which, by thrift and management, I might reasonably expect, in about

two hundred years, to be the wealthiest man in the kingdom." What would happen if all the other struldbrugs had the same ambition is not altogether clear.

The impact of longevity on saving and interest rates raises problems of economic motivation which have haunted economics for a long time. Let us take first a simple but quite unrealistic assumption, that a person saves during his working life in order to equalize his consumption in all the years of his life, including the years of retirement when he has no income. Let us suppose, then, that the individual has fifteen years of retirement without income. The following table shows what proportion of his income in each year of his working life he must save in order to provide for his retirement, leaving no net worth at the end, with various rates of interest. We see, for instance, that with a working life of fifty years at 5 percent per annum rate of interest, we need to save 4.7 percent of our income in order to provide for our old age. If the working life is 185 years, we need only save $1 in $10,000. Saving for old age, of course, is not the only motivation for saving, and indeed in an equilibrium population, saving of this kind would result in no net saving at all, as the dis-saving of the old would exactly offset the saving of those in middle life. However, the fact that in a population of Methuselahs a very large proportion of the population would in fact be in middle life and of working age means that in a market society it would be very easy to run into an under-consumption problem, and every effort would have to be made to diminish saving and see that people spent almost up to the hilt of their income.

The effect on interest rates is somewhat problematical, and indeed merely to pose the problem reveals the extraordinary deficiencies of economics in this respect. High interest rates are in a sense a subsidy for thrift, and in a world of Methuselahs, this subsidy could become very large at interest rates which are common today, as we see, for instance, by the fact that a difference in interest rates between 1 percent and 5 percent changes the lifetime accumulation of our decumulations, and inheritance. In the absence of any explicit model of the problem, however, we can only guess at the answer.

Table 1. Proportion of Income That Must be Saved to Provide for a Retirement Period of 15 Years

Rate of interest (% per annum)	0	1	2	3	4	5
Percentage income saved in working years:						
(1) Working life = 50 years	23.1	18.3	13.2	9.6	6.8	4.7
(2) Working life = 185 years	7.5	2.6	0.7	0.2	0.03	0.012

(Note: if n is the number of years lived after starting work, and s the number of years of retirement, n-s being the working life span, and i the rate of interest, the proportion of income saved in each year of working life, assuming constant income, is $a = [(1+i)^s - 1]/[(1+i)^n - 1]$.)

Methuselah above from a modest and reasonable $145,000 to an absurd $358,-000,000. It seems almost certain that if the redistributional effects of different capacities for thrift and different inheritance patterns are not to be intolerable, rates of interest would have to fall at least to the neighborhood of 1 percent and below.

The impact of longevity on the distribution of property is again a problem of enormous interest, but one which at the moment economists seem to have no apparatus to solve. It is an astonishing tribute, indeed, to the extent to which we take the average length of human life for granted, that we never work it in as an explicit variable in our models. Death is like bankruptcy; it breaks up an existing gestalt of assets which are bound together by the person, and the component parts of a divided inheritance almost certainly do not grow as fast as the asset complex did before death broke it up, especially, of course, where the deceased himself was an important element in the asset complex. In a world of Methuselahs, this event would be much rarer, hence one suspects that there would be much less redistribution from the rich to the poor in the natural course of accumulations,

All these considerations suggest that longevity is likely to present a much more serious problem for a market economy than, for instance, automation presents, when it comes to maintaining full employment on the one hand and maintaining a distribution of property which is reasonably equitable on the other. It is by no means impossible that a serious extension of longevity would make market economies quite unmanageable and unstable and that the degree of centralized planning and control would have to increase. This might be all too acceptable to the Methuselahs themselves, if there were not too many of them, who would certainly be in an admirable position to dominate all the positions of power, both political and economic, in the society. This might lead either to a stable subordination for the non-Methuselahs, or there might be revolutions, and a certain equilibrium in the length of human life might assert itself through violence.

The short-run dynamic effects might be very different from the long-run, depending very much on how the increase in longevity came about. We might suppose, for instance, as the extreme case, that the treatment for longevity was very easy and could be given to everybody, so that

almost literally, death would take a holi-
day for, say, a hundred or two hundred
years. This would be a black day for the
morticians. Furthermore, it would completely upset all existing contractual arrangements regarding pensions and an-
nuities, which are calculated, of course,
on what we think of as a normal life
table. All existing pension plans would
soon be bankrupted; old age and survivors' insurance would soon gobble up the
whole national budget; and there would
have to be a general moratorium on earlier contractual agreements. The problem
could easily be solved, of course, by
simply raising the age at which retirement
began and pension benefits were paid.
The sellers of life insurance, of course,
would enjoy a corresponding capital gain,
and this again would probably be adjusted by the renegotiation of contracts.
While there would be many difficult
technical problems involved in all this,
there seems nothing in the nature of the
case to make these problems insoluble.

If longevity is costly and can only be
given to a few people, a political problem
of some magnitude would almost certainly
arise. Is longevity a civil right? Is it an
economic good, to be appropriated by the
wealthy? Is it to go to the politically
deserving? Is it to be allocated according
to some eugenic test? These are problems
which we may be thankful we do not have
to face at the moment. The only thing
which I can think of which would make a
greater political upset is weather control,
which would almost certainly create political and legal problems quite beyond
our ability to manage.

Finally, one wonders what longevity
would do to the human condition and to
the stock of knowledge, wisdom, and
competence which is the most important
stock of the human race. If we are to
believe Bernard Shaw, we must go back
to Methuselah before the human race can
hope to better its condition, simply because, in the Pennsylvania Dutch proverb,
we get "too soon oldt and too late

schmardt." If we envisage the human
organism growing in experience and
knowledge while maintaining its health
and vigor for much longer periods of
time than it does now, the predictions of
Bernard Shaw might come true. It is certainly true that death causes an enormous
wastage and depreciation of human
knowledge, which has to be replaced
painfully and expensively in each generation. It is a somewhat frightening thought
that the whole mass of human culture is
totally lost every seventy years or there-
abouts, and has to be replaced by education and experience in that period. This
may easily put a very sharp limitation on
the total amount of knowledge that the
human race can acquire, unless there is
indeed an increase in longevity.

On the other hand, we may easily run
into the problem of the inhibiting effect
of old knowledge on the acquisition of
new. The unlearning that must often be
done if new knowledge is to be acquired
seems to be more difficult than the acquisition of the knowledge itself. The
great virtue of the institution of death is
that this is a way of unlearning, painfully
drastic, but effective from the point of
view of society. If, as Will Rogers is
supposed to have said, "The trouble with
people isn't what they don't know, it's
what they do know that ain't so," the
possibility of lifetimes of two hundred
years—or more—applied in the acquisition of negative knowledge is a little
frightening. Certainly the rate of social
evolution might easily be slowed up
rather than advanced by the possession
of such an enormous dead weight of experience. It may be, of course, that along
with the kinds of knowledge which will
be necessary to produce genuine longevity
we may also crack the problem of the
obstacles to learning, and learning drugs
may be as common as aspirin or DDT.
Still, one shudders a little to contemplate
the possibilities of organizational rigidity
which might be introduced if there were
no powerful people in a society under the

age of two hundred. Under these circumstances, youth might easily despair of ever rising to positions of power, and would dissipate its freshness and energy in folly and riotous living.

At the other end of the scale, there is Swift's hideous vision of the Struldbrugs.* Suppose longevity did not go along with the increase of knowledge and wisdom, but with a slow and progressive moral and mental decay. Under these circumstances, of course, it is improbable that we would encourage it or permit it. Nevertheless, the taste for life is so strong that if life were for sale, many would unquestionably buy it. One can perhaps visualize the extreme case in which longevity passes into immortality. The church has promised immortality for a long time. It is probably fortunate, for it and for us, that the promise has been cashed only

in hope. If you could have an operation for immortality, would you have it? How much would you pay for it? This frightening prospect now at least seems to be somewhere over the horizon. Under these circumstances, the business of departing from life would have to be a voluntary act, and we would at least begin to appreciate the enormous benefits which the institution of death has brought to mankind.

----

* "They were the most mortifying sight I ever beheld; and the women were more horrible than the men. Besides the usual deformities in extreme old age, they acquired an additional ghastliness, in proportion to their number of years, which is not to be described; and among half a dozen I soon distinguished which was the eldest, although there was not about a century or two between them." Jonathan Swift, *Gulliver's Travels*, Part Three, Chapter X (page 213 of Pocket edition, New York, 1939).

SOCIAL SCIENCES

In: *The Great Ideas Today,* R. M. Hutchins and M. J. Adler, eds. Chicago: Encyclopedia Britannica, 1965, pp. 255-284

SOCIAL SCIENCES

The year 1965 marks the twentieth year since the end of World War II. It is also the occasion of the fifth annual edition of *The Great Ideas Today*. Thus the time is ripe for taking a long and broad view of the social sciences. Therefore, instead of confining myself rather narrowly to the most recent developments in the field, as my predecessors in this review have done, I propose to attack the somewhat larger problem of the impact of the social sciences on society. In the course of doing this, I shall also have occasion to comment upon their latest developments.

Understanding of both the impact and the development of the social sciences requires some understanding of the methods that these sciences employ. These methods can be studied most clearly and briefly in the statistical images and the theoretical models which the social scientist constructs. In dealing with these subjects, in the first two sections of my review, I shall draw my illustrations from economics, which is the field I know best. I shall then be in a position to consider the impact of the social sciences as a whole upon public policy and recent work that is being done, especially in political science and economics. I shall conclude with a brief consideration of future developments for the social sciences.

The product of scientific activity is increase in knowledge, that is, a change in man's image of his universe which brings it closer to reality, whatever we mean by that. As we do not know absolutely what reality is, we can never be absolutely sure that any particular change in man's image of the world is, in fact, an increase in knowledge. The principal value of the scientific method is that it is a certain defense against error insofar as it produces images that are testable, and by the successive elimination of error we may hope that we are approaching truth.

The social sciences are seeking knowledge about society, that is, about social systems. A social system may be defined as any pattern of events that involves the interaction of two or more persons. The study of the internal constitution and behavior of persons, with which psychology is principally engaged, is, of course, an essential prerequisite to the study of social systems, and there is clearly a continuum between, say, physiology at one end of the scale and sociology at the other, within which any boundary that we draw to define the social sciences will be somewhat arbitrary.

Insofar as the social sciences change our images of social systems, they will also change our behavior and, hence, the social systems themselves. The social system does not, as it were, "stay put" while we investigate it. It changes, sometimes profoundly, under the impact of our investigation. The social scientist, therefore, unlike the physical scientist, cannot regard himself as a detached outside observer of nature but must regard himself as part of the system that he is studying.

Man's image of himself and his society has always been the most important determinant of his behavior. We might distinguish three kinds of these images: folk images, philosophical images, and scientific images. Folk images are those created and possessed by ordinary people as a result of their ordinary experience. These serve to direct a great deal of human behavior, even among philosophers and scientists. Our images of our friends and neighbors, our behavior in the street and store and even, to a considerable extent, at work, are determined by our folk images. A child growing up in the family learns to distinguish persons, learns to identify them and respond to each differently, learns how to behave in certain situations, such as at mealtimes or in a quarrel or in the bathroom, and he does this by the process of generalization or induction from his personal experience. He projects what he has experienced in the past into the future, and he lives almost wholly in a world of what William Blake calls "minute particulars."

Philosophical images go beyond the immediate experience and generalize through reflection, meditation, poetic insights, and intuition to things beyond personal experience and even to society as a whole. There are philosophical aspects to folk knowledge, as, for instance, the learning of prejudice, stereotypes, ethnocentrism, or ideological biases. At its best, however, philosophical inquiry produces "wisdom" which distills, as it were, the experience of many men, many societies, into general propositions. Unfortunately, it is the plausibility rather than the testability of propositions which leads to their survival in philosophical discourse. Great ideas, however, such as sovereignty, freedom, responsibility, legitimacy, consensus, democracy, have enlivened men's images of their social world and have had a profound influence on their behavior.

Scientific images of society are those that are testable and that can be disproved through testing. The complaint is sometimes raised that scientific images of social systems are rather trivial and not very interesting, simply because it is precisely the important concepts that cannot be tested and hence have to be classified as philosophical. There is some truth in this, for the testing of images in social systems is very difficult because of the complexity and uncertainties of the system involved. The complexity can be visualized by reflecting on the complexity of the person himself, with his ten billion neurons, and considering that a social system is the interaction of perhaps hundreds of millions of persons. The uncertainty arises partly because of random elements in social systems themselves, which cannot be predicted. The problem of gaining knowledge about a system with mixed nonrandom and random elements is very difficult, as the random elements upset our predictions of the future and also prevent us from making secure generalizations about the past, simply because we do not know how much of the past has been random.

Even in folk knowledge and the common sense of daily life, we learn to distinguish the random from the nonrandom elements in the sequence of events. If, for instance, a man's wife flies into a rage at breakfast one morning, he does not necessarily conclude that she has ceased to love him. It may just be that she had a bad night or ate something that disagreed with her. In any human relationship, there are strong nonrandom elements of stability in the image that we each have of the other and the image that we each have of the nature of the relationship. A marital relationship, for instance, has very strong nonrandom elements in it and, if it is successful, exhibits powerful forces toward equilibrium. If events that seem to contradict this equilibrium image are interpreted as random, the image itself is not much disturbed by them.

How do we know, however, whether an event is random or not? There seems to be no easy answer to this question. If we interpret random events as nonrandom, we will build into our image of the system an order that it does not possess. The human mind has enough of a "rage for order," as Austin Warren calls it, so that we have a powerful urge to "make sense," that is, impose order, on what are, in fact, random events, or, at least, random events from the point of view of some other observer. Alexander Bavelas, a social psychologist at Stanford University, has reported orally on an experiment in which he gave to a number of subjects sets of random data—random, that is, from the experimenter's point of view—and asked them to find the rule in them. Almost without exception, the subjects were able to find rules and order in the random data given them; and what is more, when they were informed after the experiment that there were, in fact, no rules, they became quite angry and insisted that the rules that they thought they had discovered must, in fact, be true. At the other end of the scale, it is also possible to interpret an event that is not random but part of a pattern as, in fact, random and insignificant, and then we are also likely to get into trouble.

If our image of the social system has a self-confirming quality, we are in still more trouble. A young man goes to a new job, for instance, and has three or four rather unpleasant experiences in rapid succession, each of which is, in fact, quite accidental. He forms an unfavorable estimate of the job situation, of his workmates, or his employer, and, as a result, he himself behaves in such a way as to confirm his unfavorable image. We must not, of course, press this principle too far. Self-confirming images are apt to operate only over short periods, and in most social systems there are more or less objective realities which eventually impose themselves on the situation. Still, we cannot exclude the possibility that a succession of random events interpreted as a system may easily have profound and long-run effects. We may perhaps here use an analogy from the physical world. A drop of water falling on a watershed will have a profoundly different history depending on whether a random puff of wind may blow it to one side or the other. On one side of the Continental Divide, for instance, it goes to the Pacific, on the other side, to the Gulf and the Atlantic. It is hardly possible to exclude the possibility that there are watershed systems and watershed points in the history either of a person or a society. Shakespeare's insight here is profound: "There is a tide in the affairs of men which, taken at the flood, leads on to fortune; omitted, all the voyage of their life is bound in shallows and in miseries" (*Julius Caesar*, Act IV, scene 3).

STATISTICAL IMAGES

Perhaps the most important contribution of the social sciences to the development of accurate images of complicated systems is the creation of what might be called "statistical images." There are two problems involved in the development of accurate images. One is the sampling problem, and the other is the problem of condensing, or indexing, large masses of information. The information output from any large system is always much more than any observer can possibly handle. If we try to take it all in, we will experience nothing but noise. Information always has to be filtered to produce knowledge. Thus, to make any sense out of the babble of conversation at a cocktail party, we must confine our attention to only one speaker and filter out all the rest. Or, to give another example, we can imagine the total confusion that would result if we were tuned in to all the radio waves that are passing through the room at the moment. The problem of sampling is how to set up an information filter with the least possible bias. If, for instance, we rely on neighborhood gossip for our information, we have a bias built into the information filter. We only get information through certain channels; other channels we neglect, and the channels that we select may easily have a bias in favor of scandal. Similarly, our information about other countries or other classes is heavily filtered in a way that tends to cut out information favorable to our opponents or to those who are different from us, and unfavorable to us.

In order to guard themselves against bias in sampling, statisticians have developed an elaborate technique for sampling information on a random basis. This is essentially the method of survey research. Here we have to be careful that we are taking the sample from a universe which is itself significant. If, for instance, we are sampling people to find their political views, it is not satisfactory to take the telephone directory as the universe from which to draw our sample, no matter how random the method by which we draw names from it, simply because people who have telephones constitute a biased sample of the whole population. They tend to be richer, for instance, or more involved with society than those who do not have telephones. A classic example of the failure of telephone sampling was the sad story of the *Literary Digest* in 1936, which had confidently predicted a Republican victory on the basis of a postcard poll, with names taken largely from telephone books. In the last twenty-five years the technique of sampling has developed to the point where a surprisingly small sample of a population can give us a considerable amount of reasonably accurate information about the whole. The Institute for Social Research at the University of Michigan, for instance, operates with national samples of only a few thousand people. This may be only one out of fifty or a hundred thousand of the total population of the United States, yet because of the care with which the samples are drawn, they produce surprisingly accurate results, as judged, for instance, by elections and censuses in which the samples are followed by counts involving whole populations or very large samples.

Two techniques have contributed greatly to the development of sampling in the last generation. One is the development of the method of area sampling, whereby people are selected for a sample according to their randomly selected location. This insures that it is the whole population that is sampled. Another important development is that of stratified sampling, by which members of the sample are selected according to a set of known distributions in the population. If we know, for instance, that only 10 percent of the population has incomes above $15,000, then only 10 percent of the members of the sample should have incomes above $15,000. An advantage of stratified sampling is that certain groups may be oversampled if there is special interest in more accurate information from these segments of a society, or if, for instance, these groups are such a small proportion of the total population that they might be missed in a completely random sample. Because we are sampling these subpopulations in a random way, we can correct in the overall estimates for any oversampling.

Once we have collected information from a sample, the next problem is how to condense it. How, for instance, do we extract the essential information from, say, three thousand long questionnaires? At this point the advantage of quantification—that is, the reduction of information to numerical form—becomes evident. The great advantage of numbers is that they can be added, subtracted, multiplied, and divided; and consequently, once information is expressed in the form of numbers, it is fairly easy to condense it into aggregates or averages. It is also possible to go one stage further and express the information in the form of a distribution, which tells us, for instance, what proportion of the population will fall below a given level of some numerical indicator.

A good example of the processes involved can be found in economic statistics. The gross national product is a concept now so familiar, even in political discourse, that it seems hard to realize that it was virtually unknown until the 1920's. Official data for the United States have only been available since 1929, and the "GNP," as it is familiarly called, only entered into the language of ordinary political discourse after World War II. The gross national product is the aggregate value in dollar terms of the total output of goods and services of an economy, compiled so as to avoid most double counting. For instance, we do not count the wheat and the flour as well as the bread: the value of the flour and the wheat is all supposed to appear in the value of the bread which it makes. There are some considerable difficulties in the concept as it is usually followed. Some of the activities of government, for instance, should probably be excluded and some of the activities of housewives included, but these criticisms aside, the concept has turned out to be extraordinarily useful in estimating not only the overall condition but the rate of change in the economy as a whole. The single number which results from this large process of aggregation (say the $622.3 billion that was estimated for 1964) summarizes an enormous mass of information. The gross national product in real terms consists not of a homogeneous sum of dollars but of an enormous heterogeneous mass of shoes and ships and sealing wax, of literally millions of goods and services of all kinds. Because, however, these goods and services are priced, or at least capable of being priced, we can express them all in terms of dollars, and we can add up the dollars into a total. If the gross national product rises, say from $583.9 billion in 1963 to $622.3 billion in 1964, we can be pretty sure that *something* has "risen," even though these two figures may hide a substantial change in the structure of output, with some things rising much more than others and some things even falling. If it is measured in constant prices and rises (in 1964 prices) from $595.3 billion in 1963 to $622.3 billion in 1964, we can be even more sure that some real total has risen.

Another statistical index, or family of indices, which is very useful, is that of the price level. This is in one sense an average of an enormous list of prices, or it can also be thought of as a ratio of aggregates, that is, the ratio of the total amount of money spent for things divided by a measure of the quantity of things bought. If the price level index rises, say from 100 to 120, we are again pretty sure that something has happened, and we are pretty sure of the direction, even though this information is condensed from an enormous list of prices, some of which have risen and some of which may even have fallen. There is a certain arbitrary element in the construction of an index of this kind, which cannot be avoided. If we are comparing two price lists in which some prices have risen and some prices have fallen, an index that weights heavily the prices that have risen and lightly those that have fallen will show a larger increase in the overall price level than an index that weights lightly the prices that have risen and heavily those that have fallen. It is even possible that two different indices constructed from the same two price lists may move in different directions; that is, one index may indicate that prices rose in a certain period and another index constructed from exactly the same data may indicate that prices fell. This is a difficulty, however, that is inherent in the fact that we are abstracting a small amount of highly significant information from a large information mass.

Once we have condensed a large mass of information into an aggregate or average, it is usually highly desirable to go back to what we have thrown away in the process of getting the condensed figure, and to examine the structures and distributions that exist within the aggregates and averages. Thus, in the case of the gross national product, we may wish to know its industrial composition, that is, how much was contributed by agriculture, by the defense industry, and so on. We are also interested in the distribution of income, that is, how are the claims on the total product divided among the population, and so on. Many different distributions of any given aggregate are possible, and it is usually a matter of judgment as to which are the most interesting and significant.

Demographic statistics give another example of the same problem of gain in significance but loss in information, in the course of aggregation and statistical manipulation. The most obvious demographic aggregate is the total population itself, and this is a figure of great interest. If we are told, for instance, that the United States has 185,000,000 persons, that China has 700,000,000, and that Iceland has 100,000, this tells us a good deal about these three countries. Two countries can have the same aggregate populations, however, and the significance of this number can be very different. In constructing an aggregate of population, we count each person—whatever his age, sex, income, occupation, level of literacy, religion, and so on—as one and one only, and the information thus obtained is valuable. However, we always want to go on to find out more about the population and especially its distributions. We want to break down the aggregate into a large number of subsets, for instance by age, sex, occupation, marital status, and a large number of other ways in which individuals differ from each other and are not merely counted as one. In a similar way we can see that a figure like crude birth and death rates is very useful and tells us a good deal. On the other hand, if we really want to appreciate its significance, we need to know, for instance, the age-specific birth rates (that is, how many children are born to women of different ages), and we need to know also the age-specific death rates (that is, the distribution of the total deaths by the age at death). For some purposes we may want to know the kind of families people are born into, and we may even be interested in the genetic aspects of the population: what, for instance, is the proportion of deficient children among those born.

It must be emphasized that while quantification is an enormous aid in the systematic condensation and indexing of large masses of information, it always involves a substantial loss of information, and some of the information lost is likely to be important. What this means is that quantitative information is not adequate to carry its own message. It always has to be interpreted, even if sometimes that interpretation is fairly obvious. The hoary jest that "figgers can't lie, but liars can figger" has an element of truth in it. It is very easy to use statistics in a misleading and propagandistic way, and no matter how they are used, they always have to be interpreted in terms of some frame of reference, that is, some larger image or model of the social system. Sociologist Amitai Etzioni has called attention very delightfully to what he calls the "Fully-Only" principle. We can take the same statistic, for instance that 10 percent of the people take a certain view, and we can express this by saying that "only" 10 percent take this view, or that "fully" 10 percent take this view. The inferences that we draw in the two cases are very different: one, that this 10 percent is unimportant, and in the second case, that this 10 percent is important. Any given figure, therefore, has to be the raw material for interpretation in a larger framework. Before the numerical image can be meaningful, there has to be a theoretical image, or at least some kind of model, that will indicate the significance of the figures.

THEORETICAL MODELS

The simplest model here is that which relates the figures to some norm, or normal value. If I say, for instance, that the rate of growth of the United States national product in the last fifteen years has been "only" 2 percent per annum, the inference is that it ought to have been larger, that 2 percent is dangerously low. If I say it has been "fully" 2 percent per annum, the inference is that this is quite satisfactory, even perhaps a bit too large.

The impact on society of the development, both of statistical images and of more sophisticated models of society, by which these images may be interpreted, can hardly be exaggerated. Every great advance in knowledge seems to have been the product of two different movements: one an improvement in measurement and observation, that is, essentially an improvement in statistical images, and the other an improvement in the model by which these images are interpreted. These two movements act and react on each other in a complex way, so that it is usually quite impossible to say which came first. Take, for instance, the so-called Copernican Revolution in astronomy, even more as it was later developed by Kepler and Newton into Newtonian celestial mechanics. This depended first of all on a profound restructuring of the model of the solar system from the earth-centered model to the sun-centered model and later from circular orbits to elliptical orbits; but it involved, also, a substantial improvement in the measurement of the positions of the planets, a movement which was begun before the invention of the telescope, for instance by Tycho Brahe, but was fully confirmed by the development of the telescope, which permitted much more accurate quantitative information about the solar system than had ever been possessed before.[1]

Similarly, what is sometimes called the Keynesian Revolution in economics[2] depends on a combination of a substantial improvement in the quantitative information about the economic system as a result of the development of sample surveys and national income statistics, coupled with an important reformulation of the fundamental theoretical model of the economic system itself. The essence of the change was not unlike the Copernican Revolution. Just as this represented a profound shift of perspective from a man-centered view of the universe to an abstract, system-oriented view, so the Keynesian Revolution represents a shift from the perspective of economic life as seen from personal experience to a system-oriented point of view that looks at the system as a whole. Thus, suppose we take the propositions which are central to the Keynesian analysis, that, first, from the point of view of a closed society, income and expenditure are exactly the same thing, and also that saving and investment are exactly the same thing. From the point of view of an individual, these propositions are not true at all. An individual can spend more than he gets or get more than he spends. He can save, that is, increase his net worth, without investing, that is, without increasing his holdings of real assets, simply by accumulating money or debts. Similarly, he can invest without saving if he simply draws down his cash and increases his real assets. For a society as a whole, however, every expenditure is simply one end of a transaction of which the other end is a receipt. The total of

1 Full documentation of the Copernican Revolution is contained in GBWW. The relevant texts are most readily found by consulting the *Syntopicon* under ASTRONOMY 2*b*.

2 John Maynard (later, Lord) Keynes' greatest book is his *General Theory of Employment, Interest and Money* (Harcourt, Brace and Co., 1936).

expenditures and total of receipts, therefore, are exactly the same thing. Similarly, in the absence of creation of money or national debt, the increase in the net worth of all private persons, that is, the total volume of saving, must be equal to the value of the increase of capital, which is the total volume of investment, as these are simply different ways of looking at the same thing.

The moment we make this shift from the person-oriented view to the system-oriented view of the economy, something becomes immediately clear which had been extraordinarily difficult to perceive before. The identity of savings and investment can also be expressed as an identity between the total output of a society (Y) and the sum of what is consumed (C) and accumulated (A), that is, $Y = C + A$. All this means is that everything that is produced in a given period either is consumed or it is still around and represents an addition to stocks. If we write this identity in the form $A = Y - C$, we have the identity of investment, that is, accumulation (A), with saving, which is income minus consumption. It then becomes apparent that *if* at any given level of aggregate output, the sum of consumption and what might be called willing accumulation is insufficient, that is, less than the aggregate output itself, there will be unwilling accumulations and the main impact of these is to reduce employment and total output. Under these circumstances total output will fall; as it falls, however, consumption falls again along with it, and the willingness to accumulate may likewise fall. Under these circumstances we get the familiar vicious spiral of depression, which may lead to an underemployment equilibrium, at which the society is not operating at its full capacity simply because it is not able to absorb in consumption and willing accumulation the output that it would produce at full capacity.

This was the condition of the Western world during the 1930's, and it seemed at that time to those who still thought of the economic system in essentially individual-centered terms to be an utterly inexplicable decay. The Keynesian theory gave a rough explanation of this decay and indicated the remedy. Consumption depends not so much on the total product itself as on what we call disposable income, which roughly is income after taxes. For any given level of output, therefore, lower taxes mean higher consumption, and higher consumption increases the willingness to accumulate. It may be possible also to increase the willingness to accumulate directly through manipulating the rate of interest and the loan market. To put the matter in another way, if the desire on the part of a society to save is too great relative to its existing investment opportunities, the opportunity to save can be given by increasing the national debt, which represents assets, that is, government securities, to the public.

The national debt exhibits perhaps better than anything else the contrast between what might be called the folk image of the economy and the scientific image. In the eyes of the folk image, debt is unqualifiedly bad, and it should be diminished at almost any cost. From the point of view of an individual, a debt is simply a liability. From the point of view of society as a whole, however, every debt is both a liability to one party and an asset to another. Similarly, the national debt, which is a liability to the government, is an asset to the people who hold it. Manipulating the national debt, therefore, which can be done indirectly by changing the volume of tax collections relative to government expenditures, is an easy way of adjusting the total volume of assets held by the public. The economist, therefore, sees the national debt as an instrument of overall social control, which can be used to prevent the economy from either slipping into deflation or into inflation. When the private sector is behaving in an inflationary manner, the national debt should be decreased; when it is behaving in a deflationary manner, the national debt should be increased. This idea of the national debt as a cybernetic mechanism for preventing a depression and insuring steady growth is something which depends on a sophisticated theoretical model of the economy for its perception and upon an adequate system of economic statistics for its consummation. The tax cut in 1964 represents a landmark, at least in American economic policy, as this perhaps is the first time that a deliberate tax policy was followed with the object of diminishing unemployment and not with the object of simply enabling the government to pay its bills. In the folk image, taxes are simply what the government has to collect in order that it may make expenditures. In the more sophisticated image, taxes can be a subtle but very powerful instrument of control of the overall level of economic activity and, properly managed, can prevent us from falling into depression.

Statistical images and theoretical models have had perhaps a somewhat less dramatic effect in the other social sciences than they have had in economics, though their influence has been by no means negligible. The rise of social work, for instance, as a profession has been associated with a shift in the image of poverty and crime as something purely and simply the responsibility of the poor and the evildoer, to be dealt with by private charity and moral exhortation, to an image of society in which both poverty and crime are seen as elements in a complex ecological picture with many determinants. We are, I suspect, still a long way from a real understanding of what are precisely those elements in social systems that produce poverty and crime, but we are at least moving in that direction, even if we have no great successes to report to date.

In the study of mental illness, likewise, we have come to realize that the incidence of mental illness in the whole society is not explained by the private history of each patient, valuable though this may be, and we are beginning to look for preventive and educational measures that will increase the incidence of mental health. Perhaps the most spectacular impact of sociology on the social system was the role that sociological investigation of the effects of segregation carried in the Supreme Court decision of 1954 that put segregated education beyond the pale of the Constitution. Even in the field of religion, the social sciences are beginning to create images beyond those that are derived from personal experience. It is significant, for instance, that the Information Service of the National Council of Churches of Christ in the U.S.A. would publish a report of a study of the relation of religious belief of various kinds to moral and ethical attitudes which is by no means flattering to the religious institution.[3] Studies of this kind can cause serious heart-searchings among religious leaders and induce them to consider carefully what *kind* of religion they are preaching.

Another place where the social sciences have made a substantial impact on the social system itself is in the management of organizations, whether these be business corporations, government offices, or even universities, labor unions, and churches. What is now called more generally management science, or more narrowly operations research, consists of a whole set of techniques for obtaining and processing information about an organization and its environment which will be of use to its decision makers. In operations research a mathematical model is constructed of some operation about which various decisions have to be made, such as, for instance, the routing of traffic through a tunnel or of materials through a plant; the production of a mix of different products from distillation or fractionation; or the planning of inventory. Various things about which decisions have to be made are reduced to quantitative form, and the mathematical function is derived by observation, experiment, or sometimes inspired guesswork. Then some variable is selected which is regarded as measuring the value of the operation, so that the "bigger the better," that is, the larger the magnitude of this variable, the better the operation. We then find at what values of all the decision quantities the maximand, or the quantity to be maximized, is at a maximum. In the model, at any rate, this represents the best position of the system, and the one that a wise decision-maker would choose. A special case of operations research in which all the functions involved are linear is called "linear programming." This has been applied with considerable success in maximization problems which involve a large number of variables and which, therefore, are not susceptible to solution by common-sense or rule-of-thumb methods. These techniques were developed first on a large scale during World War II, and they have had a great many applications in government, especially in national defense, and also in business firms.

3 Milton Rokeach, "Paradoxes of Religious Belief," *Information Service*, February 13, 1965.

Unfortunately, no general study has been made of the impact of operations research and similarly sophisticated techniques on management decisions, so that we really do not know how large this impact has been. It may be, indeed, that the decisions which are made as a result of operations research are not quantitatively very different from those that would be made by more informal and rule-of-thumb methods, but we cannot be sure of this, and one suspects that over the long pull the effects of these sophisticated methods of decision-making may be quite large in the avoidance of unnecessary waste. It must be emphasized, however, that no matter how complicated they may be, they apply only to part of a much larger social system. They, therefore, assist the human decision-making process, but, at least in the case of the larger decisions, they are in no sense a substitute for it.

The social sciences have made a considerable impact on management in a somewhat less quantitative way in the field of industrial relations and personnel management. Here the results both of observation and of experiment have given us some important propositions regarding, for instance, the relation between the nature of the communication system in an organization, the morale of the participants, and its overall productivity. This is by no means a simple relationship. Where morale is low, an improvement in morale almost always increases productivity, often quite substantially, and fairly simple changes in organizational structure and management methods from, say, an organization run as an authoritarian-line organization with orders from superiors to inferiors and no kickback, to an organization with more participation at all levels, has often produced quite startling results. On the other hand, where morale is high, a further increase in communication and participation may result in euphoria rather than productivity, and too much time may be spent in purely morale-building communications. Here again it is hard to assess the overall impact of changes of this kind; again taken over the long pull, however, they may be substantial.

Another example of the development of quantitative models of the social system which go far beyond what can be obtained through folk knowledge is the development of what is called input-output analysis, pioneered by Professor W. W. Leontief at Harvard University. This consists essentially in dividing the economy into a number of different segments or industries and studying the extent to which the output of each segment becomes input to all the other segments. We can then see what will be the effect of a change in one segment of the economy, for instance the defense industry or foreign trade, on all the others. This technique has been applied with some success in studying the impact of the creation of new industries in the course of economic development, and it has recently been applied to the study of the impact of disarmament on the economy.

THE SOCIAL-SYSTEMS CRITIQUE OF PUBLIC POLICY

In recent years there has been a rising tide of criticism in a great many fields of public policy on the grounds that decisions are mainly in the hands of people whose training is primarily in the physical sciences and engineering and who, for that reason, do not think easily in terms of social systems. No single social science can be credited with the development of what might be called the social-systems critique of policy making, but the overall impact is quite apparent. This type of criticism is noticeable in areas as diverse as flood control, irrigation, agricultural policy, public housing, urban renewal, transportation, social security, workmen's compensation, public assistance, and national defense.

It is interesting that a good deal of criticism of existing policies from the point of view of the general social systems involved has come not from the sociologists but from the geographers, who, perhaps because of their concern with overall spatial relationships, have been more open to the general social-systems point of view. There has been a good deal of criticism of our flood-control policy, for instance, on the grounds that it has been in the hands mainly of engineers, and army engineers at that, who have treated the river as an enemy, and that, hence, it has concentrated too much on dams and levees and not enough on people, zoning, and urban architecture. A flood is no problem to a river; it is, indeed, part of its way of life. If it did not have floods, it would not have a floodplain. A flood is only a problem to people, and it may be much easier to arrange things so that people conform to what the river wants to do instead of arranging things so that the river conforms to what people want to do. In practice, of course, flood control is a matter of changing the behavior both of the river and of people, and we have to conceive river and people as part of a single social system. Up to now, it must be confessed that these criticisms do not seem to have had much impact on policy, but they are so cogent that it is hard to believe that a change is not in the offing.

One could cite a number of other cases in which the failure to consider policy in terms of overall social systems leads to unexpected and frequently very unfavorable consequences. If, for instance, we conceive urban renewal as simply a matter of knocking down old buildings and building new ones that look prettier, we may easily simply transfer the problem somewhere else or, what is even worse, create what one social worker has described as "filing cabinets for live bodies," that is, localities that are neither neighborhoods nor communities, and in which, therefore, delinquency and social disorganization flourish. This does not mean, of course, that bricks and mortar are unimportant, or that architectural design and town planning are not an essential element in the building of healthy communities. Bricks and mortar and cement, however, are only the skeleton and the shell of a social system, and if we design them without reference to the social system that must inhabit them, we are almost certainly in for disastrous failures.

Another example in which the failure to regard a policy from the point of view of the social system as a whole has turned out to be unexpectedly disastrous is the movement for improved public health, as reflected, for instance, in the work of the World Health Organization. In a great many tropical countries in the years around 1950, there were highly successful campaigns for the eradication of malaria through the use of chemical insecticides, leading to the elimination of the malaria-carrying mosquitoes. The effect of this was dramatic. In many of these countries, overall mortality rates fell from somewhere in the neighborhood of twenty-five or thirty per thousand to somewhere around, or even under, ten, this often in a matter of two or three years. Infant mortality seems to have fallen even further. Birth rates, however, remained high, in some cases even increased, and as a result, not only has the overall population in many of these countries been increasing from 3–3.5 percent per annum, but this increase is heavily concentrated in the younger age groups, so that many of these countries now have more than 50 percent of their population under the age of fifteen, and the number of teen-agers entering the labor market is now almost double what it was only five or ten years ago. It is going to be extremely difficult to find places for all these teen-agers in the traditional societies of the villages. We are already seeing an explosive increase in the cities of the developing countries, some of which have been growing at rates of 12 or even 15 percent per annum. It is virtually impossible to expand employment opportunities at this rate, hence we get widespread urban unemployment, especially among young people, with its consequent dangers of social disorder and even disintegration.

Nobody is going to suggest, of course, that the reduction of mortality, especially of infant mortality, is not in itself desirable. If, indeed, a society is to have the human resources for development, it must raise its expectation of life, simply because, say, with an expectation of life between thirty and forty, people do not live long enough to make an adequate return on human investment in education and training. A developed society, therefore, practically requires an expectation of life at least in the sixties and seventies. One of the first steps toward development, therefore, should be a simultaneous reduction in both mortality and fertility. Where, however, the reduction in mortality is not accompanied by a reduction in fertility, the results can easily be disastrous. It may now be almost too late to prevent major disasters in the form of famine and social upheaval in many countries around the tropical belt. What we see here is a good example of a general principle, which is the extreme danger of concentrating on a single problem in the midst of a complex social system. The public-health specialists concentrated on a single problem, how to reduce mortality. By and large they did not regard fertility as their business. By solving one problem, however, in a partial system, they have created almost insoluble problems elsewhere. Up to a point, of course, we must have specialists, and problems must be solved piecemeal. These piecemeal solutions, however, must be made in a larger framework involving some kind of image of the general social system; otherwise piecemeal solutions may, indeed, break the larger system into pieces. There is a story of a production manager of an enterprise who said that all he wanted to do was to reduce costs, until it was pointed out to him that he could reduce costs to zero by the simple process of abandoning the enterprise altogether!

The field of economic development is a good example of an area that has received a great deal of attention in recent years, and in which the need for a general social-systems approach is widely recognized, but in which the sheer complexity of the problem and the enormous variety of cases has made any general solution very hard to find. It is widely recognized, however, that the problem of economic development cannot be solved within the framework of economics alone, even though economics has some elementary and quite essential contributions to make, such as, for instance, the proposition that if economic development requires accumulation, there must be an excess of production over consumption, or if a country fails to take advantage of certain favorable terms of trade which are offered to it, it will find development more difficult than countries which seize these advantages. It is also clear, however, that economic development is part of a much larger process of social change, and that if we are to understand it, we must understand what it is that motivates people to change, and we must understand what are the political and social institutions that encourage change, and that enable these motivations to result in action. As a result, there has been a good deal of interest, first of all in the motivations to change, in such works, for instance, as David C. McClelland's *The Achieving Society* and Everett Hagen's *On the Theory of Social Change.*

A mere study of motivation is not enough, of course. The part of the population that is motivated to change may not have the opportunity to do it, and the part that has the opportunity may not be motivated. Consequently, we cannot neglect the political structure and especially the distribution of power. This, unfortunately, seems to be a situation in which we are only wise after the event. Apart from the Marxists, who are only occasionally right, political scientists seem to have come up with remarkably little in the way of a general theory of the dynamics of power distribution. Nevertheless, we can point to economic development as an area in which the urgent needs of practice have far outrun the development of theoretical models, but where also the absence of adequate theoretical models is a severe handicap. The plain fact is that we are not being very successful in economic development, especially in the countries of the tropics, and at least part of the reason for this undoubtedly lies in the absence of adequate theoretical models and an even less adequate apparatus for collecting and processing the essential information. We have at least the beginnings of an economic information system in most countries, even though this is often quite rudimentary. We have practically no information system that will cover the psychological, motivational, ideological, and political elements of the system. A research project is now being developed, for instance, by the Department of Defense, called Project Camelot, which has as its major objective a substantial mobilization of social-science resources to study the problem of the kind of social breakdown that leads into internal war. On this subject we are starting practically from zero.

In spite of the fact that this type of criticism often seems to fall on deaf ears, and that the social sciences themselves have at most a very spotty record, at least when it comes to prediction, when one looks over the history of the twentieth century it is hard not to be impressed with signs of progress. It is particularly instructive, for instance, to contrast the twenty years after World War I, from 1919 to 1939, with the twenty years that we are just completing after World War II, from 1945 to 1965. It is not an exaggeration to say that the first period was a total failure that ended in disaster. The overall rates of economic growth, even in the developed countries, were rather low. The tropical world was still largely in the grip of colonial powers, and its development was even slower. There was a period of reasonably rapid recovery from the war in the twenties, but in the West this ended in the stock market crash of 1929 and the Great Depression of the thirties which followed it. In the Soviet Union, likewise, a period of recovery under the new economic policy was followed by the first collectivization of 1928–32, which turned out to be an even greater disaster than the Great Depression in the West, in which the Soviet Union lost half its livestock and five or six million of its people. The unemployment and disorganization of the depression years led directly to the rise of Hitler and the monstrous collapse of human decency which that represented, and the whole period ended in the bestialities of World War II, with its ruthless destruction of cities and slaughter of civilian populations on both sides.

By contrast, the twenty years from 1945 to 1965 have been relatively benign and successful, in spite of the nuclear threat and the constant menace of the Cold War. In a great many countries, the rate of economic growth has been spectacular, indeed unprecedented. Japan, out of total defeat, the loss of her empire, the destruction of her cities and her merchant marine, and the repatriation of three million overseas Japanese, went on to establish a world record for economic growth of about 8 percent per annum increase in per capita real income, sustained over the whole twenty-year period. Nothing like this has ever happened in human history before. The previous record for sustained growth before the war was about 2.3 percent per annum, attained by Japan, Sweden, and the United States from about the middle of the nineteenth century on. The case of Japan is not unique; West Germany grew at about 7.5 percent, and a number of European countries between 5 and 6 percent in this period. The United States is rather slow; indeed, in the 1950's, forty-five countries had a faster rate of economic growth than the United States, at least according to official statistics, which do not necessarily have to be believed! Even in the United States, however, growth was continuous and there was nothing like the Great Depression of the thirties. The United States achieved an enormous disarmament in 1945 without unemployment ever rising above 3 percent. Even though unemployment has tended to be uncomfortably high in recent years, running about 5 or 6 percent, we have had nothing like the disaster of the thirties. Furthermore, in the last twenty years we have seen the liquidation of nearly all the old colonial empires with the exception of the Portuguese, and even though this has created severe problems, for instance in the Congo, on the whole this remarkable transition has been achieved with little violence and to the mutual benefit of all parties. One hesitates to be too optimistic; nevertheless, it does look as if the United States and the Soviet Union are beginning to learn how to live with one another, and, even though China remains a great enigma for the future, a world war seems a good deal less inevitable in 1965 than it did in 1939.

We cannot, of course, give all the credit for the difference between these two twenty-year periods to the rising influence of the social sciences. Nevertheless, this is not a negligible factor. It is in economic policy, perhaps, that the contrast is greatest. It is an instructive exercise, for instance, to go back to the reports of the economic conferences that were held just after the first World War and to compare these with those that were held after the second. It is pretty clear that a substantial change has taken place, and that not only has our understanding of the economic system improved enormously but that also our information about it has improved. The high rates of economic growth of the last twenty-five years are by no means unconnected with the rise of Keynesian economics, of national income statistics, and of economic policies which are self-consciously directed toward what might be called a controlled market economy. It is true that a price has sometimes been paid for this in terms of inflation, but the gains are, nevertheless, substantial. One would certainly be very surprised if the Western world ever had another great depression on the scale of the thirties. The fact that the record of the controlled market economies has been distinctly better than that even of the best centrally planned, that is, communist, economies, seems to be having a marked impact on the centrally planned economies themselves, which are undergoing severe reappraisals of their economic policy and what seems to be a movement in the direction of decentralization, greater use of the market, and more individual freedom. If, indeed, we are moving into a period where ideologies can be tested by results, this would be good news for mankind.

It is still too early to say whether the development of sophisticated models and better information systems in the international system will deal with the problem of war in a way that better economic models, information, and policies have dealt with the problem of depression. Up to now, indeed, the danger of perhaps irretrievable disaster remains high. If, however, we are lucky enough to escape this for another twenty years, we may very well find that the rise of social-scientific knowledge in this field will corrode irrational nationalisms just as it seems to be corroding irrational economic ideologies. There is a race between knowledge and disaster, but in this race the longer disaster is staved off, the better chance we have of acquiring the knowledge to prevent it altogether.

DEVELOPMENTS WITHIN THE SOCIAL SCIENCES

There is a constant interaction between developments in the pure sciences and the problems perceived as important in the outside world. It is not surprising, therefore, to find that many of the developments within the social sciences themselves in the last generation have been the result of pressures generated by a sense of unsolved problems in the world outside. Where one social science tends to lag behind another, also, a sense of deficiency develops, which eventually attracts resources into it to try to bring it into line with the rest. Perhaps the most interesting example of this principle is the strong movement for the improvement of political science which has been noticeable in the last generation.

In the study of all social systems, we are constantly being brought up against the fact that the political system is at the same time one of the most important and also one of the least tractable elements in the social system when it comes to the setting up of theoretical models that are testable by refined procedures for collecting and processing information. It is hardly too much to say that it is only in the last ten years that political science has begun to move toward the kind of model construction and information collection that has long been characteristic of economics. A good deal of the stimulus here has unquestionably come from other social sciences and is a tribute to the fact that the study of social systems faces a subject matter which is so highly integrated that the specialized disciplines must be willing to learn extensively from one another if they are to function even as disciplines.

Thus, in political science, we have seen in recent years great interest in better methods of collecting information, which has come largely from political sociology, and the contacts of political science with sociologists, social psychologists, and the practitioners of survey research. Here we find, for instance, the studies of voting behavior, of opinion formation, and studies of political decision-making. In countries of regular elections, at least, political scientists have been in the curious position of having too much information about a particular moment of political behavior, namely, the vote cast in the ballot box, but very little information about all the rest of the field. The development of sample surveys of preelection behavior, for instance, by the Institute for Social Research at the University of Michigan, and also studies such as that of Professor Richard Snyder of Northwestern University on the decision-making process in the Korean crisis, all point towards substantial improvements in data collection and processing in this field.

Going hand in hand in this has been a considerable revival of interest in political theory of a fairly sophisticated kind, mainly as a result of its contacts with game theory and economics. We have, for instance, the work of Duncan Black on the theory of committee decisions, of C. E. Lindblom and R. A. Dahl and of Anthony Downs on the processes by which political decisions are made in a democracy, and by J. M. Buchanan and G. Tullock on what they call the "calculus of consent." All these attempt to apply formulations of rational behavior and optimizing concepts of decision-making, which are familiar in economics, to problems in politics. The so-called voting paradoxes have received a good deal of attention, these being situations, for instance, in which the outcome of a decision based on a voting procedure is a function of the procedure itself and the order in which matters are taken up rather than a function of the preferences of the parties. It is a symptom of the way in which the social sciences are moving toward unification that these days it is often quite hard to tell whether a book such as, for instance, Kenneth Arrow's *Social Choice and Individual Values*, is economics or political science. We could almost say that the division of the social sciences according to fields of study or according to the types of institutions studied—with, for instance, a political scientist studying states, an economist, corporations, and a sociologist, families and churches—is now breaking down, indeed has broken down. It has become clear that each social science concentrates on a certain aspect of the social system which cuts across virtually all forms of social organization, even though it may be particularly relevant to some of them. Thus the processes of decision-making are quite similar, whether they take place in a corporation, in the government, in a labor union, in a church, or in a family. If the decision has to be reached in a group or has to be accepted by a group, there are problems of compromise, accommodation, reformulation, and development of new positions which likewise take place no matter what the organization. What seems to be happening today is that besides the division according to the regular disciplines, which, to some extent at least, carves up the subject matter according to types of organizations, we seem to be getting a specialization according to certain functional processes such as decision-making, the resolution of conflict, processes of exchange, processes of threats and coercion, and so on.

Alongside these developments in political science in general, there has been a corresponding movement in the study of international systems. Part of this unquestionably is motivated by the feeling that the international system is the one which is most threatening to us today, and that unless we can solve the problem presented by the proliferation of nuclear weapons and the collapse of traditional national defense, the future looks indeed dim. As a result, there has been a certain mobilization of social-science interest in this direction which did not exist before. In the past generation it was fairly true to say that international studies were in the hands of diplomatic historians, and what might be called high-level journalists, who discussed "foreign affairs" with a certain amount of folk wisdom but with very little in the way of exact theoretical models or quantitative information. The past decade or so has seen a number of intellectual movements rather closely related and often involving the same persons, which have endeavored to close the obvious gaps and deficiencies in this field. In the first place, there has been a movement to improve the whole field of the study of international systems, first by bringing in sociologists, economists, social psychologists, game theorists, and so on, as well as political scientists, and so make the whole field multidisciplinary in character. The same sort of thing happened to industrial relations about a generation before, when it became apparent that the labor-management relationship, for instance, involved much more than economics, and that if it was to be understood and operate satisfactorily, sociology and psychology would have to be called in.

Along with the widening of the disciplinary horizons of the field, there has also come an interest in the development of mathematical models and improved quantitative information. The pioneer in both these respects was an English meteorologist, Lewis F. Richardson, whose remarkable books, *Arms and Insecurity* and *Statistics of Deadly Quarrels*, languished in microfilm for almost twenty years before they were finally published in regular form in 1960. Richardson developed a theory of arms races which he tried to test, not wholly successfully, by the application of quantitative data, and he also made important contributions toward the quantification of the history of conflict. His work often showed the marks of the gifted amateur operating in isolation, for he was at least a whole generation ahead of his time. It is, nevertheless, having an increasing influence in stimulating the present generation of researchers in this field to go beyond the folk wisdom of their predecessors as well as the folk wisdom by which the decisions in the international system are now made.

Alongside this movement for the improvement of the study of international systems has gone a closely related movement, which almost looks like the beginnings of a new science, for which the Dutch have a name. They call it *Polemologie*, that is, the science of conflict. Conflict is common to all social systems and all social organizations, whether this is economic conflict, political conflict, religious conflict, racial conflict, or international conflict. It is very hard to find any social system or any social organization that does not have conflict in it. Just as, therefore, economics abstracts from the equally universal phenomenon of exchange a theoretical system and what is beginning to be a quantitative science, so it ought to be possible to abstract a general theory of conflict from these many cases where it occurs, and it should be possible also to set up an information system which will enable us to detect where we are at any moment in any particular conflict process. Game theory is a part of this, as developed first, for instance, by John von Neumann and Oskar Morgenstern.[4] This in turn is closely related to modern decision theory. In fact, one of the standard works in the field, by Robert Luce and Howard Raiffa, is entitled *Games and Decisions*. The usefulness of game theory has been somewhat limited by the fact that its major competence had been in the field of zero-sum games, that is, games in which what one party wins, the other party loses. The extension of game theory into a general theory of conflict requires its expansion to cover the case of positive-sum games in which the total of gains and losses is positive, and these have been studied in such works as T. C. Schelling, *Strategy of Conflict*, Anatol Rapoport, *Fights, Games, and Debates*, and my own *Conflict and Defense*. There are important contributions to the theory of conflict, also, outside of game theory, as, for instance, in the economic theory of oligopoly, the theory of group dynamics (*see*, for instance, Kurt Lewin, *Resolving Social Conflicts*) and also in individual psychology, in psychoanalysis, and in the analysis of internal conflict within the person.

An important body of theory is also developing regarding what I have called "threat systems," which concerns itself with the dynamics of the way in which social systems are organized by means of threats and counterthreats. A threat relationship originates when one person or organization (call him Able) says to another (call him Baker), "You do something that I want, or I will do something that you don't want." What happens then, of course, depends on Baker's response. If Baker submits and does what Able wants him to do, a new structure of roles has been created, with Able dominant and Baker subordinate. The master-slave relationship is typical of this. On the other hand, the threat-submission

---

4 *Theory of Games and Economic Behavior* (Princeton: Princeton University Press, 1944).

pattern is also characteristic of all law enforcement and, when it is legitimized, becomes one of the most important elements in social organization. When the traffic cop says, "Pull over," we usually pull over; that is, we submit to an implied threat. If the threat is not accepted as legitimate, there may be defiance. That is, Baker says to Able, "Do your worst and see if I care." The ball is now passed back to Able. Either he has to carry out his threat, or the credibility of future threats is seriously impaired. Unfortunately, carrying out the threat is often costly. Hence, he is faced with the decision as to which of the two alternatives—that is, carrying out the threat or not carrying it out—is least costly. Another possible response to the threat is flight; Baker simply removes himself from Able's sphere of capability. Historically, this has been very important; it accounts for a great deal of human migration; and even though preachers and psychoanalysts have given this a bad press, sometimes escape is highly rational. Another possible reaction is the development of counterthreat. The system then passes into deterrence. Baker replies, in effect, to Able's original threat, "If you do something nasty to me, I will do something nasty to you." The difficulty with deterrence is that while it may operate quite successfully for a short period, it seems to have a profound long-run instability. The reason for this is that threats need to be credible, that is, believed, by the threatened party if they are to be effective, and unless they are occasionally carried out, their credibility tends to depreciate. Hence, even in a system of mutual deterrence, of which we find many examples in industrial relations, international relations, and so on, there is a certain tendency for the system to collapse into actual carrying out of threats every so often.

Along with the "pure" work in the field of conflict systems and international systems, there has been a good deal of interest in applied research in this area. Quantitatively, this is most apparent in what might be called national security research, that is, the application of sophisticated theories and models to the problem of national defense. We see this in the work of such institutions as the Rand Corporation in Santa Monica, California, and the Hudson Institute near New York City. Works that reflect this activity are, for instance, Charles J. Hitch and Roland McKean's *Economics of Defense in the Nuclear Age*, and Herman Kahn's works, especially *Thinking About the Unthinkable*. The effect of these more sophisticated approaches on actual policy is hard to determine, and its full effects may not be seen for many years. However, there does seem to be a change in the temper of the Department of Defense, for instance, in the direction of greater sophistication. Whether an institution so intimately bound up with folk images and folk ethics as the military can survive the development of sophistication without a severe crisis is another question altogether, to which I would not venture to give an answer.

There has also been a small intellectual movement in this field that has come to be known as the peace research movement, which is concerned with the application of the social sciences quite specifically to the problem of the abolition of war and the establishment of stable peace. At many points peace research and national security research overlap. In these days, certainly nobody regards war as anything but a cost to be minimized in the interest of certain other values. Nevertheless, there is a difference between those who regard it as a tolerable cost and those who regard it as an intolerable one. Or we might put the matter in another way and say that the national security research is trying to solve the problem of how to maximize national security, subject to the constraint that the probability of peace does not fall below a certain level. Peace research is asking the question: How do we maximize the probability of peace, subject to certain other values not falling below a minimum level? Thus even though the "pure" framework of international systems theory and international information collection and processing is the same for both applied fields, there are differences in values, which operate to select the problems that have the greatest interest.

We might pause to note that this difference between pure and applied research is a very general problem, which applies to all the sciences. The dominant value of pure research is curiosity, the sheer desire to know. Applied research always assumes certain other values which direct the course of the advancement of knowledge. Applied research, therefore, always implies a value system beyond that of knowledge itself, whether this is making money, increasing destructive power, or human welfare. It is a sad commentary on the human condition that such a very small amount of applied research goes to improving human welfare.

Another branch of the tree of knowledge that has shown great vitality in recent years is that of the study of information and communications. This is a field of enormous importance for the social sciences, although it goes beyond the social sciences into biology and engineering and even into the physical sciences. The pioneering work in this field was done by a happy combination of engineering and social science in the work of Claude Shannon and Warren Weaver[5] in 1949 in developing a mathematical measure of the quantity of information in a system. This measure, interestingly enough, turned out to be very similar, in fact formally identical, to the physical concept of entropy, or rather, negative entropy. As entropy is a measure of the disorder and lack of potential in a system, so information is a measure of order and potential. Another very important concept of information theory is that of the capacity of a channel of information. A unit of information is the "bit," which is short for binary unit, which is the occurrence of one event out of two equally

5 *The Mathematical Theory of Communication* (Urbana: University of Illinois Press, 1949).

probable potentialities that together exhaust the possibilities. Thus the information conveyed by the toss of a coin is one bit, assuming that heads or tails are equally probable. These relatively simple concepts opened enormous fields of research in practically all the sciences.

In the social sciences, information theory, like game theory, with which it is not unrelated, has perhaps been important mainly because of the problems it has suggested rather than because of those it has solved. Information theory operates at a level of abstraction below that of the content of information. It is thus ideally suited to the study of telephone engineering and even to certain abstract levels of social-systems analysis, where we are interested, for instance, in the problem of information overload in a quantitative sense, rather than the nature of the messages that the information system is carrying. Social scientists, however, cannot neglect the fact that when people communicate with each other, they at least have the illusion that they are saying something. In studying social systems, therefore, we are forced to go beyond the abstractions of information theory and to develop abstractions of content and knowledge. Knowledge, that is, the image of the world in people's minds, is an essential component of social systems. Human behavior cannot conceivably be understood without it. It is a structure of such immense richness and complexity, however, that it is not easy to reduce it to simple abstract concepts and measures. We do this in a rough way, of course, every time a teacher gives an examination and grades it. We do it in more refined ways with public opinion surveys, attitude studies, or what the sociologists call content analysis. Content analysis is an attempt to define variables which are characteristic of the content of a body of communicated material, such as a book, a newspaper, a letter, or a radio broadcast, and to measure these quantities by counting words or phrases that significantly embody them. Even though this method has limitations, it is another step toward improving our statistical images of the social system.

On the more theoretical or even philosophical level, we might almost distinguish a "communications school" of social scientists, who lay great stress on the importance of the communications network as the key concept of all social organization and of the behavior of all social systems. In the last generation, this position was represented mainly by the economist Harold Innis at Toronto, who saw very clearly the enormous importance of the communications network in the general phenomenon of economic development. In the present generation, we have social philosophers such as Kenneth Burke, sociologists such as Hugh Dalziel Duncan, whose *Communication and Social Order* is perhaps the nearest thing to a textbook in the field, with a very broad coverage, and, finally, an almost unclassifiable writer, Herbert Marshall McLuhan, also of Toronto. McLuhan's major works, *The Gutenberg Galaxy* and *Understanding Media*, are books of quite astonishing originality in which, indeed, the originality of both format and idea is so great that it may distract attention from the content. McLuhan's central theme is that it is not the content of communication that is so important in determining the pattern in the course of social systems as the form of the medium of communication itself. The types of social systems that develop, for instance, where the major medium is face-to-face conversation, are enormously different from those systems that have writing, and these, in turn, differ from those that have radio and television. He argues particularly that whereas print fragmented the world and led to the rise of national states, secular society, and scientific knowledge, television, because of its peculiarly intimate and domestic character, is going to create a very different kind of society, more organic, less fragmented, less rational in the sense at least of economic accounting, more like a great world village and less like the Greek city. He points out also that a society in which radio is a dominant means of communication is likely to be more tribal and much less rational than one dominated by print. He regards both Hitler and Franklin Roosevelt as essentially products of the brief radio age in the Western countries, and it is somewhat alarming to contemplate that most of the poor countries in the world are going through the radio age now. By contrast, television destroys the demagogue, as it destroyed Joseph McCarthy, simply because of its peculiar character as a medium. Anyone who paints with such a broad brush as this is bound to get many details wrong, and McLuhan's leaps of insight occasionally land him in a ditch. Nevertheless, this represents a line of thinking that is extraordinarily illuminating, and it is bound to have a substantial effect on the social sciences in the years to come.

We may, perhaps, summarize the present situation in the social sciences as follows. There is, first of all, a remarkable convergence of the different social sciences toward each other, and something like a unified social science at last seems to be emerging. This is not to say that the old divisions are disappearing. Economics, sociology, psychology, and so on, retain their ancient empires, but the growing points seem to be at the borders. It is becoming increasingly hard to classify either the social scientists or the works which they write in terms of the old classifications. This is happening, as I have suggested earlier, simply because the subject matter of the social sciences—that is, the social system itself—is highly unified, and pigeonholes like economics, sociology, and psychology are more a property of the social scientists than of the social system. We find economists, then, like Everett Hagen, studying the motivational implications of child-rearing. We find sociologists like George Homans and Peter Blau interpreting nearly all social phenomena through the generalized concept of exchange. We find economists like Duncan Black becoming political scientists, and political scientists like Gordon Tullock becoming economists, and even though there have been times when the interdisciplinary movement has become something of a foundation fad, it is still something that arises out of the sheer necessity of the problems.

This movement toward a unified social science has now got as far as to begin producing textbooks. We have, for instance, Alfred Kuhn's remarkable work, *The Study of Society*, which combines economics, sociology, and psychology in a genuinely integrated body of theory, using the concept of the transaction as the basic building block. There might be some danger that this movement toward the development of unified theory in the social sciences would produce a somewhat denatured and sterile eclecticism. My personal view is that we are in a period in which we are not only moving toward a more unified theory but also gaining substantial theoretical insights in many separate fields. Even in a field as old and staid as economics, we have seen significant developments in the theory of economic behavior, for instance in a remarkable work by Richard Cyert and J. G. March, *A Behavioral Theory of the Firm*. Economics has been breaking out of the formalism of maximization theory and realizing that such things as search processes and learning processes are essential to the interpretation, even, of the behavior of economic organizations like the firm. The work of the communications school referred to earlier does not fit neatly into any existing body of theory. It represents some genuinely new insights into the nature of the social system and the kind of abstractions that it is possible to make from it. We may find ourselves, indeed, with two bodies of rather integrated social theory—one revolving around the concept of the transaction and decision theory, the other revolving around the nature of media and the communications process. The task of bringing these together remains to be done.

Another movement that is characteristic of all the social sciences is the rapid development of quantification and mathematization, even in areas that have previously resisted this, such as political science. In economics, of course, the use of mathematics goes back a long way, at least to A. A. Cournot, 1838, and to W. S. Jevons and L. Walras in the 1870's. Econometrics emerged as a separate discipline in the 1920's and 1930's and continues to flourish even though there are some signs of diminishing returns. Mathematical sociology has now become a well-recognized discipline, as the appearance of a large textbook in the field indicates. The applications of mathematics to psychology have become very important in the past ten years or more, and in all the social sciences today a knowledge of mathematics is a substantial asset, and mathematical ignorance an even more substantial liability. As in any other movement, mathematization is sometimes carried to excess, and even though it is harder to talk nonsense in mathematics than it is in literary language, it seems to be quite possible to say nothing, and the mere fashion for mathematizing has occasionally done more harm than good. Still, the net gain on the intellectual balance sheet is very clear.

FUTURE DEVELOPMENTS IN THE SOCIAL SCIENCES

W e may perhaps conclude this survey by taking a brief look at some possible future developments in the social sciences, at least to the point of indicating deficiencies which the future may correct. The most serious deficiency in the social sciences at present is, undoubtedly, the extreme inadequacy of its present methods of collecting data, even though these methods are undergoing rapid improvement. It was barely a generation ago that we relied even for our economic data on the accidents of tax collections and customs records, and our data collection is still very far from adequate. In other aspects of the social system, a systematic and continuous data collection has hardly begun. We can consider the parallel with meteorology. The atmosphere is a very complex system, extending over the whole surface of the globe. If we are to understand it, we must have meteorological stations collecting data continuously, spaced at reasonable intervals over the whole surface of the globe, and feeding their data into a central processing agency. We are still a long way from this ideal, even in meteorology, and it is not surprising that weather prediction is so inadequate when over large areas of the globe adequate meteorological stations are absent. Just as the globe is encircled by an atmosphere, so it is enveloped in a sociosphere. The sociosphere consists of all human beings on the earth and their relations with each other, with the organizations that they create, and with their physical environment. It is dense in New York, and thin in Antarctica, but is hardly anywhere absent. If this concept seems large to the imagination, it is no larger than the reality that we have to study. Information about the sociosphere, however, is even spottier than information about the atmosphere. A remarkable little volume has recently been published, entitled *World Handbook of Political and Social Indicators*, by Bruce M. Russett *et al.*, which brings together into a single volume a good deal of the information that is available, by countries. This is depressingly small enough, but there is even less information available by regions. What is desperately needed is a network of social data stations, somewhat analogous to meteorological stations, spaced at fairly regular intervals over the human population, say one to every ten million people, which will continually collect, process, and relay social data from which we can build up a continuing image of the succession of states of the sociosphere in all its manifold aspects. The political problems of setting up an agency of this kind are not negligible. Information, unfortunately, is rarely politically neutral, and the truth is threatening to those whose power rests on the ignorance of others. Some forms of data are obviously harder to collect than others. On the whole, however, it has been the experience of social scientists that when data are gathered in a systematic, unemotional, and scientific manner, an astonishing amount can be collected. There are also a good many different methods of collecting social data. The sample survey is only one. The sampling of the whole information process of the society as it is thrown up in the mass media, in statistical reports, and in the whole mass of printed material, can provide an enormous amount of information which can be checked and processed for internal consistency. Furthermore, the very process of collecting information would reveal the gaps and would create pressures to fill them.

A system of continuous world social data collection and processing would have an enormous impact, not only on the theoretical structures of the social sciences, which would have to adapt themselves to the accumulating statistical images, but would also have an enormous impact on the social system itself. Knowledge, as we have seen, is an essential part of the social system. Any fundamental change in the knowledge about it changes the social system itself. We might expect this impact to be particularly great on the international system. This operates at present by an information processing system which seems to be positively designed to produce misinformation. On the whole, the people who make decisions in the international system in the various countries seem to be insulated even from their own social scientists, and operate by what someone has called "club knowledge"—the kind of knowledge that is derived from gossip in clubs. A quantified and carefully sampled process of data collection in this field could hardly fail to have an enormous impact, and it would go a long way toward preventing the gross mistakes and appalling dangers that now characterize it.

THE NEW KNOWLEDGE AND THE GREAT IDEAS

The question of the relation of the enormous upsurge of new knowledge which is now taking place in all disciplines to the great ideas of the past is important and also very difficult. There are two extreme views which I think we must reject. One is that the new knowledge is so enormous and so important and so new that the great ideas of the past are really irrelevant. This is a view that regards the history of thought, or indeed almost any history, as a matter of idle curiosity, suitable for the academic specialist but quite irrelevant to the great problems of the day. At the other extreme, we find the view that in regard to social systems and the understanding of man himself at least, nearly all of what can be said has been said in the past, and that our new knowledge is merely so much busy work, which adds very little to the insights of the great minds of the ages. Thus, at a conference recently, a high official of the State Department remarked that he didn't think he had anything to learn from the social sciences; that whenever he wanted to solve a problem in international relations he went back to Thucydides and read about the Peloponnesian War!

One sets up extremes, of course, to point out that the ideal must lie somewhere between them. I must confess, however, I am much more frightened by the people who think that we are still fighting the Peloponnesian War than by people who think that anything written before they went to college can be put in the ash can. We can put the matter dramatically by pointing out that where knowledge doubles every X years, the date "X years ago" divides the acquisition of knowledge into two equal parts. The knowledge of chemistry, for instance, at least as measured by the volume of publications, is supposed to double every fifteen years. Consequently, looking at it from 1965, the date 1950 divides the history of chemistry into two equal parts. Before the scientific revolution, we might reasonably suppose that it took several hundred years for knowledge to double, in which case the voices of the ancients might have as great or even greater weight than the moderns. When, however, knowledge doubles in every generation, the present becomes overwhelmingly more important than the past, and the idea that we have to go back to the past to gain our knowledge seems almost absurd.

In the case of the knowledge of man and society, the situation is perhaps a little different from what it would be in the physical sciences. In the physical sciences, for instance, folk knowledge is quite unimportant. In our knowledge of social systems, this is not so. In spite of the rise of scientific knowledge, folk knowledge is still an important part of the total, whether we wish to admit this or not. Folk knowledge, on the other hand, does not exhibit this phenomenon of continual growth, and at this level we might very well argue that Thucydides is as relevant today as he was 2,500 years ago. Certainly, the economist who goes back to Adam Smith will often find unsuspected insights which may turn out to be highly relevant to his present problems. Similarly, the political scientist who goes back to Aristotle or Machiavelli will likewise find them discussing a world that is by no means alien to his own. On the other hand, we must recognize also that the new world of information processing and collection has opened up enormous resources which were not available to the ancients or even to those of the eighteenth and nineteenth centuries. In almost all aspects of life, the twentieth century represents a unique transition and a very sharp break with the past. An awareness of the great works of the past can protect us against the fashions and fads of the moment, and it has to be confessed that in every age there are intellectual fashions. In an age of change as rapid as this, however, the past can also become an obstacle to the understanding of the new world into which we are moving, for the siren voices of the past may persuade us that the world has not changed when in fact it has changed and changed enormously. It is now truer than ever before that "what's past is prologue,"—a place to begin but not a place to linger.

THE MEDIUM AND THE MESSAGE

Review of Marshall McLuhan, *The Gutenberg Galaxy* and *Understanding Media. Can. Jour. of Econ. and Pol. Sci.,* 31, 2 (May 1965): 268-273

THE MEDIUM AND THE MESSAGE*

If, as Marshall McLuhan repeats almost to the point of being repetitious, the medium is the message, there is really no way of reviewing these two extraordinary books in a medium as linear, visual, and non-tactile as print. One might use a book as a weapon, for, as McLuhan understands very well, a weapon is also a medium and a message (*Understanding Media*, chap. 32), in which case one would simply throw the book at the reader. When I took my degree at Oxford I was literally struck by the fact that the Vice Chancellor, in conferring the degree, hit the four kneeling candidates before him solemnly on the head with a large Bible: "In nomine Patris (bang!) et Filii (bang!) et Spiritus (bang!) Sancti (bang!)" Reading these books is a rather similar experience. One is tempted to put the whole review into the form of a comic strip with balloons simply saying "Pow!," "Zowie!," and so on. Or perhaps one could simply abandon the alphabet and write a long line of asterisks, exclamation points, and question marks, like this: ! * * ! * * * ! ! * ? * ? ! * *

It is clear after reading these books that something which McLuhan will not allow me to call an explosion but which I am damned if I will call an implosion is going on in Toronto, beneath the deceptive surface of what is often regarded as a plain and provincial, even Presbyterian, exterior. The knowledgeable, however, will nod sagely to each other and murmur a magic password, "Innis." The late Harold Innis, whose stature rises as we recede from him, was perhaps the first man to realize that communication was the key to social phenomena of all kinds. The all-too-select few who have read a remarkable little magazine called *Explorations*, which came out of Toronto some years ago, realized that the Innis ferment was working mightily. Again, to vary the medium and to mix the metaphor, the McLuhan books are the skyrocket that came out of this ferment, and one feels almost that if one lit them with a match they would soar up into the sky and explode into a thousand stars.

Let me, however, try to come down to earth and explain what the books are about. *The Gutenberg Galaxy*, in spite of the fact that convention compels it to be printed as a codex, is obviously designed to be printed on a moebius strip. It has no real beginning or end, though it ostensibly begins with King Lear and ends with a significant reference to *Finnigan's Wake*, which also has no beginning or end. It has no chapters, but is divided into about a hundred sections, each of which is headed by a chapter gloss, which summarizes but is also an integral part of the section. Each of these is pretty self-contained, and

*The Gutenberg Galaxy: the Making of Typographic Man. By Marshall McLuhan. University of Toronto Press. 1962. Pp. 294. $5.95. Understanding Media, the Extensions of Man. By Marshall McLuhan. McGraw-Hill Book Company. 1964. Pp. 359. $8.75.

can be read almost at random in any order. The total effect is almost literally
that of a galaxy or a great garden of jeweled aphorisms. I can perhaps best
give the flavour of the book by quoting some of these, almost at random. For
instance, page 18, "The interiorization of the technology of the phonetic alphabet translates man from the magical world of the ear to the neutral visual
world"; 22, "Schizophrenia may be a necessary consequence of literacy"; 24,
"Does the interiorization of media such as 'letters' alter the ratio among our
senses and change mental processes?"; 26, "Civilization gives the barbarian or
tribal man an eye for an ear and is now at odds with the electronic world";
31, "The new electronic interdependence recreates the world in the image of a
global village"; 124, "The invention of typography confirmed and extended the
new visual stress of applied knowledge, providing the first uniformly repeatable
'commodity,' the first assembly-line, and the first mass-production"; 199, "Print,
in turning the vernaculars into mass media, or closed systems, created the
uniform, centralizing forces of modern nationalism"; 208, "The uniformity and
repeatability of print created the 'political arithmetic' of the seventeenth century and the 'hedonistic calculus' of the eighteenth"; 239, "Nobody ever made
a grammatical error in a non-literate society"; 251, "Typography cracked the
voices of silence."

Frankly, hopefully "gentle reader," how do you review a book like this?
Understanding Media is somewhat more conventional in form, in that it has
chapters, and does seem to have a beginning and an end. The crackling quality
of the ideas and of the style, however, remains, and it is really the same book
as *The Gutenberg Galaxy* in a slightly more conventional form, and applied
more directly to the problems of the modern world. Even so, there is a new
idea on almost every page, and the sheer density of new ideas is so great that
at the end one has a distinct feeling of having been hit over the head. The
publisher is reported to have said that nobody would read a book unless at
least ninety per cent of it was familiar, and there is no doubt that a book of
this kind, where ninety per cent of the ideas are unfamiliar to the average
reader, is exhausting. It has long been a custom of mine to take notes of the
books I read on the flyleaves at the back, and usually the page or two which
the publisher thoughtfully provides, presumably for this purpose, is ample. I
usually only jot down things which I think are somewhat new to me or significant. In McLuhan's case I find I have not only covered all the flyleaves provided, but my notes have spilled over onto an assortment of airline menus and
hotel stationery, reflecting the synthesis of two means of communication, the
airplane and the book.

Now, however, comes the sober and earthy work of appraisal. Is the *Galaxy*
a firework, exploding into stars and descending as a stick, or is there something here that shines continuously as part of the structure of the social universe? What, in other words, happens to the McLuhan message after it has
gone through the medium of the Boulding nervous system? I think my conclusion is that there is a good deal of fireworks, but in the middle of the fireworks
there are some real bright and continuing stars, in the light of which the world
will never be quite the same again. I will try to summarize in some chapter
glosses of my own.

1. A social system is largely structured by the nature of the media in which communications are made, not by the content of these communications.

This, I take it, is the central message of McLuhan, and with this proposition I think I agree almost 99 per cent. It is the invention of spoken language that differentiated man from the beasts, and enabled him to create societies, social systems, and social evolution in the first place. The invention of writing is a major mutation. Without it, urban civilizaton would have been inconceivable, even though it is not the only precondition of civilization. Thus, we must have the domestication of plants and animals, that is, agriculture, before a sufficiently large and stable food surplus appears with which cities can be fed. Men must be fed before they can write. Once they start to write, however, a whole new fabric of social life is created, and man becomes conscious of time, and the social organization extends backward into the past and forward into the future in a way it could never do in a purely oral society. Societies with alphabets do differ from those with ideographs, though perhaps McLuhan overdoes this. All languages are really ideographic. The alphabet is merely a crutch towards learning the *gestalt* patterns of whole words and sentences, though it is un- doubtedly convenient in writing dictionaries and developing lexicographical orderings. The relationship between literacy and violence forms a fascinating theme which recurs constantly in McLuhan. The letters of the alphabet are the dragon's teeth from which spring armed men. I am not sure that he is entirely right in this; I suspect rather that the alphabet and the armed men both spring from a more remote and fundamental cause, which is the rise of large-scale organization itself. The apparent peacefulness of the Neolithic vil- lage and the beastly violence of civilization may reflect merely the ability to organize violence, and even though literacy is part of the skills of organization, it is by no means the whole.

2. Media can be divided into "hot" media, which do not involve much parti- cipation on the part of the recipient, and "cool" media, in which the process of communication involves a great deal of participation on the part of the recipient. The effect of a medium on the structure of society depends very much on its temperature.

The terminology, I think, is unfortunate, but the idea is an important one, even if McLuhan runs it a little into the ground. Print is a hot medium. It is like a branding iron, imposing its own pattern on the page, if not on the mind. It is endessly repeatable; it implies abstraction. It carries man away from intimate, complex relationships, from *gemeinschaft* into *gesellschaft*, from tri- balism into nationhood, from feudalism into capitalism, from craftsmanship into mass production, from lore into science. It builds large-scale organizations because it develops abstract and simple human relationships, and permits the almost endless multiplication of messages and patterns. By contrast, speech is a cool medium, developing dialogue, response, feedback, complex and intricate patterns of personal relationships, family-centred societies, a familistic ethic, tribalism, and superstition. McLuhan argues that by far the most important thing that has happened in the twentieth century is the development of televi- sion, which is a cool medium of communication, involving a high level of participation on the part of the viewer, mainly, it would seem, because the television image is so imperfect.

It is clear that McLuhan has an enormously important idea here. On the other hand, it is not difficult to catch him out in inconsistencies, especially in his discussion of television, where he seems the least convincing. From one point of view, surely both radio and television are as hot media as print, in the sense that they do not really evoke dialogue or feedback between the recipient and the originator of messages. On the other hand, one feels that McLuhan is quite right in pointing out the enormous contrast between radio and TV. Hitler was a phenomenon of the brief radio age. On TV he would have been as ridiculous as McCarthy was. There is no doubt that TV elected Kennedy, defeated Nixon, and destroyed McCarthy, and that radio was the secret of the power both of Hitler and of Roosevelt. But this has very little to do with the hot-cold continuum, as McLuhan describes it. The real difficulty here, and it is something which is likely to distract attention from the enormous importance of McLuhan's message, is that he has tried to squash into a single dimension properties of media which require at least three dimensions for their exposition. We have on the one hand the dimension of involvement of the recipient, which is the one on which McLuhan concentrates, and this is indeed important. It accounts for a great deal of the different effects of oral *versus* written communication, or the difference between the printed page and the picture, or the difference between Renaissance and modern painting, or the difference between Mozart and Strindberg. I would like to call this dimension the *demandingness* of the media. Some media are demanding, some are undemanding. On this dimension, I suspect that print is "cooler" than McLuhan thinks. Print is not imprinted on the mind the way it is on paper. In order to effect the transmission from the printed page to the nervous system of the reader, an enormous amount of involvement is required, and the pattern of the printed page has to be translated with the aid of an enormous memory bank into a totally different pattern in the nervous system. After all, there are no letters in the brain. Demandingness here is perhaps more a function of the context of the medium than the actual physical form of the medium itself, and McLuhan often makes the mistake of supposing that it is the physical form of the medium which is significant rather than its social context.

A second dimension which McLuhan tries to squash into his single continuum is the *range* of a medium. This is closely related to the ability of the medium to develop a system of feedback from the communicatee to the communicator. A conversation, even more a dialogue, is the medium with the smallest range. It exists for the most part only at a single point in time and space, even though there is a time dimension in individual memory. The invention of writing made it possible for the present to speak to the future, and to hear from the past. It also made it possible for one man to communicate with people far beyond the range of his voice. Printing merely introduced a quantitative change in this dimension. It merely had the effect of amplifying the effect of manuscript. It is significant, I think, that in the age of print between Gutenberg and Edison, a man could communicate in visual form to many more people than he could communicate with orally. Electronics changed all this. The phonograph and the tape did for the ear what writing and printing had done for the eye. It enabled us to hear people from the past and to speak to people in the future. It also increased the potential number of people who can hear one man to include the whole population of the earth. As communication increases in range, however, it tends to lose in feedback. With increase in range, dialogue passes into monologue.

A third dimension of media is their information *density*. McLuhan hints at this many times, but never quite seems to spell it out. The concept here is close to the information theorist's concept of capacity. The information intake of the human is limited by the capacity of his sense organs. The ear has a greater capacity than the skin, and the eye than the ear. The combination of all the senses has a greater capacity than any one of them taken singly. The problem is complicated by the fact that the capacity may not be a simple additive quantity. We are interested, furthermore, not merely in the amount of information which can be transmitted per unit of time, but in the total information which can be transmitted and processed during the life of a system. There is no point in having an enormous intake of information through the senses for five minutes if it takes us five days to digest and process the information we have received. It is probably the information-processing apparatus which is the real bottleneck, not the information-receiving apparatus. The failure to realize this occasionally leads McLuhan astray. I suspect, for instance, that he puts too much stress on "synaesthesia" or the combination of the senses, and not enough on the fact that it is the processing of information in the human nervous system which is the really crucial process in the social system. In this sense it *is* the message, not the medium, which is important. The message is not just another medium, as McLuhan is continually saying, for the message consists of the processing of information into knowledge, and not the mere transmission of information through a medium.

3. Print created an "explosion" resulting in the break-up of an old integrated order into individualistic, differentiated, atomistic, mechanical human particles, producing classical economics, Protestantism, and the assembly line. Electricity creates an "implosion" which unifies the nervous systems of all mankind into a single contemporaneous whole, bringing us back to the tribal village, this time on a world scale.

This exciting theme recurs constantly in McLuhan's work. It is one of those great flashes of light which makes the surrounding world seem rather dim, and it seems almost sacrilegious to ask if this idea is true or can be tested. Print certainly had a lot to do with Protestantism and capitalism. On the other hand it also had a lot to do with the rise of the modern nation, the development of national literatures, and the break-up of the trans-national order of the Middle Ages. It is true that a book (in manuscript) created medieval Europe, and another book created Islam, and with the coming of print these old unities fragmented. Is this the result of print, however, or is it simply the result of multiplication? Surely if Gutenberg had discovered an offset process by which manuscripts themselves could simply be reproduced cheaply and easily, the effect would have been exactly the same as the discovery of print. Here again I think we see McLuhan concentrating on one dimension of a medium to the exclusion of others. Similarly with the electric implosion. It is certainly true that the rise of large-scale organization is intimately connected with the development of the telephone and telegraph and instantaneous communication. These inventions have had an enormous effect in increasing the range of media, both in terms of the distance over which dialogue could be conducted, and also in terms of the number of people to which a single person can speak. On the other hand, I would argue that electricity in itself has not had much effect on either the demandingness or the density of media in general. It has raised some and lowered others. Consequently, I have doubts about the world village. It is true, I think, that an increase in the range of media, whether this is conversations or weapons, increases the optimum scale of organization, and that we have probably now got to the point where the optimum scale of political organization is the whole world. This does not mean, however, that we are going back to the tribal village. We are going on into something quite new and strange, and even though this newness and strangeness is highly conditioned by the nature of the media that produce it, it is by no means clear that McLuhan has caught the exact relationship. It is perhaps typical of very creative minds that they hit very large nails not quite on the head.

These criticisms in no way detract from the enormous importance of these works. They should provide hypotheses for social sciences to test for a hundred years to come. One would like to see them required reading in every university. There is indeed in these days an invisible college, as de Solla Price calls it, of people who have perceived the crucial role of information processes in social systems. I am not sure that I would appoint McLuhan president of this invisible college, but I would certainly welcome him as its dean.

THE ETHICS OF RATIONAL DECISION

Management Science, 12, 6 (Feb. 1966): B-161 to B-169

THE ETHICS OF RATIONAL DECISION †

In recent years a great deal of attention has been paid by social scientists and others to the problem of the theory of decisions. The decision is a basic concept of social systems, especially in social dynamics. It represents perhaps the most important single class of *events*, an event being defined as a kind of step-function which separates one position of a social system from the next in point of time. Some events are not the result of human decision at all, such as aging or accidents; some are the results of previous decisions, such as depreciation of a previously created capital structure; but when all these are removed, there remains an important category of events which constitute a deliberate change in state of a social system as a result of human action.

The concept of a decision always implies that the change of state in question is not the only possible state, and that there is at least one other possibility. A decision, that is to say, involves choice. We imply that from any given present state, there is a number greater than one of possible alternative states in the future. We can simplify the problem by supposing that the condition that determines the future is contained in a given state, and hence the choice is among the possible "next" states of the system.

The problem of decision can then be broken down into two further problems. There is the problem of the definition of our knowledge of alternative possible states. In the initial state, we have to have some kind of image of possible future states, and it is a very interesting and quite difficult question as to how we acquire this image. There is more in this than meets the eye. Having now acquired an image of possible futures, by whatever means, in which each possible state includes what we have to do in order to attain it, the next question is how do we value these possibilities in a value ordering, so that we can choose the right one of them as superior to all the others. The principle known to economists as the principle of maximizing behavior simply states that when we are faced with a number of possibilities, we always choose that which seems to us to be best at the time. This seems like a principle of such extreme formality that it is a little surprising at first sight that it could have any use whatever. However, in the hands of economists it turns out to be quite surprisingly powerful, and it is indeed the foundation of operations research and management science, most of which consists in elaborate techniques for putting content into this otherwise contentless proposition.

The moment we state it in this way, it is clear that a decision is a process, to paraphrase a famous legal expression, "affected with the ethical interest." The

† Address presented at the 27th National Meeting of the Operations Research Society of America, Boston, Massachusetts, May 7, 1965.

ethical interest impinges on it at two points. It impinges even in the first stage when we ask ourselves, how do we come to know the range of possible alternatives, for there may be alternative ways of coming to know alternatives, and we have to make some kind of value judgment among them. At the second stage of the decision making process, in which the alternatives are subjected to value ordering, the ethical interest is clearly implied, for one of the major concerns of ethics is the evaluation of value orderings themselves. Ethics, that is, is concerned with what might be called decision problems of the second degree, that is, decision about how decisions are going to be made, and according to what principles are they going to be made.

The very use of the word "rational" in the expression "rational decision making" has ethical implications, for the problem of whether the *rational* is to be identified as the *good* is by no means a simple one. The definition of rationality itself is also by no means simple. It is customary to define rationality in terms of a set of limitations on the nature of a value ordering. It is argued, for instance, that a value ordering is irrational if it is intransitive, that is, if we prefer A to B, B to C, and C to A, or even more, if we prefer A to B, we should not at the same time prefer B to A. Even these formal definitions of rationality frequently gets us into trouble. The plain fact is that intransitive orderings are observed in real life all the time, simply because comparing pairs of things two at a time is not the same kind of process as trying to make a rank-ordering of a number of things simultaneously, even within the mind of a single individual. When we come to such things as committee and group decisions, the possibility of intransitive orderings increases substantially. In the famous voting paradoxes, for instance, those propounded by Duncan Black, and the whole set of problems associated with the name of Kenneth Arrow, it is suggested that such things as group decisions and committee decisions will often depend as much on the process or ritual by which the decision is reached as it does on the actual preferences of the individuals in the group. Even at this rather formal level, therefore, there are many difficulties in the concept of rationality.

If we take into account the cost of the decision making process itself, the concept of rationality disintegrates even further. Here the theory of the dilemma is of some importance. If we have a weak ordering of the alternatives open towards us, so that for instance there are two possibilities at the top of our rank-ordering of equal value to us, of which, however, we must choose one, we find ourselves in a difficult and painful position. If the possibilities are in fact absolutely equal in rank, then the rational decision is to be irrational and to make the selection by a random process, such as tossing a coin. Even if two possibilities are not identical but are very close to each other in our estimation, the difficulty and the cost of deciding between them may be so great that it again is rational not to be rational, and to decide the issue by random process. We could almost argue that this is what the American political system does, in the sense that where the two contending parties are really rather similar, the process of deciding between them turns out to be an almost random ritual.

A rather similar problem arises in the first part of the decision process, that is, the building up of the image of possibilities. Here, perfect knowledge is almost always too costly, and we have to be content with imperfect knowledge. This means, however, that we have the problem of search, that is, the investment of resources which might have alternative uses in expanding our image of the possibilities that are open to us. I know of no simple rational model of the process of search at all. How do we know when to stop looking for the needle in the haystack?—short of putting the whole haystack through a sieve! I recall the children's game of hide end seek, in which the group who have hidden an object tell the seeker whether he is "hot" or "cold." If there are indeed processes like this in the search procedure, we are very fortunate. Many times, however, there is nobody to shout "hot" or "cold." There may be no feedback whatever from the search until we find what we are looking for. This gets even more difficult when we are not even sure that what we are looking for exists, which is often the case in social systems. This suggests, incidentally, that existence theorems might have a profound effect on behavior because of their effect on the willingness to search. Even if we know what we are looking for, however, if we have not found it do we try, try again, or do we simply call it quits and try something else? Should we interpret failure as "too little and too late" and renew our efforts along the same lines, or should we interpret it as "too much and too soon" and divert our attention to other lines of endeavor altogether? Unfortunately there is often very little in the search situation which indicates which of these paths we should follow. One may perhaps hazard a guess that both in individual and organizational behavior, there is more tendency to beat our heads against a stone wall and to refuse to reverse the directions of search (pigheadedness) than there is to failure to persist in directions which are going to reward us at the next turn of the road (faintheartedness). I am not sure, however, that this proposition can be proved.

The problem of the calculus of probabilities when future outcomes are uncertain also presents us with a wide range of difficulties in regard to rational decision. In the first place, if we are dealing with stochastic systems, in which there are real random elements from the point of view of the observer, it is by no means easy to separate the random from the non-random elements in the system by simple observation of the sequence of events. Here we tend to fall into two opposite errors. We may interpret an event that is non-random, and is in fact built into some kind of a system, as if it were a random event, in which case we are in danger of failing to perceive the truly systematic nature of the world in which we are living. An even commoner, and perhaps more dangerous error, is the interpretation of random events as if they were in fact systematic. This results in building up an image of a system which in fact is untrue, that is, which does not correspond to the non-random, systematic character of the real world. If we add to this the fact that in social systems our images are quite often self-justifying, in the sense that they induce behavior on the part of the individual who holds them which tends to create the social system of his image, we see that rational decision-making is a very precarious system indeed, and one is almost tempted to the cynical conclusion that people are not divided into *rational* and *irrational* but into *lucky* and *unlucky*.

At this point, indeed, the ethical predispositions and images of the decision maker may have profound consequences, not only on the kinds of decisions he makes, but also on the kind of real world in which he lives. There is a famous Quaker story of a Friend who was asked by a newcomer to his community, what type of people lived there. He asked the newcomer, "What kind of people did thee live among before?" The newcomer replied, "Oh, I lived among a mean, suspicious, unfriendly, treacherous bunch of people," whereupon the Quaker replied, "Well, I am very sorry, friend, but thee will probably find the same type of people here." Going down the road, the Quaker meets another newcomer, of whom he asks the same question. "Oh," said the second man, "I lived among a fine group of people, friendly and honest, and I was sorry to leave them;" whereupon the Quaker said, "I am glad to say, friend, thee will find the same kind of people here."

Turning now to the problems involved in the selection of the value function itself, we face another interesting and difficult problem, which arises out of the development and use of what might be called value indexes. A value index, like money or money's worth, is a "measure of value," that is, it is a set of numbers arrived at by some well-defined process, which has the property that the higher the number, the higher the value of the state of the social system from which it is derived. In decision theory, we do not usually have to assume that the set of numbers of the value index represents a cardinal ordering of the underlying value function, for all we usually need is a rank ordering, that is, a set of ordinal numbers. However, every set of cardinal numbers is also at the same time a rank ordering. A value index which gives us such a set has all the properties we need, and we can easily neglect the implications of cardinality; that is, we do not have to assume that a value represented by an index of 200 is twice as great as one represented by an index of 100.

Problems arise, however, when the value index fails to maintain a 1 to 1 ordinal relation with the underlying value function, and this can also easily happen. We see this, for instance, in the familiar example of profit maximization. Profits are an extraordinarily useful value index, no matter how we measure them. Ten dollars is usually better than nine, and 10 % better than 9 %. The assumption of profit maximization, therefore, gives us a useful body of analysis in economics, the conclusions of which are certainly not wholly unrelated to the real world. Nevertheless, it is also clear that most firms do not maximize profits, mainly because at a certain point, profits tend to break down as a value index. For instance, it might well prefer a profit rate of 6 % which gives it a quiet life, good public relations, good labor relations, and so on, to a profit rate of 7 % which is less secure and which involves non-monetary disadvantages in the shape of poor labor relations, poor public relations, and so on. If profit can be sacrificed for anything, however, it is clearly not maximized; hence it cannot be taken without qualification as a value index.

The problem of a value index is of crucial importance for operations research, for the solution of any operations research problem involves the selection of a value index, the establishment of its functional relation to other variables which describe the state of the system, and a definition of that state of the system at which the value index is a maximum. If the value index which is selected does not have an ordinal relation to the underlying value function, the solutions which are reached by operations research can be severely misleading. One sees the same problem even at less sophisticated levels in what might be called the subordinate ideals of various departments in an organization. There is a famous story of a production manager who said that all he wanted to do was to minimize costs, until it was pointed out that the easiest way to do this would be to shut down operations altogether, in which case the costs would be reduced to zero. Here the fulfillment of subordinate goals can easily be inimical to the fulfillment of the larger goals and the more ultimate value system. We see this in the necessity which every organization has for compromise among departmental goals; we see it particularly acutely in the problems of the centrally planned economy; we also see it in the field of formal education, where the ultimate goal of producing educated people is often interfered with because we set up subordinate goals in the shape of grades, degrees, and so on, which are supposed to motivate people step by step towards the final goal. Thus, what might be called the subordination of subordinate goals emerges as one of the major problems of decision making in organizations.

The problem of the subordination of subordinate goals, however, also emerges as one of the major problems of ethics. One of the prime problems of ethics, as I have suggested earlier, is the evaluation of value functions themselves. This frequently takes the form of the criticism of the "insubordination" of subordinate goals, that is, a situation in which the subordinate goals become dominant and take the place of the more fundamental value function which they are supposed to represent. Even though ethical theory does not come out with any single formula for relating subordinate goals to ultimate goals, it can state with a high degree of certainty that given the complexity of the human organism, no single value index can ever serve without question as a measure of the ultimate goal. That is, in pursuing any particular subordinate goal, we must always get to the point at which we must ask ourselves, "Is a little more of this worth what we have to sacrifice in order to get it?" Obsession by single subordinate goals, whether this is money or sex or eating or even stamp-collecting, is a sign of mental or at least ethical ill health. A person who is ethically mature will constantly be weighing subordinate goals against each other and making decisions about how far to pursue each one.

The quantification of value functions into value indices, whether this is money or whether it is more subtle and complicated measures of payoff, introduces elements of ethical danger into the decision making process, simply because the clarity and apparent objectivity of quantitatively measurable subordinate goals can easily lead to a failure to bear in mind that they are in fact subordinate. The development of accounting is an interesting case in point. Before the development of double-entry bookkeeping and the fairly accurate recording of profit and loss, which began to take place in about the fourteenth or fifteenth century, presumably even merchants and still more landlords and farmers would only have very vague ideas about how profitable their operations might be. With the development of accounting, the measurement of profit became much more exact, but as a result also, certain other elements of the total value situation became less prominent and, therefore, neglected, such things for instance as morale, loyalty, legitimacy, and intimacy and complexity of personal relations. I suspect that the sociological weakness of the business community and its extraordinary inability to stand up, both to military ideologies, as witness the case of Japan, and also to socialist ideologies, arises from this fundamental deficiency. A subculture within which profit-making becomes the only criterion for decisions either must be supported by a set of institutions from outside, which can develop something like an integrative structure, such as the church or the club or the school or the state, or else it will simply collapse because of its integrative weakness. I seem to recall saying somewhere else that the only thing that is wrong with capitalism is that nobody loves it. Schumpeter makes essentially the same point, that capitalism fails in spite of its spectacular economic success because the institutions of the market do not develop an integrative system sufficient to sustain it in the face of the kind of hatred, loss of legitimacy, and criticism which arise out of pure profit-oriented decisions. This illustrates a principle of very great importance, that decisions which may seem to be rational from the point of view of a single part of the social system may in fact turn out to be disastrous from the point of view of the continuance of the social system itself.

This principle becomes even more strikingly manifested when we look at the problem of rational decision in threat systems, that is, in social systems in which threats and counter-threats are used in the organization of roles and behavior. In systems which are dominated by exchange, such as business, especially where markets are reasonably perfect, the decision maker can assume with a modicum of security that he makes the decisions in the face of an environment which will not change because of the decisions which he makes. In the case of threat systems, this is rarely, if ever, true. There is practically no analog in threat systems of the economists' concept of the perfect market. All threat systems operate under conditions analogous to oligopoly. Under these circumstances there is a strong tendency for the system to degenerate into zero-sum and negative-sum games, whereas in the exchange system, positive-sum games are prominent. The main problem with negative-sum games, however, is not how to play them well but how to avoid playing them at all; that is, how to transform the system from a threat system into either an exchange system or an integrative system. Unfortunately, the people who operate the threat system and who are supported by it have a certain vested interest in maintaining it. Hence they concentrate on the problem of how to act rationally within the threat system when frequently this is a problem that has no real solution, and effort concentrated towards replacing the threat system by a more positive-sum kind of arrangement would have much higher payoffs.

The ethical matrix of behavior, which determines the predispositions out of which the decision maker evaluates the various value systems which are open to him is of great importance in determining the width of the agenda of the decision maker. There seems to be a fundamental disposition in mankind to limit agenda, often quite arbitrarily, perhaps because of our fears of information overload. We all suffer in some degree from agoraphobia, that is, the fear of open spaces, especially open spaces in the mind. As a result, we all tend to retreat into the cosy closed spaces of limited agendas and responsibilities, into tribalism, nationalism, and religious and political sectarianism and dogmatism. Nevertheless, ethical analysis puts out a warning flag at this point. Even though there may be good reasons for limiting agenda to prevent information overload, nevertheless, limiting the agenda is always costly and is sometimes very costly, and there is something about this process which prevents us from realizing how costly it is, simply because we cannot know the cost of limiting the agenda unless we widen it, which act, of course, the very process of limiting the agenda forbids. Hence what looks like rational decisions under limited agendas often turn out to be disastrous, whether this is in business, in politics, or even in religion, and for that matter, even in science, where the deliberate limiting of agendas is at the same time often the secret of present success and an obstacle to future progress.

On the other side of the coin, there is also a considerable relationship between the capacity of a decision maker to handle large quantities of information and his ability to widen his agenda. People who have narrow agendas, the bigots, the Birchers, the Marxists, the nationalists, and the schizophrenics, are by and large people whose information processing capacities are highly limited. They retreat into narrow agendas because they cannot bear the information overload which would seem to result from wide ones. Improvements in information processing, therefore, have profound ethical significance, because they remove obstacles to that widening of agendas which is one of the major components of most ethical systems. Preaching, which has been one of the main technologies of ethics, never seems to have been very effective, beyond a certain point, and it may be that the horizons of the power of ethical ideas may be substantially extended by the development of improved methods of information processing by the individual and by the organization.

Let me conclude by illustrating these principles in the particular case of an ethical system which is at least vaguely familiar to most people in our society, that is, the Christian ethic. I am aware, of course, that there is no such thing as a single Christian ethic, and that even in the Bible we find a complex, organic historical web of interacting and often inconsistent ethical systems. By way of illustration, however, I will just pick out two classical ethical statements; the first, the injunction, "Love one's neighbor as oneself" first comes in the Old Testament and is as much a part of the Judaic as of the Christian tradition, and the second, the injunction to love one's enemies, which is more distinctively Christian, even though it has usually been regarded as a "counsel of perfection," to be admired rather than observed.

The injunction to love one's neighbor as oneself has two major implications for decision theory, the first, often overlooked, that one should love oneself. In terms of economics this means that one should maximize utility rather than minimizing disutility, a distinction which is virtually unknown to economics, but which is very important to psychology. In other words, one should move towards the best rather than moving away from the worst. This, I have argued, is the essential key to mental health. The internal conflicts and dilemmas of the utility maximizer are all of the approach-approach variety, which are easily resolved, like the dilemma of the famous donkey between the two bales of hay. The disutility minimizer constantly gets into avoidance-avoidance conflicts like the donkey between two skunks, and hence gets into insoluble dilemmas in which all rational choice breaks down.

The injunction to love one's neighbor involves a widening of agendas on the one hand and the development of an integrative system on the other. It implies in the first place that we regard our decisions as involving the total social system, and not only that part of it which revolves around our own persons. It implies, that it is to say, a kind of Copernican Revolution and an abandonment of perspective. Instead of seeing the world through our own eyes from our own position, we make the imaginative leap, as Copernicus did, and in effect see ourselves from outside. This is an injunction, therefore, which leads towards what might be called objective realism. It also, however, has profound implications for the kind of value system which we place over the world as viewed objectively. It involves a realistic appraisal of the self and its position in the world, rather than a self-denial, which I think is not really consistent with the Christian ethic, but creeps into it from the more negative religions of the East. In practice, of course, one must make concessions to perspective—the near are going to be dearer than the far, and the association of the near and dear is by no means unreasonable, especially in the light of the limits of one's power and responsibility. It is, after all, the neighbor—that is, the near one—that one is advised to love.

The question, who is my neighbor, is of course the tricky one, and this is where the love of enemies, who are also near and, therefore, neighbors, becomes relevant. There are a good many different kinds of love of enemies. There is one kind that rises out of self-hatred, as William Blake saw so clearly ("He who loves his enemies hates his friends; surely that is not what Jesus intends"). There is also a certain kind of love of enemies which might be described as political rationality. A politician doesn't have to love his friends, as they will vote for him anyway. In his policies, therefore, he moves frequently towards the position of those who *just* did not vote for him, and if his friends are really friends, they will be dismayed but will continue to vote for him. Finally, there is the kind of love of enemies which might be described as integrative behavior, which is seldom recognized as such, but of which a great many examples can be found. This sometimes is done by those who are weak in the threat system, such as the joking behavior often remarked by anthropologists and observed in many classes which are subject to discrimination, such as Negroes, Jews, and traveling salesmen. The whole study of "disarming behavior"—politeness, the handshake, the bow, the form of address, likewise falls under this category. There can also, however, be integrative behavior on the part of those who are strong in the threat system, but who recognize the essential weakness and instability of the threat system itself, and who hence are concerned to replace it by something with larger horizons.

I would suggest, therefore, that it can be shown very easily that payoffs of an ethic of love are very large. Under universal benevolence, almost all social changes are good for everybody. Why then, in spite of all the preaching, is benevolence still so rare, and malevolence so common? The answer, as I have suggested earlier, may well be the defect in our information processing system. It is our attempt to defend outselves against information overload which forces us into malevolence, prisoners' dilemmas, arms races, price wars, class wars, schisms, feuds and divorces. Management science, however, is an alternative defense against information overload. It is not inconceivable, therefore, that techniques which perhaps were originally designed with extremely limited and abstract ends in view and which look at first sight very hostile to the subtle agendas of ethical behavior may ultimately bear fruit in the development of an ethical maturity beyond what all the efforts of the moralists and the preachers have hitherto been able to achieve. I suspect this will only happen, however, if ethical theory itself can respond in depth and maturity to the opportunities which the burgeoning sciences of man now seem to offer it.

EXPECTING THE UNEXPECTED: THE UNCERTAIN FUTURE OF KNOWLEDGE AND TECHNOLOGY

In: Prospective Changes in Society by 1980 Including Some Implications for Education, E. Morphet and C. O. Ryan, eds. Denver, Colo.: Designing Education for the Future, 1966, pp. 199-215

Expecting The Unexpected:
The Uncertain Future Of
Knowledge And Technology

HOW IS PREDICTION POSSIBLE?

One thing we can say about man's future with a great deal of confidence is that it will be more or less surprising. This phenomenon of surprise is not something which arises merely out of man's ignorance, though ignorance can contribute to what might be called unnecessary surprises. There is, however, something fundamental in the nature of an evolutionary system which makes exact foreknowledge about it impossible, and as social systems are in a large measure evolutionary in character, they participate in the property of containing ineradicable surprise.

Mechanical Systems

In *mechanical* systems which have no surprise in them, we can hardly say that there is a future or a past at all, as the present is a purely arbitrary point. The best example of a system of this kind is the solar system, at least before the advent of political astronomy in the shape of man-made satellites. In the Newtonian system in which the planets are moved by angels, that is, differential equations of the second degree, the system can be moved backwards or forwards in time simply by turning the crank of an orrery. Time is reversible, and what we have is a wholly predictable succession of states of the system. The fact that such a system takes place in time is quite accidental to it. We could just as well set it out as a succession in space, as we do, for instance, when we express it as a graph.

We can express the same thing in another way. If we use the familiar sequence of Monday, Tuesday, Wednesday, etc., to denote successive states of a system, then if the state of the system on any one day depends only on its state of the day before, we say that the system is of the first degree, and it can be expressed by a difference or differential equation of the first degree. If we know, then, the constant relation between today and tomorrow, and we know what the state of the system is on Monday, we can predict its state on Tuesday. Knowing its state on Tuesday we can predict its state on Wednesday, and so on indefinitely into the future.

This is how we calculate compound interest or exponential growth. If a system is of the second order, then the state today depends not only on the state yesterday but also on the state the day before yesterday. In that case we have to know both Monday and Tuesday independently before we can predict Wednesday. If we know Monday and Tuesday, however, we know Wednesday; then we know Tuesday and Wednesday and hence we know Thursday; then we know Wednesday and Thursday and hence we know Friday, and so on indefinitely. The greater part of the solar system can be predicted with equations as simple as this, though comets, I understand, require equations of the third degree, in which case we need to know Monday, Tuesday, and Wednesday before we can predict Thursday. Having Thursday, however, Tuesday, Wednesday, and Thursday gives us Friday, and so on again. As the degree of the system increases, we need more and more initial information about it before the total description of the system and therefore prediction about it becomes possible. As we move towards evolutionary systems, we shall find that the degree of the system increases eventually to the point where mechanical predictions simply break down. If the system, for instance, has an infinite degree, which human history probably has for all practical purposes, exact prediction becomes theoretically impossible; for we could never put enough information into the system to describe it exactly. Even if we knew everything that had happened before the present, a sufficient pattern would not emerge.

Pattern Systems

There are many systems which do not possess the hundred percent predictability of mechanical systems like the solar system, but which nevertheless exhibit partial predictability in greater or less degree. If we put a chicken egg to hatch, we should be extremely surprised if it hatched into an alligator. When we see a kitten, we have a great deal of confidence that it will grow up into a cat, not a dog, if it grows up at all. Similarly, little boys almost invariably grow up into men and little girls into women, though there are a few exceptions to this rule. Similarly, when we see a skeleton steel structure, we expect to come back in a few months and see a finished building; when we see a keel in a shipyard we would later expect to find a ship, and so on over a very large range of human experiences. Probably the most respectable name for systems of this kind would be pattern-systems, as their predictability depends on the perception and recognition of a pattern which has been experienced in the past. We have watched our parents aging, so we predict that we will age ourselves in much the same way. There is a pattern of all human life from the fertilized egg to the grave, even though this pattern may be sliced off at any time by death. In a more frivolous mood I am tempted to call these systems wallpaper systems. Once we have perceived a pattern on wallpaper, we have great confidence in predicting it beyond the corner of the room that we cannot see, even though here too it might be cut off by an unexpected system break such as a door.

Just as astronomy and physics are the principal domain of mechanical systems, so the biological world is the principal domain of the pattern systems. In the fertilized egg there is a genetic blueprint for the creature that will emerge (if the process is not stopped by death), which charts within very narrow limits the growth of the phenotype, and in a very real sense creates the creature. Even if the growth of the creature is interrupted at some point by a nonfatal illness or temporary deficiencies in the food supply, the growth pattern often catches up again once the deficiency is restored. We have a great deal of confidence, therefore, in the stability of these patterns, a confidence which is rarely misplaced. The main uncertainties involved are those relating to the limits of the system, beyond which it cannot recover, for every system of this kind is subject to certain random processes which may lead to death at any time. In the mythology of the Fates, Clotho spins the pattern with great regularity; Atropos snips it at the moment of death (she is clearly the goddess of system break); and Lachesis, who measures it, is a fairly random number. Her measure is a roulette wheel with one mark on it that gives the sign to Atropos, and then—snip!

Equilibrium Systems

A third broad class of systems which admit of predictability may be identified as *equilibrium systems.* These are systems in which the dynamic processes produce a succession of states, all of which are virtually identical. Whatever sense we have of stability in the world is derived from our perception of equilibrium processes. In the short run at any rate, people stay much the same from day to day; the field, the forest, the swamp and the lake reproduce themselves season after season, year after year, in an ecological equilibrium. The stores are always full of commodities, the gas stations full of gas. Cities contain streets, public buildings, churches, schools, and houses, year after year. The university has freshmen, sophomores, professors, deans, and a president; when one goes, another takes his place. When an equilibrium is stable, we have a good deal of confidence that a disturbance will be followed by a movement toward equilibrium again. The sick man recovers, the burned city is rebuilt, the forest comes back after a fire.

An increasingly important class of equilibrium systems is what may be called *control systems,* that is, equilibria which have been deliberately contrived by man. In a house with a furnace and a thermostat we can predict the inside temperature with a great deal of confidence, even though the outside temperature cannot be predicted with any great degree of confidence. In this case we predict the future not because we know it but because we make it. Thus modern economists are not merely interested in predicting the business cycle but in controlling it, and in setting up social "thermostats" which will counteract the random and perverse processes which operate on the economy, just as a thermostatically controlled furnace counteracts changes in outside temperature. Control systems must have what is called "equilibrating feedback." When outside disturbances threaten the equilibrium of the system, it must be capable of detecting and interpreting this information and of setting in motion dynamic processes which will counteract the disturbances. Thus if we want a stable rate of growth in the economy, we must be able to perceive when the rate of growth is slowing down and be able to speed it up, or when the rate of growth is getting too large and be able to slow it down. Similarly, if we want stable peace, we have to have a control apparatus which will perceive the movement towards war and set in motion counteracting dynamic processes.

In the biological world and also in social systems, we often get patterns of succession of short-run equilibrium states, which are generally described as ecological succession. The lake fills up and becomes a swamp, finally a prairie, and then a forest. Many philosophers of history have tried to interpret human history likewise in terms of a succession of states or stages, hunting, pastoral, agricultural, and industrial, though the pattern of human history is not as clear and precise as those we find in the biological world. Insofar as we can detect these patterns of succession; however, we gain some powers of prediction.

Evolutionary Systems.

The patterns of ecological succession, however, do not help us very much when it comes to the great processes of evolution. These involve the processes of genetic mutation and ecological selection in the biological field, and parallel phenomena involving the growth of knowledge and organizations, cultures and societies, techniques and commodities, in the social field. Evolutionary theory is all hindsight; it has practically no predictive power at all. In evolutionary systems, time is not reversible nor is it arbitrary. There are indeed two systems in which time is not reversible; one is thermodynamics and the other is evolution. In thermodynamics, time's arrow points "down," according to the famous and dismal Second Law, by which entropy, that is, disorganization, continually increases, the availability of energy continually declines, potential is continuously used up, and what's done cannot be undone and can never be done again. Thermodynamics postulates a universe which starts off, as it were, with a capital and potential which it is inexorably squandering; and the end of the process is a kind of thin uniform soup in which all things are equally distributed, all at the same temperature, and chaos and old night have returned again.

By contrast, in the evolutionary process time's arrow points "up," towards the development of ever more complex and more improbable forms. Thermodyamically, it may be true that evolution is only just the segregation of entropy, that is, the building up of more and more complex little castles of order at the cost of increasing chaos elsewhere. Nevertheless, the castles of order do get more and more complex, from hydrogen to carbon to uranium, from small molecules to big molecules, to viruses, to cells, to multi-celled organisms, to vertebrates and mammals, to man, to families, to tribes, to nations, and perhaps to a world. If the evolutionary process continues, therefore, it is pretty safe to predict an increase in complexity. The nature of that complexity, however, because it is itself an information system, cannot be known in advance, at least by an organism with a merely human capacity for knowing things.

In practice, the main cause for failures in prediction is a sudden change in the characteristics of the system itself. Such a change has been called a "system break." Death, bankruptcy, and conquest are extreme forms of a system break, in which a complex system at some point simply ceases to exhibit any kind of equilibrium or homeostasis, and disintegrates. Less dramatic system breaks, however, are also common—graduation, a new job, or marriage in the case of an individual, turning points in the economy, the outbreak of war or peace in the international system, sudden changes in birth or death rates in demographic systems, and so on. The growth of knowledge and technology is as much subject to system breaks as other systems. Sometimes, for instance, there is what I have elsewhere described as an "acceleration," that is, a sudden change in the rate of growth of knowledge or productivity. Such an acceleration occurred in Europe about 1600 with the rise of science. It took place in Japan around 1868, at the time of the Meiji Restoration. As we shall see, a system break of this kind seems to have occurred in American agriculture about 1935.

System breaks, unfortunately, are very hard to detect. They are virtually impossible to predict in advance; they are even difficult to detect after they have happened for some time, because in the short run it is virtually impossible to distinguish the beginning of a new long-term trend from a strictly temporary fluctuation. Thus suppose we had a sudden increase in the birth rate which persisted for four or five years; it could still be argued (and was!) that this was only temporary. A change has to be established for a considerable time before we decide that it is permanent, and even then it can fool us.

PREDICTING KNOWLEDGE AND TECHNOLOGY

The Problem of Predicting Knowledge

The growth of knowledge is one of the most persistent and significant movements in the history of man, and, one might almost say, in the history of the universe. It is perhaps stretching the word to regard the whole evolutionary process as essentially a process of the growth of knowledge, but if we think of knowledge as a capital structure of information, that is, as an improbable arrangement or structure, we see that it is this increasing improbability of structure which characterizes the whole evolutionary process. Even the chemical atoms have "know-how" in the form of valency —carbon knows how to hitch onto four hydrogens, but not onto five. The gene unquestionably represents know-how in the form of a blueprint for the creature which it builds, and human and social development is ineradicably bound up with the growth of human knowledge, that is, with images inside the organism which correspond in some way to the world without.

Of the various processes which we have identified as permitting prediction, the growth of knowledge is least like a mechanical process and most like an evolutionary process. Mechanical projections of trends in growth rates in a system as complex as this are to be treated with the utmost reserve, though the concept of a rate of growth of knowledge which has some stability, at least in short periods, is by no means absurd. We can perceive also a certain acceleration in the growth of knowledge, that is, the rate of growth increases all the time. Thus knowledge is like a sum of capital which accumulates at continually rising interest rates. Even though the absence of any measure of the total stock of knowledge makes quantitative statements about it more akin to poetry than to mathematics, in a poetical sort of way we can hazard a guess that human knowledge perhaps doubled in a hundred thousand years in the paleolithic, in five thousand years in the neolithic, and perhaps every thousand years in the age of civilization until the rise of science. In many fields of science now knowledge seems to double about every fifteen years. It is this enormous increase in the rate of growth of knowledge which has dominated the history of the last two or three hundred years, in all aspects of human life, politically, economically, and in all forms of human organization. The domination of the world by European culture, for instance, is almost a byproduct of what may have been an accident, the fact that the mutation into science first took place in Europe.

The growth of knowledge, however, has been a subject of many interruptions and even reversals, and it would be very unwise to predict that just because knowledge has been growing at a certain rate in the past, it will continue to grow at the same rate in the future. It would be still more unwise to predict a constant rate of acceleration. We could say pretty safely, however, that the probability of growth is greater than that of decline, and that of acceleration is greater than that of deceleration.

A number of pattern systems can be detected in the growth of knowledge, especially in the spread of knowledge through education. The growth of knowledge has two aspects which can be summarized by the words education and research. Education is the spread of knowledge from one mind to another by means of communication processes between them. The communication may be one way, as when a person reads a book or sees a TV program, or it many be two way as in classroom teaching, conversation and dialogue. Thus education is a process by which what somebody knows or knew is transmitted to others. Research by contrast, is a process by which somebody gets to know something which nobody knew before. The two processes are highly intertwined. In the very act of transmitting knowledge, new knowledge is often created, which is one reason why universities combine the research and education processes. Knowledge is also lost in transmission, which is a kind of negative research, through noise and misunderstanding, which incidentally points up the great importance of dialogue and two-way transmissions if the body of knowledge is not to deteriorate in transmission.

The growth of knowledge in the individual follows a pattern which is closely related to the life pattern itself, and we hopefully suppose that knowledge increases with age. Formal education is an important part of this pattern, though it is not the only source of increase of knowledge. The growth of knowledge even in the individual is not a simple cumulative process by which information is pumped into the head and remains in a reservoir. Knowledge is a structure, and its present form always limits its possibilities of growth. Hence we get the phenomenon of "readiness" for certain kinds of knowledge at different stages of life. We get the phenomenon of wasted information input, which goes in at one ear and out the other, because it cannot latch onto anything in the existing knowledge structure. We get the phenomenon of superstition, or the development of false knowledge, as a result of the acceptance of authoritarian pronouncements and the failure of feedback; and we get the process of mutation through the imagination and testing through experience which is strikingly parallel to the evolutionary process itself, by which true knowledge grows.

The fact that the growth of knowledge has so many parallels to the evolutionary process renders it incapable of exact prediction. We can predict with some confidence that if the present system continues, knowledge will increase, not only bcause it has increased in the past but because we have a very large apparatus for increasing it. On the other hand, we run into a fundamental dilemma in attempting to predict the content of future knowledge, because if we knew the content of future knowledge, we would know it now, not in the future. That is, if we knew what we were going to know in twenty-five years, we would not have to wait twenty-five years for it. Consequently the growth of knowledge must always contain surprises, simply because the process itself represents the growth of improbable structures, and improbability always implies potential surprise. The whole idea of knowledge as a capital stock of information implies, therefore, that in detail its growth cannot be predicted. The difficulty is compounded by the fact that we know very little about the physiological structure which carries human knowledge. This difficulty, however, is less important than it might seem, for the carriers of an information structure are important only insofar as their properties limit the amount and complexity of the information that can be carried. We seem to be so far from the physical limits of the information content of the human nervous system that its physical properties can almost be neglected as a limit on the growth of knowledge.

Even though we cannot predict the specific content of future knowledge, what we know about the pattern of inputs and outputs enables us to venture at least on some probabilities. The distribution of new knowledge among the various fields and disciplines is at least likely to have some relation to the current distribution of research funds among these disciplines. Similarly the spread of knowledge in the world population is going to be related to some extent to the size of the educational industry and the funds allocated to it. I have argued elsewhere[1] that our research resources in particular are poorly allocated in the light of the importance for human welfare of the problems to which they are addressed. I have argued more particularly that the resources devoted to

---

[1]K.E. Boulding, "The Missallocation of Intellectual Resources," *Collected Papers,* Vol. III (Boulder, Colorado Associated University Press, 1973), pp. 195-200.

social systems are absurdly small in the light of the practical importance of these systems, and that whereas a failure of knowledge to advance in the physical and biological sciences for the next twenty-five years would not present mankind with any serious problems, the failure of knowledge to advance in the social sciences could well be fatal. Nevertheless we continue to devote our major effort to the physical, biological, and medical sciences and unless there is a change in this we can expect a continuation of the present imbalance in the growth of knowledge.

Predicting Technology

Many of the considerations which apply to the growth of knowledge also apply to the growth of technology. We can predict with a great deal of confidence that technology will change. In a society like ours, where a good deal of resources are devoted to improving technology, it will be very surprising if technology does not improve in the sense that it increases human productivity. On the other hand, we cannot predict the exact forms which this improvement will take, simply because again, if we could predict it we would have it now. The proposition perhaps is a little less true in regard to the spread of already known technologies to places and societies which do not yet possess them. We have already noted the distinction between education, consisting in the spread of old knowledge to people who did not have it before from people who did have it before, and research, as the development of new knowledge that nobody had before. A similar distinction can be made in regard to technology between the spread of an old technology and the creation of a new one. Strictly speaking, it is only the creation of a new technology which has to contain these elements of fundamental surprise. One might perhaps modify this proposition in the light of the fact that the transfer of technology, like the transfer of knowledge in the educational process, is itself a technology, and this too can be subject to technological change. The great problem of economic development of the poorer countries at the moment seems to be much dependent on an inability to produce an adequate technology for the transfer of technology, and of education for the transfer of knowledge. There may, therefore, be unexpected changes in the technology of transferring technology, and even this, therefore, may be subject to fundamental surprise.

While always preparing to be surprised, however, we can at least make some projections according to the simpler modes of prediction. As in the case of the growth of knowledge, even simple mechanical projections of rates of growth of technology are not meaningless. Perhaps the best general measure of the overall level of technology, in society is the index of output per man-hour. The accompanying chart from *Technology and the American Economy,* (Report of the National Commission on Technology, Automation, and Economic Progress, February 1966), page 3, shows the changes in output per man-hour for the last fifty years or so for agriculture, the private non-farm economy, and the total private economy. It is clear that we have been in a process of rapid technological advance. Output per man-hour has quadrupled in agriculture, tripled in the non-farm eco-

Indexes of Output Per Man-Hour
Total Private, Farm, and Private Non-farm Economy, 1909-65*

Output per Man-hour Index
Ratio Scale

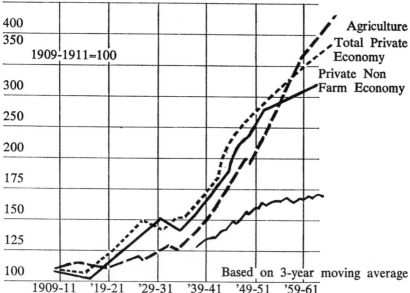

*Compiled from information provided by the U.S. Department of Commerce and Bureau of Labor Statistics, U.S. Department of Labor.

nomy, in little over forty years. If this process continues to 1980, we might expect the output per man-hour in agriculture to be almost eight times what it was around 1920, and in the private non-farm sector to be perhaps four and a half times what it was in 1920. There are no great signs of any acceleration in this process, contrary to some of the pronouncements which have been made by the more excitable writers on automation. In agriculture, indeed, we seem to have something like a system break in the mid-thirties, which could well correspond to the development of large inputs into agriculture, not only for research and development but also in price supports. It is somewhat sobering to project the index of output per man-hour in agriculture as I have done in the wavy line in the figure (which is not in the original). If agricultural productivity had continued to increase from the mid-thirties at the rate which it had followed in the preceeding twenty-five years, in the early 1960s the index would have been barely 135 or 140, by comparison with the nearly 400 which it actually reached. Nothing could illustrate better the dangers of projection, especially projection of trends, even trends which seem to have been established for quite a long period of time. Systems of this kind are always subject to system breaks, and hence the projection of existing trends should be treated with extreme reservations. Just because a boy doubles his height between the age of 8 and 18 does not mean he is going to double it again between 18 and 28, and in growth processes of any kind we have to be on the lookout for exhaustion of the original impetus which gave rise to the growth or the development of new impulses, such as the one we have just noticed in the case of agriculture.

The Qualitative Impact of Technology

We may be somewhat hesitant about the projection of quantitative trends and at the same time we may be more confident about certain qualitative and structural changes which these movements are introducing into the social system and which are likely to continue. We must first notice a phenomenon which is beginning to be of considerable importance in the American and other developed economies. This is that the more progressive sectors of the economy tend to shrink in regard to the proportion of the GNP which they generate or the amount of labor force which they absorb, relative to the technologically unprogressive sectors. This phenomenon is most striking in agriculture, where between 1930 and 1964 the proportion of civilian employment in agriculture fell from 25 percent to 7.6 percent in a little over a generation. We have managed to produce a small increase in agricultural output while reducing the absolute labor force to little more than a third of what it had been in 1929. This is an astonishing technological—and social—achievement. Even if it is repeated, however, and we continue to release people from agriculture, it is clear that the absolute numbers which can now be released are relatively small, and that though agriculture will almost certainly continue to shrink as a fraction of the economy, the resources released from it will not make the very large contribution to the non-agricultural labor force which they have made in the past, simply because there are not very many people left in it.

There is a question in many people's minds as to whether manufacturing is now about to suffer the fate of agriculture, thanks to cybernation. Manufacturing itself, however, is now not much more than 25 percent of the total labor force, so that even if the rate of technological change in manufacturing accelerates in the next fifteen years, and there are no immediate signs that it is doing this, it would be surprising if the proportion in manufacturing dropped to as little as, say, 20 percent of the total labor force. I am inclined to the view, therefore, that the great adjustment has already been made, the great adjustment, that is, out of agriculture. What has been displaced from agriculture has been absorbed largely in government, the professions, the service trades; and those who will continue to be displaced from agriculture and manufacturing will continue to be absorbed on balance in these expanding—because unprogressive—sectors. I will be a little surprised, therefore, if any spectacular change is observed in the structure of the labor force or the industrial structure of the economy in the next fifteen years, though, as I warned earlier, I am always prepared to be surprised.

Some further considerations of a qualitative kind might make the rather optimistic tone of the foregoing paragraphs seem like a very clouded crystal ball indeed by 1980 or still more by 2000. The crucial problem here is whether the development of electronics, automation, cybernation, and the whole complex of control systems does not introduce as it were a new gear into the evolutionary process, the implications of which are as yet only barely apparent. The computer is an extension of the human mind in the way that a tool or even an automobile is an extension of the human body. The automobile left practically no human institution unchanged as a result of the increase in human mobility which it permitted. The impact of the computer is likely to be just as great, and indeed of the whole world electronic network, which represents, as McLuhan has pointed out, an extension of the human nervous system and what is perhaps even more important, a linkage of our different nervous systems. It seems probable that all existing political and economic institutions will suffer some modifications as a result of this new technology; in what directions, however, it is hard to predict. That the ultimate results of this development will be benign can hardly be doubted except by those extreme pessimists who regard original sin as genetic in character and hence regard any extension of man's power as a mere increase in the opportunity to do harm. The faith that an increase in human power will be benign does depend, it is true, on certain assumptions about human teachability in ethics as well as in everything else. The very character of men's nervous system, however, assures us of his teachability, though it does not assure us that we can find ways of teaching him. At least, then, there is no theorem which drives us to a necessity for despair, even though there are plenty of occasions for a very reasonable disquiet.

We see the possible impacts of this new mode of human operation in a number of different fields. It has made the present international system, for instance, enormously threatening and so potentially destructive that it is hard to see how it can survive a generation. The day of national sovereignty and of unilateral national defense seems to be clearly over, though it may take a major catastrophe to convince us of this. As I have put it elsewhere, the world is rapidly becoming a very small crowded space ship in which men on horseback, even cowboys, cannot be tolerated. *The network of electronic communication is inevitably producing a world superculture, and the relations between this superculture and the more traditional national and regional cultures of the past remains the great question mark of the next fifty years.* For regions in which the defense industry is heavily concentrated, this question mark is particularly large, not only because of the economic adjustments which may be necessary, but because they represent prime target areas.

Another possible consequence of the qualitative changes in technology which seem to be under way is what I have sometimes called the "milk and cream" problem. Will the world separate out into two cultures, both within countries and between countries, in which a certain proportion of the people adapt through education to the world of modern technology and hence enjoy its fruits, while another proportion fail to adapt and perhaps become not only relatively worse off but even absolutely so, in the sense that what they have had in the past of traditional culture collapses under the impact of the technical superculture and leaves them disorganized, delinquent, anemic, and poor? In "creamy" societies like the United States, the "cream" may be 70 or 80 percent of the population, and the "skim milk" may be only 20 or 30 percent. The depressed sector, however, may be large enough to be threatening not only to the consciences of the rich sector but even to its security, as frustration and anger lead to violence.

On the world scale, the outlook is even darker. At the moment the separation-out phenomenon is proceeding at an alarming pace. The rich countries are getting richer at an unprecedented pace, many of the poor countries are stagnating or even retrogressing; and the difference between the rich and the poor gets larger every year. This situation can easily create dangerous instability in the international system, though perhaps because of the very poverty and impotence of the poor countries, the threat to the rich is not very great. The greater danger may be that of a stable divided world with perhaps less than 50 percent of the people having made the transition into the modern world and at least half sunk into utter misery and degradation. Such a situation could hardly persist without corrupting the cultures of both the rich and the poor, and the stability of such a system could certainly not continue forever.

Technology is an offshoot of knowledge. Hence we might expect to find something of a stable pattern between the growth of knowledge and the improvement of technology with perhaps a certain lag to account for the application of new knowledge to productive processes and also the spread of these processes throughout the economy. There is some evidence that the diffusion of knowledge into technology is taking place a little more rapidly than it used to.[2] What is difficult to identify, however, is exactly what new knowledge is going to be relevant, for a great deal of new knowledge is created in the progress of the sciences which is not relevant to technology in the immediate future and which may even never become relevant. The plain fact is that if a prediction of future technology were at all easy, there would be no money to be made in growth stocks, for the growth of the right ones would all be anticipated. The fact that fortunes are made as well as lost in new technologies suggests that the uncertainties of prediction here are very great, and that the relation between present knowledge and future technology is not really stable enough to admit of any very secure predictions.

When we add to the general uncertainties of the technological future an attempt to predict the impact on particular regions, the uncertainties become even greater. It would be even more unwise to project, for instance, constant rates of growth for a particular region than it would be for the economy as a whole. A region which is heavily devoted to, say, mining and agriculture, might expect to share in the relative decline of these industries. A region which is heavily involved in government, especially in defense, might be expected to share in the extreme uncertainty of this sector.

---

[2] See, for instance, the report of the National Commission on Technology, Automation, and Economic Progress, *Technology in the American Economy*, February 1966, pages 4 and 5.

THE IMPLICATIONS FOR EDUCATION

Perhaps the most important conclusion which emerges from this discussion for the educational system is that it should plan for surprise. This is not to say, of course, that its policies should not be based on predictions or projections, for all policies have to be directed towards the future and we must have some idea of what the future is going to be like, otherwise all rational decision is impossible. Wherever it is possible to project into the future simple dynamic systems which have had reasonably stable parameters in the past, this, of course, should be done. We do this, for instance, in population projections, which are perhaps one of the most fundamental tools of the educational planner and which are covered in other papers. We should remember even here that the population projections of the mid-1940s turned out to be completely erroneous because of a sudden change in the parameters of the system, particularly in regard to quite unexpectedly large birth rates which have persisted to this day. One would very much like to see a study of the impact of these erroneous projections of the 1940s, particularly in regard to the failure to plan for educational expansion. It would be interesting to see at what moment school systems became aware of the fact that they were going to have to provide for much larger numbers of children than they had previously expected, and how they made adjustments to these new images of the future.

In regard to the more quantitative aspects of technology, a sudden change in the rate of growth of productivity might not be felt appreciably for a few years, but in ten or twenty years the effects might be very noticeable, either in unexpected gains or unexpected declines in the growth of income.

On the qualitative side, it could well be that the most important area of possible technological change is in the field of social inventions, and it is these which might have the greatest impact on the environment of the educational system. The very strains which modern technology puts on society create a demand for social invention which did not perhaps exist before. When material technology is only advancing slowly, social invention may keep pace with it fairly easily. Thus in the course of the last three hundred years we have had such social inventions as banking, insurance, the corporation, the income tax, universal public education, conscription, social security, and even socialist states, all of which represent in a sense a response on the part of the social system to challenges presented by the growth of material technology. With the qualitative changes that seem to be taking place in material technology, new demands are placed on social invention. Certainly at some point, as per capita incomes rise, we may reach something of a watershed after which the traditional values and organizations become rapidly less capable of organizing society, and rapid social invention will be necessary. As suggested earlier, we cannot predict what these inventions will be, we can only suggest a few challenges to which some response will have to be made. We can conclude, therefore, by outlining some suggestions of possible future challenges.

1.   The American educational system in the past has been quite successful in preparing people to be middle class, to the point indeed where
middle class values permeate perhaps 80 percent of our population. The
system has not succeeded in preparing people to live useful and cheerful
lives at the lower end of the income scale, mainly because educators are
themselves middle class and hence are unsympathetic to the values of a
lower-class culture. Maybe a social invention is needed here in the
shape of an educational subsystem which will give the culture of the poor
a status of its own.

2.   American society up to now has stressed the idea of a "melting pot"
and has sought to create through public education a uniform culture. With
increased affluence and increased political skill, this ideal can now be called
into question. Can we now invent a "mosaic" society, composed of many
small subcultures, each of which gives to its participants a sense of community and identity which is so desperately needed in a mass world, and
which can at the same time remain at peace with its neighbors and not
threaten to pull the society apart? An educational system designed for
this purpose would look enormously different from what we have today.
Private education would compete on equal terms with public; we might
have something like the "voucher" scheme proposed by certain British
economists by which each child would be given a voucher which would
be exchanged for education in any school, public or private. This would
not exclude the possibility of imposing certain legal minimum standards,
but it would open up an enormous possibility for experimentation in
education, which is something we severely lack under the present system.

3.   It would not surprise me to see the educational system head for a
major financial crisis within the next few years. The tax systems by which
public education is supported tend to be regressive and inequitable, and
they only seem to be tolerable as long as the total tax collections for these
purposes are smaller than the needs of this sector of the economy. The
contrast in this regard between the public and the private sectors of the
economy is very striking, as Galbraith has pointed out so eloquently. A
great many studies have indicated that in terms of sheer rate of return on
investment, investment in education probably brings a higher rate of return than that of any competitive industry, and when we add the in-
tangible benefits, which are considerable, the argument that we are underinvesting in education as a whole and grossly underinvesting in certain
aspects of the system becomes almost irresistible. We do not need to go as far
as Dr. West[3] and propose turning the whole educational system back to
private enterprise, for there are good reasons to suppose there would be
underinvestment under these circumstances too, even more serious than
what we have at present. The fact remains, however, that access to
capital is much easier for material technology than it is for human investment, and we need social inventions to correct this. It may well be

---

[3] E. G. West, *Education and the State: A Study in Political Economy,* London: The Institute of
Economic Affairs, 1965.

that a major problem here is that we have not so much supplemented the operations of the price system in this area as destroyed it, and there is a strong case for taking a hard look at the principle that education should be universally free. Public education at all levels can easily result in the subsidization of the rich, and in view of the regressive nature of so many state and local tax systems, the public school system may even result in a redistribution of income from the poor to the rich, or at least from the poor to the middle class. If this is so, it is not surprising that taxpayers become increasingly resistant to any expansion of the educational system, and that the system operates in an atmosphere of increasing financial crisis.

4. The final problem is subtle and hard to put one's finger on; nevertheless it may be the most important problem of all. This is the problem of the role of the educational system in creating what might be called a moral identity. The obsolescence of older moral identities in the face of enormous technological change is a problem which underlies almost all others in the social system. We see this in the so-called sexual revolution; we see it in the inappropriateness of belligerent nationalist emotions in a nuclear world; and we see it also in what may be the most serious social byproduct of automation, a loss of self-respect and "manhood" on the part of those whose skills are being displaced. The greatest human tragedy is to feel useless and not wanted, and with the rise in the intelligence of machines, we may face a period in which the human race divides into two parts, those who feel themselves to be more intelligent than machines and those who feel themselves to be less. This could signalize the beginnings of a widening human tragedy which would require the utmost exercise of our skill and knowledge. I am by no means sure that this is a problem which is really upon us. It is one, however, for which we should be prepared, and in its solution the educational system would play an absolutely crucial role. It would be precisely indeed in the things which our conservatives despise as "frills" that the development of satisfying human identities may have to be found. It must never be forgotten that the ultimate thing which any society is producing is people. All other things are intermediate goods, and all organizations are intermediate organizations. No matter how rich we are or how powerful we are, if we do not produce people who can at least begin to expand into the enormous potential of man, the society must be adjudged a failure. The educational system is peculiarly specialized in the production of people, and it must never lose sight of the fact that it is producing people as ends, not as means. It is producing men, not manpower; people, not biologically generated nonlinear computers. If this principle is stamped firmly in the minds of those who guide and operate our educational system, we can afford to make a great many mistakes, we can afford to be surprised by the future, we can even afford to make some bad educational investments, because we will be protected against the ultimate mistake, which would be to make the educational system a means, not an end, serving purposes other than man himself.

THE BOUNDARIES OF SOCIAL POLICY

Social Work, 12, 1 (Jan. 1967): 3-11

The Boundaries of Social Policy

■ What distinguishes social policy from economic policy, and do we want to distinguish them? The author analyzes the aspects common to both, cites general principles of economic policy, and illustrates the contrast between an economic and a social approach to problems. A basic problem is the knowledge structure and the lack of feedback apparatus in the sphere of social policy. He suggests a council of social advisers within the Office of the President similar to the existing Council of Economic Advisors. ■

"SOCIAL POLICY" IS a vague term the boundaries of which are ill defined, but the content of which is rich. In its widest sense it would include all policies directed toward making some change in the structure of society, and since no policy could be excluded from this, social policy would simply be another name for government policy. If the term is to become meaningful, obviously it must become some kind of a subset of the larger set of policy in general. Some things must be found to distinguish it and at least mark out roughly where the boundaries lie.

A further difficulty of definition arises here because of the complexity and extreme interrelatedness of all aspects of social life and all subsystems of the larger social system. A rough distinction can be made, for instance, between foreign policy and domestic policy, or between the international system and the domestic system. Yet this distinction becomes harder to maintain all the time. Thus the war in Vietnam is affecting every aspect of American life and every aspect of domestic policy. Likewise this country's agricultural policy—which initially, at any rate, was conceived primarily as domestic—has turned out to have enormous consequences for the international system. Furthermore, there are aspects of foreign policy, such as foreign aid, that are more clearly related to certain principles of social domestic policy than to the international system as such.

One despairs, therefore, of finding any clear definition or clean boundaries. The vagueness of a distinction, however, does not destroy its importance. Almost all the great distinctions of life are vague, and in the intricate many-dimensional spectrum of social life we certainly perceive regions much as we perceive colors in the continuous spectrum of light. If we are clear, therefore, that what we are looking for is a region rather than a boundary we will save ourselves a good deal of verbal frustration.

A tricky question is whether we want to distinguish social policy from economic policy. They are obviously closely related; if they are regions they are certainly adjacent and overlapping. If there is a distinction, it is simply that of a world of discourse. There are some things about which economists talk and some things they neglect. Perhaps the best definition of economic policy is simply "that about which economists talk." It is a little unsatisfactory to define social policy as that about which economists do not talk, but unfortunately this does reflect a certain reality in the world of discourse. What economists talk about, such as prices, wages, income, unemployment, stabilization, and so on, seems to have a certain unity and coherence that the other aspects of social policy lack. It is a little unkind to say that whereas economists have models, sociologists have hypotheses, but it is not wholly untrue. Consequently social policy is not generally perceived as opposed to economic policy, as something that has clear structure and a relatively simple body of principles. In contrast with economic policy social policy looks like a sticky conglomeration of the ad hoc. It may well be, of course, that this reflects the nature of the system itself and is not, therefore, a criticism of our knowledge about it but a reflection of the realism of our image. However, in the human mind the rage for order is quite strong; the urge for intellectual tidiness can hardly be disobeyed.

COMMON THREADS

Let us then look over the spectrum of various economic and social policies and see if any common thread that unites them can be found. At one end are policies that usually are thought of as economic, such as monetary stabilization, price policy, most aspects of tax policy, fiscal policy, policies directed toward specific industries and segments of the economy, such as agriculture or public utilities, railroads, and the like. Coming a little closer to what might be thought of as social policy would be labor legislation, with the minimum wage clearly economic and policies regulating the growth and structure of labor unions more social. Antitrust policy would seem to be fairly clearly economic; policies directed toward truth in advertising and packaging or the elimination of discriminatory hiring practices would be more social. At the other end of the scale are policies that are much more social than economic, such as those relating to divorce, the treatment of children (including Aid to Families with Dependent Children), relief and rehabilitation, most of the War on Poverty, education, the exercise of religion, and so on.

It may be that part of the difficulty in defining social policy arises from the fact that in American society, at any rate, social policy is still much more laissez-faire than economic policy. By the separation of church and state it is virtually said that there shall be no policy toward religion, although the difficulties involved in prayers in public schools indicate that even the separation of church and state does not relieve us from the necessity of some policy toward religion. Similarly, in regard to education, at the national level until very recently, at any rate, the policy has been to have no policy and to leave education almost wholly to local initiative or even to private enterprise. Another aspect of policy that seems to be clearly social rather than economic is racial policy and civil rights; here the government is attempting to change overt behavior through the introduction of legal sanctions against certain types of behavior involving discriminatory practices. More fundamentally, through the educational system it hopes to change attitudes.

Finally, there is a whole range of policies toward the so-called underprivileged: relief, social security, various forms of aid to those in need, Medicare, and so on. A great deal of this is usually subsumed under the head of income maintenance, although actually the policies go far beyond the maintenance of income in a simple quantitative sense.

Going still further away from the economic we run into policies involving administration of the law, the police, criminal procedures, the protection of citizens. This finally goes beyond the field of social policy into matters of national defense and international relations.

The main question of this paper is whether there is any guiding thread through this maze of policies, agencies, objectives, and organizations that could at least help us organize our thinking about it and perhaps assist us in making evaluations. As long as everything is ad hoc, as long as every case is a special case, it is hard to make any evaluations. Any evaluation implies reducing things that are essentially heterogeneous and disparate to some kind of common denominator or measure. The desire for a simplifying principle, therefore, is not just a matter of intellectual esthetics and the rage for order; it is essential if any attempt is to be made to evaluate this enormous complex as a whole and to develop a critique that may be useful in directing further development. One could say, of course, that the only principle that is necessary is the perception of a political need large enough and vigorous enough to get itself expressed in legislation or administrative law. While this principle is no doubt realistic, it is not very helpful. It says, in effect, with Alexander Pope, "Whatever is, is right," and offers little hope of organized criticism or principles of evaluation. It may indeed be so that this will finally be all that we are left with, but it would not be absurd to at least search for some more general principle.

PRINCIPLES OF ECONOMIC POLICY

In the case of economic policy, the general principles are perhaps easier to perceive and a good deal of thought has gone into expounding them. The economist postulates what might be called the first approximation ideal for the price system, such as, for instance, that the price structure should correspond to the structure of alternative costs. To use a famous example of Adam Smith: if giving up one deer in the forest enables us to catch two beavers, then if the price in the market is not two beavers for one deer some justification for this divergence from the first approximation ideal must be made. Many such justifications are possible, of course: It may be thought that the wearing of beaver hats is unseemly and a sumptuary tax may be imposed to discourage them. It may be believed that the eating of venison is peculiarly favorable to the health and the hunting of deer may therefore be subsidized to encourage the consumption of venison. All agree that vice should be taxed and virtue subsidized, unless taxation legitimizes vice and hence encourages it or subsidization corrupts virtue. Everyone agrees also that when prices established by the market

mechanism do not reflect real costs and benefits they should be modified by regulations, prohibitions, taxes, subsidies, and grants.

On the minor detail of what is vice and what is virtue there may be wide disagreement. In actual practice this beautiful general principle does not remove as much argument as one might think. Nevertheless, the existence of the general principle is valuable and it gives the economist a sharp advantage over other social scientists when it comes to the critique of policy. This apparent advantage, however, rests partly on the fact that economists study primarily that segment of the social system that is dominated by exchange, and a system of exchange introduces the possibility of a "measuring rod"—which may be money or any other convenient commodity—by which heterogeneous aggregates of goods may be reduced to a common measure. This advantage is clearly a real one. A good deal of the apparent success of economics in producing welfare propositions rests, however, on a largely unexpressed ethical proposition that may easily be challenged—the principle of what is called the "Paretian optimum," which is that any change is for the better as long as nobody is worse off and at least one person is better off, each in his own estimation. This rests on the ethical assumption of the absence of malevolence. Unfortunately, in political and international life especially malevolence is a real factor in human behavior and people are frequently willing to damage themselves if an enemy can be damaged more.

In *The Principles of Economic Policy* this writer outlined four major objectives of economic policy, summarized as progress, stability, justice, and freedom.[1] The first two can be combined into one under the heading "stable growth," that is, a rate of growth that over the years averages some optimum rate in the sense that, at least in the estimate of the present generation, a

---

[1] Kenneth E. Boulding, *Principles of Economic Policy* (Englewood Cliffs, N.J.: Prentice-Hall, 1958).

higher rate of growth would not be worth the sacrifices involved. Stable growth means that the fluctuations of the rate of growth would be kept within tolerable limits—again, what is tolerable being rather vague. It can be defined more sharply in terms of keeping unemployment below some unacceptable level. These are fairly clearly economic goals, in the sense that they are reasonably subject to the measuring rod of money and can be measured, for instance, by the over-all growth rate of real income or real product per capita. There will be wide agreement that a zero rate of growth represents failure, a negative rate of growth disastrous failure, that 2 percent is better than 1 percent and 3 percent better than 2 percent, but there might be some hesitation as to whether 8 percent is better than 7 percent.

Even in the evaluation of economic growth, purely economic considerations may need to be modified by something that looks like social policy. Even the economist cannot afford to be wholly indifferent to the distribution of the growing income. Economists have had a good deal to say about this but the upshot of many of their remarks is that we do not know much about it. Almost everybody would agree that a growth pattern that results in a substantial rate of growth of income for 20 percent of the population but stagnation for 80 percent is not only undesirable but likely to be politically unstable, as the experience in Cuba shows. At the other extreme, a society that is so equalitarian that the fruits of progress always slip out of the hands of those who initiated the progress is in danger of inhibiting growth and stagnating, unless it can pull the Communist trick of pretending to be equalitarian and in fact creating enormous inequalities of economic power. In regard to ideal distribution, economics comes up with the excellent principle that the last dollar of income should have the same significance for everybody. Unfortunately, the absence of any interpersonal measures of significance prevents any real application of this principle except through the loose apparatus of the political process by which, for instance, such things as the schedule of a progressive income tax are determined.

CONTRAST BETWEEN APPROACHES

The contrast between an economic and a social approach to problems can be seen clearly in the case of a minimum standard of living. Virtually all societies, once they attain a certain stage of development, accept some responsibility for the social minimum below which their members should not be allowed to fall. At first this may be established in a loose and unorganized manner through mendicancy, charity, and the extended family, a system so loose that many individuals are likely to fall through the gaps. As the essential organizational skills of a society increase, however, it usually gets to the point at which, as for instance in the Elizabethan Poor Law, society itself takes some ultimate responsibility for the social minimum. As the society gets richer the social minimum tends to rise correspondingly. The purely economic approach to this problem, which has probably never existed although it is now proposed seriously in many quarters, would simply be to establish a minimum income to which every citizen would have a right, whether rich or poor, employed or unemployed, old or young, incapacitated or sturdy. From the very beginning, however, this solution has never seemed acceptable. There has been social discrimination against those who have received subsistence grants, designating them as paupers, and there has been constant fear that grants to relieve the poverty of the poor would lead to the exploitation of the productive by the unproductive. Therefore, the simple economic solution of giving people money has usually been rejected in favor of payments in kind, workhouses, and the administration of relief by social workers. Somehow, lying in the background has been the persistent idea that the recipient of charity should be deserving and that the minimum should be administered in such a way that it does not discourage self-help and self-support. This is a debate that has been carried on for a long time, at least since Speenhamland and Malthus, and we still seem to be a long way from its resolution. The very fact that the argument continues, however, suggests that there are problems of social policy that go beyond simple economic solutions.

If there is one common thread that unites all aspects of social policy and distinguishes them from merely economic policy, it is the thread of what has elsewhere been called the "integrative system." This includes those aspects of social life that are characterized not so much by exchange in which a quid is got for a quo as by unilateral transfers that are justified by some kind of appeal to a status or legitimacy, identity, or community. The institutions with which social policy is especially concerned, such as the school, family, church, or, at the other end, the public assistance office, court, prison, or criminal gang, all reflect degrees of integration and community. By and large it is an objective of social policy to build the identity of a person around some community with which he is associated. It sounds a little cynical to say that the object of this is to make the individual content with rather poor terms of trade and to persuade him to give up a lot and not get very much in return. There may be very good reasons, however, why unfavorable terms of trade at the psychological level are necessary. In the world of physical commodities terms of trade are usually favorable because exchange in this area is so efficient and is almost always a gain to both parties. What one party gives up, the other party receives. The actual cost of the transaction is small in terms of the satisfaction gained by both parties.

As we move into the more subtle exchanges that take place between persons and organizations, what one party gives up is not necessarily what the other party receives. This is seen even in the industrial relationship in the purchase and sale of labor, which is perhaps why the labor market is almost universally regarded as "social" rather than "economic." In the labor bargain, what the worker gives up is the alternative uses of his time; what the employer receives is the product of the work, which is something totally different. The possibility, therefore, of high costs in the exchange relationship is quite great in the sense that something is lost in the transfer. This is seen particularly in the political relationship, in which the terms of trade of the individual with the state are often very bad indeed. The individual gives up a great deal in terms of being taxed, conscripted, killed or injured in wars, and burdened with the guilt of murder and destruction; in return the state seems to give him little, except perhaps a bit of security and a larger identity. It is not surprising, therefore, that we have been urged to ask not what our country can do for us but what we can do for our country. The first question might prove to be too embarrassing.

Perhaps, therefore, we can identify the "grant" or unilateral transfer—whether money, time, satisfaction, energy, or even life itself—as the distinguishing mark of the social just as exchange or bilateral transfer is a mark of the economic. This means also, however, that social policy has to concern itself profoundly with questions of identity and alienation, for alienation destroys the grant system. It is this that destroys the family when one or the other partner feels that the terms of trade are not satisfactory and that he (or she) is giving a lot to the marriage and getting little out of it. It is this that leads to criminality when the individual attempts to take out of society more than he has put in, or refuses to make the grant to society of his time and energy that is necessary if he is to be a fully functioning member. By and large, it is the alienated who create social problems and the integrated who solve them. One would think, therefore, that social policy is that which is centered in those institutions that create integration and discourage alienation. The success of social policy, then, would be measured by the degree to which individuals are persuaded to make unilateral transfers in the interest of some larger group or community.

Even as one states this proposition, however, one begins to qualify it, even to deny it. Without alienation there can be no progress. If everybody is socialized into conformity with what is, nobody dares to have a dream of what might be. It is only the nonconformist who is the entrepreneur, the prophet, the artist, the creator. There are societies that have been too successful in creating integration and conformity, such as classical Chinese civilization, and have therefore tended to stagnate at the very level of perfection they have achieved. It was the disintegrated, disorganized, troubled, chaotic society of Western Europe that was the spearhead of social evolution and that produced the great mutation into science. It cannot therefore be assumed that the more integration, the more conformity, the better. In any social situation there is an optimum degree of integration. Societies that are too little integrated, too disorganized, too much ridden with factions and conflicts are incapable of creating an adequate framework of law and order and that minimum of mutual trust that is necessary for any complex development. Many societies around the world today show how the failure to achieve a sufficient degree of integration checks or even reverses economic development as resources are wasted in internal conflict and mistrust that might be devoted to improving the society's condition. On the other hand, societies are also found that are too homogeneous, in which opposition has been suppressed and in which practically everybody conforms to the prevailing culture or ideology so that each generation simply reproduces itself in the next.

PROBLEM OF THE OPTIMUM

In many ways the concept of an optimum degree of anything is unsatisfactory because it is hard to put into operation. The trouble with the Aristotelian mean is that nobody knows where it is. Nevertheless, this is a problem that is inescapable in any field of policy or behavior of any kind. We are always trying to·live precariously between the too little and the too much and are always in danger of falling into one or the other. This problem is just as important in economic policy as it is in social policy; it cannot even be assumed that higher rates of economic growth are always better. Even here there is a problem of the optimum. A society that forces itself into too high a rate of growth may pay dearly for this in terms of social disorganization, misunderstanding between the generations, and the break-up of its traditional integrative system. Fortunately for the peace of mind of the policy planner there are many dimensions of policy in which society is clearly on one side or the other of the optimum and hence there is not much doubt about the direction in which it should go. If the rate of economic growth is zero it clearly ought to be increased; if the economic fluctuations involve a great depression they should be diminished. If the lack of a sense of community results in widespread destructive strikes, riots, great personal insecurity, and war, clearly the integration of the system is what is desirable. As long as we are far below the optimum we do not have to worry about overshooting it. Certainly, as one looks at the international system one can hardly help being appalled by its cost; it is no exaggeration to say that the failure to achieve world integration may cost the human race its very existence. As we look at domestic policy, we see the high cost of the class structure, the race structure, the structure of discrimination, and here again our society seems to be so far below the optimum level of integration that it hardly seems to be possible to put too much into increasing it.

How to increase it, however, is the tricky question. As a result of a combination of theoretical models and improved information-gathering, in regard to the economy, we have some confidence that we know how to avoid depression, to improve stability, and perhaps even to increase the rate of growth. When it comes down to improving the integrative structure of society we have very little theory of the over-all system and practically no over-all apparatus for collecting, processing, and feeding back information. It is not surprising, therefore, that our efforts in the direction of social policy so often seem to be frustrated. With all the effort put into the police department, criminality seems to increase. With all that is put into work among young people, juvenile delinquency seems to increase. With all that is being put into race relations, there are more race riots. With all that is being put into the poverty program, poverty does not seem to diminish. With all that is being put into the international system, the danger of war constantly mounts. With all that is being put into foreign aid, the problem of economic development of the underdeveloped nations remains totally unsolved. With all that is being put into urban renewal, our cities seem to become increasingly disorganized. With all that is being put into family counseling and psychiatric casework, the number of divorces, disorganized families, and neglected children is increasing rather than diminishing. With all that is being put into education, even in the reduction of illiteracy we are barely holding our own.

The picture here painted is perhaps too depressing; if it is a caricature it is at least a caricature of a grim truth. In these days all who are concerned with human betterment are in danger of getting what might be called a "Canute complex"; we stand on the shore of an increasing tide of human misery and disorganization and busy ourselves frantically in sweeping it back, but for all our efforts the tide seems to creep in and in. In economic policy, at least, some of the tide is being turned back; we no longer feel the sense of despair about unemployment, for instance, that was felt in the thirties when the creeping tide of unemployment seemed to threaten society as a whole. When we come to the more subtle

things, however—criminality, delinquency, the self-perpetuating poverty subcultures, family disorganization, neighborhood decay, mental ill health and political paranoia —we feel helpless. We sweep the waves back here and there but the tide constantly engulfs us. We must learn the same lesson here that we have learned in economics, that the sources of a system are often very far from its results. Unemployment is related mainly to tax policy, not to labor policy. Similarly, it may well be that criminality, delinquency, social disorganization, divorce, race hatred, and war are related to elements in the total social information system that have not yet been identified.

THE KNOWLEDGE STRUCTURE

One thing is clear: we must look upon the total dynamic process of society as essentially a process in human learning. Even economic development is essentially a learning process. It is not merely a mechanical process of investment in piling up old knowledge; it involves learning of new skills, development of new ambitions, the widespread diffusion of new values, and often a complete reorientation both of muscles and of minds. It is even clearer that the development of social integration is a learning process. We have to be taught to love just as we have to be taught to hate. Practically nothing in human life comes naturally. It is from vague and formless biological drives and the extraordinary learning potential of the human nervous system that the intricate structure of our personalities, our identities, our values, and our communities are molded.

It is the dynamics of the knowledge structure—the total knowledge content of society, of what Pierre Teilhard de Chardin has called the "no-osphere"—that really governs all other aspects of social life.[2] It is how this total knowledge structure is transmitted and increased from one generation to the next that determines the long-

[2] *The Phenomenon of Man* (New York: Harper & Bros., 1959).

run dynamics of society. All human knowledge is destroyed by death and has to be re-established in new minds once every generation. An enormous number of agencies participate in this process of transmission: parents, teachers, peers, schools, books, conversations, mass media, sermons, speeches, jokes; every day a vast barrage of information is entering one's nervous system, modifying one's image of the world, one's values, and one's self-image. Every day, likewise, death, aging, and forgetting remove a proportionate part of the information deposit of the past. It is in this process that we must find the key to social change.

We may find, as McLuhan argues, that it is the medium, not the message, that matters, and it can certainly be argued that in our time the development of television outweighs all other factors in inducing social change by a high order of magnitude.[3] We may find also, however, that McLuhan, like everybody else who has a good idea, overdoes it, and there are some messages that are more important than the medium in which they are contained. There do seem to be great symbolic archetypes that are transmitted from generation to generation—the great myths, stories, symbols, proverbs, folklore, and now, of course, the great body of science—all of which are constantly transmitted from the old to the young in a relatively stable form. However, what it is that gives symbols their power we do not know, and until we know more about this we must constantly be prepared to be surprised by the rise of new symbolic systems.

One is almost tempted to intone a kind of litany of "Who would have thought . . .?" Who would have thought at the time that an itinerant teacher in a remote province of the great Roman Empire would have set in motion a movement that eventually became one of the world's great religions? Who would have thought that a camel driver in Arabia would have set in motion a symbolic

[3] Marshall McLuhan, *Understanding Media: The Extensions of Man* (New York: McGraw-Hill Book Co., 1964).

system that established a great civilization stretching from Spain to the Philippines? Who would have thought that a fiery old man with a beard in the British Museum would have set in motion a system that now governs a third of the human race? Considerations such as these should be at least a little humbling to the more grandiose pretensions of social science.

NEED FOR FEEDBACK APPARATUS

Nevertheless, knowledge can increase even about social systems, and as one's knowledge increases, one's capacity to control the system toward the realization of one's deeper values increases likewise. It might well be that in social policy we are on the edge of a revolution as great as that which occurred in economic policy. At the moment large numbers of people are acquiring information about segments of the system in which they operate—people such as social workers, government officials, law enforcement officers, doctors, ministers, psychiatrists, teachers, counselors, and so on—all of whom are feeding information into the system and getting information back out. This information, however, is nowhere collected, indexed, and processed into a continuing and continually modified image of society. As a result, most of it is wasted. Decisions are constantly being made on the basis of misinformation, false images of the world, or simply absence of crucial information that exists somewhere in the system but is not available. We must not be deluded, of course, into thinking that the more information the better; indeed, a fundamental principle of epistemology is that knowledge is gained by the loss of information, not by its accumulation. However, if the collection and processing of information are informed and organized by theoretical models, which in their turn are modified by the information they generate, the result is a feedback process in the information system that is the essential secret of science and of the enormous expansion in human knowledge that the scientific subculture has produced. There would seem to be no reason why processes of this kind cannot be set up in the international system and in what might be called the integrative system with which social policy essentially deals. Until some process like this is established, however, social policy will continue to be ad hoc and haphazard and its practitioners will be continually frustrated.

It has been suggested by a number of people, notably by Dr. Bernard Gross of Syracuse University, that a council of social advisers should be established in the Office of the President, somewhat analogous to the Council of Economic Advisors.[4] There is a great deal of merit in this proposal. The Council of Economic Advisors has provided a most useful focus for economic information and its application to economic policy. It represents, as it were, the "Establishment" of the economics profession within the framework of government, and exercises a constant pressure toward informed and sophisticated images of the economic system in the minds of the political decision-makers. This is not to say, of course, that the council is omniscient; it can and does make mistakes, which are inevitable in a system as complex as a total society. Even its mistakes, however, are fruitful, in the sense that there is some apparatus to foster learning from them. Perhaps the greatest significance of the council lies in the fact that it represents a process of two-way communication between the professional economist and government. As a result the professional economist himself develops a greater appreciation of the difficulties of political decision-making and becomes, one hopes, a little more humble about the advice he offers. On the other hand, whatever knowledge is contained in the minds of the professional economists is now much more accessible to the government than ever before. This factor has unquestionably played a role in preventing

depressions and in increasing the rate of economic growth.

There is no such apparatus for feedback in the case of social policy. It is nobody's business to look at it as a whole; it is nobody's business to collect information about social variables on a comprehensive scale and an integrated basis. A council of social advisers might well meet a need of this kind, although we should not blind ourselves to the fact that the task would be in the first instance much more difficult than that of the Council of Economic Advisors. The latter has been able to rely on a large information collection and processing apparatus that predated it in the Department of Commerce and in other government departments. A council of social advisers would have to pioneer almost from scratch in developing an integrated information system about social variables even though here, of course, the raw material exists in almost every government department. The success of the Council of Economic Advisors was in no small measure due to the fact that important pioneering work had been done both in the conceptual framework and in the collection of data by certain private agencies such as the National Bureau of Economic Research in New York, which pioneered in the collection and interpretation of national income statistics. It may be that before a successful council of social advisers is to be set up in government there needs to be some well-financed private agency that will pioneer in the conceptual tasks involved and in the development of new methods of collecting and processing the enormous amount of information that is required, much of which exists somewhere in the system but is simply not available. In the absence of any such private agency, however, and in the absence of any support of such an agency from private foundations, it may be that government itself will have to do the pioneering work. One thing is certain—that a great intellectual task remains to be accomplished. How it is to be accomplished only the future will reveal.

---

[4] "The State of the Nation: Social Systems Accounting," in Raymond A. Bauer, ed., *Social Indicators* (Cambridge, Mass.: MIT Press, 1966).

DARE WE TAKE THE
SOCIAL SCIENCES SERIOUSLY?

American Behavioral Scientist, 10, 10 (June 1967):
12-16. *Also in: American Psychologist,* 22, 11 (Nov. 1967)

DARE WE TAKE THE SOCIAL SCIENCES SERIOUSLY?

■ The title of this paper is a rhetorical question, designed to arouse specific expectations in the hearer. It is not couched in the language of science, but the language of oratory. It is, indeed, as inappropriate to this august gathering as a chorus girl at the first Thanksgiving dinner. I chose this, however, deliberately because it illustrates in its very form and style the problem with which I wish to struggle.

Science is one subculture among many in our society. That is a statement in the rhetoric of science itself. The concept of a subculture is a concept of the social sciences, not of the world of literature and oratory. I would find it hard to preach a fiery sermon or make a rousing political speech addressed to a subculture. It is an ugly word and in some sense an ugly concept. It involves what might be called a Copernican stance on the part of man, standing off from his own activities and his own society and observing them in Olympian detachment. I once happened to be with a group of anthropologists at a conference on the 4th of July. In the evening the fireworks were beginning to go off in the local park and one of them said, "Let's go down and see the tribal rites." The implications of this remark are profound. The anthropologist stands apart even from his own culture. The ordinary citizen probably never thinks of the 4th of July celebrations as tribal rites, any more than a tribe thinks of tribal rites as tribal rites. The citizen is unself-conscious about his national holidays and his national allegiance. The social scientist begins to see these as special cases of general principles. He participates in his own society as a participant-observer and so inevitably begins to have values different from a participant.

All the sciences are themselves a part of the system which they study. All scientists are participant-observers in their own systems. In the physical sciences, and to a somewhat lesser extent in the biological sciences, it is possible for a time to maintain the myth of non-participation, and to suppose that the scientist simply studies an empirical world which is not affected by the fact that he is studying it; even in the physical sciences, however, this myth has had to be abandoned, in the justly famous Heisenberg principle. Increasingly, the scientist is creating the universe which he studies. Physicists are producing particles unknown in nature. Chemists have produced elements unknown in nature and innumerable new compounds. The biologist produces new hybrids, new genetic arrangements and may shortly begin to intervene in genetic evolution on a massive scale. Our knowledge of ecology is likely to change the whole ecological system of the earth.

Social sciences are dominated by the fact that the social scientist and the knowledge which he creates are themselves

AUTHOR'S NOTE: Vice-Presidential Address, Section K, AAAS, Washington. D. C., December 29, 1966.

integral parts of the system which is being studied. Hence, the system changes as it is studied and because it is studied. There can be no myth of an unchanging universe with the scientist acquiring abstract knowledge about it. Economists are no longer interested in merely observing and predicting the course of the business cycle, they are interested in controlling it, even in abolishing it. The development of polls and sample surveys has profoundly changed the political system and the way in which political decisions are made. Anthropologists unquestionably have contributed substantially to the downfall of empire by revealing the cultural and artistic achievements of so-called primitive peoples. Aesthetically, indeed, in the twentieth century one might almost say that Africa has defeated Greece, and for the first time in human history, as a result of the spread of communication, a world style is emerging. The peace researchers are aiming not merely to understand the international system but to transform it through the explicit understanding of it, as economists have transformed the economy.

If science is a subculture, it must have a value system. What characterizes and distinguishes one subculture from another is its value system, that is, a set of legitimated preferences. A subculture consists of a set of people having something in common. They may have certain technologies in common. Each person in the set may have a common body of knowledge and skill. There may be a common language, a common vocabulary, and certain common life experiences. All men, however, or nearly all, have two legs, reproduce with approximately the same technology, communicate with each other through some sort of language, have a common age pattern from birth to babyhood, childhood, adolescence, adulthood, old age and death, and grow up in some kind of a kinship structure. What differentiates the cultures and subcultures of mankind is uncommon knowledge, knowledge which is common to the members of the subculture but which is not common to the rest of mankind, and uncommon values, that is, sets of preferences which members of the subculture have in common which differ from those outside it. Americans like raw power, masculinity, democratic institutions, coffee, hot dogs and french fries; whereas the Japanese like ceremony, technical skill, green tea and raw fish.

Every subculture, furthermore, has an ethic, that is, a value system for evaluating and legitimating preference systems. It is the possession of a common ethic which differentiates one culture from another and even one subculture from another. It is not enough that throughout the subculture there should be a wide preference, shall we say, for beef over ham. To a considerable extent, what creates the common preference is an ethic, that is, preference for preference systems in which beef is preferred to ham, and a feeling that those preference systems in which ham is preferred to beef are not themselves to be preferred. When there is an ethic, there is a strong tendency for the preferences of different individuals to converge. Whether there is a dynamics of convergence which itself produces the ethic or whether the ethic produces the convergence we need not now inquire.

A scientific subculture is like all others in that its constituent members share certain preferences and, likewise, an ethic. Again, whether the ethic came first and created the preferences, or whether the preferences, by converging, came to be common and so implied an ethic, is hard to determine. Probably both processes have been at work. Thus, in its European origins the scientific subculture can well be regarded as a mutation from reformed (and counter-reformed) Christian culture, and one which took over many of the ethical preferences of the culture out of which it grew. Without denying the debt of modern science to the Greeks, to Islam, to the Chinese and to the Jews, and without implying any ethnocentric superiority, for the random element in these processes is strong, the fact remains that science did not grow up as a separate subculture producing a self-sustaining expansion of knowledge either in Athens or in Baghdad, or in Peking or in the medieval ghettoes. Its founding fathers, Galileo, Copernicus, Kepler, Newton, Boyle and so on were products of a predominantly Christian culture and themselves for the most part accepted an ethic which was derived from it. More than that, it was Christian culture in its more puritan aspects, a culture in which Luther had challenged successfully traditional outward authority and in which innumerable writers hymned the praises of veracity, simplicity, purity and the testing of truth in experience. This may be one key to the mystery of why science originated in Europe and not in China, which is still a major mystery of history.

Thus, it can be argued that the ethic of the scientific subculture in considerable measure originated outside it. Just as Christianity as a cultural phylum may properly be regarded as a mutation out of Judaism, with some hybrid qualities, but inheriting the ethical system out of which it grew, so science can be regarded as a mutation out of Christianity, again inheriting, in part, the ethic of its parental matrix. Once a subculture gets under way, of course, it differentiates itself as a social species from its surroundings and it begins to develop ethical systems of its own. Science is no exception to this rule. The idea that the scientific culture is exempt from ethical principles is one which will not stand up to a moment of examination. These ethical principles, however, are fairly simple. There is, in the first place, a high preference for veracity. The only really unforgivable sin of the scientist is deliberate deception and the publication of false results. The career of any scientist who has destroyed his credibility in this way is virtually over.

Along with the preference for veracity goes a strong preference for truth. These are not the same things. Veracity is the absence of deceit and truth is the absence of error. There is a profound epistemological difference between these two phenomena. The deceiver usually knows that he is deceiving, although there is, of course, the phenomenon of self-deception. The man whose image of the world is in error obviously does not know this, for if he knew it he would not hold this particular view. The testing of error, therefore, is a much more difficult problem than the testing of deceit, and most of the aspects of the technology of science are methods that we might almost call the rituals for the detection of error.

Error is detected by the falsification of predictions. This involves the comparison of two images. An inference of the future derived from the basic image of the world which is

to be tested is then compared with an image of how the future turned out once it has become past. If there is no disappointment, that is, if the two images coincide, no error is detected, so the failure to detect error does not necessarily imply that no error exists. If the two images do not coincide, that is, if there is disappointment, then error of some kind is detected. The error might be, of course, in either of the two images and a large part of the technology of science is devoted to insuring that the error is not in the image of the past. This is done by refinement of instrumentation, careful recording, quantitative measurements and so on. There must also be defenses against error in inference, that is, in the way in which the image of the future is derived from the basic image of the world. If both these sources of error have been eliminated and there is still disappointment, the scientist is forced to revise his basic model or theory. It has been by this means, fundamentally, that science has progressed.

It should be pointed out, however, that the method by which the scientific subculture discovers error is not different in essence from the method by which error is detected in the folk culture, that is, in the ordinary business of life. We find our way to a meeting by folk knowledge, not by scientific knowledge. We had an image of where it was in our minds, we had an image of the future in which a meeting was happening, and if we had gone to the wrong place, or the right place at the wrong time, error would very soon have been revealed. It is by this kind of elimination of error that we find our way around town, that we find our way around in our personal relationships and even how we learn to drive or to ski. The thing which differentiates science from folk culture is not the method of eliminating error, but the complexity of the systems which are imagined, the refinement of the expectations and the refinement of the records by which disappointment is tested.

The social sciences differ from the natural, even the biological sciences, in that there is a good deal of quite accurate folk knowledge about the system which they study, that is, the social system. Our folk knowledge of physical or biological systems is accurate as far as it goes. In finding our way around town there is no necessity to know that the earth is a sphere, and the flat earth, which is the folk image, is quite adequate. Similarly, it is folk knowledge which enables us to procreate children without any necessity for knowing about the details of fertilization and mitosis. In these areas, however, the scientific subculture is sharply differentiated from the folk culture. If we want to navigate a satellite or produce a new drug or a new hybrid, or even explode a nuclear weapon, we do not call in the old wives. In social systems the old wives, or at least their husbands, are called in all the time. Creating a peaceful world, abolishing slums, solving the race problem, or overcoming crime and so on, are not regarded as suitable subjects for scientific technology but are regarded as fields where a pure heart and a little common sense will do all that is really necessary. Either we have no really explicit concept of social systems at all, or we regard knowledge about social systems as something which can be achieved in the ordinary business of life. In the case of simple social systems, this is true. In the case of complex systems, unfortunately, it is totally false, and many of our failures and difficulties arise from this fact. We have very little concept of what might be called social astronautics. Social astronauts who have to operate the complex social systems are sent into social space with what is the equivalent of the image of a flat earth.

There is a certain implication in the title of this paper that we do not take the social sciences seriously. This seems like rather a brash assertion when we reflect, for instance, that economics has a good claim to be the second oldest of the sciences, (after physics), having reached its fundamental theoretical formulation in 1776 at the hands of Adam Smith at a time when chemistry was still floundering in the phlogiston theory, biology and geology had not gone beyond taxonomy, the theory of evolution was 100 years off, and sociology, psychology and anthropology as separate sciences were hardly thought of. Economics, furthermore, has had a substantial impact on economic policy, not all of which has been necessarily good, but in which one can detect a continual increase in the sophistication with which the economy is guided. The English Poor-Law of 1834 may have been unnecessary and a false deduction under the circumstances of the time from what were essentially sound principles. The record of free trade is fairly impressive even if it is somewhat ambiguous, and the Keynesian economics has undoubtedly scored resounding victories. One has only to compare the miserable failure of the 20 years after World War I with the at least moderate success of the 20 years after World War II to see what difference a more sophisticated approach to economics and to economic policy has been able to make.

Judged by their impact on society, the other social sciences do not look so good. The record of industrial psychology, for instance, is not one in which one can put unbounded confidence. It has been naive about the more subtle aspects of the social system; it is not altogether exempt from the accusation of having corrupted its principles for the sake of its masters.[1] Even here there has been a learning process at work, and the surprises and the disappointments, such as the "Hawthorne effects" have at least detected a certain amount of error and contributed to an overall learning process. Clinical psychology and psychiatry likewise can only be counted as minor successes. There is not much evidence that recovery from mental illness is markedly affected by any kinds of treatment. Psychoanalysis, whatever its virtues, is much too expensive to deal with the mass problem.

Our knowledge of the learning and maturation processes in the human being is still extremely primitive. It is quite possible, for instance, that child-rearing practices based on Watsonian behavioral psychology may have actually done a great deal of damage both to individuals and to the society. The alternative methods of Dr. Spock are much more agreeable, but again we really know very little about their overall impact. All the experimentation with animals, important as it is, has not thrown much light on the complexities of the learning process when it involves the use of language and symbols. One may certainly be permitted to doubt whether all the rat psychology of the last fifty years has contributed anything toward the improvement of social policy even in the field of education. This of course is not to say it should not have been done. In exploring the tree of knowledge every promising limb should be followed at least to the point where its end is clearly in sight. One cannot help the impression, however, that in this matter we have not found the main trunk and that until we do so we will continue to be frustrated.

In even hinting that we do not take the social sciences seriously, I have no intention of belittling the large mass of important work which has gone on in them and which continues to go and which has already produced a major impact, as I have suggested in a recent essay.[2] Nevertheless, there are legitimate causes for dissatisfaction, both with the organization of the social sciences, with the amount of work which goes into them, with the quality, at least of some of its work, and by the absence of an adequate vision of the future.

The disciplinary and departmental organization of the social sciences at the moment has unquestionably arisen in response to need. There is nothing intrinsically wrong with specialization; it is, indeed, a necessity. The days of the Renaissance man are over and no one could be expected to cover even a small part of the field of the social sciences. Nonetheless,

there are good reasons for raising the question as to whether the existing types of specialization and especially the existing departmental structure is not now a handicap rather than a convenience. One reason for raising this question is that the social sciences are not really separated from each other by different levels of systems in their subject matter. Crystallography is separated from physiology by a very sharp difference in the level of the systems which are being studied, even though there no doubt may be fruitful interaction between them. Sociology, economics, political science and anthropology, however, are not distinguished by any great difference in the level of the systems which constiute their subject matter. In a real sense, they are all studying the same thing, that is, the total social system. The only real distinction of systems levels to be the difference between small systems and large. The social psychologist and the psychologist, for instance, are concerned more with the study of small systems, the sociologist and the economist more with the study of larger systems. Even this distinction, however, cuts across the existing fields and departments.

It is when we look at the overall information collection and processing apparatus of the social sciences and the theory testing procedures which depend on this apparatus that we find the greatest source of dissatisfaction. The situation is best, perhaps, in economics, where in the last 30 years or so we have developed a system of economic statistics and carefully collected sample data, which is at least adequate for gross purposes, such as economic stabilization. Even here, when we come to such problems as the impacts of changing technology of the economy, we find that the overall data is very poor indeed and we have to rely on what is essentially journalism or interesting stories about fancy machines. We also do not know enough about the distribution of income or about the impact on distribution of overall government policies at all levels. Compared with the information systems of the other social sciences, however, these are relatively minor defects. A recent work has spelled out in considerable detail the deficiencies of our present information system, even on the national level.[3]

At the international level the situation is much worse. The information collection and processing apparatus of the international system is not only inadequate, it is corrupt; it is not merely a zero, it is a minus. It is an enormous apparatus designed, in fact, to produce misinformation and to prevent feedback from inadequate images of the world so that the whole organization of the international system becomes organizationally schizophrenic, that is, the existing images of the world are confirmed no matter what happens. Information is collected without any precautions about sampling, it is processed by a system which has strong value filters which tend to filter out anything which challenges the prevailing image of the world. The one possible exception to this gloomy picture is the information apparatus of the United Nations and the related agencies, where at least the representatives of national states are exposed to each other's points of view, and where an international secretariat collects and processes information with at least a world bias. The United Nations, however, is a pitifully small organization, and though we get a lot out of it for what we put in, what we put in is so little that it cannot achieve major changes in the system. It is not surprising, therefore, that the international system is by far the most costly and the most dangerous element in the whole world social system. It costs about $150 billion a year and it produces a positive probability of almost total disaster.

One can cite many examples of policies of government in which the failure to recognize that what was involved was essentially a social system has led if not to disaster to at least gross inefficiency. Flood control is a famous example where the attempt to treat floods as a purely engineering and physical problem instead of as a parameter in the social system has led to what may be disastrous interference with the whole ecological system of the river basins, and has built into the system positive probabilities of very large-scale disasters. Floods are not a problem of a river but are indeed part of its normal way of life. They are a problem only to people and the absurd attempt to "conquer" the rivers is likely to lead to increasing disasters as people build on flood plains which cannot be protected from a hundred-year flood.

One could extend the list substantially of areas of social policy where we have made serious mistakes because we have neglected the social systems aspects of the problem, and treat social systems as if they were physical systems. Urban renewal has been thought of in primarily physical terms, and as a result has broken up communities and may easily have worsened the problem of poverty. Road building has been done largely in terms of cement, not in terms of people. Agricultural policy has been designed in terms of commodities, and while its byproducts have been favorable, from the point of view of technical development, it has done very little, again, to solve the problem of agricultural poverty. Even welfare policies, like social security, though they are obviously a part of the social system, have not been designed with any overall concepts of the dynamics of society in view, but are designed rather as measures to relieve immediate problems rather than to develop a long-range program of social change. The critics of society, unfortunately, do not seem to be much better informed than its defenders. They have romantic notions about revolutions or about how to change the existing power structure. They tend to preach and lament rather than to develop accurate and testable images of social dynamic processes. It is not surprising that under these circumstances social reform has so often proved disappointing. The prohibition movement is, perhaps, the most striking example of a large grass roots movement for social reform which failed of its objective and perhaps even made the problem worse than before because of its naiveté about social change. Whether the current reform movements are really much better only the future will show. They may be luckier than the prohibitionists, but one wonders if they are really more sophisticated.

I have suggested elsewhere almost as a kind of fantasy to illustrate the magnitude of the problem that if we made a study of the "sociosphere," that is, the total sphere of the world social system, with the same degree of seriousness with which we study the atmosphere we would need a world network of social data stations analogous to the network of weather stations. These social data stations would be engaged in a constant collection of data from their local areas by carefully sampled statistically significant methods and would transmit this data to a central agency for processing in the form of maps, indices, distributions, and other statistical images. The need for this is particularly great in the international system. It is great also however in many aspects of social policy. The information processing capability of the modern computer opens up a whole new epistemological field. It is by no means absurd to suppose, for instance, that all the records of the human race might be codified in a single computer and then searched to reveal hitherto unsuspected patterns. What we are looking for in all the sciences is repeatable patterns. We can think of the social system as if it were a four dimensional structure – three dimensions of space and one of time – a structure which may have strong random elements in it but in which also nonrandom patterns can be perceived. In a structure of such complexity, however, the pattern requires complex images, complex inferences, complex predictions and complex instruments of perception if predictions are to be compared with reality. At the moment neither our theoretical

structures, nor our inferences, nor our predictions, nor our perceptual apparatus and instrumentation in the social sciences are in any way adequate to measure up to the complexity of the social system. In this sense we do not take the social sciences seriously. We are using salt spoons to clear away snow drifts and reading glasses to study the structure of molecules. It is not surprising that up to now our results have been ambiguous.

This still leaves us with two further questions: one, *could* we take the social sciences seriously; and two, *should* we do so? I would answer both these questions with a cautious affirmative. There certainly seems to be no reason why our theoretical structure, our inferences and our perceptual apparatus should prove intractable to improvement, if we set our best minds on the problem and if we were prepared to devote economic resources to the kind of instrumentation which, say, the nuclear physicist now demands. The network of social data stations which I suggested above would probably not cost more than a billion dollars a year and the returns for this investment might be enormous in terms of disasters averted, stable peace established, and development fostered. By and large, the social sciences have not been ambitious enough to want to study the sociosphere as a totality. They have been content with the kind of professional advancement which comes from the adequate processing of small pieces of information. They have not had the larger vision of the study of the sociosphere as a totality. Economists have perhaps come closest to this, but they are handicapped by the limitations of their own abstraction, and as a result have been unable to deal satisfactorily even with such problems as the process of world development.

That we could develop much more realistic images of the sociosphere can hardly be denied. The question whether we should develop such images or how far we should develop them is not so easily answered. We cannot assume in any of the sciences that the development of more realistic and complex images of the world leaves the human value structure unchanged. Our image of value and our image of fact are symbiotic. They are part of a single knowledge structure and it is naive in the extreme to suppose that they are independent. The view that science or any other knowledge process is simply the servant of existing folk values is doomed to disappointment. Science is corrosive of all values which are based exclusively on simpler epistemological processes. The natural sciences have created an image of the world in which ghosts, witches and things that go bump in the night are so little valued that they have withered and died in the human imagination. Biology has created a world in which the folk ideas of racial purity can no longer survive. Similarly, the social sciences are creating a world in which national loyalty and the national state can no longer be taken for granted as sacred institutions, in which religion has to change profoundly its views on the nature of man and of sin, in which family loyalty and affection becomes a much more self-conscious and less simpleminded affair, and in which, indeed, all ethical systems are profoundly desacralized. There is a deep and seemingly unresolvable conflict between the ethic of science on the one hand, and the ethic of the American Legion, the United States Department of Defense, the Communist Party, the John Birch Society, the Jesuits, and the Jehovah's Witnesses on the other hand. One method by which these conflicts have been resolved in practice has been the remarkable human capacity for holding two incompatible images in the head at the same time. Up to a point these incompatibilities are even creative. It is hard, however, for an astrophysicist to be a Jehovah's Witness or for a biologist to be a racist, and it may become hard for a social scientist to be a good Russian Communist or even a 100 per cent American Liberal without strong mental reservations.

The real problem of the impact of the social sciences on

the folk culture or even on the literary culture that is dominant in the international system is that it operates in the same system as that of the folk or literary culture in which it is imbedded. Social science presents much more of a challenge and a problem to the politician than do the physical or biological sciences. In the case of the latter it is possible to maintain the fiction that the scientist should be on tap but not on top. The scientist, in other words, gives power but not values. He is merely a servant of values which are derived from other parts of the social system. In the case of the social sciences this myth is harder to maintain. It is not without reason that southern senators and the patriotic societies distrust the social scientist, for at this point there may be deep conflict between the values which are created and sustained by folk images of the world and the values which both create the social sciences and are fostered by them.

It is true, I think, of all scientists that when they become the servants of power they lose an essential element of the ethic of science itself. Here lies the fundamental dilemma. The power structure pays for the sciences, and if the sciences are to survive in any society they must find a niche in the power structure, either purchasing power or political power. How, however, do we find a niche in the power structure which does not confine or corrupt its occupant? The classical answer to this problem has been the concept of the university, a niche, as it were, specially designed to protect its occupants against the very power structure which has created it. In earlier days the church or the monastery provided such a niche. Whether niches like this can be created within the structure of government itself is one of the unsolved problems of our day. The National Science Foundation, the National Institutes of Health certainly represent an attempt to find an answer to this problem. Whether we should institutionalize the social sciences still further within this framework and create, say, a National Social Science Foundation, as is proposed,[4] is a problem which troubles the judgment and consciences of a great many who are concerned. The cloud of the "Camelot" fiasco hangs heavily over the relations between government and the social sciences, and foreshadows all too clearly the possible shape of things to come. It could well be that the kind of knowledge which would result from taking the social sciences seriously would turn out to be more threatening to traditional values and institutions even than the H bomb and bacteriological weapons. The folk knowledge itself, however, will be quite incapable of dealing with this problem, simply because it would itself represent a social system of enormous complexity. It looks, therefore, as if only the social sciences themselves could solve the problems which they themselves might create, which looks suspiciously like the principle that another little drink will cure drunkenness. Until we have drunk deeper of this particular spring, however, the dangers of a little learning may be all too apparent.

NOTES

1. See Loren Baritz, *The Servants of Power* (Middletown, Conn.: Wesleyan University Press, 1960).

2. Kenneth E. Boulding. *The Impact of the Social Sciences.* (New Brunswick, N. J.: The Rutgers University Press, 1966.)

3. Raymond A. Bauer (ed.), *Social Indicators.* (Cambridge, Mass.: The Massachusetts Institute of Technology Press, 1966).

4. See Luther J. Carter, "Social Sciences, Where Do They Fit in the Politics of Science?" *Science*, 154, (October, 1966), p. 488.

AN ECONOMIST LOOKS AT
THE FUTURE OF SOCIOLOGY

et al., 1, 2 (Winter 1967): 1-6; comment by
Talcott Parsons, 6-7

AN ECONOMIST LOOKS AT THE FUTURE OF SOCIOLOGY

It can be argued, I am sure, that economists have no business looking at the future of sociology, and I am inclined to agree, especially as I contemplate what a sociologist might say about the future of economics. Nevertheless, I am encouraged to pursue my interfering ways, partly because interfering with somebody else's business has always been regarded as a dangerous and exciting sport, and partly for a more serious reason. One of the striking things about the social sciences is that they are all studying essentially the same thing, that is, the social system. They are not divided from each other as, shall we say, physics may be divided even from chemistry by a difference in the systems level of the subject matter which they are studying. The social system is a unity; it has its own systems level and indeed if we want to divide it according to the level of complexity of systems we would probably divide it between large social systems and small social systems. This division does not correspond to any of the disciplinary divisions except insofar as anthropology and social psychology tend to concentrate a little more on small social systems whereas economics and political science tend to concentrate more on large social systems, with sociology lying somewhat uneasily in between. What divides the social sciences is not the level of complexity of the system which they study, but the nature of the abstraction from which they take their point of view. Each studies a certain aspect of the total social system from its own vantage point, but the fact that each of them is studying aspects of the same system means that the divisions among them, if they are too tight and there is not enough communication across the boundaries, can be positively harmful to an understanding of the social system in its totality. From this point of view, therefore, there is a great deal to be said for social sciences getting into each other's business, for in a way they are all in the same business, even though at different locations.

Economics looks at the total social system from the point of view of exchange, exchangeables and the production and consumption of exchangeables. It is not really very much interested in people except insofar as they produce commodities, consume commodities, push commodities around and occasionally are commodities. From the point of view of the economist the role of people towards commodities is rather like that of angels towards the planets in medieval astronomy. If they can be substituted by differential equations no harm is done and much simplicity is attained.

It is a little harder to find a core abstraction for political science in the way that exchange is the core abstraction for economics, but we can perhaps find it in the notion of legitimized threat. Elsewhere I have outlined three major role-creating relationships in society which I have described as the exchange system, the threat system and the integrative system.[1] The threat system is of peculiar concern to political science as the exchange system is to economics. It is not, however, the naked threat such as that of the bandit which is of real interest to political science, but rather the legitimated threat as exercised by the political power through the apparatus of the law and the rituals of the international system.

This leaves one with a strong temptation to identify sociology with the integrative system, that is, that aspect of social life which involves the relationships of love, loyalty and legitimation, and the structure of status, identity and community.

Sociologists themselves may object to this. They may feel in the first place that sociology is the only social science which is concerned with society in its totality and which studies the whole social system in all its relationships. This in effect would make economics and political science branches of sociology, which would not make their practitioners very happy. If sociology is to be differentiated from the other social sciences by reason of some aspect of the total social system, some vantage point, as it were, from which the social system is viewed in perspective, then the integrative system would seem to be the prime candidate. The only other candidate of which I am aware and one which perhaps would be more acceptable to sociologists themselves is that sociology looks at society from the vantage point of social structures, roles, communications and so on. The difficulty with this view as I see it is that it does not have enough content to describe the rich institutional content of sociology.

Further light perhaps can be thrown on the nature of the division among the social sciences if we look at the way in which the institutions of social life tend to be divided out among them. The economics department tends to study banks, firms, corporations and households in their aspects of spending units, that is, as sources of output and receivers of input of commodities and other exchangeables. The stock market and the financial system are regarded as almost wholly within the purview of economics and even labor unions insofar as they are regarded as institutions of the labor market, that is, organizations for arranging the terms on which labor is bought and sold. The institutions of government are considered extensively in economics departments, but only in a single aspect, that is, the exchange aspect. It is the input and output of money from government, the input of things that are bought, the government expenditure and the things which create the input of money, such as taxes and the sale of securities, which are the prime concern of the economist. Similarly, the economists are primarily concerned in the international system with trade, that is, the flow

[1]"The Relations of Economic, Political and Social Systems," this volume (IV), Ch. 13. "Towards a Pure Theory of Threat Systems," *Collected Papers*, Vol. V. See also, *Amer. Econ. Rev.*, 53:2 (May 1963): 424-434.

of exchangeables of all kinds.

The political scientist is probably more concerned with institutions as such and less with particular aspects of the society than the economist. Nevertheless it is significant that the institutions which are primarily studied in political science departments are institutions related to legitimized coercion or threat, especially institutions which have the tax power, which is a form of legitimized threat. Political scientists are more concerned with problems of structure and role maintenance than are economists; they are concerned with such things as elections, voting behavior, constitutions, transfers of power and so on. They impinge on the interests of economists when they come to discuss bargaining, even political bargaining being a phenomenon associated with exchange. While political bargaining, however, is done not so much with commodities and economic exchangeables, though these may enter into it, as with structures, positions and roles in society; perhaps it is fair to say that the economist is more interested in commodities than he is in exchange as such, commodities being readily identified goods and services rather than the vague potentialities and structures which constitute much of the object of political bargaining.

The institutions which are studied primarily in the sociology department are those of the family, the church, the law enforcement agencies, the agencies of social welfare, philanthropy, schools and perhaps the military. All these are strongly concerned with the integrative system. They are concerned with such matters as the socialization of the child into a culture, with the institutions of homeostasis by which a culture defends itself against deviants, and by the institutions of legitimation by which people are brought to accept an existing order, which is one of the major functions of the public school, the patriotic societies and the church. There are also the institutions of pure sociability, such as the lodge and the club, the institutions of sport and recreation.

This division of the institutions and organizations of the social system among the social sciences is to some extent arbitrary, though it does tend to follow the classification by aspect, that is, it is those institutions in which the exchange aspect predominates which is the study of the economics department, those in which the threat system dominates which is studied in political science, and those in which the integrative system dominates which is studied in sociology. We must recognize, however, that all institutions and organizations have all three aspects. We could, indeed, take any sub-set of the set of all social institutions which had some kind of unity, let us say, banks, and offer courses on the economics of banks, the political science of banks and the sociology of banks. In the first we would study banks as part of an exchange system with inputs and outputs of money, securities and so on, and with states or conditions of the system described largely in terms of balance sheets. In the second we would describe the legal framework of the banking system, the problems of law enforcement, the enforcement of contracts. penalties for defalcation and embezzlement, relations of banks to government at all levels and so on. In a course on the sociology of banks we would describe how banks legitimate themselves, how they become accepted as organizations, how they develop role structures, how they behave in a crisis such as a panic, how they are related to interlocking directorates with other power centers in the community, how they are related to the United Fund, to local governments, to various economic interest groups, to the schools, building trades, the real estate interests, how their decisions affect the growth of communities, what bankers talk about when they meet, who they like and dislike, and so on. We could do the same with any institution of the social system. We could certainly give short courses on the economics of the church, the politics of the family and the sociology of the national state. Some of these courses, indeed, might be a good deal more interesting than the ones which are actually given and one wonders how far the division of the institutional material among the different departments has actually distorted our view of the social system and led us to neglect some problems and overemphasize others.

Up to this point I have barely mentioned anthropology, psychology, social psychology and perhaps it would be better not to mention them at all rather than to dispose of them as briefly as I must. Psychology stands partly in the social sciences and partly out of them. It relates to the social sciences a little the way physics does to chemistry in the sense that physics is concerned with explaining the behavior of atoms whereas chemistry is concerned with their relationships. If we think of the human person as the atom of the social system, then the only thing which unites the heterogeneous cluster of almost unrelated disciplines which constitute psychology is some concern for the state, description and behavior of the individual person. At one end, however, psychology is clearly in the biological sciences as a branch of physiology trying to pry open the human black box to see what kind of wiring it contains. At the other end, clinical psychology and psychiatry are branches of practical medicine akin more to human engineering than to science. In between we have animal psychology, which is largely a branch of ethology or the study of animal behavior. Somewhere along the line also psychology is supposed to study learning, which is perhaps the most fundamental dynamic process of all social systems. Unfortunately human learning is a complex process and studies of animal learning, useful as they are, are about as helpful as an analysis of the wheelbarrow would be in understanding the operation of a racing car. In the meantime we have a certain amount of what we might call "black box theory" relating inputs to outputs but we understand practically nothing about what goes on inside as compared with the complexity of the system itself.

Social psychology focusses attention not on the individual as a piece of apparatus but as a focus or node of inputs and outputs of various kinds, that is, as a role. This is a very useful model and has thrown a good deal of light especially upon the nature and interactions of small groups. It does not necessarily help us very much when we look upon the dynamics of society in the large. Nevertheless one can certainly imagine a course in the social psychology of a bank, dealing with such problems as the communication system, how the role structures are set up, the nature of both the formal and informal organization and their relationships, the effect of physical arrangements on the behavior of customers and staff and so on.

Anthropologists have always been the gentlemen of the social sciences, and one hesitates to say anything about them at all. The major tradition has been what might be called the total study of small societies and in order to find small societies it has almost been necessary to confine these studies to societies which are regarded as primitive. The methodology of the anthropologist, which is fundamentally that of the participant observer, has been somewhat haphazard and catch as catch can, and it is not unfair to describe it as a methodology of natural history. There is nothing necessarily wrong with this and a great deal can be learned from careful observation. There are scientific dangers, however, in a lack of attention to sampling, and a quite real danger of corruption of information at the source. Even small societies can be very complex and it is easy to miss essential aspects of them, if the observer is not trained in many different fields. Writings in economic anthropology, for instance, differ very widely in quality, depending largely on whether the observer is trained in economics. Even in the simplest societies terms of trade are important and it is surprising how easy it is for anthropologists who are not taught to look out for it to miss this factor. I do not know of anyone who has given a course on the anthropology of banks, but it could be fascinating. I have argued sometimes indeed that bankers should really be studied with the techniques of Margaret Mead and that the notions of taboo, ritual and artistic convention essentially dominate the behavior of the banking system. I have never found anybody yet however who would venture on a study to be called "Coming of Age in the Federal Reserve."

As one looks at the future of the social sciences one hopefully perceives a process of convergence under way. There is increasing recognition that the social system is in fact a totality and that a study of it from any single aspect, useful as this is, is in danger of missing other aspects. A particularly striking example of this phenomenon is the general frustration which economists are beginning to feel in regard to the problem of economic development. After the peculiar abstractions of economics, it is not too difficult to develop models of economic development which look fairly reasonable, and based on these economists have gone round the world giving a great deal of advice, most of which has turned out very badly. The sensitive economist becomes aware very rapidly when he deals with almost any practical problem that it is a problem in total social systems. At this point his professional skill breaks down because he is simply not equipped to deal with many aspects of the social system, particularly those involving the total human learning process and cultural change. The interest of economists in

economic development, therefore, has forced them into rather uneasy alliances with other social sciences. A similar process could have been observed in the study of the labor movement about a generation ago, when it became clear to economists that if they were to understand the phenomenon of the labor market they had to deal with this in terms beyond the abstraction of exchange and that they had to deal with such "non-economic" problems as morale, identity, the dynamics of conflict and the politics of decision-making in organizations. At the other end of the scale we find industrial psychologists and sociologists, at least in earlier days, attempting to solve problems in the labor market without any reference at all to wages or the overall terms of trade, either of the worker or the employer. We should not forget, either, that it was economists who solved the problem of mass unemployment simply because this is a phenomenon primarily of the total market system which is squarely in the domain of the exchange abstraction.

Where then do we go from here, especially where do sociologists go? It is no doubt presumptuous for a mere economist to offer suggestions to this effect, but even in rejecting them directions may be changed. Just as a matter of personal preference, therefore, I throw out these recommendations as directions in which I would like to see sociology move in the next generation.

In the first place, at the theoretical level I would like to see sociologists take much more interest than they have done in the past in what might be called the theory of the total social system. There is something in the proposition that the sociologists are, as it were, the residual legatees of the social sciences, taking over whatever has not been allocated to the others. After economics, political science and so on have carved out their domains, the sociologist takes what is left. It is the residual legatee, however, who has the major interest in the final size of the total estate, and this very residual quality of sociology should give it a prime interest in developing the study of society as a totality. This, of course, is a much more difficult task than the study of specialties and it is not surprising that people shrink from it. If a sociologist is to be a student of the total society he must also be an economist and a political scientist, or at least he must know how to communicate with them and must know what these fields have to offer. He must also be something of a psychologist and a social psychologist, just as a chemist these days has to be something of a physicist. Nevertheless, the importance of the task is overriding and the fact that it is difficult should not prevent it being done. If sociologists as a professional group can get under the weight of it they may encourage their members to spend longer periods of training to become generalists as well as specialists, and to perform this absolutely essential role of developing an integrative study of the total social system which to my mind is one of the major priorities in the intellectual world of the next generation or so. If sociologists don't do it, who will? The economics profession is so smug and so satisfied with its own admittedly great accomplishments that it is not likely to go anywhere in the next generation. According to one of the fundamental propositions of general social systems, nothing fails like success. Political science is so split at the moment between the traditionalists and the behavioralists and seems to be so incapable of developing any adequate theoretical structures of its own, apart from what it borrows from economics, that it may be an example of the second great proposition that nothing fails like failure. It is to the sociologist, therefore, that one tends to look for the accomplishment of this task, especially if they can divest themselves of certain scholastic prejudices, and catch a vision of the magnitude of the task which is to come.

On the theoretical side, I suspect that one of the main problems of sociology is how to break away from its obsession with the economic models and its attempt to imitate the rather stultifying success of the economists. One sees in such sociologists as Parsons and Homans, for instance, an attempt to develop sociology as generalized economics, regarding exchange as the fundamental social relationship to which everything else has to be reduced. This kind of economic reductionism seems to me disastrous, even though the notion of the generalization of the concept of exchange is an important one. I am convinced, however, that the concept of exchange, no matter how broadly generalized to include all forms of bargaining, implicit and explicit, and all things which enter into bargaining, whether specifically recognized commodities or not, are inadequate to interpret the complexity of social relationships and that we must develop a much more explicit theoretical structure to deal with integrative relationships which are not really exchange but which are of the nature of unilateral transfers. It is the gift or the grant, the one-way transfer, the quid without a quo, generalize as much as we will, which seems to me the central concept of the integrative system and who is to study this if not the sociologist? It is the business of the sociologist also to warn the other social scientists of the enormous importance of the dynamics of legitimacy. Who again will study this if not the sociologists? Economists are fantastically indifferent to the concept of legitimacy. They simply assume it away and further assume that if things are profitable they will be legitimate, an assumption that is simple-minded beyond belief. Political scientists are not much better. They tend to think that power, that is, threat capability, engenders its own legitimacy, whereas the truth is that sometimes it does and sometimes it does not. I am convinced myself that the dynamics of legitimacy is perhaps the most important single key to the overall dynamics of the total social system. This may be illustrated by the simple proposition that if we lose legitimacy, we lose everything, no matter how much wealth and power we might have. It is to the sociologists, however, that we should turn for the study of this strange dynamic with its puzzling discontinuities. Yet apart from some important hints in the classical sociologists, where do we find it?

Closely related to this is the study of community and identity. Identity and its opposite, alienation, perhaps is more in the field of the psychologist than of the sociologist, though it is essentially a factor in social relations rather than in individual state or condition, simply because one's identity consists primarily in the community with which one identifies. Hence, without a community there can be no identity. The processes by which identity is learned or unlearned, however, are again very mysterious, and one looks to the sociologist for elucidation without finding very much. This problem, however, lies at the base of such practical social problems as the control of crime, the disintegration or reintegration of societies, and the very problem of war and peace itself. Why, for instance, is the human identity so extraordinarily difficult to produce? Where are the studies of the social psychology of nationalism or of other identities? At this point, one seems to shout into a very empty echoing chamber. Surely if skills to answer these questions lie anywhere, they lie with the sociologists.

All these questions are related to a still larger question which is that of the development of what might be called macrosociology or the study of the total social system in the large. The practical successes of economics have arisen largely because it developed a technique of studying the economic system as a totality and as a total parametric system, thereby revealing that in a system of this kind causes could be very distant from effects because of the mutual determination of the whole system. Hence it has become clear, for instance, that unemployment is much more closely related to fiscal and tax policy than it is to the nature of labor markets, although the nature of labor markets may have a good deal to do with inflation. It is one of the great discoveries of economics that macrosystems behave very differently from microsystems, and that the generalization from the micro to the macro is most dangerous and usually wrong. This is why what might be called the "folk economics" of the fiscal conservatives which generalizes from the personal experience into that of the total economy is apt to be quite disastrous. In economics for instance we have learned to recognize that whereas for an individual, receipts and expenditure are two quite different things, for the total society they are identical, for every receipt is also an expenditure. One feels that there must be similar propositions, especially in regard to the integrative system. The key to this problem is perhaps the development of theory and also information systems which are capable of dealing with what might be called the "macro-learning" problem. What are the processes in society by which its aggregate image of the world is created, what Teilhard de Chardin calls the "noosphere."? Until we know something about this the total dynamics of society will continue to surprise us.

Here again, however, who will investigate these problems? The economists again are boxed in by their own successes, though it may be that their failures when it comes to economic development or even the economics of war and peace may drive them out of their complacency into the development of a more general system. The political scientists likewise occupy too narrow a part of the field and are too obsessed with the processes which intrinsically may turn out to be not very important. It may not matter very much for instance who happens to occupy the powerful roles if the behavior in the role is determined by the structure which lies around it. Political scientists, like historians, are apt to be obsessed with the particular and while it is always useful to have somebody around who does this, it tends to inhibit the development of a general theory.

It may be, of course, that sociologists are running too scared to accomplish the task of producing a general social theory and it is hard to blame them altogether for this. Attempts in the past to produce general social theories have not been very encouraging, whether Herbert Spencer, Marx, Pareto, or even Toynbee and Spengler. The lack of testability, the difficulties of quantification, and the tendency for general theorists to ride some particular hobby horse as that upon which everything else depends—which might be called a clothesline syndrome—is enough to scare anybody off this particular task. Failure in the past, however, means merely that the task has not yet been accomplished. It does not say that there is no task to be accomplished and it does not say that this accomplishment is impossible. If something cries out to be done, then if at first you don't succeed, you do try, try again. You don't simply say to hell with it and try something else, which is often an entirely rational procedure.

Nevertheless, one can see that the sociology of sociology itself weights the scales heavily against the kind of development which I am advocating. In the first place, society lasts longer than sociologists. The promotions and rewards in the academic professions come from impressive short pieces of work, not from important long pieces. One of the greatest problems in the social sciences, and it may be eventually in science as a whole, is that systems which take longer than the span of human life to work themselves out are very hard to study simply because a man is dead before his results can be accomplished. It is hard enough as we know to set up a study the results of which will not be out for five years, never mind for fifty. This whole problem therefore of what might be called longitudinal study or the study of long systems, remains a largely unsolved problem of all the sciences and of the social sciences in particular where systems are very long. This is perhaps more important than it is in the physical sciences where for the most part the systems are simple and short by comparison. At this point, rather late in the game I must confess, we may have to call in the historian. If long systems are to be studied the only way to do this in the present is by studying the record of the past. It may well be that the development of computer technology opens up a whole new possibility in the study of the records of the past. Whereas previously we have had to rely on the storage capacity of the human computer for the assessment and interpretation of these records, we may now be able to employ computers of much greater storage capacity though of considerably less intelligence. The symbiosis of the

memory of the computer with the intelligence of its operator might produce quite spectacular results. It is by no means inconceivable for instance that the whole historical record of man could be placed in the memory of a single computer and analyzed to reveal relationships which no single man could possibly perceive, not because of any lack of intelligence but because of sheer lack of storage capacity.

It is not enough, however, simply to squeeze the last drop of intellectual juice out of the deposits of the past. We must improve the deposits of the future. One of the most important results of the development of the social sciences and society has been a radical transformation in the nature of the deposit of the past. This has not only increased enormously in quantity, it is improved as a sample. The records of the pre-scientific past have been preserved largely by accident. This past is an enormous jigsaw puzzle, with perhaps ninety percent of the pieces missing in quite random fashion and the task of piecing it together may even be beyond the capacity of the man-computer combination. From now on, however, we are increasingly going to find that the record of the past is more complete and more significant. The accumulation of national income statistics since 1929 for instance has had an enormous impact, not only on economics but on economic policy and on our society in general. One of the great tasks of the social sciences, therefore, is to improve the record of the present as it becomes the past so that future generations may have a better chance of knowing what actually happened in the total social system and of perceiving the regularities which one hopes underlie it and of perceiving also the random elements which likewise form an important part of its constitution. I have elsewhere advocated the establishment of a network of social data stations, analogous to weather stations which will provide a constant record of the social system in most of its aspects.[2] Without a network of weather stations and observation balloons, providing a constant series of information in time and space, the task of understanding the complexities of a system such as the atmosphere would be impossible. We are only now indeed at the beginning of the data collection or recording phase in regard to the atmosphere which may in a generation or so enable us to understand it. The sociosphere, that is, the total sphere of man and his social organizations and relationships, is even more complicated than the atmosphere. It has more severe storms and disturbances, it is more heterogeneous, it has more significant variables probably by several orders of magnitude. Yet we expect to understand this with a fragmented record of the past, collected largely by accident. Until we have something like a continually sampled and processed record of the total social system we have little hope of understanding it. This is what is described as "taking the social sciences seriously." This is, of course, a task which involves all the social sciences from all their particular points of view. The social data stations would collect economic data, political data, sociological

2"Dare We Take the Social Sciences Seriously?" this volume (IV), Ch. 26.

data, and indeed biological data. Here again, however, it seems to me that the sociologist would have a special interest in setting up a system of this kind, simply because of his greater concern with totality of society. It may take a hundred years to establish an information system of this kind. Until we do, however, social science is likely to be pre-Copernican or at least pre-Newtonian. Without the siderial time series of Tycho Brahe both Kepler and Newton would have been impossible. Wesley Mitchell perhaps was the Tycho Brahe of economics and his counterpart in the other social sciences are still to come. If the epistemological problem of understanding the social system is to be solved, however, continuous recording must come, and to this task I recommend the rising generation.

THE LEARNING PROCESS IN
THE DYNAMICS OF TOTAL SOCIETIES

In: The Study of Total Societies, Samuel Z. Klausner,
ed. Garden City, N.Y.: Doubleday and Co. Anchor Books,
1967, pp. 98-113

THE LEARNING PROCESS IN THE DYNAMICS OF TOTAL SOCIETIES

A dynamic process is a succession of states, S_1, S_2 . . . S_n, of a system at successive points in time. Dynamic systems are present if there are patterns in the succession of states. The simplest of these patterns is the difference equation, or the differential equation, but of course many other patterns are possible. We may consider the dynamic process as a four-dimensional continuum in space and time, and if there are dynamic systems, this continuum will exhibit patterns which have some property of repetition. We can think of it almost as a four-dimensional wallpaper. The present moment is a boundary in this four-dimensional continuum, from which we look backward into an image of the past, derived essentially from information contained in deposits which the past has made—fossils, writings, buildings, artifacts, and memories. Because we are able to build up an image of the past which has some sort of order and pattern to it, we are able to project this pattern to some extent into the future. The further we go from the present, of course, either into the past or the future, the less clear the patterns become. In the case of the past this is because the channels of information become fewer the further back we go. In the case of the future it is because of the presence of elements in the system which are random from the point of view of the observer, that is, which cannot be fitted into any known pattern. The proportion of

change. One of the problems in constructing an image of the past is that the patterns of change are only imperfectly known, and the further back we attempt to project anything, the more subject to uncertainty our reconstructions will be. Another great problem we face is that the information provided by the past is inevitably a strongly biased sample; biased, for instance, in favor of durability of structure, of written communications rather than the oral ones that leave no permanent record except in the memory trace. We know very little, for example, about the origins of spoken language, because they have left no clues in bones or artifacts. In the post-telephonic present, the lot of the historian has been made harder by the fact that there has been a shift from written to spoken communications in the process of decision making. Hence the record of many important steps in these processes is irretrievably lost, even though a final decision is usually embodied in permanent written form.

The development of abstract models of social systems performs a number of essential functions. It is necessary in the first place because even though the information obtained from the past may be limited, it is still so large in volume that unless there is some method of organization and selection it will produce noise rather than knowledge. As I have suggested many times elsewhere, knowledge is achieved by the orderly loss of information, not by piling bit on bit. Another essential function of the abstract model is that it enables us to detect deficiencies in the information flow itself, and to deduce what we lack from what we have. A model is something like a jigsaw puzzle: even when many of the pieces are missing we can still be aware of the fact and can have some idea of the nature of the information they would contain. However, the nature of the bias in the sample of information from the past remains a very difficult problem, one for which we may never find a complete solution.

Models of social processes may be misleading as well as helpful. If the models themselves are inadequate, they will lead the investigator to eliminate information which may be highly relevant to his problem. Conversely, they may include irrelevant information. This is the danger of all simple interpretations of history. The conventional historian, for instance, who concentrates on the dynasties and the wars that feature so prominently in the written record, is apt to miss the long, slow, unrecorded forces of population and technological changes, and even the development of economic and domestic institutions, which lie somewhere below the level of the interests of chroniclers. By contrast, the Marxist, with his excessive emphasis on dialectic, on class structure and economic interpretations of history, is apt to overlook the importance of non-dialectical cumulative processes of growth of knowledge and technology. He is likely to underestimate the significance of the autonomous dynamic processes of political, military, symbolic, and religious systems. As any single model is almost by definition inadequate and may therefore be misleading, there is much to be said for the use of several different models and an eclectic frame of mind.

The use of quantification and of mathematical models needs special attention. The great advantage of numbers is that they can be readily combined and manipulated. Hence, if a particular phenomenon can be reduced to a numerical form, it is very easy to condense large and confusing masses of information into a single index or figure. A good example of this would be the concept of the gross national product, which, with all its weaknesses, is an enormously useful tool in interpreting one of the large aggregate characteristics of a society. We are able to use it because certain aspects of social life, i.e., those connected with production, consumption, and exchange, are capable of fairly easy quantification. This is so because a price structure exists from which we can derive valuation coefficients that reduce an enormous heterogeneous mass of shoes and ships and sealing wax to a uniform number of dollars'-worth. The process of the quantification of historical data is still in its infancy, and I believe very important modifications of our image of the past will emerge from it. Nevertheless, there should be a note of warning. Like any other process of abstraction, quantification introduces into the information processing operation a certain bias in favor of precisely those elements that can easily be quantified. Ease of quantification, however, is not necessarily closely related to the importance of a phenomenon in terms of the whole historical process. It is very hard, for instance, to apply quantification to symbolic systems, or to the dynamics of ethical and religious belief. Yet these systems have a life and dynamic of their own, and history certainly cannot be interpreted without them.

To return to the main question, let us consider how far it is possible to develop an abstract description of the movement through time of a social system, in this case a large society. The first problem is that of state description, i.e., how do we develop a means of describing the state of a society at a given moment in terms at once sufficiently simple and adequately rich? Total description is obviously impossible. To describe the state of even a small society like Iceland or the Maldive Islands, would require volumes enough to fill all the libraries in the world. We must use some kind of sampling methods to select information; in order to sample we must have a universe from which to do so. Incidentally, one of the great advantages of area sampling is that the spatial universe is usually fairly well known. For most countries we have reasonably adequate maps, and a map is a beginning of any state description.

The next universe is the human population itself. Here the census is important in establishing the universe from which later samples may be made; for some purposes, perhaps, area sampling can take the place of a census. Even when we look at the human population, however, the crucial question remains how much we want to know about it. Information collection is an economic problem. It exhibits in a marked degree the phenomenon associated with scarcity. If we find out one thing, we will not find out another. It is relatively easy, although problematic, to find out a respondent's location, age, marital status, family status, etc. It is more difficult, though still possible, to learn his religious affiliations, his political preferences, and something of his range of vision in time and space. Things hard to assimilate into the information system in any quantitative way may be called the general character variables. The F-scale, as a measurement of authoritarianism, was an attempt to do something along these lines, but we do not have any very good theory about these variables; even if we did, getting at them would require long interviews of a kind which are impossible in census enumeration.

One should perhaps visualize an orderly system of information collection, beginning with a complete census for what might be called the basic universes; then descending successively to smaller samples and longer interviews, finally to extensive depth interviews with a relatively small sample of the population. An information collection process of this kind should also reveal a great deal about the social structures of the society. It would certainly yield information about organizational activity and organizations, about lines of communication, e.g., who communicates with whom. It should also be informative about population and the use of artifacts, the non-human material objects interacting with human beings, e.g., farms, machines, newspapers, radios, automobiles, etc.

One of the major problems intrinsic to the process of information collection is that of fitting the existing channels and previously gathered information into the over-all picture. A considerable amount of the normal activity of any society is devoted to collecting and processing information. One thinks of accounting, legal records, and the vast accumulation of documents common to any reasonably literate society. Most records, however, are kept for particular purposes and are not conceived of as part of a wider sample. By the next generation, thanks to the development of computer technology, we may well have developed a universalized system of information collection and processing. Such a system would have profound implications for political and personal life, in terms of problems of privacy, rights of access to knowledge, and so on. Actually, these implications are already evident.

Once we have achieved a reasonably satisfactory state description, the next task is to detect reasonably stable processes of state change. Most of these are processes of consumption and production. All states of any system are consumptive, i.e., they depreciate and decay. Persons age and die; capital depreciates and is exhausted. Knowledge is forgotten and in any case is lost with death; foodstuffs are consumed, etc.

These processes are usually governed by functions of
the state itself. Thus, if age-specific death rates are stable, the over-all death rate is a function of the age distribution. A society composed of a large proportion of
young people will have a low death rate; one having a
large number of old people will have a high death rate.
Food requirements of the human population are based
on the fact that the human being burns up a certain
amount of biological fuel and uses up certain amounts
of protein and fat in the course of living. Corresponding to these processes of consumption—and largely in-
duced by them—are the processes of production, which
may be arbitrarily divided into processes that simply
replace the consumption and restore the state to some
initial condition, and processes that go beyond mere
maintenance and raise the state itself to some higher
level. Therefore, the dynamic state of the system
largely depends on the excess of production over consumption. If births exceed deaths, the population will
grow. If the production of goods exceeds their consumption, the capital stock will increase. If the gain in
knowledge as a result of education and other information processes exceeds the loss of knowledge due to
aging and death, a society's total stock of knowledge
will increase. These are the most fundamental processes underlying the dynamic changes within the
state. If they are fairly stable and especially if they
are functionally related to the state itself, predictions
can be made about the course of future events with
some reasonable degree of probability.

We must, however, be alert to possible changes in
rates of production and consumption, and changes in
the functions relating the state to these rates. Population prediction has often been very unsuccessful because based on faulty assumptions about rates of

change, or changes in rates. In the mid-1940s, for instance, the United States Bureau of the Census was still making projections of the population that proved to be considerably underestimated with the advent of a quite unexpected and persistent jump in the birth rate after 1947. In view of the information available at earlier periods, this change can quite reasonably be regarded as a random shift in the parameters of the system. Perhaps if we had known a little more about human motivation and the relation of birth rates to income, our projections might have been more accurate.

Similarly, in economic development, a society sometimes seems to operate according to a step-function, and quite suddenly adopts new rates of production and consumption, or savings and investment. There is, perhaps, something inherently unpredictable about these step-changes. Hence, whenever systems are liable to step-change, we should avoid confusing *projections* that do not allow for that liability with *predictions* that must allow for it if they are to be useful. Sometimes these step-changes are reversible, but more often seem irreversible; they represent what I have elsewhere called a systems break. This is a most intractable kind of phenomenon to interpret in terms of the dynamics of social systems. It is particularly significant, of course, in revolutionary changes, which accounts for the difficulty of predicting revolution.

There is a whole class of related phenomena that may be called "threshold systems," which operate successfully and predictably with a set of given parameters as long as these all lie within a certain range, or inside a given threshold. However, if any one of them goes beyond that threshold, irreversible processes set in that may result in profound system change. The death of a living organism is perhaps the most striking example of a threshold system: once a certain boundary is crossed, the homeostatic processes of the system disintegrate and even its physical structure soon decays and disappears. A less extreme case could be described as transfiguration, in which the system, while retaining a certain identity through time, is so reorganized as to be virtually unrecognizable. Sometimes these processes of transfiguration are implicit in the dynamics of the system itself, as in the metamorphosis of a caterpillar into a butterfly, or an egg into a chicken. In social systems these transformations may be more random, as for instance in the transformation of the character of a firm. (The company that now produces Black Label Beer was originally a producer of mangles and then of automobiles, before it developed its present industry.) Similarly a Congregational Church may transform itself into a Unitarian one, and a state may have a Communist revolution. It is these uncertain transfigurations around which so much social conflict develops. Thus, it is both the uncertainty and apparent irreversibility of the Communist revolution that accounts for much of the emotional intensity it has engendered.

It is sometimes possible to detect continuous changes of a variable toward some recognizable threshold or crisis level, beyond which irreversible parametric change in the system will take place, either death or transfiguration. Doctors, for instance, identify the state of a sick person as "critical," in which the variables of his system are moving toward the irreversible boundary of death, or "out of danger," in which the homeostatic processes have reasserted themselves and the process toward the death boundary has been reversed. In the case of societies, soil erosion, increase in population density in limited agricultural areas, and erosion of ideologies or systems of legitimation, are examples of continuous processes which may lead to discontinuous thresholds. On the other hand, discontinuous processes, certain one-shot events, profoundly change the subsequent parameters of a social system. The introduction of a road, a school, a mission, newspaper circulation or electronic communication, may not represent any simple continuous pattern, yet may lead to system breaks in the dynamic processes.

A very difficult question is that of the importance of "key roles" in the society. Occasionally the death or removal of someone in such a key role, like Stalin, produces quite large changes in the subsequent dynamic of the society. However, there seem to be some societies, like those of Latin America, in which the latent and continuous forces are so strong that no role occupant seems to affect the dynamics of the society in any profound sense. The importance of key roles no doubt depends to a considerable extent on the nature of the societal power structure. In a pluralistic society with many centers of power, the removal of a particular role occupant makes less difference than it does in one where all the channels of power lead to a single figure at the top. It would be hard, for instance, to imagine any change in Protestantism, with its highly pluralistic organization, comparable in rapidity and magnitude with the changes introduced in the Roman Catholic Church by the late Pope John XXIII. Clearly, it should be possible to define and even to measure the significance of social role, but up to now it has been given little serious attention.

One phenomenon often overlooked is the structure and historical succession of age roles in a society. Thus, in Japan, a rebellious and radical role is quite acceptable for the student, and the casual observer might con-

clude therefore that the country will move sharply to
the left when the present student generation comes to
maturity and power. If, however, there is inherent in
the society a specific role for youthful rebellion, if the
general pattern is one of radical youth and conservative age, we should be wary of projecting the character of today's youth into the adult society of the next
generation. Even so, it is also important to identify the
operative influences on youth, for in many respects
people do not much change as they get older; the experiences of youth often determine the attitudes of
middle age. This is particularly apt to be true of trau-
matic experiences. The attitudes of the generation now
administering the United States are so deeply colored
by the Great Depression and Munich that it is almost
impossible for this generation to be realistic about the
contemporary world.

Changes in methods of child-rearing can have a profound long-range effect on the character of a population, and hence of a total society. Thus we should look
for substantial changes in the character especially of
the middle-class population of the United States, after
the introduction of new child-rearing techniques between the 1930s and 1940s. Through the impact of his
famous book on child-rearing, Dr. Spock may well be
the most influential American of the twentieth century.
We must also study very carefully the shift from family
to nursery school, especially in socialist societies, and
the possible impact of this on the character of the rising generation. Everett Hagen[1] bases his long-run dynamics essentially on the slow transformation of the
parent-child relationship as the traditional society is
threatened and invaded by ideas and people and arti-

[1] Everett E. Hagen, *On the Theory of Social Change* (Homewood, Ill.: The Dorsey Press, 1962).

facts from the developed world. This suggestion is highly plausible, but we still do not know enough about the dynamics of personality growth and change to estimate the relative importance of, say, childhood influences, influences in adolescence, and the learning processes of later life.

Perhaps the element of the social system least reducible to simple models and a trustworthy information process is the symbolic, i.e., the symbols, ideas, ideologies, theologies, myths, etc., that constitute the basis of community and around which develop deep passions and strongly held values. Most of the destructive and protracted conflicts besetting society have their origin in symbolic systems. Conflicts of interest can usually be adjusted by some bargaining process; but because they strike so deeply at the personal identity and self-image of the individual, and at the basis of community itself, conflicts of faith and ideology are extremely hard to resolve.

One of the most puzzling phenomena of history is the occasional outbreak of what might be called "symbolic epidemics"—the rise of a new religion or a new political ideology or even a new nationalism. Phenomena like the spread of Christianity or of Islam or of Communism or even of science and the world superculture exhibit many of the characteristics of biological epidemics, and it is by no means easy to identify the conditions under which they will take hold and be successful. The contagion of ideas, as far as I know, is something which has rarely been studied at the level of the total society, though there have been many studies of individual conversion. Epidemiological theory suggests that this is a phenomenon where again there are critical values of certain variables, such as the contagiousness, above which a contagion will spread among large populations and below which it will recede and reach a low-level equilibrium. What it is, however, that makes certain ideas contagious is something about which we understand very little. A study of the relative success of a rather constant missionary effort in different countries, such as that of the Mormons, would be extremely interesting.

In all these processes we can detect two major elements. One might be called the non-human element in the social system, involving such things as climatic changes, bacteriological mutations, soil erosion, etc. The second element in the system, the human element, is almost wholly concerned with the process of human learning, involving the rise or decline or transformation of the total stock of human knowledge. Up to this point in the development of the social sciences, learning has been treated largely on an individual basis. The time now seems to be ripe for the development both of theoretical systems and of empirical studies of learning on the scale of the large society, or what might be called the "macrolearning" process. The events of each day are impressed on the memories of the participants, and so add to the total structure of knowledge where the impact is positive, or subtract from it through denial, forgetting, aging, and death. If we could find some fairly simple analytical structure to portray this process, we would be far advanced toward solving the problem of the dynamics of total societies. It is not inconceivable that we might sample the information output of a particular day and employ a set of weights relating the information output to changes in the knowledge structure, or in the sum total of images of the world held by the population. We might then be able to find important clues to the more continuous and on-going processes by which the knowledge structure is changed. Then, as ever, of course we would have to be on the lookout for the step-functions and the discontinuities and system breaks. With all the difficulties, however, some genuine knowledge of the dynamics of total societies seems to be possible.

Perhaps the greatest problem in developing knowledge about total societies is the sheer difficulty, expense, and political sensitivity involved in setting up an adequate process of collecting information. Once information is collected, we have fairly good methods for processing it and interpreting it. Many of the fundamental difficulties of the social sciences, however, arise from the fact that their basic data are collected largely as by-products of other activities such as taxation, customs collection and migration restrictions. Even though an increasing amount of information is collected purely out of curiosity, it still represents a small proportion of the total. We also face the difficulty that the very collection of information and the development of knowledge about social systems is itself part of the systems, and is likely to be a crucial element in their dynamics. All decisions are made on the basis of some image of the world derived from some form of information processing. If, therefore, we introduce the collection and processing of social scientific information into the social system, we cannot expect it to remain unchanged, and the political sensitivity of such information collection and processing depends on this fact. We have been fairly successful in collecting and processing economic data on the scale of the total society, as the development of national income statistics proves. If we can structure the process on a regular, systematic, month-by-month basis for other essential social variables, it will constitute an enormous step forward towards a viable social science. I have suggested that we require a network of social data stations, analogous perhaps to the meteorological stations collecting data about the atmosphere. Without such a network, it is hard to see how really substantial knowledge collection processes about the "sociosphere" can be developed. This is probably a task for the United Nations rather than for any merely national agency, because the collection of knowledge, like any other social process, has to be legitimated if it is to be continuous. The experience with Project Camelot illustrates the difficulty of legitimating any major information collection and processing operation merely through the agency of national institutions. It is the basic illegitimacy of the nation-state itself outside its own borders that is the real problem; a world system of social data collection and processing must be legitimated by world organizations.

TECHNOLOGY AND THE INTEGRATIVE SYSTEM

In: Today's Changing Society, A Challenge to
Individual Identity, Clarence C. Walton, ed.
New York: Inst. of Life Insurance, 1967, pp. 57-73

Technology
and the
Integrative System

History in general, and human history in particular, is a very complex pattern in four dimensions, three dimensions in space and one of time. The study of social dynamics attempts to find patterns in this structure which are repeated almost the way the patterns are repeated in wallpaper. If we can find such patterns then we have a fair chance of making predictions. If we can find stable relationships between things which we want to control and things which we cannot control we may be able to extend our area of control and actually mold the future rather than predicting it. We do this molding of the future every time we make a plan, for part of the determinants of the future is the image of the future which we have at the present.

This complex pattern in space-time that we call history is not homogeneous. It has, indeed, a structure which might be compared to a layer cake. A number of different social systems or patterns can be postulated, each of which has a certain dynamic of its own, in the sense that its own future is in part derived from its own past in a fairly regular, stable way, within which, also, each of these parallel systems affects the others. We might illustrate this in Figure 1 where the lines A, B and C represent three parallel systems. A, for instance, might represent the economic system, B the political system and C the religious system, each of which has a certain independence of its own as reflected by the horizontal arrows, but each of which also interacts with the others, as repre-

sented by the diagonal arrows, so the total process is a result partly
of each system pursuing an independent course of its own, partly
a result of each system acting upon others. Thus the process of
economic development has a certain dynamic of its own in which
the present character of the economy in regard to investments and
the distribution of resources has a great deal to do with determining
what the economy is going to be like next year or even in ten years.
On the other hand, the economic system is always subject to influences from other systems, from the political system or from the
religious system. A new government or a religious reformation may
profoundly affect the development of the economy. Each of these
other systems likewise has a certain integrity of its own, and it is
likewise affected by the economy. The society which is having
rapid economic development will find that both its political and
its religious structure are profoundly affected by this fact.

Figure 1.

Social systems as a parallel series

of interacting dynamic systems.

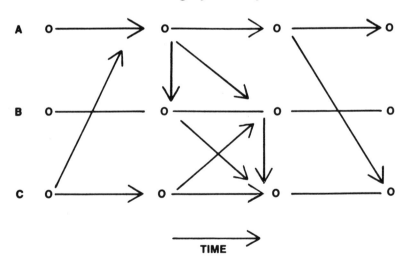

Exactly how we define the "layers" of the layer cake is to some extent arbitrary. The layers are not clearly defined in nature and at the edges especially they merge into each other so that it is certainly not easy to say, for instance, where the economic system ends and the political system begins. For purposes of analysis, however, it is useful to define certain broad areas of the social system as quasi-independent sub-systems and to discuss the inter-action among them. This paper will concentrate on two of these sub-systems of great importance, both of which have a great deal of independence in the sense that the horizontal arrows of Figure 1 represent strong relationships and the future of each system is determined in considerable measure by its own past. Both systems also have very strong impacts each on the other. These two systems are the technological system and the integrative system. Neither of these is easy to define, especially at the edges; each of them however is a system with a good deal of independence.

The Technological System

The technological system is that aspect of society which is concerned with human artifacts both material and social and of the interactions of humans with artifacts, largely in the process of producing more artifacts. We think of technology in terms of tools, implements, machines and the ways of using them. We think of it also in terms of human skills, roles and organizations. A state, a church or a corporation is as much an artifact as a weapon, an altar or an account book. The history of technology is a history of the increasing complexity, variety and number of human artifacts, starting with primitive tools such as chipped flints, arrows and spears, early dwellings, clothing. We work up to agriculture, metallurgy, wheeled vehicles, ships, roads, domesticated animals, villages, cities and empires, money, credit and banking. This process finally leads in the present day to electrical and nuclear power, railroads, airplanes, computers, nuclear weapons, missiles, nation states and the United Nations.

As we define it, technology seems to include almost everything. Within this larger process of social evolution we want to distinguish material technology on the one hand and social technology on the other. Even material technology has a certain dynamic of its own.

We can treat human artifacts as if they were an evolutionary species with populations, birth rates, death rates, the birth of an artifact being its production and its death its consumption. Thus in the past 60 years the world has become largely populated with large four-wheeled metal bugs with detachable brains, called automobiles. These constitute a social species, with its own genetic apparatus: wombs in the shape of automobile factories; sperm in the shape of ideas in the heads of engineers; death in the form of final passage to an automobile graveyard; and even a certain amount of resurrection in the shape of spare parts and steel scrap. The mutation which produced the automobile has had a profound effect on the whole ecological system of the world and has altered the numbers of almost all other species both biological and social. It has diminished the number of horses, increased the number of supermarkets, increased the areas devoted to roads, increased peculiar roadside vegetation, altered the pattern of forest fires, polluted the atmosphere and increased the lead content of the top level of the oceans by several orders of magnitude. The automobile, furthermore, is a good example of the inner dynamic of material technology. It could not possibly have been developed much earlier than it was, for at least 200 inventions had to precede it, such as the vulcanization of rubber, the fractionation of oil, and so on. Once these inventions had been made it would have been hard to prevent the automobile. The fact that is so often noted in the history of technology that certain inventions are made quite independently by different people in different parts of the world at about the same time is a very clear proof of the independence of the dynamic of material technology, given a certain social climate and certain payoffs in the social system.

The Integrative System

What I call the "integrative system" is much less familiar than the technological system, for the idea that the integrative system exists at all is a fairly new one. Nevertheless I am prepared both to define and defend a "layer" of the total social system which deserves this name. The integrative system then is that part of the total social system which deals with such matters as status, community, identity, legitimacy, loyalty, love, respect, dignity, acceptance and so on, and of course the negative aspects of these variables, alienation, hostility, exclusion, malevolence, hatred, disloyalty, illegitimacy and so on. In this country especially, we have not taken these aspects of social life very seriously. We have regarded them either as purely personal and eccentric, like young lovers in the park, or we have taken them for granted, and assumed, for instance, that power and wealth always creates its own legitimacy. This, I think, is a grave error, and contributes more than anything else to the frustration of our policies and the extremely unsatisfactory nature of our present political life. This is nowhere more evident than it is in Viet Nam where we are under the illusion that threat capability will create its own legitimacy whereas in fact it does not. With 10 times the military power that the French had in Viet Nam we find ourselves quite incapable of achieving the kind of stable, independent and democratic society that we desire, simply because we cannot achieve legitimacy, and the very extent of our power destroys any legitimacy we might have.

The Grants Economy

As a first approximation the integrative system may be defined in terms of extent and structure by what I have called the "grants economy." A grant is a unilateral transfer or sacrifice from one person or social unit to another, without anything passing in return. Exchange, by contrast, is bilateral transfer in which A gives something to B and B gives something to A. A grant or unilateral transfer from A to B can only take place if there is an integrative relationship between them; that is, if A in some sense identifies with B and regards him as being in the same community of interest with himself. When we give a dime to a beggar out of pity, there is a low level integrative relationship, the level, perhaps of common humanity, which is not very strong but which does exist. A study of the grants economy, even in money terms, would tell us a lot about the structure of the world integrative system. It would reveal, for instance, that the national state is by far and away the most powerful integrative system, for the grants which the state makes to its own citizens far exceed in magnitude any other grants. In most well organized and developed national states the internal grants of the state to its own citizens are at least of the order of magnitude of 10 percent of the gross national product. Foreign aid is usually well below one percent of the gross national product. Internal charity and philanthropy, religious gifts and missionary endeavors and so on are not much more than this.

A study of the grants economy would further reveal the integrative weakness of many systems which make a good deal of show of integrative rhetoric. Class, for instance, is extraordinarily weak as an integrative system. The workers of the world do not unite. World socialism is very weak as an integrative system. The Russians, for instance, did practically nothing for the Chinese, in spite of the fact that they ostensibly had the same ideology so it is not surprising that the Chinese are so angry with the Russians! Here we have an example of where the inability of an ostensibly integrative system to create a grants economy in effect produced an integrative split. The Russian contribution to Chinese development was about one cent per Chinese per annum, and even this was in the form of a loan which the Chinese had to pay back when they were under particularly difficult circumstances. The Russians were prepared to do a good deal for the Uzbeks because Uzbekistan is in the same national state as the Russians; that is, the Soviet Union. They did virtually nothing for the Chinese and have actively exploited East Germany, in spite of the supposedly ideological community. The strongest national integrative system, as a matter of fact, was the old French Empire. The French gave a much larger proportion of their gross national product in foreign aid into their old Empire than any other country.

Grants in money or commodities are not of course the whole story, for there are many other forms of sacrifice, culminating of course in the sacrifice of life itself, which is the most extreme measure of an integrative relationship. "Greater love hath no man than this, that he lay down his life for his friend." Grants can also be made in the shape of time and energy and unpaid work. They may be measured indeed by "terms of trade" which are in some sense below normal. If people give a lot to something and get very little out of it, then presumably they are giving a grant and this is both a measure and a symbol of an integrative relationship. The dynamics of a system of this kind is often very peculiar. Sacrifices — to use a term which is more general than grants — are at the same time both the measure of an integrative relationship and also sometimes its cause. If we once start making sacrifices for something we find it very hard to admit to ourselves that the sacrifices have been in vain. Hence, sacrifices tend to be self-justifying in that they create the integrative system which justifies them and in the interests of which they are made. This is why the blood of the Martyrs is the seed of the Church and the blood of the soldiers the seed of the state. We feel that we cannot "let down" those who have made sacrifices in the past with whom we identify. The sacrifice of life has a peculiar emotional intensity, as the extreme magnitude of the integrative relationship, and it is not surprising that many sacred institutions have originated in human sacrifice. One thinks of the religion of the Aztecs, of Moloch, of the ancient Chinese burials, and their modern equivalent in the national state, which demands constant sacrifice of young men on the battlefield in order to maintain the love and the loyalty which people bear towards it. Moloch is not only one of the most ancient of gods, but one of the most persistent.

In the course of the development of the integrative system the discovery is always made that vicarious or substitutional sacrifice performs most if not all of the functions of real sacrifice. The victims in the graves of the monarchs of early civilizations are replaced by statues and figurines. Animal sacrifices and scapegoats replace the human sacrifices of ancient religions. The purely symbolic sacrifice of the Mass replaces even the animal sacrifices of the temple. Similarly, we may perhaps think of the development of foreign aid as the beginnings of substitutionary sacrifice in the national state and we may hope, perhaps, that as the national state as an institution matures the time will come when it will seem perfectly appropriate to sacrifice money for it but absolutely absurd and indecent to sacrifice human life the way we do today. It will then seem preposterous that anybody should be asked to die for his country, just as nobody is now asked to die for his religion or his lord.

The Unity of the Integrative System

We could spend a great deal more time in developing the concepts of the integrative system. Enough has been said, however, to suggest that it exists, that it is a social reality of great importance and that it has a certain unity of its own. Its internal dynamic produces a time pattern something like an escarpment. The origins of all integrative systems are obscure, but once they begin, however, they develop a dynamic of their own. Sacrifices which are made create a further sense of integration which enables the objects of these sacrifices to command still more sacrifices. These create a greater sense of integration with rising integrative relationship and rising sacrifices, until finally we reach the top of the system, until it is at the height of its power and extent and then frequently it collapses quite suddenly in a surprising debacle. The temples are suddenly deserted, the monarch is abandoned and the empire is destroyed. Sacrifice is piled on sacrifice until suddenly at some point it seems too much, and at that point the whole system collapses abruptly.

This pattern of cumulative unilateral sacrifice leading to collapse, however, is fortunately not the only pattern of the system. There is another pattern which might be described as reciprocity. Reciprocity is superficially like exchange and is often confused with it. It differs from exchange, however, in that whereas exchange is a conditional relationship reciprocity is unconditional. In exchange A gives something to B on the condition that B gives something to A, and vice versa. In reciprocity A gives something to B.unconditionally whether B gives anything to A or not and similarly B gives something to A unconditionally whether A gives anything to B or not. Thus while we have mutual and bilateral transfers as in an exchange these transfers have the quality of grants or sacrifices which pure exchange does not. A very good example of reciprocity is the exchange of Christmas presents, which is a very important ritual in the reaffirmation of the integrative system of the family and the intimate friendship group, even though the terms of trade here are important. One who never gives any Christmas presents will pretty soon find that he doesn't get any. The fact that it is an exchange of gifts which is supposed to be unconditional is of great importance in creating the integrative affect. This is why an exchange of money, for instance, is much less satisfactory than an exchange of commodities in developing an integrative relationship. The growth of reciprocity, fortunately, does not follow the pathological pattern which the growth of unilateral sacrifices is apt to do. It produces a pattern of healthy mutuality and equality of status whereas the pattern of sacrifice produces hierarchy, organizational schizophrenia and paranoia and eventually unstable organization. Thus, if we simply say, "Ask not what America will do for you, ask what you can do for your country," this is a symbol of a "sacrifice trap" which will eventually lead to too much sacrifice for the country and eventual collapse of the national integrative system. Suppose now we contrast our reactions to the phrase, "Ask not what General Motors can do for you, ask only what you can do for General Motors." We see the difference between an organization with a strong integrative system like the national state and an organization which is almost purely within the exchange system like a corporation.

The trouble with the corporation and indeed with almost all purely economic organizations is that everybody has good terms of trade with them. We do ask what General Motors can do for us and the answer is, "Quite a lot." If we are employed by it, it gives us good wages; if we buy from it, it gives us automobiles. As a result, however, of existing in a purely exchange environment it creates a very weak integrative system. One of the problems of General Motors is that nobody loves it much, hence it is ultimately very vulnerable to shifts in the integrative system which would deny it legitimacy. The only answer to this seems to be a system of reciprocity which combines the virtues of the exchange system, which are very great, with the development of an integrative structure. I am not suggesting that we should have Christmas all the year round but we do need to think about how we can introduce some of this element into the system. It may be, for instance, that the trading stamp is an interesting example of the introduction of something that looks like a Christmas present into a system which otherwise would be pure exchange.

In the case of the national state also, even though a citizen perhaps should not ask too loud and clear, "What can my country do for me?," the country should ask itself very loud and clear what it can do for its citizens. The whole meaning of democracy and the collapse of the legitimacy of monarchy and the absolute state rests upon the principle that a system of pure sacrifice is unstable and even the state must develop reciprocity. That is, the terms of trade of a citizen with his country is a very important question, and how much he gets for what he gives is a highly legitimate social value. Even if we are not allowed to ask this ourselves, somebody should ask it for us. The whole theory of the democratic state indeed is that if the existing government does not provide good terms of trade for its citizens and gives them a good deal in terms of what they give to it, it should be voted out. On the other hand, it may also be that reciprocity is the real key to a healthy integrative relationship. Perhaps we should indeed give to our country unconditionally and it should give unconditionally to us.

There seems to be an almost inevitable paradox about reciprocity in the sense that even though the exchange of gifts is unconditional, the terms of trade in past exchanges is significant in determining the willingness of people to enter into future exchanges. If the terms of trade for any party to a reciprocal arrangement are bad and persistently bad, this may eventually destroy the integrative system on which the reciprocal relationship depends.

Interaction Between the Two Systems

The interactions between the technological system and the integrative system represented by the diagonal or even vertical arrows of Figure 1, are extremely complex and enormously important. We cannot hope to do more than hint at some of the possibilities here. The relations are profoundly reciprocal. The dynamic properties of the technological system depend in considerable degree on its integrative matrix, likewise the development of technology produces enormous effects on the system of loyalties, legitimacies, and affections. Here we can only illustrate some possible connections.

We tend to take the enormous technological dynamic of Western society in the last 300 years very much for granted. Nevertheless, it is one of the most puzzling phenomena in human history. Suppose we ask ourselves the question, for instance as Joseph Needham has done, why the great mutation into science and science-based technology took place in Europe and the Atlantic world and not in China? Up to the year 1600 there can be little doubt that China was the center of the human race. It was indeed the Middle Kingdom. Most of the important technological developments in the first 1600 years of the Christian era originated in China and arrived the total pattern involving these random elements increases as we move into the future, and the possibility of predicting becomes less; that is, the subjective probability which we might attach to any particular image of the future becomes less as the future becomes more remote and as we look further and further into it.

Our ability to develop and perceive patterns in the past depends on two things, the information channels which extend back into the past and our ability to develop abstractions, that is, models, with which to filter, arrange, and interpret the information received from the past. Such information is carried by those objects or structures that exhibit some kind of stability through time, e.g., rocks, fossils, buildings, monuments, inscriptions, books, records, and memories. If we know the law of dynamic change of a structure, then we can project its present condition into the past and know what it was like at various dates in the past. Thus an archaeologist can take a ruin and reconstruct it as the building it must once have been; he can even deduce many things about the nature of the culture that produced it, since there are certain regularities in the transformation of buildings into ruins. Similarly, ancient texts can be reconstructed because there are certain consistencies of textual corruption through copying. In the case of Carbon 14 dating, we use a constant process of radioactive decay to project an existing structure back into the past, thus establishing the date when atmospheric carbon was captured by the object in question. In the case of rocks and fossils, there may be no decay at all, and we can project their existing structure for hundreds of millions of years into the past.

This, however, is only a special case of the general principle of projection by means of known patterns of in Europe often some 300 years later. Eighteenth century European intellectuals regarded China as the most advanced, developed and civilized country in the world. The history of the last 300 years, however, has been written largely in terms of the fact that Europe made the breakthrough into modern science, whereas China did not, and is now desperately trying to catch up with this 300-year lag. The reasons for this difference are still very obscure, but many of them unquestionably lie in the nature of the integrative system in the two societies. It may well be that China was too well integrated to permit a revolution in knowledge. It was administered by a bureaucracy, recruited by public examination, and hence always open to able and ambitious young men, who could thus enter the system and become part of the establishment. There was really only one central power and one central loyalty. There was no separation of church and state. The magistrate performed the functions of the priest. A powerfully unified system of loyalty and affection was created with the study of the classics and the pursuit of Confucian ideals. This integrative system was powerful enough and integrated enough so that alternative systems, whether Christianity or Islam, could make no real headway against it. Buddhism and Taoism degenerated into purely popular religions, incapable of challenging the established order of the society.

Europe by contrast was deeply divided not only into separate nation states but divided as to church and state, with a long, early tradition of conflict between the Pope and the Emperor, and the further split caused by the Reformation and the Counter Reformation. The Roman Church might try to suppress Galileo, but what was impiety in one place could become piety in another. Hence in this fractured integrative system it was possible to develop a small sub-culture almost in the interstices of the fractures themselves. It was committed to veracity, without fear of novelty, liberated from the tyranny of intellectual authority, devoted to the testing of realities and to the reality and importance of the natural world. There are many puzzling aspects still of this phenomenon; nevertheless, it is clear that the nature of the integrative system had an enormous impact. China had an Un-Chinese Activities Committee for too long. It created too much loyalty, too much commitment to the established ways and established orders. In Europe disloyalty was easier. Luther was disloyal to the Pope;

the Prince was disloyal to the Emperor. There was indeed no universal loyalty and hence man's mind was free for loyalty to the truth which is the foundation of scientific advance.

Coming closer to our own day, we can see many cases in which the spread of the science-based technology is hampered by the nature of the integrative system of particular countries and societies. India is a strong case in point, where the traditional integrative system of the Indian village is enormously strong. In a caste society everybody has a place. Hence it is very hard to find a place for the innovator who indeed is often seen as a threat to the highly integrated established order. In India, indeed, it seems that innovation is largely confined either to those who have broken out of the established order through contact with Western education or to those who are refugees from Pakistan and hence have been forced out of their traditional established order. In Latin America again we see an integrative system which this time perhaps is too weak to create the matrix within which a successful transition to science-based technology can be achieved. Internal conflict and the inability to achieve any political synthesis in the society has led to rule by the military, which is rarely friendly toward technological development. Here again all generalizations should be looked on suspiciously, but the notion of an interaction between the integrative system and the technological system is of profound importance and needs much further study.

The Dynamics of Technology

On the other side, the dynamics of technology have a constant impact on the integrative system. Illustrations could be multiplied almost indefinitely. One looks, for instance, at what I have elsewhere called the "organizational revolution;" that is, the rise in the size of organizations of all kinds which began about 1870. This is directly related to certain technological changes in the system of communications — the telephone, the telegraph, the mimeograph, the dictaphone — and also certain social inventions, especially in the form of organization of the executive and the division of labor in bureaucracies. All this has permitted an enormous increase in the optimum size of the organization and has created such organizations as General Motors, the United Auto

Workers, the American Association for the Advancement of Science, the American Medical Association, the United States Department of Defense, the Soviet Union, and even the Metropolitan Life Insurance Company. This produces all sorts of change in the integrative system. The kind of loyalty which people have to a small organization is very different from what they have to a large one. The integrative system of a small family firm is very different from that of a large corporation. It is not surprising that as the size of the organization grows we see movement from status to contract, a movement perhaps from reciprocity towards contractual exchange. On the other hand, growth of organizations produces a profound change in the interrelations between them. We move from something like perfect competition into oligopoly, not only in the relations of firms but also in the relations of states. This profoundly affects the nature of the structure of legitimacy.

The technological revolution in communications, as McLuhan has suggested, is producing an enormous impact, not only on forms of organization but on the whole spirit and structure of society including the whole nature of the learning process, which is the most fundamental process in all social dynamics. The development of television, for instance, which can be regarded on the whole as pure offshoot of the dynamics of technology, has had an enormous effect on all aspects of human life: on the family, on politics, on the nature of rhetoric, on drama and the arts and on formal education. It upsets traditional societies everywhere and has played a large part in creating this remarkable generation of young people which we now have with us, who have been raised all their lives on TV. By introducing, as it were, a competitive source of information into the home to the parents, it produces profound changes in psychological development. We are certainly going to have to rewrite psychoanalysis as a result of the TV set. It destroys the intimacy of the local or even the national community and moves us a long way towards the "spaceship earth," which is such a remarkably apt symbol of the world to come.

Another illustration of the impact of technology on the integrative system is the enormous impact of the automobile. Here again we have something which came mainly out of technological evolution which has profoundly changed the structure of our cities, the nature of the family, the nature of human intercourse, even the structure of retailing. Even after 60 years of experience of what it has really done to us hardly anybody knows. In a very real sense it has destroyed the city as an integrative system. It has intensified the class structure at one end of the scale while it has destroyed classes at the other end. It has helped create a society with a very large middle class and a very intractable small poverty sub-culture. It has changed the nature of crime and police. It has affected the birth rate and has tended to destroy both the bachelor and the extended family. The principal unit of social behavior is now the nuclear family that can fit into a car.

Military technology has had an enormous impact on the structure of the international system. Probably the most important agent in destroying the feudal system was gunpowder. The terms of trade of the baron with his retainers became too unfavorable for the retainers once gunpowder was invented and the baron could offer them no real protection. In a very real sense, therefore, gunpowder led to the destruction of feudal loyalties and the rise of loyalties to the national state. It seems highly probable that the development of the nuclear weapon and the missile with a range of half the earth's diameter will do for the national state what gunpowder did for the feudal baron. It makes it only conditionally viable from a military point of view and this in the long run will destroy its sacred character. When it becomes clear that your country can do nothing for you in the way of defending you, the question of why you should do anything for it becomes perfectly sensible and it is quite possible that the national state in the next 100 years or so will go the way of the monarchy and the empire, in the sense that if it is to retain its legitimacy it will have to abandon its power, that is, its threat capability. Paradoxical as it may seem, unilateral disarmament may be the only really adequate method of national defense. All this again results essentially from the impact of technology on the integrative system and again all propositions in this area must be regarded as highly tentative. All we can be sure of is that the impacts will be large.*

The impact of scientific technology on religion is another area in which a good deal has been written but on which not very

---

* I have deliberately avoided the problem of automation and the impact of computers, mainly because so much has been written on it and so little is known about it!

much is known. It is clear, of course, that the scientific image of the universe has profoundly affected religious ideologies in regard to cosmology and even in regard to ethics and the nature of man himself. Dante may well have half believed in the geography of hell and of purgatory. We now know, however, that at least purgatory is not at the South Pole, because we have been there. The Copernican Revolution profoundly destroyed the old cosmology of the Christian Church, the old three-story universe, with hell in the basement, earth on the first floor and heaven in the attic. Similarly, the impacts of modern medicine have forced a profound revision in religious teaching in regard to sex and birth control. Death control and birth control indeed are part of the same package. The scientific point of view, furthermore, by introducing historical criticism of the sacred books and by its general elevation of empirical testing over traditional authority, has had a corrosive effect on totalitarian religion. Nevertheless religion has survived all these adversities and shows no signs at all of disappearing. In the United States, church membership is at an all time high, with some 64 percent of the population, and has risen fairly steadily for nearly 200 years. In Europe it is Christian democracy that picked up the pieces after the collapse of fascism. Even in the socialist countries the church exhibits astonishing vitality and the moderate persecution to which it has been subjected seems to have purified it. In Japan there have been many new religions in the last 100 years and new forms of Buddhism in particular are showing great vitality. All this may seem very surprising to those who are still in the age of 18th century enlightenment, as so many intellectuals are, but it is a fact of the world that has to be taken into account and is evidence of the extraordinary ability of religion to adapt itself to the implications of technological and scientific change.

Status and Contract

It should be clear that these interactions are so complex that anyone who offers a single key to them is likely to be faced with the fact that there are far too many locks to open and that no single key will fit them all. Sir Henry Maine, for instance, saw the great movement of history as one leading from a society of status to one of contract, that is, a society in which roles were assigned mainly through the integrative system to one in which roles are assigned largely through exchange. There is, of course, something in this view, especially as we contemplate the rise of capitalism and the decline of feudalism.

The rise of the insurance industry itself is a very interesting example of this principle. In what my children call the "olden days," in which they think I was born, the only insurance policy was one's status in the integrative system as a parent or as a monk or as a feudal retainer. Today the formalization of insurance has largely replaced status as the principle method of providing for accidents and old age. Nevertheless, the rise of socialism, not only in socialist countries themselves, but in the development of the welfare state in the capitalist world, is a reflection of a certain breakdown in the exchange mechanism and to some extent a return to status. The Social Security contract is of a slightly different order from that which we have with a private insurance company. It arises out of our status as citizens in a society, not as a contract with a private organization. The "retreat," if indeed it is, from contract back to status, which we see in the socialist countries is even more striking. An enormous appeal has to be made to the solidarity of the individual with the society and to his concern for the future, if more naked forms of coercion are to be avoided in getting at the product. Socialism indeed is an interesting example of the extraordinary difficulties of integrative development. It arises as an ideology in large measure out of protest against what are perceived to be the inequities of the system of pure exchange. Also out of a yearning for a society in which people did things for love rather than for money, in which the grubbiness of trade was replaced by the altruism of unselfish service and in which, as it were, the whole of society became one big happy family. Unfortunately, abolishing the market and free exchange and the private property on which these stand does not automatically create an integrative society. The history of socialist societies is a grim illustration of how the search for larger integration can easily lead into a retreat into coercion as the grim record of Stalinism, or the even grimmer record of Hitler testifies. Even National Socialism was a search for an integrative system, however nationalistic and exclusive, and was motivated by some of the same dissatisfactions with liberal capitalism which gave rise to communism.

I have done little more in this paper than to suggest an enormous field of inquiry. We know very little about the integrative system, even less than we know about the dynamics of technology, and we do not even know very much about that. I am convinced, however, that it is precisely in the interaction of these two great dynamic systems that the understanding of the main dynamics processes of society must lie. In this country we are fairly sensitive to the dynamics of technology. We are, however, extraordinarily insensitive to the dynamics of the integrative system. We have something that might be called integrative policy in, for instance, racial policies, educational policies, and the bare beginnings of an integrative policy in the international system, through such things as cultural exchange. We do not, however, have any clear concept of the integrative system as a whole. I have been trying to persuade people for many years that we should study love just as seriously and intensely as we study anything else. This suggestion is usually met with jeers. We seem to be thoroughly indoctrinated with the view that anything which is preached about cannot be taken seriously. We may never make a costlier mistake, and all our technological and economic success may go down the drain if it produces a society which is incapable of love, incapable of attracting an uncoerced loyalty and incapable of establishing or maintaining its own legitimacy.

THE "TWO CULTURES"

In: *Technology in Western Civilization,* Vol. II,
Melvin Kranzberg and Carroll W. Pursell, Jr., eds.
New York: Oxford Univ. Press, 1967, pp. 686-695

The "Two Cultures"

In 1959 C. P. Snow, English scientist, scientific administrator, and novelist, delivered a series of lectures later published under the title *The Two Cultures and the Scientific Revolution*. This book introduced a new phrase—the two cultures —into currency and stimulated widespread discussion of the role of science in modern life. It was Snow's argument that modern culture was becoming increasingly bifurcated between the traditional literary or humanistic culture and the increasingly important scientific culture, in which he included technology. He excoriated the upholders of the humanistic culture for their snobbish refusal to recognize that science itself had, in the modern period, become a valid culture demanding recognition in the present world. Custodians of the literary culture answered, somewhat snippishly, that there was only one culture, and that scientists by and large did not have any culture.

Snow's concept of the polarization of modern society is, of course, oversimplified. There are, in fact, not two but many subcultures with which we must deal, and deciding how to bring about communication among them is a general rather than a specific need. One may know how to make a rocket go up without knowing where it should come down, but to separate completely the two knowledge systems may be fatal to mankind. Somehow, integration must be achieved.

THE CONCEPT OF CULTURE

The word "culture" is itself used in different senses in ordinary speech and in the social sciences, and leads to some confusion. In ordinary speech, we often use it to mean those aspects of human life which involve a cultivated taste, especially in the arts. We think of culture in terms of opera, art galleries, classical music, good taste in architecture, furniture, or dress, and so on. To call a person "uncultured" is a form of abuse, implying that he has unrefined tastes or does not belong to the cultural elite.

In the social sciences, however, and especially in anthropology, the word culture is used simply to refer to a social system in all its aspects. The culture of the Hopi Indians, for instance, consists of their language, norms of behavior, forms of organization and community structure, family and kinship patterns, technology and methods of production, and so on. In this sense, then, culture means the general description of a society as a total system, and in this sense everyone is part of a culture of some kind, for no human being can exist in isolation from others. Even Robinson Crusoe carried with him the artifacts, memories, and knowledge of his own culture, though in isolation he began to modify the culture he possessed.

We often use the word "subculture" to mean a sub-system within a larger social system, and we use this term again as a total description. Thus, we find occupational subcultures. Truckers, for instance, have a pattern of life, even of speech, which is very different from that of doctors. There are organizational subcultures. A school, a hospital, a city, or a neighborhood will develop certain patterns of its own, even though it shares patterns of speech, behavior, and organization with other groups in the society in which it is embedded.

Although they all have some apparatus for preventing change and maintaining the old patterns, cultures and subcultures continually change. The very fact that human beings are born, age, and die, forces change; furthermore, some processes of learning, whether a result of inputs of information from outside the culture or the result of internal information generation, likewise lead to change. Where, however, the existing structures and patterns of a culture are highly valued by the persons who belong to it, change will be resisted, and will be interpreted as "bad." Thus the university continually tries to maintain the quality of its staff, its integrity, and academic freedom; a nation resists threats from outside or internal challenges to its legitimacy; a family, too, will resist attempts to undermine the mutual affection of the members; and so on. The overall dynamics of a culture is the result of the interaction of the forces making for

change and the countervailing forces making for stability. Perfect stability and
equilibrium is unknown in nature, though some systems, such as the solar system, approximate it. No biological or social system even comes close to perfect
stability. We have to judge the "health" of a system by its ability to maintain
desirable patterns of change. What we mean by "desirable," however, raises
large issues which cannot be adequately discussed here.

THE "SOCIOSPHERE"

Social systems, then, consist of people, the roles they occupy (that is, the patterns of behavior they exhibit), and the inputs and outputs which go into these
roles and the channels they follow. The inputs and outputs may be material, as
when raw materials and people go into a factory and produce automobiles, or
they may be inputs and outputs of information. A role in a social system, then,
can be thought of as a transformer of inputs into outputs.

The role occupant does not have to be a person; it may be a machine, a combination of a person and a machine, or a group of persons in combination with
a group of machines. Some inputs modify the transformation process itself, and
create a different input-output relationship. Some material inputs may do this,
in which case we think of them as investment. Information inputs also do this
when they create new knowledge and new ways of transforming inputs into
outputs.

On the whole, the *information* inputs and outputs, and the knowledge they
create, dominate social systems, and even biological systems. Though the availability of sources for *material* inputs and outlets for material outputs considerably affects the operation of a system, the role of information and knowledge
in social systems can hardly be overestimated. Even something we consider
physical capital, such as a machine, is really a knowledge structure imposed on
the material world which began as a knowledge structure in the human mind.
Material inputs and outputs set limits and boundaries on the system, but information makes the system function.

We can picture the entire social system, then, as a "sociosphere," almost like
the biosphere or the atmosphere, which consists at any one moment of all the
people in the world, all the roles they are occupying, all the knowledge inside
their heads, all the lines of communication among them, all the commodity
flows among them, all the material capital (the houses, factories, machines, and
so on) with which they work, and the organizations in which they participate.
Change in the sociosphere comes partly from the accumulation of material capital, more fundamentally from the accumulation of knowledge, which will determine what people can do. Even when material capital is destroyed it can be
recreated if the social system of which it is a part is unimpaired. We see this,
for instance, in Japan, where the cities destroyed in World War II are now re-

built and thriving; we see it in a city such as Leningrad or the central part of Warsaw, which has been rebuilt exactly as it was. These examples show very clearly how the information and knowledge aspects of a culture dominate its material substructure.

SCIENTIFIC KNOWLEDGE AND FOLK KNOWLEDGE

The last three hundred years have seen an enormous change in the sociosphere, mainly because of the development of a relatively small human subculture known as science. Science specializes in the cumulative increase of knowledge. This cumulative increase, can, of course, be traced back a·long way. Only in the last three hundred years, however, has the increase of knowledge become, as it were, a specialized trade, making it possible now to distinguish between what is often called "folk knowledge" and "scientific knowledge."

Folk knowledge is acquired in the ordinary experience of life, and a great deal of it is useful. We all have images in our mind, for instance, of the geography of our house, school, or local community; we know about the members of our family and our friends, and the people with whom we have day-to-day, face-to-face contact; and we learn many things in ordinary conversation from our friends and relations; and so on. None of us, indeed, could operate for a single day without folk knowledge.

In pre-scientific societies, almost all knowledge is folk knowledge; and the knowledge capital of the society is transmitted from generation to generation largely through the family, by word of mouth, and face-to-face contacts. The introduction of writing about five thousand years ago profoundly modified this process and probably introduced an irreversible change; for once language can be written down, the past can speak to the future, and the knowledge capital of a society is no longer dependent on the fragile memories of old men.

The processes by which knowledge is acquired—whether folk knowledge or scientific knowledge—are essentially alike. In both cases, true images of the world in our minds can be derived only by the successive elimination of error. There is no way in which we can compare directly the image of the world that we have in our minds with the world as it presumably exists outside us. We have the opportunity to detect error after we make an inference regarding some message or input of information anticipated in the future, for when the future date arrives we can compare the expected input with the actual input. If these do not correspond, obviously something is wrong. (Even when they correspond, this does not necessarily mean that we are right. We may have made a correct prediction by accident.) Disappointment, however, forces us to reexamine the situation, and we can usually do one of three things: (1) we can reject the present message, which is inconsistent with our expectations, and say it was a false message; (2) we can, on the other hand, reject the inference which gave rise to the expectations—and with each of these choices our basic image of the world remains unchanged; (3) if, however, we can neither reject the inference nor the message, we must revise our image of the world, for we have then detected an error.

This process goes on all the time, even in ordinary life in the accumulation of folk knowledge. Suppose, for instance, I have an image in my mind of where the post office is located, and go to mail a letter and discover it is no longer there. My disappointment forces me to reorganize my image of where the post office is. I don't try to mail a letter in a nonexistent mailbox on the grounds that it has always been there and therefore must still be there. I don't reject the evidence of my senses and say I must be going blind because I can't see the post office. In a simple case like this, the error-detection process operates extremely well and produces genuine knowledge.

As we move away from the kind of systems involved in ordinary daily life to larger and more complex systems, whether in the physical or the social world, folk knowledge becomes less and less reliable. Folk knowledge, for instance, tells us that the earth is flat. Ordinarily this assumption will not get us into much trouble if we don't travel for long distances. Even in driving about the United States, for instance, a flat road map is quite adequate, and we do not usually have to take into account the curvature of the earth. The scientific image of the earth as a spheroid can be developed only by much more accurate inferences and observations than ordinary life provides—and such scientific images are essential if we are going to be an astronaut, for to believe then that the earth is flat, will get us into very serious, indeed fatal, trouble!

THE N-CULTURES

The "two-cultures" problem arises because within the educated community there seem to be two subcultures, two constellations of communication networks, that do not interact very much with each other—the scientific, engineering, and technological subculture on the one hand and the literary, artistic, and perhaps political subculture on the other. The problem of communication between the two is perhaps more acute in European countries than in the United States because of the nature of the European educational system, which forces specialization at an early age. Even in the United States, however, the problem is real, although it would be more precise to call it the "n-cultures" problem. It is not merely that we have only two non-communicating cultures; we have a great many of them.

It is one of the fundamental principles of economics that specialization without trade is useless, for the farmer would freeze and the tailor would starve. The same principle applies to the world of information and knowledge. Specialization permits greater productivity in a particular field and a particular line of knowledge, but if it is not accompanied by exchange and even by a class of people who specialize in intellectual exchange, the bits of specialized knowledge do not add up to a total knowledge structure for mankind. And within the scientific community, the inability of specialists to communicate with specialists in a different field hampers the progress of the various specialties and also the total growth of knowledge. In part, this problem has been handled in the sciences by the development of what might be called interstitial fields such as physical chemistry or biophysics. It is countered, also, by the development of good scientific journalism, such as we find, for instance, in *Science,* the magazine of the American Association for the Advancement of Science, or in the *Scientific American.* The value of publications of this kind can hardly be overestimated. Nevertheless, the n-culture problem remains, and the fact that politicians, businessmen, artists, writers, poets, musicians, engineers, and scientists, often move in non-intersecting circles means that each may have knowledge and skills that are important to others but which are unavailable because of the lack of communication.

The social sciences can play a crucial role in bridging the gap which exists among the various cultures, and especially the two-culture gap between the humanistic and literary kind of knowledge and scientific knowledge. The social scientist himself is in a key position as a part of the systems he studies. He can not only approach the study of social systems from the point of view of an outside scientific observer—taking careful observations, making careful measurements, making predictions by mathematical or logical inference, and then seeing whether these are confirmed or falsified; but he also has an "inside track." The physicist has never been an atom or an electron; but the social scientist has participated himself in a great many social systems. Genuine knowledge can be derived from the inside track, and indeed provides many of the hypotheses and insights which the social scientists may then proceed to test by more rigorous methods.

Literary and humanistic studies represent a process of reflection and sifting of the accumulated records of folk knowledge. As such they represent a scholarly type of knowledge which is intermediate between the unsophisticated folk knowledge of ordinary life and the more testable images of science. Humanistic knowledge is in no sense to be despised; indeed, if one wants to understand the human being, a reading of Sophocles or Shakespeare may instruct us more than the latest psychological experiments. I have elsewhere defined science as the art of substituting unimportant questions which can be answered for important questions which cannot. This wisecrack clearly belongs to the humanistic subculture and is pretty hard to test. Nevertheless, it contains elements of truth; and as we move from the humanities through the "soft" into the "hard" sciences, we often find that our knowledge becomes less significant as it becomes more exact.

The technologist who is so absorbed in his own technique that he has no time for that expansion of his personal experience and, if we like, folk knowledge,

which comes from acquaintance with the great literature of the world, or who
has a mind so completely oriented toward verbal and mathematical symbols
that he cannot appreciate the messages of art, music, or religion, will fail in his
own technique, no matter how good it is. Somewhat in the mood of the former
wisecrack, I once defined an engineer as a man who spends his life finding the
best way of doing something which shouldn't be done at all. This indeed is always the danger of the technician. It is what is known in the technical language
of programming as sub-optimization. The problem is summarized by the story
of the engineer who said all he wanted to do was to reduce costs, until it was
pointed out that costs could be reduced to zero by the simple process of shutting down the plant and liquidating the enterprise.

THE ROLE OF THE SOCIAL SCIENCES

Perhaps one of the most important questions which faces mankind at the present time is whether the increase and spread of knowledge in the social sciences,
of a testable and cumulative kind, can meaningfully affect the decision-making
processes of governments, businesses and large organizations, and of individuals
and households. There is a good deal of evidence, indeed, that it can, and that
as we acquire more knowledge of the relationships, the significant variables,
and the magnitude of the parameters of social systems, we will be able to avoid
the disastrous consequences which failure to understand these systems has often
caused in the past. The record of famine, depression, war, and social collapse,
which has characterized past history, is at least in part a product of human
decision-making and inadequate technologies.

We still do not have the social technology capable of creating a world social
system in which men can live out their lives with the expectation of peace,
plenty, and the fulfillment of their potentialities. The technology here must be
thought of not only in terms of machines and material inventions, but also in
terms of social inventions, such things as government itself, the United Nations,
decision-making through consent, and such homely things as a deductible-at-
source income tax, which was probably one of the major social inventions of
the 20th century.

Economics is the oldest of the social sciences, and indeed one of the oldest
of all the sciences, having developed its basic theoretical structure under Adam
Smith in 1776, before the development of scientific chemistry. It is not surprising, therefore, to find that the impact of the social sciences on social systems
is most apparent in the application of economics. The great economic development of the last two hundred years in Western countries itself is not unconnected with the profound insights of Adam Smith regarding the social and
developmental function of the price system.

If we contrast the twenty years between the two world wars, say from 1919-
39, with the twenty years after the Second World War, 1945-65, we see a

remarkable difference. The first period saw the Great Depression in the West and the disastrous First Collectivization in the Soviet Union, and it ended with Hitler and the Second World War. In the second period, there has been no major depression, though some small ones; rates of development in many countries have been unprecedented, indeed, two or three times what they were before the Second World War; a large number of colonies have become new nations, and some of these have started on the road to development. It would be both immodest and untrue to attribute the whole difference between these two periods to the growth of economic knowledge. Nevertheless, the rise of better information systems as reflected in national income statistics and a certain frame of theoretical reference provided by Keynesian economics has made a noticeable contribution to the difference between the two periods.

The international system has barely begun to feel the impact of the accumulating knowledge of the social sciences, but this, perhaps, is the next field of advance. It is still largely true that international systems operate by folk knowledge; and the gap between the two cultures, in this case between the developing science of international systems and the folk knowledge of the major decision-makers, is wide and hard to bridge. The information collection and processing system, on which the decisions of states are made, is primitive in the extreme as judged by scientific standards. Indeed, one could hardly do better, if one were setting up a system for producing misinformation and false images, than the system which relies extensively on diplomats and spies. There is a problem of sampling here, and also a problem of what is called the "value filter," which screens out information which is unacceptable to the recipient. In the scientific community there are defenses against these corruptions of the information system. In the international system, unfortunately, these defenses are still very primitive. It is not surprising, therefore, that the international system is so appallingly costly, and that it operates so badly.

A world system that spends $140 billion on the war industry and still gives no real security to the world must be reckoned a failure, and the problem of how to devise a better system for doing what unilateral national defense can no longer provide is one of the major tasks of mankind. The intellectual effort going into the solution of these problems, however, is at present much smaller than it should be; and we are certainly not going to solve them with the kind of resources which are now being applied. Still, some progress is being made, and the abolition of war does not seem so utopian an objective as it did a generation ago.

SPACESHIP EARTH AND THE HUMAN BEING

There are long-run problems facing the human race which may be very difficult to solve. We do not yet, for instance, have a stable, high-level technology. Our existing technology is based on fossil fuels and ores, and is thus limited; we will be all right for a hundred years, or perhaps two hundred, but within strictly historic time we may face a totally exhausted earth. Fortunately, a technology based on the concept of Earth as a self-contained spaceship is by no means impossible, and indeed seems to be on the way. This would involve placing man in a self-perpetuating cycle, drawing on the atmosphere and the oceans as the only basic resource, and importing energy either from the sun or from nuclear fusion on the earth.

For the spaceship society, we must also achieve population control, which we are a long way from accomplishing. We do not even know how large a population the earth could support in a stable, high-level economy. One hopes for the sake of the unborn that it will be large, for world population is all too likely to go to six billion by the end of this century, and we are not likely to catch it before then.

A final problem related to the problem of the two cultures is that of human development, that is, the full development of human potential in terms of the enjoyment of life, variety of experience, sensitivity of concern, appreciation of beauty, love, affection, community, and so on. The very concept of development implies some ideal or at least some direction of change which we regard as ideal, by which we can measure achievements.

The social sciences can, perhaps, help here by expanding our knowledge of what men have in fact regarded as ideal, and by attempting to explain the circumstances under which one set of ideals becomes prevalent. Our ideals themselves are derived largely from people we have known, imagined, or encountered in literature, poetry, religion, and art. We can, perhaps, find out something about the relation of prevalent ideals to the survival of societies and subcultures; or we can study the way in which its ideals affect the character of a society. Where, for example, there is an exaggerated ideal of masculinity, where the status of women is low, or where achievement goes into rivalry rather than into production, economic development may be hampered. The social sciences study the relation of these ideals to the nature and development of a society. The ideals themselves, however, come out of the folk culture or out of humanistic culture. This is true even for science itself, which has ideals of objectivity, dispassion, honesty, and so on. These ideals come not from science itself, though they are the prerequisites for the development of science.

A PROBLEM OF CHOICE

There are questions here that the framework of science and technology cannot answer. No matter how far we go in technology, all that technology gives us is power; and power without an objective is meaningless and ultimately self-destructive. This is an area scarcely penetrated as yet by the social sciences. We have, therefore, to rely a great deal on the humanistic vision expressed in poetry, art, and religion. We can grow in knowledge and begin to apply the human mind to the critique of the *ends* of man and his social systems, just as we can to the improvement of *means*.

Thus the increase of power technology produces raises all the more insistently those questions about the "chief end of man" which religion and philosophy, poetry and the arts, have always raised. When we are impotent, the question of whether we want the wrong things hardly arises; we cannot get them anyway. As our power increases, the question of *what* we want to do with it acquires overriding importance. At this point even the social scientist must take a back seat, for such knowledge is perhaps unobtainable, and wisdom is all that we have left.

THE DYNAMICS OF SOCIETY

Bell Telephone Magazine, 47, 3 (May-June 1968): 4-7

THE DYNAMICS OF SOCIETY

During the past year we have witnessed many student demonstrations against the presence of corporate recruiters on campus. The picketing of business executives seeking to hire bright young students is highly visible and perhaps symptomatic of deep unrest.

What is not visible, but probably more important, are the bull sessions and conversations which go on in dormitories and fraternities in which the merits of various careers are explored. Unfortunately, we have no way of knowing what happens there. We do know, however, that fundamental values are established much more by communication from peers than from superiors, and our general ignorance of communications among peers is a great handicap in predicting future values and attitudes.

My main interest in recent years has been what might be called the long-run dynamics of society. In this connection I have come to the conclusion that while the interaction among different elements in the social system is so complex and intense that no one element completely dominates the others, the dynamics of *legitimacy* dominate practically everything, including the dynamics of power and wealth.

By legitimacy, I mean two closely related aspects of society. One is internal legitimacy, which is roughly equivalent to morale or nerve. This is the conviction on the part of the actor or decision-maker that his role and activities are justified in his own eyes. Without this sense of inner justification, his sense of being "O.K.," action is paralyzed and roles cannot be performed. For an individual, as well as an organization, a loss of nerve is a prelude to collapse.

The other aspect of legitimacy is external legitimacy. This is the conviction on the part of the people who surround the decision-maker that his role and actions are justified. Internal and external legitimacy are closely related and each tends to create the other. A man who has a strong sense of his own legitimacy will create the same feeling in others. Similarly, sup-

port on the part of others around us confirms us in our own justification. Conversely, a man who loses his sense of legitimacy internally will soon create external doubts in the minds of others. A man who loses his external legitimacy will soon receive indications that challenge his internal morale.

There are at least seven sources of legitimacy, whether internal or external. These may be listed briefly as:

1. Positive payoffs. This is probably the most important element in the long run, but may be surprisingly unimportant in the short run.

2. Sacrifices or negative payoffs. These create legitimacy because of their association with personal identity. If we make sacrifices for something, we find it hard to admit that these sacrifices have been in vain and hence we build up the legitimacy which will justify the sacrifices. This frequently produces a phenomenon I call the "sacrifice trap," in which an institution exploits its legitimacy by demanding still more sacrifices, until finally the demand for positive payoffs reasserts itself and the whole process collapses.

3. Age. Legitimacy may be derived from newness or antiquity. There is often a sag in middle age.

4. Mystery and secrecy. The veil of the temple, the mysteries of finance, the clandestine spy, and classified information give an aura of legitimacy.

5. Symbols, rituals and other specialized communicators of legitimacy. Pomp and splendor, noble buildings, military parades and so on are part of the system of legitimating communications.

6. Association with other legitimacies. Legitimacies rub off on each other. The association of church and state is a good example.

7. Expectations fulfilled or disappointed. This has a special dynamic significance. Unexpected payoffs, either positive or negative, have a weight far beyond

Nobody expects the president of AT&T, for example, to get up and say, "Ask not what AT&T can do for you, only ask what you can do for AT&T." We ask what AT&T can do for us.

realized expectations. Unexpected rewards enhance the legitimacy of the rewarder.

If there has been a decline in the legitimacy of the corporation, either in its internal morale or in any of its external environments, we must look to one or another of the seven sources of legitimacy to analyze the problem. If, for example, there are difficulties of recruitment — if there is evidence, as there seems to be, that the attitude of the present generation of college students toward careers with corporations is less favorable than it was, say, ten or twenty years ago — then a very important clue to this phenomenon is the analysis of legitimacy. It is not necessarily the only clue. A particular corporation, for instance, may have difficulty recruiting simply because of its payoffs: because it does not pay enough, or the conditions of work are not satisfactory.

Where the phenomenon is as general as this one seems to be, however, one suspects that the problem is deeper than that of relative economic reward, and we must look at the dynamics of legitimacy if we are to find a clue for its solution. We can run down the seven sources then to see how they apply to the corporation.

It is clear that positive payoffs, even in quite crude economic terms, are an important element — perhaps *the* most important element — in establishing the legitimacy of the corporation. It has been the capacity of the corporation, in general, to offer good terms of trade for its employees and management, and at the same time offer reasonably good terms of trade to its customers, which has created the greater part of its legitimacy.

The very extent of its positive payoffs, however, has meant that the corporation is not able to rely on sacrifices for legitimacy. In other words, the corporation is not a sacred institution, for it is only sacrifice that creates sacredness. There may be some sacrifices at the executive level — the long hours, the ulcers, the geographical mobility, and public invisibility of the corporation executive — but these are compensated for by financial rewards. There may be some sacred allegiances to particular organizations, especially on the part of the top executives whose identity is closely related to the organizations which they control, but even here the sacred elements are very weak by comparison with, say, the church or the armed forces.

Nobody expects the president of AT&T, for example, to get up and say, "Ask not what AT&T can do for you, only ask what you can do for AT&T." We ask what AT&T can do for us. We demand favorable terms with it, whether as employees or as consumers, or even as investors, and if AT&T cannot provide these favorable terms, we go somewhere else. Competition, indeed, demands absolute disloyalty and a total lack of sacredness.

In the case of the corporation, we can pass over lightly age, mystery and secrecy, and symbols and rituals as sources of legitimacy. It may owe a little of its legitimacy to mystery — the mystique of finance and corporate management or the myth of the mysterious supermen in the board room — but we would be ill-advised to put much faith in this. On the whole, the corporation is a workaday beast, plodding along doing useful things in a bright weekday light. It is not very romantic and not really mysterious. Likewise, it owes little of its legitimacy to charisma or ritual, and — by comparison with a high mass, a military parade, or even a graduation — the annual meeting of a corporation is a pretty pale affair. Nor does it owe a great deal of its legitimacy to the trappings of dress, architecture, and language.

In regard to age there may be a problem. Most

The older generation is utterly bewildered by the rejection of its achievements and its ideals by the unspeakably young.

corporations are now rather middle-aged. They neither have the excitement of youth, nor the great reservoirs of legitimacy that come from age. Middle-age, however, sits more lightly on the organization than it does on the individual, and you can hardly place this as a major factor. If the corporation is indeed in the trough of middle-age, the future looks good. If it can stick around a bit longer, it will become an almost unbreakable habit.

The sixth source of legitimacy — that is, association with other legitimacies — may be very important but also hard to assess. Here, of course, the major association is with the state, for the corporation draws practically no legitimacy from the church. The corporation is a creature of the state, at least in the legal sense, and in so far as it is incorporated in the state and regulated by it, some of the legitimacy which is attached to the state rubs off on the corporation.

Where the legitimacy of the corporation has been challenged (as it has been, for instance, in the name of socialism) the corporation has often attempted to regain legitimacy by closer association with the state.

There are a number of levels of this intimacy, beginning at one end with simple incorporation, going on to regulation, from there to the independent public corporation, then to the socialized industry, and finally to the Soviet Trust. The real difference between capitalist and socialist organizations is in their methods of legitimation, not in their structure. AT&T, for instance, which is legitimated by incorporation and regulation, is not very different from a socialized telephone company in its internal structure and organization, even though it differs somewhat in the nature of the environment, the degree of independ-

ence, the nature of the capital markets, and so on. There is a great deal of evidence that socialization results in the diminution of the actual payoffs. And when it comes to economic development, a regulated private monopoly like AT&T, leads the field when it comes to payoffs for everybody.

Positive payoffs, however, are only one source of legitimacy and they may not be sufficient. The state has an extraordinary advantage in that it provides us legacies of various kinds in what I call the "grants economy." In its negative aspects, however, the state taxes us, conscripts us, sometimes commits in our name unspeakable atrocities (Auschwitz, Dresden, et. al.), and can involve us in an enormous sacrifice trap. The association with particularly unpleasant aspects of the national state unquestionably diminishes the legitimacy of the private corporation.

The problem of the legitimacy of the corporation in the minds of college students is complicated by the existence of a quite unusual "generation gap." There is always, of course, a war of youth against age, the only class war that seems to make any sense. But it is also a war that youth cannot win without becoming old and regretting its victory.

At the present moment, however, the conflict between youth and age is unusually intense for several reasons. In the first place, we have had a revolution in childrearing dating roughly from the Second World War and symbolized by Dr. Spock. The present generation of middle age people who are running things was raised on Watsonian principles under which they learned very rapidly that nobody loved them. This "loveless generation", as it has been unkindly called, was further traumatized in its youth and may deserve the name of the traumatized generation. The present middle-age generation was not picked up in its cradle; the First World War hit it in childhood; it graduated from college into the Great Depression; it was caught by the Second World War; and its children are rebellious.

By contrast, this generation of college students was

Perhaps the most critical question of the next generation will be the relative legitimacy of private versus governmental organizations.

raised in infancy on what is called a demand schedule, its parents read Dr. Spock or, if they were very erudite, Gesell, and were permissive in their child raising. These young people have lived all their lives on a rising market. They are the untraumatized generation, almost at times frighteningly tender.

It is not surprising that under these circumstances a generation gap of unusual magnitude has opened. The older generation is utterly bewildered by the rejection of its achievements and its ideals by the unspeakably young.

The hippies are only the extreme manifestation of this phenomenon, exhibiting an odd kind of secular Franciscanism in revolt against the loveless world of their elders who, they say, are intent on power, realism, and the roasting of children with napalm. But one gets the impression that the hippies are only the fringes of a frighteningly new, large and solid country of youth, more affluent and more personally secure than its fathers, yet perhaps in danger of rejecting some of the very things which have permitted it to come into existence. One begins to wonder, indeed, what is the optimum of youthful trauma.

Youth, of course, has no future and one should not be too disturbed by its manifestations. But we cannot simply assume that the youth of today are going to be just like us oldsters in thirty years. There is a difference. It is a result of difference in the whole life experience of the generations. The difference will perpetuate itself.

In *The Achieving Society*, David McClelland has pointed to the enormous importance of changes in childrearing in creating sociological "faults," and in changing the whole tone and history of a society.

We should be on the lookout for something like this in our own society. Adaptations are possible, but what we are trying to adapt to is the subtle and little understood dynamics of legitimacy.

Perhaps the most critical question of the next generation will be the relative legitimacy of private versus governmental organizations. In the last hundred years, on the whole, private organizations have been defending themselves against rising tides of legitimacy of public organizations. This has been reflected in increased public control, public ownership, and, in an extreme form, the socialist state.

It may be that this long tide is now turning. The horrors of the threat system as embodied in the national state are raising questions about the previously unquestioned legitimacy of the national state. The payoffs of the national state in a nuclear age seem to be declining, even though its sacredness as measured by accumulated sacrifices is enormous. (Who would dare tell a mother of any son who died on the battlefield that he has died in vain?)

Once the sacredness of the sacred institution is challenged, it becomes very hard to defend. It may be, therefore, that looking at the long pull the legitimacy of the private corporation may best be protected by actually stressing its privateness, its serviceability, its harmlessness.

The question of associating with legitimacies other than the national state is at least worth thinking about. Association with the church certainly seems farfetched, although historically religion has been a very powerful legitimator.

The United Nations is another source of legitimacy: I have argued that if corporations — especially those which operate internationally — were wise, they might well seek United Nations charters. And although it may seem ridiculous at the moment to associate the corporation with flower power — rather than fire power — flower power may win out in the long run.

Now is the time for corporations to evaluate their sources of legitimacy. There is no easy answer. ☐

WHAT CAN WE KNOW AND TEACH ABOUT SOCIAL SYSTEMS?

Soc. Sci. Educ. Consortium Newsletter,
Univ. of Colo., No. 5 (June 1968): 1-5

WHAT CAN WE KNOW AND TEACH ABOUT SOCIAL SYSTEMS?

My thesis is that the principle task of education in this day is to convey from one generation to the next a rich image of what I call the "total earth." The universe we can leave for the next generation but for this generation the prime task is to convey the idea of the earth as a total system. This is an idea around which one can organize a whole educational process, not only in the social sciences but all the other sciences and the arts and the humanities as well.

We start with the concept of the earth as a series of approximately concentric spheres, such as the lithosphere, the hydrosphere, the atmosphere and the biosphere. Finally we have what I have been calling the sociosphere, or the anthroposphere, which is the sphere of man and all his activities. In our day the sociosphere is becoming increasingly dominant over the others. Thanks to it the evolution of the elements is now continuing where it seems to have left off four or six billion years ago. The sociosphere is beginning to affect the biosphere very rapidly and it will be surprising if in the next generation man does not get his busy little fingers into the business of genetic evolution. We might even recreate the dodo and the dinosaur and then go on to the imaginary animals, the centaurs and the fauns. This is the kind of world for which we might have to prepare our children.

Toward A Unified Social Science

If we look closely at the various social sciences it becomes clear that they are all studying the same thing and are all operating at the same systems level. This is not true of all the sciences; thus the crystallographer studies the world at a different systems level from that of the physiologist and the physiologist from that of the social scientist. But the economist, the political scientist, the anthropologist, the sociologist, and the social psychologist, even the historian and the human geographer, are all really studying the same thing, which is the sociosphere, that is, the three billion human beings, all their inputs, outputs, interactions, organizations, communications, and transactions.

The different social scientists of course study the sociosphere from different points of view. We also carve up the set of organizations and institutions; thus economists study banks, anthropologists tribes, political scientists governments, sociologists families, and so on. In this matter we should do some trading around. It would be fun to have anthropologists study banking on the ground

that bankers are really a savage tribe. The economist has already been moving in on the family, which we call a spending unit. Political scientists have already begun to look at the political structure of the corporation and the game theorists have even begun to move in on moral philosophy. All this is much to the good, but it has not yet affected our teaching very much and the way we divide up the field can easily result in a great deal of misapprehension at the level of the students who do not see that all institutions are part of the totality.

Thus I agree with Dr. Alfred Kuhn[1] that we are moving very rapidly toward a unified social science, simply because we are all coming to realize that the sociosphere itself is a unity, and offers a single system to be studied. This does not deny the usefulness of such abstractions as economic systems, the international system, or what I have recently been calling the integrative system which is that aspect of the sociosphere which deals with such matters as status, community, identity, legitimacy, loyalty, and love. We must somehow manage to teach the students that all these systems have a certain structure and dynamic of their own, that they also all interact very strongly with each other, and that they are all indeed abstractions from a total system of reality.

What I am arguing for is, frankly, a general systems approach to education. I have some prejudice here, being one of the founding fathers of the Society for General Systems Research. I think of general systems not so much as a body of doctrine as a way of looking at things which permits the perception of the world as a totality and fosters communication among the specialized disciplines.

A system can be defined as anything which is not chaos, and by this definition earth is clearly a system in spite of large random elements. The task of learning is to perceive what is chaos and what is not chaos in the world around us. It is important both to perceive order where it exists and not to perceive it where it does not, for that leads us into superstition.

The Dynamics of Systems

All real systems are dynamic; that is, they exist in four dimensions, three of space and one of time. What we are trying to do in the learning process is to try to perceive the continuing patterns in this four-dimensional solid. This is really what education is all about. This does not preclude the use of equilibrium systems which are special cases where a pattern in space-time repeats or produces itself. We cannot of course visualize four dimensions directly. It is very useful, however, to visualize two dimensions of space and one of time. Thus we can visualize the earth going around the sun as a kind of spiral tapeworm, the cross-section of which in the plane of space is roughly circular.

There are four easily distinguishable types of pattern in the space-time continuum which correspond to four types of dynamics. The simplest kind is simple dynamics such as Newtonian celestial mechanics, which really involves the perception of stable relationships between today and tomorrow or between today, tomorrow, and the next day. These relationships can be described by difference or differential equations. If regularity of this kind persists we can easily project it into the future as we perceive it in the past. Thus if we have a stable relationship between today and tomorrow, we have a difference equation of the first degree. Then if we know the state of the system today we know it tomorrow; if we know it tomorrow we know it the day after and so on indefinitely into the future. Examples of such projections would be growth at constant rates, such as compound interest, population projections, and so on. In social systems we have to be careful about such projections because the differential equations are usually not stable as they are in the solar system. The astronomer is fortunate in that the planets are moved by angels which are extremely well behaved, whereas in social systems things are moved by people who are not well behaved, and if our projections are mistaken for predictions we can be led badly astray.

A famous example of projections that were falsified were the projections of the U.S. Bureau of the Census in the middle 1940's according to which the United States would have a stable population of about 180 million by the 1980's. Between 1945 and 1947 indeed we had a "system break," in which the basic parameters of the demographic system shifted in such a manner as to give us a much larger rate of population expansion than had been expected. I would very much like to see a study of the impact on the educational system of this country of planning based on these quite false projections. Almost everybody in the 1950's found themselves with much larger numbers of children to educate than they expected. Thus, when constants are not constant, as they frequently are not in social systems, we have to learn to take predictions based on constant parameters with a great deal of reserve.

The Life Cycle Pattern

A second dynamic pattern is what I have called the "wallpaper principle." If we see a wallpaper with a regular pattern we have a good deal of confidence that the pattern continues under the mirror and behind the furniture or even beyond our field of vision. Similarly, we can see the space-time continuum as a four-dimensional wall paper in which our field of vision is cut off abruptly at the present. If, however, we perceive the beginnings of past patterns we may reasonably expect them to be projected into the future. Perhaps the best example of this principle is the life cycle. Up to now, at any rate, man has shared with all other living creatures a very regular life pattern. A person's age is probably the most important single piece of information about him. We know that if he is one year old he will look like a baby and if he is ninety he will look like an old man. This pattern may, of course, be upset by the growth of biological knowledge in the next generation or so and we may be in a great danger of immortality. This would present

the human race with probably the greatest crisis it has ever had to face. Who, for instance, would want to be an assistant professor for five hundred years? What makes life tolerable, especially for the young, is death, and if we do away with this we are in real trouble. It is just as well that at the moment this is something we do not have to worry about.

Life cycle patterns are found in human artifacts, such as automobiles, buildings, and so on. The concept is less applicable to social organizations which often have the capacity for self-renewal. Neither organizations nor civilizations are under the necessity of aging, although this does sometimes happen. The fact that people die, however, means that organizations can renew their youth as the old occupants of powerful positions die off and younger occupants take their place. We do not seem to be able to do this with neurons.

Mutation and Selection

A third type of dynamic system is that of evolution and learning. These can be put together because they are essentially the same thing. Even biological evolution is a learning process by which matter is "taught" to form itself into more and more improbable structures as time goes on. Similarly, human learning involves the construction of more and more improbable images in the mind. Both these processes take place by mutation and selection.

One of the difficulties with evolutionary theory is that it is hard to put content into it. It is a beautiful vision but it has extraordinarily little predictive power. There is a good reason for this, for any dynamic system which has information or knowledge in it as a fundamental element is inherently unpredictable. It has to have what I call fundamental surprise. Thus, if we could predict what we are going to know in twenty-five years we would know it now, and if we could predict the result of a research project there would be no need to do it and you could not get any money for it.

The Decision System

The fourth dynamic process is of peculiar importance in social systems, and might be called the decision system. We can see the movement of the social system through time as a kind of "decision tree" in which we keep coming to decision points at which there are a number of possible futures and select only one of these. Our decisions, however, depend on values and in man values are almost wholly learned. Instincts are quite literally for the birds. A decision tree therefore is a curiously unstable dynamic structure which is hard to predict. Decision theory states that everybody does what he thinks best at the time, which is hard to deny. The tricky problem is how do we learn not only what are the real alternatives, but also what values we place on them. It is true that we move toward the higher payoffs, but the trick is that we learn what the payoffs are only by moving toward them. The economist tends to assume that decision-making is a maximization process, something like getting to the top of a mountain. On the other hand, if we had to deduce the mountain from the behavior of people who climb it, which is the theory of revealed preference, the theory becomes dangerously close to the proposition that people do what they do, and it does not require much theory to tell us this, no matter how elegant the mathematical language in which it is wrapped. The situation is even worse than this because in actual decisions we are not climbing a real mountain, but an imaginary mountain, and a mountain furthermore which is like a featherbed and falls in as we get to the top of it. We learn to like what we get as well as to get what we like.

One way out of this morass is to look for structures which determine decisions because perhaps they determine the information flows and corrupt or purify information as it flows up through an organization. When hearing Lawrence Senesh's delightful poem about cities I could not help adding a verse to it as I felt that the last verse was a little too Pollyannish to be realistic.[2] Here is my version of the last verse:

> The reason why cities are ugly and sad
> Is not that the people who live there are bad;
> It's that most of the people who really decide
> What goes on in the city live somewhere outside.

This simple structural fact throws a great deal of light on the whole dynamics of urban decay. At this level we have to admit that we do not know very much, although there do seem to be possibilities of knowing a great deal more in the future.

Ecological Equilibrium

How, then, does all this apply to teaching about the social system? I have been rather cool about equilibrium systems simply because a realistic appraisal must regard them as special cases of the general dynamic process. Nevertheless, as an economist I cannot throw them away because in many cases this is all we have and they are in any case a useful intellectual stepping-stone to an appreciation of a more complex dynamics. Somewhere in the teaching business, therefore, we have to tell people about equilibrium systems and we can even point to actual phenomena in society and also in the biosphere, perhaps even in the atmosphere where something like a quasi-equilibrium exists. Thus the notion of ecological equilibrium is a tremendously important concept which we must get over to the student at some point. Here I endorse Alfred Kuhn's theory that ecology is the beginning of wisdom in a great many spheres.

Somewhere in the schools we must get the idea across that society is a great pond, and just as in a pond fish, frogs, vegetation, and chemicals all interact to form a reasonably stable equilibrium of populations, so in society we have rough equilibrium at any one moment of interacting populations of criminals, police, automobiles, schools, churches, supermarkets, nations, armies, corporations, laws, universities, and ideas. The ideal time for formalizing this concept would seem to be in high school algebra when the student is studying simultaneous equations. The essential proposition of ecological equilibrium is that if everything depends on everything else and if there is one equation of equilibrium for each population, we have n-equations and n-unknowns which with a bit of luck may have a solution in which the equilibrium size of each population is consistent with the size of all the others. The fact that ecological systems do exist in nature means that sometimes these equations can be solved. Boulding's first law is that anything which exists is possible. It is surprising how many people do not believe it. There must be some ecological equations therefore which have a solution and this is worked out in the pond and the prairie and the forest and likewise in the city, the nation and the world. Even in the primary grades we could get something of this idea across.

Homeostasis and Ecological Succession

It is a big step from the concept of ecological equilibrium to the concepts of homeostasis and cybernetics by which equilibrium is maintained through a dynamic process. It should not be difficult for children even in grade school to understand the thermostat and go on to see that the body regulates many processes in a similar way. Social organizations are similarly full of homeostatic mechanisms by which disruptive change is resisted and role occupants are replaced.

Recently in Poland I saw an example of the homeostasis of beauty. Many ancient buildings in Poland which were destroyed during the war have been rebuilt exactly as they were before; large parts of Warsaw have been rebuilt stone by stone, street by street, house by house, church by church, and palace by palace. The Russians did the same thing with Leningrad. Here the image of a city perpetuates itself in society because decisions are made on the basis of an idea of beauty from the past. The astonishing recovery of nations such as Japan and Germany after a destructive war is a good example of how an old equilibrium reasserts itself.

The next concept beyond that of ecological equilibrium and homeostasis is that of ecological succession in which the equilibrium is gradually changed by irreversible movements. This gets us right into the developmental process and into the theory of evolution, both biological and social. Mutation is a process by which new equations are introduced into the ecological system; selection is the process by which these equations result either in a new solution or in a rejection of the new populations. Likewise in the learning process, information put into the old structure of ideas, either coming from outside or generated from within, is a mutation which may be rejected or which may restructure the content of the mind into a new ecological pattern.

Teaching and Learning

We still have a long way to go before we can begin to understand the human learning process even though real progress is being made in this direction. We have even further to go before we can understand the process of education, which is by no means the same thing as learning. One of the things which is most puzzling is why some people survive the educational process and some do not—in the sense that after they have gone through formal education they never seem to learn anything again. The main object of formal education should be to teach people how to continue learning, yet as educators we fall very far short of this idea.

Recently I read a delightful statement that the year 1910 was a crucial year in human history because this was the year in which the medical profession began to do more good than harm. I wonder whether the teaching profession has reached this watershed yet. In the past I am sure we have often done more harm than good. I am almost certain that the government has not reached the point of doing more good than harm. Every time Congress adjourns I draw a huge sigh of relief in that a damaging process has been temporarily suspended. Yet, as a teacher, I wonder if I am any better. The most depressing experience I ever had as a teacher was once while standing in the commencement procession at a little college where I was teaching, I overheard one senior say to another, both of them splendid in their caps and gowns, "Well, that is the last time I am ever going to have to crack a book." I almost tore my hair in despair. How often, with our grades and quizzes and exams, assignments and curricula and all this do we destroy the learning process in our attempts at forced feeding?

Priorities In The Social Sciences

I would like to conclude by looking at some possible content areas of high priority in the social sciences which could contribute toward the larger ends which we have in view.

My first suggestion as to content is the comparative study of relatively stable cultures, most of which, of course, comes out of anthropology. A good deal of anthropology is at the level of natural history rather than analysis—interesting stories about strange people—but it does at least give the student the idea that there are many ways of doing things besides his own, and so opens up worlds of culture beyond his own back yard. It is important even for young children to have a feeling that there are a great many ways of doing things. I am convinced that if a thing is worth doing it is worth doing wrong, or at least worth doing in many ways. The curse of the British educational system in which I grew up was the idea that there is a right way to do everything. I have a vivid memory of a British mother at a swimming pool making her children absolutely miserable by saying all the time, "Swim properly, swim properly," while our children just swam cheerfully. The Russians are even worse than the British when it comes to the appalling concept of propriety, for there even ideas have to be "correct." Anthropology undermines propriety because it shows there are many different kinds of stable systems.

Even in complex social systems the student should be able to perceive certain stabilities and capacities for regeneration. Students can be made to perceive that the recovery of a society after a disaster, the regeneration of a limb of a star fish, and even the return of the liquor industry after prohibition are all examples of similar systems of regeneration and homeostasis.

Once we have established the idea that there are stabilities in equilibria we can then go on to dynamics, to developmental systems, and into concepts of economic and political development and ideological change. One of the unfortunate effects of Marxism and the cold war has been a polarization of views on the matter of dialectics. The communists cannot admit that there are any non-dialectical systems and we find it hard to admit that there are dialectical ones. This is disastrous, because obviously there are both and we need to see the total social dynamic process as a complex interaction of dialectical and non-dialectical elements. As a result of our polarization on this matter, both parties have developed unrealistic attitudes towards conflict. The dialecticians idealize it, whereas in this country we tend to suppress it because of our lack of confidence in our ability to manage it. We ought to be able to train people to feel that a well-managed conflict is a beautiful thing, and should not be suppressed. On the other hand, a badly-managed conflict can be disastrous for all parties. This is something which formal education does not seem to teach very well.

The institutions of formal education also seem to be insensitive to a very profound conflict which can neither be suppressed nor allowed to get out of hand between that part of the educational system representing the "super-culture"—the culture of science, airports, and universities which is pretty uniform all around the world—and the local, national, and folk cultures within which many

institutions including elementary and secondary education still largely rest and by which they are supported.

An interesting example of this conflict at the moment is the tension which has been created between the universities and the Selective Service System over the issue of ranking. This is an issue which seems to have acquired a symbolic value far out of proportion to its intrinsic importance precisely because it is a symbol of the conflict between the super-culture of the university and the folk culture of Selective Service. This is a conflict which should not be resolved, although it does need to be managed.

Facts: How Many and What Kind?

One final question which puzzles me a good deal about formal education is what people should know in the way of plain old facts. General principles are obviously not enough. If you live in California you need to know that Sacramento is the capital, although you may not need to recall immediately what is the capital of Chad. We have never asked ourselves seriously what is the minimum that people need to know in the way of factual material. In the light of the knowledge explosion this question becomes more important all the time, for it becomes almost criminal to teach people things they do not really need to know, if this prevents them from learning things they do need to know. On this point I have four very tentative suggestions.

In the first place, we need to know something about the order of magnitude of the factual world. It is often more important to know orders of magnitude than it is to know about particular details. Thus, people ought to know in this country that agriculture is only 5% of the gross national product. We ought to know that the world war industry is equal to the total income of the poorest half of the human race. We ought to know that Japan in recent years has had a rate of economic development of 8 per cent per annum per capita, whereas the United States has had about 2½ per cent. We ought to have some idea as to what the "real maps" of the world look like. We often stuff students with names and dates and general principles, but there is an intermediate area of orders of magnitude that is neglected by everybody. Even in universities there is an incredible ignorance about the orders of magnitude of the world.

The second point is that it is often more important to know where to find information than to have it in your head. This is one point where my own formal training was sadly deficient. When I was at Oxford, for instance, the catalog of the Bodleian Library was written in elegant eighteenth century longhand in enormous and rather inaccessible volumes. This no doubt accounts for the fundamental Oxford principle that it is much easier to think something up than to look it up. In this day and age, however, we must teach people how to search for information. Computers and information retrieval are going to revolutionize the process of search. But in order to use information systems, one must have a certain amount of information to start with.

A third suggestion is that we need to give people factual information—at least on an order-of-magnitude basis—about the shape of the space-time continuum in which they live. This is history-geography, which to my mind should be the same subject, history being only geography in four dimensions. From the point of view of total earth, formal education does a poor job on this, mainly because it is deliberately distorted to create an artificial national image. Thus students are surprised when they learn that medieval Europe was a peninsula on the edge of the civilized world, and that even at the time of the Roman Empire the Han Empire in China was probably superior in knowledge and technology. After about 700 A.D. there is little doubt that the most developed country was China, that Islam was the second layer of development, and Europe the third. In that period most advances in technology started in China and came to Europe by way of Islam. This is not the impression that we produce in our school system, and white Americans, at any rate, ought to know that their European ancestors were by no means top dogs, and that in the Middle Ages it would not be wholly unfair to categorize them as slowly emerging hillbillies.

The Limitations of Personal Experience

My fourth objective for formal education is to develop a lively appreciation of the nature and necessity of sampling and a distrust of purely personal experience. One of the fatal weaknesses of Deweyism is that while theoretically it emphasized starting from where the student is, in practice it often resulted in an emphasis on *being* where the student is. If where he is is in a backyard at West Lafayette, Indiana, where is that? The really interesting thing is not where you are but where you are not and the purpose of education is to get you from where you are to where you aren't. This is why a purely empirical bias in the culture can be very dangerous because it results in a bias of the attention toward what exists, whereas the things that do not exist are much more numerous and perhaps more important. Even in the evolutionary process many of the most interesting things were

those which did not survive and we need to know why they did not.

One of the greatest political problems arises from the tendency of people to generalize from their own personal experience to propositions about society as a whole. Formal education should teach people that their personal experience, important as it is to them, is a very imperfect sample of the totality and we must give people an idea of *how* to sample this totality.

What formal education has to do is to produce people who are fit to be inhabitants of the planet. This has become an urgent necessity because for the first time in human history we have reached the boundaries of our planet and found that it is a small one at that—the space ship earth. This generation of young people have to be prepared to live in a very small and crowded space ship earth. Otherwise they are going to get a terrible shock when they grow up and discover that we have taught them how to live in a world that has passed away. The nightmare of the educator is what Veblen called "trained incapacity" and we have to be constantly on the watch that this does not become one of our main products.

1. Alfred Kuhn. *The Study of Society: A Unified Approach.* Homewood, Illinois: Richard D. Irwin, Inc., and The Dorsey Press, Inc., 1963.
2. Lawrence Senesh. *Our Working World: Cities at Work.* Chicago: Science Research Associates, Inc., 1967. p. 14. The last verse of Senesh's poem reads:

> If cities will be
> Rich, exciting, and bold,
> Using and treasuring
> New things and old,
> Safe, pleasant places
> For work and for play,
> The people who live there
> Must make them that way.

THE FIFTH MEANING OF LOVE: NOTES ON CHRISTIAN ETHICS AND SOCIAL POLICY

Lutheran World, 16, 3 (July 1969): 219-229

The Fifth Meaning of Love—*Notes on Christian Ethics and Social Policy*

All behavior involves choice and all choice involves preference, i.e., an ordering of possible alternatives according to rank—first, second, third, etc. If we choose *one* out of a set of alternatives this implies that it ranks first.

An ethical system is a set of preferences or rank orders of alternatives which is believed to be applicable to more than one person. Tastes are preferences which apply only to an individual and which he does not apply to others. This is why there is no disputing about tastes. I may prefer green tea to black tea, but this has no ethical significance unless it matters to me whether somebody else prefers green tea to black tea. An ethical system then is preference about preferences or ranking of rankings. If I say "everybody", or even if I say "you", should prefer green tea to black tea, I am making an ethical statement.

There are two primary sources of ethical statements. The first may be called the economic or prudential ethic and the second the heroic ethic. The economic ethic tends to justify and to universalize preferences by appeal to calculations related to the future, or what economists call cost-benefit analysis. The simplest and commonest form is in terms of monetary calculations as when, for instance, we try to compare the advantages of two dam sites.

The heroic ethic by contrast arises out of an expression of the identity of the individual concerned. This is Luther: "Here I stand and I can do no other." It is the Charge of the Light Brigade, "theirs not to reason why, theirs but to do or die." It is expressed principally in three aspects of human life—the religious, the military and the sporting. The saint like St. Francis who urges us to give and not to count the cost, to labor and ask for no reward, the president who urges, "ask not what your country can do for you, only ask what you can do for your country", and the sportsman, the mountaineer who risks his life to climb a mountain "because it is there", are all examples of the heroic value system. This only becomes an ethic if it is applied to others. It can only be applied to others if we assume that a group of people have the *same* identity. It is because there is a communion of saints that saintly values become ethical. It is because there is a Light Brigade that all its members are expected to sacrifice themselves. Sport is more a matter of taste, but even here people are "expected" to be achievers, especially on teams.

Ethical theory goes to the third level of ranking and ranks ethical systems themselves. For the purposes of this essay let us suppose that the most attractive ethical theory is that which supposes that the main ethical task of mankind is to achieve a proper balance between the heroic and the economic ethic. The purely economic man is a clod, the purely heroic man is a fool. Somewhere we have to maintain a precarious balance between the two apparently contradictory ideals.

The central concept of the Christian ethic is love, just as the central concept of Christian theology is the assertion that God is love. Love is a word of many meanings and before we can examine its ethical implications we must analyze its possible meanings. There are at least five:

1. Love may simply mean desire or strong preference. "I love" may simply mean "I want", as in the expression "I love pancakes".
2. Love may mean mutual desire—"I want you, you want me". Sexual love has a strong element of this.
3. Love may mean an emotion of affection. It may refer to the emotional tone of a desire—warm rather than cold, expressive rather than restrained, and so on.
4. Love may mean benevolence, i.e., good will towards another. We have benevolence if our perception of an improvement in the condition of another improves our own condition. Malevolence is the opposite. We are malevolent if the perception of a worsening of the condition of another improves our own condition. Selfishness is the knife edge between benevolence and malevolence in which we are indifferent to the perception of the change in the welfare of another. Selfishness is actually very rare.
5. The fifth meaning of love is expressed by the Greek word *agape*, sometimes called "Christian love". The concept is found in some other religions, such as Buddhism. This may be defined as universal benevolence. It includes the love of enemies which is a peculiar characteristic of the Christian ethic. It may arise, as in Buddhism or Jainism, with an identification of the self with the totality of things so that benevolence extends to all forms of life or even to inanimate objects. Christianity has tended to limit benevolence more to human beings or animals associated with man. Christian love does not go very far towards the mosquito!

An ethic of love is itself a combination of economic and heroic elements. The economic case for love is quite strong. Benevolence is what game theorists describe as a positive sum game, it makes everybody better off. Malevolence makes everybody worse off. Love produces love. Even exchange, which is based on selfishness, makes everybody better off. If, therefore, we can reinforce the learning of benevolence by theological argument, the economic gains may be very substantial. Furthermore, it seems much easier for "natural man" to learn malevolence than benevolence so that anything which reinforces the learning of benevolence is all to the good.

The ethic of love also has strong heroic elements. In Christianity this arises out of the identification of the individual with the figure of Christ who is himself a heroic figure. Nearly all religion is a mixture of the economic and the heroic, promising at the same time rewards in heaven for good behavior on earth and also urging self-abandonment to a heroic ideal. On the whole, "higher" religion tends to be heroic, rather than economic, as we find it, for instance, in the Book of Job: "Though he slay me, yet will I trust in him: but I will maintain mine own ways before him." (Job 13:15). See also Habakkuk 3:17: "Although the fig tree shall not blossom . . . yet will I rejoice in the Lord." Without this heroic aspect of love, benevolence would soon decline from its many disappointments, for benevolence will increase only as love persists which is not requited. This, however, is the essence of the fifth meaning of love. It is only as love is willing to sacrifice and to withstand disappointments that it tends to propagate itself in the world.

Every generation of Christians must reinterpret the Christian ethic to meet the needs of their own day. The following problems particularly call for interpretation in the modern world:

1. The application of the Christian ethic to the international system.

2. The particular problem of the "cold war" and the ideological conflict between socialism and capitalism, often called the "East-West" conflict.

3. The problem of development, especially in the tropical belt of poor countries. This is sometimes called the "North-South" problem, but it applies even within the rich countries to their own poor.

4. The problem of discrimination—the division of mankind into classes, castes, races and sexes of different degrees of status and power.

5. The special problems of economic life.

6. Sexual behavior and the family.

7. Education and the transmission of the knowledge structure. The "war of the generations" probably comes under this heading.

8. Styles of life—the hippies, the Bohemians, the "squares".

9. The problem of large-scale organizations.

10. The role of religion and the church.

In each of these we can detect a spectrum of "ethical positions", ranging from the heroic on the one side to the economic on the other.

Ethical problems of the international system involve attitudes towards war and peace, towards the national state, towards international organizations, etc. At the heroic end of the scale we have Christian pacifism which rejects all war as illegitimate and inconsistent with Christian love, especially with love of enemies. At the other end of the scale we have the Niebuhrian or Lutheran doctrine of accommodation with the demands of the national state in the interest of "justice". The relations of the Christian church to the armed forces and to the whole institution of war remain very ambiguous. On the one hand, the official church is no longer willing to give its unqualified blessing to mass murder as it has done in the past. On the other hand, it is hung up by an unwillingness to relinquish its organizational and spiritual ties to the national state. The choice between being a good Christian and a good American or a good German is too hard for it!

The Christian church straddles the East-West conflict and is indeed one of the forces leading to its amelioration. The church has adjusted itself to capitalism in the West and to socialism in the East. It is clear that the church can survive under either system. Official socialist doctrine is more hostile to the church than is capitalism. On the other hand, some of the moral pressures of socialism, such as dissatisfaction with the cash nexus, with the apparent inequality and selfish-ness of capitalist society, and the desire for a more familistic approach to economic life, have come directly out of Christianity. Toynbee has described Marxism as a "Christian heresy" and certainly Marxism cannot be understood except as a social mutation out of an essentially Judeo-Christian culture. On the other hand, there is also in the Christian ethic a strong prejudice in favor of personal freedom and equality. Love can only take place between people who are independent and equal in status. A hierarchy, therefore, which is indispensable in the socialist societies, is unfavorable to the development of love. Nevertheless, Christian socialism is the heroic aspect of the Christian ethic in this field, demanding a society in which people do the common things of life for love and not for money. Christian capitalism recognizes that too great a burden should not be placed on love, and that in a society in which exchange and private property bear the brunt of producing and distributing commodities, love can flourish more than in a totalitarian centrally-planned state.

In the perspective of the next hundred years the North-South problem may loom much larger than the East-West problem. At the moment most of the countries of the temperate zone, all around the world, are on what might be called the "main line" of development, with the poorer ones developing faster than the rich ones, but with all of them gravitating rapidly towards high per capita incomes. In the meantime, however, the countries of the tropical zone for the most part are not only poor but have slow rates of development so that the world is increas-ingly separating out into a rich temperate zone and a miserably poor tropical zone. A gospel of universal love cannot contemplate with any satisfaction a world which is separating out in this way. Nevertheless, the problem is not an easy one and cannot be solved merely by gifts or extensive foreign aid, even though where this is well done it is a great help. The real problem is one of social reorganization within the poor countries to the point where they can accept modernization and at the same time retain a strong traditional culture. The difficulty here is that some traditional cultures like that of Japan are friendly towards moderniza-tion whereas some like that of India are profoundly hostile towards it. Here the revolutionaries are "heroic" and the developmentalists, "economic".

The problem of the division of the world into classes, castes, races, and sexes, characterized by various degrees of power and weakness presents very difficult ethical problems. The Christian ethic has produced a strong long-run tendency towards equalitarianism simply because love can only really take place between equals. In all earlier civilizations, however, hierarchy, domination and oppression seem to have been inevitable characteristics of the very fabric of society. It is only in the modern world with the development of a science-based technology that any-thing approaching an equalitarian society has become technically possible. There is, therefore, a long-run drive towards a society in which all people, no matter what their color, religion, ancestors, sex or occupation, shall have in some real sense equal status. This means the end of domination by the male in the family, by the priest in the church, by imperialist powers in the international system, by hereditary aristocracies or self-perpetuating elites in political life, by particular racial or religious groups, and so on. The actual dynamic by which equality is increased, however, is by no means always clear. In all societies, the powerful have power. All organizations tend towards hierarchy, authority and subordination. One answer to this problem is sheer complexity and the more complex the society the better the chance any individual has of getting out from under oppressive domination. Where there is a great variety in status and occupation, the more niches, the more ladders, the more mobility, the less oppressive the society will be. The Christian ethic clearly regards all men as equal in status in the sight of God. This recognition, however, seems to be compatible with great inequality of status in the sight of man, even in Christian societies. A very difficult question which is becoming of great importance is the extent to which equality can be achieved on an individual basis and the extent to which it has to be achieved by the organization of subordinate groups. This is a problem faced by such diverse phenomena as the labor movement, the Black Power movement, student power, anti-colonialism, nationalism, women's rights, and so on. On the whole, the United States has been following the theory of equality through individual mobility, which may not be wholly realistic. The possibility that this may have to be supplemented, at least by bargaining among groups, must receive careful consideration.

The ethical problems involved in economic life are extremely complex but are closely related to the ethical issues of the cold war, as the confrontation of the two systems revolves to a considerable extent around the organization of economic life. Economic life deals mainly with exchange and with exchangeables and the very fact that both parties benefit in an exchange, makes it low in moral affect. It produces neither hate nor love, though it does depend for its continued existence on fairly high levels of honesty, trust, fulfillment of promises and so on, all of which might be called the prudential or economic virtues. That part of economic life which has the most moral affect is what I have called the "grants economy", i.e., the system of one-way transfers of exchangeables. An exchange is a two-way transfer. I give you something, you give me something. A grant is a one-way transfer. I give you something, you don't give me anything in the way of an exchangeable. Grants much more than exchange reflect the moral or "integrative" structure of society. The critical issue of the cold war may very well be whether the exchange economy should be dominant but modified by a system of grants or whether the grants economy should dominate, modified by a system of exchange; the first, of course, corresponding to the capitalist and the second to the socialist system. An important ethical problem here is that whereas exchange does imply equality among the exchangers—and therefore is at least compatible with love, even if it does not produce love—a grants system always implies hierarchy and inequality, the grantor always having a higher status than the grantee. In light of this fact, "doing good" may not necessarily be a very high Christian virtue unless the consequence is to produce greater equality of status. Thus, poverty can only be solved in the long-run by increasing the productivity or the terms of trade of the poor, not only by giving them perpetual grants. This does not rule out proposals like the negative income tax, or even the guaranteed annual income which has at least the advantage of creating equality of status. One of the great problems of economic policy is that a great deal which is justified on the grounds of supporting the poor in fact ends up with the rich. A good deal of "social democracy" at least seems to be something of a fraud. This is especially true in the United States where a great deal of the grants economy is "wasted" on the rich, as for instance agricultural subsidies, educational subsidies, and so on.

The ethical problems regarding sex, the family and procreation have seldom seemed more acute. The ideal of Christian marriage is under sharp attack. A sensate society sees no reason why sex should not be indulged in as long as it gives pleasure, or why marriage should be regarded as a lifetime obligation. This whole issue is caught up also with the problem of having children. The ethic of unlimited procreation is being sharply challenged in a world that is getting more and more crowded, and population control (not mere birth control) is seen as an absolute necessity in the world of the future. In the modern world it seems increasingly important, first to set forth both in precept and in practice the ideal of a Christian family as a "colony of heaven", a little principality, or perhaps a domestic democracy, within which love is fostered and in which husband and wife grow old together in a constant process of spiritual maturation and in which children receive an experience which teaches them to be truly human and enables them in turn to set up similar families. It must be made clear I think that unlimited sexual freedom is a poor preparation for the creation of a family based on the fifth meaning of love. Nevertheless, it must also be recognized that great changes are underway and that some of the ancient legitimacies which are being threatened may need to be questioned, especially those which may have been based on the blind fear of sex. On the other hand, the Polyannaish view that there is nothing to fear in sex at all is equally unrealistic. The church has an inescapable responsibility for the legitimation of sexual life. The problem of population control is not being faced by the church at all, yet it is both very difficult and of enormous importance. The crucial problem here is how to reconcile the social control over population growth, which is going to be absolutely necessary in a "spaceship earth", with the very proper sense that we have that this is an area in which individual freedom is very precious.

The problem of education and the transmission of knowledge from one generation to the next is becoming of acute importance with the continued increase in the total stock of knowledge and the very real danger of cultural loss from one generation to the next if the legitimacy of these transfers is lost. The "war between the generations" is probably as intense today as it has ever been, partly because of the very rapid pace of change. The older generation is now being rejected as having received its education in a world which has largely passed away. Nevertheless, love between the generations is of enormous importance in sanctifying the transmission of knowledge, without which the human race would fall backward in its developmental process. The problem of how to reconcile the difference in status between the old and the young with the equality implied in Christian love is critical. Student unrest is but a symptom of this much larger problem and the Christian community may have a role here which it has hardly yet begun to recognize.

Part of the "war between the generations", but something which also goes beyond it, is the problem of recognizing the possibility of different styles of life. Do we want a society which will tolerate and recognize many different styles—the Amish, the hippies, the artist-Bohemians, the "squares", the suburbanites, and so on? Can everybody do his own "thing" without impinging too much on the freedom or the identity of others? Does love imply making people over in our own image or does it imply recognizing and respecting them for what "they are"? On the other hand, what people are is what they have learned to become and we cannot be indifferent to these learning processes. Can we have a "mosaic" society with many different cultures and styles all held together by mutual respect and benevolence? What are the limits of toleration? How far should we tolerate practices and subcultures which are detrimental to health or liberty?

The rise of large-scale organizations since about 1870—such as the great corporation, labor unions, military organizations, and even socialist states—has presented a whole new set of ethical problems. There are now only about eleven countries with a gross product, as measured by total sales, larger than the gross product of General Motors Corporation. The gross products of most of the smaller socialist countries are about the same magnitude as that of General Electric Corporation. The United States Department of Defense is a centrally-planned economy larger in its total budget than the total economic product of the Peoples' Republic of China. In this world of Goliaths how can the integrity and dignity of the individual David be secured? There are two traditional solutions to this problem. First, the market, especially the labor market, which gives individual persons a choice of employer and a choice of "niches" in which they can make a living and a life; and second, the vote, by which individuals can exercise some choice in the selection of the occupants of political roles. The increase in the optimum size of organizations of all kinds has taken place in the last hundred years largely as a result of certain inventions in communication (such as the telephone), or in organization (such as division of labor in the executive task), not as a result of any self-conscious movement. This sheer increase in size, however, threatens both the two traditional solutions to this problem. Large business organizations threaten to control the market and are not adequately controlled by it. Large political organizations make the individual voter impotent, and even in the smaller countries there has been a strong movement towards military dictatorship. Galbraith has drawn a contrast in his book, *The New Industrial State*, between the "accepted sequence" in which organizations are supposed to be guided by customers in case of business, and voters in the case of governments; and the "revised sequence" in which businesses persuade customers, through selling, to take what businesses want to produce, and governments "sell" their citizens on what governments want to do. This is a problem which has always been with us, but which is intensified by the rise of large-scale organization. There is a great need in the modern world, therefore, for new forms of "checks and balances", by which different types of organization can each check the power of the other in the interest of the welfare of individual persons.

A great many of these problems revolve around the relative roles in the development of society of the three great organizers of social development—the threat system, the exchange system, and the integrative system. Disagreement about the relative proportions that these three should occupy is at the base of a great deal of argument between the Marxists and the non-Marxists, between the radicals and the conservatives. All social systems involve all three elements, though in varying proportions. An armed force, for instance, is primarily concerned with threat. It usually conscripts men into it, i.e., does not rely on the labor market. It uses the threat system to get its inputs of personnel, and its internal organization relies heavily on threats and on punishments, not on rewards. And, of course, its main product is threat capability, i.e., the capacity to destroy things which other people value. On the other hand, even an armed force has to rely on exchange for many of its inputs: it conscripts men but it does not usually conscript commodities; it purchases its equipment and it even pays something to its men. It also relies heavily on certain integrative relationships and it employs chaplains or communist political officers, depending on the prevailing religion, who arouse loyalty and identification of the individual with the objectives of the organization. Similarly, a bank operates largely in the field of exchange. Its relations with the outside world consist almost wholly of exchange, and it attracts its labor force from the labor market by paying them what is necessary to attract them. On the other hand, it also relies on an underlying threat system in the law for the enforcement of its contracts, the punishment for embezzlement, and to a certain extent the discipline of its employees. It also must have an integrative system, in the sense that the people who run it and who work for it must be convinced of its legitimacy and the rightfulness of its place in the structure of society. A monastery or utopian community may rely for its continued existence mainly on "love", i.e., on integrative relationships and on the identification of its members with the purpose of the community. Nevertheless, even the most idealistic community has always behind it the threat of expulsion of unsuitable members. It has to engage in exchange with the rest of society unless it can create enough identification with its purposes to persuade the outside world to give it the inputs of commodities which it needs. Even in its internal relationships there has to be a certain element of justice in distribution in the sense that members who feel they are giving too much and getting too little are likely to become discontented and destructive to the community.

There would probably be a high measure of agreement right across the spectrum of political opinion, from the revolutionaries to the conservatives, that in the course of social development there is diminution in the threat component of the social system and an increase in the integrative component. The threat system is usually regarded as a bad thing in itself, justified only by its consequences. Integrative relationships are usually regarded as good in themselves. Exchange is in a curiously neutral position. It is perhaps because of this that there is such wide disagreement about its moral value. The socialists, the revolutionaries, and the romantics tend to despise it, perhaps because they are more "heroic" than "economic". Conservatives and liberals in the older sense of the word tend to elevate exchange and the institutions of the market to a high moral virtue. This is a conflict which is very hard to resolve simply because it does involve the internal tension between the heroic and the economic ethics.

I am inclined to argue myself that there is too much of the heroic ethic in the socialist and revolutionary countries, and that this has a very high social cost in terms of refugees, in terms of the destruction of the simple, joyful things of life, in terms of the corruption of the arts, and in terms of the whole style of life which seems to be esthetically false, giving high emotional affect to things which should be commonplace and constantly destroying the whole esthetic tone of the society. Because of this I do not regard myself as a socialist.

Nevertheless, one must also recognize that there are corresponding vices in capitalist market-type societies. The ethical neutrality of exchange can easily lead into a vulgarity of life and over-emphasis on the monetary measure and a starving of the heroic and integrative aspects of life. This starvation of the heroic aspects of life often takes its revenge, in market-type societies, in the development of monstrously perverse forms of heroism and of integrative relationships, such as we saw in Germany under National Socialism, or in nineteenth-century Western European imperialism, or in the kind of romantic imperialism that is represented by the United States war in Vietnam. These are terrible perversions of the heroic and the integrative relationships and it may not be an accident that they developed in market-dominated societies. It is clear that we have a problem here that nobody has solved, that still requires a great deal of social invention. None of the existing ideologies come even close to solving it.

This raises the question of social planning and "social self-consciousness". The essence of self-consciousness is to have an image of the future which is realistic in the sense that it can be fulfilled at least with a high degree of probability. I write these words in July in Colorado, I have a "plan" to be in Frankfurt in August to discuss this paper, I expect the fulfillment of this plan to have a high degree of probability, even though I recognize that it may not be fulfilled, that all sorts of accidents could happen. In the last hundred years, thanks in part one must confess to Karl Marx, the idea of social self-consciousness has evolved in the minds of men. This is the idea that a whole society, or at least a large number of its members, or at worst a small elite within it, could have an image of the future of that society which has a high probability of being realized, through the activities of the members of that society in the present. Planning involves a decision between alternative futures which guide the activity of the present. Thus, at the personal level, the fact that I now plan to be in Frankfurt in August means that I must make plane reservations, I must cancel certain other engagements, and so on. A farmer who plans to grow wheat must plow his land and plant seed and do those things which are necessary now in order to get a crop later. Similarly, a society which plans a certain rate of economic development will have to do certain things in the present.

Planning, however, always requires what might be called "practical knowledge" of the dynamics of the system which produces the future. In the case of the farmer, this requires knowledge of agronomy and of certain "production functions", as the economist would say, which provide the link between present behavior and future results. In the case of a total society we are still very ignorant of its production functions and its general dynamic regularities. Consequently, we are always being painfully surprised. We make plans for the future and we act in the present, but our image of the future is not fulfilled. There is indeed almost a law of irony in social planning, that everything that we do will turn out differently from what we expected. The idealism of the Russian Revolution produces a Stalin. The "Thousand Year Reich" under Hitler ended in disaster. After the defeat of Germany and Japan in the Second World War came an extraordinary outburst of economic development in these countries, which is leading them to surpass their victors. Economic planning in most of the poor countries has resulted in corruption and almost certainly a diminution in the rate of economic growth. The "great leap forward" in China turned out to be a great leap backward, or at least sideways, and the plans have been fulfilled negatively. Planning for national defense often results in national disaster. We could multiply the instances almost indefinitely.

The failures of social planning are not merely the result of inadequate social theory, such as Marxism or the theories of economic development in western countries. It is due to something more fundamental which is the fact that in any system involving knowledge as a crucial variable, exact prediction is intrinsically impossible. We can see this clearly if we ask ourselves, "could we predict what we are going to know in twenty-five years?" Obviously the answer is "no", because if we could predict it, we would know it now, we would not have to wait twenty-five years. It is because the growth of human knowledge is the dominant dynamic process of the social system that it must have, what I have elsewhere called, an element of "fundamental surprise". This does not mean that planning is useless or impossible. It simply means that all images of the future have a degree of probability which is less than one. Hence an essential element in planning is being prepared to be surprised. In other words, we must be flexible, adaptable and prepared to change our image of the future constantly, as the present moves towards it. This is perhaps one reason why the socialist countries are introducing greater and greater elements of market freedom into their society, simply because a completely centrally-planned economy finds it extremely hard to solve the administrative problem of flexibility and adaptability. A rigid plan easily becomes a straightjacket rather than a compass or a map.

Are we then to conclude that what is happening now is a dialectical synthesis of ideologies, that the Marxist thesis has produced its modern development antithesis (in many Japanese universities there are two departments of economics, a "Marxist department" and a "modern department") and that what we are seeing now is something of the synthesis between these two? This is a pretty pattern and there may be something in it. However, my personal view is that the dialectical patterns of history are essentially subordinate to the non-dialectical patterns, the principal one of which is the accumulation of securely-based practical knowledge. This is a process much more like the growth of a coral reef than it is like a dialectical conflict. It is this process which would carry us beyond dialectics and beyond ideology into a firmly-established practical knowledge of the dynamics of society.

Finally we must consider the role of the church and the Christian community in developing and interpreting its own ethic and also in being challenged by this ethic. In the history of Christianity, Christ has been in constant dialog with his church. The church itself in its own practices has often fallen short of the ethic which it preached. One of the consequences of the ecumenical movement is that the church is being forced back on its origin, for Christ is the *only* thing which all these incredibly diverse Christian churches have in common. The challenge of the gospel Christian ethic to the Christian church itself, therefore, is perhaps one of the most interesting problems which it faces. We see this most strikingly in the enormous upheaval which is now going on in the Catholic church. The Protestants, though backward, will not be immune to "modernization". The critical question is whether the Christian "phylum", as Teilhard de Chardin calls it, still has evolutionary potential. Can it adapt itself to the modern world without losing its identity and indeed be leaven in the enormous lump of the twentieth century?

THE INTERPLAY OF TECHNOLOGY AND VALUES: THE EMERGING SUPERCULTURE

In: *Values and the Future, The Impact of Technological Change on American Values,* Kurt Baier and N. Rescher, eds. New York: The Free Press, 1969, pp. 336-350

THE INTERPLAY OF TECHNOLOGY AND VALUES

The emerging superculture

It has been pointed out by B. L. Whorf and a number of writers that one of the problems of those who are trained to think in Indo-European languages is that nouns tend to be substituted for verbs. There seems to be something about the subject-predicate-object structure of the sentence in these languages which inhibits us from talking about activity as such, and which leads us into reification, that is, talking about processes as if they were things. Both the words "technology" and "values" are examples of this peculiar linguistic difficulty. Whether there is any such "thing" as a value it is hard to know in the absence of any secure knowledge about the physical or physiological substructure of the valuation and choice processes of the human nervous system. For all I know, love may be coded into one chemical and hate into another; but up to now at any rate we have not been able to identify these structural forms. What we observe is not values but valuation, that is, an activity which may be inferred from the study of behavior, guided by introspection on the choice process.

Similarly, technology is not a thing. It is also a process, a complex set of ways of doing things with both human and material instruments. Again, perhaps, as a thing it may be represented by some as yet quite unknown structure in somebody's head in terms of knowledge. Up to now at any rate, this carrier cannot be observed directly, and what we observe in technology is people applying means to secure ends.

Among social scientists, economists have probably paid the most attention to the problems involved both in the choice process and in the processes of technology. Oddly enough, the problems are formally rather similar. In his attempt to describe the process of choice, the economist has postulated a utility or welfare function according to which every relevant state of the field or social system is given an ordinal number which indicates an order of preference, first, second, third, and so on. In what is called a strong ordering, each state of the field is given a unique ordinal number; in a weak ordering, different states of the field may have the same ordinal number, in much the way that students may be bracketed in a class list. As the economist sees it, then, the problem of valuation is that of ordering a field of choice and then selecting the first on the order of preference. This is the famous principle of maximizing behavior, as it is called, which is simply a mathematical elaboration of the rather obvious principle that people always do what seems to them best at the time. It has always surprised me, as I have remarked elsewhere, that such a seemingly empty principle should be capable of such enormous mathematical elaboration. It can only be given content, of course, if there are some information processes by which the preference field can be spelled out and the preference function described. Where the field which is to be ordered consists of a set of possible exchanges under a given system of exchange opportunities or prices, certain broad properties of the preference function, at least, can be deduced from the observation of differences in behavior in response to different price systems. This is what is called the "theory of revealed preference." Theoretically, we suppose that we can deduce the preference function of an individual from the differences of his observed behavior under different price structures. In practice, of course, because of the sheer difficulty of observing the behavior of the same individual under different price structures, what we observe is some kind of aggregate behavior of the behavior of different individuals under different price structures, and we deduce from this some kind of aggregate or average preference function. If the preference functions of different individuals are not widely dissimilar, there is some justification for this procedure.

Just as preferences, or the valuation process, is described by economists as a utility function, so technology is defined by a production function. The forms of these two functions, in fact, are highly similar, in fact virtually identical. A production function relates physical inputs of some kind to physical outputs of some kind. In this case, the field consists of all possible or relevant combinations of inputs and the function describes the quantities of outputs which are associated with each combination of inputs. It tells us, for instance, that with quantity x of labor and y of land we will get z of potatoes. In the case of the production function, we can frequently assume not merely ordinal numbering of the product but cardinal numbering. In the case of the utility function, all we know is that of two combinations of inputs, one gives more utility than the other if it is preferred. In the case of the production function, we can usually measure the product directly so that we know not only that one combination of inputs gives more potatoes than another, but we know how much more, and we know, indeed, how great a quantity of potatoes is given in each combination of inputs. Oddly enough for the purposes of price theory, this richness of information about the production function is unnecessary, and all we really need to know to determine the equilibrium price structure is whether any given combination of inputs gives us more, less, or an equal amount of product than another.

Figure 1, which is very familiar to economists, illustrates the two concepts. Here we suppose two variables, say inputs in the state of the system, measured along OA and OB. We then postulate a function in the third dimension, of which the curves C_1, C_2, etc. are contours. These are called isoquants in the case of the production function, in which, shall we

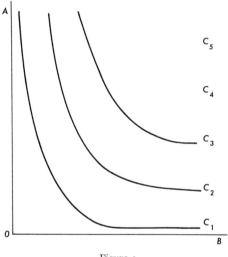

Figure 1

say, OA measures the quantity of labor, OB the quantity of land, and all combinations on one of the isoquants represents a given quantity of product. In the case of the preference function these are called indifference curves, and represent all combinations of two inputs to which the decision maker is indifferent, that is, which have the same utility. Utility can be thought of as the product of the decision making process, much as potatoes are the product of a production function; and the form of the two functions is likely to be very similar. In the case of the utility function, however, the indifference curves are given merely ordinal numbers so that we know which of any two indifference curves represents the higher utility and is the more preferred. In the case of the production function, the isoquants can be given a cardinal number representing the actual quantity of product.

In elementary economic theory it is generally assumed that both the utility or preference functions on the one hand, and the production functions on the other, are given factors in the social situation. As a first step in the process of analysis, this is quite legitimate, for it is important to deduce the consequences of any given set of preferences and technologies. The moment we try to make the system dynamic, however, it becomes very clear that neither the preferences nor the technologies are given, for they are both derived from a learning process which itself is dependent on the very dynamics of society which we are investigating. This proposition that both values, that is, preference functions, and technologies or production functions are learned is the key to any dynamic theory of society, though unfortunately we know far too little about the learning processes involved. Values and technologies, preference functions and production functions, interact to produce a price system, a system of exchange opportunities, not only in the narrow sense of a system of commodities with which economics usually concerns itself, but in the large sense of the whole social system of terms of trade, that is, the totality of what we give up for what we get. The concept can even be broadened to include what I have elsewhere called the grants economy and the integrative system, by which we give and receive unilateral transfers; for these, too, depend on preference functions and identifications which must be learned.

Because of the greater richness of information which seems to be available at the level of the production functions, the learning process can perhaps be perceived more easily there. Even if we look at a technology as relatively simple as that of peasant agriculture, it is clear that the whole process by which inputs are transformed into outputs is one that must exist in the mind of the producer before any production process will be set in motion. We will not plant seeds unless we have some image in our mind of a process of production by which certain activities of plowing, planting, weeding, fertilizing, and so on will eventually produce a harvest. Men lived on top of rich soil long before they ever thought of devoting it to agriculture, and unless there is an image of a whole productive process in their minds, the sequence of steps required for the process will not be carried out. The same simple principle is true of the most complex industrial process. An automobile, for instance, originates in the mind of the engineers and designer; it develops as a set of detailed blueprints and information which organizes an assembly line, and its production requires an enormous amount of communication of specialized knowledge. All human artifacts, indeed all capital, can be regarded as human knowledge imposed on the material world. All processes of production originate in the minds of men and have to be maintained in the minds of men if these processes themselves are to continue. Even the perpetuation of the simplest productive process requires the transmission of an elaborate body of knowledge from one generation to the next, for all human knowledge is lost every generation by the sheer processes of death. Learning is not something which can be done once and for all; it is something which must be repeated to the last detail in every generation, if existing processes are even to continue.

Production functions are not merely transmitted from one generation to the next in an educational process, for what might be described as a net learning process goes on which actually improves them in a developing society. What we call economic development, indeed, is largely a learning process by which improved production processes are learned. Two rather distinct processes are involved here: first, the innovative process by which a new image of a production process is created in the mind of someone which existed in no other mind previously; and second, the educative process by which the image of a production process in one mind is transmitted to another. Both of these are necessary if there is to be development. If there are no innovative processes and education is successful, the knowledge of each generation will be transmitted unimpaired to the next. We should not overlook the possibility of degenerative processes, in which the knowledge of one generation is impaired in transmission to the next, and in which therefore technology declines and productive processes become less productive. The rate of technological development depends almost entirely on the amount of resources which a society devotes to the innovative process and to the educative process. Of these, the innovative process is the most mysterious. We do not really understand the sources of human creativity. Many societies have existed and continue to exist in which all attention is concentrated on the process of transmitting unimpaired the images of one generation into its successor. A good example of this would be the traditional Indian village, or shall we say the Amish society of the United States. The object of the educative process here is to produce children who are exact replicas, in their images, of the parents. We can be pretty sure that innovation will not be carried on unless it is rewarded, and in traditional societies, where the innovator is looked upon with suspicion or even horror as one who violates the ancient dignities and destroys the sacred patterns of the society, innovation is not likely to be successful.

It is a proposition for which there is a good deal of historical evidence that the innovator is likely to be one who is in some sense a "refugee," that is, who is in a degree an alien in the society and yet who has a role and a status that can be accepted. The refugee in the literal sense, that is, one who has been driven out of his previous home and who has sought refuge in another society, is no longer bound by the traditional ways of doing things because his traditional environment is no longer around him. On the other hand, because he is an alien in the society to which he goes, peculiarities of behavior are tolerated in a way that the native does not enjoy. It is not surprising, therefore, that in India and Pakistan it is the refugees who have been vigorous entrepreneurs. It is not surprising also to see the important innovative role that groups like the Jews or the Parsees, the Syrian and Lebanese traders, the Chinese outside China, and other displaced peoples have played in the whole process for world development. There may also be "internal refugees" as well as external ones, the noncomformists like the Quakers and Methodists in England, who played a disproportionate role in the first Industrial Revolution of the eighteenth century, the Samurai, especially the Ronin or masterless Samurai in nineteenth century Japan, the Calvinists in Europe, and so on. These are people who might be described as internal aliens, who are in some sense alienated from the established patterns of the societies in which they live, but who nevertheless have a recognized status as nonconformists and dissenters, which gives them, as it were, license to innovate.

Innovation, of course, is useless unless it is supplemented with a fairly large investment in the educative process. There is no point in having innovations unless they can be imitated. This educative process, of course, is by no means confined to formal education, although as technologies become more complex the role of formal education in transmitting them becomes more important. Even in complex societies like the United States, however, a great deal of the educative process by which innovations are transmitted through the population is quite informal. Transmission takes place by word of mouth or simple observation, through advertising and commerical propaganda, in face to face groups, and so on. The rate of transmission throughout a society of successful innovations depends, of course, to a considerable extent on the value system in the society, and particularly its willingness to innovate. A society which regards all old things as good and new things as bad will be unlikely to innovate in the first place and even if there are innovations, they will take a long time to establish themselves. A society which has the reverse value system, in which new things are regarded as good simply because they are new and old things as bad just because they are old, will put a high value on innovation and innovations will spread rapidly.

The last observation illustrates a principle of the utmost importance, that values and technologies constantly interact on each other in the dynamic processes of society because both are created and transmitted by a common learning process. The learning of values, that is, of preference functions, is less obvious, perhaps, than the learning of technologies;

nevertheless, all societies devote a noticeable amount of resources to the process of the transmission of preference functions from one generation to the next, and societies differ enormously in their tolerance of innovation in preference functions. It is clear that there is a certain genetic base for preference functions, but in the case of man, this represents a very small proportion of the total. In the insects and even the birds, the preference functions seem to be generated almost wholly by genetic processes, that is, the genes or genetic structure contains an information code which builds certain preferences into the phenotype which it creates. An oriole has a strong *preference* for building oriole nests, but this preference is not learned from its parents, it is built into the bird by its genes. The same seems to be true of insects, although in the highest insects like the bees there does seem to be a certain process of communication and education. For the most part, however, even the bee does not have to learn how to be a bee it simply *knows* how to be a bee. As we move towards the mammals and still more towards the primates, the proportion of the value structure which is learned increases. A kitten learns in part how to be a cat from its mother, not from its genes. Monkeys, it would seem, have to learn even such things as sexual behavior from their parents. As we move to man, instincts, that is, the value system which is built in by the genetic system, shrink to a very small proportion of the total. We do seem to have a genetic value system at birth which includes such things as high preference for milk, warmth, and stimulation and low preferences for loud noises, falling, and hunger; but on this slim genetic base we finally achieve preferences for transubstantiation or atheism, surplus value or free private enterprise, oysters, raw fish, olives, alcohol, chastity, and self-immolation. Genetics provides only the vaguest of drives. It seems fair to say today that there are no instincts in man in any detailed sense of the term, and that practically the whole of his value structure is learned from parents, from teachers, from his peers, from the mass media, and from information inputs of all kinds which pour into him both from outside and from within and continue perhaps even in sleep. From the moment of birth, we are the recipients of enormous inputs of information, out of which we gradually build our image of the world in regard to space, time, causality, the future, and values. Our preference functions are not innate; they are a product of our total information input, operating, perhaps, within certain guidelines laid down by our genetic inheritance. The old problem of the relation between hered-ity and environment has never been solved, it has simply been laid aside because we do not know how to answer it at present. That genetics imposes certain predispositions is very plausible, but it is clear also that in the mass, whatever individual peculiarities may be due to individual differences in genetic structure tend to cancel themselves out, and that the value systems of a culture are transmitted in the processes of that culture by the information inputs which the culture generates. There is nothing, for instance, in the genetic composition of a Japanese American that prevents him from becoming 100 percent American in culture. If he is only 99 percent American, it is because certain physical difference affect a little the way he is treated and the information inputs which he receives. Apart from this slight difference, however, the Nisei will learn to like coffee and eggs and bacon for breakfast as over against the rice, raw egg, and soup of his Japanese cousin, who may be genetically identical.

At this point I believe I can detect a subterranean rumble from the moral philosophers, who are likely to object to what seems to be my identification of values with valuation, and of valuation with preference and choice. Surely, some of them will argue, the choice between good and evil, right and wrong, is qualitatively different from the choice between bacon or sausage for breakfast; and still more, they may argue, concepts of utility or preference functions cannot account for problems of freedom, justice, and still less for mercy, pity, peace, and love. I am not altogether unsympathetic to their indignation against what must seem like economics' imperialism, that is, the attempt on the part of economics to take over not only all the other social sciences but moral philosophy as well. Nevertheless, I am prepared to defend my identification of the problem of values with the problem of preference, though I will gladly concede to the moral philosopher that this can operate on a number of different levels. Thus, while economics tends to assume a preference function, the moral philosopher raises the question of the choice among preference functions themselves. What I think this means in terms of the dynamic process of society is that the learning processes by which we learn our preference functions are not simply arbitrary, nor are they purely relative and culture-bound, but that there are certain selective processes which are in a real sense universal. It seems to be a plain fact of observation that cultural and moral relativism of a pure sort tends to break down when it is pressed too far. It is all very well for the relativist to observe that it is very interesting that some people eat their grandmothers and some do not, but that no one should pass any moral judgment on this interesting difference of behavior. When, however, somebody proposes to eat *him*, there is some tendency for relativism to break down. What we have to recognize here is that in the processes by which we learn our preferences, there are certain information inputs and certain sources of information which are peculiarly salient and effective in the formation of preferences. Preferences are always learned from a reference group, as the social psychologists call it. This may be, in the first instance, the family group with which the individual identifies early, even though the identification, as psychoanalysts have pointed out, is often ambiguous. All societies have produced religious and educational institutions which also are salient in establishing preferences, but these preferences are subject to innovation just as the production function is subject to innovation. The Aztecs had strong preferences for human sacrifice and rather messy religious rituals. Under the joint challenge of the Conquistadores and the Jesuits, Spanish baroque churches celebrating a symbolic sacrifice were substituted in the preference system for the human victims. The relative role of the Conquistadores and the Jesuits in this is almost as difficult to estimate as the role of heredity and environment. We can be pretty sure, however, that one without the other would not have been very effective. In other words, it was a complex mutation-selection process by which old values are challenged by new values, old technologies by new technologies, and indeed these two processes are not very different. The images in the minds of the living, both of preference functions and of production functions, have to be transmitted from generation to generation. In the course of transmission the images are changed, and they both may be changed by innovation or mutations, some of which prosper and spread through the minds of the living, and some which do not.

The problem of the complex interaction between our preferences and the technologies is rendered particularly acute in the present epoch by the fact that we have been going through enormous changes in both technology and values, that is, in our images of what inputs produce what outputs on the one hand and our images also of what states of the system are preferable to others on the other hand. The Great Transition, as I have called it elsewhere, which began with the rise of modern science around the end of the sixteenth century and which continues with ever accelerating change up to today, is a change in the state of man as great, if not greater, as in the change from the neolithic village to urban civilization; and I have described as the change from civilization to post-civilization, civilization being the state of man typified, shall we say, by the Roman Empire or by the poor countries such as Indonesia today. (Certainly if the Roman Empire were around today we would regard it as an extremely poor country and would be giving it aid on a large scale.) This great transition was preceded by a long period of accelerating folk science and folk technology, a period also of slow but continuous change in values and preferences. In the West we can date this preparatory period roughly from the fall of Rome and the rise of the great monastic orders; in China it can be dated from a little earlier, perhaps the beginning of the Han Empire. The so-called Industrial Revolution of the eighteenth century in England and Western Europe represented essentially the culmination of this process of folk technology. It owed very little to science, even though science, as it were, was developing underneath it. The steam engine and the spinning jenny are not in essence very different from the printing press and the clock. The theory of the steam engine, for instance, which is thermodynamics, did not develop until the early nineteenth century, and the steam engine itself clearly owed nothing to it. In the latter half of the nineteenth century, however, the science-based industries began, which could not have developed at all without the previous development of a certain branch of science. Of these, the chemical industry was the first, the electrical industry the second, the biological industry the third, and the nuclear industry the somewhat premature fourth. Today in the developed countries, more than half the economy is producing products and using methods which would have been virtually inconceivable a hundred years ago. Never in the whole course of human history has there been a change as rapid at that which has taken place in the last hundred years.

In this great transition there has been a constant interplay between changing technologies and changing values, both of these being an integral part of the larger process of change in what Teilhard de Chardin calls the "noosphere" or the totality of images of the world in the minds of the living. The interaction between values and technologies is so complex that it is quite impossible to say which precedes the other. It is a hen and egg problem in n dimensions. It seems fairly certain, for instance, that there were changes in values, that is, preference systems, which were a necessary prerequisite for the rise of science, in the direction of introducing higher preferences for change, for the authority of nature rather than the authority of sacred books and ancient writers. These changes in values, however, were not unconnected with certain preceding changes in technologies, for instance the rise of the money economy, development of accounting, and the subsequent opportunities for more rational behavior in the light of better information. A strong case can be made out, indeed, that in the origins of science it was the machine that preceded the scientific or mechanical image of the world. The clock, for instance, preceded the Copernican-Newtonian image of the solar system as the great clock; the water pump preceded the discovery of the circulation of the blood, just as the steam engine preceded thermodynamics. The development of the more elaborate folk technology imperceptibly changes the values of the society which used it, and by giving man a little power over the material world perhaps increased his desire for knowledge about it.

On the other hand, there are also changes which occur fairly spontaneously within the system of values and preferences. The Max Weber thesis of the impact of the Reformation and especially of Calvinism on economic activity and technology is well known. Once the authority of the Pope had been challenged and a high value has been placed in the Protestant countries on successful dissent, the legitimation of dissent in general is a fairly easy step. The legitimation of dissent, as we have seen, is an essential element in the innovative process; therefore innovation must be legitimated if it is to be rapid. It is not surprising, therefore, that Luther's initial break with Rome was accompanied by the more radical Anabaptists and followed by Calvin, George Fox, John Wesley, and the more radical religious reformers. It is not surprising either that it was out of this radical nonconformity that the great changes in economic institutions and technology of the seventeenth and eighteenth century largely developed. In this case, the development of a religious value system which stressed the immediacy of personal experience as over against the authority of a pope or even a king, which stressed veracity as a high virtue and which also stressed simplicity of life and thriftiness and the sacredness of the material world, should provide the groundwork for enormous changes in knowledge and technology.

These considerations perhaps throw some light on the puzzling question of why the breakthrough into science and the technology that is related to it and based upon it took place in Europe rather than in China. The great work of Joseph Needham on Chinese technology has opened our minds in the West to the fact that at least up to 1600, the folk technology of China was considerably ahead of that in the West, and that indeed many of the essential developments in the western part of the old world were not only anticipated in China, sometimes by hundreds of years, but in many cases actually derived from China. This seems to be true, for instance, of such things as the stirrup, on which so much of the medieval aristocratic culture was based, which reached Europe from China or Tibet by about the eighth century. Such essential technologies as that of clockwork and printing were likewise discovered in China long before they were discovered in Europe, although here the actual connection is more obscure and the European discoveries may be independent. The exact relation of innovation to imitation remains one of the mysteries of human history.

In spite of the fact, however, that China had been the superior of the West for so long and unquestionably was still the superior of the West, shall we say in 1600—from 1600 on Europe takes an enormous spurt forward under the impact of the rise of modern science, whereas China proceeds in the old slow pace of folk technology. It may be indeed that China was too successful (one very fundamental principle of social science is that nothing fails like success). Perhaps the very disjointed and disintegrated structure of Europe, with its many centers of power, its religious and national divisions, its separation of ecclesiastical from political power, and at the same time its active network of trade and communication (the result partly of its long coastline and waterborne traffic), made that fraction of difference which carried Europe over the watershed into science. China, at any rate did not make this transition. This fact has dominated the history of the last 300 years.

As we compare Europe with China, the subtle and constant inter-action between values and technology again becomes apparent. In the fifteenth and sixteenth centuries, for instance, as the Ming voyages, indicate, China clearly had the technology to explore the world and to expand its culture, and the fact that it did not do so is almost certainly due to the value systems of its rulers, which favored withdrawal, stability, and staying at home. By contrast, the Spanish and the Portuguese, in what might be described as the last great burst of the Crusades, discovered and colonized America to the West, and Eastward as far as the Philippines and Japan. This was indeed the moment of globalization, the moment in human history at which the earth ceased to be a great plain and became a sphere. All this, indeed, was before the rise of science, but the high values and rewards given to adventure, exploration, and discovery from, say, 1450 to 1600 in the West, unquestionably helped to create the value system which later gave rise to Galileo and his successors. The hens of value produced the eggs of technology; the eggs of technology the hens of value, in an ever-increasing, ever-expanding process of increasing complexity.

By way of conclusion, or perhaps an epilogue, let us take a brief, speculative glance at the implication for future values and perhaps even for future technology of the great transition through which we are now going. Its most obvious and immediate impact is the separation out in the world of two cultural systems, the superculture on the one hand and traditional cultures on the other. It is hardly too much to say that all the major problems of the world today revolve around the tension between these two cultural systems. The superculture is the culture of airports, throughways, sky-scrapers, hybrid corn and artificial fertilizers, birth control, and universities. It is worldwide in its scope; in a very real sense all airports are the same airport, all universities the same university. It even has a world language, technical English, and a common ideology, science.

Side by side with the superculture, and interpenetrating it at many points, are the various folk cultures, national, religious, ethnic, linguistic, and so on. The tensions between the superculture and traditional cultures are felt at a great many points. We see it, for instance, in the international system, where the superculture has given the traditional cultures of the national states appalling powers of destruction which are threatening the whole future of man. We see it in race relations, where the superculture moves towards uniformity, the absence of discrimination, and differentiation by roles rather than by race or class or other ascribed category. We see it in education, where formal education tends increasingly to become the agent of transmission of the superculture, leaving the transmission of folk culture to the family, the peer group, and more informal organizations. We see it in religion, where the superculture tends towards the secular and traditional culture preserves the sacred.

At a great many points, these tensions between the superculture and traditional cultures produce challenges to traditional values and even disintegration of these values. Family loyalties are replaced by loyalties to larger and more abstract entities; national loyalties are eroded by inconsistencies between the national state and the world order which the supercultural requires; religious loyalties are eroded by new views of man and the universe; political loyalties are eroded by new images of the social system arising out of social sciences.

The picture, however, is not merely one of constant retreat and erosion of traditional values in the fact of the superculture. There is also the transformation and regeneration of traditional values under the impact of the superculture. A strong case can be made, indeed, for the proposition that the superculture itself does not generate the values and preferences which will support it, perhaps because of the very fact that it has to be transmitted through channels of formal education of a more or less authoritarian kind. Traditional culture, on the other hand, is transmitted through the family, the peer group, and intimate relations which are capable of creating much more intense value commitments and stronger preferences than the more abstract and cold-blooded relationships of the superculture. We do not feel towards the airport or the chemistry textbook the degree of emotional involvement that we have with the family, the nation, or the little brown church in the wildwood.

As an integrative system, the superculture is really very weak. Fellow scientists kill each other in national wars almost as enthusiastically as co-religionists. Scientists have not raised money very much to help other scientists, and while they have a certain sense of occupational community, this does not usually go much beyond the rather tenuous bond of the professional association. People die for their countries, even for their faith, but very few people have died for biochemistry. Up to now at any rate, therefore, the ethical values of mankind on the whole have arisen out of the traditional cultures rather than out of the superculture. There is something to be said for the proposition, indeed, that it is only countries which have strong traditional cultures and as a result strong ethical systems which are able to create or adapt to the superculture, and that where the traditional culture is weak, the society will have great difficulty in making adjustments to the superculture. Japan is perhaps one of the best examples of a society in which the traditional culture is very strong and in which it generates principles of ethical judgment and behavior which are friendly to the superculture and which permit it to develop at an enormous rate. In a greater or lesser degree, this is true of all the successfully developing countries. It is by contrast those countries in which the traditional culture cannot adapt itself and produces values which are unfriendly to the superculture that development is most difficult. The contrast between Japan and India in this respect is most instructive. In some cases the traditional culture has proved so incapable of adaptation to the impinging superculture that it has been virtually destroyed. This seems to be the case in China, and to a smaller extent in the other socialist countries.

From the point of view of this paper, communism is a curious phenomenon which represents on the one hand a vehicle for bringing traditional societies into the superculture and which expresses many of the values of the superculture, such as education, equality of status for women, the abolition of castes, and so on. On the other hand, ideologically it represents what is really a prescientific view of society, and its results in a curious fixation of the socialist countries on the attitudes and ideologies of the nineteenth century. Ideologically it is a kind of folk science lying somewhere between an unsophisticated folk image of society on the one hand and empirically based scientific concepts on the other. At certain points, therefore, it may assist, and at other points it may hinder the transition and adaptation of a society to the superculture.

The inability of the superculture to produce adequate values of its own and the adaptability of certain aspects of traditional culture is reflected strongly in the continuing strength of the religious institution in the developed societies. This is nowhere more striking than in the United States, which is at the same time perhaps the furthest advanced towards the superculture and yet is also a society whose history has been characterized by the rise of the numerical strength and power of the churches. What we seem to face in the future, therefore, is a very complex set of mutual adjustments, in which an adapted traditional culture transmitted in the family, the peer group, and the church will create ethical values and preferences which are consistent with the world superculture. If the superculture simply destroys the traditional culture in which it is embedded, it may easily destroy itself. On the other hand, if the traditional culture does not adapt to the superculture, it too may destroy itself. This is a precarious balance, and not all societies may achieve it. The costs of a failure to achieve it, however, are very high, and there is great need, therefore, for widespread self-consciousness about the nature of the problem, and a willingness to put resources into solving it.

THE TASK OF THE TEACHER
IN THE SOCIAL SCIENCES

In: *Effective College Teaching: The Quest for Relevance,*
William H. Morris, ed. Washington, D.C.:
American Council on Education, 1970, pp. 104-123

The Task of the Teacher
in the Social Sciences

TEACHING AS A SOCIAL SYSTEM

All human development, and one is tempted to add, all evolutionary development of any kind, is essentially a process of learning. Formal education, which might be defined as those learning processes which are assisted by a teacher, is only part of the total learning-process, and it must be evaluated in the light of the total process. This is particularly important in learning about social systems, because a great deal of what we know about social systems is learned outside of formal teaching. It is learned from members of the families in which we grow up, from playmates, schoolmates, comic books, television, and so on. We cannot become human without learning a good deal about the social system in which we find ourselves. Any formal teaching about social systems, therefore, must take as its background fairly complex images of society and of social relations, which are built up in the ordinary experience of life.

A good deal of this "folk knowledge" of social systems lies below the level of reflective thinking. We learn the appropriate behavior for different social groups, very much as we learn to walk, without much self-conscious theory of what we are doing. Folk knowledge of social systems, however, does express itself consciously in a body of "popular wisdom" in the form of aphorisms and proverbs. These represent a rich, though by no means systematic and consistent, body of folk wisdom about human relations. The very inconsistency—as expressed, for instance, in "Out of sight, out of mind" and "Absence makes the heart grow fonder"—may well reflect the richness, complexity, and inconsistency of the social system itself. Even the social sciences rely in part on the folk knowledge of the social scientists. Nevertheless, as the social scientists move toward maturity, they tend to diverge in their content more and more from the body of folk wisdom.

We have somewhat the same problem in the physical and biological sciences. Here, however, the scientific knowledge is more remote from folk knowledge and can be built up from its own foundations. Thus the fact that what we learn in school about the solar system seems to contradict our daily experience does not bother us very much, for the contradiction can fairly easily be resolved. In social systems, however, the habit of generalizing from personal experience is so widespread that contradictions between "common sense" and the more sophisticated image of the world that comes out of scientific inquiry are not so easy to resolve. Nevertheless, it is the principal task of formal education in schools and colleges to expand the student's image of the world beyond his personal experience and to give him an image which encompasses the total system of the earth or even the universe.

The awkward mixture of folk and formal knowledge that constitutes even the sophisticated images of the social system may still give the teacher of the social sciences a certain advantage, in that the process of teaching and learning is itself part of the social system. Neither the physicist nor his students have ever been in—or even seen—an electron, nor has the biologist ever been in a cell, but both the teacher and the student of social systems have participated actively in many social systems of many different kinds. This potential advantage is by no means always exploited, for formal training in the social sciences does not always result in sensitivity in the interpretation of particular social systems in which the social scientist operates. Not only are the conclusions of research on the transfer of training very depressing, but the behavior of social scientists and their professional associations does not always reflect high standards of sophistication. Nevertheless, one hopes (perhaps foolishly) that the teacher in the social sciences should be in a particularly good situation to develop some concept of what he is doing as part of a larger social process. It is to be hoped, then, that he may perceive the teaching and learning process itself as essential to all social systems, as the process by which is transmitted and expanded that stock of knowledge on which all the other activities of a society are based. One hopes, again, the teacher of the social sciences, therefore, is perhaps in a better position than other teachers to visualize his impact. This impact is not merely the immediate product of the class that he is teaching but consists of what happens to his students, to himself, and to the social systems in which they participate for the rest of their lives as a result of their experiences in class. The teacher may then see that the main purpose of formal education is to facilitate the student's continuation of learning throughout his life. Education does this in a number of ways. It gives the student a vocabulary that will enable him to understand further communications and so continue his learning beyond the limits of the classroom. This vocabulary may include not only words but also mathematical and statistical symbols. It includes also conceptual contexts which should enable the student to fit further communications into a structure of increasing knowledge.

TEACHING AND LEARNING

The study of human learning is likely to be an extremely important area in the social sciences in the next generation and should produce marked changes in the practice of teaching. Teaching at all levels today is a skill based more on folk knowledge than on any explicit scientific knowledge of the learning process, and, while folk knowledge is real knowledge in the sense that with its aid we have obviously succeeded in teaching people something over the centuries, it has limited horizons of development, which were almost certainly reached long ago. It is doubtful whether teaching today is much more effective in transmitting knowledge than it was in the schools of Athens. It is possible that we are on the edge of a substantial advance that should make teaching in this generation a peculiar challenge and delight. Thus if a teacher, especially in the field of the social sciences, can be aware that his classroom is a social system and that his teaching is also a form of research that may contribute to the advance of knowledge in this area, its significance is all the more enhanced.

We need to break down the view that teaching and research are totally unrelated activities. It is not only that teaching may be a form of research in human learning but also that the act of teaching forces a reexamination of the subject matter being taught, no matter what it is. Every good teacher learns as he teaches. This indeed is one of the miracles of teaching; it is not a form of exchange in which the teacher loses what the student gains but an extraordinary act of development in which, after the class, not only the student knows more but the teacher knows more. Teaching should also continually force a reexamination of the subject matter that is being taught, for the difficulties in transmitting subject matter from teacher to students come very frequently from a defect in the content of what the teacher is trying to transmit. It is much easier to believe nonsense than it is to teach it, and the very act of trying to teach nonsense becomes a self-correcting force.

EVALUATIVE FEEDBACK

One would hope to see considerable progress in the next generation in the integration of evaluation into the learning process. Little as we know about human learning, one of the principles that seems to be emerging is that evaluative feedback is a crucial element in all modifications of the image of the world. Evaluative feedback is crucial in folk learning. Thus, a child learns his native language largely by the selective responses of his parents and the people around him. When he starts babbling, he soon learns to select the sounds that are received with favorable responses, those on which, as it were, he gets an A, and to reject those which produce no response or unfavorable responses. Similarly, we learn to find our way around town because if our image of the world does not correspond to reality we get unfavorable evaluative feedback, often very quickly. If we go to the grocery store and it has moved, our disappointment produces a rapid learning process. Similarly, we learn who are our friends and enemies, we learn that immediate responses are not always wise ones, and we learn what gets us into trouble and what does not. The method of science, likewise, is essentially the method of organized evaluative feedback. It is only through the failure of predictions that science progresses.

It is only in the classroom that evaluation is sharply divorced from the learning process. The student does not learn easily why he has failed. Indeed, often he does not even get back his examination papers. The whole secret of programmed learning, insofar as there is one, is precisely to build evaluative feedback closely into the learning process, so that every time a student does anything it may be evaluated and the evaluation fed back to him. Programmed learning, however, is not the answer to all our problems. There are many learning processes, those which involve the structuring of complex images of the world, in which we have to learn to operate without much positive feedback or reinforcement for long periods. The mysterious processes by which the slow building up of vocabulary and grammar eventually leads to fluency in a language or by which little bits of learning eventually add up to mastery of a musical instrument are very little understood. Out of boredom or out of a sense of being insulted or out of a loss of personal dignity, programmed learning—if it is too picayune—may discourage people from learning. A good deal of the function of the teacher is to cheer students up, to encourage the discouraged, and to keep alive the students' sense of dignity and worth in a process that often destroys self-confidence and the sense of personal worth.

One hopes, therefore, that a substantial area of research in the effect of examinations, tests, grades, and other evaluative devices of the learning process will be developed in the next generation. We must evaluate evaluation itself as an element in a total social process, which is important not only in the learning process of the student who is being evaluated but also in the learning process of other people, both peers and superiors in the social matrix, with whom the student may be related.

All examinations and tests evaluate much more than knowledge of the subject matter. They also evaluate such things as a student's ability to solve puzzles, to write essays, to speak coherently, to organize material, to operate under stress, even the all-important ability to get away with things. If tests do not measure what they are supposed to measure, then decisions based on the results will be incorrect. The evaluation of the overall capacity of persons is a particularly delicate operation, and teachers should at least try to be conscious of what they are doing.

A peculiar difficulty in understanding the theory of the human learning-process is that we learn not only "facts"—that is, images of an external world—but also tastes, ethical values, and capacities for future learning. It is easy to see that our developing image grows toward "values" and that in some sense all learning is "wishful learning"; that is, we learn to see the world the way we do because it pays off. On the other hand, we learn about the payoffs themselves; for we do not come into the world like the birds, with a complete apparatus of genetically formed values. The values that we learn, furthermore, affect our capacity for further learning. If we learn that we cannot learn, or that we are "no good," we will not learn in the future. This is a system that defies the present skills of the systems analysts. It means, however, that we must be cautious about misinterpreting evaluative feedback, important as it is; for evaluative feedback, if it is poorly constructed, can easily destroy the capacity to learn. How do we distinguish between the kind of feedback which says, "I made a mistake, which I can correct," and the feedback which says, "I made a mistake, therefore I am no good, and I will continue to make mistakes." It may well be that the real difference between good and bad teaching lies precisely in differentiating between various kinds of evaluative feedback.

A NEED FOR RESEARCH

At the moment, the social sciences are very poorly organized to carry on research in the teaching-learning process. In graduate schools the gulf between research and teaching has gotten so wide that hardly any of the regular social science departments will tolerate a Ph.D. thesis in the teaching of its subject. Schools of education, unfortunately, often occupy the lowest position in prestige in the whole academic community. This is perhaps in part because of their use of the police power to force prospective teachers to take required courses and perhaps in part because of the general location of education in the grants sector of the economy, which tends to make it a field unremunerative by comparison, say, with law or engineering. Whatever the reason for this low status, it is nothing short of a disaster. Some persons believe that we might get along without good lawyers, who are engaged, after all, mainly in redistributing old property and resolving personal disputes. Some also believe that in these days we might even get along without good doctors, for the improvement in public health and the increase in the expectation in human life have been accomplished mainly by people outside the medical profession. If, however, we cannot transmit the knowledge that is in the heads of one generation into the heads of the next, society will inevitably decay. In any scale of social priorities, therefore, teaching should obviously stand very high. It is indeed a major challenge to the social sciences to find out why teaching and the study of teaching do not have a higher prestige and, perhaps, to recommend measures to correct this serious defect in our social system.

The first step toward a new science of learning and teaching would be, as it has been in many sciences, to develop a better "natural history." At the moment, each teacher is isolated in his classroom. Over the course of his life, he probably learns a good deal out of sheer experience. He learns that some things work and some things do not. If he is a good teacher, he will get a fair amount of feedback from his students and will modify his procedures accordingly. At the moment, however, there is practically no way by which this individual knowledge can be disseminated. The biological sciences owe a great debt to bird watching, even if bird watching is not strictly a science. Class watching, however, is regarded as a degrading business to be indulged in only by those who are supervising student teachers. In university teaching, especially, any outside intervention in the classroom is regarded as a deep threat to status, and resistance to it almost reaches proportions of paranoia.

There are, however, some hopeful signs. Some progress is being made by economists in reporting experiments in the teaching of economics, thanks in part to the Joint Committee on Economic Education and the Committee on Teaching of Economics of the American Economic Association. Similar progress is being made in other social sciences. The new *Journal of Economic Education* (vol. 1, no. 1, fall 1969) will be useful in opening up a new discourse. One possible means of freeing the teacher from the isolation of his classroom is the development of team teaching, even if this takes only the basic form of two colleagues teaching a single class. This perhaps is less threatening than having observers from outside, and if two people teach the same class, at least they will have something to talk about, and a conversation between them may attract others.

Outside Influences on Teaching

Three influences coming from outside the profession may affect the teaching process in the next generation, but exactly what the impact will be is hard to predict.

STUDENT UNREST

The first of these is the increasing student dissatisfaction and unrest. This is, in part, no doubt a consequence of the general disorders of our day and reflects what is perhaps a general unhappiness of the academic community with the draft, the rising power of the military, an "imperialistic" national image which seems more appropriate to an earlier period, and the increasing use of violence by the police. At least part of the student dissatisfaction, however, is directed specifically at the teaching and learning experiences to which they are subjected, and one must honestly confess their complaint is not wholly without foundation. A dean once told me that the one excuse he had never had a faculty member give is that he had to spend time preparing for his classes. The sheer economics—of the universities especially—gives strong marginal payoffs to research and writing and even to speaking outside the classroom, whereas the only reward for professors who spend a lot of time in teaching is, to quote W. S. Gilbert, "the gratifying feeling that our duty has been done." When we reflect how meager are the payoffs, we must realize it is a tribute, indeed, to the moral integrity of university faculties that teaching does not disintegrate even below its present level.

If student dissatisfaction can be channeled into some positive schemes for the improvement of teaching, it may well be one of the fortunate by-products of an otherwise rather calamitous era. Certainly the efforts at student evaluation of courses, which a good many universities now tolerate, could perhaps be linked up with a program of research and development in teaching that would make these evaluations less casual and more reliable. We are all aware, of course, that a popular teacher is not necessarily a good one and that many students are not able to identify their best teachers until they have been out of school for ten years or so. Still, popular teachers are frequently good ones, and there is probably some correlation between popularity and the capacity for inspiring students to learn.

EDUCATIONAL HARDWARE

The second outside effect on the teaching-learning process is likely to result from a massive attempt by manufacturers to introduce hardware—teaching machines, computer-assisted instruction, audiovisual aids and the like—into the teaching process. If the teaching profession remains passive in the face of this onslaught, it may well be disorganized by it, and the result will be disheartening, if not disastrous. We could easily see a parallel to the experience of the medical profession with commercial drug houses, the positive features of which are constantly being threatened by the incapacity of the medical profession to control its own inputs of information. It is not easy to see an answer to this problem. The teaching profession is not going to be able to control the research and development that are going into teaching devices. The only control, indeed, would come from a well-organized program in research in teaching that could act toward the teaching machines as, shall we say, the critics toward a play. In view of the reliance of the teaching profession, especially at the elementary and secondary levels, on compulsory schooling—and even on the use of the police power in the accreditation of teachers—a little commercial admixture into the occupation may not be wholly a bad thing, for if people can make money out of something honestly, there is continual pressure for improvement. Nevertheless, whatever beneficial effects the hardware revolution, if that is what it is going to be, can produce are likely to be much augmented if the teaching profession is organized to handle it and to criticize.

A great deal depends here on having a positive theory of teaching that can take (or leave) hardware in the light of testing, refining, and revising the theoretical structure. The great danger of hardware is that it tends to concentrate on specific and particular performances and behavior and by its very nature cannot be concerned with the total development of the individual. It is argued that hardware will relieve the teacher from burdensome and unnecessary duties and leave him free to concentrate on the great personal task of developing the total personality of the student. This sounds fine, but one has one's suspicions, and a nightmarish future in which the teacher becomes primarily an electronic repairman and the students all turn into well-trained rogues and clods is not inconceivable. It may be, of course, that the hardware will not be efficient enough to justify its cost. The teacher, as someone has said, is a nonlinear computer of enormous capacity produced initially by entirely unskilled labor, and the economics of biology in the long run may outrun the economics of mechanical and electrical engineering. Here, however, we must simply wait and see and be prepared for the unexpected.

CONTENT AND ORGANIZATION OF SOCIAL SCIENCES

The third, and perhaps in the long run the most important, effect on the teaching of social sciences is likely to come from the content and the organization of the social sciences. The change in the content of the social sciences as time goes on obviously affects what is taught. One is reminded of the old story about the alumnus who visited his old department and found that the questions that were being asked on the examinations were the same as those that he had answered a generation ago. He was reassured of progress, however, by the professor, who explained that while the questions might be the same, the answers were now different. Certainly in the last fifty years there has been a marked change in the answers. For instance, in economics the Keynesian system has triumphed, in psychology the instincts have been abandoned, in political science quantification is no longer a dirty word.

From the point of view of the teacher, perhaps one of the major questions of the next generation is whether the social sciences will exhibit any convergence or reorganization. The existing division into economics, political science, sociology, anthropology, psychology, and so on is the result of a long historical process with at least some random elements in it. Whatever may have been past justifications for the existing division, we should not necessarily assume that these will persist indefinitely. In fact, all social sciences are studying the same thing, that is, the total social system.

This might be called the "sociosphere" by analogy with the biosphere or the atmosphere. It consists of all three billion human beings; their inputs and outputs of commodities and information associated with them; the roles which they occupy and the organizations constructed out of these roles; the symbols, images, and knowledge embodied in their nervous systems; and so on. Social systems are differentiated fairly sharply from biological systems by the importance of information, symbols, and consciousness in them. There is a real difference in systems level between the study of the social system and, say, even the study of human physiology. The social sciences, however, are not divided from each other by differences in systems level, but by the fact that they abstract somewhat different elements and concentrate on different parts of the social system. Thus, economics concentrates on exchange and exchangeables and on how the social system is organized through exchange. It concentrates heavily on those organizations and institutions that are concerned primarily with exchange, such as banks, corporations, and public finance agencies. Political science concentrates primarily on institutions that are organized through legitimated threat, such as governments. Sociology deals primarily with integrative relationships and tends to take institutions that concentrate on community and solidarity—and their opposites—such as the family, the church, crime, the military, and so on. Anthropology, historically, has concentrated on the study of small societies and especially of primitive societies. Psychology concentrates on studies of the behavior of individual organisms; social psychology, on behavior of small groups.

The arbitrary nature of the existing divisions of the social sciences is reflected first in the fact that almost any attempt to characterize them will produce substantial protest from the practitioners. Thus, economists will protest that what they are really studying is the allocation of resources under conditions of scarcity. On the other hand, political scientists want to get into this one too and define political science as an authoritative allocation of resources through public institutions. Sociologists will complain that economists have no monopoly on the concept of exchange and that social exchange is an essential characteristic of sociological systems. Anthropology, at least in the guise of social anthropology, pushes its claim towards larger and larger societies. Another aspect of the arbitrariness of the present divisions is that the differences within the existing disciplines are probably greater than the differences between them. This is especially true of psychology, which is an extraordinary aggregation of almost unrelated studies close to physiology and ethology at one end and into clinical psychology and "literary psychoanalysis" at the other. It could be argued, indeed, that in the systems level there is a fundamental difference between the "micro" and the "macro" in virtually all the existing disciplines.

In defense of the existing structure of the social sciences, one can only say that each of the disciplines creates a subculture, the members of which can talk fairly easily to each other, but not easily to those in other disciplines. If, however, the existing disciplinary structure does not in fact represent the most useful mode of division, the development of these disciplinary subcultures is an all the more damning indictment. We can hardly take much satisfaction in the reflection that the training of social scientists has become so highly specialized that each field has tended to create a little world of discourse of its own with high protective tariffs against intrusions from other fields. In the universities especially, the fact that the major political power rests with the departments and the professions they represent means that attempts to teach a unified social science are regarded with suspicion or even with contempt. Each discipline tends to live within itself and to think that there is not much that it has to learn from others. The economist, for instance, is not trained to think of economics as simply a contribution to a larger system but tends to think of it as something completely self-contained and unrelated to other disciplines. A case perhaps can be made for this attitude at the graduate level, where the tricks of the trade have to be learned, but at the high school or undergraduate level, this intellectual isolationism can be disastrous. There is great need for teachers who can respect their own disciplines and at the same time give the student a sense of the totality out of which he can abstract some particular segment. An occupational disease of the academic is that of mistaking an abstraction for reality, and this is particularly dangerous in the social sciences.

A serious problem for teaching in the social sciences is created by the fact that the lower the grade level of the student, the more difficult the question of content. At the graduate level there is not much of a problem, as the student has to learn the current, detailed content of his own profession. At the level of freshman or sophomore courses, which are supposed to be more general, the problem of content is acute. It is a deplorable aspect of the American tradition in higher education that these lower-level courses are usually taught by younger faculty members, who are the most ill prepared to teach them. The German tradition, in which the elementary courses in the subject were usually taught by the senior professor, has much to recommend it, and universities should not be above using economic incentives to persuade senior members to teach elementary courses.

In the high schools and grade schools, the problem of content in the social sciences becomes all the more acute and, apart from some fine work like that of Lawrence Senesh, social science pays little attention to what should be taught in the lower grades. At the high school level, some attention is now being paid to the problem, but with practically no coordination among the different social scientists. What is desperately needed here is an elementary, general social science of adequate content, but there is literally no apparatus in the professions or in the schools for producing one. If anything, the interest of university people in the high schools is contributing to even further fractionation of social science. Economists are pushing economics, sociologists are pushing sociology, and so on, with potentially disastrous results.

A word should be said here for geography and history, each of which has an ambiguous, but highly important, relation to the social sciences. Geography has a strong claim to being the principal integrator of all the sciences, insofar as it studies the earth as a total system. The fact that it is already well-established in the lower schools suggests that it could play a key role in introducing concepts of the social system in the first twelve grades. Unfortunately, it suffers as a discipline from some lack of organized contact with the social sciences and also from a quite unwarranted feeling of inferiority. It can provide an important link between the social sciences and the biological and physical sciences, and one can visualize a curriculum in which all the sciences are organized in an essentially geographical setting.

History as a discipline straddles the social sciences and the humanities and should indeed provide an important link between them. The historical record, in the larger sense, is the raw material from which all science must come, and the record of human history and experience is the great mine of information from which the precious metals of understanding have to be extracted by an enormous process of orderly sifting and rejection of information. The historian's skill in appraising, sifting, condensing, and interpreting the deposits of the historical record is an essential part of the general search for stable patterns and interpretative theories. Here again, if social science is to be taught in the first twelve grades, a great deal of the teaching must be done in the name of history, a kind of history which creates real understanding of both the necessities and the accidents of the total social process. The sociosphere, after all, is a four-dimensional body with three dimensions of space and one of time. The historian is absolutely necessary to the filling out of the fourth dimension. The social scientists, however, can perform a crucial role in discovering the patterns within the "noise."

It is not easy to be optimistic about the progress, at least in the next generation, of the social sciences toward an integrated body of content. Nevertheless, if there is one element in the social system itself that will push us towards this seemingly utopian goal, it is the pressure of teaching and the pressure of teachers. We have already noted the impact of teaching on the content of what is taught. One would like to stir up a revolt of the teachers, and especially teachers below the graduate level, against the unsatisfactory nature of much of the content that they are expected to teach. Here again the need for a marriage of teaching and research in a single learning process has never been more clear.

The Social Sciences as a Sensitive Area

One of the most critical problems facing the institutions and the practitioners of formal education is the relationship of these institutions and persons to the world around them, which largely pays for them and yet is apt to be dominated by a folk culture with images of the world very different from those which prevail within the walls of the school or college. This problem is perhaps more nearly acute today than at any other time in human history, simply because we are in an enormous transition in the state of the human race, largely as a result of formal education and its offshoots in science. Under these circumstances, the tension between the values and images of the academic and scholastic community and those of the outside world is likely to be severe. The physical sciences and the biological sciences had to fight this battle somewhat earlier. On the whole, they won it. No longer does the outside world consider a school teaching Copernican astronomy or Einsteinian physics or Darwinian evolution to be a threat, though we sometimes forget that this was a long, hard battle and that until a recent court decision there were still two states where the teaching of evolution was formally, if ineffectually, prohibited by law. Nowhere in formal education does anybody have to teach that the earth is flat. In the social sciences, however, the equivalent of the flat-earth image is still very powerful, and people who hold such views are naturally upset by the heretical views which their children bring home from school. The kind of sophisticated images that are involved in such things as the Keynesian economics, the modern theory of the international system, or the sociology of education or religion would create tensions with less sophisticated counterparts even if no value problems were involved. All this puts the teacher of the social sciences into a peculiarly difficult position and makes the ethical problems of teaching, which arise in all disciplines, acute.

The social sciences thus occupy an area that is much more sensitive than that of the physical or biological sciences. They deal with matters that are controversial, political, and of great importance to people in their daily economic, political, and social lives. At many points the findings and concepts of the social sciences tend to run counter to those of the folk culture, and it is not surprising that opposition is aroused. These matters cannot be ignored by the teacher, for in the first place they are an essential part of the social system that he studies and teaches, and in the second place his students quite rightly come to the social sciences in the hope of finding light in the dark political, social, economic, and ethical controversies of their own day. At least part of the student dissatisfaction in universities, which is showing some signs of getting into the high schools, arises from the conviction that students are not receiving the help they need in finding what is relevant to their own problems, both personal and political. Students feel a strong need to know more about such problems as the draft, the war, urban decay, poverty, racial discrimination, taxation and public expenditure. The teacher of the social sciences simply cannot pretend that these problems do not exist. Neither can he claim that the social sciences give simple and unequivocal answers to them.

DIFFERING VALUE SYSTEMS

The problem arises partly, as we have seen, because the value system of the scientific and academic communities tends to be different from that of the world around them. Science first arose in a small European subculture, which developed an unusual value system putting a high value on curiosity, openness, and veracity and a low value on any authority but that of evidence. These values are not characteristic of many folk cultures or even of many fairly well developed political cultures. They are not characteristic, for instance, of the international system, where secrecy rather than openness is the rule, power is more highly valued than truth, and veracity is valued only if it serves the purposes of power. In the business community, in the labor movement, and even in the church, the system of ethical priorities may differ in quite important respects from the ethical system of science. The teacher of the social sciences especially must be self-conscious of these matters and is under an almost Hippocratic obligation to encourage the growth of a similar self-consciousness in students. Self-consciousness in any shape, however, may be the enemy of certain folk values. I recall, for instance, being in the company of some anthropologists on the Fourth of July when the fireworks were starting in the town square and overhearing one say to another, "Let's go down and see the tribal rites." A good, simple-minded patriot might well be scandalized at hearing his sacred observances compared to tribal rites. The acids of self-consciousness, however, are always eating away at traditional legitimacies, and as one of the principal objects of the social sciences is to create social self-consciousness, the threat to ancient legitimacies, which this postulates, may be quite real.

SOCIAL SCIENCES AND ETHICS

One of the most delicate and important problems in social science is its relation to ethical principles and practices. There is little agreement, indeed, on the nature of its responsibility for them. There are those who argue that this is something that should be left entirely to the folk culture, that formal education has no responsibility for the development of ethical principles for the inculcation of ethical conduct, and that the social sciences have no more responsibility for this than do any other fields. This view seems to me unrealistic. In the first place, it is virtually impossible to change the "image of fact" in the mind of a person without at the same time changing his image of value. Our evaluations of the world and our preferences depend on our total view of what the world is like. If a student learns in the family that the earth is flat, we cannot teach him in school that the earth is round without creating a whole set of readjustments of his value system, for if he believes his school teacher he will have to adjust to the fact that his parents are in error. He will have less respect for the opinions of his parents, whatever respect he may have for their persons, and his whole value system is very likely to take a subtle shift, for he is very likely to have less respect for his family's preferences in general. The great debate about indoctrination, which has been going on in educational circles for two generations, cannot be resolved by pretending that we can have a value-free education.

A further problem arises, as we have noted above, because science itself has a strong ethical base and cannot exist without strong ethical principles, which may easily run into conflict with the ethical principles of the culture around it. Any kind of epistemological process involves some kind of payoff. Human learning, indeed, is inconceivable without a set of preferences. Wherever there is a set of preferences that is assumed to have some sort of universal validity, or at least to go beyond those tastes that are purely personal and about which there is supposed to be no disputing, an ethical system is involved. Knowledge without ethics, and education without ethics, are therefore inconceivable. The principle that scientists and educators simply take their ethical systems from the community around them is untenable. This forces the question: Does the social scientist, as representing that segment of the intellectual, scientific, and educational community that specializes in the study of social systems, have a special responsibility for the formulation, or even the propagation, of ethical principles that are appropriate for the educational enterprise? This is a view which most social scientists would reject, probably on the grounds that their concern is only with what is, not with what ought to be. This, however, assumes a naive epistemology. We cannot get to know things simply by comparing our images with reality, for as Hume pointed out a long time ago, this cannot be done; images can only be compared with images. The scientific method is not a method of discovering truth. It is a method for organizing feedback from error and so, if hopes are realized, for approaching truth by progressively eliminating error. The proposition that we should eliminate error, however, is an ethical proposition, one indeed which can even be called into question; for the proposition that under some circumstances ignorance may be bliss is not one that can be disproved easily, if at all.

Furthermore, the society's ethical principles profoundly affect its preferences, its decisions, its behavior, and hence its dynamic course. Even the social scientist who eschews admonition and exhortation, or thinks he does, cannot avoid studying the impact of the ethical principles on society, for these are an essential part of his subject matter. What is more, insofar as he is interested in teaching and learning as a social system, he should have a special interest in the ethical principles that are appropriate to this social system because he is a participant in it. If he believes in self-improvement and in improving his own performance as a teacher, he should be willing to scrutinize his own behavior, not only in the light of the general folk ethic to which he adheres, but in the light of his image as a social scientist studying the teaching-learning process.

The Quakers have developed an ingenious method of collective ethical analysis in their *queries,* a set of loaded questions intended in these days primarily for self-examination but also continually revised to meet the consensus of the group. Thus, the query has a certain advantage over the *commandment,* in that even the query itself may be questioned. Hence, it leads to ethical analysis rather than to dogma. The following queries for teachers are therefore intended to provoke ethical analysis, and they are, of course, relevant to all teachers. Social scientists, however, may have a peculiar responsibility for seeking further knowledge about the implied social system.

1. Do I abuse my position of superior status to the student by treating him as a moral or social inferior?

The problem of the relevance of the status structure of the classroom, or more generally the problem of the teacher-student relationship, to success in the teaching-learning process is one that needs much further study. To a certain extent the teacher-student relationship, by its very nature, is hierarchical, in that a teacher is supposed to know more than a student or at least he is supposed to teach the student more than the student teaches him. In an unbalanced exchange of this kind, hierarchy always arises. Furthermore, in the organization of education the teacher is usually in a superior position in the threat system. He can threaten a student with failure as a student much more effectively than the student can threaten him with failure as a teacher. He grades the student, the student does not usually grade him. This is the kind of situation in which arises the possibility of abuse. We need to know much more about the effect of exploitation of status on the learning process. We need to know more, for instance, about the effects of bullying and sarcasm in blocking learning. On the other hand, it is also possible that too much emphasis on equality of status between the teacher and the student, by making the student inattentive or disrespectful and unwilling to accept what the teacher has to say, may also diminish the effectiveness of the learning process. One of the principal research problems here is the measurement and detection of these status attitudes. At the moment they are never clearly defined in the evaluation of the teacher, and because of this many teachers who do enormous damage to the learning process may be employed.

2. Am I careful to avoid using my authority to force factual accep-

tance of propositions which may be only opinion or hypothesis? Do I tolerate honest disagreement? Would I be pleased if I were ever proved to be wrong by a student?

This question is closely related to the first. The authority of the teacher, because he is also the examiner or judge, is dangerously great, and the teacher may be unwilling to accept challenge to his authority, either from his students or from the world around him. It is part of the myth of science that authority comes only from the "real world," not from authoritative persons, past or present. It is not easy for any kind of scientist to convey this in the classroom where the status symbols—the desk, the podium, the blackboard—all reinforce the authority of the teacher rather than the authority of the subject matter itself. One could visualize some interesting experimental work in this field with a view to finding out what kind of teaching produces the scientific ethic and what kind produces the authoritarian ethic.

3. Do I express my overt or covert hostility to my students in my teaching? Am I irritated by student failure, or am I quick to detect and encourage growth in knowledge and understanding, however slow or imperfect?

This query raises the question of the personality of the teacher, rather than of his attitude toward status, although the two are clearly related, for hostile people have a strong tendency to seek authoritarian status. It would be interesting to know whether teaching attracts more hostile personalities than other occupations. We might well find that teachers are sharply bimodal, that some are attracted into the profession because they find the transmission of knowledge pleasurable. These people are likely to be friendly, rather than hostile, toward the student. Others, however, may enter the profession because they have failed elsewhere. One recalls Bernard Shaw's unkind crack "Those who can, do. Those who cannot, teach." Teachers who are frustrated executives or politicians are very likely to work out their frustrations and hostilities on the students, and this may be damaging to the learning process. Here again, an instrument which would detect this kind of hostility and frustration would be of great value, for the teacher who is both hostile and authoritarian may be enormously damaging.

4. Am I myself interested in the subject matter that I am teaching? Do I enjoy learning more about it, and do I carry over to the student my own enthusiasm for the subject?

There is a widespread belief that a teacher's enthusiasm for his subject can compensate for a good many deficiencies in his technique. A famous example of this was John R. Commons of the University of Wisconsin, who is reported to have been a very poor lecturer; yet he inspired a whole generation of students who were active, for instance, in developing the New Deal and who in many ways changed the face of America. The negative proposition is probably more easily demonstrated than the positive one; certainly the teacher who is bored with his own subject makes life miserable for his students as well as for himself. For this reason, there is much to be said for rotating courses among teachers, so that nobody teaches the same course for too long.

5. Do I convey to my students both the setting and the significance of my subject matter, so that it appears neither isolated nor irrelevant?

This query is closely related to the previous one, though it covers a slightly different point. A teacher may often be enthusiastic about his own particular speciality, without himself appreciating adequately where it stands in the great republic of learning and what its broad significance may be. There is a certain division of opinion here between those who favor orderly presentation of subject matter and those who believe that the main function of the teacher is to digress, assuming that the textbook is usually orderly enough and that the function of the teacher is to introduce a little creative disorder by showing the student that no subject is as tidy as it seems.

6. Do I convey to the student the necessity for intellectual discipline and a sense of the need for hard work on difficult intellectual tasks if the practical problems of our society are to be solved?

This query should perhaps be particularly addressed to idealistic teachers who have idealistic students. Good will is a complement, not a substitute, for good knowledge. Likewise, euphoria is a very poor substitute for truth. While dullness has a strong claim to being considered as the most deadly sin of the teacher, excitement in itself is not always a virtue, for it may distract people from doing the hard, slogging work that is always necessary for the mastery of a difficult subject. There is a delicate problem of balance here. The teacher, especially in the social sciences, can easily discourage the idealist too greatly by pointing out the extraordinary difficulties that lie in the way of good social change. Like Hamlet, we need to avoid being "sicklied o'er with the pale cast of thought." The teacher in the social sciences, especially, has to walk a difficult tightrope between the kind of despair and atrophy of the moral sense that sometimes comes from overintellectualization and the hyperactivity that can easily be destructive of those who are both morally aroused and proudly ignorant.

7. Do I convey to the student the importance of technical skill and, at the same time, leave him problem-oriented rather than technique-oriented, the master and not the servant of the skills which he has acquired?

This query, again, is closely related to the preceding one, but it is addressed to what is the particular vice of the social sciences, especially of economics. Techniques usually arise in response to problems, and certainly one needs to encourage the use of the best intellectual tools. On the other hand, techniques tend to have a certain life of their own and to become ends in themselves. This is particularly true of advanced statistical and mathematical techniques. Furthermore, the ability to use a technique and to develop technical skill becomes a point of professional pride and a measure of professional achievement. This is dangerous if it leads to an evaluation on the basis of ability to manipulate existing techniques, rather than from the point of view of ability to struggle with the "real world." The danger of technique-oriented education is that it creates what Veblen called "trained incapacity"—persons who are trained exclusively in techniques prefer to do only the things that can be done with the techniques that they have learned rather than to tackle jobs that may be more important but that are unresponsive to their existing tools, like a surgeon insisting on using his scalpel to dig away a snowdrift. The teacher often tends to underrate what he does not understand and overrate what he does understand, and it is hard for him to walk a tightrope between these two extremes.

8. Is my relation to other teachers one of cooperation in a great common task of transmitting and extending the knowledge structure of society, or am I jealous and suspicious of others? Am I conscious of my citizenship in the academic community? Do I insist on doing only those things that will lead to my personal advancement?

This query raises large and difficult issues. Advancement in the academic community rarely comes from good teaching. Still more rarely does it come from doing the necessary "menial" intellectual labor of the academic community. In the absence of an economic system that rewards good teaching directly there is great necessity for constant reiteration of the ethical principles of what constitutes good citizenship in the academic community. Communities, however, may be subject to "ethical strain" where the organization of the community, and especially of the reward structure, does not conform to real interests and productivities. Ethical strain is a much neglected area in the social sciences—indeed, the concept is hardly recognized. We are becoming intensely aware of it, however, in such problems as economic development, relations with government, and the power structure in general. Hypocrisy, subterfuge, and corruption are visible symptoms of ethical strain. The social sciences may perhaps make an important contribution to solving this problem by pointing out that the answer to ethical strain may not lie in stepping up the level of exhortation and preaching. It may lie, rather, in reorganizing the institutions and the payoffs of society itself. This is as true inside the academic community as it is outside it. It is one of the paradoxes of the social sciences, indeed, that whereas social science is used to study practically every tribe and every form of human organization and relationship, the one great unstudied area is the university itself, perhaps because it is too close to home. A much more serious social science study of educational organizations than we have had in the past should clearly be on the agenda for the future.

9. Do I have a proper sense of my own dignity as a teacher and researcher, and do I have an equivalent sense of the dignity of all those with whom I come in contact?

This query perhaps summarizes all the others. Unless the teacher has a sense of his own worth and of the importance of his task, he should be doing something else.

I am content to leave the matter at this point and to conclude with a personal testimony that for thirty-five years I have found teaching, with all its frustrations and difficulties, to be a very good life, and I expect the situation to continue in the future.

TECHNOLOGY AND
THE CHANGING SOCIAL ORDER

*In: The Urban-Industrial Frontier: Essays on Social
Trends and Institutional Goals in Modern Communities,*
David Popenoe, ed. New Brunswick, N.J.: Rutgers Univ. Press, 1969

Technology and the Changing Social Order

When we look at the larger dynamics of society as it is spread out in human history it is by no means easy to tell where technology leaves off and society begins. The world social system, which I have sometimes called the "sociosphere," consists of all three billion human beings, the knowledge and skills that they possess, the roles that they occupy and the organizations in which they participate, plus the changes in all these things and the actions and interactions, the inputs into and outputs from all these "behavior units," both of commodities and of communications. This is a very large and complex system. We must not forget to include within it also all human artifacts and certain relevant parts of the physical environment. It is not easy to distinguish a part of this system and call it "technology." Technology is certainly much more than the artifacts, the houses, machines, tools, automobiles, etc., which surround people and which people use. It consists also of the skills and habits of people who use these artifacts, for the artifacts themselves are useless unless people know how to use them. In this sense we have to think of the individual human being as himself in large part an artifact, the genetic contribution toward which many have been made by almost completely unskilled labor, but in which the skills and knowledge are largely acquired by processes which themselves involve investment in skill and knowledge. If we think of technology therefore as ways of doing things, it is very hard to draw any line between what is technology and what is society. The two concepts seem almost identical. There is a technology for praying as well as for plowing, for producing poetry as well as producing potatoes, for controlling fears as well as for controlling floods.

Even if we succeed in differentiating, shall we say, material technology from the rest of society it is evident that the interactions between the two segments of the social system, that is, between what we have defined as technology and the rest of it, are so intimate and complex that we are still really dealing with a single system. Even if one is the chicken and the other is the egg, it is hard to tell which is which, for they succeed each other with such rapidity that they blur. Society produces technology, technology produces society in an endless mesh of action and interaction.

No matter how we define the technological segment of the social system it is clear that behind all technological and social change is the process of increasing human knowledge. Even the set of human artifacts, what the economist knows as "capital," consists in a very real sense of human knowledge imposed and impressed on the physical world. Every artifact originated in an idea in some human mind. It has been created because of some human skill both in production and in organization. However, artifacts help to produce and increase knowledge just as knowledge produces the artifact. The invention of writing, for instance, and the artifacts that permit it, such as clay tablets, papyrus, paper, styluses and pens, permitted the storing of human knowledge on a scale previously impossible. With writing, the past can speak to the present and the present to the future, and mankind becomes integrated into a much larger knowledge structure than is possible with merely oral communication. The invention of printing enabled existing written knowledge to be propagated to a much larger portion of the population than previously. The invention of radio and television as McLuhan has suggested makes the world into a single village, or perhaps only into a single mob. As knowledge increases it becomes embodied in artifacts, memory banks of books and libraries, and increased human skills which permit an even more rapid increase. It is this fact of increase leading to still more rapid increase that creates the peculiar dynamic instabilities of social systems and that has created in our day what may be described as a "knowledge explosion."

The progressive increase of knowledge which is so characteristic of social systems, at least beyond a certain point of take-off
in the neolithic, represents as it were a gear change in the whole
evolutionary process. All evolution, whether biological or social,
is a process whereby mutation and selection lead to increasingly
complex and improbable structures. It is only stretching the
meaning of the word a little to say that as we move from
hydrogen to helium, from the large molecule to the virus, from
the virus to the cell, or from the cell to the many-celled organisms
and from these to the vertebrates and from these to man, there
is an increase in knowledge at each step. What is going on in
the social system, therefore, is merely an acceleration of the total
process of evolution, created by the extraordinary capacity for
knowledge of the human nervous system.

We can, if we wish, make a distinction between pure knowledge and technology, the former being simply "know-what" and
the latter being "know-how." This distinction, however, like that
between technology and society itself is arbitrary and not easy
to draw and each process leads so much into the other that we
again have a chicken-egg blur. Nevertheless, one can perhaps
point to a certain watershed in history which I would put about
1860, some would put it perhaps a hundred years earlier, before
which the dominating force in technological change was what
might be called folk knowledge and folk technology arising out
of the practical and ordinary experiences of mankind, and after
which the enormous dynamic inherent in the specialized process
of increase in scientific knowledge became dominant and pulled
technology along behind it.

We can certainly trace in the last 10,000 years, or even before,
a slow but accelerating process of improvement in folk technology. The great irreversible step was the domestication of
crops and livestock and the invention of agriculture. According
to one authority, this increased the average life span from about
thirty-two years to thirty-eight. This meant a substantial reduction in the rate of consumption of knowledge by death and hence
permitted a slow, steady increase both in technological skill and
in an unsystematic but useful folk knowledge of materials, plants,
animals, minerals, chemical reactions, and so on. The rise of
metallurgy, the development of writing, the so-called urban
revolution, involving the rise of cities, all seem to have followed

directly from the food surpluses that agriculture permitted. Civilization, especially imperial civilization, indeed may even have been a setback in the sense that it often reduced the average length of life, created a highly stratified society and confined reading and writing to small priestly classes who were often much more interested in the perpetuation of their own privileges than in the extension of knowledge itself. There is a good deal of evidence, for instance, that it was the collapse of the Roman Empire in the West that started off a new surge of improving technology after four hundred years of technological stagnation. The Christian monastic orders seem to have played an important role both in the development and spread of technological improvements. Christianity, by reason of its humble origin among carpenters, fishermen, and tentmakers, undoubtedly raised the status of common labor and of the artisan. Its emphasis on the reality and sacredness of the material world also opened the way for technological improvements. These factors seem to outweigh the impact of the ascetic spirit and the eschatological world view which by themselves would be unfavorable to development.

Constantine seems to have marked the end of the Roman stagnation and the beginning of a long slow improvement in pre-scientific technology which culminated in the so-called industrial revolution of the eighteenth century. It was only in the West, of course, that Christianity was important. In the same period China had an even more rapid rate of development than Europe, and from about the time of Christ to the sixteenth century China was not only the most developed society technologically but also was the source of many technological exports to the West.

The rise of science as a separate and legitimated subculture eventually introduces a higher gear again into the rate of technological evolution. The significant date here is 1660, the foundation of the Royal Society in London, for it represents the legitimation of the scientific subculture. The eighteenth century saw the early beginnings of the impact of science on technology; the reciprocating steam engine probably owed something to Boyle's Law, although the real theory of the steam engine, that is, thermodynamics, did not come along until 1824, almost one hundred years after the steam engine itself. I am inclined myself to regard the development of the eighteenth century as the culmination of the long growth of folk technology, though one must admit that the successful steam engine was a very great step forward. This represented the first time that man had actually created a source of power instead of simply utilizing the powers of nature around him, as in the water wheel or in the windmill, which, incidentally, came surprisingly late, the first recorded mention being about 1180.

It was not until 1860, however, that science-based technology really began to get under way with the development of the chemical industry, which would have been quite impossible without Dalton and Kekulé. A little later comes the electrical industry, which would have been impossible without Faraday, Ohm, and Clark-Maxwell. An even more striking example, of course, is the nuclear industry, which would have been impossible without Bohr and Einstein. We now seem to be on the edge of an enormous expansion of industries based upon biology, of which the spectacular rise in the productivity of agriculture in the last generation may be only the foretaste.

Rates of development in earlier periods of course cannot be measured exactly and must be in part a matter of speculation. It at least illustrates the enormous order of magnitude of the change through which we are going, to suppose that whereas in the paleolithic period it is doubtful whether knowledge doubled in fifty thousand years, in the neolithic period it may have doubled in two thousand years, in the period of civilization it may have doubled every thousand years or less, and in the modern world in many sciences it doubles every fifteen or twenty-five years. We see this process reflected also in the rise of per capita income, which is closely related to the stock of knowledge. In the paleolithic period it may be doubted whether the per capita income changed at all in a hundred thousand years, if indeed the concept has any meaning. After the invention of agriculture and in the age of civilization it may perhaps have doubled every one to three thousand years. In the eighteenth and early nineteenth centuries in the advanced countries it may have doubled in a hundred years. From 1860 on we are on firmer statistical grounds. In the most rapidly developing countries, such as Sweden, Japan, and the United States, the per capita income doubled every thirty years. In Japan since 1946 the per capita real income has approximately doubled every eight years. By comparison we may note incidentally that it took the United States thirty-five years before 1966 to double its per capita income, but the United States is now rich enough perhaps to be a slowpoke. The change even from the nineteenth to the twentieth century in this regard, however, is highly significant. At the best nineteenth century rates of development the children were twice as rich as the parents. At the Japanese rate of development the children may be six times as rich as the parents, and it is not surprising that in Japan they say that it is not only that the parents cannot understand the children, the sophomores cannot understand the freshmen! Whether society can stand a rate of development so enormous without shaking itself apart still remains to be seen.

Even if we do not separate technology sharply from the rest of society we may distinguish within both technology and society a number of subsystems, each of which has a certain dynamic of its own but each of which also interacts with the others. I am suspicious of any monistic interpretation of history that seeks to argue that any one of these subsystems dominates all the others. Neither material technology, as Marx thought, nor a religious and moral technology, as Max Weber suggested, nor biological, genetic, or racial determinants necessarily dominate the others. We can think of history as a kind of layer cake in which a number of different layers run side by side through time, each with a dynamic of its own, and yet each from time to time profoundly penetrating and interacting with others. One layer, and a very thick layer, is that of material technology, consisting of human artifacts, and the way in which human beings interact with them. This layer has undoubtedly a good deal of independence. We can see, for instance, how the automobile could not have come along much before the end of the nineteenth century because the technological prerequisites were not fulfilled, in the shape, for instance, of rubber technology for the tires, fine machining for the cylinders and pistons, gasoline for the fuel, electrical technology for the spark, and so on. On the other hand, we can also see, especially after the event, that when all these prerequisites have been fulfilled the probability of inventing the automobile was very high indeed. Once the automobile is invented we are not surprised to find a substantial pressure for the improvement of road technology, and we would certainly not be surprised to find a decline of the horse and the horse-based technologies.

Material technology indeed frequently proceeds by a kind of dialectical process with a continuous temporary imbalance in which one invention creates an imbalance in the system in the form of particular scarcities that stimulate another invention to correct the imbalance. The development of spinning and weaving seems to have been an interesting example of this principle. Each improvement in spinning would create a demand for improvement in weaving, and each improvement in weaving would create a demand for improvement in spinning.

Parallel to the development of material technology we have also the development of what might be called social technology. Social artifacts and social inventions are just as real and may be even more important than material artifacts and material inventions. The invention of representative government, for instance, which is a slow process stretching over the centuries, enormously increased the capacity and power of the state and its ability to legitimate its actions. The social invention of the corporation in the eighteenth and nineteenth centuries had an enormous effect on economic development and on the scale of economic organizations without which a great many of the technical developments of the nineteenth and twentieth centuries would have been impossible. Social inventions often have consequences far beyond their intent. A good example of this is the deductible-at-source income tax which was invented almost as a by-product of war finance, but has turned out to be a very powerful social stabilizer, introducing a cybernetic element into the economy that can check both inflation and deflation, especially if the tax is progressive. In an inflation taxes rise currently faster than incomes as people move into the upper brackets which creates government surpluses and checks the inflation; in the case of deflation taxes decline faster than incomes which produces government deficits and stops the deflation. This simple little device may have done more to create the economic success of the post-World War II period than any amount of specific planning.

A very important segment of the stream of social technology which perhaps deserves a label as a subsystem of its own is the stream of ideological and moral invention. Religious and ideological systems tend to have a certain dynamic of their own, following a kind of corruption-reformation cycle. The rise of a new ideology often has profound effects on all other social systems.

These symbolic mutations are virtually impossible to predict and
we do not understand very much about what it is even that
makes for survival. Why, for instance, did Christianity survive
in late Roman times, when Mithraism did not? Why did Islam
and the Koran appeal so much to the Arabs and the desert
peoples, and Christianity and the Bible appeal more to people in
moist temperate climates? How do we account for the extraordinary impact of an almost unreadable book such as Marx's
Kapital or a curious work like the *Book of Mormon?* How do we
account for something like the spectacular rise of Soka Gakki in
modern Japan, in which a small obscure sect of Nichiren Buddhism suddenly blooms into a powerful quasi-political organization of three million people! We have to confess, I think, that we
know very little about the dynamics of symbolic systems, and we
must always be prepared to be surprised by them; that they have
a dynamic of their own, however, can hardly be doubted.

Many other subdivisions of the social system could undoubtedly be identified. The three mentioned above, however, which
we might perhaps call material technology, social technology,
and moral technology, serve to illustrate the complexity of the
interaction among the subsystems. The material here is so rich,
indeed, that we must content ourselves with a few examples.

An example which is peculiarly relevant to the purposes of
this symposium is the close relationship between agricultural
technology and the rise of cities. It is only the development of a
food surplus from the food producer, made possible by agriculture, that created the conditions for the existence of cities at all.
Food surplus alone, however, is not enough. There have been
many societies with a food surplus and no cities. The rise of cities
demands essentially social inventions, probably indeed moral and
ideological inventions. The social invention is the development
of political structures of legitimated coercion. These in turn are
related closely to the development of religious ideologies to assist
in this legitimation. In the age of classical civilization the cities
produced very little to exchange for the food that the food producer gives them. Civilization quite literally is founded on agriculture and exploitation. The exploitation, however, is itself a
social invention without which the material technology would
have quite different results.

The scientific revolution has had an enormous impact on agriculture. The so-called "agricultural revolution"—development of the turnip, of artificial grasses, and the four-course rotation which intertilled crops made possible—began in Western Europe at the end of the seventeenth and beginning of the eighteenth century. Even though this movement, like the "industrial revolution," was also in a way prescientific, it laid the foundation for almost all subsequent development. It increased the food supply, it particularly increased the supply of proteins through better animal feed, it improved animal breeding, it diminished mortality, especially infant mortality, and was perhaps the major factor in the enormous expansion of the northwest European peoples in the following two or three centuries. Here again the technological developments would have been unsuccessful if it had not been for the enclosures, that is, the creation of unified farms, which is really a social invention. As we move into the period of true scientific technology we find a social invention in the United States, the land-grant college, playing an enormous role in the spectacular improvements in agricultural technology of the last hundred years and the subsequent release of a large proportion of the agricultural labor force to manufacturing and to tertiary industries.

It is irresistibly tempting to note a few more examples of the interaction of material and social technology even though they may be a little exaggerated. The stirrup and the rein, for instance, reached Europe after the fall of Rome, almost certainly from China by way of Central Asia. The impact of this apparently simple and obvious invention was enormous. Without it chivalry and the whole apparatus of medieval knighthood would have been much more difficult, for it is hard to have a knight who cannot stay on a horse. The Romans, indeed, could not do anything very energetic on horseback without falling off. A similar connection can be made between the horse collar (which arrived in Europe about the same time, or perhaps a little later) and the great agricultural and building improvements of the tenth and eleventh centuries. The Romanesque and even the Gothic cathedral are a direct outcome of the increased agricultural surplus and draft power that resulted from the horse collar, together, again, with some social inventions, like the three-field system. Eventually, indeed, it has been argued, the horse collar abolished slavery simply because a horse that could pull things was so much better at slave work than a man. The sternpost rudder is another example of what seems like a very obvious invention which came very late. It is first noted in China in the eighth century and in Europe at the end of the twelfth century. It undoubtedly had enormous consequences in enabling ships to travel much longer distances, and it played a great role in the expansion of Europe around the Cape of Good Hope eastward to Asia and across the Atlantic to America. Given a rudder so that he could set a course and steer in a reasonably straight line, it was hard to see how Columbus could miss America.

It is clear that many examples can be cited in which the stream of material technology seems to have been the prime mover in historical development. Other examples can be given, however, as we have seen above, in which social, economic, and political inventions were the prime movers, and led to expansions in material technology. It is hard to evaluate social inventions such as the patent system, but there is little doubt that it has had a marked effect on the acceleration of material invention. Similarly, social inventions such as public education and, in more recent years, organizations like the National Science Foundation are examples where social invention has had enormous consequences on the material world. Man's adventure into outer space, indeed, is a result not of the dynamics of material invention so much as a peculiar dynamic of conflict and emulation between two great powers.

The impact of invention in the moral, religious, ideological, and symbolic sphere is harder to trace, but there can be little doubt that at times it has been enormous. The impact of Islam, for instance, in creating a great civilization within which the scientific achievements of the Greeks were preserved at a time when they might easily have been lost in disorganized Europe undoubtedly advanced technology in the material world. The thesis of Max Weber regarding the impact of Protestantism and especially of Calvinism not only on social inventions such as capitalism but on material inventions which this in turn generated is well known, even if in detail it is open to criticism. The impact of Marxism on the spread of science-based technology has been very substantial even if it has not produced any great innovations in its own right. Further examples could be multiplied, and the principle of mutual interaction of the different levels of technology seems to be secure. Nevertheless the impact or even the very existence of social and moral technologies frequently is unrecognized or at least underestimated, and it can hardly be emphasized too strongly that these stand at least on a par with material technology in the total social process.

In all this complex hurly-burly of interacting systems what do we identify as the "social order" which is supposed to be the second main theme of this essay? Just as we had considerable difficulty in separating technology from the total social system we may find some difficulty in defining the social order in a way that does not take in practically everything. Nevertheless, if we wish to identify a portion of the social system which is particularly relevant to the problem of social order we may perhaps identify a segment of the social system that I have come to call the "integrative system." This is the segment of the social system that deals with such matters as community, identity, status, legitimacy, loyalty, and love. This is a recognizable and identifiable segment of the social system, even though, like all other segments, it shades off into others and is in constant interaction with the other segments. It has, furthermore, a certain inner dynamic of its own, as well as receiving inputs and giving outputs to other systems. The problem of the rise of ideological systems and the social institutions based on them which we have noted above is closely connected with the problem of the dynamics of legitimacy and community. In spite of my previous warnings against making any particular segment of the social system dominant, I find a strong temptation to argue for the dominance of the integrative system over the others, and especially for the dynamics of legitimacy as the key to almost anything else that goes on in social dynamics. The argument is simply that no institution can survive the loss of legitimacy in either of its two major senses, inward legitimacy in the sense of justification on the part of the people who operate the institution, and outward legitimacy or acceptance on the part of the people who constitute its environment. Legitimacy grows slowly and it can collapse quickly. It may be produced by age, by charisma, by appropriate symbolic rhetoric, by linkages with other legitimacies, and also by sacrifice, for we cannot deny the legitimacy of what we make sacrifices for without a threat to our own identity. Legitimacy, however, can collapse very quickly, once

an institution ceases to pay off in some sense. Thus in Europe
the legitimacy of absolute monarchy collapsed, between 1640
and 1920, and the monarchs who survived did so only by abandoning their political power and becoming "mere" symbols of
legitimacy. Similarly, in the twentieth century the legitimacy of
empires collapsed. The Reformation, over a large part of Christendom, led to the sudden collapse of the legitimacy of the Pope,
perhaps because he tried to hang on to temporal and spiritual
power too long!

There are interesting questions regarding the technology of
the integrative system as we see it in the organization of religion,
the establishment, and legitimation of the institution of the family,
and the great amount that is invested in the legitimation of the
national state, through education and the public sacrifice of
soldiers. It is interesting to look at political institutions primarily
in terms of the technology of legitimation, although considerations of space make it illegitimate for us to pursue this theme
much further.

What is clear is that there are large mutual interactions between the integrative system in its various aspects and the other
continuing dynamic systems of society. Changes in material technology profoundly affect the integrative system. Thus it seems
plausible to link the development of gunpowder and firearms
with the loss of legitimacy of the feudal baron and the city-state.
The rise of the affluent society and the impact of science-based
material technology has profoundly changed our attitudes toward
the legitimacy of wealth and poverty. Marxism may well have
been propagated by the railroad and destroyed by the automobile. Here again one can only make examples and give suggestions, for the relationships are enormously complex.

In conclusion, can one draw any lessons from what may seem
a rather grandiose argument, for the problem which is the immediate concern of this symposium, which is the future of the city?
The most obvious moral to be drawn from the above argument
is of course that the city must be regarded as a total system.
Today it is unquestionably reeling under the impact of the gallop-
ing dynamic of material technology. The automobile especially
has turned the city inside out and is destroying its center, as
vacant urban-renewal lots in a great many cities testify, and is
turning the ecological pattern of the city from the fan or the

TECHNOLOGY AND THE CHANGING SOCIAL ORDER   505

spoked wheel to the doughnut and the loose ring or net structure
of ribbon development. The airplane, television, radio are creating the world city, an integrated network of communications
based on airports and mass communications, while locally the
surrounding tissue decays into ghettos and slums. The need for
moral invention is clear. We have here a magnificent example of
the principle of disproportion, where inventions in material technology have created an enormous need for balancing inventions
in the social and moral order. What these inventions are going
to be, however, is hard to predict. Indeed, if we could predict
them we could have them now, and there would be no need to
invent them!

It is a familiar thesis that one of the major problems of the city
arises because it cannot expand its territory into the surrounding
suburbs. Hence the central city decays because both its potential
leadership and the tax base which that leadership might use in
rehabilitation is lost to the central city in the course of the flight
to the suburbs. The central city therefore falls back into more
and more social disorganization with a vicious cycle of deterioration, further loss of tax base, further flight of leadership outside
and so on. I cannot resist quoting a verse on the subject which
emerged in my mind at another conference recently:

> The reason why cities are ugly and sad
> Is not that the people within them are bad,
> But that most of the people who really decide
> What goes on in the city live somewhere outside.

It is easy enough to perceive the problem but it is much more
difficult to perceive the answer. Do we look, for instance, for an
expansion of the city organization into the suburbs and the surrounding territory, to bring back the lost leadership to the city
organization as it expands into the greater metropolitan area, like
Toronto or Miami? Or do we abandon the concept of the city
altogether as wholly inappropriate to the modern world, organize
a world city quite self-consciously on a national or even an international basis and then break up the old central cities into
twenty or thirty suburbs in the hope of restoring the lost sense
of community at the local level for the residual local issues?

All this is highly speculative. It merely points up the fact that
in the case of the urban problem we have an example of dis-

proportional development, with material technology having developed such an enormous dynamic that it has created an unusual need for imaginative social and moral technology which in this particular instance seems to be lagging. The question of what philosophical, religious, and ideological framework can sustain the urban world is very intriguing and also very difficult. The great world religions grew up in the age of civilization when on the whole rural life predominated and the city was seen primarily as exploitative. Christianity is a good example of this principle. Its imagery is that of the shepherd and the sheep, the sacrificial lamb, the sower and the seed, the bread and the wine, and though of all the world ideologies it seems to be the one at the moment that is most adaptable and most conscious of the necessity for change, it still does not find it easy to adapt itself to the urban world. Some of the success of communism may perhaps be attributed to the fact that it was born in the British Museum in the middle of the then largest city in the world and that it is urban to the point of being antirural. Its antirural bias, indeed, has been a real handicap to those countries which it dominates, for they have all tried to urbanize on an inadequate rural technological base, and the antirural bias has at least to bear part of the responsibility for the socialist failures in agriculture. Even in America the rural ideology is very strong. Jeffersonian democracy, rural virtue, and the family farm are deep in our political mythology, and our failure to come to grips with the problem of poverty in the cities and of urban disorganization is perhaps a hangover from our rural past. It is at this point that moral invention seems desperately necessary to give hope and significance to a drive in the direction of a better urban world.

I might end therefore on a note of mild economic optimism that where there is a demand there usually eventually develops a supply, and though the principle which I call the principle of fundamental surprise pertains in the prediction of moral invention as in any other, that is, if we could predict it we would have it now, it does not seem unreasonable to look for moral and social inventions in whatever surprising places they may arise as a key to the ongoing development of this urban world. The problem that these inventions have to solve, however, is a tough one and it lies at the heart of a great many of the difficulties of our society. It is a problem fundamentally in the nature of personal identity. In our society it is fairly easy to develop a national identity which is reinforced by the public schools and many other agencies of society. It is fairly easy also to develop what might be called a personal identity in the family, in the small peer group, in the immediate occupational environment, and so on. Many of the problems of the city rise because it requires a strong sense of identity with a community that lies somewhere between the nation and the family or the peer group. This intermediate identity seems very hard to develop, especially in a society as mobile as ours in which people ordinarily do not stay all their lives in the places in which they were born and hence do not develop a strong sense of identity with a particular locality. It may be that there is no answer to this problem at the level of the urban community and that we must seek the answer in a reformation either of the national or personal identities, or maybe both. How this reformation can come about, however, is a mystery which only the future can reveal.

THE ROLE OF LEGITIMACY
IN THE DYNAMICS OF SOCIETY

University Park, Pa.: Pennsylvania State Univ.,
Center for Research, College of Bus. Admin., 1969, 13 pp.

THE ROLE OF LEGITIMACY IN THE DYNAMICS OF SOCIETY

The problem of legitimacy, and especially of the dynamic processes by which legitimacy is acquired or lost, is one of the most important single elements in the whole intricate process of the social system. Nevertheless, the study of legitimacy is surprisingly neglected, and there is very little general realization among social scientists, especially among economists, of its importance. There is good reason for this neglect. When legitimacy is granted, we tend to take it for granted. It becomes part of that unquestioned substructure of social life which we never think about at all because it is never questioned. The highest degree of legitimacy indeed is precisely that which is never thought about. Legitimacy, therefore, only comes into view, as it were, at precisely the moment when it is most likely to disappear. In this respect, it is a bit like the metal sodium, which bursts into flame when it is exposed to air; therefore, it is never found in a state of nature, but has to be found in a highly artificial environment. To vary the metaphor, legitimacy is like the air that we breathe; we only notice it when it is not there.

The essence of legitimacy is *acceptance*. It exhibits two forms — internal legitimacy and external legitimacy. Internal legitimacy means the acceptance of a person in his own role or his own identity as essentially satisfactory and worthy of continuation. It is thus equivalent to morale or "nerve," in the sense of the expression "a loss of nerve." Here again it is highly significant that we only notice nerve when we have lost it; otherwise we take it for granted. External legitimacy means acceptance of a role, a person, an identity, an organization, or an institution by those other people who constitute its significant environment. Internal and external legitimacy are, of course, very closely related, for each tends to create the other. A reigning monarch who is constantly surrounded by people who believe in his power or even his wisdom is likely to acquire a good deal of self-confidence and internal legitimacy as a result. The person who is thought to be no good by everybody around him soon comes to accept that judgment. On the other side of the relationship, a person who has an unshakable self-confidence and an overwhelming sense of his own personal legitimacy is apt to inspire confidence in others and soon creates the external legitimacy which is necessary for his operation.

The significance of legitimacy lies in the fact that without it no continuing social operation or continuing role or organization is possible. A temporary organization can be created without legitimacy. A bandit, for instance, creates a highly temporary social organization at gun point which results in temporary roles of giver and receiver. If he collects money every week, however, he will either have to be a rent collector or a tax collector. The role of the victim will have to be legitimated.

There are complicated relationships between legitimacy and legality. One of the principal functions of the law is to establish legitimacy. The two concepts are not the same. Law, for instance, may be regarded as illegitimate by large numbers of people, in which case it usually becomes unenforceable and a dead letter. Decisions of judges are not always regarded as legitimate, as they may not be, for instance, in a colonial situation. The mere forms of the law are not sufficient for the resolution of conflicts. This is one of the problems in international law; it is apt to be deficient in general acceptance. On the other hand, law does tend to create the legitimacy which supports it. Organizations which do not create the legitimacy necessary to support them tend to disappear, so there is a strong process of natural selection to produce strong correlations among law, constitutionality, and legitimacy. Nevertheless, this relationship is not infrequently broken, as, for instance, in revolution. We can say, however, with some confidence, that any institution requires a minimum degree of legitimacy before it can function. Either this minimum must be created by the institution, or it must be created elsewhere in the system. Legitimacy, therefore, is not merely a matter of following rules, as, for instance, in the succession of a monarch or the election of a president or legislature, because there is always a further question as to whether the rules themselves are legitimate. Having a rule of almost any kind is a factor which tends to create legitimacy, but it is by no means always enough.

We have seen many examples in history of institutions where

legitimacy has been eroded, often leading to the collapse of the institutions, though at the summit of their power they seem to be almost impregnable. The great fallacy of taking legitimacy for granted is that men tend to think that wealth (exchange capability) or power (threat capability) are self-legitimating, that is, capable of providing their own legitimacy. Sometimes this is true, sometimes it is not. Predictions of social systems which neglect any conscious consideration of legitimacy occasionally have produced quite disastrous mistakes. Historically, legitimacy is what business cycle theorists call a "lead variable." Its movements, if they could be identified, would tend to foreshadow both the rise and the fall of the institutions to which they refer. The only exception to this rule would be where some institution declined for purely external reasons or even accidental reasons; the very fact of its decline might then destroy its legitimacy.

Thus the institution of a hereditary monarchy and indeed the hereditary principle in general have tended to lose legitimacy over the last three or four hundred years, and with the loss of legitimacy comes the eventual loss of power. A king might be the head of a paper organization, but if people did not accept him and obey him his power would soon be eroded. Likewise, wealth can easily be destroyed, as in a socialist revolution. The underlying fluctuations of the legitimacy of parliamentary and representative institutions of government can largely foreshadow constitutional changes. Thus, with the decline in the legitimacy of the monarchy the legitimacy of parliamentary and democratic institutions rose. In some cases, however, the effectiveness of representative legislatures and the rise in the legitimacy of military organizations have led to military takeovers and dictatorships. These in turn often find their legitimacy eroded with the result that representative government is restored.

The whole concept of empire is an interesting example of the long-run erosion of legitimacy, with the rise of legitimacy of the concept of self-government and self-determination. The European empires, for instance, were quite indestructible in 1910. The fact that they have so largely disappeared from the scene is not the result of any conquest, but primarily the result of the disappearance of legitimacy, both internal and external. The imperial powers found themselves faced not only with a denial of their legitimacy on the part of their colonial peoples, but also with the increasing denial of legitimacy of empire on the part of their own people.

An illustration of the importance of legitimacy may be found in the reflection that institutions sometimes have to abandon power or even wealth in the interest of preserving it. A very good example of this would be the constitutional monarch. For the most part, only those monarchs have survived who have abandoned their political power and have become themselves symbols of legitimacy. This is clear evidence that in the long run legitimacy dominates power. One might put it simply by saying that if you lose legitimacy, you lose everything.

In understanding the dynamics of the process of legitimation and delegitimation we must look to the sources of legitimacy, what it is that makes people accept an institution, a person, or an organization. Why do some people accept themselves so wholeheartedly when other people do not? The sources of legitimacy are quite varied and we can distinguish a number of them, though they may not all pull in the same direction.

In the first place, there can be no doubt that one of the major sources of legitimacy is positive payoffs. What the payoffs are is another question and a very difficult one; an important aspect of it is how we learn to accept some things as payoffs and other things as not. We can put this question out of sight at the moment. However, suppose there is an institution which develops payoffs in terms of human welfare, and especially, one has to say, in terms of the welfare of the powerful. This institution is likely to increase and to retain its legitimacy. On the other hand, an institution which ceases to promote human welfare will tend to lose legitimacy, at least in the long run. The monarchy is a good example of this principle. In the state of society which might be described as early civilization, the hereditary principle provides a useful method of conflict resolution about competing contenders for power; it is likely to diminish the costs of conflict and hence have substantial payoffs. The hereditary principle, however, has a great flaw in that genetic inheritance is relatively unimportant, by comparison with experience and learning, in determining ability and character. The eldest son of a good king all too often turns out to be a bad king. Indeed, a crown prince growing up in the shadow of a good king is often likely to become a bad one when he comes to the throne.

As society became more complicated, and as the duties of government became more onerous and it became more of a necessity to have able people in positions of power, the net payoffs to the hereditary principle declined. Because it was inherently a poor method of selecting role occupants, the negative payoffs gradually became more important by comparison with the positive payoffs in the heredity principle's ability to resolve conflicts. As other methods of conflict resolution were devised, such as elections, the payoffs to the hereditary principle became even more strongly negative, and it very rapidly lost its legitimacy. As it lost its legitimacy, the monarchs who tried to hang on to their power and privileges in face of the increasing complexity of society frequently lost their heads; only those survived who bowed to the winds of change and became constitutional monarchs.

The second source of legitimacy may seem to be quite contradictory to the first, and indeed it introduces a number of very odd phenomena into the dynamics of the social system. This second source is *sacrifice* or negative payoffs. We make sacrifices for people and things we love, with which we have a strong personal identification, or with which our personal identity is deeply involved. Thus a parent makes sacrifices for his children because he identifies with them. They represent hopefully a piece of himself, as it were, continuing into the future. Similarly, a man may identify with his country or with his church, even with his corporation, employer, or trade union, as these organizations provide him with an identity which he would not otherwise possess. Sacrifice, however, is not only justified by an existing identity with the object or institution for which the sacrifice has been made. It frequently creates its identity which justifies it. Anything that we have made sacrifices for we feel almost compelled to identify with; otherwise the sacrifices would have been in vain, and this may be a threat to our internal legitimacy. At the low end of the moral scale, this is a fool persisting in his folly, because to admit that it is folly would be to admit that he is a fool, and this he cannot do without destroying his internal legitimacy. At the upper end of the moral scale, this is the martyr going cheerfully to death for his faith, the soldier dying for his country, the mother sacrificing for her child or even "Greater love hath no man than this, that a man should lay down his life for his friends." A sacrifice then becomes one of the most subtle, delicate, unstable, noble, and foolish sources of legitimacy. It represents the noblest heights of heroism and the lowest depths of folly attainable by man. Involved in it is what I have elsewhere called the "heroic" value system, which emphasizes the risk of sacrifice as the most ennobling activity of man and which contrasts with the "economic" ethic which counts cost and asks for reward, and hence stresses the positive payoffs.

In spite of both its reality and its virtues, sacrifice as a source of legitimacy is in grave danger of creating a perverse dynamic which can easily lead to drastic diminutions in human welfare. I have called this perverse dynamic the "sacrifice trap." If we have once made a sacrifice for any object, we find it hard to admit, without a threat to our personal identity, that the sacrifice was in vain and the object not worth the sacrifice. Consequently, any institution which even by accident has been able to evoke sacrifice is often thereby enabled to create legitimacy which will enable it to demand more sacrifice in the future. Many early religions and priesthoods, for instance, have been based on the principle of sacrifice, even of humans, which is the ultimate sacrifice. If the sacrifice is questioned, the guardians of the sacrificial object (whether this is a priesthood or a military and political caste) can always counter any arguments. They can say that the past sacrifices could not have been in vain, therefore future sacrifices will not be in vain either, even though the ultimate payoffs which the sacrifices may be intended to produce may be extremely dubious or even negative. Thus the guardians of sacrifice from the Aztec priesthood to the current patriots have always been in a good position to demand more and more sacrifices. Eventually, however, as more and more sacrifices are demanded, the demand for positive payoffs begins to dominate. A house of cards sometimes collapses almost overnight. Suddenly the emperor has no clothes, the altars are neglected, and perhaps someday somebody will give a war and nobody will come.

Beside these two major sources of legitimacy (that is, positive and negative payoffs) we should mention other subordinate sources which in particular cases may be very important. Thus, a third source of legitimacy is *age*. Age frequently has a curiously nonlinear relationship to legitimacy. New things tend to be legitimate simply because they are young and new-fashioned. Their benefits lie mainly in the future, and even though they frequently involve sacrifices in the present, they have not yet been found out! Thus they benefit from both the major sources. The new fashion, the new style, the kitten, the child have a legitimacy which is simply a function of youngness. As people, styles, and institutions get older, however, their legitimacy frequently tends to decline; it reaches a minimum in middle age, when things become old-fashioned, out-of-style, old-hat, and so on. If they can survive this trough, however, they sometimes pass into the period where legitimacy rises with age. From being old-fashioned, they graduate to being elder statemen. With institutions, especially, age seems to convey increasing legitimacy in itself, though it does not always suffice to overcome the decline of legitimacy, for instance, due to declining payoffs. As one looks at the enormous legitimacy of the Pope, however, or the emperor of Japan, one sees how institutions can pile up, as it were, a great reserve bank of legitimacy which not even the Borgias in the one case, or disastrous military defeat in the other could exhaust. On the other hand, even very ancient institutions sometimes run out of legitimacy and disappear.

Another important source of legitimacy might be described by the term *dignity*. This consists of symbolic communications which create acceptance because they are symbols of impressiveness. The crown of the monarch, the wig of the judge, the gown of the scholar or the preacher, the cope of the priest, the tails and white tie, the old school tie — and even the miniskirts and the long hair and beard of the hippie — are symbols which convey status, identity, and a plea to somebody, as it were, for acceptance and legitimacy. When somebody is dressed impressively and feels impressive, his internal legitimacy is also enhanced, and when other people see him they also are impressed and his external legitimacy is enhanced. As in the case of age, however, the relationship is sometimes nonlinear. The overdone attempt to impress can have quite the reverse effect from what is intended. The rich garments of the priest produce puritan reaction; the finery of the soldier makes him eventually look ridiculous; the ostentation of the rich produces rebellion among the poor; and even the gown of the scholar produces derision among the students. In our day especially, traditional symbols of legitimacy are strongly under attack. We all run to disguise ourselves in the uniform of the common man as his legitimacy rises.

Architecture, like clothing, is another important symbol of legitimacy. The great cathedral may maintain legitimacy for the church which owns it, even when the doctrines which produced it have faded. The Roman pillar, the dome of the Capitol, all the architectural brocade which adorns our public buildings again says to the world, "I am important, I am!" A society which feels uneasy about its legitimacy, perhaps because its payoffs are not as good as they might be, runs to monuments. One recalls Ozymandias, Augustus, Napoleon, Stalin, and even Washington. Often it has been noticed that the biggest monuments are built just at the moment before legitimacy collapses or declines, like St. Peter's, Versailles, New Delhi, and the Palace of the League of Nations. It is indeed often a sign of increasing legitimacy that the symbols of legitimacy are played down — the young illegitimate university has to build an expensive Gothic campus that pretends to be heir to the Middle Ages, but as the university becomes securely legitimate as an institution it builds shoebox buildings, devoid of the most elementary ornamentation. Banks are a particularly good example of an institution which in early days at least felt obliged to impress the public with marble palaces and Corinthian columns. Architecture, if we care to look at it critically, will provide sermons in stone at almost every main corner.

One finds the same principle also in language and literary style — the verbosity of the law may have come, as Adam Smith suggests, from the fact that lawyers have been paid by the word, but it is also an attempt to be impressive, to create legitimacy by impressing the unlearned with big words. One reflects uneasily that a science with very obvious payoffs, such as physics, does not have to bother with an elaborate vocabulary beyond its needs, whereas sociology often seems to indulge in impressive verbiage beyond the call of duty.

A fifth source of legitimacy which does not seem to be encompassed by the others might be called *charisma*. This is the capacity of an individual to inspire enormous confidence in himself and his own mission and to convey this sense of more than earthly authority to others. The founders of religions, the saints, or the prophets have this character beyond all others, for there is no source of acceptance so powerful as conviction that one derives one's legitimacy from a divine source. Political leaders, however, have had this trait in considerable degree, and even business leaders are not exempt from it. It is something which defies analysis, yet is of enormous importance in human history and in the development of what might be called symbolic systems. It is unpredictable: no one knows where it will strike next, and it is often not apparent at first. Many great religious leaders, especially, have died unnoticed by the great or powerful whose powers they were frequently to destroy eventually by the creation of a new legitimacy in which the old ruling class could not participate. Great artists, actors, and singers likewise possess this peculiar quality to a degree, and every young man in love has felt himself touched, however briefly, by its wings. For the social scientist, however, it remains one of the distressingly random elements in the social process, and while we may perhaps define various circumstances under which a new charismatic movement is likely to arise, we can never be sure that it will. In the dynamics of legitimacy a place must be found for a concept which might be called "sacred history," which might be defined as a succession of improbable events which create a powerful image of some kind of order, which in turn creates an organization and a community with great capability for transmission to successive generations, and which therefore sets in motion a "phylum" of social evolution. Christianity, Islam, Communism, and nation-states are examples of such great phyla of human history. Their origins remain of necessity inaccessible to the scientific vision.

We might define the sixth source of legitimacy as *mystery*. Closely related to charisma, it is not quite the same thing, for mystery can be contrived, while charisma cannot. Legitimacy is enhanced by the veil of the temple, the dim religious light of cathedrals, the mysteries of classified information, and the aura of secrecy which surrounds the operations of the national state in its relation to others. The closed doors of smoke-filled rooms at political conventions, the secrecy which surrounds board meetings of corporations, and even the secrecies and mysteries of sex and family life are all elements contributing to legitimacy. One might add the mathematical formulæ of the physicist, or even of the econometrician, for at least part of the legitimacy of science arises because ordinary people do not understand it. Like many of the other elements, however, mystery also may have a nonlinear relationship to legitimacy — if it is overdone, the person who is supposed to be impressed may reject the whole business as mumbo jumbo. The mystery that is not wholly mysterious seems to be ideal. It is the things that we "see through a glass darkly" that really impress us.

A seventh, combined, factor which affects legitimacy — perhaps more in the sense of destroying it than of creating it — is honesty, trust, confidence on the one side, and deception and disappointment on the other. Perhaps nothing destroys legitimacy so rapidly as the perception of having been betrayed. Nothing is more essential to the maintenance of legitimacy than the avoidance of this perception. Exactly what it is that creates the perception of having been deceived is not easy to say. Politicians, for instance, seem to be able to survive a great deal of disappointment on the part of the electorate and a remarkable amount of lack of fulfillment of promises. Perhaps one of the reasons for the steady persistence of otherworldly religions is that there is not much feedback from otherworldly promises, so that whatever disappointments there may be are not reported. A this-worldly ideology, however, is likely to get into serious trouble if its promises are not fulfilled. This may well be one of the reasons for the present crisis in the Communist world. It is perhaps why, also, the "revolution of rising expectations" in the tropical countries is potentially very dangerous for existing institutions and power structures; when these expectations are disappointed, as they are all too likely to be, the legitimacy of those who made the promises or gave rise to the expectations will be severely called into question. The intensity of the current crisis of the Democratic Party in the United States is all unquestionably due to a sense of betrayal on the part of many of its former adherents. Reaction to disappointment, however, is not always a sense of betrayal; sometimes it is a sense of having bad luck. Perhaps a certain amount of advice to the sovereign emerges from these considerations: if he wishes to preserve his legitimacy, he should be careful to stress the random elements in the success or failure of his programs.

An eighth source of legitimacy consists of *association*. An institution which has insufficient legitimacy may acquire more through association with institutions which have a sufficient amount. What is mysterious is that two institutions by themselves may be somewhat deficient in legitimacy, but may increase the legitimacy of both by associating with each other. A very important example of this phenomenon is the association of the state with the church, which is extremely common in almost all societies. Religion, as we noted earlier, is a very powerful source of legitimacy in that the divine is clearly more legitimate than the human. An association with the divine therefore leads to an increase in legitimacy of the person or the institution which is aspiring to this relationship. The edifices and the rituals of religion may be designed in the mind of the worshipper to serve the glory of God, but incidentally they are also likely to increase his own legitimacy, both internal and external. At the human level, church-going almost inevitably reinforces the internal legitimacy of the church-goer, which in turn, as we have seen, tends to increase external legitimacy. The state has always had a desperate need of legitimating the threat system on which it mainly rests, and it therefore finds the church a useful ally in persuading people to accept the legitimacy of the political institution. Thus, religion can be both a stimulant and an opiate of the people; it can both challenge and reinforce the legitimacy of an established political order.

Interaction between the dynamics of legitimacy and other dynamic processes in the social system is the key to the total dynamic process of the system. The structure of legitimacy provides a framework without which it is difficult for any of these other processes to go on. Consider, for instance, the process of accumulation of knowledge and the enlargement of what Pierre Teilhard de Chardin has called the "noosphere." This depends very much on the existence of institutions for the expansion and transmission of knowledge, such as schools and universities, which are accepted as legitimate. If these institutions lose their legitimacy the whole process of expansion of knowledge can be seriously interrupted as it has been time and time again in human history. Another example would be the process of economic development, which depends very largely on the ability of a society to legitimate certain institutions and practices. This legitimation often comes from quite remote sources which have very little to do with its eventual consequences. Thus, as Max Weber pointed out, the development of a Protestant, or what would be better called a Puritan, ethic in Europe by legitimating hard work and thrift and the accumulation of property for primary religious reasons had as a by-product the development of the whole first period of capitalist expansion. The phenomenon of socialism is likewise the result of a loss of legitimacy of certain institutions such as the stock market, capital markets in general, and private property in the means of production. The development of threat systems, likewise, is strongly linked with their ability to achieve both internal and external legitimacy. Naked threats are merely destructive; it is only as the threat system is dressed up with a legitimizing activity of law and political institutions that it becomes capable of creating frameworks for large-scale development. A society of bandits stagnates or else it regresses.

The other elements of the dynamic social system also have strong interactions with the structure of legitimacy. The social system is an ecological system in which almost everything affects everything else and there are no simple one-way causative relationships. Where the economic system is successful and where the institutions of exchange produce economic development and increasing income, there is, as it were, a reservoir of payoffs with which legitimacy may be bought. Paradoxically, however, the very success of economic institutions may threaten their legitimacy simply because of the absence of sacrifice. We feel a much stronger attachment to our parents, who punished us, and the state which taxes, threatens, and conscripts us, than we do towards General Motors or the Federal Reserve System, which merely provide goodies. This is a central thesis of Schumpeter in his *Capitalism, Socialism and Democracy*, in which he argued that the very success of capitalism was likely to undermine it, because the calculating, rational frame of mind which the market created would undermine the legitimating institutions such as the family, the church, and even the aristocracy, all of which provide a framework of legitimation within which the exchange system can function. This problem has taken a curious turn in the socialist countries, where one of the current problems is how to legitimate exchange and the private property which an exchange system requires, within the framework of the socialist society, simply because exchange has very good payoffs as an organizer of social life as compared with the threat system and authoritative allocations.

There is not time in a short paper to work out the details of these relationships. The question as to which is the dominant element in social dynamics cannot really be answered here; in fact it is not altogether clear how the question should be asked. The concept of a dominant species in an ecological system is not unreasonable in the sense that a pine forest, for instance, will have a very different ecological pattern of other species—birds, other plants, and insects—than will a deciduous forest; there is some sense in saying that the tree is the dominant species of the forest. Similarly, man is unquestionably the dominant species of the cities and suburbs, and only those things survive that can live with him. In a rather similar sense, I would argue, without being quite sure of the matter, that legitimacy is the dominant species of the social ecosystem in the sense that whatever cannot establish itself as legitimate is quite likely to disappear. This does not mean, of course, that exchange and threats are unimportant. It does mean, however, that the form depends a great deal on the institutions and the dominant patterns by which legitimacy is established or destroyed. Because of the complex interaction of other elements of the social system of legitimacy itself, we cannot simply use the ecological analogy and say that legitimacy is the dominant social species. It is probably wise to regard the ecosystem of society as one in which no single social species or group of species is really dominant.

THE FUTURE AS CHANCE AND DESIGN

Pub. in German as "Die Zukunft als Moglichkeit."
Bauwalt, 50 (15 Dec. 1969): 1807-1811

The Future as Chance and Design

Two closely related properties of the human organism distinguish man from the lower animals and have led to the evolution of social systems.   The first is linguistic capacity, or communication by means of symbols and abstractions.   The second is the development of complex and extended images of the future, which govern behaviour. Man, indeed, might be described as a conscious teleological system, a teleological system being one in which behaviour is governed by a structure of information or "blueprint" which is in some way related to the future, rather than by simple stimuli from the past.   All biological systems have an unconscious teleology as expressed in the genetic structure, which is, as it were, a blueprint for the growth of the organism. Only man, however, as far as we know, in this part of the universe, has a conscious image of the future which directs his behaviour.   I am composing this paper in February in Boulder, Colorado because I have an image of the future which involves delivering it in London in September.

Because of the importance of the image of the future in determining human behaviour, man has always had an incurable wonder about the future.   If our behaviour is directed towards the future, we obviously need to know what the future is going to be like.   It is clear, however, that knowledge about the future cannot possibly be derived from experience, for it is essential to the very concept of the future that it has not been experienced yet.   Knowledge of the future, therefore, can only be derived from abstract images of total processes in space and time which are derived from our experiences of the past.   This is why there is such a close relationship between the human capacity to abstract and to communicate through symbols and the development of complex images of the future.   The only way in which we can have any knowledge of the future is by perceiving design in the past, which we then project into the future on the assumption that the past designs will persist.   I have sometimes called this the "wallpaper principle", for if we perceive a pattern on the wallpaper, we have a great deal of confidence that it persists behind the pictures and the furniture where we cannot see it.   If we think of the real world as a kind of four-dimensional wallpaper with three dimensions of space and one of time, the future part of it is cut off sharply from our immediate perception by the impenetrable barrier of the present.   We are standing in the corridor of time with an impenetrable curtain in front of us.   Nevertheless, we can look back down the corridor, for a record of the past is with us in the present, and if from this record of the past we can perceive patterns in the corridor we may be justified in projecting these patterns through the curtain which divides us from the future.

The first patterns that we are likely to perceive are the cyclical ones - day and night and the return of the seasons.   We have an immense confidence, in front of which philosophers have frequently prostrated themselves, that the sun will rise tomorrow. In the Temperate Zone at least seed time and harvest roll around with majestic constancy.   One wonders indeed whether the greater orientation to the future among people living in the Temperate Zone, as opposed to those in the Tropics, is not due to the experience of the seasons.   At the equator one day is very much like the next. The further north we go, the more striking becomes the succession of the seasons and the more aware man is that he is always waiting for something - "If winter comes, can spring be far behind?"

Another obvious cyclical pattern is that of the moon which gives us the month and pre- sumably the week - the Sabbath after all is the moon's quarter.   Then in long clear nights in the desert or at sea man perceived the planets and discovered even more complex cycles in their movements.   It is not surprising that out of all this developed astrology, for by contrast with the inconstancy and uncertainty of human life, the great smooth revolutions of the spheres seems like a divine perfection which could surely be turned to human advantage.   Even though astrology turned out to be a pseudo science in many ways it laid down the foundations of the sciences to come, for it did direct man towards the perception of design as the only foundation of knowledge about the future.   Celestial mechanics, furthermore, gave man an extraordinary confidence in himself and in his own epistemological powers.   A creature that was able to predict eclipses within a fraction of a second could hardly dismiss himself as negligible. Celestial mechanics, indeed, has had an enormous impact on all the other sciences, not all of it desirable, for the methods which lead to success in one system may not be those which are successful in others.   Economists, for instance, are still mainly at the stage of celestial mechanics.   They are still building mechnical models, re- cording the movements of economic planets, of prices and incomes, and trying to find stable differential equations of a reasonable degree.

Celestial mechanics is the most spectacular example, but by no means the only case of what I have called simple dynamics, that is, systems which project into the future because they are able to discover stable relationships among successive states of the system in time.   The simplest form of these stable relationships is the difference equation, which relates successive terms of a sequence, and its college educated cousin the differential equation, which is really the same thing in a more elegant form.   It was Newton's discovery of "fluxions", that is, the differential calculus, which really made celestial mechanics possible.   The equations of celestial mechanics are almost uniformly cyclical.   In ordinary life, however, we constantly make use of non-cyclical projections as, for instance, when we are walking or driving a car.   We constantly direct our behaviour to where we think people are going to be in the next few seconds because we project their movement, assuming, for instance, constant velocity.   We may be even more elaborate and project constant acceleration, that is, a constant rate of change in velocity.   If we leave money in a bank to accumulate compound interest, we anticipate exponential growth.   The decisions in the financial system, indeed, are profoundly affected by exponential rates of growth all the time. Here again, we see the perception of design in the past projecting into the future.

As we move into the biological world, we find another pattern, derived from our exper- ience with the past, which we project into the future.   This is what is sometimes called the "creode", which is the pattern in time of development of the living creature from a fertilized egg to childhood and maturity, and eventual decay and death.   We predict that a kitten will grow up into a cat with extraordinary confidence, provided it does not come to an untimely end, for never in human experience has a kitten grown up into a dog.   In human life, too, the pattern of ageing is extraordin- arily regular, though, of course, there is some individual variation.   For at least the firsty twenty years or so of life, however, we classify people by age and put those of the same age in the same grade, we retire almost everybody between sixty-five and seventy, and we do not allow anybody to be President of the United States before he is thirty-five on the grounds, no doubt, that you can't trust anybody under that age. Youth, as I am constantly telling my young friends to their annoyance, is one thing that we know has no future. Because of this we have developed a concept of a career which is indeed an artificial creode, designed for the totality of a single human life, extending through time.

The creode is different from mechanical patterns of the future because it is programmed, that is it is a teleological system. What makes the kitten grow up into the cat is the fact that the fertilized cat's egg which was its origin contained a blueprint for this development in the shape of the genes. These have a remarkable capacity for reproducing themselves without change through a process which resembles three-dimensional printing. Sometimes, indeed, something goes wrong with the printing process and we get a mutation. These are almost always unfavourable; for it is always easier to lose information in a structure than it is to gain it. It is this loss of genetic information of the cell which probably produces cancer. We have rather similar processes in society in which individuals fail to receive the imprint of society in which they are growing up and become deviants. Deviance, however, may be the price we have to pay for evolution, for it is only because there is some possibility of transforming genetic structure that we have any possibility of developing favourable mutations. We see this also in society. It is a "defect" in the transmission of social information which permits the development of criminals on the one hand and prophets and inventors on the other. This does not mean, of course, that there is no possibility of increasing the proportion of favourable mutations and diminishing the proportion of unfavourable ones. It does mean, however, that in a zeal for the elimination of deviants that we had better be careful that we do not also eliminate development.

This brings us to the next great pattern that we perceive in space and time which is evolution. This is a grand design indeed, a pattern which extends from the first mutation by which hydrogen becomes helium, through the evolution of the elements, the compounds, the macro-molecules, the viruses, the cells, the multi-celled organisms, animals, men, families, tribes, nations, corporations, to the United Nations, and so on. We see the same process in human artifacts from the flint axe to the computer. What we have here is a pattern of increase in organized complexity that results however in eventual decrease. There seems to be, however, a fundamental difference between the process of evolution and the processes of the creode. The creode is quite clearly and distinctly a teleological system and cannot be understood in the absence of a preexistent plan. The model of biological evolution which assumes a random mutation of the genetic structure and selection of the resulting phenotypes, according to the principles of ecological equilibrium and succession is not teleological, that is, according to this model, we do not have to assume a blueprint at the beginning of process. Whether this model is adequate or even "true" is another question altogether. The record of the past is so fragmentary, incomplete, and biased that one would be extremely hesitant to identify any model which we can construct at this stage of the game with universal and absolute truth. I think we have to say that we simply do not know whether the evolutionary process is teleological, though a non-teleological model of mutation and selection will explain a great deal of it. Any system in which an increase in complexity, even if produced by random processes, can perpetuate itself will be an evolutionary system and will be a system in which organised complexity increases with time, as W. R. Ashby (1) has pointed out.

Once the process of biological evolution produced man, by whatever mechanism, a whole new evolutionary process began to take place in the human nervous system, an apparatus which has an enormous potential for the development of new forms of complexity. This new evolutionary model was human learning, which also proceeds by a process of mutation and selection. The human nervous system is capable of creating and maintaining "images", that is, complex informational structures which represent "the world", that is, a totality of reality both inside and outside the organism. Because of the capacity of the organism for perceiving information through the senses, and also for receiving information in symbolic form through language, these internally produced images produced by the "imagination" are constantly subject to critical selection and only those which survive certain tests persist. Thus, I may be imagining somewhere in the vast networks of the cortex that I am in a great palace and I may also be imagining that I am in my little study. My eyes tell me that the image of the palace is false and the image of my study is true, but my eyes are not so much creating the image as criticizing it. This, indeed, is the essence of the modern theory of perception. We develop not only images of the space around us but images of space and time and, what is even more important, of relationships. These images are constantly being selected through the process of disappointment, that is, the failure of an image of the future to be fulfilled. If I go up to a lady I think is my wife and kiss her fondly and it turns out to be a stranger, a rapid learning process goes on.

Failure to learn, or learning things that are not so, that is, the development of negative knowledge, can come through failure either of mutation, as imagination, or more likely through a failure of selective process. The trouble with disappointment is that it is often not selective enough. It tells us what is wrong, but does not tell us what is right. It is, however, fundamental to the epistemological process that we learn not by the perception of truth, but by the perception of error. We have to make a leap of faith that the successive elimination of error leaves us with more and more truth, though I think there is no way of proving this. It is by this process of elimination of error, however, that we learn even what I have called "folk knowledge", that is, the things that we learn in our ordinary experience of life. The processes of scientific epistemology are not really any different. We learn in science also through disappointment. The difference between folk knowledge and scientific knowledge lies only in the complexity of the images involved and the subtlety of the disappointments, as our image of possible futures becomes more and more complex through theory, and our disappointments become more subtle through instrumentation.

The capacity of the human nervous system for emitting and receiving information in symbolic form, that is, through language, has permitted the development of what Teilhard de Chardin calls the "noosphere", that is, the gossamer web of knowledge or images of the world as it exists in nervous systems and other structures over the face of the globe. In some sense, this can be considered as a single system in spite of the fact that it is mostly embodied in discreet human bodies. Recorded knowledge outside the human nervous system is artifacts, books, tapes, and so on should also be considered as part of the noosphere, although not an independent part. It is only within the human nervous system that the noosphere can grow and develop. If all humans were to disappear from the earth, the libraries would be meaningless and useless unless some other intelligence appeared which could interpret them. The growth in the noosphere itself has been accelerated at various times by evolutionary developments. Thus, writing permits communication from the past and the development of records which are larger than any single human brain could store.. Printing augments the quantity of recorded information and disseminates it very widely. The phonograph record and the tape permit the storage of oral information and the computer has augmented again the storage and processing capacities for information. It is one of the peculiarities of an evolutionary system that it accelerates, because the evolutionary process itself produces structures which are capabale of changing it. Social evolution is a particularly striking example of this principle. This is what I have sometimes called the "gear change principle", that evolution as it proceeds develops by its own process "higher gears" which then make the process go faster. We see this even in biological evolution where evolution went into higher gear, for instance, with the development of life and still more with the development of man. We see many examples of this in social evolution.

The most significant gear changes in social evolution have been the development of increased capacities for design. The word "design" in English has a double meaning, even perhaps a double entendre. It means in the first place simple patterns, as we might speak about the design on a fabric or a wallpaper. It means also what might be called a teleological pattern, that is, an image of the future which governs present behaviour. Design in this sense is an image or blueprint for something that may not even yet exist, but which comes into existence because of the design. We see this phenomenon in a primitive level even in the lower animals. The behaviour of a dog chasing a rabbit can only be explained by the theory that there is a rabbit inside the dog as well as outside it, and that the dog's behaviour is very largely determined by the inside rabbit, that is, its image of the rabbit in its own nervous system. Even in this sense, even a dog has a "design" for catching the rabbit. This design, however, is below the level of self-consciousness.

The emergence of self-consciousness is an evolutionary gear change of first importance. We do not really know when individual self-consciousness emerged in man. The paleolithic cave paintings certainly suggest that it emerged a long time ago and that this was closely related to the development of language. Unfortunately, at this point the record of the past is hopelessly lost. Nevertheless, it seems not implausible to suppose that the great breakthrough from the paleolithic into the neolithic, with the invention of agriculture and the domestication of crops, animals, and even the human male, was associated with a quantum-like increase in human self-consciousness. Without this it is difficult to see how man could have invented agriculture. Just how it came about, however, is a profound mystery. Once this step had been taken, however, the pace of social evolution increased enormously. Man lived through one hundred thousand years of the paleolithic with hardly any perceptible change in culture. The step from the neolithic into civilized society, even though in some ways it may have been a retrogression in the welfare of the ordinary human being, took place very soon after the invention of agriculture and the next great breakthrough into science took place, geologically speaking, almost immediately after.

It is only in the last hundred years or so that we have experienced still another breakthrough into what might be called "social self-consciousness". Before the nineteenth century almost everybody regarded the social system and culture in which they lived as a fact of nature, neither to be questioned nor changed. This was as true of the powerful figures of society as it was for the humble. The powerful might make decisions - like starting a war or passing laws - which would affect the relative position of people within the society but nobody ever thought of changing society itself. Social self-consciousness, that is, the awareness of society itself as a system, may perhaps be detected as far back as Machiavelli, begins to be noticeable in Adam Smith and Malthus, and is highly developed in Marx. I happen to think that Marx's image of society has almost fatal defects in it, but this perhaps is less important than the fact that he had a self-conscious image of social transformation which he was able to propogate. Whether we are Marxists or not we have to recognize today that the attitudes of all societies towards their own development, for instance, is vastly different from what it was one hundred years ago. In past centuries the images of society were largely confined to the present and the past; today, all societies tend to have strong images of a future different from the present into which they hope to go. This might be called perhaps the development of social design, which is a more accurate word than "planning".

It is probably no accident, however, that the word "designing", as in the expression "a designing woman", has strong overtones of disapproval. Just as someone has said, "People are more apt to be planned against than planning". So while it is very nice to be a designer it is also possible to be designed against and to become the object of somebody else's design. This is one of the most critical and difficult problems in the evaluation of social systems. The noosphere and the social system or "sociosphere" which it sustains and develops is unquestionably in some sense a unitary system, but it is not and cannot be an organism, and the coporations, the nations, and other bodies which constitute the organs and subsystems of the sociosphere cannot be thought of, except metaphorically, as persons.

In any evaluation of social systems, therefore, the principle of the sovereignty of the individual person is of paramount importance. Just as libraries, which may be storehouses of information, do not contain any knowledge in the absence of people, so organizations and social systems, although they may be instruments of good and evil, joy and pain, ecstasy and agony, hope and despair, do not experience these things and are totally incapable of being human; this is why the word "designing" has unfavourable connotation. It is all very well to be a designer, but it is often quite unpleasant to be designed. One cannot, of course, set up an abstract principle that human beings should always be designers and should never be designed. Every society designs its children to grow up and become members of it. This is precisely what the sociologists mean by socialization. The very concept of coming of age, however, suggests that there must be strong limits on the extent to which adults can be designed. We do, of course, use adults as means; the whole concept of a labour force, indeed, would be impossible without it. Whenever somebody is hired to do something, he is used as a means for some other end. Nevertheless, we feel quite rightly that this relationship must be a restricted one and should be hedged around with all kinds of safeguards against the abuse of the person and the exercise of illegitimate power. We are still a long way from having solved this problem.

It may seem perhaps that when we are designing things rather than people we are exempt from the unfavourable aspects of the word "designing". We should not be too sure of this, however; things are extentions of people. A man's clothes are as much a part of his personality as his skin and his automobile is just a mobile suit of armour. A man's house, also, is clothing at a somewhat greater distance from him than his garments, but nevertheless an integument which is also part of his personality. We cannot assume, therefore, that we can design artifacts in the absence of people, although the fact that it is much easier to push things around than to push people around gives almost all planners a strong bias in favour of cement. The problem, indeed, of how to design without having "designs on" must be regarded as one of the major unsolved problems of the human race. We have partial solutions in the market and the institutions of exchange which achieve a sort of equality by allowing people to exploit each other. We have a partial solution in the political organs of democracy but we still live in a world in which too many people are pushed around and there is still too sharp a distinction between the designers and the designed, between the planners and the planned.

Nevertheless, the solution to the problem is not less design or less conscious effort to move into consciously desired futures, as there is no way back to the Eden of the unselfconscious. When we look at the evolutionary process, moreover, we see the great changes have come by the developments of the design of designers. We see this even in biological evolution where the genetic structure is in effect a design for producing an organism capable of further design. We see the same principle operating in social evolution where the development of universities, research institutes, and the like represents social mutations which are themselves capable of generating many more mutations. The subculture of science, indeed, could almost be described as a design for designers and its enormous success in increasing human knowledge is precisely the result of the development of a subculture which was specialized towards this end. In contemplating the present discontents of the world, therefore, which could almost all be interpreted as a failure of design, we ask ourselves "Where are the institutions that can produce the designers themselves?"

As we look around the world, we see that these institutions have been very unevenly produced. In the last hundred years, for instance, we have an enormous technological change in agriculture, especially in the United States, but also in Japan and the countries of the Atlantic community. This success has not been shared in anything like the same degree by the socialist countries, where agriculture remains remarkably unproductive. In the United States, at least, this success unquestionably goes back to the Morrill Act of 1862 which established the land-grant colleges. Because of this the agricultural sector of the economy became closely linked with the scientific subculture. We had agricultural chemistry, agricultural biology, agricultural economics, rural sociology and so on, all of which helped to create an atmosphere in which the scientific community and the agricultural community exhibited a remarkable symbiosis.

In other fields of life this has not happened and it is precisely in these areas that we are faced with threatening deficiencies of design. The first of these areas is the inter-national system which is still operated pretty much on the level of folk knowledge, and where the impact of the scientific community has, if anything, made the system more expensive and less tolerable than it was before. The very existence of the world-war industry of some 160 billion dollars is a clear indication of the unsatisfactory design in the international system. The amount of effort which is going into producing a better design, however, is miniscule. It is doubtful if more than a few hundred people around the world are seriously engaged in this task.

Another example of the failure of designs for design is in the building industry. No one to my knowledge ever set up anything like a land-grant college for the building industry. As a result it has continued in an essentially pre-scientific atmosphere. There is virtually nothing that might be called building physics, building chemistry, building biology, building economics or building sociology, as there is in agriculture. As a result the building industry has not only been stagnant technologically, apart from a few inputs which have come in the way of new materials from the manufacturing sector, but it is isolated from current developments not only in the physical and biological but also in the social sciences. It still remains largely at the level of "folk knowledge". It is not surprising, therefore, that our cities are in such a deep crisis, for this in part is a crisis of the whole structure of the building industry, though it also represents a deep failure of political design.

To some extent this is a failure of schools of architecture themselves, which have not, like agriculture, become part of the ongoing stream of science, and especially have neglected the social sciences almost completely. Departments of architectural economics or sociology, for instance, as far as I know, are virtually non-existent. The architects cannot be wholly blamed for the state of affairs, though one can hardly help feeling that there has been a certain failure of vision in the profession. There has been a failure also, however, in the general perceptions of society and especially in the political structure, which has paid far too much attention to food and not enough to shelter.

I have been suggesting, therefore, that what we need is a series of Morrill Acts for the building industry around the world which will set up what I have been calling "Ubis" or Universities of the Building Industry, or perhaps we should be more general and call them universities of design. The existing schools of architecture might be the core of these institutions, though it may be difficult to reform these institutions and might almost be better to set up entirely new ones. If, however, the schools of architecture could be expanded in this way, they might play an extraordinarily important role in uniting the arts and the sciences, and providing communications between them. Up to now the tradition of architecture has been more in the fine arts than it has been in the sciences, although with the development of functionalism one gets the feeling that it has abandoned even that. In the past generation architecture has been imaginative and creative; in some ways indeed it has been a great period, but it has also been at heart very frivolous in the sense that architects have not been willing as a group to go through the painful and painstaking process of testing their creativity, but have develop-ed their own internal standard for what is good and what is bad. A friend of mine is doing a study of social consequences of prize architecture.   This may well reveal that these are all too frequently designs for disaster, and that the people who have to live in the structures which architects admire pay a very heavy cost in human terms for this privilege.

I suppose what I am suggesting is a kind of third order mutation to redesign the institutions that design the designers of designers.   This may sound ambitious but it is, I think, the only response which is likely to deal with quite extraordinary crises of our times.

Note: (1)   W. Ross Ashby.   "Principles of the Self Organizing System".
Heinz von Poerster and George W. Zoto, eds. <u>Principles of Self Organization</u>.   New York: Pergamon Press, 1962.   Pp. 255-278.

THE FUTURE OF PERSONAL RESPONSIBILITY

Amer. Behavioral Scientist, 15, 3 (Jan.-Feb. 1972): 329-359

The Future of Personal Responsibility

The problem of this paper is one of the most subtle and difficult in the whole of social dynamics. It may very well be insoluble with the present techniques of social science. The principal purpose of this paper, therefore, is to make clear the nature of the problem and the sort of things we might have to know if we were to solve it.

THE CONCEPT OF PERSONAL RESPONSIBILITY

The title implies a twofold problem. The first is the general problem of prediction or projection into the future. There are a number of different ways of doing this, and we will examine the more important ones in light of the specific problem of the future of personal responsibility. The second is the nature of the dynamic system we are trying to define. Personal responsibility is a vague, though very important, concept. Though all have a vague idea what we mean by it, I know of no attempt to define it exactly, to measure it, or even to get indicators as to its increase or decrease. The social science literature on the subject is sparse. In a recent symposium (Wertheimer, 1970), the index, under Responsibility, Personal, simply says, "See Conformity." Also see Boulding (1954). The pronouncements of the World Council of Churches have consistently dealt with what we call the "responsible society," but this rhetoric, attractive as it is, does not seem to produce any study of the concept by social scientists. We are starting, therefore, practically from scratch.

We can read "responsibility" as a characteristic either of a person or of certain types of behavior. In the first case, we might ask if a particular person is very responsible, somewhat responsible, not particularly responsible, somewhat irresponsible, or very irresponsible? Most of us could probably decide to scale our friends and acquaintances this way, and we could conceivably aggregate these scales to get a measure of the responsibility characteristic of the whole population or the total society. However, the responsibility concept itself has a number of dimensions and is not a simple scalar.

In my 1954 article, I indicated that there are at least two different concepts—responsibility *for* and responsibility *to*. Responsibility "for" related to the degree to which an individual, whether acting on his own behalf or on behalf of some group or organization, made decisions in light of his perception of the effects of these decisions on others beyond himself or his immediate group. The first of the matters here is the idea of the power of a person—that is, the extent to which his decision in fact affects small or large numbers of other people. It is in this sense that the President of the United States has more power than a poor old-age pensioner. Power itself has two dimensions—objective and subjective. That is, there is the real effect which the decision of one person has on other people, and then there is his subjective image of that effect, for a man may mistake the extent of his actual power.

Another important dimension of responsibility is benevolence or malevolence. A person is benevolent if he perceives an alternative which increases the welfare of another as increasing the value of that alternative. He is malevolent if he perceives that increasing the welfare of another diminishes the value of that alternative. Selfishness is simply the zero point on a scale of benevolence-malevolence, and I have argued that we can measure malevolence or benevolence by the "rate of benevolence"—how much one person would give up to perceive that another person is better off by a dollar. A negative rate of benevolence, of course, indicates malevolence; a zero rate, selfishness. The interrelations of power and benevolence are extraordinarily complicated. If a malevolent person exercises power to destroy his enemy, is he being responsible?

Another significant dimension is the laziness/hard-working dimension. Irresponsible people are lazy; responsible people are hard-working. There is an implication here about having power but not exercising it.

A responsible person sometimes acts irresponsibly, and an irresponsible person, responsibly. It is much easier to observe behavior than it is to observe personality; we usually arrive at the concept of a personality from the observation of some sort of consistent behavior: A responsible person is someone who usually behaves responsibly. A good many organizational devices in society, however, are designed to persuade people to act responsibly whether their personalities are responsible or not, so that it would not be wise to pay too much attention to personality to the exclusion of behavior. Nevertheless, insofar as behavior is a product of a person's image of his own identity, which I have argued is an important aspect of human behavior, then obviously the forces which determine a person's image of his own identity are important in determining his behavior, whether the image corresponds to objective reality or not.

We are particularly concerned here with the learning of values and identities, which is, unfortunately, something we know very little about. We may start life with certain genetic values—such as a liking for being warm, dry and cuddled rather than for being cold, wet, and lonely—and our other values are added to this as a result of a very complex process of information input, filtering, and feedback. Some values are learned by simple association: We like mother, so we like mother's values. Sometimes a child rebels and rejects his parents' values. Sometimes the sour grapes principle operates—what we cannot get, we decide we do not want; sometimes, however, if we cannot get something we want it all the more. Popular wisdom reveals very clearly that the process of learning values is extremely unstable. The phenomenon of imprinting in animals certainly exists in humans. The right input at the right time creates a strong value set. It is not surprising that it is as hard to make predictions as it is to define indicators in a system which is so inherently precarious in its dynamic path.

Out of this precarious process of human learning, some people and institutions emerge as more responsible than others. Some rhetorical systems and some clusters of values emerge as more powerful than others, in their effects on the minds of men. Fashion is a nice example of a particular pattern's "population explosion" in this great field of human minds. Fashions thrive and decay in ideas, ideologies, and theologies, as well as in clothes. In mid-eighteenth century, religion seemed to be dying out in the Western world, incapable of propagating itself on the bare prairies and in the bright sunshine of the Enlightenment. Methodism in the eighteenth century and evangelical revivals in the nineteenth completely changed the picture. Religion grew like a great forest, sheltering all sorts of unlikely sects. The rise of religion indeed has been one of the most striking phenomena in the history of the United States, something which the Founding Fathers certainly never contemplated (see Figure 1). The rise of Communism since 1848 has been just as spectacular. On the dry plains of dialectical materialism, however, again the strange green shoots of religion have sprouted, and the socialist countries may well repeat U.S. history in this matter.

It is fairly easy to identify the growth of organizations, even of ideologies and ideas, but it is difficult to identify something

Figure 1
CHURCH MEMBERSHIP AND SUNDAY SCHOOL
ENROLLMENT AS A PERCENTAGE OF THE POPULATION

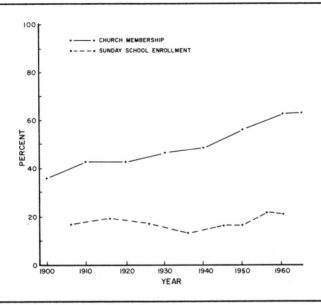

SOURCE: Elise Boulding and Patricia Trainer, "Quality of Life, U.S.A.: Costs and Benefits of Urbanization and Industrialization, 1900-1970." Proceedings of the Institute of Environmental Sciences, Second Annual Session, **Environmental Awareness,** edited by Malcolm Lillywhite and Cassandra Martin (Denver, Colorado: Martin Marietta, 1971), p. 8.

as subtle and fundamental as personal responsibility. This is almost like trying to identify particular amino acids in the genetic structure of a forest. While particular species of trees, grasses, and fungi are easy to identify, the individual genetic structures which underly the whole require the most refined and difficult analysis. We must not be surprised, therefore, if it seems almost impossible to answer the question of more or less personal responsibility, say, in the United States today than it was ten or fifty or a hundred years ago. It is much easier to say whether there are more or fewer Catholics or Methodists, Republicans or Democrats, chiropractors or gas station attendants, or any of the other easily recognizable species of social life.

Even the general social indicators in this area are inadequate. We ought to get some inkling from crime statistics. Though the incidence of some forms of crime seems to be rising steadily (Figures 2-5), we do not know if this is simply better reporting. Divorce, another indicator, has exhibited a surprisingly small upward trend, though in the last two or three years it has jumped sharply (Figure 6). A rise in divorce, however, may not mean that people are less responsible in marriage, but that society has become more tolerant of correcting mistakes. Statistics of health and disease, likewise, are dubious indicators.

Figure 2
SELECTED UNITED STATES CRIME RATES

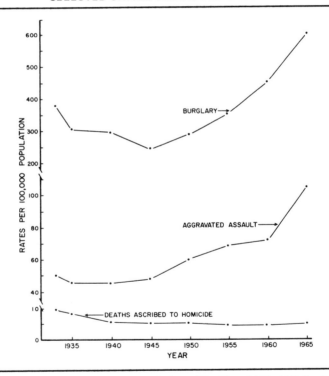

SOURCE: Elise Boulding and Patricia Trainer, "Quality of Life, U.S.A.: Costs and Benefits of Urbanization and Industrialization, 1900-1970." Proceedings of the Institute of Environmental Sciences, Second Annual Session, **Environmental Awareness,** edited by Malcolm Lillywhite and Cassandra Martin (Denver, Colorado: Martin Marietta, 1971), p. 12.

Figure 3
TRENDS IN JUVENILE COURT DELINQUENCY CASES
AND CHILD POPULATION 10-17 YEARS OF AGE, 1940-1966
(SEMI-LOGARITHMIC SCALE)

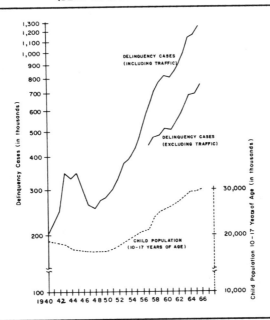

SOURCE: U.S. Department of Health, Education and Welfare, Social and Rehabilitation Service, Children's Bureau. **Juvenile Court Statistics,** 1906. Children's Bureau Statistical Series 90, 1967.

Figure 4
POPULATION-BASED RATES OF JUVENILE COURT DELINQUENCY
CASES, 1940-1966 (PER 1,000 POPULATION, 10-17 YEARS OF AGE)

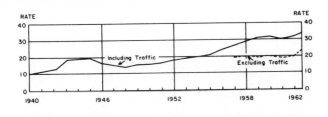

SOURCE: Elise Boulding and Patricia Trainer, "Quality of Life, U.S.A.: Costs and Benefits of Urbanization and Industrialization, 1900-1970." Proceedings of the Institute of Environmental Sciences, Second Annual Session, **Environmental Awareness,** edited by Malcolm Lillywhite and Cassandra Martin (Denver, Colorado: Martin Marietta, 1971), p. 12.

The remarkable conquest of premature mortality in the last hundred years reflects technology rather than responsibility, although it may reflect an increasing sense of community responsibility in good water supplies and sewage; this also reflects certain scientific spinoffs, like penicillin and insecticides. Mental hospitals, like tuberculosis sanitoria have been emptying, but this is likely a result of a drug revolution, rather than of any moral change.

It is frequently asserted that there has been a shift from personal or individual responsibility to social responsibility. Statements of this kind, while they are frequent, are very hard

Figure 5
SUICIDE, HOMICIDE AND ACCIDENT RATES
IN THE UNITED STATES

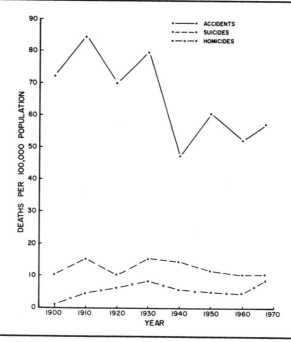

SOURCE: Elise Boulding and Patricia Trainer, "Quality of Life, U.S.A.: Costs and Benefits of Urbanization and Industrialization, 1900-1970." Proceedings of the Institute of Environmental Sciences, Second Annual Session, **Environmental Awareness,** edited by Malcolm Lillywhite and Cassandra Martin (Denver, Colorado: Martin Marietta, 1971), p. 6.

Figure 6
DIVORCE RATES: UNITED STATES, 1920-68

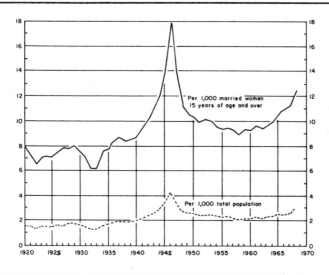

SOURCE: Public Health Service, **Monthly Vital Statistics Report**, Vol. 19, No. 10, Supplement (2), January 26, 1971 (Washington, D.C.: U.S. Government Printing Office), p. 1.

to document. A possible index here is the rise of what is now being called the "grants economy"—that is, that segment of economic activity which consists of one-way transfers of exchangeables, by contrast with the "exchange economy," a two-way transfer of exchangeables. It is not always easy to tell a grant from an exchange, for many things that look like grants may be deferred exchanges, but a useful operational definition is that the grant diminishes the net worth of a grantor and increases that of the grantee, whereas an exchange merely rearranges the ownership of assets, but does not change the net worth of either party. The proportion of the economy consisting of grants has substantially increased in the twentieth century. Figure 7 shows the rise in government transfers. The difficulty with grants as an indicator of social responsibility, however, is that they may originate from two different sources—either from threats, as when a bandit says "Your money or your life," or when the tax collector says "Pay your income tax or we will put you in jail," or from gifts, which arise from some sense of community or identity, as when parents sacrifice for their children or people without children vote for school bonds and school taxes.

Another significant indicator which is somewhat related to the grants economy is the rise of government in the economic system (see Figure 8). Government in the United States—federal, state, and local—has risen from 8.3% of the economy in 1929, to 22.6% in 1970. A great part of this rise, however, has

Figure 7
TOTAL GOVERNMENT TRANSFER PAYMENTS AND
PURCHASE OF GOODS AND SERVICES AS A PERCENTAGE
OF GROSS CAPACITY PRODUCT

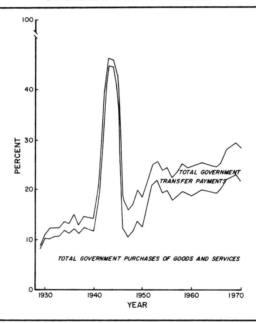

SOURCE: **Economic Report of the President** (Washington, D.C.: U.S. Government Printing Office, 1971); **Facts and Figures on Government Finance** (New York: Tax Foundation, Inc. 1971). Gross Capacity Product from K. E. Boulding, "The Impact of the Defense Industry on the American Economy," **Adjustment of the U.S. Economy to Reductions in Military Spending,** edited by Bernard Udis. Prepared for the U.S. Arms Control and Disarmament Agency, ACDA/E-156, December, 1970, pp. 399-433.

Figure 8
STATE AND LOCAL GOVERNMENT, FEDERAL CIVILIAN,
FEDERAL DEFENSE, AS A PERCENTAGE OF
GROSS CAPACITY PRODUCT

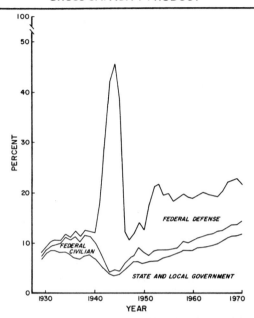

SOURCE: **Economic Report of the President** (Washington, D.C.: U.S. Government Printing Office, 1971); **Facts and Figures on Government Finance** (New York: Tax Foundation, Inc. 1971). Gross Capacity Product from K. E. Boulding, "The Impact of the Defense Industry on the Structure of the American Economy." Adjustment of the U.S. Economy to Reductions in Military Spending, edited by Bernard Udis. Prepared for the U.S. Arms Control and Disarmament Agency, ACDA/E-156, December, 1970, pp. 399-433.

been in national defense, which is much more a function of the international threat system than it is of any sense of community. In fact, it is a symbol of the absence of world community, and may be, as in the case of the Vietnam War, highly destructive for the national community. The rise in civilian government, from 7.6% of the economy in 1929 to 11% in 1939 to 14.7% in 1970 is by no means spectacular, though it does suggest an increase in the significance of the national community. The rise in government might simply be interpreted as a result of increasing income, public goods being "superior goods" in the economist's language—that is, goods which are demanded more by the rich than by the poor. Hence, a general rise in income would lead us to expect a shift toward public goods, just as there is a shift toward housing and transportation and away from food and clothing with rising incomes. There is certainly no evidence in the economic statistics, therefore, for any massive shift in consciousness or in personal responsibility. Most people in this country continue to work to earn incomes, to marry, to buy houses, and have children, much as their grandfathers and great-grandfathers did. The fringe of Reich's Consciousness III is still very small indeed. Hippies and radicals are certainly not more than one percent of the population, if that.

THE APPROACH FROM THE FUTURE

In the first part of this paper, we tried to look at the concept of personal responsibility from the point of view of its place in the total social system. We have by no means found satisfactory definitions and indicators. We may be able, however, by looking directly at the general problem of projecting the future, to better identify the kind of system involved in trying to project the future of personal responsibility. We will consider in turn four general types of systems and projections. All projections of the future, of course, involve the perception of patterns of some kind in the space-time continuum of the past, so that we then suppose the same kind of regularity to be continued into the future. I have sometimes called this the "wallpaper principle." If wallpaper has a regular pattern, we have a great deal of confidence in projecting it in the space behind the pictures and the furniture, even though we cannot see it. Similarly, we perceive the past as a kind of four-dimensional wallpaper, the patterns of which we suppose continue beyond the veil of the present into the hidden future. The four types of patterns we shall consider may be called: (1) mechanical, (2) leading signal, (3) equilibrium, and (4) controlled systems.

Mechanical patterns are patterns which can be described by simple difference or differential equations, in which variables exhibit either constant rates of change or constant rates of change of rates of change, and so on, or in which the system is a stable function of what it was like yesterday, or yesterday and the day before. The spectacular predictive success of celestial mechanics depends on the fact that the movements of heavenly bodies can be described in terms of difference or differential equations of a low degree with constant parameters. The simplest such systems are projections of linear trends. These are very rare in nature, except for rather short periods of time, and assumptions of linearity are rarely justified and easily get us into very serious trouble. Relations involving difference equations of the second and third order are commoner. Celestial mechanics, for instance, rarely involves more than third-order differential equations. Growth curves which merely assume constantly declining rates of growth will carry us quite a long way, and so on.

A category of somewhat neglected mechanical systems might be called "catastrophic systems," in which there are sharp discontinuous changes. The overturning of an iceberg would be a good example. The ice above the surface melts at a different rate from the ice below the surface, each of these being moderately simple mechanical systems related to surface area and the temperature of the surrounding air or water. If, however, the underwater part of the iceberg melts faster, at some point the center of gravity of the ice moves above that of the displaced water, and the whole iceberg moves to another position. We see something like this occasionally in social systems, for instance, in revolution or in the change in "war moods," from peace to war or from war to peace (Richardson, 1960).

When we are looking at something as subtle and complicated as personal responsibility, mechanical dynamic models have to be used with great care. Linear projections are certainly most dangerous, and we should always be on the lookout for "iceberg" models. The extraordinary shift in mood on the American campuses, for instance, between the anger and frustration of 1969-1970 to the astonishing calm of 1970-1971 is a case in point. A reverse shift, however, can take place at any time, for the structure of legitimacy is likely to be an "iceberg" system, and sudden reversals in legitimacy are not uncommon.

A second group of projection models might be described as the "leading signal" models. Whenever we observe in the past a constant time sequence between two events or series of events, observation of only the first, makes it reasonable to expect the second to follow. When we see a flash of lightning, we usually expect to hear thunder in a second or two. This is, of course, a special case of mechanical models, but it frequently has applicability where the actual mechanics of the model are not really understood. Economists have long searched for leading indicators in business cycles without much success, perhaps because of instability in the actual mechanics of the system.

Leading signals are extremely useful, even though we do not really understand the overall mechanics of the system, in biological growth—what the biologists call a "creode." This is any living organism's pattern of development from its origin in the fertilized egg or the seed to its death and dissolution. These patterns exhibit a remarkable regularity, even though we do not really understand their detailed mechanics. Kittens always grow into cats, never into hippopotamuses. However, we have to be particularly careful in applying any biological analogies to social organizations, simply because the two systems have essentially different mechanics.

One leading signal which may be of considerable importance, particularly in the anticipation of catastrophes, is the perception of inconsistencies or structural deficiencies in existing systems. The phenomenon of cognitive or moral dissonance is of particular importance where, for instance, the same people hold logically inconsistent positions. Such inconsistencies, of course, may persist for a long time through the compartmentalization of life—Sundays and weekdays, verbal expressions versus actual behavior, and so on—but, as far as there are inconsistencies, the system cannot be regarded as really secure, especially if the inconsistencies are growing. A good example of this would be the inconsistency between domestic and foreign behavior. One of the great forces making for change in the United States at the moment is the increasingly perceived inconsistency between the sort of behavior considered acceptable domestically and the sort which is accepted in Vietnam. The attempt to unify a society by a common enemy often results in an increase in the internal tensions and factional conflicts within the society itself. Especially when we are dealing with the dynamics of legitimacy, the perception of inconsistencies and dissonances may be an extremely important cue for subsequent change.

A third major area of systems of future projection is that of equilibrium systems. If a system has a position of equilibrium, then it is not so important to know the exact dynamics of the system, because any disturbance will be followed by a return to the equilibrium position. A ball in the bottom of a bowl is a classical example. It is not surprising that all sciences have sought for equilibrium models, if only because true dynamics are so difficult that equilibrium is accepted gratefully as a substitute, though really stable equilibria are virtually unknown in nature. Even the moon, which remained in almost perfect equilibrium until man violated its deathly peace, receives meteorites and cosmic dust. The earth, of course, has been a disequilibrium system for three or four billion years, simply because it has experienced evolution, and evolution is a disequilibrium process. We never go back again to where we were.

Nevertheless, there are enough temporary equilibria in nature to make the concept useful. We have, for instance, the homeostasis of the human body, which is a useful concept in physiology. The body maintains a large number of variables at an approximately constant level—for example, blood temperature, calcium content, sodium content, and so on—disturbance either way from the equilibrium level causes powerful dynamic forces to bring the system back to equilibrium. Even the homeostasis of the body is only temporary, for all living organisms are subject to the irreversible processes of maturation and aging. A total population, however, may be in approximate equilibrium with constant numbers in the different age groups, even though the individuals change, age, and die. At a more complex level, we may postulate equilibrium in ecosystems— that is, systems of interacting populations, each of which has an equilibrium size that depends on the size of all the others. A pond is a good example. If we take out, say, 20% of the population of a certain fish, it will usually not be long before the population is back to its previous level.

Society exhibits similar ecological equilibria. There is a well-known equilibrium of the relative price structure, with a given technology and tastes. Even after a thousandfold inflation, a pound of butter tends to be worth about ten pounds of bread. After the disturbance of a war, say, there is a strong movement for "back to normalcy."

How then does this apply to something like personal responsibility? It is certainly not unreasonable to suppose that any given culture will produce a certain "equilibrium personality," or an equilibrium distribution of personality types. The many studies of culture and personality, more popular some twenty years ago than now, reflect an equilibrium system of this kind. The culture in which he grows up produces the child's learning experiences, which produce the personality distribution of the adult population, which, in turn, perpetuates the culture. This may be a true equilibrium system, because divergences from the cultural norm are not rewarded, but conformity to the norm is. Margaret Mead's delightful study of the Arapesh and the Manu are classic examples. There may be good reasons for the decline in interest in studies of this kind, in that they do not throw much light on the crucial problems of irreversible change, both in culture and in personality. The difficulty with equilibrium theory is that it may divert our attention from the more fundamental disequilibrium processes, like evolution, also at work in the world. The ball displaced too much from its equilibrium position in the bottom of the bowl will go over the edge into another bowl and is unlikely to return to its previous equilibrium. We have seen a good many examples in recent years of irreversible culture change, particularly under the impact of the "superculture" in the modern world. The old culture of Hawaii, for instance, was simply abandoned, or at least radically transformed, under the impact of the missionaries, the traders, and the American government. Some cultures, like that of the Plains Indians in the United States, simply disintegrated under the impact of modern society into dependent and anomic Indian reservation cultures. Some young people revolt against the culture of their middle-class parents and become hippies, drug addicts, or members of religious sects.

In this welter of change and discontinuity, can anything be said about personal responsibility? One hopes that there are certain detectable equilibrium tendencies in the search for satisfactory personal identity. Independence, competence, and the sort of extended self involved with and concerned for others, are very widely regarded in different types of cultures as implying a satisfactory identity, whereas dependence, incompetence and self-centeredness are widely regarded with disfavor. We must recognize, however, that there are many different subcultures, each of which tends to create an equilibrium personality type of its own. There is also ecological shift among subcultures, as some grow and some decline.

One of the things which creates strain in society is inconsistency or disproportion between the types of personality required to fit the role structures of the society and the types of personality actually produced by the society's various subcultures. If the personality-producing agencies of society—the family, the educational system, the mass media, the church, and the peer groups—are producing a distribution of personality types for which the society has no demand, we are obviously in for trouble, for expectations will be created which cannot be fulfilled.

Even though equilibrium theories may sometimes divert attention from real dynamic processes, there is one use of them which is, as it were, a halfway house, between statics and dynamics. This is what economists call "comparative statics"— that is, the comparison of two equilibrium models which differ by a change in some parameter of the model from one time period to another. A good deal of economic theory is comparative statics. This type of analysis is frequently very useful, provided that its limitations are recognized.

A particularly significant application for the problem of this essay is the equilibrium of the age distribution in society, an equilibrium we can postulate for a population if we know the specific death rate at different ages. In the last hundred years, this has changed dramatically because of the spectacular reductions in premature mortality—that is, mortality before seventy. As a result, the age distribution in our own, and in most other developed societies, has changed from the "triangle" which used to characterize most societies, with the largest numbers in the lowest age groups and the numbers in each increased age group declining in almost linear proportion. In a society in which mortality is very small before the age of seventy, the age distribution will be rectangular rather than triangular, with about equal numbers of people in each age group to the "allotted span," with perhaps a small triangle "penthouse" in the upper age groups. Figure 9 illustrates this phenomenon for the United States.

The consequences in this change may be profound, and we have not as yet become aware nor defined them, simply because the change is so recent. The dilemma it poses for society is that hierarchies, whether of organization or of status, are almost universally "triangular," with a small number of people in the upper slots and a large number of people in the lower ones. If the age distribution is "triangular," then those few young people who survive into middle and old age have a pretty fair chance of finding themselves in superior hierarchical or status roles. When almost everybody survives into old age, as in our

Figure 9
DISTRIBUTION OF THE POPULATION OF THE UNITED STATES, BY AGE AND SEX: 1870 to 1969

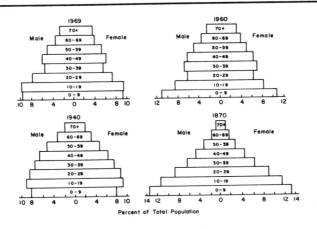

SOURCE: Bureau of the Census, **Current Population Reports,** Series P-25, No. 441, March 19, 1970 (Washington, D.C.: U.S. Government Printing Office), p. 1.

own society, finding hierarchical and status structures which correspond to this age distribution becomes a problem of acute difficulty, and may, indeed, be one of the most important in our own society, though hardly anybody is yet aware of it.

Many of the problems, indeed, that we associate with the present "youth culture," of the generation gap and so on, may simply reflect a half-conscious awareness of the problem of a rectangular age distribution. Our present behavior is determined very much by our image of our own future, our image of what might be called the "probable total life pattern." Figure 10 postulates three of these patterns. By way of illustration, on the vertical scale of each, we measure some sort of "value" of the person, which is a composite of income, status, self-esteem, respect, and so on, and we postulate different ways in which this may fluctuate over the whole life. Diagram a represents a pattern in which there is an overall steady rise to a plateau in old age; this may perhaps be regarded as the most satisfactory. Diagram b is a pattern in which the value of the person reaches

Figure 10
PERSONAL VALUE PATTERNS OVER THE LIFE CYCLE

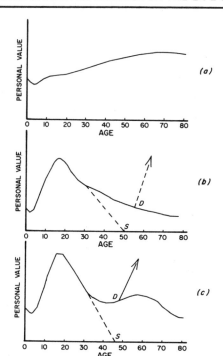

a maximum in his youth and declines thereafter. Diagram c shows a maximum in youth with a trough in middle age and a rise toward old age. If, at any point, value declines to zero, as at S, there will be suicide.

Development of personal responsibility is going to depend a great deal on the kind of total life pattern anticipated. Pattern a is optimum for the development of personal responsibility—the individual always has something to look forward to which is better than what he presently has. He has an optimistic image of the future, and he has every incentive to plan for this. Indeed, of the major dimensions of the **personal** responsibility syndrome is the length of time for which **decisions** are taken, and

THE FUTURE OF PERSONAL RESPONSIBILITY

this may depend very much on the expected life pattern. Under pattern b we cannot expect to find much personal responsibility; we expect to find a youth culture devoted to eating, drinking, and being merry, simply because tomorrow its members will be worse off. Case c is interesting, because its impact depends very much on the ability of individuals to survive and see beyond a trough in their personal valuations. Adversity may be destructive, or it may be creative, depending very largely on the extent of "hope"—that is, of a perception of some better state beyond the adversity, providing incentive to survive. This perhaps explains what otherwise might seem a paradox, that eschatological and other-worldly religions, like Jehovah's Witnesses or Seventh Day Adventists, have produced a remarkable amount of personal responsibility and an unusual competence in dealing with temporary adversities and with the problems of life in this world, because their image of the future translates the personal catastrophe of death—or even the social catastrophe of the last judgment—into the hope of a glorious future in heaven. Thus, in diagrams b and c, if D represents death, in the case of those with the lively hope of a better world to come, the personal value takes off in the direction of the arrows so that even through a long decline in this life, "hope of glory" sustains personal responsibility.

Many of the problems of personal responsibility today, therefore, arise because medical science has reduced premature mortality to the point where many individuals now visualize a life pattern very much like that of diagram b. The other-worldly hope, the only thing to make it bearable, is now largely confined to fundamentalist and millennialist sects, which, although growing, are still a rather small proportion of the total population. Under these circumstances, as previously suggested, we have a pathological youth culture, devoted to the sensate world and the pleasures of the moment in sex and drugs. The problem, furthermore, is an intractable one, for we are certainly not going back to the triangular age distribution. It is hard to construct rectangular hierarchical distributions. The idea of having just as many people at the top as there are at the bottom would be somewhat threatening to most organizations, and the whole concept of the "span of control" implies a triangular hierarchy. Status, likewise, is a tricky thing to organize, although we may modify status by the sheer multiplication of organizations. The elderly janitor in the corporation may be the Lord High Potentate of the lodge or the senior vestryman of his church. Another possibility is the manipulation of income structures, so that income rises with age. In the middle class, it generally does which is probably one reason the middle class is associated with the long-term images of the future and with personal responsibility. In the working class, incomes frequently reach a peak in youth and decline thereafter. Redistribution of income from youth to age, therefore, may be highly desirable, though it is doubtful whether it would be as popular as it deserves to be.

Another equilibrium concept which may be of great importance in creating an image of the future is that of some long-run equilibrium or stationary state. Economists from the days of Adam Smith have maintained an interest in the "stationary state," the equilibrium condition of society at the end of the process of economic development. No process of development and growth can go on forever, either in the individual or in society, and it is possible to perceive certain patterns which lead to the eventual slowing down of growth and the developing of an equilibrium state. A stationary state, of course, has no growth of population and no growth of capital; every item in the structure of society, whether people or commodities, is simply replaced as it is consumed. There has been a recent revival of interest in the problems of the stationary state as a result of the realization that the existing type of "linear economy," which runs from mines to dumps, cannot go on forever, and that in the course of the next century or so mankind will face a fundamental transition into what I and some others have been calling a "spaceship earth." This will be a small, closed, limited, planetary society, almost certainly dependent on solar energy for its input or power, and it will have to recycle virtually all its materials into a circular economy, in which the dumps become the mines.

In the spaceship, we cannot afford to have population growth, organized violence, wars, revolutions, or a great many of the things which constitute human history, simply because of the precariousness of the total extended system. The ethic of the spaceship has to be very different from that of the cowboy on the Great Plains. This imminent "closure" of the human environment is a profound psychological change in the state of mankind. When I was a boy, there were still white spaces on the map where nobody had ever been. Today there are none, and even though the resources of the earth are far from being fully explored, the great age of expansion, exploration, and development is clearly coming to an end. The consequences of this for personality, ethics, religion, the family, the nation, the corporation—indeed for all human institutions—will be profound. Human culture developed on a psychologically flat earth—that is, on an infinite plane, always with somewhere to go over the hill, always with a frontier, a place for escape. The transition from the infinite plane to the closed, limited, round ball of spaceship earth is a psychological transition whose bare beginnings we have only just encountered. The spaceship earth economy is still at least a hundred, perhaps five hundred, years off, but its shadow falls across our own times, and may well be the partial cause of the present crises of legitimacy. The decline in the legitimacy of war, such a striking phenomenon of the last fifty or sixty years, is not only a reflection of the increasing vulnerability of all societies and the disappearance of what I have called the "unconditional viability" of nation-states; it also reflects the fact that, whereas war might have been tolerable on Matthew Arnold's "darkling plain—where ignorant armies clash by night," it is quite intolerable in the finite, precarious confines of the spaceship, where failure to cooperate brings disaster. Some of what may seem a decline in traditional virtues, therefore—of patriotism, masculinity, and feminity, aggressiveness, and so on—may be a dim recognition that we are moving into an environment in which these virtues can easily become vices.

One widely current illusion about the future needs to be dispelled. This is the illusion of great future affluence and leisure, an image obtained by an illegitimate mechanical projection of constantly increasing productivity. We are all familiar with the image of the future popularized by writers like Robert Theobald, Buckminster Fuller, and the late Norbert Weiner, who should have known better, of societies in which clever machines do all the work and hence in which everybody enters the leisure class. The great problem of the future in such a society is what to do with leisure. A future of this kind cannot wholly be ruled out, but I regard it as highly improbable. In the last hundred years, we have been going through a period of rapidly increasing labor productivity, mainly as a result of the application of physical sciences to processes of production. This is an impulse which is bound to exhaust itself sooner or later. The sharp decline in the rate of productivity increase in the United States since 1967 may be only a temporary phenomenon, but we will simply have to wait and see, for it may well represent something fundamental. There is no evidence to date that automation creates any great increase in labor productivity as a whole. The overall impact of computers has certainly been much less significant than, say, the impact of the automobile a generation or so before.

I have been arguing indeed that there is a quite high probability the great age of change is approaching an end, that the peak period of change was my grandfather's life, say, from 1860 to 1920. I have certainly seen much less change than he did. Today's most probable image of the future is not one of accelerating technical change, but rather one in which the gains of the last hundred years are consolidated and in which there is only a slow increase in productivity—at least in the rich countries—in which there is some catching up on the part of the poorer countries, in which the international system becomes relatively stable, and in which the world of one hundred years from now looks surprisingly like the world of today, except for a greater awareness of the limitations of the earth and the exhaustion of resources. This image of the future is shocking to many people today, who may, however, be making the mistake of mechanical projection of the trends of the last hundred years, without perceiving that all growth systems move toward some sort of temporary equilibrium. All sorts of things could happen, of course, to upset this prediction of greater stability in the next hundred years, such as a nuclear war, a worldwide epidemic, crop failure, a major breakthrough in the creation of artificial life or artificial intelligence, or even the development of an antigravity machine, but my personal view is that the probability of any of these is quite low. Nevertheless, "false" images of the future may have a profound effect on present behavior, and we run into the further difficulty that some images of the future are self-justifying, and that both pessimistic and optimistic images have some tendency to be realized. All of us in some degree tend to create our own image of the world, and the same is true of societies. The only unforgivable sin is despair, because it is so completely self-justifying.

The fourth and last type of system which gives us a chance of predicting the future might be called the "controlled system," where the future is deliberately built into the system itself. We can predict the temperature of a thermostatically controlled room with confidence, but we cannot predict the temperature outside with any confidence at all. This is because inside the room we have constructed an apparatus to create a known future by constructing a cybernetic system. There are many examples of such systems in social life. If the exchange rates between currencies of two countries, for instance, are "pegged" either through a mutual gold standard or through agreements between the central banks, we can predict with great confidence what these exchange rates will be as long as this apparatus continues, whereas an uncontrolled market is as unpredictable as the weather. The Dow Jones or any similar average of stock prices is essentially unpredictable, but if we set up a stock exchange equalization fund to stabilize it, we could predict its future with great confidence. What we are doing is constructing equilibrium systems, and we are still a very long way from having finished this job. We now have something like a cybernetic system for preventing depressions, though it may not be adequate to prevent a repetition of the disastrous process that went on from 1929 to 1932. We do not have any adequate cybernetic mechanism to ensure stable international peace, nor do we have an adequate mechanism to prevent moral decay. All these are tasks for social invention in the future.

Not all controlled systems are equilibrium systems. We also have controlled dynamic systems, which are what we call "plans." The architect's blueprint in the construction of a building plays much the same role as does the genetic structure in the growth of a living organism from a fertilized egg. We predict the future in this case because we "planned it that way." Similarly, an investment plan in the case of a corporation or, what is not really very different, the plan of a socialist state, is an attempt on the part of the people in the present to impose their will on the future. Plans, however, imply knowledge of dynamic systems which frequently we do not have, so it is not surprising that they are frequently not fulfilled. Even when they are not wholly fulfilled, however, they are still very important as "leading signals," as it is possible to make some sort of assessment not only of the plan itself, but also of the capacity of the planning organization to carry it out.

On large moral issues, like personal responsibility, we have little in the way of social policy at the level of contrived equilibria, at the level of plans, or at the level of strategies. In any given culture or subculture, the generally accepted standards of morality constitute a kind of homeostatic norm, in the sense that individuals who deviate markedly from this norm will encounter censure or the sanctions of society and hence may be pushed back toward it. Society has all kinds of homeostatic apparatus in the attempt to control deviance. Deviance is usually not reduced to zero, but to some tolerable level below which it does not seem worthwhile to reduce it. Thus, we do have a seemingly unpalatable concept of an optimum degree of crime. Reduction below some level is not worth the expenditure, and if it expands beyond the optimum, crime reduction agencies will come into play. In the United States, the tolerance of crime seems to have been rising. Thus, as Figure 11 shows, we have substantially diminished the proportion of the gross national product devoted to police and fire protection in the last forty years, mainly due to the impact of World War II. This

Figure 11
STATE AND LOCAL GOVERNMENT – POLICE AND FIRE
AS A PERCENTAGE OF GROSS CAPACITY PRODUCT

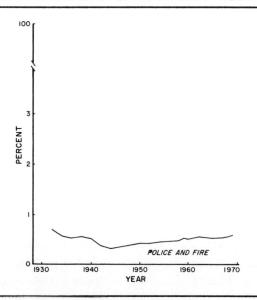

SOURCE: **Economic Report of the President** (Washington, D.C.: U.S. Government Printing Office, 1971); **Facts and Figures on Government Finance** (New York: Tax Foundation, Inc. 1971). Gross Capacity Product from K. E. Boulding, "The Impact of the Defense Industry on the American Economy," **Adjustment of the U.S. Economy to Reductions in Military Spending,** edited by Bernard Udis. Prepared for the U.S. Arms Control and Disarmament Agency, ACDA/E-156, December, 1970, pp. 399-433.

may not be so much the result of conscious decision as a result of the creation of substantial pressures on state and local government by the growth of war industry. The police are among the vulnerable elements in the budgets of these governments, simply because they have no real pressure group behind them, and nobody loves them very much. Still, presumably, there has been some sort of decision, or at least lack of decision in this matter, which may actually be perfectly rational. It may well be, for instance, that riots are much cheaper than the amount of policing required to prevent them. Just as there is an optimum amount of crime, so there is an optimum amount of civil disturbance, which acts as an emotional safety valve and as an informal method of urban renewal.

One complicating factor here is that there is a constant change in the norms, frequently under the pressure of deviance. If there is a norm from which everybody deviates, it is not a norm. Frequently, also, something regarded as a norm in one subculture is not in another, and, in the kind of ecological competition of subcultures, one may grow and another decline, so that the overall norms change. Norms indeed, often originate in small subcultures which then grow in importance until they finally dominate the society. The rise of Christianity from the Roman Empire is a case in point; so is the rise of scientific norms in the present era. Prohibition is an interesting example of a norm that failed.

The problem of social norms is complicated by the fact that, in some areas of life, it does not matter very much what decisions we make, and in other areas it matters a great deal. This is what I have sometimes called the "mesa principle," illustrated in Figure 12. We supposed the horizontal axis represents some quantity about which we have to make decisions, say, how much alcohol to take. The vertical dimension measures the value of this decision—that is, whether it is better or worse. Economists have frequently assumed that this function is a "Matterhorn" rather like the dotted line in

Figure 12
TYPES OF DECISION FUNCTIONS

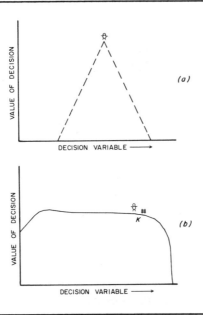

diagram a of Figure 12, with one point clearly better than all the others, which we try to attain. In fact, however, the value function may be quite flat or mesa-like over a considerable part of its range, as in diagram b with all choices about equally good. On the other hand, the mesa may have a cliff, as at the point K, where the decision can lead to disaster. The ideal "no-nos" of conventional morality are fences in front of these cliffs, necessary because the individual may have no good information system to tell him where the cliffs are, falling over them, the worst possible method of learning about them, would be easy. On the other hand, we then run into the danger that fences may not be built in the right places, and if we build fences where there are no cliffs, people will climb over them, find that there are no cliffs on the other side, and may deduce from this that there are no cliffs at all, then go a little further and fall over one. It is very important, therefore, not only to put fences where there are cliffs, but not to put them where there are none. This is a difficult problem in information about social systems.

In the area of moral norms, neither planning nor strategy has been very successful. Generally, we tend to accept norms as given and try to find methods of enforcing them, rather than discuss how we might plan for changing the norms themselves. We run into difficult problems here about what are ultimate and what are proximate norms and how far the achievement of proximate norms may interfere with the achievement of ultimate ones. The proximate norms of getting good grades may interfere with a student's education, which is the ultimate norm; the proximate norm of national defense may interfere with the ultimate norm of national survival or human survival; the proximate norm of law enforcement may interfere with the ultimate norm of crime reduction, and so on. There are grave problems here in the reality-testing of images of social systems, clearly insoluble in this brief essay.

If this paper seems to sound an uncertain trumpet, it is because we really do not know what battle we are engaged in. There is a good deal of confused anxiety at the present time about personal responsibility and possible decay of norms or increased deviance from norms which seem to have served us very well in the past. These changes, however, as we have seen, are hard to assess and even harder to predict. The kind of systems with which we are dealing—such as the dynamics of legitimacy, change in norms, and so on—are not well behaved, predictable systems, but are subject to all sorts of discontinuities, sudden transformations, and shocks, as well as having certain underlying continuities. If there is any message which emerges out of this analysis, it is first that we should beware of appearances. Sometimes, though not always, what looks like an increase in deviance is, in fact, a change in norms, which itself may have to be assessed according to more fundamental norms. The second message is that, when it comes to the future, the most important thing to prepare for is the unexpected.

The evolutionary race goes to the adaptable, not to the well-adapted, to those who can learn, not to those who know. One of the most dangerous things in any decision-making is to have an illusion of certainty in an uncertain situation. In any situation, there is an optimum degree of commitment. The overcommitted are apt to commit themselves to the wrong thing, and the undercommitted to wallow in an everlasting dither. The ability to detect this optimum is perhaps one of the principal characteristics of leadership in any field.

THE SCHOOLING INDUSTRY AS A POSSIBLY PATHOLOGICAL SECTION OF THE AMERICAN ECONOMY

Rev. of Educ. Res., 42, 1 (April 1972): 129-143

THE SCHOOLING INDUSTRY AS
A POSSIBLY PATHOLOGICAL SECTION
OF THE AMERICAN ECONOMY

The schooling industry may be described as the segment of an economy that maintains the institutions of formal education—kindergartens, schools, colleges, universities, and so on. One should really include private schools, technical schools, occupational schools and perhaps, a little more doubtfully, training programs in industry, especially where these have independent organizations. As a segment of the American economy, the schooling industry now represents between 6% and 7% of the total, having risen from somewhat under 3% in the last thirty years. It is now a larger segment of the American economy than agriculture, and there are good reasons for supposing that it will continue to grow at least until the end of the century.

Like the war industry, which is the segment of the economy that produces what is purchased with the military budget, the schooling industry is supported mainly through public or private grants (that is, one-way transfer payments) rather than by the sale of services in an open market. The war industry, incidentally, at 8% is not much larger than the schooling industry.

I have used the term "schooling" rather than "education" deliberately; "schooling" is what is done in schools and other places of formal education, whereas "education" is a much larger phenomenon that includes all human learning. The education industry would include not only schooling but also a great deal of child rearing, travel, books, newspapers, television, radio, public speeches, meetings, churches, indeed, all situations in human life where some kind of change is effected in the cognitive structure of the human nervous system. Machlup (1962) has devised an even larger concept that he calls the "knowledge industry" ; this includes not only all forms of human learning, but also entertainment and any situation where some kind of communication passes from one human being to another. Machlup in

1962 estimated the knowledge industry as some 29% of the American economy, compared with the 7% that is devoted to schooling. What happens to the schooling industry, therefore, must always be considered in the light of the larger educational and knowledge industry of which it is an essential part, but still only a part.

Products of the Schooling Industry

Knowledge

The schooling industry has a number of peculiarities. In the first place it is producing a product, or rather a set of products, that are hard to define, measure, and even to identify. Its first product is *knowledge*, that is, changes in the cognitive structure of the nervous system of particular individuals, which increase that structure in extent and hopefully in realism (that is, in correspondence with some outside reality). An unlettered lady from Appalachia who was asked if she had ever heard of France said, yes, she thought it was a place somewhere the other side of Asheville. Every person who has been through the eighth grade probably knows that France is a country on the eastern side of the Atlantic Ocean, that its people speak a language called French, and so on, even though 99% of the people who have this knowledge may never have been to France. Without schooling our knowledge is confined very largely to what our unaided senses bring into us, and it is therefore confined to our specific environment. One of the major purposes of schooling is to expand knowledge into the larger environment that includes the whole earth and indeed the universe, and to expand it also back into time far beyond the direct personal experience of the individual, so that he knows not only about his own contemporaries, but about people who lived thousands of years ago and thousands of miles away.

The quantity of knowledge acquired by any person can be investigated by examination, that is, by asking questions to which the person has to respond. Examinations, we all know, are imperfect samples of the knowledge of any one person, but they are usually better than nothing. A frequent criticism of schooling is that its only product is examinations and examination results. There certainly are types of schooling, perhaps less important than they used to be, that are directed towards passing examinations rather than acquiring knowledge; in such cases the measure is usurping the thing it is supposed to measure. I am not sure, however, that this criticism is a very severe one, for the ability to pass an examination is certainly positively related to the amount of knowledge the examinee possesses, and furthermore is in itself a skill that is not valueless.

Skills

This suggests that the second product of schooling is *skills*, which is not quite the same thing as knowledge. I can have knowledge about France without knowing how to get there, or without this knowledge requiring me or even enabling me to do anything at all. There are many kinds of knowledge, however, such as literacy, knowledge of other languages, and knowledge of practical skills, that are of importance mainly because they enable the possessor to do things that otherwise he would not be able to do—to read, to write, to make pottery, to weld, to mend clothes, or to do any of the innumerable things life requires of us. There is a certain tendency among psychologists especially to identify knowledge with skill under the impact of behavioral notions.

This identification seems to me to be unwarranted, but we could always get around it by defining knowledge as the skill in passing examinations and a skill as the ability to do other things. It is possible, however, to have knowledge without skill; it is not possible to have skill without knowledge, even though the knowledge may be at the level of the lower nervous system rather than at the higher (as for example, the kind of knowledge required to play tennis). It should be noted that schooling usually includes this nonverbal kind of knowledge, especially in the athletic department and in vocational education. Know-how, however, is just as surely knowledge as know-what, and it is just as surely a legitimate part of schooling. The teaching of practical morality, incidentally, can easily be regarded as a kind of skill. It is the know-how of getting along in the particular society in which one is placed. This also is clearly a part of schooling.

Custodial Service

The production of knowledge and skill may be regarded as the most legitimate products of schooling. There are, however, other products that are not usually mentioned as often, and that perhaps have a certain flavor of illegitimacy about them; they are, nevertheless, important in determining the willingness of the society to expand or contract the schooling industry. One of these less legitimate, or perhaps merely less recognized, products is *custodial service*, or "childsitting." In an industrial urban society, especially, children are something of a nuisance to their parents if they are around the house underfoot all day. By taking the children off their parents' hands and by moving young people off the streets and into high schools and colleges, the schools perform a public service somewhat akin to the garbage collector. They remove sources of disutility and segregate them away from the rest of the society, at least for certain hours during the day. This releases parents for productive activity of some kind, either in a job or in preferred leisure-time activities. The actual economics of the schooling industry may be more closely related to this by-product than to its main products of knowledge and skill.

The willingness of people to raise their school taxes is remarkably enhanced by a school system shutting down for a few weeks and delivering the children to the tender mercies of their parents and the streets, or even by going on double sessions so that the children are released into the outside world at unusual times. It may be indeed that the great virtue of the traditional summer vacation, even though it may have originated in an earlier agricultural age, is that by the end of the summer the willingness of adults to get children back to school is considerably augmented. A wise school district indeed will always put up its tax votes just before Labor Day. I would very much like to see a study of the success of school bonds and millage increases related to the time of year in which they are voted on.

The custodial role of the school industry, while it has undoubted positive aspects in releasing adults from the worry and inconvenience of having children and young people around them, also has considerable social costs, which we are only just beginning to realize. It is impossible to exercise custodial care of any group of people without segregating them. We see this, for instance, in the most extreme form in prisons, which are optimistically called reformatories but which are usually schools for crime. It is likewise impossible to segregate children and young people in schools, colleges, and universities without creating a "youth culture," which may easily become pathological. In all human societies, until about the last hundred years, schooling was the privilege of a very small elite, typically perhaps not more than 1% of the population. Most children lived around the house with their parents; when they became young people they lived in an essentially adult world, working with adults and developing a "youth culture" only in their free time, which was not very much.

By 1900 most Western countries had virtually all children up to the age of fourteen in the schools. In the United States we have gone from about 10% of the corresponding age group in high schools in 1900 to about 80% today, with an even more striking proportional increase in students in college. This is an absolutely unprecedented change in the condition of society, the full consequences of which have by no means been worked out. Some of the consequences, of course, are very desirable, in the shape of a much better-informed and highly-skilled population. Other consequences, however, in terms of segregated youth cultures, may be quite undesirable, and such youth cultures may produce startling social changes, perhaps considerably for the worse, in the next thirty years. The "generation gap" that is so much observed and is unquestionably pronounced today is precisely a result of the fact that the older generation, as it were, is a product of an age in which schooling was much more a privilege, whereas the younger generation takes it for granted and perhaps therefore values it less.

Certification

Another slightly disreputable, but extremely important, product of the schooling industry is *certification*. A high school diploma and a college degree are worth something in the job market, and these equivalences have been studied in some detail. Certification, of course, is not the same thing as either knowledge or skill, although it is presumably positively correlated with these desirable products, even though the correlation may not be as high as we would wish. Certification is like the stamp on a coin. Once it is the certificate that has become important, rather than the knowledge or skill which it is supposed to represent, there is always danger of inflation. A high school diploma today, unless one looks behind it to the actual course of study that has been taken, is a very different thing from what it was in 1900. It now may represent a great deal more semi-vocational skills in such subjects as basket weaving and shop than it does knowledge of even quite small segments of the universe. The rise of students to political power in the colleges and universities is almost certain to result in an inflation of the college degree. After all, if one can get certification with less work this looks like an improvement in productivity. The only physical product of the teacher is a grade sheet and the only physical product of the school or college is a piece of paper, or maybe parchment or vellum, with some sort of certification inscribed on it.

Certification may be overvalued as well as undervalued. It may be an inflated measure of the achievement that it is supposed to certify, but it may also be overvalued, especially in the job market, as a surrogate for detailed inquiries into the real capabilities of the job applicant. High school diplomas are frequently required for jobs of a relatively unskilled nature, which clearly do not require the high school experience as a prerequisite for their performance. The same may be said of college degrees. I frankly do not know what can be done about this. It is a very puzzling question in social policy. Some of the imperfections in the labor market that raise very serious problems (especially in American society) such as hindering us from achieving full employment without inflation, may be attributed to the overemphasis placed on certification. On the other hand, unless there is some distinction between the certified and the uncertified, the incentive to obtain certification is considerably lowered and, if the incentive to acquire knowledge and skill is less than the incentive to acquire certification, certification may be the major avenue in society through which a demand for knowledge and skill is encouraged. I am afraid I do not hold the optimistic view that in the absence of any reward structure young people will spontaneously engage themselves in the arduous and frequently unpleasant task of acquiring knowledge and skill. Just what the optimum relative reward structure should be, however, is a very difficult problem that we are still a very long way from solving.

Community Activity

A fifth, and more positive product of the schooling industry is that its institutions are often the focus for *community activity*. The high school, especially in an American community, often plays something of the role that the church did in the Middle Ages as a focus for the community; a symbol of its pride; and a place where people gather for school concerts, school plays, and so on; or as a center for adult education. This is a positive aspect of the schooling industry that is often overlooked by its critics.

Schooling as a Grants Economy

The second great peculiarity of the schooling industry is that its revenue, unlike that, say, of the steel industry, is not derived from the sale of its product in the market (except in relatively small segments of the industry) but is derived mainly from what I have been calling the "grants economy," that is, by essentially one-way transfers. A "grant" differs from an exchange: An exchange represents a reciprocal transfer of conventionally equal values, so that in an exchange the net worth of the exchanging parties does not change in total, although their assets change in structure. In a grant, however, the net worth of the granting party is reduced and the net worth of the grantee is increased in the moment of the transaction. Outside of a rather small private sector of adult education—such as Berlitz language schools, secretarial schools, and so on, where the student himself buys the education out of his own money and the product of the school can therefore be considered as being sold in a market—the schooling industry is almost wholly financed by grants, either public or private. Even in the case of private schools, it is usually parents who pay the bills and the children who receive the schooling, so that what we have in fact is a grant of money from the parent to the school and a grant of schooling from the parent to the child.

In the case of the public schools, the grants element is even clearer. Taxes are a grant from the taxpayer to the taxing authority, in the sense that when a person pays his taxes his net worth diminishes and that of the recipient increases. Schools may be financed directly out of school taxes, in which case the school system itself is the taxing authority and there is no intermediary, or they may be financed by grants from other taxing authorities, such as states or cities. In any case, the persons who receive the product—whether this is knowledge, skill, custodial care, or certification—are not the people who pay for it. This divorce between the recipient of the product and the payer of the bills is perhaps the major element in the peculiar situation of the industry that may lead to pathological results. It is hard to resist quoting from Adam Smith (1937) at this point, who held a low opinion of a situation in which the producers of a product were effectively divorced from its consumers:

> Those parts of education, it is to be observed, for the teaching of which there are no public institutions, are generally the best taught. When a young man goes to a fencing or a dancing school, he does not indeed always learn to fence or to dance very well; but he seldom fails of learning to fence or to dance. The good effects of the riding school are not commonly so evident. The expence of a riding school is so great, that in most places it is a public institution. The three most essential parts of literary education, to read, write, and account, it still continues to be more common to acquire in private than in public schools; and it very seldom happens that any body fails of acquiring them to the degree in which it is necessary to acquire them [p. 721].

Productivity of the Schooling Industry

Is Progress Possible?

The schooling industry—and one might even add the whole educational industry to this—is notoriously unprogressive when it comes to productivity. It is hard indeed to measure the productivity of the industry. A rough measure of its backwardness relative to the rest of the economy, however, may be gathered from Table 1, in which the

TABLE 1

A Comparison of the Growth of the Schooling Industry with the Increase of Its Physical Product

Year	Total School Expenditure as a Percentage of Gross Capacity Product	Percent of "Children" (Age 5-19) in School Year	Index of Terms of Trade of "Schooling"
1930	3.3	.80	100
1940	2.7	.85	77
1950	2.9	.91	77
1960	4.7	.90	127
1969	6.0	.93	156

schooling industry as a percentage of the total product (in current dollars) is compared with almost the only measure of its physical product that we have: the number of school years as a proportion of the school population. It will be seen that the schooling industry as a proportion of the total economy has risen much faster than its physical product, suggesting that there has been a substantial increase in the "real price" of education, that is, in education's terms of trade, which has almost doubled since 1950. This is to be expected if it is an industry that is not increasing in productivity as fast as the rest of the economy, because the sheer pressures of the labor market will force up wages in the schooling industry to something comparable to the rest of society, and if productivity is not increased this means that the real price of schooling will have to increase in order to pay the increase of real wages and other costs.

Whether we regard this as "pathological" or not depends on our estimate of the extent to which the failure of the schooling industry to increase its productivity is something fundamental and unavoidable in the nature of the industry itself, or whether it is related to the particular form of social and economic organization that the industry possesses. I frankly know of no way to make a very accurate judgment in this matter. If there is in fact no way in which the productivity of the schooling industry can be increased, in the sense that there are simply no other possible techniques that would result in, let us say, more knowledge and skill acquired per real dollar of expenditure, then there is nothing pathological about the present situation, just as there is nothing pathological in the inability of a human being to jump a hundred feet up into the air. I use knowledge and skill, incidentally, as the measures of productivity, simply because the custodial function obviously is not capable of any increase in productivity, except at the sacrifice in the increase in knowledge and skill. We could, I suppose, simply build very cheap huts in which we keep young people under sedatives all day. Indeed, where the attitude of the public toward education is primarily concerned with its custodial aspect, this is often the real meaning of "cutting out the frills," of the classroom being a cheap and respectable sedative.

The certification aspect, also, can only be subject to pathological changes in productivity if it is unrelated to the development of knowledge and skill. The kind of certification that consists of a diploma from Groton, Eton, or Harrow may have very little to do with knowledge, though it may have something to do with the skill of belonging to the upper class. It is, however, the kind of certification that is incapable of generalization without defeating itself. There is a good deal of evidence indeed that high prestige universities, colleges, and schools produce certification rather than knowledge and skill, in the sense that it is only in certification that they have a comparative advantage over the low prestige institutions, who seem to produce about as much knowledge and skill as the high prestige ones. This all the more underlines the principle, however, that certification is not subject to developments in productivity, and from this point of view it is only productivity in knowledge and skill that is significant.

One would have to be a very great pessimist indeed, however, to believe that no further improvements in the productivity in schooling in terms of knowledge and skill per real dollar expenditure could possibly be achieved. It may well be that the major obstacle to any substantial increase in this productivity is the absence of any adequate theory regarding the nature and machinery of the human learning process. Almost all that we really know about human learning could probably be put on a page. We know it may be discontinuous; that it exhibits problems of "readiness" rather like the imprinting phenomenon that is well documented in some animals; that it is related to the system of rewards and punishment in the perception of payoffs; that knowledge tends to grow towards the payoffs. On the other hand, we also have to learn what the payoffs are, so that this makes the whole process remarkably unstable dynamically. We know that emulation sometimes produces greater productivity and sometimes produces less, and we don't know very much about when it does one and when it does the other. We know a little about reinforcement and the acquisition of skill; we know astonishingly little about the acquisition of knowledge and concepts; and we know still less about motivation towards the acquisition of knowledge.

It is this absence of a basic theoretical framework that I think makes most educational research have the fatal quality of lack of cumulative additivity, so that we are by no means sure that we really know much more about how to educate people than we did, say, fifty years ago, in spite of all the educational research that has been done. Educational practice exhibits fashions and cycles, but one does not get the impression that it has the kind of strongly increasing trends in productivity that some other industries do. The trouble here is that it is impossible to predict technical change. It is, in particular, impossible to predict undiscovered ideas; otherwise, we would have them now. It is, therefore, extremely hard to estimate the potential for increasing productivity of any industry, and it is particularly hard in the case of education, where there is very little history of increasing productivity, so that we do not even have any trends to project.

What I think one can assert is that if an increase in productivity were better rewarded than it is now, the probability of productivity increase would certainly be greater, even though there is no way of knowing by how much. The present system certainly militates against any increase in the productivity of education. Educators receive their incomes mainly, let us be frank about it, from the by-products of custodial care and certification, and if an educator develops an exceptionally productive method of increasing knowledge and skill he is not likely to be particularly well rewarded for it. The same goes for educational institutions. There is really no way in which the educational "firm," that is, the school district—even the private school, or the college, or the university—can make the public aware of any substantial increase in its own productivity and so increase its share of the market. In industries in which the revenue is derived mainly from the sale of a product to people who directly consume it, if the product is not good people will not buy it, subject to some modifications of this proposition by the arts of Madison Avenue. If a firm discovers a substantially improved method of production that increases its productivity, it can sell its product cheaper so that it will have a competitive advantage and will expand. We even have a patent law to give people property in innovations; this is presumably more in the public interest than secrecy, which would be almost the only other alternative.

In the schooling industry, by contrast, price competition is very ineffective. The difference in price, for instance to the parent, of private schools versus public schools, or private universities versus state universities, is a striking example of the dominance of certification over knowledge and skill, for there is very little evidence that private schools or private universities produce a much better knowledge product than many of their public equivalents. There are outstanding teachers at all levels of education who inspire an abnormal proportion of their students to go on to acquire increasing amounts of knowledge and skill. In the words of W. S. Gilbert, their reward all too often is "the satisfying feeling that our duty has been done," and though this internal satisfaction may be substantial reward it is neither patentable nor duplicable.

One of the most frustrating things about the schooling industry indeed is the apparent almost-total incapacity of good teachers to be able to pass on this particular skill to others. There is a parallel in many other fields including, for instance in music. Music schools can teach the elements but they cannot undertake to produce a great artist, and the great artist is quite incapable of explaining to anybody else how he uses his skill in a way that would enable him to transmit the skill to others. In the schooling industry, however, the difference in productivity between the great teacher and the mediocre one may be large. The bad teacher, furthermore, may have a negative productivity that leads to a positive destruction of motivation and ambition in the student. One sometimes suspects indeed that the main problem of the schooling industry is how to keep out of it those teachers who have negative productivity and who destroy the incentives and the identity of their students.

Increasing the Productivity of Schooling

The Commercial Approach. The question then remains, "Are there any organizational devices which might be applied to the schooling industry which would encourage the growth of genuine productivity?" A considerable number of suggestions to this effect have been made; none, I think, have really been proved. Popular terms these days, of course, are "performance contracting" and "accountability," as expressed particularly in the contracting of education out to private firms. Theoretically one might suppose that a firm that developed unusually productive techniques would be able to patent these and would have remarkable competitive advantage. There are, however, real difficulties that cannot be laid wholly to the traditional conservatism of the teaching profession. One can certainly expect teachers who have been comfortably inefficient not to like the risk of occasionally rather plush competition. The objections of the teaching profession, however, may not be entirely a result of blind conservatism and the defense of special interests. The very peculiarities of the schooling industry make it unfit to be treated as if it were a simple commercial operation like the production of fat hogs.

It is not merely that students are extraordinarily complex pieces of apparatus and that we do not really know what it is that induces them to perform, except very superficially; but, what is more important, schooling is something that almost always takes place in a community setting. This is something that is not always realized by technicians, and the destruction of the community of the school or even of the classroom, imperfect as it is, can easily be disastrous to the total development of the student. Schooling on a slick assembly line basis may produce "results" in the short run, but it could easily have disastrous long-term consequences of which at present we know very little, and perhaps care less. I am not saying that these more subtle phenomena could not be taken care of by commercial enterprises. I am just saying that the atmosphere of commercial enterprises is very different from those in an educational institution, and that the fulfillment of clearly defined short-run objectives may easily be contrary to certain very important and large long-run objectives that are hard to pinpoint but have been developed over long years of experience in what might be called the "folk knowledge" of the schooling industry.

The Voucher Plan. Another proposal that is receiving some favorable attention at the moment is the so-called "voucher plan," by which the student rather than the school is subsidized. In this plan the student is given a voucher of so many dollars a year that he can exchange for education at any recognized establishment. We have had experience with something like this, of course, under the GI Bill of Rights, so it is not wholly unfamiliar. That experience was by no means adverse, even if it did produce a few fly-by-night educational operations. The great virtue claimed for the voucher plan is that it permits the student (or parent) greater freedom of choice in the selection of schools; it also forces the schools to compete for students so that here, again, a school that achieves a greater productivity may be able to attract a larger number of students and hence will expand. Likewise, methods that have proved themselves in one place will have to be imitated in others if the competing institutions are to survive. There is enough logic in this proposal to make it seem worth a try and some experiments in this direction are now being proposed.

This proposal also meets with substantial opposition from the educational establishment. In this case, however, one is a little afraid that the opposition of the establishment is not wholly unrelated to its unwillingness to move out of a highly protected market, for which after all it can hardly be blamed. Perhaps the principal argument against the voucher plan is that it would permit too much variety in education (would permit, for instance, the development of parochial schools and subcultural schools of all kinds), and that it would fragment the society. In the United States, especially, we have always visualized the educational system as an Americanizer, especially for the enormously diverse subcultures that have populated this continent. In the early days one could make a strong argument for this point of view. Today, however, the society seems well-enough established that it can afford diversity; indeed it may be more threatened from an enforced conformity than it is from a tolerated diversity. If the state retained the power of licensing the approved schools that could compete for students, this would seem to be enough regulatory capacity to deal with any extreme cases that went beyond the bounds of the acceptable middle ground of public and private custom.

The voucher plan would still leave the revenue of the school systems pretty much in the hands of the grants economy, especially the public grants economy. It would permit the development of supplementary markets at the edges, where parents who wish to add a little extra would be able to do so. It might be argued that this would interfere with the equalizing function of the public school system. This, however, is not too strong an argument even now, simply because of the geographical segregation by income that permits the rich suburbs to have expensive school systems and the poor areas to have poor systems. If the voucher were generous enough it could act as an equalizer far beyond the extent of the present system, although it is a little doubtful whether this would be politically feasible. The great problem here is the problem of the grants economy in general, in that its total size reflects the strength of the community and the willingness of individuals within the community to sacrifice for public goods, especially those they may not enjoy personally.

The Grants Economy. There are several reasons for supposing that the grants economy, especially as applied to the schooling industry, is likely to run into increasing difficulty in the next few decades. One reason for this is the changing age composition of the population. As the birth rate declines and as the older age groups fill up we may find that the proportion of the population that consists of parents with children is quite likely to decline, particularly once the present "bulge" of births from 1947 to 1961 has passed through their age of childbearing, which is now just beginning. A voting population that is heavily weighted towards those past childrearing, or even those before it, is less likely to vote large sums of money for the schooling industry whether directly through a public school system or indirectly through a voucher plan.

The Economics of the Schooling Industry

It may well be, therefore, that we will have to look for some way of getting the educational industry out from under the grants economy, or at least to get a larger proportion of it into something that looks more like a market exchange economy than it does now. One very interesting proposal for this which I have been calling the Killingsworth proposal, originated by Professor Charles Killingsworth of Michigan State University (1963, 1967). This proposal is to set up educational banks, federally financed, that will lend the student the full cost of his education. The loan would be repaid by a surcharge on his income tax for the rest of his life. This scheme is particularly valuable perhaps for college and beyond, as in this case education is very clearly an investment to the individual as well as to the society, and there seems to be no reason why an appropriate financial system should not be devised to take care of what is essentially a private investment. We cannot, of course, use the chattel mortgage system, as this would put too great a burden on the individual whose income does not happen to be increased by his education. If an individual's income is increased by his education, however, there seems to be no reason why he should not use part of this increase to pay for the education itself. In a rough way, of course, this is what already happens in so far as the progressive income tax is used to finance education. Actually, however, at present the finance of education comes far too much out of regressive local taxes, especially property taxes, so that all too often it is the poor who are really subsidizing the education of the rich and the middle classes.

The Killingsworth proposals are not so appropriate at the high school level or below, mainly because we have the ideal of educating everybody up to this level; in this case education is no longer a privilege that provides a higher income, but a kind of standard base that is, as it were, a ticket of admission to the system in general. For some time to come, however, higher education is likely to be an investment for the individual, and under these circumstances something like the Killingsworth proposal seems to me sensible and perhaps almost the only way of averting a major economic crisis in colleges and universities in the next generation.

In any consideration of the economics of the schooling industry it must never be forgotten that it always is embedded in the larger educational enterprise, much of which is conducted in the family. One of the most striking of all educational statistics is the relationship between the number of years of schooling obtained by any individual and the number of his siblings on the one hand, and the educational level of his parents on the other. The larger the family, the poorer the educational achievements of its members; the poorer the educational achievement of the parents, the poorer the educational achievement of the children. This effect is probably more significant in determining the distribution of education and even its total quantity than all the reforms we might make in the schooling industry (Duncan, 1968). These relationships relate perhaps to the demand for education rather than to its supply or to its productivity, but they do suggest that the self-perpetuating character of poverty subcultures and large family subcultures may be the greatest source of what might be called "educational wastage," that is, unused capacities for knowledge and skill. We certainly cannot rest content with the present situation in seeking for a solution of the very difficult problems that lie ahead however; we must look at the educational industry or even the knowledge industry as a whole, as well as that part that is comprised of schooling. Otherwise, we may find ourselves trying to provide a supply for which there is quite inadequate demand and we may find ourselves destroying the subcultures within our society that actually keep the schooling industry alive and prospering.

It now looks as if we are at the beginning of a great outburst of research in educational matters, something which is long overdue. Our educational statistics and the whole information system in this regard are woefully inadequate, as we all know. The theoretical basis in human learning, as I have suggested, is even more inadequate. Nevertheless, it does seem to be an area where a substantial intellectual effort would have very substantial results; I myself would put it as virtually the highest priority of our society in the next generation.

NEW GOALS FOR SOCIETY?

In: Energy, Economic Growth, and the Environment.
Sam H. Schurr, ed. Baltimore: John Hopkins Univ. Press,
for Resources for the Future, 1972, pp. 139-151

New Goals for Society?

The thing in pollution we most need to know
Is, where does it come from and where does it go?
One major idea in the pot must be tossed,
That things may be missing, but never are lost.
Most chemical elements cannot be changed.
They can't be destroyed, they are just rearranged.
So clean water and air, and, indeed, your clean shirt,
Are obtained by the wise segregation of dirt.
So if our research is to bear healthy fruit,
The critical question is what to pollute.
One policy matter is clear; the polluter
Should not be allowed to become a commuter.
And as long as industrial systems have bowels
The boss should reside in the nest that he fouls.
Economists argue that all the world lacks is
A suitable system of effluent taxes.
They forget that if people pollute with impunity
This must be a symptom of lack of community.
But this means producing a mild kind of love
So let's hope the eagle gives birth to a dove.

The idea that society could have goals of any sort is a fairly modern one. I am not familiar with any intensive study of the history of the idea, and it is far beyond the scope of this paper to produce one. The rise of social self-consciousness and the idea that society itself might have an image of the future into which it could proceed is unfamiliar in classical civilization. For the Greeks, the future was in the hands of essentially random fates, and the idea that the society could decide what it was going to be like in 100 years would have been thought of as outrageous hubris, certain to call down almost immediate retribution from the gods.

In the Old Testament one finds a concept of a conditional future: Obey the Law and prosper; disobey the Law and be clobbered—and even this idea suffered substantial modification as a result of disappointments. Josiah was a good king and was clobbered; Manasseh was a bad one and prospered. The Babylonian captivities spiritualized the Jews' concept of social causation, and the Greek and Roman conquests pushed it toward eschatology and the messianic hope, a concept that also was dominant in early Christianity, where the individual goal was salvation and the social goal was simply to wait until the end. We see this view surviving vigorously to our own day in the Seventh-Day Adventists and similar cultures.

The idea that society in the secular sense might have patterns in time that could be detected, and hence have an image of its own future that might be realized, can perhaps be traced back to Machiavelli, but the idea of society as a developing process, with regularities that can be detected and a future that can be projected must be attributed to Adam Smith and classical economics. The "magnificent dynamic," as Baumol[1] calls it, the great scheme of secular processes by which a society accumulates knowledge, population, and capital and moves toward the stationary state, is as dramatic and magnificent in its own way as the great scheme of salvation in Christianity as we see it in Dante or Milton. Marx, however, is perhaps the first writer who seized upon the idea of a social dynamic, in this case a modified Hegelian dialectic, and turned it into a rhetoric for social change. The Marxist image, curiously enough, is perhaps closer to Christian eschatology than it is to Adam Smith, for it has a Garden of Eden in Primitive Communism, a "fall" in the invention of private property and primary accumulation, "sin" in the expropriation of surplus value by private property owners, a "last judgment" in the Revolution and the expropriation of the expropriators, and the Kingdom of Heaven on Earth in the Communist society to follow.

[1] William J. Baumol, *Economic Dynamics* (3rd ed., Macmillan, 1970).

By contrast, Adam Smith, Ricardo, and Malthus are more deterministic and more pessimistic, though the very formulation of the iron laws of the dismal science held open the possibility of breaking them. Thus, Malthus's dismal theorem that if the only checks on population growth were starvation and misery, then the population would grow until it was miserable and starved, can be expressed in the cheerful form that if something other than starvation and misery can be found to check population growth, the population does not have to grow until it is miserable and starves. All the classical economists were well aware of this potential cheerfulness underneath the gloom. To be cheerful, however, one has to understand the iron necessities of social life and social relationships, and that understanding has to be widespread enough for even political decision makers to understand it and act accordingly.

The development of images of the social future and of social self-consciousness, however, does not necessarily mean that society and those who make decisions on its behalf set goals, especially ultimate goals, for society to achieve. We really know very little about the future, and the further we look into the future the vaguer it gets. Even a self-conscious society, therefore, does not really proceed toward well-defined goals; it tries rather to proceed from day to day in a direction it perceives as "up"—"up," for some strange reason, meaning "better." This is perhaps why most of the social goals literature, such as that produced by President Eisenhower's Commission on National Goals,[2] for example, tends to have a slightly unreal and otherworldly quality. This is true even in the socialist countries. If one tries to talk to Communists about what they mean by Communism, which is supposed to be the ultimate goal toward which they are tending, they also become very fuzzy and unreal. No description of heaven, whether in another world or in this one, has ever sounded very convincing. There are very good reasons for this. Any statement of ultimate goals inevitably involves a projection of the growth of human knowledge, and this by definition is impossible, for if we could project knowledge we would know it now.

Another reason for rejecting the concept of social goals as inadequate is that the path that can be taken toward goals is itself subject to evaluation. Means are not evaluatively neutral. In some respects, means are more subject to evaluation than ends, and the doctrine that the ends justify the means is justly abhorred. I recall writing a verse inspired by Ward's study, *Goals of Economic Life*,[3] that

[2] *Goals for Americans*, The Report of the President's Commission on National Goals and Chapters Submitted for the Consideration of the Commission, Administered by the American Assembly, Columbia University (Prentice–Hall, 1960).

[3] Alfred Dudley Ward, ed., *Goals of Economic Life* (Harper, 1953).

went: "Oh where does economics tend, when end is means and means is end?" The whole distinction between ends and means becomes extremely difficult to maintain, when in a sense all ends are approximate and are means to something else. Even in the rituals of the Planning, Programming, and Budgeting System, the ends that are defined are usually quite arbitrary and are in fact always means to something else. There is a great deal in the Kantian ethic that every person should be treated as an ends rather than as a means. Even though it is never really possible to carry this out fully in practice, extreme violations of this principle, such as the Communists have sometimes practiced, destroy the legitimacy of the very ends of those who are so careless and indifferent to the means. Belief in an overriding social goal that justified any and every means was precisely what destroyed the legitimacy of the Communist party in the United States and is now very rapidly destroying the legitimacy of an aggressive American foreign policy.

It brings us closer to realism when we abandon the "social goals" concept and concentrate simply on what might be called a "dynamic evaluation function," which is simply a way of trying to describe "which way is up." To those eagle-eyed soaring souls who want to base every action on some splendid glimpse of a distant glorious future, this may seem like chickening out. The awful truth is that most of us are chickens, not eagles, and we could even take some evangelical solace in Newman's great hymn: "Keep Thou my feet;/ I do not ask to see the distant scene:/ one step enough for me." Even the kindly light that enables us to see the next step, however, is often remarkably dim, and in many social systems we do not really know whether we are going up or down.

What is implied here, of course, is a social welfare function, which we might perhaps better call an evaluative function, such as $V = f(a, b, c, \text{etc.})$. All we need for V is a set of ordinal numbers so that the higher numbers indicate a better state of the world, but what is inside the bracket is nothing less than the universe, or at least that part of it that most immediately concerns us. The difficulty here is that no general evaluative index, such as V, exists. That is, there is no single social indicator of which it can be said "the bigger the better" unequivocally.

If indeed we are to take the doctrine of the Aristotelian mean seriously, then all particular relationships between the indicators of the universe within the bracket of the function and the value indicator V will be nonlinear and will exhibit a maximum so that when an indicator is small, an increase in it will be "good," that is, will increase V, but as it gets larger it will reach a certain point where the impact on V is zero, and beyond that point an increase in the indicator diminishes V and is "bad." This could well be true even of something like the gross national product (GNP) per capita, or of any other measure of wealth. When the people are poor, it is obviously good if they become richer; but if the rich get richer they may merely become corrupted—an undesirable result that will cause V to decline with an increase in riches. Similarly, with an index like the expectation of life—when this is very low, an increase is clearly good; when it reaches, let us say, seventy or eighty, it is by no means clear that an increase in expectation of life is a good thing. It may easily become a bad thing. This essential nonlinearity of the social evaluation function makes these evaluations very difficult and opens up all sorts of possibilities of disagreement. This is particularly true of the more subtle qualities of a society, such as individual freedom, if we could index them. At what point, for instance, does freedom become license? At what point does equality become leveling? At what point does justice need to be turned into mercy, and so on?

Another source of difficulty in the development of social evaluation functions is the difficulty of estimating the interrelationships among the various items of the argument—a, b, c, and so on. Because of the enormous interrelatedness of the social system, it is very hard for any one of these items to go up without something else going down. The famous economic principle that none of the best things in life are free applies also to the social evaluation function in the sense that an increase in almost anything that is regarded as good, that is, an increase in it increases V, is likely to be accompanied by an increase in something else that is "bad," which decreases V, or a decrease in something else that is good, which also decreases V. Almost the whole pollution-environmental problem is summed up in the proposition that all goods are generally produced jointly with bads.

As we increase electric power, which is good, we also increase air pollution, destroy the beauty of the landscape with overhead wires, and use up irreplaceable fossil fuels, all of which are bad, but we diminish more polluting forms of power, which is good. The total evaluation thus becomes very difficult, partly because of psychological censoring processes that suppress information about bads and partly because of failures of the price system to put negative prices on negative commodities. There is thus a constant tendency to overestimate the goods and to underestimate the bads in these joint processes, and hence to indulge in processes of production that produce too many bads per good. Almost the only answer to this problem is to increase the visibility of the bads by better social indicators and by what might almost be called "Naderometers," or visible fuss.

There is no adequate name for decisions that involve and affect large numbers of people. Perhaps we might call them "macro decisions." It does not seem quite correct to call them "political decisions," because many decisions that affect large numbers of people, such as those made by the directors of large corporations, are not political in the ordinary sense of the word, yet they may affect more people than do the decisions of government bodies. A very important aspect of social dynamics is the process by which the evaluative functions of powerful decision makers are created and changed, for all decisions are made by evaluating alternative futures, according to some evaluation function.

The law and the prophets of decision theory can be summed up in the simple proposition that everybody does what he thinks is best at the time; then the question arises, however, the best for whom? There is a real distinction between "private" decisions, which are believed to be best for a particular individual, organization, or segment of society, and "public" decisions, which are supposed to be guided by what is best for society as a whole. There is, of course, an enormous literature, especially in economics, on the question of the circumstances under which what is best for the part is also best for the whole. The general conclusion found in this literature might be described as the law of parametric invariance. The simplest example of this is the economist's theory of perfect competition, in which each individual finds that all the exchange ratios with which he is faced cannot be affected by his own behavior. Even the economist's theory of natural liberty, however, soon becomes riddled with exceptions, particularly when we introduce threats, malevolence and benevolence, community, interdependence of utilities, and so on, so that a general theory of correspondence between public and private decisions still seems a long way off.

In any theory of social process, however, we must recognize that there is an enormous process of influencing the evaluation functions of powerful people who make macro decisions, whether these decisions are private or political. This may take place through persuasion, a process that goes on continuously in all organizations and also between organizations—in intimate chat, in committee discussions, in lobbying, in the mass media, and so on. When the processes of persuasion do not produce unanimity, social rituals, such as voting, may have to be invoked in order to achieve political decisions. If we define a ritual as an arbitrary procedure approved by everybody in the group concerned, it does not seem to be stretching the use of the word to use it to describe voting procedures—the majority rule, the two-thirds voting rule, or even nonvoting procedures, such as the choice of the occupants of political roles by lot, as in ancient Greece, or by hereditary succession. The great social significance of ritual is that it is usually easier to reach unanimity on ritualistic procedures than it is on substantive issues, and that hence the ritualistic procedures can be used to resolve conflicts where there is no agreement on substantive issues.

We by no means have exhausted the processes that are involved in acting on the welfare functions of powerful people. Threat processes are certainly important and are an element in persuasion. A man who commands a powerful bloc of votes that he can withdraw is apt to have a more persuasive rhetoric than one who does not. It must also be recognized that threats in the absence of a proper rhetorical matrix can easily backfire or produce counterthreat rather than submission. The exchange system, likewise, is significant in these processes. At its crudest, this is bribery and corruption, and a good many powerful people in history have been persuaded to change their evaluation functions by payments under the table.

It has been pointed out also by political analysts, such as David Easton,[4] that more subtle and legitimate exchange processes are also usually at work—such things as logrolling and the generalized exchange of political favors for support. In a society like the United States, which has a powerful voting ritual that commands almost universal acceptance, a critical factor in achieving political power is the identification of that cluster of evaluation functions that will command a majority of the electorate. This may easily result in curious inconsistencies or even intransitivities in the evaluation function, for instance, of the president, simply because the easiest way to get a majority of votes is to have a lot of people voting for one for different reasons. Hence, a candidate whose evaluation function is very clear and definite is less likely to be successful than one who creates a generalized impression of benign personality. A language that is blessed with enough ambiguity, so that it can mean a lot of different things to different people, can also be a powerful resolver of conflict.

These political considerations are taking me considerably beyond the original scope of this paper, and I must return to consider the problem of the impact of ultimate goals, or at least the vision of these goals as held by a significant number of significant people, and of the present evaluation functions that, as I have argued, really govern present behavior. I threw social goals out of the window in order to make way for the social evaluation function. Now I can sneak them in again by the back door. Certainly it cannot be denied that the prevailing vision of the future, either social or personal, has a profound effect on the evaluation function of the present.

Thus, if the prevailing image of the future is that of an otherworldly paradise, which all the great world religions have fostered in some of their phases, the general impact is to deny all social goals except that of toleration of the religion and support of the existing order. For certain kinds of religions, Marx's accusation that religion is an opiate of the people has some validity. There are times, however, when the prevailing ideology, whether religious or secular, becomes expansionist and comes to have an image of the future in which the existing structure spreads beyond its present boundaries. Expansionism is a persistent yet still very puzzling aspect of human history, as reflected in missionary religions and also in political imperialism. Nobody understands why some cultures become expansionistic and some do not. What is still more puzzling is why expansionism collapses, as it often does, very suddenly. It is within present lifetimes that British audiences, for instance, were singing Elgar's "Land of Hope and Glory," with its incredible couplet: "Wider, still and wider, may thy bounds be set,/ God who made Thee mighty, make Thee mightier yet"—a sentiment that

[4] David Easton, *A Systems Analysis of Political Life* (Wiley, 1965).

could only draw embarrassment from a modern British audience. Christianity, Islam, and Buddhism, likewise, have had periods of great expansionism and missionary endeavor and periods of withdrawal and support of the status quo.

Expansionism, however, is not the same thing as an image of future social change. Presumably the participants in all rebellions and uprisings have had some such image in mind. But as a major factor in social change itself, persuasive images of future social change became significant only after the eighteenth century. It is curious that even in the eighteenth century the image of the past, especially the ancient history of the Greeks and Romans, was frequently used to create and to legitimate expectations of the future, as in the American and the French Revolutions. The tremendous impact of Marxism on the world has unquestionably been because Marxism provided an image of social change as a legitimation of revolution and of treason against established orders. Revolutions, however, because of the randomness of the forces they unleash, almost inevitably produce changes that are very different from those in the minds of the original founders. Indeed, I have argued that revolutions have to be interpreted as disturbances in the course of the development of social evolutionary phyla, which frequently divert these phyla from their original potential.

More significant than revolutions, therefore, are the nonrevolutionary images of social change, such as those of the British Fabians and the American Institutionalists—even, one should add, the Prohibitionists—which had a very profound effect on policies and the evaluation functions of whole decades of subsequent decision makers. To a considerable extent the Fabians at the turn of the century wrote the history of Britain for the subsequent fifty years.

The effect of a vision of ultimate goals on immediate evaluation functions and decisions is by no means always benign. The disaster of the first collectivization of agriculture in the Soviet Union in the 1930s was a clear example of certain very long-run ultimate goals taking precedence over any kind of immediate pragmatic solution of problems. In the case of the United States, the disaster of Vietnam may well be the result of certain long-run images of the international system, derived from past experiences, such as Munich, which may not be at all applicable in the present situation. It is all too easy to keep one's eyes on the stars and then fall into the ditch. Nevertheless, it is also true that without vision the people perish; hence the development of ultimate goals and images of future society, which are not only persuasive and dramatic but realistic as well, is a very high priority for human survival.

We are now witnessing a fundamental shift that might be described without exaggeration as one of cataclysmic proportions in man's image of his own future. I have described this as a shift from "the great plane" to "the spaceship earth." Until very recently, man has inhabited, psychologically, a virtually unlimited flat earth. There has always been somewhere to go over the horizon, some boundary to the known world beyond which there were further worlds to explore. Now this long period of human expansion has suddenly come to an end, actually, in my own lifetime. Even when I was a boy, there were still white places on the map of the globe where no man had ever been. Today there are none. The space enterprise has, if anything, accentuated the smallness of the earth and the loneliness of man. This beautiful blue and white ball is clearly the only decent piece of real estate in a very long way and we are stuck with it. We have had a period of enormous expansion in the last 200 years, in which, for instance, the growth of human knowledge has almost certainly increased natural resources much faster than man has used them up. Nevertheless, there is now a brooding sense that this cannot go on forever, or indeed for very long as historical time is counted, and that within, say, 100 years, or at most 500 years, a very radical change has to be made in man's technology and in all probability in his social system, his culture, and in his image of himself as he makes the transition into the small, tight, closed, crowded, limited spaceship earth, which will almost certainly have to rely on inputs of solar energy for its power and will have to recycle virtually all materials for its goods. We are moving toward the end of the linear economy that goes from mines and wells to dumps and pollution. The circle must be made complete. All the excreta of man's activities must be transformed, and this by inputs of solar power, into goods again.

This image of the future has a grim air of physical necessity about it. We are living in just so big a house and there are only so many things that can be done with it. The psychological impact of this shift has barely begun to be felt. I think many of what look like pathological aspects of the current youth culture may be a symptom of further changes to come. Young people, after all, are more sensitive to the future than oldsters, simply because they are going to live in it longer. My own personal concern about the twenty-first century is strictly abstract, since I will be quite surprised if I reach that century, whereas young people today will live well into it.

Closely connected with this vision of a spaceship earth is a slowly gathering realization that perhaps the really great age of change is now over, that economic growth, or at least its technical basis, is slowing down and is likely to slow down even further. I have been teasing audiences by saying that I thought the great age of change was my grandfather's life. When I look back on my childhood in the 1920s, the world does not seem terribly different; there were automobiles, electricity, the beginnings of the radio, telephone, the movies, and with one or two exceptions, like television, plastics, and antibiotics, what I have seen in my lifetime is more of the same. By contrast, my grandfather, looking back in 1920 on his childhood in 1860, looked back on a wholly different world—without electricity, without automobiles, without airplanes, without movies, without telephones, without anything that we think of as constituting modern life, and his life as a boy was certainly not very much different from that of his grandfather or his grandfather or his grandfather.

In the United States since 1967 we have seen a very sharp decline in the rate of increase of gross productivity, that is, GNP in real terms divided by the total employed labor force, including the armed services (table 1). We have had periods like this in the past so that it is hard to tell whether this is a temporary phenomenon or the beginnings of a long-run trend, but it certainly suggests why

Table 1. Rate of Increase of Gross Labor Productivity in the United States, 1961-1970

Year	Gross labor productivity change from previous year (*percent*)
1961	1.90
1962	4.70
1963	2.59
1964	3.19
1965	3.81
1966	3.43
1967	0.21
1968	2.58
1969	0.35
1970	−0.88

we managed to have both unemployment and inflation in 1970, with the economy geared to increases in money income to take advantage of expected increases in productivity that did not materialize. Even over the last forty years economic growth in the United States has not been spectacular. It took thirty years to increase real per capita disposable income by 50 percent. This might underestimate welfare somewhat, since it does not take account of public goods, but even on the most optimistic assumptions, we are certainly not much more than twice as rich as our grandfathers. Furthermore, many of the factors that have permitted increasing incomes in the last thirty years are not repeatable. One of these is the remarkable release of manpower from the increase in productivity of agriculture, which has now brought agriculture down to 6 percent of the labor force so that even if agricultural productivity doubles in the next generation only 3 percent of the labor force would be released for other things. As productivity in particular occupations increases, the proportion of the economy in industries that are improving declines, and the proportion in productivity-stagnant industries, such as education, government, medicine, and so on, increases. It seems highly probable, therefore, that there will be a substantial decline in the rate of increase in gross productivity in the next few decades.

A sharp decline in the rate of population growth is also very much in the works for the United States and indeed for the whole temperate zone. Fertility in the United States has declined so dramatically from 1961 that a little further decline will bring Americans to a net reproductive ratio of 1. It seems, therefore, that the United States is much closer to what might be called ZPPG, that is, Zero Population and Productivity Growth, than anyone could have conceived ten or twenty years ago.

It is a fundamental principle of futurology that all projections are wrong, including mine, and certain events, of course, could postpone the coming of the spaceship earth and could lead to a longer period of productivity growth, though not perhaps of population growth. I have been able to think of only three changes, all of which seem to have rather low probability, that could drastically change the picture. These are artificial life, as a result of the developments of molecular biology; artificial intelligence, as a result of the development of computers—or even a breakthrough on the understanding of natural intelligence and human learning; and the gravity shield (a substance or process that would block the force of gravity), which would drastically change the whole power picture. None of these, however, seem at all probable in the next 50 or 100 years, with the possible exception of the first.

The image of the future outlined here is bound to have a profound effect on the evaluation function of all kinds of decision makers, an effect that will increase as we move further into the future. It implies a high value on modesty rather than grandeur. There is no room for "great societies" in the spaceship. It implies conservationism to the point of conservatism rather than expansionism. It implies a high value on taking things easy, on conflict management. There is no place in the spaceship for men on white horses and very little room for horsing around. We cannot afford to have war, revolution, or dialectical processes. Everything must be directed toward the preservation of precarious order rather than experimentation with new forms. We have to stress equality rather than incentives, simply in order to minimize uncertainty and conflict. It is important to realize that the case for equality may not rest at all on the concepts of social justice. Equality, indeed, denies at least one principle of social justice—that distribution should be in rough proportion to desert—for under an equalitarian regime the deserving get less than they deserve and the undeserving get more, assuming at least something like a normal distribution of deservingness. Nevertheless, there may be a case for equality that rests not at all on social justice but on the sheer demand of the system for stability. A just society that provided incentives for virtue might simply prove to be too unstable.

If all this sounds rather depressing, it is intended to be. Economists have never been very cheerful about the stationary state, and a permanent, planetwide stationary state, from which there seemed to be no possible means of escape, might be a very depressing prospect indeed. What is even more depressing is that a stationary state (ZPPG) might not even be stable, simply because of the intensification of conflicts within it.

In the progressive state, conflicts can be resolved fairly easily by progress itself. The poor can get richer without the rich getting poorer. In the stationary state, if the poor are to get richer, then the rich must get poorer, and what is even more frightening, if the rich are to get richer, they can only do so by increasing their exploitation of the poor, and since the rich may be the most powerful, they may have strong incentives to do this. Thus, the banished specter of exploitation, which progress made obsolete, is reintroduced into the world. The dialectical processes to which a stationary state would be exposed would thereby become much more acute and might easily destroy the state's precarious equilibrium, in war, revolution, social upheaval, the decay of all legitimacies, and a Hobbesian nightmare of retrogression in the war of all against all. As Adam Smith said prophetically, the declining state is melancholy.[5]

As long as I am being pessimistic, I might as well go the whole way. Let me suggest, therefore, that the romantic socialism of the Mao–Castro variety, which seems at the moment to both the capitalist world and the "business socialist" camp of the Soviet Union and Eastern Europe to be an embarrassing blemish on the face of at least a moderately rational earth, may turn out to be more significant than we think, as a legitimation of economic stagnation. These societies still make some sort of pretense that they are engaged in economic development. A genuinely equalitarian society, however, in which reward is completely divorced from performance of any kind is extremely unlikely to have very much increase in productivity. It will be like Adam Smith's Oxford University, which was a society remarkably equalitarian among the Fellows, in which rewards were completely divorced from productivity; which, being celibate, certainly had zero or negative population growth; which had zero productivity growth; and which therefore should be the beau ideal of any thorough-paced ecologically minded advocate of Consciousness Three. One can even visualize the scientists lingering in these future stable societies like the despised clerics of C. P. Snow's Cambridge, as the unhappy practitioners of a departed religion of truth in a society devoted entirely to propaganda and agreeable illusion. In a mood that was not intended to be congratulatory, I once defined Maoist economics as the substitution of euphoria for commodities. In the stationary state, one has a haunting feeling that this trick might be highly valuable.

I cannot bear to end on a note of unrelieved gloom, and even the practitioner of the dismal science knows that every dismal theorem can be restated in a more cheerful form. My natural glandular optimism, therefore, always reasserts itself in moments like these. I do have considerable optimism about what might be called the "middle run" of the next 100 years, if we are lucky. The chance of nuclear war I think is quite low, although large enough to be very uncomfortable. There are distinct signs that sheer social self-consciousness is beginning to solve the population problem, for even Communists, Catholics, Fundamentalists,

---

[5]"The progressive state is in reality the cheerful and the hearty state to all the different orders of the society. The stationary is dull; the declining melancholy." Adam Smith, *The Wealth of Nations* (Modern Library, 1937), p. 81.

and Traditionalists will be forced to come to terms with the blunt logic of Malthusian arithmetic. Many of our immediate environmental problems are soluble, I think, in the sense that the particular environments of urban areas, for instance, can be noticeably improved—they have been in many places—with the aid of relatively simple social devices that give negative commodities negative prices. The resource exhaustion problem is very unpredictable because of the unpredictability of human knowledge. Still, we use such a fantastically small proportion of our current input of solar energy, it would be very surprising if this could not be vastly improved, and we have put so little thought into large-scale recycling that it would be surprising if this also could not be enormously improved. We are not operating here within tight limits of human capacity but within very wide limits.

The ultimate question of whether a stationary state would be bearable, or even stable, depends a great deal on the human capacity for social invention. One might even have an optimistic image of the present period of human expansion as a kind of adolescence of the human race, in which man has to devote a large proportion of his energy and information to sheer physical growth. Hence, we could regard the stationary state as a kind of maturity in which physical growth is no longer necessary and in which, therefore, human energies can be devoted to qualitative growth—knowledge, spirit, art, and love. One might even romantically regard the twenty-first century as symbolizing the achievement of this maturity. Fortunately for us, we have to leave most of these problems to our descendants. All we can really do is to wish them well, to leave them a little elbow room, and to guide our current evaluation functions somewhere toward the minimax of being on the safe side.

THE MEANING OF HUMAN BETTERMENT

Nebraska Jour. of Econ. and Bus.,
10, 2 (Spring 1971): 3-12

THE MEANING OF HUMAN BETTERMENT*

The behavior of all living things involves something like a process of evaluation, an assessment of different states of the world as either better or worse. Even the simplest one-celled organism, such as the amoeba, prefers a piece of food to a piece of stone. It accepts the food and rejects the stone. In more complex forms of life the state of the world, or conditions which are evaluated, also become much more complex. The dog, for instance, prefers not only food to no food, but prefers being with his master to being with somebody else, which is really a very complicated idea.

Man, the most complex form of life we know, has an image of the world which extends far beyond his immediate environment and his personal experience. Most of us now, for instance, have an image of the far side of the moon, which we have never seen with our own eyes, because we have seen it in photographs. Our evaluations likewise go far beyond our immediate comfort and welfare. It is true that we warm ourselves when we are cold and eat when we are hungry, but we may sacrifice either of these, we may be willing to be both cold and hungry, for our own future or the future of our children, for the future of our own society, or for the future of all mankind.

There seems to be a general principle that as evolution proceeds, either in the biological or in the social world, the field, as the mathematicians say, over which evaluations are made—the totality of things which are evaluated—becomes wider and wider. Primitive man evaluates only his immediate personal environment. Modern man evaluates the whole system of the world. He evaluates the conditions of the whale in the ocean, the atmosphere, and all mankind, even perhaps the condition of the moon. Nature has no such values, except perhaps those of survival. There are many more extinct species than there are species alive today, so nature obviously has no favorites. Man may care about the possible extinction

---

*This paper was presented as the Gerald L. Phillippe Memorial Lecture at the University of Nebraska-Lincoln, March 8, 1971, under the title "How Things Go From Bad to Worse; The Theory of Deteriorating Systems."

of the whale, not only because it serves his needs by providing whale oil, but because he can enjoy directly contemplating the richness and variety of living species, and therefore he cares about things which do not care about him at all.

Evaluation, however, produces conflict. Of two states of the world, let us say A and B, one person may say that A is better than B and another may say that B is better than A. The more complex the field over which evaluations are made, the more likely, perhaps, is conflict to occur. Conflict, however, is itself part of the state of the world which we evaluate. It is possible, therefore, that if two people get into conflict about whether state of the world A is better than state B, they may end up in state of the world C, which is worse for both of them. The problem of conflict resolution, or conflict management—the development of institutions and habits that will minimize the cost of conflict—is therefore of great importance for all society.

It must be emphasized that all evaluations are essentially subjective. Thus any evaluation is a property or act of a single human mind. It always involves statements, such as "I think that A is better than B." This is not to say, however, that evaluations are either arbitrary or random. The process of evaluation and the capacity to perform evaluations are things which we learn in human life. We build on a very small base of genetic values. A newborn baby already has a value system built into its organism by the genes, such as a preference for milk or a preference for being dry. Then there are some values which are more easily learned than others, and the fact that all individuals grow up in society, without which we would not be human at all, means that everyone tends to learn the values of the people around him.

Society tends to separate into subcultures consisting of groups of people who have similar values or evaluation processes. We define a subculture, indeed, as a group of people who share similar evaluation processes. Economists have devised certain measures of objective value, such as per capita real income, on the assumption that at constant prices an increase in the dollar value of something always represents betterment or improvement. As rough approximations such measures are useful, but they do not always correspond to real subjective values. Thus the problem of learning values and the methods by which they are learned is a very important one in any society.

Welfare economics has developed certain tests for measuring whether the state of society A is better than the state of society B on the assumption that individuals are indifferent to perception of an increase or diminution in the welfare of others. This is the assumption of selfishness. On this assumption, economists suppose that condition A is better than condition B if under A some people feel themselves to be better off and nobody feels himself to be worse off. This is unrealistic. Actually we must reckon with the fact that people are not indifferent to the welfare of others and are usually either malevolent or benevolent.

Benevolence means that one person's perception that another is better off increases his evaluation of his own welfare. (If A perceives that B is better off, then A is pleased.) We sacrifice for our children, for instance, because we identify their welfare with our own. This means that we are benevolent toward them. Malevolence is the converse. It is the willingness to sacrifice in order to perceive that someone else is worse off, which also unfortunately is a very common element in human nature. Malevolence and benevolence are learned, however, just as other values are learned. One of the things that is a little puzzling in the human process is why, when benevolence is so clearly beneficial to all (I help you, you help me, and we all go up together) and malevolence is so clearly injurious to all (I beat you down, you beat me down), malevolence is so absurdly popular and easy to learn.

It is clear that there can be no simple or single answer to the question of whether state of the world A is better than state of the world B, either for an individual or for mankind as a whole. Some people prefer socialism, others prefer capitalism. How are we to evaluate these things? If there were any simple answers, we would not have cold wars or political parties. In fact, there would be little for politicians to do. Nevertheless, we can evaluate procedures for resolving these conflicts in terms of their cost, and this is one of the major tasks of political life. Political decisions could almost be defined as those made on behalf of society as a whole and involving evaluations of the position of the total society.

Cost-benefit analysis, even of socialism and capitalism, is not an inconceivable procedure. Any critique of political decisions involves two things. The first is a realistic analysis of their consequences, which is by no means easy. We must have some idea of the exact condition of world A and the exact condition of world B. This requires a social science which perhaps is beyond our capacity at the moment. The second is an evaluation of these conditions according to what economists have come to call "shadow prices"—a set of evaluative weights given to different parts of the total state or condition of the world. Thus, suppose state A contains a lot of X and a little of Y, and state B contains a lot of Y and a little of X. If X is a very important good to us, we are more likely to evaluate state A as better than state B. If Y is a very important good to us, we are more likely to evaluate state B as better than state A.

Much of the ideological conflict in the world today arises out of divergent evaluations of different elements in different systems. If one attaches great importance to order, equality, stability, and conservatism, he is likely to be a socialist. If another attaches great importance to freedom, vulgarity, excitement, and change, he is likely to be a defender of capitalism.

It is easy to come to the very depressing conclusion that, at least with the present techniques of the social sciences, no simple quantitative answer can be given to the question of whether condition A of society is better or worse than condition B. Nevertheless, it is possible to identify certain qualitative characteristics of society that are likely to lead to clearly deteriorating systems on the one side or improving systems on the other. Thus tentative conclusions may be reached as to what it is that makes a society go from bad to worse, or from bad to better, in the evaluation of most of its members. Society's chief concern should be that it go from bad to better, rather than from bad to worse. In this paper eight such deteriorating or, conversely, improving systems, that is, adverse or beneficial processes in society, will be identified. The eight processes of deterioration will first be defined, then means of correcting or avoiding them will be discussed.

The first of these is *consumption*. This is the process by which something recognized as good becomes smaller. The depreciation of capital, the exhaustion of resources, soil erosion, forgetting what one has learned, and the obsolescence of ideas are examples. Closely related to consumption is pollution, which is the increase of things that are recognized as bad, such as air and water pollution, congestion, and the spread of disease and superstition.

The second process is *overload*. As the utilization of any given structure increases, a point may be reached at which there is a very sudden increase in some form of consumption or pollution. A highway, for instance, can take a certain body of traffic easily, but beyond a certain point congestion arises, and traffic may virtually stop. A river, lake, or even the oceans, may take a considerable amount of pollution up to some point at which the self-cleaning processes are destroyed. Even the human organism beyond a certain point of information overload becomes pathological and falls into mental ill health.

The third process may be called *linkages*. This is the joint production of "goods" and "bads" together. In most processes with which we are familiar we produce both. We put up with pollution because we want the goods or services that come with it.

The term *invisibilities* seems appropriate for the fourth process. These are the small evils which individually perhaps are imperceptible or which seem not to be worth bothering about, but which easily accumulate into larger ones. Automobile exhaust fumes, small doses of cumulative poisons, small acts of lying, slander, or dishonesty would be examples.

The fifth process may be designated *knowledge failures.* This process involves failure in the creation or transmission of realistic images of the world and success in the transmission of unrealistic images. True knowledge is a good that must be propagated. Error and superstition are, as it were, knowledge pollution, which unfortunately can also be propagated, since we often fail to create truth and succeed only in creating error.

Conflict mismanagement is the sixth process. This is the development of conflict which makes everybody worse off. There are many examples. Such mismanagement occurs when conflicts escalate and arms races result. Often it develops from a system of deterrence, which may be stable over short periods but always tends to break down in the long run.

The seventh process, referred to earlier, is the process of increasing *malevolence*—the development and learning of social relationships in which people try to do each other harm rather than good.

The eighth process may be termed *reward failures.* If the production of good things is not rewarded and the production of bad things is, then human activity will be distorted toward the production of bad things and away from the production of good things. One aspect of this process is a failure of the price system to reward the good things and to penalize the bad. Another aspect is the failure of the public economy to provide for public goods, that is, those things which cannot be provided through the market system. There is a similar problem in dealing with public "bads," like pollution. These problems, incidentally, if they are not handled well, may be just as severe in socialist as in capitalist societies. Because no existing ideological system is really capable of handling them at the moment, development of quite a new set of social and political institutions may be needed to deal with them.

Each of these eight deteriorating systems has a counterpart in an appreciating or an improving system in which things go from bad to better, rather than from bad to worse. The solution to the problem of the deteriorating system, therefore, always involves finding an improving system which can counteract or offset the deteriorating one.

In the first process, the obvious offsetting activity to consumption is production, which is any process by which goods and good things are increased and, by an easy extension of the term, any process by which bad things are diminished. Depreciation of capital can be overcome only by new investment which replaces the old. Exhaustion of resources is overcome, in part at any rate, by increased knowledge, which discovers new resources, even though this process cannot go on forever in a limited earth. Soil erosion is countered by soil conservation. Pollution can be checked by changing processes of production to those which produce more "goods" and fewer "bads," or which utilize waste products by turning them into something useful. Congestion can be solved either by inducing people to disperse into less populated areas or by increasing the capacity of the more populated ones to handle dense populations.

The second process, overload, is perhaps just a special case of the consumption-production problem, but it has the additional difficulty that it may occur suddenly and without warning. A highway, for instance, may carry a certain load of traffic easily, but with one more car or truck on it everything jams up. The solution is either to expand the capacity of the system—build wider roads, install more telephone lines, innovate new technology, create, a better organizational structure, or even improve the teaching process—or, on the other hand, to diminish the load by the lessening of activity, to change values toward more inactive processes, or to transfer activity to other and less used capacities.

The third process, linkages, is a peculiarly difficult problem which accounts for a great deal of the production of bad things in the world. For instance, we want electric power, but its production also produces air and stream pollution. We want automobiles, which give us status, speed, and mobility, but also give us accidents, death, and pollution. We want national independence and security, very good things, but attempts to achieve them produce a system which is continually disintegrating into war and which extorts enormous costs in defense. The world defense industry is 200 billion dollars a year, an enormous "bad," which the human race can ill afford. The only solution is a change in the methods of production of all sorts, not only of economic goods like electric power, which we should be able to produce with less pollution, but also of many things like security, order, justice, all of which have bad counterparts. The problem here is partly that of awareness, because we tend to be more aware of the "goods" than of the "bads" which accompany them, and partly also, as will be noted later, a failure of the reward structure.

Process four, the problem of invisibilities, is closely related to the problem of linkages. For instance, each automobile produces so little pollution that it is not noticed, but the accumulation of all these little bits of pollution produces something very bad indeed, especially in cities like Los Angeles. Another important example of invisible dangers is found in the population problem. One little baby does not seem to make any difference, but a million little babies do. The problems involved in unilateral national defense are also rather similar. Each nation makes only a small contribution to world instability, but all together may move toward disaster. Here again improved technology may be a part of the solution. Another part is to make the invisible things visible, by the increase of awareness. The solution may involve governmental actions, as will be pointed out later, to change the reward structure by penalizing the production of "bads" through the tax system. Governmental action often creates "bads" of its own, however, unless it is guided by a realistic view of the nature of the problem and supported by an informed public opinion.

Process five is fundamental, because behind nearly all deteriorating systems is some kind of knowledge failure, some kind of failure in the human learning process. The most extreme case of this that comes to mind is the end of the Mayan civilization in Central America, where it appears that some catastrophe, perhaps a revolution, killed off all the people who had in their heads the accumulated knowledge of the society, which then apparently collapsed overnight. Remains still exist of great cities in the jungle with huge stone calendars which simply end on a certain date. People still live in the jungles, but they live a primitive kind of life.

This same process appears less dramatically in the deteriorating culture of the poverty areas of many cities, particularly those which have received a great migration of rural people. Family links are broken by this migration. Because grandparents, who transmit the traditional wisdom of the society, are left behind on the farm, the children grow up not only knowing nothing of the folklore, nursery rhymes, poetry, and wise sayings of the traditional society they left behind, but also frequently incapable of adapting to the new culture of the cities.

An extreme case, of course, would be a society which destroyed its educational system. It would revert to a much lower level in one generation as the people who had in their heads the knowledge necessary for the society died off and were not replaced by younger people with the same or greater knowledge. Educational systems are necessary because knowledge in the heads of any particular individual depreciates and is subject to consumption as people get old, become forgetful, and eventually die. Societies have also been swept by epidemics, we might say, of religious or of political superstition. One thinks particularly of Nazi Germany or of Mao's China, where superstition in the form of the "little red book" has swept over the country almost like an epidemic disease. Such superstitions can impose severe damage on societies. These are cases of knowledge failure. The only answer is to develop social processes which reward truth and penalize error. This is a problem which has been largely solved in the scientific community, but which in society at large still demands solution.

The next two systems are really special cases of knowledge failure or failure in the human learning process. Process six is the mismanagement of conflict, which easily can result in all the conflicting parties becoming worse off. A injures B, so B injures A, so A retaliates, so B retaliates, and so we go on with everybody getting worse off. We see this in the family, for instance. Children of all ages are always getting into fights, which make all the participants worse off. The same thing appears in industrial relations where in an early stage we often find that unions and employers are bent on damaging each other, with the result that everybody becomes worse off.

This is one of the costs of a dialectical process, which can sometimes be very injurious to a society. There are two possible solutions. One is the growth of knowledge on the part of both A and B, and also a change in their values, which will deter them from trying to gain short-run advantages that will ultimately leave both worse off. This might be thought of as the development of maturity in conflict relations. It is only as people mature that they learn how to manage conflicts without the process of mutual damage. They learn that if one does something nasty to the other the latter will retaliate and both will be worse off. We all must learn these skills in the management of conflict and the limitation of mutual damage.

The second solution to this problem is the development of third-party intervention. In the case of children, the parents intervene and separate them so that they cannot hurt each other. In industrial relations, we have conciliation, mediation, and arbitration. In internal quarrels, we have civil law, which is a device to prevent people from hurting each other. But we are still a very long way from learning these skills of conflict management in the international system, which is extremely badly managed and very expensive. In many countries the internal political system is also inadequate, and internal conflict is much too costly.

Process seven, the development of malevolence or ill will, is closely related to the last two, and is also a process in human learning. Malevolence, like benevolence, is learned. There is little that is genetic in either love or hate. If malevolence develops, therefore, it is a result of a learning process.

The rate of malevolence may be measured by how many dollars A would sacrifice in order to perceive that B is a dollar worse off. That is, if one person would pay 20 cents to see that another is worse off by a dollar, then his rate of malevolence is 20 percent. The rate of malevolence of the United States toward Vietnam appears to be about 400 percent. That is, we damage ourselves $4 in order to damage the Vietnamese by $1.

The converse of malevolence, of course, is benevolence, in which A would sacrifice in order to perceive that B is better off. As suggested earlier, one of the paradoxes of human life is that, while it is clear that benevolence leads into improving systems and malevolence into deteriorating ones, malevolence is so surprisingly popular and so easy to learn. It is practiced between nations, between political parties, and sometimes even between husband and wife.

One of the most interesting and perhaps most unexplored problems in human psychology is precisely what the structures and devices are in society by which malevolence is learned so easily. This anomaly is partly a result of failure in the process of rearing children, which is the only really significant process of production in society that is left entirely to unskilled labor. An unskillful parent easily produces pathological identities in the children which make them prone to malevolence. Certainly some people are malevolence-prone, as it were, just as others are benevolence-prone, but what makes the difference is not clear. It does appear, however, that failure in conflict management easily produces not only malevolence but mutual malevolence. There can be conflict without malevolence, but a conflict easily produces it, and then the malevolence itself intensifies the conflict. Here again, the only answer is understanding of the development of processes and institutions in society which do produce benevolence. There appears to be little real understanding of this. The preachers have preached about it for a long time, but no one seems to understand very clearly the exact conditions under which benevolence is produced.

The last process may be the most important of all. Behind nearly all deteriorating processes are failures of human learning, both in developing realistic images of what the world is like, and in developing mature values toward it. Failures in all forms of production are related to this. All these failures are in turn related to the general structure of rewards and punishments in society. When we are looking at the question of how people learn the things they do and how the structure of social organization is related to learning, it is clear that the structure of rewards and of punishments, which are simply negative rewards, is of enormous importance. Reward is the perception of something good which happens to a person because he does something. Punishment, or negative reward, is something bad which happens to someone as a result of his doing something. Thus one may be rewarded in the form of a monthly paycheck for being a professor and for this reason do the things he has to do in order to be a professor; on the other hand, he may never have been rewarded for robbing banks, and for this reason he never engages in this activity.

The price system—the whole structure of relative prices—produces a set of rewards and punishments. It rewards people who produce something that has a high price; it punishes, relatively, people who produce things that have a low price. Such rewards and punishments profoundly affect human behavior. The system of "grants"—one-way transfers of economic goods—rewards those who get the grants, or at least does not reward those who do not get them, and punishes those who get negative grants, like bombs. We learn according to the rewards and punishments given by our parents, friends, and teachers.

The whole structure of human knowledge grows toward rewards and away from punishments. We see the world the way we do and learn to value it the way we do because it pays us to do so. If, then, we are rewarded for learning error or for producing "bads," or for developing malevolence, a society is more likely to fall into deteriorating systems. Things are likely to go from bad to worse. The great problem of political, social, and economic organization in society, then, is precisely the problem of how to establish a total reward system which encourages the spread of truth, realism, and the production of "goods" rather than "bads."

No existing theory or ideology of society comes close to achieving the ideal suggested here or appears at all capable of solving the problem of mankind in the next hundred years. Nationalism is a failure. Capitalism in the raw sense is a failure. Socialism is a dismal failure. It has not achieved human liberation and has created societies which are no better than any others. The awful truth that must be faced today is that we do not know how to organize society for human betterment. There is an enormous task ahead of mankind in developing the kind of society, the kind of knowledge, the kind of social organization, which protect man from deteriorating systems, which protect him from the illegitimate and foolish use of power, and which encourage betterment rather than deterioration. This is a task to which all of us can dedicate the rest of our lives.

INDEX OF NAMES

SUBJECT INDEX